Truth

A JOURNEY FROM DARKNESS INTO LIGHT

"You will know the truth,
and the truth will make you free."
– John 8:32

R. JOHN ANDERSON

EachDay.org | Walking Towards Christ Jesus

FOR GOD SO LOVES THE WORLD, AND YOU TOO!

Visit our website at: https://eachday.org

Copyright ©2018, 2021 Holy Spirit Prints. All Rights Reserved. No part of this publication may be reproduced, reprinted, distributed, transmitted, or used in any manner, in any form or by any means, electronic, mechanical, or otherwise, without prior written permission from the publisher.

The Message of Truth, v1.07
(También disponible en Español – *La Palabra de Verdad*)
Published by: Holy Spirit Prints. https://holyspiritprints.com
11700 W. Charleston Blvd., Suite 170-136
Las Vegas NV 89135

All Scripture quotations unless otherwise marked are taken from the NEW AMERICAN STANDARD BIBLE® Copyright © 1960, 1962, 1963, 1968, 1971, 1972, 1973, 1975, 1977, 1995 by The Lockman Foundation. Used by permission. http://www.lockman.org

Scripture quotations marked (ESV) are from The Holy Bible, English Standard Version® (ESV®), copyright ©2001 by Crossway, a publishing ministry of Good News Publishers. Used by permission. All rights reserved.

Scripture quotations marked (KJV) are taken from the KING JAMES VERSION, public domain.

Cover Photo Copyright ©R. John Anderson. All Rights Reserved.
https://rjohnanderson.photo

ISBN: 978-1-7339384-8-8

TABLE OF CONTENTS

ACKNOWLEDGMENTS v
INTRODUCTION vi

PART I: GOD, HUMANITY & SIN 1

1.0 God Created 2
1.1 Male And Female 16
1.2 It Was Very Good 22
1.3 Science vs. The Bible 24
1.4 Humanity & Sin 35
1.5 We Are All Sinners 42
1.6 The Coming Great Day Of Judgment 48

PART II: OUR HOPE 78

2.0 Who Is Jesus Of Nazareth? 79
2.1 Is Jesus Really God? 95
2.2 Was Jesus Really Raised From The Dead? 102
2.3 The "Good News" Of The Gospel 117

PART III: THE NEW TESTAMENT PLAN OF SALVATION 136

3.0 The Path To Eternal Life 137
3.1 Believe In Jesus (By First Hearing the Gospel Message) 150
3.2 Repent Of Your Sins 155
3.3 Confess Christ 158
3.4 Be Baptized 162
3.5 You Are Born Again 169

PART IV: THE WAY OF A CHRISTIAN 176

4.0 Walking In The Way 177
4.1 Living In The Spirit 195
4.2 Obedience 212
4.3 Bearing Fruit (The Role of Works) 222
4.4 Persevering In Faith 246
4.5 Some Encouragement 266
4.6 The Peace Of God 276
4.7 The Kingdom Of God 291
4.8 The Wisdom Of God 302
4.9 The Armor Of God 309
4.10 The Power Of Prayer 318
4.11 Holy, Holy, Holy 331
4.12 All Things Made New 335
4.13 Now Go And Tell Others 342

PART V: NEXT STEPS 350
5.0 The Strait And Narrow Path.. 351
5.1 Choosing A Bible.. 354
5.2 Reading And Studying The Bible... 362
5.3 Start Memorizing Verses... 367
5.4 Finding A Church.. 370
5.5 Utilizing Technology.. 380
5.6 Changing Your Worldly Habits.. 382
5.7 Changing Your Entertainment Habits.. 397
5.8 Attending A New Believer Class.. 400
5.9 Finding Your First Bible Study.. 402
5.10 Being A Berean... 403
5.11 Essential First 30-Days Activities... 405

PART VI: BEWARE THE WOLVES 408
6.0 Be Not Deceived... 409
6.1 The "Theory" Of Evolution 439
6.2 Satan (The Devil) Is Just A Myth 440
6.3 Annihilation After Death.. 441
6.4 "Soul Sleeping"... 443
6.5 Hell Isn't Real 445
6.6 The Doctrine Of "Original Sin".. 446
6.7 Sabbath Keeping 451
6.8 Abstaining From Certain Foods... 455
6.9 False Teachings On Baptism 457
6.10 Saying A "Sinner's Prayer" Saves You 464
6.11 You Are Saved By "Faith Alone/Only".. 465
6.12 Once Saved Always Saved 471
6.13 Predestination 473
6.14 Calvinism 474
6.15 The "Secret Rapture"... 476
6.16 The "7-Year Great Tribulation" Period.. 477
6.17 Dispensational Premillennialism 477
6.18 Dispensational Postmillennialism 482
6.19 A Third Temple 483
6.20 Distortions Of Matthew 24 485
6.21 Modern/Popular Eschatology 485
6.22 Bizarre Interpretations Of The "Mark Of The Beast"............................... 486
6.23 The "Two Witnesses" Of Revelation.. 490
6.24 Predictions Of Jesus' Return 490
6.25 Lucifer As The Devil... 491
6.26 All Bible Prophecy Must Be Literally Fulfilled 491
6.27 The "One True End-Times Church".. 492
6.28 Universalism 492
6.29 Ecumenism 492
6.30 You Get A "2nd Chance" After Death... 493
6.31 Roman Catholicism Masquerading As Christianity................................... 493

6.32 The "KJV Only" Bible Movement 495
6.33 Demonic Possession/Exorcism Today 498
6.34 Touching Vipers (Snakes) 498
6.35 Speaking In Tongues Today 499
6.36 Miracle Healers Today 499
6.37 The "Prosperity Gospel" 500
6.38 A "Second Filling" Of The Holy Spirit 500
6.39 Feet Washing 501
6.40 Mormonism Masquerading As Christianity 501
6.41 Denominationalism 502
6.42 12-Step Recovery Programs 506
6.43 Jesus Already Returned In A.D. 70 507
6.44 Mystical Signs Before/Predicting Christ's Return 507
6.45 Interpreting Symbolic Or Figurative Language Literally 507
6.46 Aliens And The Nephilim 511
6.47 Cults That Deny Christ 511
6.48 Salvation Is A Free Gift Of God, So No Action Is Required 513
6.49 A Christian No Longer Sins 514
6.50 The Nicene Creed 517

PART VII: CLOSING ITEMS 520

7.0 Questions & Doubts 521
7.1 Psalm 1 522
7.2 Psalm 2 522
7.3 Psalm 23 523
7.4 Psalm 31 523
7.5 Psalm 34 524
7.6 Psalm 46 525
7.7 Psalm 69 526
7.8 Psalm 91 528
7.9 Psalm 107 529
7.10 Psalm 116 531
7.11 Psalm 145 532
7.12 My Testimony 533
7.13 Helpful Resources 536

BENEDICTION 540

ACKNOWLEDGMENTS

I would like to thank Wayne Jackson of Christian Courier for his wonderful and accurate writings and Jason Jackson of Christian Courier and Tyler Kirkpatrick of Oakey Boulevard Church of Christ for their thoughtful review, comments, and suggestions. Thanks to Ashley Young for her help in the preparation of the cover layout. Special thanks to The Lockman Foundation for their faithful work in providing the NASB Bible translation along with permission to use it in this book – we often take for granted the work of those who make the various Bible translations available to us today but let us be mindful of the extraordinary amount of work that goes into preparing any translation for our use, without which I would not be able to do this book. And thanks above all to the Lord Jesus Christ for His extreme patience, love, mercy, grace, and lovingkindness towards me. Truth be told, I easily could have died a sinner long before I ever got to do this work for the Lord.

INTRODUCTION

Many do not realize that the Bible is actually "God's Love Story" written for mankind, and it is filled with the glorious promise of hope along with a spectacularly triumphant ending! But it is up to each of us to choose that hope and our eternal destiny – for we are all born with an immortal spirit which lives on forever; the only question is where. Our spirit doesn't die; only our fleshly body does, for we will one day shed this body made from dust. Therefore, we each have a free-will choice to make, which determines whether we will spend eternity with God in heaven or with Satan and the angels who sinned in hell.

GOOD NEWS

This book presents the "good news" (Luke 2:10) of the Bible (the gospel "message [word] of truth") from start to finish – Genesis to Revelation. It also helps you understand how we got here in this fallen world today full of disease, death, war, murder, and other sinful behaviors that cause misery to the human race – humanity has fallen into sin by disobeying God. The good news is that Jesus "did not come [the first time] to judge the world, but to save the world" (John 12:47) from sin, to be "the Light of the World" (John 8:12), and to rescue us from "the dominion of darkness" (Colossians 1:13) and bondage under sin, Satan, and death. For "just as through one man [Adam] sin entered into the world, and death through sin" (Romans 5:12), another Man (Jesus) "gave His life for us" (1 John 3:16) to redeem (purchase) us back from sin: "for God so loved the world, that He gave His only begotten Son, that whoever believes in Him shall not perish, but have eternal life" (John 3:16).

BUT JUDGMENT DAY APPROACHES

The Bible tells us that "God is love" (1 John 4:7) and that He is holy and righteous. But we also read that He is a God of justice and that He will bring all sin to judgment on the great Day of Judgment to come: "When the Lord Jesus will be revealed from heaven with His mighty angels in flaming fire" (2 Thessalonians 1:7), i.e., He comes the second time. Jesus came to Earth the first time as a humble and sacrificial servant to save you from sin; when He returns, it will be in power and glory for judgment and to restore creation to a state of perfection – without sin, suffering, or death. Only those who are able to stand before God on that great Day righteous and blameless (i.e., not guilty of sin) will be granted eternal life with God in heaven. It is only through belief and faith in Christ that you can be declared righteous in the sight of God and saved to eternal life, if you so choose. This Day is also called the "Day of the Lord" (1 Thessalonians 5:2) and the "Day of Eternity" (2 Peter 3:18). On this great Day, God will judge all unrighteousness (sin) for all eternity, and all sin will be completely and finally eradicated from God's creation.

And on this Day, everyone will stand before God to give an account of themselves: "For we must all appear before the judgment seat of Christ, so that each one may be recompensed for his deeds in the body, according to what he has done, whether good or bad" (2 Corinthians 5:10). Nothing that has been done or whispered in secret will be hidden; in fact, "there is nothing covered up that will not be revealed, and hidden that will not be known. Accordingly, whatever you have said in the dark will be heard in the light, and what you have whispered in the inner rooms will be proclaimed upon the housetops" (Luke 12:2-3).

Those who stand righteous (blameless, morally pure, free from guilt or sin, declared "not guilty" of sin, justifiable) on that Day of Judgment will enter into eternal life in heaven (paradise) – for eternal life can only be found in the presence of God, who creates and sustains all life. Those who die in sin (through their own choice) will be banished to hell, which is a real literal place of "outer darkness" (Matthew 22:13), "away from the presence of the Lord and from the glory of His power" (2 Thessalonians 1:9) where there will be "weeping and gnashing of teeth" (Matthew 22:13), with the memory of their (unforgiven) sins searing into their consciousness for all time. That is the torment of hell. Nothing sinful will be permitted to enter heaven in the presence of God when He restores His creation to righteousness.

This Day of Judgment will arrive when most are not expecting it – it will start just like any other normal day, but then just "like a thief in the night" (1 Thessalonians 5:2), without any further warning, it will be here. The only warning you will receive is from reading the Bible, reading books like this one, and listening to those who share the gospel "message of truth" with you (Ephesians 1:13). Be not deceived, for there are no more signs and wonders in the sky, nor signs in the stars and moon (astrology), nor any Bible prophecy remaining yet to be fulfilled before the arrival of this great and awesome Day of the Lord.

Like a charging grizzly, this Day of Judgment is rapidly approaching. And just like an encounter with a charging grizzly, the consequences will be eternally devastating for those who are unprepared for the encounter. If you were staring down a grizzly bear in a life-or-death situation, wouldn't you want the truth, the whole truth, and nothing but the truth on how to handle it? In an analogous fashion, this book gives you the truth of the gospel message, which will allow you to stand before God on that Day, righteous, blameless, and holy with your sins forgiven and justified to eternal life in heaven.

What a glorious day this will be for the saints (those who are in Christ), and what a terrifying day this will be for everyone else (the lost). Know that God in His infinite wisdom, love, mercy, and grace has provided a way for you to stand righteous before Him on that Day. The only way you can stand righteous before God is through the forgiveness of sin by accepting Jesus Christ as your Lord and Savior, "for there is one God, and one mediator also between God and men, the man Christ Jesus, who gave Himself as a ransom for all" (1 Timothy 2:5-6). Jesus said, "I am the way, and the truth, and the life; no one comes to the Father but through Me" (John 14:6), and "there is salvation in no one else; for there is no other name under heaven that has been given among men by which we must be saved" (Acts 4:12). Furthermore, there is no "second chance" to accept Christ after death, for "it is appointed for men to die once and after this comes judgment" (Hebrews 9:27) – and your judgment will stand for eternity.

And contrary to what the world teaches, death is not your ending – you don't disappear into nothingness; you are not "annihilated" after death. We read in Scripture that we are born with an immortal spirit that will live on even after the body dies. In fact, death is the doorway to eternity, when you put off this old self, this earthly vessel, your fleshly body (tent) with its corrupt (sinful) nature and inherit a new glorified eternal (immortal) body! It is written, "there shall certainly be a resurrection of both the righteous and the wicked" (Acts 24:15). So, everyone who has ever lived will be raised immortal – those who died in righteousness will remain righteous for eternity (eternal life), and those who died in sin will remain sinful for eternity (eternal death). Your spiritual state, either righteous or sinful, is sealed at your death – again, there are no "second chances" to change it after you die.

I WANT YOU TO BE FULLY INFORMED

It is written: "My people are destroyed for lack of knowledge" (Hosea 4:6). To get eternal life, we must look to the Holy Bible to tell us what we need to do to be saved on that Day so that we are not caught unaware or unprepared. The Holy Bible, the "word of life" (Philippians 2:16), declares to us the pure and accurate truth (knowledge) that saves us to eternal life – for God "desires all men to be saved and to come to the knowledge of the truth" (1 Timothy 2:4) so that no one is lost in judgment. So I am trying to leave no stone unturned in presenting the correct and complete gospel message to you.

You will read Who our hope is: "Jesus of Nazareth" – "the Christ of God," the one "living and true God," the Lord "our Savior." Christ is not His last name – Christ means the "Messiah" or the "Anointed One" of God. And the "good news" part of the gospel is that through belief in Christ, you can stand holy and blameless before God on that Great Day of Judgment with your sins forgiven (pardoned) and receive eternal life. You can hear God pronounce a verdict of "not guilty" (of sin) for you, along with "well done, good and faithful servant…Enter into the joy of your master" (Matthew 25:21 ESV) – for it is God Who is both your Judge and your attorney! And Jesus Christ is God. How amazing is that!

While the gospel message proper is the hope that is found in Jesus Christ in the New Testament of the Bible, one must start all the way back at the beginning in Genesis, where the foundation of the Gospel message is laid, and we learn about God, His creation, humanity, sin, and the fall, and this fallen world we now find ourselves in. Indeed, Jesus was mentioned even in the very first chapters of the Bible (Genesis 3:15). If you don't understand how we (mankind) got to the place where we needed a Savior (Jesus), you won't fully appreciate what He did for you (and me). So, this book also starts at the very beginning (in Genesis) with information to help you understand how we "got here": why we find ourselves today in this fallen world, rampant with disease, destruction, disasters, death, famines, wars, lying, cheating, stealing, murder, and other sinful behavior, and why we need a Savior. I then lead you through the gospel message as given in the New Testament.

> In Him, you also, after listening to the message [word] of truth, the gospel of your salvation—having also believed, you were sealed in Him with the Holy Spirit of promise, who is given as a pledge of our inheritance, with a view to the redemption of *God's own* possession, to the praise of His glory. – Ephesians 1:13-14

GOD IS NOT A GOD OF CONFUSION

I want to spend a moment setting up the proper mental framework for you to evaluate the gospel message presented herein. You see, I didn't believe in the Bible, or "faith," or "religious" stuff myself either – for many years. I was trained as a scientist, a physicist. I needed to use logic, reason, and intellect, even when approaching the subject of Christianity. I didn't think it (the Bible) could possibly be true or that it was supported by a vast ream of hard scientific data. However, <u>by reading with an open mind</u> what Christian scientists have to say on various topics (e.g., evolution, dinosaurs, carbon dating, etc.), I came to realize that there were other (very valid) scientific viewpoints than what I had been taught all my life from secular books, schools, and institutions – from preschool all the way on up through university level! It was then that I started to see how the lies I'd been told since childhood had programmed me for disbelief – in effect, I had been brainwashed (by man) from childhood against the truth of the Bible and against God. And I didn't even realize it!

Contrary to many peoples' beliefs, becoming a Christian doesn't mean you abandon your reason, logic, and intellect and "blindly believe" in Jesus. God is a God of logic, wisdom, reason, and understanding, not a God of confusion (see Isaiah 1:18, Proverbs 3:19, Jeremiah 10:12, 1 Corinthians 14:33). God is not asking you to take a leap of faith in the dark about His Son Jesus Christ. In fact, much light has been given to you, so you can and should come to the decision to accept Jesus as your Lord and Savior only after carefully evaluating all the facts, evidence (scientific, historical, archaeological, literary, etc.), and eyewitness testimony that is available. You do this just like any modern jury of law would in reaching a verdict.

Matthew Henry, a nonconformist minister and author in England from 1662-1714, writes: [1]

> First, Intelligent hearers; they hear the word and understand it; they understand not only the sense and meaning of the word, but their own concern in it; they understand it as a man of business understands his business. God in his word deals with men as men, in a rational way, and gains possession of the will and affections by opening the understanding: whereas Satan, who is a thief and a robber, comes not in by that door, but climbeth up another way [by deceiving you through lies, half-truths, and distorting Scripture].

In fact, the evidence given in the Bible (and outside the Bible) supporting its inerrancy along with the reality of Jesus Christ (as God, resurrected from the dead) far supersedes the "beyond a reasonable doubt" burden of proof level that would be required by a modern jury in a court of law to arrive at a consensus verdict, even in the most severe of capital punishment cases! It is by reviewing all available information that you then make an informed, logical, rational decision to accept Scripture as God's Word and truth and to accept Jesus Christ your Lord and Savior if you so choose.

Like you almost surely do, I had literally hundreds of questions about the Bible and Christianity. But I confronted my questions and doubts head-on, with an open (but rational and logical) mind, and that is what I ask you to do. I cannot present all the evidence herein to try to convince you that the Bible and Christianity are true, but I can give you an overview of it and walk you through the main thread of the Bible so that you understand the big picture and the main questions of "why" and "Who" and "how." The rest is up to you and God. There are links to resources on our website with more information on the scientific, historical, geological, archeological, and other evidence of biblical truth. Please research further anything you have questions or doubts about. Don't let those questions and doubts discourage you from taking a serious look at what the Bible says. Dig into them; tackle them head-on — for it's your own eternal life which is at stake here!

I urge you to seriously contemplate the enormity of eternity. For we all are, each of us, rushing towards that great Day of Judgment, where we must stand before the Lord and give an account of ourselves. We can be saved from judgment and condemnation

---

[1] Henry, Matthew. *Exposition of the Old and New Testaments*, London. 1706-1710/1721.

only through Jesus Christ. This is a matter of choosing eternal life or eternal death. We each have that choice to make (Joshua 24:15).

Always remember that we serve a God of love, who "is love" (1 John 4:8), "who is patient toward you, not willing for any to perish, but for all to come to repentance," (2 Peter 3:9), "who wants all people to be saved and to come to the knowledge of the truth" (1 Timothy 4:4) and who "take[s] no pleasure at all in the death of the wicked, but rather [desires] that the wicked turn from his way and live" (Ezekiel 33:11). It is God alone who is from eternity past to eternity future. You too can have eternal life offered by "the living and true God" (1 Thessalonians 1:9 ESV), the Lord Jesus Christ. He offers it as a gift to all, and to you – so "let the one who hears say, 'Come.' And let the one who is thirsty come; let the one who desires, take the water of life without cost" (Revelation 22:17).

WHY "YET ANOTHER" GOSPEL BOOK

Scripture says that we are to worship the Lord "in spirit and truth" (John 4:24): meaning the Lord's truth as given in Scripture itself, not man's truth. So, if you are new to Christ and this gospel message, please realize that we are to approach God by and through His truth only as given in Scripture, not man-made opinions, schemes, or false teachings. It is very easy, especially for someone new to the gospel message, to be confused about which is which. For we've had centuries now (over 2,000 years!) of man-made false teachings, fanciful interpretations, catechisms, rites, rules, rituals, ceremonies, "traditions," myths, wild-speculation, superstition, mysticism, fake prophecies, and a myriad of sectarian and denominational divisions (Gnosticism, Montanism, Manichaeism, Monasticism, Docetism, Arianism, Sabellianism, Paganism, Mysticism, Nestorianism, Pelagianism, Rationalism, Apollinarianism, Monophysitism, Eutychianism, Adoptionism, Catholicism, Protestantism, Reformed Protestantism, Arminianism, Calvinism, Adventism, Modernism, etc. ad nauseam'ism), and dozens upon dozens of false doctrines, false gospels, and theological systems and frameworks made up by man, committees and institutions all piled up one on top of another and masquerading as so-called "Christianity," obfuscating the pure truth of the gospel "that was once for all *time* handed down to the saints" in Scripture. Whew!

Further compounding the situation is the absolutely staggering amount of noise generated by the secular world, with its God-denying media and institutions trying to drown out the gospel message and the name of Jesus altogether by creating even more false teachings which masquerade as science, but which are in reality fake science. We are being fed today fake news, fake science (e.g., The "Theory" of Evolution), fake entertainment (e.g., lip-synced performances, so-called "reality" but scripted TV), fake food (e.g., margarine, "meat substitutes"), fake body parts (e.g., vanity cosmetic surgery), fake economics (e.g., Keynesian Economics, debt as an asset), fake (and fraudulent) accounting (e.g., non-GAAP reporting, off-balance sheet items), fake money (e.g., fiat currencies), fake "religions," fake prophecy and yes, even fake gospels (e.g., lukewarm, apostate so-called "Christianity").

These false teachings are being shouted today 24/7/365 (i.e., nonstop) in blaring volume from both secular media sources as well as so-called "Christian" pulpits, broadcasts, books/authors, movies, publications, and even seminary schools. And we are gradually conditioned by repeated, frequent, and persistent marketing propaganda (for that is exactly what it is) to accept the fakes (the false teachings) as the real thing and even begin to believe them in place of the real. The exact same thing has happened to Christianity over the last 2000 years - we have been gradually trained and conditioned to accept and even believe that the fakes are the real thing, and in many cases, we cannot even tell the difference anymore!

This is a very sad state of affairs as very few today are even able to recognize true Christianity as defined in Scripture, and people are more confused today than ever before by all the false teachings as well as by seeing an almost endless stream of hypocritical pretenders proclaiming to be "Christians" parading before and all around them. Many today aren't even sure who is a true Christian or what a true Christian church even looks like, nor how to truly accept Christ. Also, know that true Christianity isn't achieved through the performance of "religious" rites, rituals, "traditions," or ceremonies, nor does it live in a church building.

So, when I use "Christianity" in quotes, it's because many groups and so-called "Christian" churches are "neglecting the commandment of God" and "teaching as doctrines the precepts of men" (Mark 7:7-8). They are not teaching the Christianity "that was once for all *time* handed down to the saints," but the doctrines of their own opinions – for they have either added to, taken away from, or distorted what is written in Scripture. Some of these "Christian" groups are well-meaning but simply misguided, while others intend to deceive. Sadly, many who are lost or new to Christ simply give up when confronted with so many differing and conflicting teachings – which all claim to be true Christianity (but are not)!

I experienced many of these false teachings (both secular and "Christian") firsthand as I began my own journey. This is why I believed "yet another" book explaining the gospel needed to be written. It's time for a good dose of solid food – the truth of the New Testament Gospel as it was given to and practiced in the apostolic era (in the years just after Christ's death). As it is written: "Beloved, while I was making every effort to write you about our common salvation, I felt the necessity to write to you appealing that you contend earnestly for the faith that was once for all *time* handed down to the saints" (Jude 3). If you will, "I am A VOICE OF ONE CRYING IN THE WILDERNESS" of modern, liberal, corrupt, apostate, lukewarm, dead, pretend "Christianity": "MAKE STRAIGHT" the gospel of our Lord and Savior Jesus Christ!

THE TRUE AND CORRECT GOSPEL

So as much as I wanted to only present the simple and true Word of God as given in Scripture, in the world we find ourselves today, I must not only teach you this truth, but I must also prepare you to face a dizzying array of false teachings, false doctrines, and dogmas invented by man. A good child of God must not only know the Word of God, but they must also know what is not the Word of God. After all, it was in this fashion that Satan deceived Eve, and then Adam, in the Garden of Eden, leading to the downfall of humanity (Genesis 3). So be not deceived...there will be many who try to trick you out of the path to eternal life!

A whole section of the book called "Beware the Wolves" addresses popular false teachings that are absolutely rampant and widespread today. The sad fact that it is also the longest section of the book shows you just how extensive and pervasive these false teachings really are. I am very direct in addressing the false teachings of man, and I hope you can respect that – I am doing it for your eternal good, so you are not deceived and "come short of" eternal life (Hebrews 4:1)! I give you the correct gospel straight up, without sugar-coating it, watering it down, or making liberal concessions. We are not trying to get doctrine "close enough" or "good enough" or "almost right" – the goal is to get it 100% exactly right in agreement with what is written in Scripture.

You will see as we go forward on the path to eternal life that you will have to fight off this massive avalanche of false teachings at <u>each and every step</u> of the way - first from the secular God-denying world which tries to stop you from believing in God altogether, and then even further, from the false so-called "Christian" churches trying to "trick" you out of your eternal salvation. Amazing! You will be confronted by false teachings, such as:

- You are saved by "faith alone/only,"
- That a Christian is "once saved, always saved" no matter what they do or how they subsequently live after accepting Christ,
- Calvinism (i.e., "Reformed" Protestantism) – a whole framework of false teachings from top to bottom,
- We are born in "original sin,"
- Saying the "the sinner's prayer" (nowhere found in the Bible) at one time in your life somehow magically saves you to eternal life,
- Being baptized isn't essential for salvation because it is a "good work" of man,
- And many others!

It is staggering and frustrating to see. But if you want eternal life, you must be a warrior in Christ and blast through every single one of them! Each of these false teachings seeks to turn you out of the path of truth or turn you away from Christ. They are snares and traps of man set up for you, orchestrated by Satan – the Devil and "the ruler of this world." You conquer them first by accepting Christ in truth and then by the power of Christ living in you, and you must never stop "growing in the grace and knowledge [understanding]" of the Lord Jesus Christ, each day of your life. Truth be told, writing this book has been hugely rewarding for me. If you want to learn something, read a book on it; but if you want to really understand something, write a book on it. Writing this book has helped me weed out any false beliefs I had.

MY OBJECTIVES

My overall goal is that if someone has only a Bible and this book, that I have explained the gospel "message of truth" well enough to enable them to accept Christ and get all the way to eternal life. Therefore, the primary objectives of this book are threefold:

1) Present the gospel message from start to finish (without false teachings) to those who have not yet heard it and to those who may have heard it but who have not yet come to believe in Christ. I hope this book helps you better understand the hope that can be found in the Lord Jesus Christ,
2) Help the professing Christian who is not worshiping the Lord "in spirit and truth" (John 4:24) to identify any false teachings or false beliefs in their faith and return to the pure gospel message "that was once for all *time* handed down to the saints" (Jude 3:1) in New Testament Scripture, and
3) Serve as a handbook of sorts to which the born-again Christian can refer to from time to time as they walk with Christ, and also use to explain the gospel message to others around them. Consequently, there is a fair amount of overlap among

some of the chapters as I've designed each chapter so that it can also serve as a study guide that could be used separately; and, if you're like me, it often helps to have something explained more than once, perhaps in a couple of different ways (Philippians 3:1). I also hope to help you to avoid making the same mistakes I made when starting out in faith by being a gullible baby Christian and succumbing to all sorts of false teachings.

I have attempted to present the "message of truth" in a methodical manner, building "line upon line" and "precept upon precept" (Isaiah 28:10 ESV), for that is how we are to learn. I ask you to forgive any deficiencies in literary style or prose as I am not a trained or professional writer; I am just an average guy trying to explain the gospel message to you as best I can. For those who are new to the Bible, God, His Son Jesus Christ, and the gospel message of hope, I have tried not to assume much prior knowledge. I have tried to lead you step by step from the very beginning. For those who have already accepted Christ, I hope that this book serves to refresh your love of Christ and also helps you correct any false beliefs or interpretations that you may have which are not in agreement with Scripture.

It is also important to understand what the purpose of this book is not; it is not the purpose of this book to:

1) Convince you that there is a God (i.e., that God exists),
2) Convince you that the Holy Bible is inerrant (without error) and true and that it is indeed the Word of God,
3) Convince you that the first chapters of creation in Genesis are true,
4) Convince you that Jesus Christ was a real person. However, I do show you what Scripture says about Jesus (e.g., remember He still lives!) and that He did, in fact, claim to be God, despite the claims of modern liberals and skeptics,
5) Be an apologetics work for Christianity – I'm simply going to state the truth that is given in Scripture,
6) Be a complete rebuttal for the myriad false teachings you will encounter; I'm simply trying to provide awareness of the false teachings, along with enough information about them, so you are not deceived.

It is also not possible in a book of this size to go into all the nuances of faith and Christian doctrine – the main objective is to give you an accurate and truthful saving knowledge of the gospel message itself. Besides, it is by your own continued study of the Word that you will "grow in the grace and knowledge [understanding] of the Lord" (2 Peter 3:18) and "press on to maturity" (Hebrews 6:1) as a Christian.

THE WORD OF GOD IS LIVING AND ACTIVE

Please remember that my words are only the non-inspired words of a mere man – Scripture is the full and final authority on all matters. Indeed, it is not my words that give power, life, and authority to this book; it is the Scripture verses themselves. So, please do not skip over the verses I've included in each chapter – for it is they which have the power of life! At the risk of making the book lengthier, I have included the full text for all Bible verses; I did this because some readers may not have a Bible handy when reading this book. Similarly, I've included more verses in each chapter than you might first think necessary; I've done this for two reasons:

1. As mentioned, some reading this book may not have a Bible, and,

2. One must consider what Scripture has to say in aggregate on any topic (Psalm 119:160) to avoid false teachings and false doctrines, which arise when one picks and chooses some verses and ignores others on any particular topic.

In some verses, I have added comments in brackets [e.g., words here]. I have done this only to help with context and reading. I'm not adding to Scripture, but I'm clarifying some things at times because the verses are being used without the full contextual setting in which they appear in the Bible. You will also find that many verses pertain to and are repeated across multiple chapters. These repetitions have been done purposely to make the respective chapters complete within themselves. Please also realize that Scripture is multi-faceted, whereby the same verse applies to multiple topics, hence another reason for the repetition.

Thank God we have the wonderful writings of prior saints and servants of God available to us today, so we may learn from, build on and stand upon them. From this standpoint, we are the most blessed generation in history, having come after many wonderful saints (and martyrs) before us, and it is wise to learn from them (Romans 15:4). Those of us who are living at a time and place with abundant access to God's Word and freedom to be a Christian should at the very least be diligent enough in our own studies to get the gospel "message of truth" correct and free from false teachings – those who face tribulation, persecution and even death in the name of the Lord Jesus Christ deserve no less from us.

It's an honor, a privilege, and a blessing to write a book like this. I'm very grateful for being given the opportunity to do it and for His unbelievable slowness to anger, His lovingkindness, and His seemingly endless patience with me. At some particular times, you realize the full weight, authority, and power of the Living Word, which you are being asked to handle and represent – it can be quite emotional. For the Word of God is "living, active and sharper than a two-edged sword" (Hebrews 4:12) – yes, it is alive! It is the power of eternal life.

> Blessed *be* the God and Father of our Lord Jesus Christ, who has blessed us with every spiritual blessing in the heavenly *places* in Christ, just as He chose us in Him before the foundation of the world, that we would be holy and blameless before Him. In love He predestined us to adoption as sons through Jesus Christ to Himself, according to the kind intention of His will, to the praise of the glory of His grace, which He freely bestowed on us in the Beloved. In Him we have redemption through His blood, the forgiveness of our trespasses, according to the riches of His grace which He lavished on us. In all wisdom and insight He made known to us the mystery of His will, according to His kind intention which He purposed in Him with a view to an administration suitable to the fullness of the times, *that is*, the summing up of all things in Christ, things in the heavens and things on the earth. In Him also we have obtained an inheritance, having been predestined according to His purpose who works all things after the counsel of His will, to the end that we who were the first to hope in Christ would be to the praise of His glory. In Him, you also, after listening to <u>the message of truth</u>, the gospel of your salvation— having also believed, you were sealed in Him with the Holy Spirit of promise, who is given as a pledge of our inheritance, with a view to the redemption of *God's own possession*, to the praise of His glory. – Ephesians 1:3-14

How then will they call on Him in whom they have not believed? How will they believe in Him whom they have not heard? And how will they hear without a preacher? How will they preach unless they are sent? Just as it is written, "HOW BEAUTIFUL ARE THE FEET OF THOSE WHO BRING GOOD NEWS OF GOOD THINGS!"

However, they did not all heed the good news; for Isaiah says, "LORD, WHO HAS BELIEVED OUR REPORT?" So faith *comes* from hearing, and hearing by the word of Christ. – Romans 10:11-17

THE PROMISE OF ETERNAL LIFE AWAITS

And lastly, we should greatly heed the warning that is given to us in Scripture that there comes a time when God will no longer strive to reach those who have hardened their hearts beyond the point of no return:

> Then the LORD said, "My Spirit shall not strive with man forever, because he also is flesh." – Genesis 6:3

Yes, today, this very day that you are reading this sentence, is the day of (your) salvation – should you so choose. Do not keep putting it off, for you may not get tomorrow. While the patience of God is massive in waiting for people everywhere to repent and turn to Him, it will not last forever:

> And working together *with Him*, we also urge you not to receive the grace of God in vain— for He says,
>
> > "AT THE ACCEPTABLE TIME I LISTENED TO YOU,
> > AND ON THE DAY OF SALVATION I HELPED YOU."
>
> Behold, now is "THE ACCEPTABLE TIME," behold, now is "THE DAY OF SALVATION." – 2 Corinthians 6:1-2

May God richly bless you with wisdom and understanding of the "message of truth." And may you choose to walk each day towards eternal life with God and His Christ Jesus. Amen.

– In Jesus Christ, R. John Anderson

PART I:

GOD, HUMANITY & SIN

1.0 GOD CREATED
(There is a God)

In the beginning God created the heavens and the earth. – Genesis 1:1

In the Beginning. Realize that there is a Creator, the Lord God of Hosts, who "created the heavens and the earth" and everything in it. He created everything in seven (7) literal days – not over millions or billions of years as evolutionists claim. Furthermore, life itself did not just randomly "evolve" out of a sea of primordial goo by a "stroke of lightning" accident, as the evolutionists would also have you believe.

The truth is that God brought all things into existence – the universe, the Earth, and you and me! He did this by simply speaking His Word! This is recorded in the very first verse of the Bible:

> In the beginning God created the heavens and the earth. The earth was formless and void, and darkness was over the surface of the deep, and the Spirit of God was moving over the surface of the waters. Then God said, "Let there be light"; and there was light. – Genesis 1:1-3

> The LORD founded the earth by wisdom,
> He established the heavens by understanding. – Proverbs 3:19

> "YOU, LORD, IN THE BEGINNING LAID THE FOUNDATION OF THE EARTH, AND THE HEAVENS ARE THE WORKS OF YOUR HANDS." – Hebrews 1:10

Then God "breathed" life into man and woman, as explained in the next chapter. Imagine the staggering power in such statements; the enormity of the above statements should make you stop in wonder, awe, and amazement at what a big, great, powerful, and awesome God He is.

Christianity believes in one God – i.e., that there is only one Being with the nature of divinity/deity. God is not a "force" as some new-agers like to claim – He is a real spiritual Being, with feelings, emotions, actions, love, laws, and also justice. God introduces Himself in the very first verse of the first book of the Bible and is identified by the word "Elohim" (ĕlôhîym or אֱלֹהִים in Hebrew, theos or θεός in Greek), which conveys the quality or nature of being divine – i.e., having the essential nature of deity:

> In the beginning God [אֱלֹהִים, ĕlôhîym] created the heavens and the earth. – Genesis 1:1

God's name is subsequently given as "YHWH" (or "YHVH") in the original Hebrew texts of the Old Testament:

> This is the account of the heavens and the earth when they were created, in the day that the LORD [יְהוָה, YHWH, yehôvâh, Yahweh] God [אֱלֹהִים, ĕlôhîym] made earth and heaven. – Genesis 2:4

> And God spake unto Moses, and said unto him, I am the LORD [יְהוָה, YHWH, yehôvâh, Yahweh]: And I appeared unto Abraham, unto Isaac, and unto Jacob, by the name of God Almighty, but by my name JEHOVAH [יְהוָה, YHWH, yehôvâh, Yahweh] was I not known to them. – Exodus 6:2-3 (KJV Translation)

God spoke further to Moses and said to him, "I am the LORD [יְהוָה, YHWH, yehôvâh, Yahweh]; and I appeared to Abraham, Isaac, and Jacob, as God Almighty, but *by* My name, LORD [יְהוָה, YHWH, yehôvâh, Yahweh], I did not make Myself known to them." – Exodus 6:2-3 (NASB Translation)

The name of God, "YHWH," called the tetragrammaton (i.e., four letters), means "to be" (e.g., "I exist") – indicating God's self-existent, eternal nature, for He has no beginning and no end (Revelation 1:17, 22:13). "YHWH" is rendered in various English Bible translations in several ways (you see two translations KJV and NASB above), including:

- JEHOVAH (JEHOVAH, Jehovah, Yehovah, yehôvâh),
- LORD or LORD or GOD (all caps or small caps),
- Yahweh (or Jahweh).

Since God's name "YHWH" is unpronounceable, the words "Jehovah" and "Yahweh" have been constructed (made up) by adding vowels (in the first case from "Adonai") to the "YHWH" tetragrammaton in order to make the name pronounceable. So for example, where you see "LORD God" in Scripture (e.g., Genesis 2:4), this reads as "YHWH (Jehovah, Yahweh) Elohim" ("yehôvâh ĕlôhîym" or "יְהוָה אֱלֹהִים"). Matthew Henry writes on Genesis 2:4: [2]

> In these verses, I. Here is a name given to the Creator which we have not yet met with, and that is *Jehovah* - the LORD, in capital letters, which are constantly used in our English translation to intimate that in the original it is *Jehovah*. All along, in the first chapter, he was called *Elohim - a God of power;* but now *Jehovah Elohim - a God of power and perfection,* a finishing God. As we find him known by his name Jehovah when he appeared to perform what he had promised (Exo 6:3), so now we have him known by that name, when he had perfected what he had begun. *Jehovah* is that great and incommunicable name of God which denotes his having his being of himself, and his giving being to all things; fitly therefore is he called by that name now that heaven and earth are finished.

The word "Adonai" (ădônây, meaning Lord or Master) is also used for God, which is rendered as "Lord" (standard capitalization) in English Bibles. So, for example, where you see it written "Lord GOD," this reads as "Adonai YHWH" ("ădônây yehôvâh"):

> Abram [Abraham] said, "O Lord [ădônây] GOD [יְהוָה, YHWH, yehôvâh, Jehovah], what will You give me, since I am childless, and the heir of my house is Eliezer of Damascus?" – Genesis 15:2

God's name is also given in expression (idiom) form as "I AM WHO I AM" (or "I AM THAT I AM"), or simply "I AM":

> Then Moses said to God, "Behold, I am going to the sons of Israel, and I will say to them, 'The God of your fathers has sent me to you.' Now they may say to me, 'What is His name?' What shall I say to them?" God said to Moses, "I AM WHO I AM"; and He said, "Thus you shall say to the sons of Israel, 'I AM [היה, hâyâh, havah] has sent me to you.'" – Exodus 3:13-14

---

[2] Henry, Matthew. Exposition of the Old and New Testaments, London. 1706-1710/1721.

An idiom is an expression that has a meaning which cannot be understood by the individual words. This expression could be translated as "I will become whatsoever I may become," again denoting God's essential self-existent eternal nature of "being" or "He who becometh." In effect, the expression "I AM" explains what the name "YHWH" means – God is externally self-existing and "the same yesterday and today and forever" (Hebrews 13:8).

Additionally, the word "Elohim" is plural, and we understand today that God exists as three Persons: Father, Son (Jesus Christ), and Holy Spirit (or Holy Ghost). Each Person is fully God and also fully One Themselves. God uses plural pronouns (Us, Our) in Old Testament Scripture when referring to Himself. This concept of a Holy Trinity (One God, Three Persons) is extremely difficult for us to comprehend fully. In fact, our finite mortal minds cannot even begin to approach God's infinite mind, nor His infinite knowledge and wisdom, for it is written:

> "For My thoughts are not your thoughts,
> Nor are your ways My ways," declares the LORD.
> "For *as* the heavens are higher than the earth,
> So are My ways higher than your ways
> And My thoughts than your thoughts." – Isaiah 55:8-9

Wayne Jackson writes on the subject of the Triune Godhead:[3]

> It is also clear that the Scriptures teach that there is a personal distinction between those individuals identified in the New Testament as the Father, the Son, and the Holy Spirit, and these persons are in some sense **three**.
>
> Study very carefully the following passages in which the persons of the divine Godhead are distinguished: Matthew 3:16-17; 28:19; Luke 1:35; John 14:26; 15:26; 2 Corinthians 13:14; Ephesians 2:18; 4:4-6; 1 Peter 1:2; Jude 20-21; Revelation 1:4-5.
>
> It is obvious that these inspired verses reveal three separate persons.
>
> Furthermore, additional biblical data reveal that each of these three persons is God—i.e., each possesses the quality or nature of **deity**. The Father is deity (Ephesians 1:3), as is the Son (Hebrews 1:8), and so also the Holy Spirit (Acts 5:3-4).
>
> Any elementary student of logic knows perfectly well that the Godhead cannot be both one and three without a logical contradiction being involved—if the adjectives "one" and "three" are employed **in the identical sense**.
>
> But the fact of the matter is, they are not used in the same sense. There is but **one** divine **nature**, but there are **three** distinct **personalities** possessing that unified set of infinite qualities. Thus, there is no contradiction at all.
>
> Without a recognition of the above principle, some Bible passages would be difficult to harmonize.

Yes, God is the great "I AM." He is the "Lord of hosts." He is not bound by time and space as we are in this physical universe. Nothing can surprise Him or catch Him off guard. He is omniscient (all-knowing – past, present, and future); nothing is hidden from Him, and there is nothing that He doesn't know. He is omnipresent (everywhere

---

[3] Jackson, Wayne. "The Biblical Doctrine of the Godhead." *ChristianCourier.com*. Access date: May 16, 2019. https://christiancourier.com/articles/1488-biblical-doctrine-of-the-godhead-the

present simultaneously). He is omnipotent (all-powerful) – nothing is impossible with God. He "upholds all things by the word of His power." It is He who created and sustains all life – without God, there can be no life. He is majesty defined. "God is love" itself (1 John 4:8). Amazing!

But above all, God is "HOLY." Holy means sacred and morally perfect (pure) – there is not even the smallest or most infinitesimal amount or trace of impurity, evil, wicked thought, action, or character defect in Him. His holiness is beyond anything we can imagine; please do not underestimate this fact. Our human minds often fail to ascribe to God His proper holiness, while we simultaneously grossly underappreciate how bad even the most trivial/minor of sins are when compared to a Holy God. The depth and breadth of His holiness are hard for us mere mortal humans to fully comprehend. It is even important for those of us who are trying to lead others into truth to be diligent about this matter, daily humbling ourselves before God and reminding ourselves of His unimaginable holiness and glory. It is altogether too easy to become complacent and treat Him casually and not with the honor and respect that He deserves.

Many choose to focus solely on the fact that the Bible tells us that "God is love" and completely ignore that Scripture also clearly tells us that He hates sin and that He is a God of justice – He is perfectly just (righteous, correct, perfect in rule of law). Scripture abundantly warns us that He will therefore bring all sin into judgment on the Great Day of Judgment (explained in detail in an upcoming chapter).

GOD IS SPIRIT

He is not a material being like we humans are and like the physical universe is – the world around us that we can see, hear, touch, taste, smell, and feel. Scripture tells us that everything we see around us in this physical material universe was actually created out of things that are unseen, out of spiritual things. And it is only God who can reveal spiritual things to us, and He does so through the Holy Bible, the inspired Word of God:

> By faith we understand that the worlds were prepared by the word of God, so that what is seen was not made out of things which are visible. – Hebrews 11:3

> "God is spirit, and those who worship Him must worship in spirit and truth." – John 4:24

Here are some things Scripture says about the creation of this world:

> By the word of the LORD the heavens were made,
> And by the breath of His mouth all their host.
> He gathers the waters of the sea together as a heap;
> He lays up the deeps in storehouses.
> Let all the earth fear the LORD;
> Let all the inhabitants of the world stand in awe of Him.
> For He spoke, and it was done;
> He commanded, and it stood fast. – Psalm 33:6-9

> For in six days the LORD made the heavens and the earth, the sea and all that is in them, and rested on the seventh day. – Exodus 20:11

> All things came into being through Him, and apart from Him nothing came into being that has come into being. – John 1:3

> Thus declares the Lord who stretches out the heavens, lays the foundation of the earth, and forms the spirit of man within him. – Zechariah 12:1

> For by Him all things were created, *both* in the heavens and on earth, visible and invisible, whether thrones or dominions or rulers or authorities—all things have been created through Him and for Him. – Colossians 1:16

> "'Ah Lord GOD! Behold, You have made the heavens and the earth by Your great power and by Your outstretched arm! Nothing is too difficult for You.'" – Jeremiah 32:17

> For thus says the LORD, who created the heavens (He is the God who formed the earth and made it, He established it *and* did not create it a waste place, *but* formed it to be inhabited), "I am the LORD, and there is none else." – Isaiah 45:18

> "Of old You founded the earth;
> And the heavens are the work of Your hands.
> "Even they will perish, but You endure;
> And all of them will wear out like a garment.
> Like clothing You will change them and they will be changed.
> "But You are the same,
> And Your years will not come to an end." – Psalm 102:25-27

> The earth is the LORD'S, and all it contains,
> The world, and those who dwell in it. – Psalm 24:1

> Do you not know? Have you not heard?
> The Everlasting God, the LORD,
> the Creator of the ends of the earth
> Does not become weary or tired.
> His understanding is inscrutable. – Isaiah 40:28

Those who mock God and refuse to believe that He exists because "science can't prove it" fail to understand this fact. God is worshiped in spirit – "no one has seen God at any time" (John 1:18). It takes faith to find God, for it is written that "without faith it is impossible to please Him, for he who comes to God must believe that He is and that He is a rewarder of those who seek Him" (Hebrews 11:6); but it is also written that "You will seek Me and find Me when you search for Me with all your heart" (Jeremiah 29:13).

The Bible provides overwhelming evidence for Him, and many other areas provide supporting evidence that what the Bible says is indeed true: areas such as archaeology, geology, historical documents, eyewitnesses, and even scientific studies. So, God is not without evidence and witnesses as to His existence, for He has revealed Himself to us through 1) Evidence as seen in nature of Creation, 2) His Holy Word the Bible, and 3) through His Son Jesus Christ – so we are "without excuse" in denying Him (see Romans 1). The Bible was supernaturally given to us through human writers inspired by the Holy Spirit. It is without error (in the original language manuscripts) and without contradiction. It was given to us over the span of several thousand years as God progressively revealed Himself to us, and His plan for Creation unfolded in human history.

The Bible also states that it is the spiritual world that is eternal, not the material world. The material world we see around us (the Earth, Sun, Moon, stars) and everything that we taste, touch, smell, hear and see is not eternal. Furthermore, this material world (i.e., Earth) is in the middle of a raging spiritual war, with the forces of evil led by Satan (the Devil) and his servants on one side and God and His saints (servants) on the other side (this is explained more fully in subsequent chapters).

God dwells in unimaginable, unapproachable light. He appears in the brightest, purest white light you've ever seen, or ever imagined, not an impure light as from a lightbulb or the sun. Imagine something a million times brighter or purer – a white so pure it cannot even be described, only felt. That light cannot be approached by any man or woman at this time, due to our fallen state, our current fleshly bodies, and our sin; or, in other words, God says: "you cannot see my face, for man shall not see me and live." But a time is coming when we will see His face!

Scripture also tells us that "God is love" and that this perfect, just, holy, loving, and merciful God desires to have a relationship with His created beings (us) – and with you! I realize how hard it is to conceptualize and rationalize such enormous statements and such an enormous, powerful, awesome, and splendid God, but it is written that "you will find Him if you search for [seek] Him with all your heart and all your soul"!

God rules the universe (all of Creation) by His rule of law, and we are His creatures. As you will also read in subsequent chapters, it is sin, resulting from pride and disobedience to God which separates man from God at the present time (although there is hope and a cure for the sickness of sin). It is pride and arrogance which causes man to refuse to see and acknowledge his own sin and that there is a God: And man doesn't want to be told what to do. Man doesn't want to bow down to anyone or anything – he wants to be his own God! But one must discard the wisdom of man (the wisdom of this world) to see God, for it is but mere foolishness before God:

> Let no man deceive himself. If any man among you thinks that he is wise in this age, he must become foolish, so that he may become wise. For the wisdom of this world is foolishness before God. For it is written, "*He is* THE ONE WHO CATCHES THE WISE IN THEIR CRAFTINESS"; and again, "THE LORD KNOWS THE REASONINGS of the wise, THAT THEY ARE USELESS." – 1 Corinthians 3:18-20

Only God, through His Spirit, can reveal the things of God:

> Now we have received, not the spirit of the world, but the Spirit who is from God, so that we may know the things freely given to us by God, which things we also speak, not in words taught by human wisdom, but in those taught by the Spirit, combining spiritual *thoughts* with spiritual *words*.

> But a natural man does not accept the things of the Spirit of God, for they are foolishness to him; and he cannot understand them, because they are spiritually appraised. – 1 Corinthians 2:12-14

EVIDENCE OF GOD

Scripture states that man "suppresses the truth [of God] in unrighteousness" (Romans 1:18) and that all men are "without excuse" in denying the existence of God:

> …that which is known about God is evident within them [each of us]; for God made it evident to them. For since the creation of the world His invisible attributes, His eternal power and divine nature, have been clearly seen, being understood

through what has been made, so that they are without excuse [with regards to denying that there is in fact a God]. For even though they knew God, they did not honor Him as God or give thanks, but they became futile in their speculations, and their foolish heart was darkened. Professing to be wise, they became fools, and exchanged the glory of the incorruptible God for an image in the form of corruptible man and of birds and four-footed animals and crawling creatures. – Romans 1:19-23

Scripture also states that nature itself provides evidence of God, is a witness for the existence of God, and that the voice of that witness has gone out "through all the earth" for all to hear:

[Paul and Barnabas, apostles]…saying, "Men, why are you doing these things? We are also men of the same nature as you, and preach the gospel to you that you should turn from these vain things to a living God, WHO MADE THE HEAVEN AND THE EARTH AND THE SEA AND ALL THAT IS IN THEM. In the generations gone by He permitted all the nations to go their own ways; and yet He did not leave Himself without witness, in that He did good and gave you rains from heaven and fruitful seasons, satisfying your hearts with food and gladness." – Acts 14:15-17

The heavens declare the glory of God,
and the sky above proclaims his handiwork.
Day to day pours out speech,
and night to night reveals knowledge.
There is no speech, nor are there words,
whose voice is not heard.
Their voice goes out through all the earth,
and their words to the end of the world. – Psalm 19:1-4 (ESV)

If you look all around you, you will see the wonderfully synchronized majesty of creation, God's Creation – the Sun, Moon, and stars all designed and put in their places just so to work perfectly to support life here on Earth, the Earth's axis tilted just so for seasons, the Moon put in exactly the right distance from the Earth for its impact on tidal forces and oceans, the Earth at just the precise distance from the sun to allow water which sustains life – not too close so that the sun evaporates all the oceans and not too far so that all water isn't frozen solid.

When you look with an open mind, you can see all this as evidence that this world was created by intelligence. Furthermore, the laws of Physics are exact and precise – the law of gravity, the laws of motion, the laws of thermodynamics, etc. The laws of logic are just as precise. So are the laws of mathematics. These laws did not "evolve" out of goo, so where did they come from? God created these physical laws to govern His universe and life. "For God is not *a God* of confusion" and disorder, but of order and intelligence – and the physical laws of the universe represent that order and design.

The "Theory of Evolution" (notice, it's not called the Facts of Evolution) false teaching (and fake science) causes many to disbelieve in God and doubt the Bible – before they even begin to read it! That is the intent of that false teaching/fake science. The very real forces of evil know that if you don't believe the very first sentence(s) of the Bible, you will not read or believe the rest! That is why "evolution" is one of the first and biggest false teachings that you encounter when trying to present God and the

The Message of Truth

gospel message, for we are brainwashed since birth to believe the lie of evolution, which is spread nonstop, 24/7/365 (literally every day and night, all day long) from every media outlet on the planet, shouted out at the highest volume level possible, and taught all the way from preschool on up through university level and beyond!

You will see that this pattern repeats itself throughout this entire book – for every single step I take in presenting the gospel "message of truth" to you, there are corresponding false teachings (lies, deceptions, and snares of man) set up to stop you at that step from believing and continuing on to eternal life. At the end of each chapter is a list of the false teachings that you must confront to move forward and continue on the path towards eternal life. Also, know that you will face the lies and false teachings of man not only from the secular God-denying world but also from within the church itself – from those who profess to be Christians! Many "Christian" churches, pastors, and teachers are not teaching what is written in Scripture; this book identifies many of those false teachings for you, so you are not deceived.

And contrary to what many believe or have been taught to believe, science does not disprove God or the Bible; more information on this subject is given in the upcoming chapter on Science vs. the Bible. In fact, the more science discovers and advances and the more we learn about God's creation – the more it confirms the truth of the Bible! And if you are honest with yourself, you must admit that everything you see around you in the physical world says order and intelligence – and it says so very clearly. You actually must suppress that truth and evidence to deny there is a God.

Matthew Henry writes on Genesis 1:1:[4]

> Atheism is folly, and atheists are the greatest fools in nature; for they see there is a world that could not make itself, and yet they will not own there is a God that made it. Doubtless, they are without excuse, but the god of this world (Satan) has blinded their minds.

No, this world did not come about gradually over millions or billions of years, nor did life "evolve" randomly out of goo and mud puddles. God simply "spoke" – and it was. Amazing! If you're looking for a "big bang" to start the universe, let me tell you right now that it doesn't get any bigger than that! Don't you want to know more about this God?

We will come shortly to the matter of why creation isn't perfect (any longer) and why there are earthquakes, floods, and other natural disasters as well as disease and death in the world today (hint: those are all because of the sinful actions of man, not God).

FALSE TEACHING(S) YOU WILL ENCOUNTER:

- Atheism (there is no God)
- The "Theory" of Evolution (and millions of years for earth history)
- Satan (the Devil) is just a myth
- The Bible is simply fictional "myths, folklore, and poetry"
- God is simply some kind of "force" or "a state of inner being" or an "inner feeling"

---

[4] Henry, Matthew. *Exposition of the Old and New Testaments*, London. 1706-1710/1721.

RELATED SCRIPTURE:

…God, who gives life to the dead and calls into being that which does not exist. – Romans 4:17

Thus the heavens and the earth were completed, and all their hosts. By the seventh day God completed His work which He had done, and He rested on the seventh day from all His work which He had done. – Genesis 2:1-2

Then Moses said to God, "Behold, I am going to the sons of Israel, and I will say to them, 'The God of your fathers has sent me to you.' Now they may say to me, 'What is His name?' What shall I say to them?" God said to Moses, "I AM WHO I AM"; and He said, "Thus you shall say to the sons of Israel, 'I AM has sent me to you.'" – Exodus 3:13-14

The fool has said in his heart, "There is no God." – Psalm 14:1

Rather, let God be found true, though every man be found a liar. – Romans 3:4 [Note: These verses speak to things like the lies of the "theory of evolution" and those who deny that there is a God.]

Lord, You have been our dwelling place in all generations.
Before the mountains were born
Or You gave birth to the earth and the world,
Even from everlasting to everlasting, You are God.

You turn man back into dust
And say, "Return, O children of men."
For a thousand years in Your sight
Are like yesterday when it passes by,
Or *as* a watch in the night. – Psalm 90:1-4

O LORD, our Lord,
How majestic is Your name in all the earth,
Who have displayed Your splendor above the heavens! – Psalm 8:1

And blessed be His glorious name forever;
And may the whole earth be filled with His glory.
Amen, and Amen. – Psalm 72:19

Bless the LORD, O my soul,
And all that is within me, *bless* His holy name.
Bless the LORD, O my soul,
And forget none of His benefits;
Who pardons all your iniquities,
Who heals all your diseases;
Who redeems your life from the pit,
Who crowns you with lovingkindness and compassion;
Who satisfies your years with good things,
So that your youth is renewed like the eagle. – Psalm 103:1-5

God, after He spoke long ago to the fathers in the prophets in many portions and in many ways, in these last days has spoken to us in His Son, whom He appointed heir of all things, through whom also He made the world. And He is the radiance of His glory and the exact representation of His nature, and upholds all things by the word of His power. – Hebrews 1:1-3a

For the things which are seen are temporal, but the things which are not seen are eternal. – 2 Corinthians 4:18b

…for the form of this world is passing away. – 1 Corinthians 7:31b

For God is not *a God* of confusion… – 1 Corinthians 14:33

Oh, the depth of the riches both of the wisdom and knowledge of God! How unsearchable are His judgments and unfathomable His ways! For WHO HAS KNOWN THE MIND OF THE LORD, OR WHO BECAME HIS COUNSELOR? Or WHO HAS FIRST GIVEN TO HIM THAT IT MIGHT BE PAID BACK TO HIM AGAIN? For from Him and through Him and to Him are all things. To Him *be* the glory forever. Amen. – Romans 11:33-36

Great is our Lord and abundant in strength;
His understanding is infinite. – Psalm 147:5

"But an hour is coming, and now is, when the true worshipers will worship the Father in spirit and truth; for such people the Father seeks to be His worshipers. God is spirit, and those who worship Him must worship in spirit and truth." – John 4:23-24

[God]…who alone possesses immortality and dwells in unapproachable light, whom no man has seen or can see. – 1 Timothy 6:16

The one who does not love does not know God, for God is love. – 1 John 4:8

Then Moses said, "I pray You, show me Your glory!" And He said, "I Myself will make all My goodness pass before you, and will proclaim the name of the LORD before you; and I will be gracious to whom I will be gracious, and will show compassion on whom I will show compassion." But He said, "You cannot see My face, for no man can see Me and live!" – Exodus 33:18-20

Then said I, Woe is me! for I am undone; because I am a man of unclean lips, and I dwell in the midst of a people of unclean lips: for mine eyes have seen the King, the LORD of hosts. – Isaiah 6:5 (KJV)

"How great are His signs
And how mighty are His wonders!
His kingdom is an everlasting kingdom
And His dominion is from generation to generation." – Daniel 4:3

"*It is God* who removes the mountains, they know not *how*,
When He overturns them in His anger;
Who shakes the earth out of its place,
And its pillars tremble;
Who commands the sun not to shine,
And sets a seal upon the stars;
Who alone stretches out the heavens
And tramples down the waves of the sea;
Who makes the Bear, Orion and the Pleiades,
And the chambers of the south;

Who does great things, unfathomable,
And wondrous works without number." – Job 9:5-10

"But now ask the beasts, and let them teach you;
And the birds of the heavens, and let them tell you.
"Or speak to the earth, and let it teach you;
And let the fish of the sea declare to you.
"Who among all these does not know
That the hand of the LORD has done this,
In whose hand is the life of every living thing,
And the breath of all mankind?" – Job 12:7-10

"He stretches out the north over empty space
And hangs the earth on nothing.
"He wraps up the waters in His clouds,
And the cloud does not burst under them.
"He obscures the face of the full moon
And spreads His cloud over it.
"He has inscribed a circle on the surface of the waters
At the boundary of light and darkness.
"The pillars of heaven tremble
And are amazed at His rebuke.
"He quieted the sea with His power,
And by His understanding He shattered Rahab.
"By His breath the heavens are cleared;
His hand has pierced the fleeing serpent.
"Behold, these are the fringes of His ways;
And how faint a word we hear of Him!
But His mighty thunder, who can understand?" – Job 26:7-14

"Behold, God is exalted, and we do not know *Him*;
The number of His years is unsearchable.
"For He draws up the drops of water,
They distill rain from the mist,
Which the clouds pour down,
They drip upon man abundantly.
"Can anyone understand the spreading of the clouds,
The thundering of His pavilion?
"Behold, He spreads His lightning about Him,
And He covers the depths of the sea." – Job 36:26-30

Seek the LORD while He may be found;
Call upon Him while He is near.
Let the wicked forsake his way
And the unrighteous man his thoughts;
And let him return to the LORD,
And He will have compassion on him,
And to our God,
For He will abundantly pardon. – Isaiah 55:6-7

"At this also my heart trembles,
And leaps from its place.
"Listen closely to the thunder of His voice,
And the rumbling that goes out from His mouth.
"Under the whole heaven He lets it loose,
And His lightning to the ends of the earth.
"After it, a voice roars;
He thunders with His majestic voice,
And He does not restrain the lightnings when His voice is heard.
"God thunders with His voice wondrously,
Doing great things which we cannot comprehend.
"For to the snow He says, 'Fall on the earth,'
And to the downpour and the rain, 'Be strong.'
"He seals the hand of every man,
That all men may know His work.
"Then the beast goes into its lair
And remains in its den.
"Out of the south comes the storm,
And out of the north the cold.
"From the breath of God ice is made,
And the expanse of the waters is frozen.
"Also with moisture He loads the thick cloud;
He disperses the cloud of His lightning.
"It changes direction, turning around by His guidance,
That it may do whatever He commands it
On the face of the inhabited earth.
"Whether for correction, or for His world,
Or for lovingkindness, He causes it to happen.

"Listen to this, O Job,
Stand and consider the wonders of God.
"Do you know how God establishes them,
And makes the lightning of His cloud to shine?
"Do you know about the layers of the thick clouds,
The wonders of one perfect in knowledge,
You whose garments are hot,
When the land is still because of the south wind?
"Can you, with Him, spread out the skies,
Strong as a molten mirror?
"Teach us what we shall say to Him;
We cannot arrange *our case* because of darkness.
"Shall it be told Him that I would speak?
Or should a man say that he would be swallowed up?

"Now men do not see the light which is bright in the skies;
But the wind has passed and cleared them.
"Out of the north comes golden *splendor*;
Around God is awesome majesty.
"The Almighty—we cannot find Him;

He is exalted in power
And He will not do violence to justice and abundant righteousness.
"Therefore men fear Him;
He does not regard any who are wise of heart." – Job 37

Then the LORD answered Job out of the whirlwind and said,

> "Who is this that darkens counsel
> By words without knowledge?
> "Now gird up your loins like a man,
> And I will ask you, and you instruct Me!
> "Where were you when I laid the foundation of the earth?
> Tell *Me*, if you have understanding,
> Who set its measurements? Since you know.
> Or who stretched the line on it?
> "On what were its bases sunk?
> Or who laid its cornerstone,
> When the morning stars sang together
> And all the sons of God shouted for joy?" – Job 38:1-7

Bless the LORD, O my soul!
O LORD my God, You are very great;
You are clothed with splendor and majesty,
Covering Yourself with light as with a cloak,
Stretching out heaven like a *tent* curtain.
He lays the beams of His upper chambers in the waters;
He makes the clouds His chariot;
He walks upon the wings of the wind;
He makes the winds His messengers,
Flaming fire His ministers. – Psalm 104:1-4

"I am the Alpha and the Omega," says the Lord God, "who is and who was and who is to come, the Almighty." – Revelation 1:8

And the four living creatures, each one of them having six wings, are full of eyes around and within; and day and night they do not cease to say,

> "HOLY, HOLY, HOLY *is* THE LORD GOD, THE ALMIGHTY, WHO WAS AND WHO IS AND WHO IS TO COME." – Revelation 4:8

You will seek Me and find *Me* when you search for Me with all your heart. – Jeremiah 29:13

"Worthy are You, our Lord and our God, to receive glory and honor and power; for You created all things, and because of Your will they existed, and were created." – Revelation 4:11

So Paul stood in the midst of the Areopagus and said, "Men of Athens, I observe that you are very religious in all respects. For while I was passing through and examining the objects of your worship, I also found an altar with this inscription, 'TO AN UNKNOWN GOD.' Therefore what you worship in ignorance, this I proclaim to you. The God who made the world and all things in it, since He is Lord of heaven and earth, does not dwell in temples made with hands; nor is He served by human hands, as though He needed anything, since He Himself gives to all *people* life and breath and all things; and He made from one *man* every nation of mankind to live on all the face of the earth, having determined *their* appointed times and the boundaries of their habitation, that they would seek God, if perhaps they might grope for Him and find Him, though He is not far from each one of us; for in Him we live and move and exist, as even some of your own poets have said, 'For we also are His children.' Being then the children of God, we ought not to think that the Divine Nature is like gold or silver or stone, an image formed by the art and thought of man. Therefore having overlooked the times of ignorance, God is now declaring to men that all *people* everywhere should repent, because He has fixed a day in which He will judge the world in righteousness through a Man whom He has appointed, having furnished proof to all men by raising Him from the dead." – Acts 17:22-31

For the wrath of God is revealed from heaven against all ungodliness and unrighteousness of men who suppress the truth in unrighteousness, because that which is known about God is evident within them; for God made it evident to them. For since the creation of the world His invisible attributes, His eternal power and divine nature, have been clearly seen, being understood through what has been made, so that they are without excuse. For even though they knew God, they did not honor Him as God or give thanks, but they became futile in their speculations, and their foolish heart was darkened. Professing to be wise, they became fools, and exchanged the glory of the incorruptible God for an image in the form of corruptible man and of birds and four-footed animals and crawling creatures. – Romans 1:18-23

But the LORD is the true God;
He is the living God and the everlasting King.
The earth quakes at His wrath,
And the nations cannot endure His indignation. – Jeremiah 10:10

For they themselves report concerning us the kind of reception we had among you, and how you turned to God from idols to serve the living and true God. – 1 Thessalonians 1:9 (ESV)

If you seek Him [God], He will let you find Him. – 1 Chronicles 28:9

1.1 MALE AND FEMALE

God created man in His own image, in the image of God He created him; male and female He created them. – Genesis 1:27

God Created Humanity. God created and breathed life into mankind, first through Adam and Eve, in the perfect Garden of Eden:

> Then the LORD God formed the man of dust from the ground, and breathed into his nostrils the breath of life; and the man became a living person. – Genesis 2:7

Man is a created being, not the creator. We were created out of the dust of the ground, but we are also created in the image (likeness) of God – meaning we all (each of us) have an immortal spirit. Some think of this as our soul; for the purpose of this book, spirit and soul can be considered the same.

> Then God said, "Let Us make man in Our image, according to Our likeness; and let them rule over the fish of the sea and over the birds of the sky and over the cattle and over all the earth, and over every creeping thing that creeps on the earth." God created man in His own image, in the image of God He created him; male and female He created them. – Genesis 1:26-27

> All came from the dust and all return to the dust. – Ecclesiastes 3:20

> "Because from it [the ground, dust] you were taken;
> For you are dust,
> And to dust you shall return." – Genesis 3:19

We are the property and possession of the Lord; we are not our own. He owns us; all of us:

> The earth is the LORD'S, and all it contains,
> The world, and those who dwell in it. – Psalm 24:1

Many will refuse to accept this fact and therefore deny the Lord. Please do not make that same mistake. It is only pride that leads man to take that position, and pride leads to death. The Lord is the potter, and we are just clay vessels:

> But now, LORD, You are our Father;
> We are the clay, and You our potter,
> And all of us are the work of Your hand. – Isaiah 64:8

> Just as a father has compassion on *his* children,
> So the LORD has compassion on those who fear Him.
> For He Himself knows our form;
> He is mindful that we are *nothing but* dust. – Psalm 104:13-14

It is God who sustains all life everywhere; for without God, there is no life:

> The Spirit of God has made me,
> And the breath of the Almighty gives me life. – Job 33:4

> Your steadfast love, O LORD, extends to the heavens,
> your faithfulness to the clouds.

> Your righteousness is like the mountains of God;
> your judgments are like the great deep;
> man and beast you save [sustain, give life to], O LORD. – Psalm 36:5-6 (ESV)

> ...yet for us there is one God, the Father, from whom are all things and for whom we exist, and one Lord, Jesus Christ, through whom are all things and through whom we exist. – 1 Corinthians 8:6 (ESV)

> ...one God and Father of all who is over all and through all and in all. – Ephesians 4:6

> He is before all things, and in Him all things hold together. – Colossians 1:17

> And He is the radiance of His glory and the exact representation of His nature, and upholds all things by the word of His power. – Hebrews 1:3

The Bible explains and teaches us the ways of God, which lead to life; all other ways ("the ways of man") lead to eternal death. Thankfully, we serve a God of love, who "is love." In the Bible, you will also read that God is a "jealous" God; that confused me greatly at first because I've only known jealousy as destructive negative human emotion. But that phrase actually means that God has zealous, burning, and passionate love for us; He desires that we seek only Him, not the things of man or this world, nor worship idols made of gold, silver, bronze, stone, or wood – for it is only He who provides life. He jealously guards us, and this is why we are told to seek Him with "all our heart, all our minds, and all our soul."

Contrary to popular opinion and false teachings, you do not pass away into "nothingness" (annihilation) after death – while your earthly body will die, your spirit will live on forever! As explained in the previous chapter, this physical world is not all there is as materialists proclaim; and this life is not all there is. Furthermore, everyone who has ever lived will be resurrected in immortal bodies! The state of your spirit at death (sinful or righteous) determines where you will spend eternity. For a detailed treatment of this topic, please see another book we publish called *Beyond the Tomb* by H.M. Riggle (Church of God, pastor, evangelist and author, and president of The Gospel Trumpet Publishing Co., 1933-1946). It covers your eternal soul and destiny in great detail and provides solid biblical support. A snippet from that book is given below on the origin of man:[5]

> The question was once asked, "What is man?" This is a subject which should occupy our minds and be considered with much careful study. We have acquired knowledge along nearly every line of study in God's vast creation; therefore, it is reasonable that we should know ourselves. Man's problems are of eternal moment, for he is destined to live long after this heavens and earth have passed away (Isaiah 65:17; Isaiah 66:22; 2 Peter 3:12-13; Revelation 21:1-4). Eternal verities are his.
>
> It is not my purpose to undertake to solve this question from a scientific standpoint; I shall treat it purely from the Bible standpoint. The Word of God is the only Book that lifts the veil which separates this material world from the future and eternal state and gives us a clear view not only of the present but of the future. Its teaching is plain. It gives us a clear solution of what man is, and what his eternal destiny will be. Being a Divine revelation, its teachings can be relied upon and are

---

[5] Riggle, H.M. (1929/2018), Beyond the *Tomb*, (The Gospel Trumpet Company/Holy Spirit Prints).

perfectly safe to accept. Jesus said, "The Scriptures CANNOT BE BROKEN," and what He said is authentic.

King David said, "I am fearfully and wonderfully made" (Psalm 139:14). Man is the crowning work of God's creation. He stands upon the highest pedestal of all earthly creatures, on a much higher plane than the beasts which perish. "Thou hast crowned him with glory and honor. Thou madest him to have dominion over the works of thy hands" (Psalm 8:5-6).

Physically—we are "fearfully and wonderfully made." While the elements that compose the human body are practically the same as those found in the lower animals, man in his physical organism is far superior. Our body is a congeries [collection] of wonders and mysteries, so finely, delicately, and exquisitely made that its beauty, symmetry, utility, and form places us far above the other creatures about us. But man's superiority does not lie in this alone.

Mentally—we are "fearfully and wonderfully made." Man has the power to plan, think, reason, learn, and to know. This is the vital force back of every earthly achievement—the power of ideas, the might of reason. By it we have discovered the mysteries that surround us in earth and sky. A materialist once argued with me on this point and declared that he had absolutely no superior qualities above the other animals. I told him that if I believed as did he, I would go to the barn and take my place in a stall with the horses and cows. Or I would send the donkey to school and college and invite my dog and jersey cow into the office to keep books and do business. Why not? A moment's reflection here should suffice.

Materialists deny that we possess a spiritual, conscious entity (eternal soul) separate and distinct from the body. They claim our life here and now is all there is and that when we die, we become nothingness.

Just stop and consider what the mind of man has accomplished. He ransacks [searches through] the galaxies above; tells us the number of the stars and unlocks the mysteries of the heavens. He delves into the strata of the rocks and in the stone-book [geologic record] of nature he reads the history of the ages. He blasts the rocks unshaken by ages and hurls their ponderous masses into the air as easily as a child tosses up a tennis ball. He tunnels the mountains, bridges the mighty streams, builds great ships that plow the briny deep, and circumnavigates the globe. He flies around the world and over the top of the earth like an eagle. He girdles the earth with a belt of wire, and as swift as thought flashes his messages from pole to pole, and even without the wire on the waves of the ether [air, e.g. radio, satellite] he accomplishes all this. He discovers the forces of nature, harnesses them, and starts the wheels of machinery all over the world. He is capable of intermingling with all wisdom, and of receiving continuous supplies of advanced knowledge. All this positively differentiates us from the brutes [beasts or animals, the word is not derogatory, just the language of that time] and allies us with Deity. But above all this—

Morally and spiritually—we are "fearfully and wonderfully made" (Psalm 139:14). The first man Adam "was made a living soul" (1 Corinthians 15:45). We are moral as well as physical beings. We stand associated with two worlds. Through our physical nature we take our place in the material world and we are affiliated with the things of earth, while through our moral and spiritual nature we are associated with the environments of the spiritual and eternal world.

Thus, we are beings accountable to God, who is the Creator of all things in heaven and in earth. These natures of ours are distinguished through a moral sense, a perception of right and wrong; and we shall never be divested of this to all eternity. We are capable of choosing the evil or the good, of understanding the difference, and this choice is our own act, making us wholly responsible. Our life here and our destiny hereafter are determined by a *choice* and a *course,* and the consequences. "To whom ye yield yourselves servants to obey, his servants ye are to whom you obey" (Romans 6:16). We choose our master and the service we render. We are blessed with astounding possibilities for time and eternity, and this lays upon us a fearful responsibility.

These facts distinguish man from the other creatures of this lower world. And such a wonderful being could not possibly be the result of mere chance. He must be the work of an infinite, independent, all-wise Creator. Life cannot generate itself; it must come from pre-existing life. The Bible testimony on this point is clear: "Know ye not that the Lord he is God: it is he that hath made us, and not we ourselves; we are his people, and the sheep of his pasture" (Psalm 100:3). "For in him we live, and move, and have our being. ... For we are also his offspring" (Acts 17:28). "Have we not all one Father? Hath not one God created us?" (Malachi 2:10). "Let us kneel before the Lord our maker" (Psalm 95:6). "The rich and poor meet together: the Lord is the maker of them all." (Proverbs 22:2). "For thy Maker is thine husband; the Lord of hosts is his name" (Isaiah 54:5).

Now, the opposite of this reasonable truth is the modern materialistic teaching of [the theory of] evolution that links man to the lower forms of life and makes him a lineal descendent [direct line of ancestry] of the brute. These guessers who base their belief on what they themselves style a mere "hypothesis," would have man come up through hundreds of millions of years from a common ancestry or blood relationship with the spider, elephant, toad, horse, lizard, cow, worm, ape, hummingbird, cat, dog, snail, monkey, giraffe, and what not. It is a thousand times easier to believe the Bible account of creation that we are "THE OFFSPRING OF GOD." How plain and simple is the language! "So God created man in his own image, in the image of God created he him; male and female created he them" (Genesis 1:27). ...

Jesus taught this truth in the clearest manner: "And fear not them which kill the body, but are not able to kill the soul: but rather fear him which is able to destroy both soul and body in hell" (Matthew 10:28). "And I say unto you my friends, Be not afraid of them that kill the body, and after that have no more that they can do. But I will forewarn you whom ye shall fear: Fear him, which after he hath killed hath power to cast into hell; yea, I say unto you, Fear him" (Luke 12:4-5). If the body were the soul men could kill that. If by soul is meant merely the physical man, men can kill him. If by soul is simply meant physical life, man can take that from us. But here Jesus plainly taught that the soul of man is indestructible by material forces. Man can kill the body, but "he CANNOT KILL THE SOUL." So, when the body dies the soul still lives. Then it is immortal.

This clear teaching of Christ's announcing the separability of the soul from the body and of the fact that the death of the body does not involve the extinction of the soul, has troubled and perplexed our materialistic friends not a little, and it is surprising how much time and space they devote in their writings to explain away the force of its meaning. But with all their labor, Matthew 10:28 stands unshaken and mocks their efforts. One of their own materialistic writers, J. P. Ham, in his work *Life and Death*, says, "Nothing more is implied than that the soul is distinct from the body." Good for Ham. While he denies its immortality, he admits what is fatal to the whole materialistic teaching— "the soul is *distinct* from the body." And, may I add, Matthew 10:28 as clearly teaches that the soul survives the death of the body. Uriah Smith in *Here and Hereafter* (pp. 109-116) argues that soul here means "the life which is to come." He quotes Matthew 16:25, "Whosoever will lose his life for my sake shall find it." That is, we may lose our present life in martyrdom or death for Christ's sake and gain it again in the resurrection. That would make Matthew 10:28 read, "Fear not them which kill the body, but are not able to kill the life which is to come in the resurrection." This is certainly a new definition of the term soul and does not at all give a correct exegesis of this scripture.

I quote Dr. Adam Clarke: "We find that the body and the soul are distinct principles, for the body may be slain and the soul escape; and secondly, that the soul is immaterial [spirit], for the murderers of the body are not able, have it not in their power, to injure it." The import of Christ's words cannot be mistaken. He expressly asserts that man consists of both soul and body, and that the soul survives the death of the body and continues in a state of consciousness when separated from the body. The soul and body do not perish together at death. Jesus taught that all of us possess souls which come not under the power of men but are subject to the power of God alone.

The next chapter will help you understand more about God, humanity, and sin and also explain the fallen world we see all around us today.

FALSE TEACHING(S) YOU WILL ENCOUNTER:
- Atheism (there is no God)
- The "Theory" of Evolution (and millions of years for earth history)
- Satan (the Devil) is just a myth
- The Bible is simply fictional "myths, folklore, and poetry"
- Annihilation after death
- You get a "2nd chance" after death

RELATED SCRIPTURE:

Then the LORD God said, "It is not good for the man to be alone; I will make him a helper suitable for him." Out of the ground the LORD God formed every beast of the field and every bird of the sky, and brought *them* to the man to see what he would call them; and whatever the man called a living creature, that was its name. The man gave names to all the cattle, and to the birds of the sky, and to every beast of the field, but for Adam there was not found a helper suitable for him. So the LORD God caused a deep sleep to fall upon the man, and he slept; then He took one of his ribs and closed up the flesh at that place. The LORD God fashioned into a woman the rib which He had taken from the man, and brought her to the man. The man said,

"This is now bone of my bones,
And flesh of my flesh;
She shall be called Woman,
Because she was taken out of Man."

For this reason a man shall leave his father and his mother, and be joined to his wife; and they shall become one flesh. – Genesis 2:18-24

Thus declares the LORD who stretches out the heavens, lays the foundation of the earth, and forms the spirit of man within him. – Zechariah 12:1b

O LORD, our Lord,
How majestic is Your name in all the earth,
Who have displayed Your splendor above the heavens!
From the mouth of infants and nursing babes You have established strength
Because of Your adversaries,
To make the enemy and the revengeful cease.

When I consider Your heavens, the work of Your fingers,
The moon and the stars, which You have ordained;
What is man that You take thought of him,
And the son of man that You care for him?
Yet You have made him a little lower than God,
And You crown him with glory and majesty! – Psalm 8:1-5

For You formed my inward parts;
You wove me in my mother's womb.
I will give thanks to You, for I am fearfully and wonderfully made;
Wonderful are Your works,
And my soul knows it very well.
My frame was not hidden from You,
When I was made in secret,
And skillfully wrought in the depths of the earth;
Your eyes have seen my unformed substance;
And in Your book were all written
The days that were ordained *for me*,
When as yet there was not one of them. – Psalm 139:13-16

O LORD, how many are Your works!
In wisdom You have made them all;
The earth is full of Your possessions. – Psalm 104:24

1.2 IT WAS VERY GOOD

God saw all that He had made, and behold, it was very good. – Genesis 1:31

Initial Creation Was Perfect. Just as God Himself is holy, righteous, just, true, and perfect, you must also realize that the Bible states that God's initial creation of this Earth (and the Garden of Eden, and mankind as well as all animals and plants) was also perfect – without sin, suffering, disease or death. God "is love," and He declared that His creation was "very good." God would not declare anything "very good" if it were not perfect in His own mind, which must also reflect His own character. And when "God, who cannot lie" tells us that through Scripture, we know it is true.

Now you may be thinking to yourself: "But what I see around me shows disease, suffering, killing, and death!" You're also probably thinking: "What I've learned and seen proof of is that it took millions of years for us to evolve to this point." Additionally, you may be thinking: "Well, what I see around me doesn't match what is in the Bible!" You look around at the reality we find ourselves in and wonder how could there ever be a God, or how can God be called "good" and "loving" with what we see in the world today?

If so, I empathize with you greatly; for the longest time (many years, decades even), I also didn't believe in God because of what I saw around me in this fallen, sinful world. But you mustn't make the mistake of blaming God for what you see around us – this fallen world and the reality that we find ourselves in now resulted from man's actions. What we see around us today is not what God initially created. We are currently seeing things through the veil of sin and the curse; we cannot see things clearly here in this fallen world.

In fact, what we see today is just a mere foggy glimpse of what initial creation was like, as if looking through a dark and dimly lit veil. What we see today is a result of a "curse" being put on creation by God, but that was done as a result of the sinful actions of man, and it was done out of love and for our benefit: so that we would not live forever in a sinful state of separation from Him by taking and eating of the "Tree of Life" that was in the perfect Garden of Eden. This matter of humanity and sin is covered more fully in the upcoming chapter on Humanity and Sin. But first, we must deal with the commonly held belief that science has disproven the Bible (and therefore God).

FALSE TEACHING(S) YOU WILL ENCOUNTER:
- Atheism (there is no God)
- The "Theory" of Evolution (and millions of years for earth history)
- Science disproves the Bible (see next chapter)

RELATED SCRIPTURE:

God saw all that He had made, and behold, it was very good. And there was evening and there was morning, the sixth day. – Genesis 1:31

The LORD God planted a garden toward the east, in Eden; and there He placed the man whom He had formed. Out of the ground the LORD God caused to grow every tree that is pleasing to the sight and good for food; the tree of life also in the midst of the garden, and the tree of the knowledge of good and evil.

The Message of Truth

Now a river flowed out of Eden to water the garden; and from there it divided and became four rivers. The name of the first is Pishon; it flows around the whole land of Havilah, where there is gold. The gold of that land is good; the bdellium and the onyx stone are there. The name of the second river is Gihon; it flows around the whole land of Cush. The name of the third river is Tigris; it flows east of Assyria. And the fourth river is the Euphrates.

Then the LORD God took the man and put him into the garden of Eden to cultivate it and keep it. The LORD God commanded the man, saying, "From any tree of the garden you may eat freely; but from the tree of the knowledge of good and evil you shall not eat, for in the day that you eat from it you will surely die." – Genesis 2:8-17

"The Rock! His work is perfect,
For all His ways are just;
A God of faithfulness and without injustice,
Righteous and upright is He." – Deuteronomy 32:4

And one called out to another and said,

> "Holy, Holy, Holy, is the LORD of hosts,
> The whole earth is full of His glory." – Isaiah 6:3

O give thanks to the LORD, for *He is* good;
For His lovingkindness is everlasting. – 1 Chronicles 16:34

But the lovingkindness of the LORD is from everlasting to everlasting on those who fear Him,
And His righteousness to children's children. – Psalm 103:17

For His lovingkindness is great toward us,
And the truth of the LORD is everlasting.
Praise the LORD! – Psalm 117:2

…for God is love. – 1 John 4:8

For the anxious longing of the creation waits eagerly for the revealing of the sons of God. For the creation was subjected to futility, not willingly, but because of Him who subjected it, in hope that the creation itself also will be set free from its slavery to corruption into the freedom of the glory of the children of God. For we know that the whole creation groans and suffers the pains of childbirth together until now. And not only this, but also we ourselves, having the first fruits of the Spirit, even we ourselves groan within ourselves, waiting eagerly for *our* adoption as sons, the redemption of our body. – Romans 8:19-23

1.3 SCIENCE VS. THE BIBLE
(Or Creation vs. Evolution)

Let God be found true, though every man be found a liar. – Romans 3:4

You Have Been Brainwashed. Before we can continue further, we must deal with some of the false teachings of man which are masquerading as "science"– for many people are mistakenly under the impression that science has disproven the Bible because that is what they have been taught and heard their entire life. This claim has become a deafening onslaught of propaganda and brainwashing (and that's exactly what it is!), repeated often and continuously, causing many to doubt the Bible, and in particular, to doubt the very first book of the Bible called Genesis, and even more specifically, the very first sentence(s) of Genesis.

However, nothing could be further from the truth. The reality is that just the opposite is actually true – every advancement and discovery in science (and in other fields such as archaeology) has, in fact, served to prove further that the Bible is indeed true! It is sad today to see the brainwashing that is done since the time we are wee infants in the educational system. We are brainwashed to be prejudiced against God from our earliest cognizant development moments and educational levels. Man sure can be a strange and illogical creature; for he will endlessly chase after myths and nonsense like looking for the mythical "Fountain of Youth" or trying to find the secret to eternal life from science when all he has to do is look to God who gives eternal life freely to all who seek Him!

What you need to realize is that the earth is in the middle of a raging war. Now I'm not talking about the endless wars waged by man which cause so much suffering, but we are in a spiritual war with the forces of God and good on one side and evil on the other side (led by Satan, his evil spirits, and men who do his work): "for our struggle is not against flesh and blood, but against the rulers, against the powers, against the world *forces* of this darkness, against the spiritual forces of wickedness in the heavenly *places*." Please understand that this war is not a physical war fought with guns and knives and swords, but a spiritual war fought with the tools outlined in Scripture (lies, false teachings, and deceptions, but also prayer). Please do not be deceived, these spiritual forces of darkness and evil are very real even though you cannot see them, and they are firmly set against you in spiritual warfare trying to get you to end in eternal death – for they oppose all that is good and of God. They do not want you to obtain eternal life!

And their very first line of defense is to get you to doubt the Bible! They know that if they stop you at that point, you won't go any further! One major retailer even placed their Bibles in the fiction section of books – I kid you not! That's how determined they are to convince you that the Bible is not true. The second greatest weapon they use against you is false teachings – both from the secular God-denying world and also from within the fake so-called "Christian" churches.

Friend, please realize that all your life, you have been the victim of anti-God brainwashing, propaganda, and lies/distractions of man; they are designed to lead you away from God, away from Christ, and away from eternal life! The knowledge of the truth given in Scripture, which I give to you in this book, is essential in countering the false teachings. That is why I'm so adamant in this book about calling out and identifying these false teachings for you.

Many of these false teachings masquerade as "science" and "theories" of man, but which are, in fact, fake science. You are told that these "theories" are true and proven by scientifically measured facts when they are instead mere illusions and deceptions of man brought to you by the secular world and its institutions. For example, you have been taught, and very likely believe, that all of the following are true and established "facts" of science:

- Doesn't evolution disprove the Bible? (or how can the seven (7) literal days of creation in the book of Genesis possibly be true?)
- What about the dinosaurs? Don't they disprove the Bible? (and didn't an asteroid kill them off millions of years ago?)
- Don't fossils prove millions of years and disprove the Bible?
- Doesn't carbon dating prove millions of years and disprove the Bible?
- Don't tree growth rings prove millions of years and disprove the Bible?
- Don't erosion prove millions of years and disprove the Bible?
- Doesn't natural selection disprove the Bible?
- Doesn't science prove that there were many "ice ages" over millions of years and disprove the Bible?
- Doesn't light red-shift prove millions of years and disprove the Bible?
- Don't animals having sharp teeth disprove the Bible?
- Doesn't the "Big-Bang Theory" disprove the Bible?
- Noah's flood is just a myth; isn't a worldwide flood impossible?

However, the answer to these and many other commonly accepted (without challenge) "scientific" questions is a resounding: no! In particular regarding evolution, by their very own admission, evolutionary "scientists" acknowledge and admit that their own "theory" cannot even explain where life first came from! Only the Bible gives us the answer. Nonetheless, the lies and cries of "millions of years" continue to emanate loudly and often in blaring volume trying to drown out the truth of the Bible, so you must continually be on guard for it.

As you see from the headline verse to this chapter, the truth is actually opposite to what man claims; in fact, the truth (and rule) is that if something man says disagrees with or contradicts the Bible, then it is man who is wrong, not the Bible! While science can help us understand the physical world through its theories and measurements, it tells us absolutely nothing whatsoever about the spiritual world, about God, angels, heaven, and hell, or even life and death. Only the Bible tells us what truth in such matters is.

CREATION VS. EVOLUTION

One teaching, in particular, the "Theory of Evolution" (along with its attendant theories of "millions/billions of years" for earth history), is so widespread, popular, believed by many, and shouted from the rooftops in staggering volume day and night from every single media outlet on the planet that you have been exposed to this teaching since you were an infant and may not even realize it is just a "theory" of man! Please note that it is called the "<u>Theory</u>" of Evolution, not the "Facts" of Evolution! That's right, it's just a "theory" of man, although they try to pass it off as fact, as hard science, when it is nothing of the sort. This fake science is front and center as you encounter these first chapters on God's creation; in effect, the subject of science vs. the Bible is commonly manifest as the particular argument of creation vs. evolution.

I really do know and empathize with what you're experiencing if you doubt there is a God and that His initial Creation was good, pure, without sin, suffering, and death. As a scientist myself (physics), I also struggled mightily with these questions about evolution, the age of the earth, etc. – how could it all be possibly created by a God in a mere literal seven (7) days? How could all the "facts" (or so I was told) of evolution and millions of years be wrong? I had to sort through hundreds of my own questions and doubts on these matters before I could come to believe that there really is a God and that He is good and loving! I mean, how can "science" be wrong? And believe me, when I question and doubt something, I do it like the best of them. When I have questions, there are literally hundreds and hundreds to be answered! So, I am speaking from personal experience on this subject.

The subject of science vs. the Bible is such a vast area that I can only highlight some of the key areas in this book; but know that there are many good and knowledgeable articles, studies, and research on this subject written by very competent, highly trained and respected Christian scientists and scholars who have studied mountains of evidence and data which show clearly that science has not disproven the Bible. Many scientists, who are also Christians, have studies and research those atheistic scientists (and their sponsoring institutions) just don't like, want to hear, or want you to hear. So that information is suppressed (or ignored) in schools or discredited by atheistic groups, so the information can be harder to find.

There isn't space here to refute all these theories of man, presented as scientific "facts," but I encourage you to consult some of the reference materials listed at the end of this book. Our website also lists many questions and answers (Q&A) in the area of science vs. the Bible, with links to articles, papers, studies, and research. The website Q&A covers many of the most common stumbling blocks and false teachings of man in the area of science that cause disbelief.

DO YOU HAVE AN OPEN MIND?

To find the truth about this world, the universe, heaven, hell, eternity, your eternal soul, and God, are you:

1) Prepared to be open-minded and consider new information? Are you ready to objectively evaluate factual information and to consider that you have been lied to (and brainwashed) for so many years? Are you really open to considering that the biblical view on science and creation (and other matters) MAY indeed be accurate?
2) Willing to concede that there even is a God? The modern and so-called enlightened man thinks that his science is the final authority and basis for all understanding and justification, but that simply isn't the case. Even the ancient Greeks, with all of their sophistication and knowledge, believed in a God; they just didn't know "which" God, so the Apostle Paul pointed them in the correct direction:

> So Paul stood in the midst of the Areopagus and said, "Men of Athens, I observe that you are very religious in all respects. For while I was passing through and examining the objects of your worship, I also found an altar with

this inscription, 'TO AN UNKNOWN GOD.' Therefore what you worship in ignorance, this I proclaim to you. The God who made the world and all things in it, since He is Lord of heaven and earth, does not dwell in temples made with hands; nor is He served by human hands, as though He needed anything, since He Himself gives to all people life and breath and all things; and He made from one man every nation of mankind to live on all the face of the earth, having determined their appointed times and the boundaries of their habitation, that they would seek God, if perhaps they might grope for Him and find Him, though He is not far from each one of us; for in Him we live and move and exist, as even some of your own poets have said, 'For we also are His children.' Being then the children of God, we ought not to think that the Divine Nature is like gold or silver or stone, an image formed by the art and thought of man. Therefore having overlooked the times of ignorance, God is now declaring to men that all people everywhere should repent, because He has fixed a day in which He will judge the world in righteousness through a Man whom He has appointed, having furnished proof to all men by raising Him from the dead." – Acts 17:22-31

3) Willing to challenge what you hear? Are you simply accepting the word of man without challenging it? Do you believe anything you hear if it comes from someone dressed up in a nice and expensive suit with an intimidating title, or who has lots of important-sounding initials placed before or after their name? Or worse, are you accepting as truth what you read on social media and the Internet these days?

Yes, in large majority, people generally tend to simply accept almost anything they hear presented as "science" without doing due diligence and challenging it to see if it is actually true. This goes for Christians as well as anyone else. For example, Wayne Jackson, who has written for and edited the Christian Courier since its inception in 1965, writes this regarding the general public reaction to the "Jesus Bones" so-called "science" a few years ago:[6]

> **Those Bogus "Jesus Bones"**
>
> Society has just been treated to the almost-yearly attempt of entertainment exploiters, who seek to line their pockets with "filthy lucre" by hitching a ride on the reputation of Jesus Christ.
>
> It would be a laughable, though stupid enterprise, were it not for the fact that so many gullible souls ingest any trash that purports to have the endorsement of "science." Never has the reputation of "science" been so low.
>
> There is nothing new that is "scientifically credible" in this story. The knowledge of these "bones" has been around for more than a quarter of a century — scarcely raising an eyebrow.

From the introduction, I remind you just how far the deceptions of man (and fake science) go – in fact, nearly everything today is fake:

---

[6] Reference: Jackson, Wayne. "Those Bogus 'Jesus Bones'." ChristianCourier.*com*. Access date: March 12, 2019. https://christiancourier.com/articles/1342-those-bogus-jesus-bones

Further compounding the situation is the absolutely staggering amount of noise (and even more false teachings) generated by the secular world, with its God-denying media and institutions trying to drown out the gospel message and the name of Jesus altogether by creating even more false teachings which masquerade as science, but which are in reality fake science. Yes, we are being fed today fake news, fake science (e.g., The "Theory" of Evolution), fake entertainment (e.g., lip synced performances, so-called "reality" but scripted TV), fake food (e.g. margarine, "meat substitutes"), fake body parts (e.g., vanity cosmetic surgery), fake economics (e.g., Keynesian Economics, debt as an asset), fake (and fraudulent) accounting (e.g., non-GAAP reporting, off-balance sheet items), fake money (e.g., fiat currencies), fake "religions," fake prophecy and even fake gospels (e.g., lukewarm, apostate so-called "Christianity").

These false teachings are being shouted today 24/7/365 (i.e., nonstop) in blaring volume from both secular media sources as well as co-called "Christian" pulpits, broadcasts, books/authors, movies and publications. And we are gradually conditioned by repeated, frequent and persistent marketing propaganda (for that is exactly what it is) to accept the fakes (the false teachings) as the real thing, and even begin to believe it in place of the real.

But when you stop listening to the theories, myths, "traditions," and fables of man and start to seek knowledge, wisdom, and truth from the Lord via His Word, then you will start to get real wisdom and knowledge; and you will be blessed with understanding and start to see the lies and deceptions of man clearly. However, until you do that, you will simply keep chasing more theories, myths, and fables of man. I know it sounds harsh reading that, but it's the truth! That is why Scripture tells us "The fear of the LORD is the beginning of knowledge [and wisdom]" (Proverbs 1:7).

I must also confess to being gullible by formerly believing much of this fake science, but now I know the truth - and here is the important part: I no longer sit in ignorance believing the nonsense of man. I've seen the change in myself after realizing that man isn't the ultimate authority on matters – the Lord is. And when you accept that God (not man) has truth, a light goes off, and you have a "wow, what I've been taught all my life isn't so much proven by science after all" moment! You will then realize that on these essential matters, God is truth, and men are not. Are you ready to trust God's wisdom on these essential and eternal matters over man's? It is written: "There is a way which seems right to a man [his notions, myths, theories, superstitions, opinions, traditions, etc.], but its end is the way of death" (Proverbs 16:25) and "let God be found true, though every man be found a liar" (Romans 3:4). Only God and His Word and His Wisdom lead to life; trust in God's holy Word.

GOD IS NOT A GOD OF CONFUSION

Now please don't misunderstand what I'm saying in this chapter. God is not against science, only the "fake science" invented by man. Science in and of itself is good and was created by God; it is a fantastic tool which God gave us to enable us to better our condition and help humanity, when used for good. In fact, we even read that God created and designed this universe using logic, wisdom, reason and understanding:

> The LORD by wisdom founded the earth,
> By understanding He established the heavens. – Proverbs 3:19

> ...for God is not *a God* of confusion. – 1 Corinthians 14:33

The Bible tells us that wisdom, God's wisdom, was around before the world existed, and it is by that very wisdom that He created this world we now live in. Yes, even the laws of nature themselves were created from God's wisdom:

> "The LORD possessed me [wisdom] at the beginning of His way,
> Before His works of old.
> "From everlasting I was established,
> From the beginning, from the earliest times of the earth.
> "When there were no depths I was brought forth,
> When there were no springs abounding with water.
> "Before the mountains were settled,
> Before the hills I was brought forth;
> While He had not yet made the earth and the fields,
> Nor the first dust of the world.
> "When He established the heavens, I was there,
> When He inscribed a circle on the face of the deep,
> When He made firm the skies above,
> When the springs of the deep became fixed,
> When He set for the sea its boundary
> So that the water would not transgress His command,
> When He marked out the foundations of the earth;
> Then I was beside Him, *as* a master workman;
> And I was daily *His* delight,
> Rejoicing always before Him,
> Rejoicing in the world, His earth,
> And *having* my delight in the sons of men." – Proverbs 8:22-31

Additionally, He upholds this very universe and all things in it by His Word, so it was God who created science in the first place! He created the things that we know today as the laws of mathematics, the laws of physics, the laws of thermodynamics, the laws of logic, etc., from His wisdom. So, God does not ask us to discard logic and reasoning when evaluating research and science, whether for or against the Bible. God gave us logic and reasoning to use wisely, but we must allow Him to direct us to the truth. Are we ready to be led by God into truth, wisdom, and understanding? Are we humble enough to be taught and receive truth, even when we think we know better, and may even think we know more than God Himself?

The book of Job is most enlightening on this matter; I've included a few chapters from it in the verses at the end of the chapter. They show the Lord really laying it on Job thick and heavy and squarely putting him back in his place again for thinking he was wiser than God. The Lord showed him that it was He who created, ordered, and maintains all things, and notice that God used matters of creation and the physical and natural world as examples of His wisdom. While lengthy, it's worth reading in its entirety.

And finally, after reading some of the materials I have suggested (I sincerely hope you do), you will see that there are many valid interpretations of "scientific data" which agree with the Bible. You will also find that there is a whole body of scientific knowledge and facts that have been kept hidden from you. You may be wondering why you haven't heard or been taught any of this stuff in school? I'll let you ponder the answer to that...but I now see that much of what secular science and textbooks and colleges taught me was just "theories" and even brainwashing, all designed to make God opaquer and harder to find.

Please realize that nearly all schools, colleges, universities (and even seminaries!) are run and controlled by extremely liberal secular God-denying entities which are directly opposed to Christianity. The textbooks we are taught from are also under their control, being published by secular entities. Staggering! Astounding? …. Hard to believe? Impossible, you say? But that's a true statement, and the facts are out there; you can easily look up the ownership of many of these institutions and review their board members.

I mentioned this earlier, but it bears repeating, so I want to close with it again: Do you know why they spend so much energy and effort to try to stop you from believing the very first sentences of the Bible? It is because they know that if you don't believe the first sentence(s) of the Bible, you won't believe or read the rest of it either. And make no mistake, the "they" are ungodly men who are under the control of Satan, the Devil, whether they like to think so or not, and they do not want to see you coming to God, and His Christ, and to eternal life. This is the front line in the spiritual battle for human souls.

So please do not judge matters (and God) and form beliefs based only on what you see today in this fallen world and by what you have been taught as "science." See truth; seek God's wisdom. This is why the Lord has given us the Bible – so we know the truth, even when it's hard to see in this fallen world. The Bible transcends both space and time. It is God's Holy Word, given to guide those who will listen. For God is before all, created all, in all, through all, for all, after all, and above all things! Amen!

In the next chapter, we get back on track presenting the gospel message and learning more about why God cursed creation, which explains the fallen world we see around us today with sin, suffering, disease, and death.

FALSE TEACHING(S) YOU WILL ENCOUNTER:
- Atheism (there is no God)
- The "Theory" of Evolution (and millions of years for earth history)
- Satan (the Devil) is just a myth
- Science disproves the Bible

RELATED SCRIPTURE:

Rather, let God be found true, though every man *be found* a liar, as it is written,

> "THAT YOU MAY BE JUSTIFIED IN YOUR WORDS,
> AND PREVAIL WHEN YOU ARE JUDGED." – Romans 3:4

There is a way *which seems* right to a man,
But its end is the way of death. – Proverbs 14:12

The fear of the LORD is the beginning of knowledge;
Fools despise wisdom and instruction. – Proverbs 1:7

Trust in the LORD with all your heart
And do not lean on your own understanding.
In all your ways acknowledge Him,
And He will make your paths straight.

Do not be wise in your own eyes;
Fear the LORD and turn away from evil. – Proverbs 3:5-7

For the word of the cross is foolishness to those who are perishing, but to us who are being saved it is the power of God. For it is written,

> "I WILL DESTROY THE WISDOM OF THE WISE,
> AND THE CLEVERNESS OF THE CLEVER I WILL SET ASIDE."

Where is the wise man? Where is the scribe? Where is the debater of this age? Has not God made foolish the wisdom of the world? For since in the wisdom of God the world through its wisdom did not *come to* know God, God was well-pleased through the foolishness of the message preached to save those who believe… Because the foolishness of God is wiser than men, and the weakness of God is stronger than men. – 1 Corinthians 1:18-21,25

Listen to counsel and accept discipline,
That you may be wise the rest of your days. – Proverbs 19:20

How blessed is the man who finds wisdom
And the man who gains understanding. – Proverbs 3:13

Let no man deceive himself. If any man among you thinks that he is wise in this age, he must become foolish, so that he may become wise. For the wisdom of this world is foolishness before God. For it is written, "*He is* THE ONE WHO CATCHES THE WISE IN THEIR CRAFTINESS"; and again, "THE LORD KNOWS THE REASONINGS of the wise, THAT THEY ARE USELESS." – 1 Corinthians 3:18-20

Then the LORD answered Job out of the whirlwind and said,

> "Who is this that darkens counsel
> By words without knowledge?
> "Now gird up your loins like a man,
> And I will ask you, and you instruct Me!
> "Where were you when I laid the foundation of the earth?
> Tell *Me*, if you have understanding,
> Who set its measurements? Since you know.
> Or who stretched the line on it?
> "On what were its bases sunk?
> Or who laid its cornerstone,
> When the morning stars sang together
> And all the sons of God shouted for joy?
>
> "Or *who* enclosed the sea with doors
> When, bursting forth, it went out from the womb;
> When I made a cloud its garment
> And thick darkness its swaddling band,
> And I placed boundaries on it
> And set a bolt and doors,
> And I said, 'Thus far you shall come, but no farther;
> And here shall your proud waves stop'?

"Have you ever in your life commanded the morning,
And caused the dawn to know its place,
That it might take hold of the ends of the earth,
And the wicked be shaken out of it?
"It is changed like clay *under* the seal;
And they stand forth like a garment.
"From the wicked their light is withheld,
And the uplifted arm is broken.

"Have you entered into the springs of the sea
Or walked in the recesses of the deep?
"Have the gates of death been revealed to you,
Or have you seen the gates of deep darkness?
"Have you understood the expanse of the earth?
Tell *Me*, if you know all this.

"Where is the way to the dwelling of light?
And darkness, where is its place,
That you may take it to its territory
And that you may discern the paths to its home?
"You know, for you were born then,
And the number of your days is great!
"Have you entered the storehouses of the snow,
Or have you seen the storehouses of the hail,
Which I have reserved for the time of distress,
For the day of war and battle?
"Where is the way that the light is divided,
Or the east wind scattered on the earth?

"Who has cleft a channel for the flood,
Or a way for the thunderbolt,
To bring rain on a land without people,
On a desert without a man in it,
To satisfy the waste and desolate land
And to make the seeds of grass to sprout?
"Has the rain a father?
Or who has begotten the drops of dew?
"From whose womb has come the ice?
And the frost of heaven, who has given it birth?
"Water becomes hard like stone,
And the surface of the deep is imprisoned.

"Can you bind the chains of the Pleiades,
Or loose the cords of Orion?
"Can you lead forth a constellation in its season,
And guide the Bear with her satellites?
"Do you know the ordinances of the heavens,
Or fix their rule over the earth?

The Message of Truth

"Can you lift up your voice to the clouds,
So that an abundance of water will cover you?
"Can you send forth lightnings that they may go
And say to you, 'Here we are'?
"Who has put wisdom in the innermost being
Or given understanding to the mind?
"Who can count the clouds by wisdom,
Or tip the water jars of the heavens,
When the dust hardens into a mass
And the clods stick together?

"Can you hunt the prey for the lion,
Or satisfy the appetite of the young lions,
When they crouch in *their* dens
And lie in wait in *their* lair?
"Who prepares for the raven its nourishment
When its young cry to God
And wander about without food? – Job 38:1-41

"Do you know the time the mountain goats give birth?
Do you observe the calving of the deer?
"Can you count the months they fulfill,
Or do you know the time they give birth?
"They kneel down, they bring forth their young,
They get rid of their labor pains.
"Their offspring become strong, they grow up in the open field;
They leave and do not return to them.

"Who sent out the wild donkey free?
And who loosed the bonds of the swift donkey,
To whom I gave the wilderness for a home
And the salt land for his dwelling place?
"He scorns the tumult of the city,
The shoutings of the driver he does not hear.
"He explores the mountains for his pasture
And searches after every green thing.
"Will the wild ox consent to serve you,
Or will he spend the night at your manger?
"Can you bind the wild ox in a furrow with ropes,
Or will he harrow the valleys after you?
"Will you trust him because his strength is great
And leave your labor to him?
"Will you have faith in him that he will return your grain
And gather *it from* your threshing floor?

"The ostriches' wings flap joyously
With the pinion and plumage of love,
For she abandons her eggs to the earth
And warms them in the dust,
And she forgets that a foot may crush them,

Or that a wild beast may trample them.
"She treats her young cruelly, as if *they* were not hers;
Though her labor be in vain, *she* is unconcerned;
Because God has made her forget wisdom,
And has not given her a share of understanding.
"When she lifts herself on high,
She laughs at the horse and his rider.

"Do you give the horse *his* might?
Do you clothe his neck with a mane?
"Do you make him leap like the locust?
His majestic snorting is terrible.
"He paws in the valley, and rejoices in *his* strength;
He goes out to meet the weapons.
"He laughs at fear and is not dismayed;
And he does not turn back from the sword.
"The quiver rattles against him,
The flashing spear and javelin.
"With shaking and rage he races over the ground,
And he does not stand still at the voice of the trumpet.
"As often as the trumpet *sounds* he says, 'Aha!'
And he scents the battle from afar,
And the thunder of the captains and the war cry.

"Is it by your understanding that the hawk soars,
Stretching his wings toward the south?
"Is it at your command that the eagle mounts up
And makes his nest on high?
"On the cliff he dwells and lodges,
Upon the rocky crag, an inaccessible place.

"From there he spies out food;
His eyes see *it* from afar.
"His young ones also suck up blood;
And where the slain are, there is he." – Job 39:1-30

Then the LORD said to Job,

"Will the faultfinder contend with the Almighty?
Let him who reproves God answer it."

Then Job answered the LORD and said,

"Behold, I am insignificant; what can I reply to You?
I lay my hand on my mouth.
"Once I have spoken, and I will not answer;
Even twice, and I will add nothing more." – Job 40:1-5

1.4 HUMANITY & SIN
(A Fallen World – Sin, Suffering & Death Enter)

The LORD God commanded the man, saying, "From any tree of the garden you may eat freely; but from the tree of the knowledge of good and evil you shall not eat, for in the day that you eat from it you will surely die." – Genesis 2:16-17

Man Disobeyed God. When God created man, He gave man free will to choose who to believe and obey, for without free will, there can be no love (i.e., a robot pre-programmed to perform a set of commands is not love). Satan, the devil, tempted Eve (and thereby Adam) in the Garden of Eden to disobey God by eating the fruit of the one forbidden "Tree of the Knowledge of Good and Evil." Satan tricked them by deliberately misquoting God's Word, twisting it in a way that creates doubt or invites temptation through lust of the flesh; that is how he deceives – for he is described as "the father of lies."

But it was a deliberate and willful choice by Eve and then Adam to disobey God's rules and eat the forbidden fruit. Scripture tells us that Eve saw that the fruit was a "delight" to her eyes – she wanted to have it despite God having forbidden it (she lusted after it). God gives us rules for our good, our protection, and our well-being so we can have life and have it "abundantly." We don't always fully understand why some rules are given but know they are for our good because God is a good and loving God.

The consequences of that act of disobedience were severe, as we see in the world today, for it is through this initial act of disobedience that sin, suffering, and death entered the world. Before they disobeyed God, they could be with God in the Garden of Eden; after sinning (disobeying), they were separated from God and cast out of the Garden – due to sin.

Now you may be wondering what or who this "Satan" is. Please realize that we are not alone in this universe. God also created angels (spiritual beings). And while the Bible doesn't tell us precisely when angels were created or how many there are, it does tell us they are created beings, and we can make some intelligent guesses about such matters. However, those details are not fundamental to the gospel message, and I don't want to get sidetracked with them here; they also do not alter the reality that we find ourselves in, which is: Satan was a chief angel who rebelled against God, and some of the angels followed him in rebellion. So today, there are good angels who obeyed God (these are called "ministering spirits" and work for the good of God) and evil spirits (fallen angels and demons) who follow Satan.

Satan and his evil spirits stand against anything that is good and of God, and since humans were created in the image of God, Satan stands against us. Make no mistake; Satan is a real spiritual being who is described as your "adversary," "tempter," and "accuser." He wants you to have eternal death; he does everything he can to deceive you out of the path to eternal life with God. He is not some fanciful cartoon character in red tights with a pitchfork – that illusion is created to deceive many by causing them not to take him seriously!

So please don't ignore Satan because you cannot see him, for he is very real. And he deceives people by obfuscating the truth of Scripture, by telling lies, half-truths, and distorting (misquoting) Scripture. Satan is "the father of lies," deceptions, and illusions. Here's an analogy to help you understand this: we don't have to know where the Law of Gravity came from, or even need to understand it completely, to know that it is very real indeed, and there are dire consequences for ignoring it!

Consequently, the Earth and this world we live in is actually a spiritual battleground between the forces of good vs. evil. Do not mistake this all as just a myth or fable, for it is written in God's Holy Word:

> Now the serpent [Satan] was more crafty than any beast of the field which the LORD God had made. – Genesis 3:1

> Now there was a day when the sons of God came to present themselves before the LORD, and Satan also came among them. The LORD said to Satan, "From where do you come?" Then Satan answered the LORD and said, "From roaming about on the earth and walking around on it." – Job 1:6-7

> Be of sober *spirit*, be on the alert. Your adversary, the devil, prowls around like a roaring lion, seeking someone to devour. – 1 Peter 5:8

> Then Jesus was led up by the Spirit into the wilderness to be tempted by the devil. – Matthew 4:1

> "Now the salvation, and the power, and the kingdom of our God and the authority of His Christ have come, for the accuser of our brethren has been thrown down, he who accuses them before our God day and night." – Revelation 12:10

> The one who practices sin is of the devil; for the devil has sinned from the beginning. The Son of God appeared for this purpose, to destroy the works of the devil. – 1 John 3:8

> Finally, be strong in the Lord and in the strength of His might. Put on the full armor of God, so that you will be able to stand firm against the schemes of the devil. For our struggle is not against flesh and blood, but against the rulers, against the powers, against the world forces of this darkness, against the spiritual *forces* of wickedness in the heavenly *places*. Therefore, take up the full armor of God, so that you will be able to resist in the evil day, and having done everything, to stand firm. Stand firm therefore, HAVING GIRDED YOUR LOINS WITH TRUTH, and HAVING PUT ON THE BREASTPLATE OF RIGHTEOUSNESS, and having shod YOUR FEET WITH THE PREPARATION OF THE GOSPEL OF PEACE; in addition to all, taking up the shield of faith with which you will be able to extinguish all the flaming arrows of the evil *one [Satan]*. And take THE HELMET OF SALVATION, and the sword of the Spirit, which is the word of God. – Ephesians 6:10-17

> "You are of *your* father the devil, and you want to do the desires of your father. He was a murderer from the beginning, and does not stand in the truth because there is no truth in him. Whenever he speaks a lie, he speaks from his own *nature*, for he is a liar and the father of lies." – John 8:44

> Submit therefore to God. Resist the devil and he will flee from you. – James 4:7

So, this initial act of deliberate, willful disobedience by Eve, and Adam, in choosing to believe Satan over God was the fall of humanity and this world – this is why we read in Scripture: "through one man sin entered into the world, and death through sin" (Romans 5:12). Scripture also tells us that God banished man from the

Garden of Eden and set a curse on this world as a result of this act of disobedience. As explained below, God did this out of love for us, not out of hate or malice. This curse was the result of disobedience, the result of sin, which introduced disease, suffering, and death into this world. It makes this world that we see today different from the one God initially created ("in the beginning"), which He described as "very good." Therefore, we live in a fallen and sinful world, which is exactly what we see around us today. So, please don't blame God for creating what we see in this fallen world today – the sin, suffering, and death we see all around us; this is the work of man, resulting from disobedience to God. God gave man a) sovereignty over this world and b) free will. It is man, therefore, who is responsible.

God had clearly warned Adam and Eve that "in the day that you eat from it [the forbidden Tree of the Knowledge of Good and Evil] you will surely die." They did die spiritually that very day due to sin. Recall from a prior chapter that we were created in God's image, which means every person is created with an immortal, eternal spirit. Scripture also tells us that sin results in (spiritual) death and separation from God. And while their physical death didn't occur instantly, they did also physically die at a later time (we all do). So, it was this act of disobedience that introduced physical death and decay into the world.

The curse and banishment from the Garden of Eden were done to prevent Adam and Eve (and others after them) from eating of the "Tree of Life," which was also in the Garden, as doing so would have given them eternal life – but remember after they had disobeyed God, they were now in a sinful state (spiritually separated from God), so they would have been eternally separated from God (eternal death). That is why God acted for our protection, out of love – so we would not be condemned to eternal death, for God wants us, each of us, all of us, to be with Him forever in eternal life. Please do not make the mistake of underestimating the importance of your spirit and your spiritual state, for it is what is eternal! It is even more important than our current fleshly, corruptible (mortal) bodies!

But it gets even worse. For when Adam (after Eve) deliberately chose to believe Satan over God and eat from the one forbidden tree, the dominion of the Earth was in effect legally deeded over to Satan. Satan became "the ruler of this [fallen] world," the "god of this age [world]," and the "prince of the power of the air" (until Christ defeated him on the cross). So great was the consequence of disobedience to God and the sin that resulted that God actually had to redeem (buy back, purchase) man from sin and from ownership by Satan and death, so we could once again enter paradise (heaven) with Him. God in His mercy, love, grace, and kindness has provided a way for man to become "righteous," which means to be without sin (i.e., spiritually reconciled with God); He has provided a way for our sins to be forgiven, so we can again have eternal life with Him. That is the essence of the gospel message which this book is presenting to you. Each of us will choose eternal life (with God) or eternal death (separation from God). Those who end up in hell will do so as a result of their own choosing; God doesn't "send" anyone to hell – man sends himself there, and man chooses that destiny out of free will. Hell was not even created for man! Scripture tells us that hell was "prepared for the devil and his angels who followed after him." The Bible also clearly tells us that hell is a very real place of "eternal punishment" and "torment" – it is not a myth. This is covered in more detail later in this book.

The following excerpt by H.M. Riggle from *The Christian Church, Its Rise and Progress* is helpful: [7]

> As a result of the fall of man into sin back at the foundation of the world, Adam and Eve lost Paradise, holiness, eternal life, and the companionship of God, and reaped sorrow, misery, and death. Moreover, all their posterity fared the same result, and the whole world was enshrouded in darkness and sin. In this period, we are told, "death reigned"; that is, spiritual death, which came as a result of universal sin. Man stood in the attitude of a guilty violator of God's holy and infinite law, and hence was under an infinite penalty. Since the broken law was eternal, the penalty for its violation was eternal. The justice of God demanded that man suffer for his disobedience. God's immutability demanded that the penalty of his law be executed. To lift the penalty, he would have been obliged to abolish his law; but since that law was "holy, just, and good," he could not abolish it and yet be the God of law and order. Thus, man seemed eternally and hopelessly lost.
>
> But mercy rejoiced against judgment. The infinite love of God for lost humanity brought His infinite wisdom and knowledge into action. That wisdom, which is far beyond our comprehension, yes, "past finding out," schemed a way of escape, a plan of salvation. It was by providing an atoning sacrifice in the person of His own Son. This secured deliverance from the awful penalty and made the salvation of a lost world possible.

It's also helpful at this point to look at the full exchange between Satan and Eve as recorded in Genesis 3:

> Now the serpent [Satan] was more crafty than any beast of the field which the LORD God had made. And he said to the woman, "Indeed, has God said, 'You shall not eat from any tree of the garden'?" The woman said to the serpent, "From the fruit of the trees of the garden we may eat; but from the fruit of the tree which is in the middle of the garden, God has said, 'You shall not eat from it or touch it, or you will die.'" The serpent said to the woman, "You surely will not die! For God knows that in the day you eat from it your eyes will be opened, and you will be like God, knowing good and evil." When the woman saw that the tree was good for food, and that it was a delight to the eyes, and that the tree was desirable to make *one* wise, she took from its fruit and ate; and she gave also to her husband with her, and he ate. Then the eyes of both of them were opened, and they knew that they were naked; and they sewed fig leaves together and made themselves loin coverings.
>
> They heard the sound of the LORD God walking in the garden in the cool of the day, and the man and his wife hid themselves from the presence of the LORD God among the trees of the garden. Then the LORD God called to the man, and said to him, "Where are you?" He said, "I heard the sound of You in the garden, and I was afraid because I was naked; so I hid myself." And He said, "Who told you that you were naked? Have you eaten from the tree of which I commanded you not to eat?" The man said, "The woman whom You gave *to be* with me, she gave

---

[7] Riggle, H.M. (1912), *The Christian Church, Its Rise and Progress*, (The Gospel Trumpet Company), Prestonsburg KY.

me from the tree, and I ate." Then the LORD God said to the woman, "What is this you have done?" And the woman said, "The serpent deceived me, and I ate." The LORD God said to the serpent,

> "Because you have done this,
> Cursed are you more than all cattle,
> And more than every beast of the field;
> On your belly you will go,
> And dust you will eat
> All the days of your life;
> And I will put enmity
> Between you and the woman,
> And between your seed and her seed;
> He shall bruise you on the head,
> And you shall bruise him on the heel."
> To the woman He said,
> "I will greatly multiply
> Your pain in childbirth,
> In pain you will bring forth children;
> Yet your desire will be for your husband,
> And he will rule over you."

Then to Adam He said, "Because you have listened to the voice of your wife, and have eaten from the tree about which I commanded you, saying, 'You shall not eat from it';

> Cursed is the ground because of you;
> In toil you will eat of it
> All the days of your life.
> "Both thorns and thistles it shall grow for you;
> And you will eat the plants of the field;
> By the sweat of your face
> You will eat bread,
> Till you return to the ground,
> Because from it you were taken;
> For you are dust,
> And to dust you shall return." – Genesis 3:1-19

Notice how Satan deliberately tries to deceive Eve, hoping to spiritually and eternally kill all of the human race which was just being born. He was trying to trick Eve into doubting God, doubting that God was good, and also trick her into disobeying God. This is one reason we are admonished strongly to really, deeply know "the word of God" which is "the message [word] of truth" as it is actually given in Scripture, free from the false teachings of man (and Satan)! God gave us His Word so we can have life, not death. But we must know His Word; we must treasure it, and we must read, study, and pray (meditate) on it. This reinforces why I'm so adamant about pointing out all the false teachings of man so you can avoid them – they are all distortions of Scripture. They are designed to trick you out of eternal life, just like Satan tricked Eve.

And finally, understand that we each choose our own destiny, for we each choose who to follow – either God or Satan. There are no other choices. Even when you deliberately make no choice, you have thereby chosen Satan, for unless you have chosen God and eternal life (through His Son Jesus Christ), you have rejected Him and will suffer eternal death, which is separation from God with Satan and his evil spirits (fallen angels and demons) in hell forever.

In the next chapter, we will see that we are each individually responsible for our own choices – God gave each of us free will. We cannot blame Adam and Eve (or Satan) for our own free will actions and resulting disobedience and sin. We will also see that God plans to judge all sin and restore His creation to a state of paradise – that happens on the great Day of Judgment. That is why we need a Savior, for we are all dead (spiritually) in sin, eternally separated from God due to our own sinful actions unless something (or Someone) cleanses us from that sin. That also is the hope of the gospel message!

FALSE TEACHING(S) YOU WILL ENCOUNTER:
- Atheism (there is no God)
- The "Theory" of Evolution (and millions of years for earth history)
- Satan (the Devil) is just a myth
- Science disproves the Bible
- Annihilation after death

RELATED SCRIPTURE:

Therefore, just as through one man sin entered into the world, and death through sin, and so death spread to all men, because all sinned. – Romans 5:12

Then the LORD God took the man and put him into the garden of Eden to cultivate it and keep it. The LORD God commanded the man, saying, "From any tree of the garden you may eat freely; but from the tree of the knowledge of good and evil you shall not eat, for in the day that you eat from it you will surely die." – Genesis 2:15-17

For the wages [payment, penalty] of sin is death, but the free gift of God is eternal life in Christ Jesus our Lord. – Romans 6:23

For the anxious longing of the creation waits eagerly for the revealing of the sons of God. For the creation was subjected to futility [the curse – sin suffering, disease, death], not willingly, but because of Him who subjected it, in hope that the creation itself also will be set free from its slavery to corruption into the freedom of the glory of the children of God. For we know that the whole creation groans and suffers the pains of childbirth together until now. And not only this, but also we ourselves, having the first fruits of the Spirit, even we ourselves groan within ourselves, waiting eagerly for *our* adoption as sons, the redemption of our body. – Romans 8:19-23

We know that we are of God, and that the whole world lies in *the power of* the evil one. – 1 John 5:19

And you were dead in your trespasses and sins, in which you formerly walked according to the course of this world, according to the prince of the power of the air [Satan], of the spirit that is now working in the sons of disobedience. – Ephesians 2:1-2

Now the deeds of the flesh are evident, which are: immorality, impurity, sensuality, idolatry, sorcery, enmities, strife, jealousy, outbursts of anger, disputes, dissensions, factions, envying, drunkenness, carousing, and things like these, of which I forewarn you, just as I have forewarned you, that those who practice such things will not inherit the kingdom of God. – Galatians 5:19-21

"Then He will also say to those on His left, 'Depart from Me, accursed ones, into the eternal fire which has been prepared for the devil and his angels.'" – Matthew 25:41

But I am afraid that, as the serpent deceived Eve by his craftiness, your minds will be led astray from the simplicity and purity *of devotion* to Christ. – 2 Corinthians 11:3

1.5 WE ARE ALL SINNERS

Therefore, just as through one man sin entered into the world, and death through sin, and so death spread to all men, because all sinned. – Romans 5:12

For All Have Sinned. We read in the last chapter that it was by the disobedience of Eve, and then Adam, that sin entered the world, and through sin death. The Bible tells us that the penalty of sin is death, which is separation from God. Unless corrected, this state of spiritual death will last for eternity, for your soul/spirit (again, I'm using those words interchangeably herein) will live on forever. Life can only be found in the presence of God – for it is only God who gives and sustains life.

Therefore, realize that you're a sinner, and it is this sin that separates you from God. It is exactly at this point that many will ask: "Hey, why am I being held responsible for the choices [sin] of Adam and Eve? I wasn't even alive then!" We aren't – Scripture is clear that we are each responsible for our own choices, actions, and sins after reaching the age of accountability.

Now even after noting the above, the next thing many will ask/wonder (as I did at first) is: "Hey, I don't think I'm a sinner! I'm a pretty good person!" But I ask you to evaluate your own life and actions honestly. Have you <u>ever</u> in your entire life even once: lied, cheated, stolen, deceived someone, hurt someone, even killed someone, etc.? Those are examples of sins of commission. But there are also sins of omission (see James 4:17), which are things you didn't do but should have, such as: helping the needy or poor, standing up for the afflicted, speaking truth in witnessing, etc. These are all acts of a sinner, yes? Furthermore, did Adam make you do any of those things? No, I didn't think so.

And if you're like me, I bet you can tell very quickly when someone sins against you, yes? And they can tell when you've sinned against them. And if you're truly honest with yourself, you cannot claim that you've never ever in your entire life sinned against someone, can you? And if you can't even declare that you are sinless in front of man, how much more will you be unable to claim that you are sinless before a Holy God, the Almighty Lord, who knows all things, even the hidden things unseen and unsaid!

Please also do not make the fatal mistake of thinking that, well, "it's just a little tiny unimportant or harmless sin, so this can't separate me from God and keep me from heaven, right?" What we see as sin is not what God sees as sin: We grossly underestimate the seriousness and severity of even the smallest, tiniest sin when compared to an unimaginably holy and just God. What we think is the severity of sin is not what God says is the severity of sin. What we think should be the punishment for our sin(s) is not what God says is the punishment for sin(s). It is only from what is written in the Word of God that we must come to an understanding of sin. What we think doesn't really even matter on the subject; what God says on the subject is all that matters. I hope that makes sense to you.

Wayne Jackson writes:[8]

> The Bible clearly teaches that God is an absolutely holy Being (Isaiah 6:3; Revelation 4:8)—i.e., he is utterly separate from evil. His holiness is demonstrated

---

[8] Jackson, Wayne. "Why Would a Loving God Send Us to Hell?" *ChristianCourier.com*. Access date: March 9, 2019. https://christiancourier.com/articles/1563-why-would-a-loving-god-send-us-to-hell

in numerous narratives in the Scriptures. At Sinai, the chasm between God and sinful Israel was underscored vividly (Exodus 19:12-25). The tabernacle arrangement, with its holy place and most holy place (the abode of God [Exodus 25:22]) certainly was designed to instruct the Hebrews relative to Jehovah's holy nature (Exodus 26:33).

The Lord's holiness not only suggests that he cannot commit sin personally (James 1:13), it also means that he cannot ignore rebellion as if it had never happened. The prophet Habakkuk declared to Jehovah: "Your eyes are too pure to look upon evil [i.e., favorably]; you cannot tolerate wrong" (1:13, NIV). God takes no pleasure in wickedness (Psalm 5:4), and those who indulge themselves therein will be recipients of his vengeance (11:6-7). The Bible affirms that the outpouring of divine wrath on the ungodly is, in fact, a "revelation of the righteous judgment of God" (Romans 2:5; emphasis added).

Sin Separates from God

When humanity chose to sin, it made the decision to be separated from the holy Creator. The prophet clearly stated: "[Y]our iniquities have separated between you and your God, and your sins have hid his face from you" (Isaiah 59:2). In biblical parlance, "death" generally denotes a separation of some sort. When the spirit departs the body, the body is dead (James 2:26). Similarly, when a person enters a state of sinfulness, he becomes spiritually dead (Ephesians 2:1), for, by that act, he has determined to separate himself from God. Remember, the initiation of this estrangement was not forced on us by our Maker; it is totally human responsibility.

We simply cannot fully comprehend the true nature and severity of our sin in this fallen world, but one day, we will see all sin for the true abomination and horror that it really is. The true weight of sin will then be realized and understood by all, even those who claim they don't need or believe in God. Once again, please realize that it is not shameful to admit that you are a sinner before God; remember, He already knows that – He knows all things! It actually takes strength of character and courage and humbleness of heart to confess that you're a sinner. What truly is shameful is remaining in your sins, which is almost always due to stubbornness and pride.

It's also vital at this point to address one popular false teaching called "original sin." This false teaching claims that we are born in sin as babies. However, Scripture is clear that we are not born in "original sin" and that babies are not born sinners. This false teaching comes about (primarily) from a misinterpretation of several Bible verses (e.g., Psalms 51, 58). The reason this "original sin" false teaching is so important to address is that many will use the excuse of: "Hey, if I was born a sinner, then I'm not responsible for what I do!" What they are actually saying is: "Since God made me the way I am, I'm not responsible!" But be not deceived, the "original sin" teaching is not true, and this false teaching can lead you to eternal death! This "original sin" false teaching is covered in more detail in the Beware the Wolves chapter; please read it now if it is a sticking point for you in proceeding.

We also do not "inherit" sin from our parents, neither father nor mother. Scripture is very clear that we are each responsible for our own actions and sins, which we decide to do after reaching what the Bible calls the "age of accountability" (see Romans 1:20, Numbers 14:26-29, Deuteronomy 1:39). This age isn't precisely defined in Scripture, although the age that God used when leading the ancient Hebrews out of Egypt and through the wilderness into the promised land of Canaan was twenty (20) years old (see Numbers 14). Those over the age of 20 were decreed to die in the wilderness due to their unbelief; those under that age were spared and continued on to go into the Promised Land. I'm not dogmatic about this particular age, and from what I can find, read and study on the matter, no one knows the exact age except God Himself. Suffice it to say, at some point in our life, we all reach the age where we know right from wrong, yes? And after that age, all of us are responsible for our own sins.

So, continuing on, please be honest with yourself; it's not Adam who is to blame for your sins, is it? – you chose to do them (as did I). I hope that you see that you are a sinner, as am I, yes? This is a vitally important step before proceeding. A failure to admit (or accept) that you are indeed a sinner stems from pride, and pride leads to death. It's no shame to admit that you're a sinner; we all are! All of us in this fallen world have an unclean heart (described as "deceitful," "sick"), unclean thoughts and motives, "unclean lips," and unclean actions. The Bible tells us that "there is none righteous, not even one" (Romans 3:10-11). Every one of us who has ever lived is a sinner – except one Man, the Son of God, the Man Christ Jesus.

The Bible also tells us that God will put an end to sin once and for all; He will not let man continue in a state of rebellion forever. While God is holy, loving, and patient beyond measure, He is also just, and He will judge all sin. He will eradicate sin forever and once again restore His creation to a "very good" state of paradise (i.e., perfect, Genesis 1:31) – where there is no more sin, suffering, and death (Revelation 21:4). This brings us to the coming Great Day of Judgment, which is discussed in the next chapter.

FALSE TEACHING(S) YOU WILL ENCOUNTER:
- The Doctrine of "Original Sin"
- Satan (the Devil) is just a myth
- Annihilation after death
- You get a "2nd Chance" after death
- "Soul Sleeping"

RELATED SCRIPTURE:

Therefore, just as through one man sin entered into the world, and death through sin, and so death spread to all men, because all sinned. – Romans 5:12

For the wages [penalty] of sin is death, but the free gift of God is eternal life in Christ Jesus our Lord. – Romans 6:23

…for all have sinned and fall short of the glory of God. – Romans 3:23

As it is written,
> "THERE IS NONE RIGHTEOUS, NOT EVEN ONE;
> THERE IS NONE WHO UNDERSTANDS,
> THERE IS NONE WHO SEEKS FOR GOD;
> ALL HAVE TURNED ASIDE, TOGETHER THEY HAVE BECOME USELESS;
> THERE IS NONE WHO DOES GOOD,
> THERE IS NOT EVEN ONE."
> "THEIR THROAT IS AN OPEN GRAVE,
> WITH THEIR TONGUES THEY KEEP DECEIVING,"

"THE POISON OF ASPS IS UNDER THEIR LIPS";
"WHOSE MOUTH IS FULL OF CURSING AND BITTERNESS";
"THEIR FEET ARE SWIFT TO SHED BLOOD,
DESTRUCTION AND MISERY ARE IN THEIR PATHS,
AND THE PATH OF PEACE THEY HAVE NOT KNOWN."
"THERE IS NO FEAR OF GOD BEFORE THEIR EYES." – Romans 3:10-18

For all of us have become like one who is unclean,
And all our righteous deeds are like a filthy garment;
And all of us wither like a leaf,
And our iniquities, like the wind, take us away. – Isaiah 64:6

For since the creation of the world His invisible attributes, His eternal power and divine nature, have been clearly seen, being understood through what has been made, so that they are without excuse. For even though they knew God, they did not honor Him as God or give thanks, but they became futile in their speculations, and their foolish heart was darkened. – Romans 1:20-21

And you were dead in your trespasses and sins, in which you formerly walked according to the course of this world, according to the prince of the power of the air, of the spirit that is now working in the sons of disobedience. – Ephesians 2:1-2

"The heart is more deceitful than all else
And is desperately sick;
Who can understand it?
I, the LORD, search the heart,
I test the mind,
To give to each person according to his ways,
According to the results of his deeds." – Jeremiah 17:9-10

For from within, out of the hearts of people, come the evil thoughts, *acts of* sexual immorality, thefts, murders, *acts of* adultery, deeds of greed, wickedness, deceit, indecent behavior, envy, slander, pride, *and* foolishness. – Mark 7:21-22

Jesus said to them, "*It is* not those who are healthy who need a physician, but those who are sick; I did not come to call the righteous, but sinners." – Mark 2:17

Therefore, to one who knows *the* right thing to do and does not do it, to him it is sin. – James 4:17

Pride *goes* before destruction,
And a haughty spirit before stumbling. – Proverbs 16:18

There is a way *which seems* right to a man,
But its end is the way of death. – Proverbs 14:12

Why do you boast in evil, O mighty man?
The lovingkindness of God *endures* all day long.
Your tongue devises destruction,
Like a sharp razor, O worker of deceit.
You love evil more than good,
Falsehood more than speaking what is right. *Selah.*

You love all words that devour,
O deceitful tongue.

But God will break you down forever;
He will snatch you up and tear you away from *your* tent,
And uproot you from the land of the living. – Psalm 52:1-5

The fool has said in his heart, "There is no God."
They are corrupt, they have committed abominable deeds;
There is no one who does good.
The LORD has looked down from heaven upon the sons of men
To see if there are any who understand,
Who seek after God.
They have all turned aside, together they have become corrupt;
There is no one who does good, not even one. – Psalm 14:1-3

I prayed to the LORD my God and confessed and said,

"Alas, O Lord, the great and awesome God, who keeps His covenant and lovingkindness for those who love Him and keep His commandments, we have sinned, committed iniquity, acted wickedly and rebelled, even turning aside from Your commandments and ordinances. Moreover, we have not listened to Your servants the prophets, who spoke in Your name to our kings, our princes, our fathers and all the people of the land." – Daniel 9:4-6

Do not be deceived, God is not mocked; for whatever a man sows, this he will also reap. For the one who sows to his own flesh will from the flesh reap corruption, but the one who sows to the Spirit will from the Spirit reap eternal life. – Galatians 6:7-8

"Enter through the narrow gate; for the gate is wide and the way is broad that leads to destruction, and there are many who enter through it. For the gate is small and the way is narrow that leads to life, and there are few who find it." – Matthew 7:13-14

Why should *any* living mortal, or *any* man,
Offer complaint in view of his sins?
Let us examine and probe our ways,
And let us return to the LORD.
We lift up our heart and hands
Toward God in heaven. – Lamentations 3:39-41

The LORD'S lovingkindnesses indeed never cease,
For His compassions never fail.
They are new every morning;
Great is Your faithfulness.
"The LORD is my portion," says my soul,
"Therefore I have hope in Him."
The LORD is good to those who wait for Him,
To the person who seeks Him.
It is good that he waits silently
For the salvation of the LORD. – Lamentations 3:22-26

Be gracious to me, O God, according to Your lovingkindness;
According to the greatness of Your compassion blot out my transgressions.
Wash me thoroughly from my iniquity
And cleanse me from my sin.
For I know my transgressions,
And my sin is ever before me.
Against You, You only, I have sinned
And done what is evil in Your sight,
So that You are justified when You speak
And blameless when You judge. – Psalm 51:1-4

1.6 THE COMING GREAT DAY OF JUDGMENT

For we will all stand before the judgment seat of God.
For it is written, "AS I LIVE, SAYS THE LORD, EVERY KNEE SHALL BOW TO ME,
AND EVERY TONGUE SHALL GIVE PRAISE TO GOD."
So then each one of us will give an account of himself to God. – Romans 14:10-12

The Coming Great Day of Judgment. The Bible tells us that not only is God a God of love ("for God is love"), but He is also "holy" and a God of justice (perfect in "righteousness" and the rule of law), and that He will punish (judge) all sin (that has ever been committed). This is a pretty weighty chapter and not a topic of popular appeal, for His love is often stressed, and His justice is often ignored or downplayed. But it is one we must address and go through in detail to avoid being deceived, for Scripture warns us to be ready for Christ's return at any moment (e.g., right now) – for that is also the great Day of Judgment.

Scripture tells us that He will bring all sin to a conclusion on this Day of Judgment – which is also referred to as "the great and awesome Day of the Lord," the "day of Christ Jesus," the "end of this age" and the end of time itself. On this Day, God will judge all sin that has ever been committed in the world, and sin will be eradicated, banished from His creation forever, and creation will be restored to its rightful and perfect state – where there is no more curse and no more sin, suffering or death. It is here, if you will allow the analogy, where we meet the grizzly bear depicted on the cover of this book – are you prepared for the encounter?

This will be the most awesomely hopeful or dreadful Day for all mankind in all of human history. Which of those it is depends on how you are able to stand before the Lord on that Day, when we will all stand before the Supreme Court of the Lord for "it is appointed for men to die once and after this comes judgment." We will all be called to give an account for everything we've ever said and done; in fact, all the deeds of man over all of human history will be made known and judged. No one who has ever lived – past, present, or future – will escape this Day of Judgment:

> For we must all appear before the judgment seat of Christ, so that each one may be recompensed for his deeds in the body, according to what he has done, whether good or bad. – 2 Corinthians 5:10

On this Day, God will judge our motives as well as our actions, for "He [God] knows the thoughts of man"; nothing, no matter how dark or secret, can be hidden from God. For it is written: "nothing is hidden that will not become evident, nor anything secret that will not be known and come to light," and "whatever you have said in the dark will be heard in the light, and what you have whispered in the inner rooms will be proclaimed upon the housetops," and "then each of us will give an account of himself to God," so "that each one may be recompensed for his deeds in the body, according to what he has done, whether good or bad." It's only pride and arrogance that cause one to think he or she can hide anything from God, who is Creator of all. You (and I) will have to answer for every single sinful thought, word, deed, action, and motive we have ever had, said, or done. All sin will be judged by a holy, righteous, and just God for what it truly is. He will make no mistakes in judgment either, for He knows all things.

We will all be gathered before Christ on that Day – those who died in sin by rejecting Christ (the lost) will be gathered on "His left," and those who died in righteousness (the saved, who are covered by the blood of Christ) will be on "His right." As explained in previous chapters, your spirit is eternal – it lives on fully conscious even after your body dies. When Christ returns for Judgment Day, the spirits of all those who have died will be reunited with their new resurrected eternal bodies; and those alive at Christs' return will be "changed in an instant" into their new eternal bodies. The Bible tells us that both the saved and the lost will be resurrected in eternal bodies! You do not pass into nothingness at death, and the wicked (the lost) are not extinguished into nothingness after judgment (the false teaching of annihilation).

At Judgment, "books will be opened" (in which every thought, word, motive, action, and deed you have done in your life is recorded), and then "EVERY KNEE SHALL BOW TO ME, AND EVERY TONGUE SHALL GIVE PRAISE TO GOD," also written as: "at the name of Jesus every knee will bow, of those who are in heaven and on earth and under the earth, and that every tongue will confess that Jesus Christ is Lord, to the glory of God the Father," for Jesus is the Lord God Himself. Even those who did not believe in God and His Christ will bow down and declare Jesus as Lord, to the glory of God. Then judgment will happen. Scripture says that Jesus will be our Judge, but get this, He will also be the attorney for those who have accepted Him! Wouldn't you like to have the Judge also as your Attorney? How amazing is that! This is explained in the upcoming chapters on the "good news" of the gospel.

The saved, those who died righteous (forgiven of sin by accepting Christ) and justified (by being obedient to the commandments of Christ), will hear the verdict of "NOT GUILTY" (of sin) and hear "Well done, good and faithful servant," "enter into my rest" in heaven with God and His holy angels forever. The lost, however, those who died in sin by rejecting Christ, will hear the verdict: "GUILTY" (of sin). Scripture also tells us that the penalty for sin is death; the guilty will hear the Judge say, "I never knew you; depart from Me, you who practice lawlessness," and they will then be thrown "into the eternal fire [hell] which has been prepared for the devil and his angels who followed after him" for all eternity, where they "will pay the penalty of eternal destruction, away from the presence of the Lord and from the glory of His power." This is called eternal death, for life can only be found in the presence of God. Only the righteous will enter heaven with God in eternal life; nothing and no one sinful can enter heaven with God.

HELL IS A REAL PLACE OF TORMENT

Make no mistake; hell is a real place, and those who die in sin will be banished there forever, away from the presence of God. It is described as a place of "eternal fire," a "lake of fire and brimstone," but also one of "outer darkness" and a place "of torment" where there is "weeping and gnashing of teeth." Hell was "prepared for the devil and his angels who followed after him"; it was not created for man. However, when man chooses to remain in sin (by his own free will – the result of pride and stubbornness), his destination is the same as the devils. Wayne Jackson writes: [9]

---

[9] Jackson, Wayne. "Why Would a Loving God Send Us to Hell?" *ChristianCourier.com*. Access date: March 9, 2019. https://christiancourier.com/articles/1563-why-would-a-loving-god-send-us-to-hell

Hell: The Ultimate Separation

Inspiration describes the penalty of hell as "the second death" (Revelation 20:14), which suggests that it is the ultimate separation from God. This is emphasized forcefully in several New Testament passages. In the parable of the virgins, those unprepared virgins who "slept" (i.e., died), when awakened by the coming of the Bridegroom, wanted entrance into his presence, but the door was shut, and they were denied that association (Matthew 25:1-13).

Unprofitable servants will be "cast out" and will hear the Lord exclaim: "Depart from me" (Matthew 25:41). Paul expressed it like this. Those who know not God and who obey not the gospel, "shall suffer punishment, even eternal destruction from the face of the Lord and from the glory of his might" (2 Thessalonians 1:9; emphasis added). This abiding separation from God is but a continuation of the estrangement that the rebel cultivated in this life. The Lord is not responsible for such a reckless decision!

The Horror of Separation from God

How is it possible to describe the spiritual state of being banished from the presence of the supreme Being of the universe? Being alienated from Jehovah is the ultimate experience of horror. It is a separation from everything that is pure and good, everything that is right and wholesome, and everything that makes for joy and tranquility. It is, however, a spiritual experience, and since the human mind operates on the plane of the material, we really are not prepared to appreciate the gravity of such a circumstance. Hence, God has employed appropriate symbolism to describe the agonies of hell.

The spiritual abode of the wicked is a state of pain, trouble, and sorrow (Psalm 116:3). It is characterized by shame and contempt (Daniel 12:2) and is a realm of affliction (Jonah 2:2). Hell is a place of outer darkness where there is weeping and the gnashing of teeth (Matthew 25:30)—a sphere of eternal fire (Matthew 25:41) where the "worm" (a figure for gnawing anguish) does not die (Mark 9:48).

The wicked are described as being beaten with stripes (Luke 12:47-48). They are recipients of God's wrath and indignation, they experience tribulation and anguish (Romans 2:8-9), and they suffer punishment as a manifestation of the Lord's vengeance (2 Thessalonians 1:8-9). Hell is a place of utter torment, where no rest ever is known (Revelation 14:10-11).

While it would not be an expression of responsible exegesis to literalize the figures of speech cataloged above, one must never forget that the symbolism is designed to emphasize the terror of being abandoned by God. Moreover, the figures doubtless do not do justice to the actual reality of this eternal nightmare.

The torment of hell comes with the eternal memory and regret of one's sins searing into their consciousness for all time; for on Judgment Day, everyone will have finally seen their sin (and their sinful nature) fully revealed for what it really is, and they will also have seen God for who He truly is – a patient, merciful, loving, righteous and unimaginably holy God. The lost will have seen the true glory of God and heaven revealed right in front of them, as if almost able to reach out and touch it and grasp it themselves, but they will then realize they are barred from entering such glory for all eternity because of their unforgiven sin. Those condemned to hell will be fully conscious and alive in spirit, and they will have all eternity to regret that they rejected the free gift of eternal life which God offered to everyone. They will see that God was "patient toward you, not wishing for any to perish but for all to come to repentance"; they will see that He tirelessly, mercifully, and continuously reached out to them over the course of their lives, trying to save them from "the wrath [judgment] to come." They will then have all eternity to think, "what if" I had only listened. Oh, that is the searing torment of hell – and it will all be self-imposed.

This is such an important topic that I want to include what some other writers have said on the subject. Wayne Jackson writes: [10]

The Nature of Gehenna

There are several important truths regarding the punishment of Gehenna that the Bible student must consider.

Body and Soul

Gehenna is a state that involves both the resurrected body and the soul. First, note that unrighteous people will be resurrected from the dead, just as the saints will (Jn. 5:28-29; Acts 24:15). Then, observe that Christ clearly indicated that the body, as well as the soul, will be subjected to the agonies of Gehenna (Mt. 5:29-30; Mk. 9:43-48; Mt. 10:28).

Consciousness

Gehenna involves a state of awareness. It is very important that this point be made, because there are those who allege that hell will consist in the wicked being annihilated (C. Pinnock, 40 [11]; cf. LaGard Smith, 1988 [12]). In their view, the occupants of Gehenna will eventually cease to exist. This concept is flawed indeed.

First, when the Lord affirmed that God will "destroy" both body and soul in Gehenna (Mt. 10:28), he employed the word apollumi (used about 92 times in the New Testament). It is translated by such terms as "destroy," "perish," "loss," and "lost." The term does not suggest the sense of annihilation.

When the prodigal son was in the far country, he was "lost" (apolollos), i.e., estranged from the blessings of his home, but he was not annihilated. Jesus affirmed that he came to save that which stands lost (apolollos). The perfect tense describes a present condition which has resulted from previous activity. The Lord did not come to save folks who were in a state of non-existence!

"In every instance where the word apollumi is found in the New Testament, something other than annihilation is being described" (Morey, 90 [13]).

Regarding apollumi, Vine notes: "The idea is not extinction but ruin, loss, not of being, but of well-being" (211). [14]

---

[10] Jackson, Wayne. "The Use of 'Hell' in the New Testament." *ChristianCourier.com*. Access date: March 9, 2019. https://christiancourier.com/articles/406-use-of-hell-in-the-new-testament-the

[11] Pinnock, Clark (1987), "Fire, Then Nothing," *Christianity Today*, March 20.

[12] Smith, F. LaGard (April, 1988), "A Christian Response to the New Age Movement," Pepperdine University Lectureship, Tape 3. See: *Christian Courier*, Oct., 1992, 21-22.

[13] Morey, Robert (1984), *Death and the Afterlife* (Minneapolis: Bethany).

[14] Vine, W.E. (1991), *Amplified Expository Dictionary of New Testament Words* (Iowa Falls: World).

Thayer defines apollumi, in connection with Matthew 10:28, as follows: "to devote or give over to eternal misery" (64). [15]

Second, the Bible employs a number of expressions to describe the emotional state of Gehenna, which can only imply the concept of conscious agony. It is depicted as a place of "unquenchable fire" (Mk. 9:44) — fire being a metaphor for "the extreme penal torments which the wicked are to undergo after their life on earth" (Thayer, 558).

Jesus spoke of Gehenna as a place "where their worm dies not" (Mk. 9:48). The never-dying worm is a symbol of the unending "torment of the damned" (Arndt/Gingrich, 765). [16]

The Lord describes Gehenna as a place of "eternal punishment." The word rendered "punishment" is the Greek kolasis. Note the following statement from the patristic document known as 1 Clement (A.D. 95). "… [The Lord] does not forsake those that hope in Him, but gives up such as depart from Him to punishment [kolasis] and torment" (XI).

Punishment implies consciousness. It would be absurd to describe those who no longer exist as being "punished." The wicked will be "tormented" with the fire of Gehenna (cf. Rev. 14:10-11). Torment certainly implies awareness (cf. Rev. 9:5; 11:10).

Finally, we would raise this question: If the condition of the rich man in Hades was one of "anguish" (odunao – "to suffer pain"), though it involved only the soul, does it seem likely that the ultimate punishment of Gehenna, which involves both body and soul, would entail less?

H.M. Riggle in *Beyond the Tomb* writes this on hell: [17]

We shall come then to the direct question: What will the eternal punishment of the lost consist in and of, or what will be its nature? We believe the Bible clearly teaches that it is a state of endless, irrecoverable misery and conscious suffering.

First, *torment.*

"And when he was come to the other side into the country of the Gergesenes, there met him two possessed with devils, coming out of the tombs, exceeding fierce, so that no man might pass by that way. And, behold, they cried out, saying, What have we to do with thee, Jesus, thou Son of God? art thou come hither to torment us before the time?" (Matt. 8:28-29).

In Thayer's Greek-English Lexicon *basanizo,* the verb form for the Greek noun translated "torment" is: "To vex with grievous pains of body or mind, to torment." *Torment*— "That which gives pain, vexation, or misery. Extreme pain, anguish, the utmost degree of misery, either of body or mind. To torture, hence to put to extreme pain or anguish, to inflict excruciating pain and misery."— *Webster.* The text describes a man possessed with a legion of demons. At the

---

[15] Thayer, J.H. (1958), A Greek-English Lexicon of the New Testament (Edinburgh: T.&T. Clark).

[16] Arndt, W.F. & Gingrich, F.W. (1967), Greek-English Lexicon of the New Testament (Chicago: University of Chicago).

[17] Riggle, H.M. (1929/2018), Beyond the Tomb, (The Gospel Trumpet Company/Holy Spirit Prints).

approach of Christ, the devils cried out, "Jesus, thou Son of God: art thou come hither to torment us before the time?" On this Dr. Adam Clarke remarks: "They knew there was a time determined by the divine Judge, when they should be sent into greater torment." Torment awaits these devils beyond the judgment, and this text proves that they are fully cognizant of the fact. That is why they "tremble" (James 2:19). They did not say to Jesus, "Do not annihilate us," but "I adjure thee by God, that thou torment me not" (Mark 5:7). Further proof that this will be their awful punishment is found in Rev. 20:10: "And the devil that deceived them was cast into the lake of fire and brimstone, and shall be tormented day and night forever and ever."

This hell of torment was "prepared for the devil and his angels," and the wicked will be cast into the same place and state (Matt. 25:41). So, *torment,* and not obliteration, awaits the guilty. After death, the Rich Man "lift up his eyes, being in torments" (Luke 16:23). He cried for mercy, begged for water, and said, "I am tormented in this flame" (Luke 16:24). He called his abode "this place of torment." Hell, then, is not a state of non-existence, but a place of torment, suffering. This was not said of the moldering corpse that had been buried on earth, but it was the state and condition of a man whose spirit was alive in the eternal world. ...

Second, *tribulation and anguish.*

"But unto them that are contentious, and do not obey the truth, but obey unrighteousness, indignation and wrath, tribulation and anguish, upon every soul of man that doeth evil" (Rom. 2:8-9).

Paul's theme here is the "righteous judgment of God" that all men must face in the final "day of wrath." Read the context. The Divine penalty upon the ungodly is "indignation and wrath," and its effect upon them is not annihilation but "tribulation and anguish." Tribulation here means pressure—extreme anguish and excruciating pain. The anguish simply intensifies the other. The idea conveyed is that of extreme suffering. ...

Fifth, *suffering vengeance of the Almighty, who is a consuming fire.*

"Suffering the vengeance of eternal fire" (Jude 7). This is the opposite of blotting out of existence. When God rained fire and brimstone upon Sodom and Gomorrah, the buildings, etc., were reduced to ashes; but the wicked inhabitants of those cities who committed fornication, "going after strange flesh" (Jude 7), are "suffering the vengeance of eternal fire." The fire of Divine wrath is upon them and will be forever. This is not annihilation, but a perpetual suffering.

Sixth, *the punishment of loss, or deprivation.*

"Depart from me, ye that work iniquity" (Matt. 7:23). "What a terrible word! What a dreadful separation! Depart from me! From the very Jesus whom you have proclaimed, in union with whom alone is eternal life to be found. For, united with Christ, all is heaven; separated from him, all is hell."—Dr. Adam Clarke. "Depart from me, ye cursed" (Matt. 25:41). "And these shall go away" (Matt. 25:46). "Bind him hand and foot, and take him away, and cast him into outer darkness; there shall be weeping and gnashing of teeth" (Matt. 22:13).

In life salvation was within their reach; they could have secured it and have become qualified for the enjoyment and companionship of God, and of the good and pure of all ages: but they disdained it, refused it, and disqualified themselves for the holy society of heaven. Now, since by their action such chose to be separated from the holy and redeemed hosts of heaven, they must be associated with the impure and unholy in both character and doom. An utter severance and banishment from the presence of the Lord, and an abode and association with demons and the refuse of all ages is the necessary consequence of all the workers of iniquity, and this is the eternal misery of the damned.

There is for them no other alternative. This doom is deprivation of eternal life, endurance of God's displeasure, and an utter rejection and banishment from the society of Jesus and the blessed in heaven. This state is final. He shall "sever the wicked from among the just" (Matt. 13:40-43, 48, 50). Eternal separation from God. "This is the second death" (Rev. 20:14). "When once the master of the house is risen up, and hath shut to the door, and ye begin to stand without, and to knock at the door, saying, Lord, Lord, open unto us; and he shall answer and say unto you, I know you not whence ye are: then shall ye begin to say, We have eaten and drunk in thy presence, and thou has taught in our streets. But he shall say, I tell you, I know you not whence ye are; depart from me, all ye workers of iniquity. There shall be weeping and gnashing of teeth, when ye shall see Abraham, and Isaac, and Jacob, and all the prophets, in the kingdom of God, and you yourselves thrust out" (Luke 13:25-28). "And while they went to buy, the bridegroom came; and they that were ready went in with him to the marriage: and the door was shut. Afterward came also the other virgins, saying, Lord, Lord, open to us. But he answered and said, Verily I say unto you, I know you not" (Matt. 25:10-12). Barred from heaven forever. Here we have a glimpse of the soul's eternal loss.

"Blessed are they that do his commandments, that they may have right to the tree of life, and may enter in through the gates into the city. For without [outside] are dogs [the morally impure], and sorcerers [those who practice occult crafts, use altering drugs, etc.], and whoremongers [sexually immoral, fornicators, molesters, adulterers], and murderers, and idolaters, and whosoever loveth and maketh a lie" (Rev. 22:14-15).

Here are some of the saddest statements to be found in the Bible. The place is where time and eternity meet and eternal destinies are apportioned to all men. "They that were ready went in," "through the gates into the city"—heaven. Then "the door was shut," and the whoremongers, idolaters, liars, and all characters of the lost were "thrust out," left "without," lost, ruined, cursed, damned, and in torment. "There shall be weeping and gnashing of teeth." What a disappointment and sense of misery when heaven's door, the door of mercy and opportunity, is forever closed, and the lost hear the awful sentence, "depart," and find themselves in "outer darkness."

"Here we have the misery of the unjust and impure, and the happiness of the righteous and holy. It connects time with eternity. The character wherewith we sink into the grave at death is the very character with which we shall reappear on the day of resurrection. The moral lineaments [distinctive features or characteristics] which are graven on [deeply imprinted or carved into] the tablet of the inner man, and which every day of an unconverted life marks deeper and more indelible [cannot be removed] than before, will retain the impress they have received unaltered by the transition to the future state of our existence. Propensity is strengthened by every new act of indulgence; any virtuous principle is more firmly established than before by every new act of resolute obedience to its dictates. Then the hell of the wicked may be said to be already begun, and the heaven of the virtuous. The one has a foretaste of the wretchedness before him, the other of the happiness before him. The inward sense of dishonor which haunts and humbles the sinner here is but the commencement of that shame and everlasting contempt to which he shall awake hereafter. In stepping from time to eternity he carries in his own distempered bosom [sinful or sick heart] the materials of his coming vengeance along with him. He will carry his unsanctified habits and unhallowed passions thitherward. When probation is over, character is unalterably fixed, and there is but one probation."—*T. Chalmers, D.D.*

Eternal torment, tribulation, anguish, damnation, shame and contempt, suffering the vengeance of Almighty God, cast into outer darkness, barred from God's presence and heaven forever, weeping, wailing, gnashing of teeth, "where their worm dieth not, and the fire is not quenched"—such is the Bible description of the nature of future punishment. What the realities will be, only fallen angels and the wicked shall ever know.

"Pray always, that ye may be accounted worthy to escape all these things that shall come to pass, and to stand before the Son of man" (Luke 21:36).

One last point about hell needs to be stressed: it is eternal in duration. This is also a topic that many don't like to discuss or preach on – yet Scripture is clear. In fact, the same Greek word that is used to describe the eternal duration of the saints in heaven is also used to describe the eternal duration of the punishment of the wicked in hell. No one argues that the saints won't have eternal life in heaven, yet they argue that the very same word, when used referring to the wicked in hell, doesn't mean the same thing! This is horribly inconsistent logic. H.M. Riggle writes in *Beyond the Tomb*:[18]

THE PUNISHMENT OF THE WICKED WILL BE TO ALL ETERNITY

Eternity is well expressed in the following text: "From everlasting to everlasting, thou art God" (Ps. 90:2). There are three words which in our English Bible in their true sense signify eternity and are so used in the Scriptures. They are *everlasting, eternal,* and *forever,* from the Greek *aionios.* Forever is also translated from *aiona.* I shall here submit the definition of *aionios* by some of the standard Greek lexicons:

- "Everlasting; perpetual; eternal."—*Pickering*
- "Without end, never to cease, everlasting."—*Dr. Thayer*
- "Everlasting, eternal."—*Liddell and Scott.* Also *Donnegan*
- "Everlasting, perpetual."—*Youge*
- "Without end; perpetual and interminable."—*Schleusner*
- "To eternity."—*Cremer*
- "Indeterminate as to duration; eternal; everlasting."—*Baxter*

---

[18] Riggle, H.M. (1929/2018), *Beyond the Tomb*, (The Gospel Trumpet Company/Holy Spirit Prints).

- "Unlimited as to duration; eternal, everlasting."—*Greenfield*
- "Ever enduring; perpetual; everlasting; implying eternity; without end."—*Robinson*
- Aiona— "forever," is defined by Robert Young in his Analytical Concordance— "To the ages of the ages." From this we learn that when our translators rendered aionios as "everlasting" and "eternal," and aiona as "forever," and they had solid grounds for doing so.
- Everlasting— "Lasting or enduring forever, eternal, endless."—*Webster*
- Eternal— "Everlasting, endless, immortal."—*Webster*
- Forever— "Throughout eternity, endless."—*Webster*

I shall now give a number of texts where the Greek word is aionios and the English rendering is everlasting:

- The righteous "shall inherit *everlasting* life" (Matt. 19:29).
- "In the world to come, life *everlasting*" (Luke 18:30).
- "The end *everlasting* life" (Rom. 6:22).
- "The *everlasting* kingdom" (2 Pet. 1:11).
- "The *everlasting* God" (Rom. 16:26).
- Now, we read— "Some to shame and everlasting [Greek Septuagint—aionion] contempt" (Dan. 12:2).
- "Cast into everlasting fire" (Matt. 18:8).
- "Depart from me ye cursed, into everlasting fire, prepared for the devil and his angels" (Matt. 25:41).
- "And these shall go away into everlasting punishment; but the righteous unto life eternal" (Matt. 25:46).

As long as God Himself shall exist, and as long as He shall have dominion and a kingdom, the wicked will suffer "contempt and shame everlasting"; "everlasting punishment" in "everlasting fire." The same word that measures the endless existence of God Himself, of His kingdom, dominion, gospel, and the life and felicities of the righteous in heaven, measures the duration of the punishment of the wicked in hell. There is no appeal from this fact.

IS ETERNAL PUNISHMENT FAIR?

Many refuse to believe that a loving God will sentence anyone to eternal punishment in hell. As I've written, we grossly underestimate the nature of sin; we will see sin for what it truly is on Judgment Day. We are thinking from the standpoint of our puny, finite human minds; we do not see sin as God sees it. We also tend to stress (or focus on) the fact that God is loving while dismissing the fact that God is also righteous and just – and He, therefore, must bring all sin into judgment.

We must also remember that God "desires all people to be saved and to come to the knowledge of the truth" so that none are lost in judgment, and He has provided a way for each and every person to inherit eternal life. It is only by their own free-will choice that anyone ends up in hell. God doesn't send anyone to hell – they send themselves there!

Scripture also tells us that hell will have varying degrees of punishment. Those who received greater light and exposure to the truth of God and His Christ Jesus and the message of salvation, but still reject it, will have a harsher punishment to bear. This speaks directly to us today as we have the most widespread access to the gospel "message of truth" in all of history, and with that comes a responsibility to respond to it.

Wayne Jackson writes:[19]

> Many religionists who deny the biblical teaching of the eternal, conscious torment of hell do so strictly on emotional grounds. They reject everlasting punishment — not because they have carefully studied the scriptural evidence, and have arrived at their convictions on an intellectual basis — but because, in their view, eternal punishment just "doesn't seem fair." How could a just God punish forever someone who has only rebelled a brief period on earth?
>
> There are several things to be said in response to this.
>
> First, how could a just God eternally reward someone who has only served him the limited span of an earthly existence? No one seems to have a problem with that!
>
> Second, the Bible makes it abundantly clear that our loving God has never been of the disposition to delight in the possibility of a single soul ending in hell.
>
> "The Lord is not slack concerning his promise, as some count slackness; but is longsuffering to you-ward, not wishing that any should perish, but that all should come to repentance" (2 Pet. 3:9).
>
> He does not wish that anyone perish. The term "wishing" (ASV) or "willing" (KJV) reflects a present tense participle, emphasizing a sustained benevolence on the part of the Creator. Note that.
>
> The fact is, hell was initially prepared for Satan and his angels (Mt. 25:41), not humans. The Lord has made every possible provision so that humanity might avoid eternal punishment. Who can fault the justice of God in the light of Christ's death?
>
> Third, eternal separation from God is a matter of human determination. Paul defends the justice of God in imposing destruction upon rebellious men in his letter to the Romans:
>
> "What if God, willing to show his wrath, and to make his power known, endured with much longsuffering vessels of wrath fitted unto destruction" (Rom. 9:22).
>
> The apostle describes the inmates of hell as "vessels of wrath fitted unto destruction." Albert Barnes notes that "fitted" suggests that these subjects of divine wrath are those "whose characters are such as to deserve destruction."
>
> Further, if "fitted" is viewed as a middle voice form (which is possible; cf. Vine), then the sense would be that these folks "prepared themselves for destruction" (Arndt & Gingrich, Greek Lexicon, 419). Note these points.
>
> Fourth, God's justice is evidenced in the fact that judgment of hell will be rendered proportionate to the degree of one's guilt. Consider the following passages:
>
> "But I say unto you, it shall be more tolerable for Tyre and Sidon in the day of judgment than for you. And thou, Capernaum, shalt thou be exalted unto heaven? thou shalt go down unto Hades: for if the mighty works had been done in Sodom which were done in thee, it would have remained until this day. But I

---

[19] Jackson, Wayne. "Romans 9:22 - Is Eternal Punishment Fair?" *ChristianCourier.com*. Access date: March 9, 2019. https://christiancourier.com/articles/617-romans-9-22-is-eternal-punishment-fair

say unto you that it shall be more tolerable for the land of Sodom in the day of judgment, than for thee" (Mt. 11:22-24).

"And that servant, who knew his lord's will, and made not ready, nor did according to his will, shall be beaten with **many stripes**; but he that knew not, and did things worthy of stripes, shall be beaten with **few stripes**. And to whomsoever much is given, of him shall much be required: and to whom they commit much, of him will they ask the more" (Lk. 12:47-48).

"…of how much sorer punishment, think ye, shall he be judged worthy, who hath trodden under foot the Son of God, and hath counted the blood of the covenant wherewith he was sanctified an unholy thing, and hath done despite unto the Spirit of grace?" (Heb. 10:29).

"Be not many of you teachers, my brethren, knowing that we shall receive heavier judgment" (Jas. 3:1).

Fifth, it appears that the fate of the wicked is justified in that even punishment seems to produce no change in their character. It is amazing that the rich man, in a state of torment (Lk. 16:23ff), though requesting relief, and soliciting a warning for his earthly brothers, never expresses a word of repentance for his disobedience, nor does he plead for the opportunity to leave his abode in order to dwell with God and his people. That speaks volumes. Make a notation to that effect.

THERE ARE NO "SECOND CHANCES" AFTER DEATH

There are only two great families on Earth, and everyone who has ever been born and will be born belongs to one or the other. You are either in the family of those who are "of their father the devil" or the family of those who are of God through Christ. You belong to one family or the other – there is no other option. In fact, if you say to yourself: "Well, I'm just not going to choose either…" you're only deceiving yourself, for by default when you do that, you are "of their [your] father the devil," for he is "the ruler of this world." By not choosing, you have chosen to remain in sin and therefore implicitly chosen who you follow. You can choose whether or not to be a friend of Jesus in this life if you want, but realize that if you do not want Jesus in this life, you won't have Him in the next life either – which is eternal.

Also, your spiritual state (of sin or righteousness before God) is fixed (set in stone, permanently unchangeable) at the time of your death for all eternity and determines your eternal destiny. There are no "second chances" after you die, as it is written:

> And inasmuch as it is appointed for men to die once and after this *comes* judgment.
> – Hebrews 9:27

There will be no continued lengthy appeals process after the verdict is read, as there can be in the courts of this world. You either die in sin or in righteousness, period. Those who are in sin (unrighteous) at the time of death will remain in sin for eternity; those who die righteous at their death will remain righteous for all eternity. You must prepare to meet God while you are alive in this life, not after you die.

If you die before Christ returns, it is fixed at your death; if you are alive when Christ returns, it is fixed at that instant when Christ appears on the Day of Judgment. If you are covered by the blood of Jesus, your sins are forgiven and forgotten as "far as the east is from the west," blotted out for all eternity, and get this – Jesus will also be your Attorney pleading your case before God on Judgment Day! But if you are not covered by the blood of Christ, you will have to be your own attorney and plead/argue that you are holy and righteous before Almighty God Himself. But friend, understand that Scripture tells us that "THERE IS NO RIGHTEOUS PERSON, NOT EVEN ONE." Even one little teensy tiny sin ever committed by you will condemn you as guilty of sin. Remember, nothing can be concealed before God at that time.

As mentioned, Jesus will be your judge (remember He is God), for "all Judgment has been given to the Son [Jesus]." Why? Because He became a man unto death (the man Jesus of Nazareth, the Christ of God), and He was tempted in all things as we are, so he knows what we have gone through here in this fallen world. This makes Him our "mediator" (between man and God) and also a fair and impartial judge. He experienced what we do in this fallen world, and yet He remained perfect and sinless unto death. He was victorious over sin and death and the power of the devil – He defeated sin, Satan, and death at the cross, for us!

God will make no errors in judgment. Jesus' judgment on that great Day will be perfect, righteous, and true. His justice won't be flawed like human vengeance. Neither will He be swayed by claims of innocence or excuses, nor clever arguments of counsel, nor the subtle twisting or even omission of facts as so often happens in the courts of this world. Claiming ignorance will not be an excuse either, for we are all called to "accurately handle [rightly divide] the word of truth," and this is why Scripture admonishes us strongly to "grow in the grace and knowledge of the Lord," which we do by reading the Bible (see Acts 17:22-32, Romans 4:15, Leviticus 5:17-18, 2 Peter 3:18, 2 Timothy 2:15). And no, the "devil made me do it" excuses won't hold on Judgment Day either, for "God is not mocked."

JUDGMENT WILL LAST FOR ETERNITY

Remember, your spirit lives on forever – it is eternal. The only unknown is whether it will live on in heaven or hell. The judgment rendered by God on this great Day will stand unchangeable for all eternity – and eternity is a very (*very*, ***very***) long time! Our finite human minds simply cannot begin to comprehend it properly. The best words we can find to express it can only begin to touch on the enormousness of eternity. Matthew Henry writes:[20]

> Note, the reason why people are so eager in the pursuit, and so entangled in the pleasures of this world, is, because they do not know, and believe, and consider, the eternity which they are upon the brink of. Did we know aright that all these things [of this material world] must shortly be dissolved, and we must certainly survive them, we should not set our eyes and hearts so much upon them as we do.

H.M. Riggle in *Beyond the Tomb* writes this about eternity:[21]

> In Isaiah 57:15, it is said that God "inhabiteth eternity." This is the only text in the Bible where the word "eternity" occurs. It is one of the greatest and most comprehensive words in any language. In life, we are the subjects of Time. We are told, however, that the day is approaching when an angel shall swear "by him that liveth for ever and ever that there shall be time no longer" (Revelation 10:6). This

---

[20] Henry, Matthew. Exposition of the Old and New Testaments, London. 1706-1710/1721.
[21] Riggle, H.M. (1929/2018), Beyond the Tomb, (The Gospel Trumpet Company/Holy Spirit Prints).

means eternity. Time has a beginning and ending. It is a fragment of eternity. It might be likened to a small island in the midst of the ocean. Gradually its sands are washed away by the mighty billows [waves] which sweep against its shores. By degrees it is being washed away until at length—God only knows how soon—the billows of eternity will sweep over and wash away the last sands of time, and nothing will remain but eternity. Time is a measured portion of duration. Moments, hours, days, weeks, months, years, centuries, and ages, measure time. But eternity! No cycle of years can measure it. It is a boundless ocean, a shoreless sea, or as Paul expresses it, a "world without end." It is without beginning or ending. It takes ten hundred thousand years to make a million; a thousand million to make a billion; a thousand billion to make a trillion; a thousand trillion to make a quadrillion; a thousand quadrillion to make a quintillion; a thousand quintillion to make a sextillion; a thousand sextillion to make a septillion, a thousand septillion to make an octillion; a thousand octillion to make a nonillion; a thousand nonillion to make a decillion (which when expressed in numerical form looks like this very, very large number: 1,000,000,000,000,000,000,000,000,000,000,000). But even this vast number does not express eternity.

Let us suppose that a bird comes from a far distant planet, making one trip in each decillion years. It carries away as much water in its tiny beak as it can contain. The length of time required by that bird thus to transfer to the distant planet all the waters contained in the springs, rivers, lakes, and oceans, would not measure eternity. After carrying away all the waters, suppose the bird still continues its journeys to earth, coming but once in a decillion of years, and carries away in its tiny beak a grain of sand from the seashore, or a bit of dust. That bird could carry away the entire globe on which we live, and yet eternity would not be measured.

Dear reader, you are going to eternity. We shall all soon be there. Death is the gateway each of us must pass through, and death fixes our destiny either in heaven or in hell. You are now forming a character for eternity. You are sowing seed, the harvest of which you must there reap. Now is the only time to prepare.

God inhabits eternity; it is His palace. When we attempt to span the marvels and glories of this divine dwelling-place, with its illimitable [without limits] corridors of space, we are lost in amazement. In the "high and holy place"—heaven—beyond galaxies, and stretching into immensities and infinities, God "inhabiteth eternity." As already expressed, the only way we finite creatures can form an idea of eternity is by going step by step up to the largest measures of time we know of, and then on and on, till we are lost in wonder. Eternity is vaster than the vastest.

"A perpetual duration which has neither beginning nor end."—*Charnock*
"Beyond is all abyss, eternity, whose end no eye can reach."—*Milton*
"Oh, if we could tear aside the veil, and see but for one hour what it signifies, to be a soul in the power of an endless life, what a revelation would it be."—*Horace Bushnell*
"Eternity has no gray hairs. The flowers fade, the heart withers, man grows old and dies, the world lies down in the sepulcher of ages, but time writes no wrinkles on the brow of eternity."—*Bishop Heber*

"Sow the seeds of life; and in the long eternity which lies before the soul, every minutest grain will come up again with an increase of thirty, sixty, or a hundredfold."—*F. W. Robertson*

To the above, I add my own comment on eternity:

The strange thing about eternity is that
it rushes at you very slowly at first,
almost imperceptibly…
and then suddenly,
all at once
it's here!

FALSE TEACHINGS ABOUND IN THIS AREA

Many people (and even most Christians!) are looking for more signs and wonders to appear (e.g., in the skies above, Sun, Moon, and stars, etc.) so they will know when the end-time is drawing near, thinking that they will have more time to get ready to meet God when they see these signs start to occur. You will therefore hear it loudly (and repeatedly) proclaimed that all these events must happen before Judgment Day arrives:

- The "Secret Rapture" of the Church: the taking away of believers into heaven with the lost "left behind" here on earth, along with
- A coming "Antichrist" world nationalistic/political figure, and
- A new "Third Temple" built in Jerusalem, and
- The "New World Order/One World Government," and
- The "Mark of the Beast" (i.e., a 666 tattoo, barcode, chip implant, or whatever the imagination conjures up), and then
- A "7-Year Great Tribulation" period where world forces under "The Antichrist" battle Israel, and then even further
- The "Battle of Armageddon" (often portrayed as a planet-wide nuclear war), and all that still further followed by
- A "Thousand-Year Millennial Reign of Christ on Earth from Jerusalem" where the nation of Israel rules over the entire world.

Or if not those, then something like these:

- We are still waiting for the "great apostasy" to happen first (the falling away referred to by Paul in 2 Thessalonians 2:3), or
- "Worldwide peace on earth" must happen before Christ returns, or
- Other fantastical and mystical prophecies of man (such as the arrival of "Planet X" or "Aliens in Antarctica"), or
- Insert {whatever worldly or political event you want here}

From a Biblical perspective, those are all false teachings – every single one of them! Sadly, many people believe them. And even sadder, many professing Christians who claim to know Scripture also believe them. As indicated in the book of Revelation, there will continue to be endless wars, famines, and pestilence at various times and places until Christ returns; but such are simply due to the continued sinful behavior and actions of fallen man and this fallen world. The false teachings above have no basis in Scripture.

It is also not surprising that on this topic (Christ's return and Judgment Day), you encounter a veritable avalanche of false teachings, for they are all designed to trick you out of eternal life. They are created by Satan and furthered by those men who do his bidding here on earth. The false teachings pose a grave danger to both the non-believer and also the believer – for they cause one to procrastinate. For the non-believer, the false teachings may cause you to procrastinate in accepting Christ for salvation, as you think to yourself: "Well, when I see you 'raptured away,' then I'll start to take all this Bible and Jesus stuff seriously." For the believer, the false teachings may cause you to procrastinate in sharing the gospel message in urgency with your friends and loved ones, for you may also think to yourself: "Well, when you see me 'raptured' away, then you'll finally start to take all this Bible and Jesus stuff seriously." So, the false teachings are all traps, created to deceive man into thinking there is always more time…just a little more time…and still more time. But one day, Judgment Day will have arrived, and you will not be ready.

While the "evolution" false teaching is primarily brought to you by the secular God-denying world, be aware that many of the false teachings related to Christ's return and Judgment Day are brought to you by those who appear to be "Christians": Christian churches, denominations, pastors, publications, books, movies, etc. They are what Scripture calls "wolves in sheep's clothing," and they can be just as deadly to your eternal life! If you listen to what modern (liberal, apostate) Christianity is teaching on this subject, or even worse, what is blaring out in stunning and deafening volume from the secular media world, you will be deceived. Even those who do not even believe the Bible and haven't ever read it seem to want to tell you all about Bible prophecy and what it means. It is amazing to watch Christians listen to and believe what secular sources give as their interpretation of Scripture, and in particular, Bible prophecy! Astounding!

These false teachings are covered in more detail in the Beware the Wolves chapter, but I wanted to mention a few of them here in passing so you are aware of them. Let us now proceed with the truth of what Scripture actually tells us about Christ's return and Judgment Day…

JUDGMENT DAY WILL ARRIVE WITHOUT WARNING

Because of the false teachings which abound, many are under the impression that they will have more time to prepare for the coming of Judgment Day (the "day of the Lord") – that they will be able to see more "signs and wonders" in the skies and heavens (and on Earth) and thereby know when it is getting closer, so they can start to take all this "Jesus stuff" seriously. But is this what Scripture actually says? Let us take a look; it is written:

> Now as to the times and the epochs, brethren, you have no need of anything to be written to you. For you yourselves know full well that <u>the day of the Lord will come just like a thief in the night. While they are saying, "Peace and safety!"</u> then destruction will come upon them suddenly like labor pains upon a woman with child, and they will not escape. But you, brethren, are not in darkness, that the day would overtake you like a thief; for you are all sons of light and sons of day. We are not of night nor of darkness; so then let us not sleep as others do, but let us be alert and sober. – 1 Thessalonians 5:1-6

The Message of Truth

Know this first of all, that in the last days mockers will come with *their* mocking, following after their own lusts, and saying, "Where is the promise of His coming? For *ever* since the fathers fell asleep, all continues just as it was from the beginning of creation." For when they maintain this, it escapes their notice that by the word of God *the* heavens existed long ago and *the* earth was formed out of water and by water, through which the world at that time was destroyed, being flooded with water. But by His word the present heavens and earth are being reserved for fire, kept for the day of judgment and destruction of ungodly men.

But do not let this one *fact* escape your notice, beloved, that with the Lord one day is like a thousand years, and a thousand years like one day. The Lord is not slow about His promise, as some count slowness, but is patient toward you, not wishing for any to perish but for all to come to repentance.

But the day of the Lord will come <u>like a thief, in which</u> [that very day, not 7 years, or 1000 years later!] the heavens will pass away with a roar and the elements will be destroyed with intense heat, and the earth and its works will be burned up. – 2 Peter 3:3-10

"But of that day and hour no one knows, not even the angels of heaven, nor the Son, but the Father alone. For <u>the coming of the Son of Man will be just like the days of Noah</u>. For as in those days before the flood they were eating and drinking, marrying and giving in marriage, until the day that Noah entered the ark, and they did not understand until the flood came and took them all away; so will the coming of the Son of Man be. Then there will be two men in the field; one will be taken and one will be left. Two women *will be* grinding at the mill; one will be taken and one will be left.

"Therefore be on the alert, for you do not know which day your Lord is coming. But be sure of this, that if the head of the house had known at what time of the night the thief was coming, he would have been on the alert and would not have allowed his house to be broken into. For this reason you also must be ready; <u>for the Son of Man is coming at an hour when you do not think</u> *He will*.

"Who then is the faithful and sensible slave whom his master put in charge of his household to give them their food at the proper time? Blessed is that slave whom his master finds so doing when he comes. Truly I say to you that he will put him in charge of all his possessions. But if that evil slave says in his heart, 'My master is not coming for a long time,' and begins to beat his fellow slaves and eat and drink with drunkards; the master of that slave will come on a day when he does not expect *him* and at an hour which he does not know, and will cut him in pieces and assign him a place with the hypocrites; in that place there will be weeping and gnashing of teeth." – Matthew 24:36-51

For after all it is *only* just for God to repay with affliction those who afflict you, and *to give* relief to you who are afflicted and to us as well <u>when the Lord Jesus will be revealed from heaven with His mighty angels in flaming fire</u>, dealing out retribution to those who do not know God and to those who do not obey the gospel of our Lord Jesus. These will pay the penalty of eternal destruction, away from the presence of the Lord and from the glory of His power, when He comes to be glorified in His saints on <u>that day</u>, and to be marveled at among all who have believed—for our testimony to you was believed. – 2 Thessalonians 1:6-10

But now Christ has been raised from the dead, the first fruits of those who are asleep. For since by a man *came* death, by a man also *came* the resurrection of the dead. For as in Adam all die, so also in Christ all will be made alive. But each in his own order: Christ the first fruits, after that those who are Christ's <u>at His coming, then</u> *comes* <u>the end</u>, when He hands over the kingdom to the God and Father, when He has abolished all rule and all authority and power. – 1 Corinthians 15:20-24

We see that Scripture clearly tells us that Christ's return will be like "a thief in the night," "at an hour you do not expect," while they (nearly everyone) are saying "peace and safety" going about their worldly business as usual, "in which" (that very day) "then *comes* the end" and "the heavens will pass away with a roar and the elements will be destroyed with intense heat, and the earth and its works will be burned up." Scripture is abundantly clear that this great Day of Judgment will happen on the same day as Christ's return (His Second Coming, i.e., advent).

Please note the repeated warnings that Christ's return happens when least expected by the overwhelming majority of humanity and His return occurs "quickly" [i.e., suddenly, rapidly], "like a thief in the night." Any teaching to the contrary is false. The only thing that precedes (and announces) the Lord's return is the final "trumpet of God," the "last trumpet" of the "seventh angel" of Revelation, which sounds immediately before:

> For this we say to you by the word of the Lord, that we who are alive and remain until the coming of the Lord, will not precede those who have fallen asleep. For the Lord Himself will descend from heaven with a shout, with the voice of *the* archangel and with the trumpet of God, and the dead in Christ will rise first. Then we who are alive and remain will be caught up together with them in the clouds to meet the Lord in the air, and so we shall always be with the Lord. – 1 Thessalonians 4:15-17

> Behold, I tell you a mystery; we will not all sleep, but we will all be changed, in a moment, in the twinkling of an eye, at the last trumpet; for the trumpet will sound, and the dead will be raised imperishable, and we will be changed. – 1 Corinthians 15:51-52

> "But when the Son of Man comes in His glory, and all the angels with Him, then He will sit on His glorious throne. All the nations will be gathered before Him; and He will separate them from one another, as the shepherd separates the sheep from the goats; and He will put the sheep on His right, and the goats on the left.

> "Then the King will say to those on His right, 'Come, you who are blessed of My Father, inherit the kingdom prepared for you from the foundation of the world. For I was hungry, and you gave Me *something* to eat; I was thirsty, and you gave Me *something* to drink; I was a stranger, and you invited Me in; naked, and you clothed Me; I was sick, and you visited Me; I was in prison, and you came to Me.' Then the righteous will answer Him, 'Lord, when did we see You hungry, and feed You, or thirsty, and give You *something* to drink? And when did we see You

a stranger, and invite You in, or naked, and clothe You? When did we see You sick, or in prison, and come to You?' The King will answer and say to them, 'Truly I say to you, to the extent that you did it to one of these brothers of Mine, *even* the least *of them*, you did it to Me.'

Then He will also say to those on His left, 'Depart from Me, accursed ones, into the eternal fire which has been prepared for the devil and his angels; for I was hungry, and you gave Me *nothing* to eat; I was thirsty, and you gave Me nothing to drink; I was a stranger, and you did not invite Me in; naked, and you did not clothe Me; sick, and in prison, and you did not visit Me.' Then they themselves also will answer, 'Lord, when did we see You hungry, or thirsty, or a stranger, or naked, or sick, or in prison, and did not take care of You?' Then He will answer them, 'Truly I say to you, to the extent that you did not do it to one of the least of these, you did not do it to Me.' These will go away into eternal punishment, but the righteous into eternal life." – Matthew 25:31-46

This "last trumpet" will be not some "secret rapture" as the false teachers claim, but an extraordinary event that will be visible and known to everyone who has ever lived (both the living and the dead) – yes, even the dead will be raised to see it. Everyone will then clearly see and know that the Lord Jesus Christ is returning in "power and great glory," "revealed from heaven with His mighty angels in flaming fire." And when this trumpet sounds, people will instantly know that their eternal destiny has been sealed, and that it's too late to change it. For those not covered by the blood of Christ, their hearts will tremble and fail, as they "hid themselves in the caves and among the rocks of the mountains; and they said to the mountains and to the rocks, 'Fall on us and hide us from the presence of Him who sits on the throne, and from the wrath of the Lamb; for the great day of their wrath has come, and who is able to stand?'," trying to hide from the presence of God as they finally realize their sinful nature, and "the mountains melted like wax at the presence of the LORD, At the presence of the Lord of the whole earth." These "mountains" are all the things of this world, the institutions and governments and everything created by man along with his endless lust for fame, power, and fortune, which will all be revealed to be absolutely worthless before the Lord on this great Day.

The first time Jesus came to Earth, He came humbly and meekly as a baby and a suffering servant to die on the cross as an atoning sacrifice for our sins; the next time He comes/returns, He will come in full power and glory as Lord God Almighty to execute judgment. And when Jesus returns, it will not be to start a "1000-year millennial" reign on here Earth; no, the great Day of Judgment will have arrived! For it is written: "At His coming, then comes the end, when He hands over the kingdom to the God and Father." The time of this Day has been fixed beforehand by God, and only He knows when it will occur. You have read that only those who have prepared ahead of time (during their own lifetime) to meet the Lord on that Day can stand with the hope of eternal life; there are no "second chances" after death!

There will be no more signs or wonders to seek, nor other specific political, social, economic, or nationalistic agendas, wars, or special natural disasters before Judgment Day arrives. There will be no more signs and wonders in the heavens (sun, moon, stars) or anything else to come along which will reveal the nearness of Christ's return and Judgment Day. If you are looking to the stars, blood moons, mystical signs and wonders (i.e., astrology), or false teachings of man, you will be deceived and not ready for it!

I'm here to correctly tell you that there is not a single Bible prophecy remaining to be fulfilled before Christ returns! No further warnings will be given before the "Lord Jesus will be revealed from heaven with His mighty angels in flaming fire" for everyone to see, those alive on the Earth and even those under the earth and under the sea (the living and the dead), "dealing out retribution to those who do not know God and to those who do not obey the gospel of our Lord Jesus." It could be today, or tomorrow, or the next day!

Yes, all Bible prophecy has already been fulfilled, even from the book of Revelation, except for the events of (and subsequent to) Christ's return – which is also the great Day of Judgment. Said differently for the avoidance of any doubt: the very next prophetic Bible event to occur will be Jesus appearing in skies of fire above for all to see at the start of the great Day of Judgment. Yes, you read that right. Be not deceived! Sadly, that statement will come as a shock and surprise even to many professing Christians and pastors who claim to know Scripture. Were Christ to appear today in skies of fire, the vast majority of the Christian church (at least from what I've seen of it here in America) would be just as shocked and surprised as the lost! Brother or sister in Christ, that just should not be!

Again, I say, be not deceived by the "wolves" and false teachers which abound today trying to trick you (and your friends and loved ones) into thinking there is more time, always just a little more time... These false teachings are designed (by Satan) to trick you into thinking that you can just wait until the next {...insert whatever national, political, or social event you choose here...} happens, and then you can begin to take all this "God and Bible stuff" seriously. But there will not be more time. When Christ returns, it will be for the great Day of Judgment.

The chapter of Matthew 24, referred to as the Olivet discourse, is often grossly misinterpreted to support the various false teachings. Matthew 24:1-35 applies only and specifically to the events leading up to (and of) A.D. 70 and the "great tribulation" of the Jews under the Romans (the destruction of Jerusalem). Separately, Matthew 24:36-51 and Matthew 25 (given below) refer to the end of time, which is at Christ's second coming, which is also the Day of Judgment.

THE WORLD IN AWFUL SLEEP ("As in the days of Noah")

We are also told that Christ's return (and Judgment Day) will be "as in the days of Noah." In the days of Noah, by the Spirit of Jesus, Noah preached the coming judgment by flood for 120 years; all the while God patiently waited for others to come to repentance! During this entire time, Noah was building the ark – but no one listened! That's right: not even one single person (outside of his own family) listened to the warning given over 120 years until it was too late! But then, suddenly one day, the skies opened, and the flood began: "While they are saying, 'Peace and safety!' then destruction will come upon them suddenly like labor pains upon a woman with child, and they will not escape." It is exactly the same prelude today – we are preaching that judgment is coming and that it grows very near. But is anyone listening? Similarly, in Sodom and Gomorrah, one day started just like all the rest had for as long as they could remember, but then suddenly, "the LORD rained on Sodom and Gomorrah brimstone and fire...out of heaven" in judgment.

Wayne Jackson writes on this critically important subject:[22]

Jesus' teaching regarding the Second Coming

The illustrations introduced by Jesus to insure preparedness for his Second Coming preclude the possibility of signs being given to determine the time of that event.

In a number of vivid historical illustrations, the Lord declared that no time indicators would be given to signal his Return; rather, the Judgment Day would catch men unawares.

Note the following:

1. As the people of Noah's day continued business as normal "until the day" that the flood came, "so shall be the coming of the Son of man" (Matt. 24:38,39).
2. The people of ancient Sodom were unaware of the impending disaster until "the day that Lot went out from Sodom," even so "after the same manner shall it be in the day that the Son of man is revealed" (Lk. 17:28-30).
3. Christ declared that he would come at an unexpected time, even as a thief does. "If the master of the house had known in what watch the thief was coming, he would have watched, and would not have suffered his house to be broken through. Therefore be ye also ready; for in an hour that ye think not the Son of man cometh" (Matt. 24:43,44; cf. 1 Thes. 5:2; 2 Pet. 3:10).
4. The parable of the virgins in Matthew 25 surely teaches the lesson of constant preparation, for the bridegroom will come at the most unexpected time [the midnight hour — a most surprising time for a wedding!].

There is nothing in Matthew 24 that lends support to the theory that Christ gave some signs that would herald the end of the world.

Jesus' own words

One of the most persuasive points demonstrating that the Lord gave no signs by which the end of time could be calculated is the affirmation of verse Matt. 24:36. "But of that day and hour knoweth no one, not even the angels of heaven, neither the Son, but the Father only."

The argument is devastating: though Jesus gave the signs of Matthew 24:4-14 [pertaining to the destruction of Jerusalem in A.D. 70], not even he knew when the time of his Second Coming would occur. It must therefore be obvious to anyone (save those totally deceived) that the signs of Matthew 24 [verses 1-35] can in no way be employed to figure the time of the Lord's Return!

Does it not seem odd that modern "prophets" can read Matthew 24 and predict the time of the end of the world; yet not even he who spoke the message was able to so decipher it?!

There are no signs concerning the time of the end of this age. Let us strive, therefore, to be always prepared for the Lord's Return, or death, whichever comes first.

---

[22] Jackson, Wayne. "Are There 'Signs' of the Second Coming of Christ?" *ChristianCourier.com*. Access date: March 9, 2019. https://christiancourier.com/articles/551-are-there-signs-of-the-second-coming-of-christ

It is exactly similar today; I repeat to be abundantly crystal clear without any ambiguity whatsoever: no further warnings will be given! Why am I being so adamant about making this point? It is because, by far and away, the biggest danger I think people face today is complacency. In addition to the false teachings previously mentioned, the abundance, comforts, and convenience of modern life, which abound in large measure today (though not in all places, of course), can lull you into a sense of complacency (on top of procrastination) about ensuring your own eternal destiny – always thinking to yourself, well, there's more time, more time, always more time. Remember, Satan and his forces of evil are very real, and they mean to totally destroy you! You are falling directly into their trap by thinking that! That trap leads to eternal death!

In times of the early church and its persecution (under the Roman empire and also under the Papacy), when you were going to be thrown into the lion's den, sawed in half, burned at the stake, or torn to pieces by wild beasts if you confessed Christ, you very quickly and surely sorted out your true faith and allegiance, and you did so with finality! It is well worth reading *Foxe's Book of Martyrs* and *The Church History* by Eusebius to learn more about the persecutions early Christians faced. With the comforts and conveniences of modern life, a person today can easily procrastinate in coming to a decision to accept Christ - delaying it one day at a time and relying on false teachings which say there is "more time" before Jesus returns, until one day, it will be too late. For you will have either died or the great Day of Judgment will have arrived suddenly, and you will not be ready to stand before God. We don't have any sense of urgency today.

In prior times (dispensations), God spoke through visions, dreams, and prophets; but today, God speaks to us through His Word. And just as God's instruction and prophecy had ceased for approximately 400 years before Christ was born in Bethlehem, likewise today, all prophecy (secret or otherwise) and explicit communication and new revelation from God to the world have again ceased until Christ's second coming. We are not to expect further messages, communications, or revelations from God, nor secret visions or prophecies or new prophets – the canon of Scripture has been sealed up and completed, Genesis to Revelation. Just as we are not to look for another yet to come (Christ was It), we are not to look for any new revelations from God. Therefore, if someone today claims to have a new "secret" message or revelation from God, we know that such claims are not in agreement with Scripture.

And just "as in the days of Noah," when he preached about the flood judgment to come, today we preach "the message of truth" to all who will hear. One day, however, Christ "will be revealed from heaven with His mighty angels in flaming fire," and the Great Day of Judgment will have arrived. You are getting all the warnings and signs right now that you will ever get from reading this book and also hearing others preach "the message of truth" to you. We are also not to look for another to come, for Jesus Christ was the Messiah, the Savior – in Him God was fully revealed to us.

Please don't keep waiting for the next worldwide cataclysm event to be "sure" that the Bible (and Christ) is for real. Scripture is abundantly clear that in the last days (which is this gospel/church age we are now in), the world will simply continue to get worse and worse, with men growing colder and colder, meaner, more hateful and sinful, with wars, famine, and pestilence occurring from time to time and in various places:

> But realize this, that in the last days difficult times will come. For men will be lovers of self, lovers of money, boastful, arrogant, revilers, disobedient to parents, ungrateful, unholy, unloving, irreconcilable, malicious gossips, without self-control, brutal, haters of good, treacherous, reckless, conceited, lovers of pleasure rather than lovers of God, holding to a form of godliness, although they have denied its power; Avoid such men as these. For among them are those who enter into households and captivate weak women weighed down with sins, led on by various impulses, always learning and never able to come to the knowledge of the truth. Just as Jannes and Jambres opposed Moses, so these *men* also oppose the truth, men of depraved mind, rejected in regard to the faith. But they will not make further progress; for their folly will be obvious to all, just as Jannes's and Jambres's folly was also…Indeed, all who desire to live godly in Christ Jesus will be persecuted. But evil men and impostors will proceed *from bad* to worse, deceiving and being deceived. – 2 Timothy 3:1-9,12-13

Yes, the world is in awful sleep regarding all of this; it's staggering to see people go to great lengths and effort to plan their next weekend sporting event or vacation, but they won't even lift a finger or spend the smallest amount of time to plan and prepare for their own eternity. The verses above match the world today exceedingly well as the world marches on in awful sleep, ignoring and blatantly mocking God, pursuing its own worldly self-interests, lusts, desires, idols, fame, fortune, and the ways of man, and suppressing the truth of Jesus Christ. Matthew Henry writes:[23]

> We find the world of mankind here very careless: All the earth sits still, and is at rest, while all the church is made uneasy, tossed with tempests and not comforted. Those that are strangers to the church are secure; those that are enemies to it are successful. … It is sad to think what a deep sleep the world is cast into, what a spirit of slumber has seized the generality of mankind, that are under God's wrath and Satan's power, and yet secure and unconcerned! They sit still and are at rest.

H.M. Riggle writes in *Beyond the Tomb* about the "red lights of warning" that God waves in front of us, warning about hell:[24]

> Sin acts on the soul as deadly drugs do on the body. Opium, cocaine, morphine, alcohol and chloroform deaden and numb the sense of feeling. People under the influence of these drugs are not conscious of pain and are dead to the things about them. Just so, sin hardens the heart and turns it to stone. "But after thy hardness and impenitent heart treasurest up unto thyself wrath against the day of wrath" (Rom. 2:5). "They have made their hearts like an adamant stone" (Zech. 7:12). We read of some whose conscience is "seared as with a hot iron" (1 Tim. 4:2), and who are "past feeling." This well describes the condition of multitudes all about us, unawakened and impenitent. The solemn exhortation to the church is: "Let us not sleep as do others, but let us watch and be sober" (1 Thess. 5:6).
>
> Satan, like "a strong man armed keepeth his palace [the unregenerate soul of man]" (Luke 11:21). He is a "prince of this world" (John 14:30), "ruler of the darkness of this world" (Eph. 6:12), the "god [little "g"] of this world" (2 Cor. 4:4),

---

[23] Henry, Matthew. *Exposition of the Old and New Testaments*, London. 1706-1710/1721.

[24] Riggle, H.M. (1929/2018), *Beyond the Tomb*, (The Gospel Trumpet Company/Holy Spirit Prints).

and holds dominion over countless millions of human beings. He reigns in their hearts and lives, controls, holds fast, destroys, ruins, blights, disqualifies, and throws over them his hellish opiates and lulls them to sleep in carnal security. He hangs up the curtains of deception and delusion decorated with unclean visions, and fills the affections with worldliness, pride, and vanity. Here in the human heart is his throne, and here he is exalted, served, and yielded to, so that he sways his scepter over the mind, heart, and life.

He keeps possession by blinding folks so they do not see themselves. He pulls down the blinds and shuts out the light so that his subjects are insensible to the gracious things of God and to their own danger. "For the heart of this people is waxed gross, and their ears are dull of hearing, and their eyes have they closed" (Acts 28:27). Such folks are very much alive and active in worldly affairs and in the business of sin but they are dead to God. God speaks in thunder-tones, but they hear not. He swings red lights of warning across their pathway, but their eyes are closed. A thousand blessings fall around them, but they have no taste nor desire for these, unconscious to the "things that belong to their peace." With the transplendent light of the gospel shining all about them they "sit in the valley and shadow of death" (Ps. 23:4). [Editor's note: We are to walk THROUGH the valley of the shadow of death, not sit and stay and dwell there!]

This is a state of great danger and of grave peril. A person sound asleep cannot defend himself against the thief or assassin. In a burning building, unless awakened, he is sure to perish. Every lost sinner is in a worse condition than a sleeping man in a structure all in flames. He is blind to eternal dangers. Deaf to the Spirit's voice, deaf to the roar of approaching storm, deaf to the rumblings of hell beneath. The thunder and lightning grows more loud and vivid. Death is at the door. Satan, the murderer of souls, is ready to strike a dagger at his heart. The casket in which he will be buried is now in the undertaker's rooms, and the tools that will dig his grave are waiting; and yet he slumbers on. Great God, awaken the slumbering souls of men.

Yes, we are on the very brink of eternity. It could happen the very day you are reading this. I have explained that you cannot prepare for your eternity after you die – for your spiritual state is sealed at death. You must prepare right here, right now, in this life. I cannot help you once the "seventh angel" sounds the "trumpet of God" ("the last trumpet") and Jesus returns; I can only help you now by warning you and showing you in upcoming chapters of this book how to be saved to eternal life through Christ. I can only help you today, not when you see me on the great Day of Judgment. The preaching of this "message of truth" is the only warning you will get. If you, or your friends or loved ones, have not yet accepted Christ as your Lord and Savior, it is written that "now [today] is the day of salvation"; "let him who has ears to hear, hear"! Use today wisely knowing you may not get tomorrow – as the great Day of Judgment may have arrived. Please do not delay in your contemplation of this matter of eternal moment.

I hope you are sensing my urgency and outright emotional plea in this chapter; I can do no more than that to encourage you to take all of this seriously and do so today. We read in 2 Peter 3:3-10 (above) that the only reason that the Day of Judgment has not come already, and you are still able to read this book at this time on this day, is because the Lord is (unbelievably) patient towards mankind (and me, and you) out of His abundant lovingkindness, mercy, and slowness to anger. His judgments are delayed

The Message of Truth

so that more people can have time to come to repentance and turn to Him – so that you can still have time to turn to Him.

But just "as in the days of Noah" and in the days of Sodom, the time will come when Time itself is up and Judgment Day arrives. Matthew Henry writes on Revelation 22:20-21: [25]

> If any say, "Where is the promise of his coming, when so many ages have passed since this was written?" let them know he is not slack to his people, but long-suffering to his enemies: his coming will be sooner than they are aware, sooner than they are prepared, sooner than they desire; and to his people it will be seasonable. The vision is for an appointed time and will not tarry. He will come quickly; let this word be always sounding in our ear and let us give all diligence that we may be found of him in peace, without spot and blameless...It is an awful thought, and enough to make the hole world to tremble, that eternal damnation immediately follows upon the death of an impenitent sinner.

BE ON THE ALERT (THE EVENTS OF THAT DAY WILL HAPPEN QUICKLY)

And finally, in the book of Revelation, we read several times that Jesus says he is "coming quickly" and that we must "be on the alert":

> "And behold, I am coming quickly. Blessed is he who heeds the words of the prophecy of this book." – Revelation 22:7

> "Behold, I am coming quickly, and My reward *is* with Me, to render to every man according to what he has done." – Revelation 22:12

> He who testifies to these things says, "Yes, I am coming quickly." Amen. Come, Lord Jesus. – Revelation 22:20

> "Watch out, stay alert; for you do not know when the *appointed* time is. *It is* like a man away on a journey, *who* upon leaving his house and putting his slaves in charge, *assigning* to each one his task, also commanded the doorkeeper to stay alert. Therefore, stay alert—for you do not know when the master of the house is coming, whether in the evening, at midnight, or when the rooster crows, or in the morning— so that he does not come suddenly and find you asleep. What I say to you I say to all: 'Stay alert!'"– Mark 13:33-37

You have already read that Jesus' return will be sudden and unexpected and will catch many unprepared. The word "quickly" in the verses above is the Greek "tachu," which conveys the idea of swiftly (occurring rapidly), with haste or suddenly (by surprise). The warning given here is that we must prepare now, today, this very day for Jesus' return and the Great Day of Judgment. We must not procrastinate or delay in making sure that we can stand before God holy and blameless on that Great Day. If you have not prepared beforehand (either before you die or before Christ returns), there will be no time to prepare later. When "Jesus is revealed with all His holy angels in skies of fire," it will be too late to prepare, for the events of that Day will unfold quickly (rapidly).

---

[25] Henry, Matthew. *Exposition of the Old and New Testaments*, London. 1706-1710/1721.

Note that the word "quickly" in the verses above does not mean, as some falsely teach, that the great Day of Judgment and Christ's return was to occur soon after (temporally) the apostles lived (i.e., that Jesus return and the Day of Judgment already happened in A.D. 70); that is the false teaching of "preterism."

OUR HOPE

So far in this book, we have seen how God's creation came about, along with the origin of humanity. We then saw the disobedience of man and the introduction of sin, suffering, and death into the world – and we saw that we are all sinful. In this chapter, we have looked forward to the great Day of Judgment – the climax of humanity and the end of time itself. It might be at this point you are feeling a little discouraged, like there is a heavy weight or burden placed on you, and there is no hope; we have been under the bondage of sin heading towards inescapable judgment. You might be thinking: if we are so sinful, fallen, and separated from God, what can I possibly do?

But know there is good, even great news ahead, for God "desires all people to be saved and to come to the knowledge of the truth" so that none are lost in judgment, and He wants all to choose to have eternal life with Him. The Bible explains how we each can become "without sin" and stand before the Lord on the Day of Judgment holy and blameless through grace and the gift of God. In fact, it's not at all about what you need to do or about what you can do of yourself; it's about what Someone has already done for you! I think you can guess by now that Someone is Jesus Christ. We'll cover shortly how you can know Jesus and decide to accept Him as your Lord and Savior (if you want to) – for it is He alone who can save you from sin and judgment. And only He can give you eternal life.

In the next section of the book, we, therefore, start on the path of hope towards redemption from sin and eternal life – the "good news" part of the gospel message. I hope very shortly you will come to see the relentless love of God towards you as it is written:

> "For God so loved the world, that He gave His only begotten Son [Jesus Christ], that whoever believes in Him shall not perish, but have eternal life." – John 3:16

So, let's get started on the path to redemption and eternal life…

[Note: But first, I hope you notice the veritable AVALANCHE of false teachings below that center on the topic of Christ's return and Judgment Day! Someone or something (hint: Satan) really, *really*, **REALLY** doesn't want you to take Judgment Day seriously, and to do so today…this should make you start to wonder if there really is something to all this God, Jesus, Heaven, and Hell stuff after all…yes?]

FALSE TEACHING(S) YOU WILL ENCOUNTER:

- Atheism (there is no God)
- The Bible is simply fictional "myths, folklore, and poetry"
- Satan (The Devil) is just a myth
- Annihilation after death
- Hell isn't real
- Man can earn salvation through good works or by being a "good person" (or even buy it with money)
- Dispensational Premillennialism

- Dispensational Postmillennialism
- Universalism (i.e., any name, or any religion, even one you make up, or even no belief at all, can save you to eternal life)
- You get a "2nd Chance" after death
- Distortions of Matthew 24 (the Olivet Discourse)
- Modern/Popular Eschatology (we are waiting for a "Third Temple" to be built, or the "Battle of Armageddon" to occur first, or "the Antichrist" person to arise, or Gog and Magog, or "signs and wonders" in the skies, or the "Secret Rapture," or the "7-Year Great Tribulation" period, and other bizarre interpretations of the book of Revelation…all false)
- Predictions of Jesus' return (setting dates)
- Jesus already returned in A.D. 70 (Preterism)
- Bizarre interpretations of the "Mark of the Beast" (i.e., 666)
- Aliens and the Nephilim
- and many others!

RELATED SCRIPTURE:

"Therefore having overlooked the times of ignorance, God is now declaring to men that all *people* everywhere should repent, because He has fixed a day in which He will judge the world in righteousness through a Man [Jesus] whom He has appointed, having furnished proof to all men by raising Him from the dead." – Acts 17:30-31

And inasmuch as it is appointed for men to die once and after this *comes* judgment, so Christ also, having been offered once to bear the sins of many, will appear a second time for salvation without *reference to* sin, to those who eagerly await Him. – Hebrews 9:27-28

"Truly, truly, I [Jesus] say to you, an hour is coming and now is, when the dead will hear the voice of the Son of God, and those who hear will live. For just as the Father has life in Himself, even so He gave to the Son also to have life in Himself; and He gave Him [Jesus] authority to execute judgment, because He [Jesus] is *the* Son of Man. Do not marvel at this; for an hour is coming, in which all who are in the tombs will hear His voice, and will come forth; those who did the good *deeds* to a resurrection of life, those who committed the evil *deeds* to a resurrection of judgment." – John 5:25-29

For we will all stand before the judgment seat of God. For it is written,

> "AS I LIVE, SAYS THE LORD, EVERY KNEE SHALL BOW TO ME,
> AND EVERY TONGUE SHALL GIVE PRAISE TO GOD."

So then each one of us will give an account of himself to God. – Romans 14:10b-12

"Repent, for the kingdom of heaven is at hand." – Matthew 3:2

For this reason also, God highly exalted Him [Jesus], and bestowed on Him the name which is above every name, so that at the name of Jesus EVERY KNEE WILL BOW, of those who are in heaven and on earth and under the earth, and that every tongue will confess that Jesus Christ is Lord, to the glory of God the Father. – Philippians 2:9-11

Accordingly, whatever you have said in the dark will be heard in the light, and what you have whispered in the inner rooms will be proclaimed upon the housetops. – Luke 12:3

For the eyes of the LORD move to and fro throughout the earth that He may strongly support those whose heart is completely His. – 2 Chronicles 16:9

Or do you think lightly of the riches of His kindness and tolerance and patience, not knowing that the kindness of God leads you to repentance? But because of your stubbornness and unrepentant heart you are storing up wrath for yourself in the day of wrath and revelation of the righteous judgment of God, who WILL RENDER TO EACH PERSON ACCORDING TO HIS DEEDS: to those who by perseverance in doing good seek for glory and honor and immortality, eternal life; but to those who are selfishly ambitious and do not obey the truth, but obey unrighteousness, wrath and indignation. – Romans 2:4-8

"As for me, I baptize you with water for repentance, but He who is coming after me is mightier than I, and I am not fit to remove His sandals; He will baptize you with the Holy Spirit and fire." – Matthew 3:11

For the wrath of God is revealed from heaven against all ungodliness and unrighteousness of men who suppress the truth in unrighteousness, because that which is known about God is evident within them; for God made it evident to them. For since the creation of the world His invisible attributes, His eternal power and divine nature, have been clearly seen, being understood through what has been made, so that they are without excuse. For even though they knew God, they did not honor Him as God or give thanks, but they became futile in their speculations, and their foolish heart was darkened. Professing to be wise, they became fools, and exchanged the glory of the incorruptible God for an image in the form of corruptible man and of birds and four-footed animals and crawling creatures.

Therefore God gave them over in the lusts of their hearts to impurity, so that their bodies would be dishonored among them. For they exchanged the truth of God for a lie, and worshiped and served the creature rather than the Creator, who is blessed forever. Amen. – Romans 1:18-25

For God will bring every act to judgment, everything which is hidden, whether it is good or evil. – Ecclesiastes 12:14

But the LORD abides forever;
He has established His throne for judgment,
And He will judge the world in righteousness;
He will execute judgment for the peoples with equity. – Psalm 9:7-8

For the LORD is our judge,
The LORD is our lawgiver,
The LORD is our king;
He will save us. – Isaiah 33:22

God is a righteous judge,
And a God who has indignation every day [against the wicked]. – Psalm 7:11

He summons the heavens above,
And the earth, to judge His people. – Psalm 50:4

And men will say, "Surely there is a reward for the righteous;
Surely there is a God who judges on earth!" – Psalm 58:11

Let the heavens be glad, and let the earth rejoice;
Let the sea roar, and all it contains;
Let the field exult, and all that is in it.
Then all the trees of the forest will sing for joy
Before the LORD, for He is coming,
For He is coming to judge the earth.
He will judge the world in righteousness
And the peoples in His faithfulness. – Psalm 96:11-13

And the heavens declare His righteousness,
For God Himself is judge. *Selah.* – Psalm 50:6

You caused judgment to be heard from heaven;
The earth feared and was still
When God arose to judgment,
To save all the humble of the earth. *Selah.* – Psalm 76:8-9

Rise up, O Judge of the earth,
Render recompense to the proud. – Psalm 94:2

It was also about these men *that* Enoch, *in* the seventh *generation* from Adam, prophesied, saying, "Behold, the Lord came with many thousands of His holy ones, to execute judgment upon all, and to convict all the ungodly of all their ungodly deeds which they have done in an ungodly way, and of all the harsh things which ungodly sinners have spoken against Him." – Jude 1:14-15

Then Jesus said to His disciples, "If anyone wishes to come after Me, he must deny himself, and take up his cross and follow Me. For whoever wishes to save his life will lose it; but whoever loses his life for My sake will find it. For what will it profit a man if he gains the whole world and forfeits his soul? Or what will a man give in exchange for his soul? For the Son of Man is going to come in the glory of His Father with His angels, and WILL THEN REPAY EVERY MAN ACCORDING TO HIS DEEDS." – Matthew 16:24-27

Or do you not know that the unrighteous will not inherit the kingdom of God? Do not be deceived; neither fornicators, nor idolaters, nor adulterers, nor effeminate, nor homosexuals, nor thieves, nor *the* covetous, nor drunkards, nor revilers, nor swindlers, will inherit the kingdom of God. Such were some of you; but you were washed, but you were sanctified, but you were justified in the name of the Lord Jesus Christ and in the Spirit of our God. – 1 Corinthians 6:9-11

"But for the cowardly and unbelieving and abominable and murderers and immoral persons and sorcerers and idolaters and all liars, their part *will be* in the lake that burns with fire and brimstone, which is the second death." – Revelation 21:8

See to it that you do not refuse Him who is speaking. For if those did not escape when they refused him who warned *them* on earth, much less *will* we *escape* who turn away from Him who *warns* from heaven. And His voice shook the earth then, but now He has promised, saying, "YET ONCE MORE I WILL SHAKE NOT ONLY THE EARTH, BUT ALSO THE HEAVEN." This *expression*, "Yet once more," denotes the removing of those things which can be shaken, as of created things, so that those things which cannot be shaken may remain. Therefore, since we receive a kingdom which cannot be shaken, let us show gratitude, by which we may offer to God an acceptable service with reverence and awe; for our God is a consuming fire. – Hebrews 12:25-29 [Note: Sin will be consumed, destroyed, at the end of time (this church, gospel age) on the Day of Judgment, for God is holy]

It is a terrifying [fearful] thing to fall into the hands of the living God. – Hebrews 10:31 [Note: This verse applies to those who die in sin, who are not covered by the righteousness of Christ on the Day of Judgment. This is explained in upcoming chapters.]

And the devil who deceived them [all those who followed him instead of Christ] was thrown into the lake of fire and brimstone, where the beast and the false prophet are also; and they will be tormented day and night forever and ever.

Then I saw a great white throne [on the great Day of Judgment] and Him who sat upon it, from whose presence earth and heaven fled away, and no place was found for them. And I saw the dead, the great and the small, standing before the throne, and books were opened; and another book was opened, which is *the book* of life; and the dead were judged from the things which were written in the books, according to their deeds. And the sea gave up the dead which were in it, and death and Hades gave up the dead which were in them; and they were judged, every one *of them* according to their deeds. Then death and Hades were thrown into the lake of fire. This is the second death, the lake of fire. And if anyone's name was not found written in the book of life, he was thrown into the lake of fire. – Revelation 20:10-15

…and nothing unclean, and no one who practices abomination and lying, shall ever come into it [New Jerusalem], but only those whose names are written in the Lamb's book of life. – Revelation 21:27

"Let the one who does wrong, still do wrong; and the one who is filthy, still be filthy; and let the one who is righteous, still practice righteousness; and the one who is holy, still keep himself holy." – Revelation 22:11

Do not be deceived, God is not mocked; for whatever a man sows, this he will also reap. For the one who sows to his own flesh will from the flesh reap corruption, but the one who sows to the Spirit will from the Spirit reap eternal life. – Galatians 6:7-8

How blessed is the man who does not walk in the counsel of the wicked,
Nor stand in the path of sinners,
Nor sit in the seat of scoffers!
But his delight is in the law of the LORD,
And in His law he meditates day and night.
He will be like a tree *firmly* planted by streams of water,
Which yields its fruit in its season
And its leaf does not wither;
And in whatever he does, he prospers.
The wicked are not so,
But they are like chaff which the wind drives away.
Therefore the wicked will not stand in the judgment,

The Message of Truth

Nor sinners in the assembly of the righteous.
For the LORD knows the way of the righteous,
But the way of the wicked will perish. – Psalm 1

The LORD is righteous in all His ways
And kind in all His deeds.
The LORD is near to all who call upon Him,
To all who call upon Him in truth.
He will fulfill the desire of those who fear Him;
He will also hear their cry and will save them.
The LORD keeps all who love Him,
But all the wicked He will destroy. – Psalm 145:17-20

Let the sea roar and all it contains,
The world and those who dwell in it.
Let the rivers clap their hands,
Let the mountains sing together for joy
Before the LORD, for He is coming to judge the earth;
He will judge the world with righteousness
And the peoples with equity. – Psalm 98:7-9

"Heaven and earth will pass away, but My words will not pass away." – Mark 13:31

PART II:

OUR HOPE

(Jesus Christ of Nazareth)

2.0 WHO IS JESUS OF NAZARETH?

For unto us a child is born, unto us a son is given: and the government shall be upon his shoulder: and his name shall be called Wonderful, Counsellor, The mighty God, The everlasting Father, The Prince of Peace. – Isaiah 9:6 (KJV)

This Jesus of Nazareth. At the close of the previous chapter on the great Day of Judgment, we ended with a promise of hope to come – so that we can stand before God on that Day of Judgment, holy and blameless, and be declared "NOT GUILTY" of sin. I also indicated that we would be moving from a position of bondage under sin, suffering, and death towards redemption and eternal life. We read in Scripture that God "desires all people to be saved and to come to the knowledge of the truth" so that none are lost in judgment, and that He has provided a way for everyone to obtain eternal life through a "Savior":

> For a child will be born to us, a son will be given to us;
> And the government will rest on His shoulders;
> And His name will be called Wonderful Counselor, Mighty God,
> Eternal Father, Prince of Peace. – Isaiah 9:6

> "BEHOLD, THE VIRGIN SHALL BE WITH CHILD AND SHALL BEAR A SON, AND THEY SHALL CALL HIS NAME IMMANUEL," which translated means, "GOD WITH US." – Matthew 1:23

> But the angel said to them, "Do not be afraid; for behold, I bring you good news of great joy which will be for all the people; for today in the city of David there has been born for you a Savior, who is Christ the Lord. This *will be* a sign for you: you will find a baby wrapped in cloths and lying in a manger." And suddenly there appeared with the angel a multitude of the heavenly host praising God and saying,
>
>> "Glory to God in the highest,
>> And on earth peace among men with whom He is pleased." – Luke 2:10-14

> This is good and acceptable in the sight of God our Savior, who desires all men to be saved and to come to the knowledge of the truth. – 1 Timothy 2:3-4

> "Truly, truly, I say to you, he who hears My word, and believes Him who sent Me, has eternal life, and does not come into judgment, but has passed out of death into life." – John 5:24

> Truly, truly, I say to you, he who believes has eternal life. – John 6:47

> "As Moses lifted up the serpent in the wilderness, even so must the Son of Man be lifted up; so that whoever believes will in Him have eternal life. For God so loved the world, that He gave His only begotten Son, that whoever believes in Him shall not perish, but have eternal life. For God did not send the Son into the world to judge the world, but that the world might be saved through Him. He who believes in Him is not judged; he who does not believe has been judged already, because he has not believed in the name of the only begotten Son of God." – John 3:14-18

> In the beginning was the Word, and the Word was with God, and the Word was God. He was in the beginning with God. All things came into being through Him,

and apart from Him nothing came into being that has come into being. In Him was life, and the life was the Light of men. The Light shines in the darkness, and the darkness did not comprehend it. – John 1:1-5

I pray that the eyes of your heart may be enlightened, so that you will know what is the hope of His calling, what are the riches of the glory of His inheritance in the saints, and what is the surpassing greatness of His power toward us who believe. *These are* in accordance with the working of the strength of His might which He brought about in Christ, when He raised Him from the dead and seated Him at His right hand in the heavenly *places*, far above all rule and authority and power and dominion, and every name that is named, not only in this age but also in the one to come. – Ephesians 1:18-21

So, to proceed further, we must first know Who this "Son of God," this "Son of Man," this "Eternal Father," this "Prince of Peace," this "Savior," this "Immanuel," this "Redeemer," this "Word," and this "Christ" is. Scripture says that we must "believe in Him" to be forgiven of our sins and stand righteous (blameless, morally pure, free from guilt or sin, declared "not guilty" of sin, justifiable) before God on the great Day of Judgment and saved to eternal life. The Bible tells us that this "Son of God" is Jesus Christ – "Jesus of Nazareth." Of course, there are many opinions, myths, and man-made distortions about who Jesus was (and still is), but we will give the truth as stated in Scripture. Please also note that this chapter's title doesn't say "Who Was Jesus," for He is alive this very day! Yes, He lives! Let's learn more about Him.

"Jesus of Nazareth," "the Christ of God," is a man who lived approximately 2000 years ago. Christ is not His last name; it is a title meaning "anointed one," "anointed by God," or "the Messiah." Christ and anointed are the same word in Greek and the same as "messiach" or "Messiah" in Hebrew. Jesus (Ἰησοῦς, Iésous) is the transliteration of the Greek name Joshua (Jehoshua, Yeshua) in English. Jesus was born in Bethlehem and raised in Nazareth.

Jesus' genealogy is given in the books of Matthew and Luke. Luke traces His legal genealogy back to Adam ("the first man") on His father's side (Joseph), while Matthew traces His biological genealogy back to Abraham on His mother's side (Mary). Jesus was a Jew; He was born and lived under Mosaic law – the Old Testament law given through Moses to Israel and the Jews after they were brought out of bondage (slavery) in Egypt by God.

Scripture says Jesus was supernaturally born of "a virgin" (Mary), that He lived a holy, pure, and sinless life, and that He died on the cross as an atoning sacrifice for your sins, indeed, for the sins of all who choose to call on His name! Scripture says that God raised Him to life after three (3) days and that He [Jesus] is right now "seated at the right hand of God [the Father]" in heaven, ruling as King in His kingdom.

His life was documented and confirmed by many eyewitnesses (the twelve disciples and many others) who testified and wrote as to what they saw, heard, and experienced, many living with Him during His three-year ministry on earth. Even skeptics and atheists concede that there is overwhelming historical evidence that the man "Jesus of Nazareth" did indeed live exactly as told in Scripture.

Jesus Christ was "God manifest in the flesh," God incarnate – fully man but also fully God. He is our Lord and Savior and our King, and it is through Him, and Him alone, that we have salvation:

And the Word [Jesus] became flesh, and dwelt among us, and we saw His glory, glory as of the only begotten from the Father, full of grace and truth. – John 1:14

Now when Jesus came into the district of Caesarea Philippi, He was asking His disciples, "Who do people say that the Son of Man is?" And they said, "Some *say* John the Baptist; and others, Elijah; but still others, Jeremiah, or one of the prophets." He said to them, "But who do you say that I am?" Simon Peter answered, "You are the Christ, the Son of the living God." – Matthew 16:13-16

Then Peter, filled with the Holy Spirit, said to them, "Rulers and elders of the people, if we are on trial today for a benefit done to a sick man, as to how this man has been made well, let it be known to all of you and to all the people of Israel, that by the name of Jesus Christ the Nazarene, whom you crucified, whom God raised from the dead—by this *name* this man stands here before you in good health. He is the STONE WHICH WAS REJECTED by you, THE BUILDERS, but WHICH BECAME THE CHIEF CORNER stone. And there is salvation in no one else; for there is no other name under heaven that has been given among men by which we must be saved." – Acts 4:8-12

Opening his mouth, Peter said:

"I most certainly understand now that God is not one to show partiality, but in every nation the man who fears Him and does what is right is welcome to Him. The word which He sent to the sons of Israel, preaching peace through Jesus Christ (He is Lord of all)—you yourselves know the thing which took place throughout all Judea, starting from Galilee, after the baptism which John proclaimed. You know of Jesus of Nazareth, how God anointed Him with the Holy Spirit and with power, and how He went about doing good and healing all who were oppressed by the devil, for God was with Him. We are witnesses of all the things He did both in the land of the Jews and in Jerusalem. They also put Him to death by hanging Him on a cross. God raised Him up on the third day and granted that He become visible, not to all the people, but to witnesses who were chosen beforehand by God, that is, to us who ate and drank with Him after He arose from the dead. And He ordered us to preach to the people, and solemnly to testify that this is the One who has been appointed by God as Judge of the living and the dead. Of Him all the prophets bear witness that through His name everyone who believes in Him receives forgiveness of sins." – Acts 10:34-43

Paul, a bond-servant of Christ Jesus, called *as* an apostle, set apart for the gospel of God, which He promised beforehand through His prophets in the holy Scriptures, concerning His Son, who was born of a descendant of David according to the flesh, who was declared the Son of God with power by the resurrection from the dead, according to the Spirit of holiness, Jesus Christ our Lord… – Romans 1:1-4

And the testimony is this, that God has given us eternal life, and this life is in His Son. He who has the Son has the life; he who does not have the Son of God does not have the life. These things I have written to you who believe in the name of the Son of God, so that you may know that you have eternal life. – 1 John 5:11-13

And we know that the Son of God has come, and has given us understanding so that we may know Him who is true; and we are in Him who is true, in His Son Jesus Christ. This is the true God and eternal life. – 1 John 5:20

For the wages of sin is death, but the free gift of God is eternal life in Christ Jesus our Lord. – Romans 6:23

H.M. Riggle writes in The Christian Church: Its Rise and Progress: [26]

The Morning Light Is Breaking.

While the world was shrouded in darkness, and no prophet's voice could be heard; while Israel, with a few individual exceptions, was engulfed in sin and idolatry, forsaken of God; while the then known world was under the rule of pagan Rome, and heathenism held sway in the hearts of men everywhere—suddenly there appeared "one crying in the wilderness" and saying, "Repent ye: for the kingdom of heaven is at hand." After four hundred long years of silence, a prophet appeared, yea, more than a prophet. John, the looked-for Elias, the harbinger of a new day, was now preparing the way for Messiah to begin His ministry. "There was a man sent from God whose name was John. The same came for a witness, to bear witness of the light" John 1:6-7. Of John and his work, the angel told Zacharias this: "And many of the children of Israel shall he turn to the Lord their God. And he shall go before him in the spirit and power of Elias, to turn the hearts of the fathers to the children, and the disobedient to the wisdom of the just; to make ready a people prepared for the Lord" Luke 1:16-17. Zacharias said of him, "And thou, child, shalt be called the prophet of the Highest: for thou shalt go before the face of the Lord to prepare his ways; to give knowledge of salvation unto his people by the remission of their sins" Luke 1:76-77.

This was the dawning of a new day, the breaking forth of earth's most glorious day—the day of salvation. The prophets foresaw this, and spoke of it as a clear morning. Isaiah foretold it in these words: "The burden of Dumah. He calleth to me out of Seir, Watchman, what of the night? Watchman, what of the night? The watchman said, The morning cometh, and also the night: if ye will inquire, inquire ye: return, come" Isa. 21:11-12. Dumah signifies silence. This was the time of silence from Malachi to Christ. The inquirer asks, "What of the night?" namely, What time of night is it? The watchman cried, "The morning cometh." This morning was the clear morning of the Christian era. "For, behold, darkness shall cover the earth, and gross darkness the people: but the Lord shall arise upon thee, and his glory shall be seen upon thee. And the Gentiles shall come to thy light, and kings to the brightness of thy rising" Isa. 60:2-3. This time of darkness was the night of Judaism. But it was foreseen that the Lord could arise and that His glory would be seen. This refers to the ushering in of the better dispensation. The coming of Christ was to be a beautiful sunrise, and the Gentiles were to come to the brightness of His rising. "But unto you that fear my name shall the Sun of righteousness arise with healing in his wings; and ye shall go forth, and grow up as calves in the stall" Mal. 4:2.

---

[26] Riggle, H.M. (1912), The Christian Church, Its Rise and Progress, (The Gospel Trumpet Company), Prestonsburg KY.

The Pristine Glory—The Ushering in of a Clear Day.

In fulfillment of these predictions, Christ came the Sun of righteousness, and ushered in a clear day. "Weeping may endure for a night; but joy cometh in the morning." Nineteen centuries ago a babe was born in the stable of an inn, in the Roman province of Judea. At this time Caesar Augustus was an absolute sovereign. With unlimited power, he ruled over three hundred millions of people, comprising the Roman empire. Such power no mortal ever swayed before. Little did this proud ruler of all the world then known dream, as he sat upon his throne in gorgeous apparel, that a newborn Babe who was slumbering in a manger, in the town of Bethlehem, in far-off Syria, and whose infant cries were mingled with the braying of donkeys, the lowing of cattle, and the bleating of goats—little, I say, did this mighty sovereign dream that this lowly infant was destined to establish a religion and kingdom before which all the glory and power of the proud Caesars would fade away. But, dear reader, it was so. At the birth of that Babe the bells of heaven rang and all the angels worshiped. The glad news was at once wafted from heaven to earth that this was the "Saviour…Christ the Lord." Shepherds on the Judean hills heard the angels sing the glad refrain, "Glory to God in the highest."

"Through the tender mercy of our God; thereby the dayspring [sunrising, margin] from on high hath visited us, to give light to them that sit in darkness and in the shadow of death, to guide our feet into the way of peace" Luke 1:78-79. The advent of the Saviour was a beautiful sunrising. "The people which sat in darkness saw great light; and to them which sat in the region and shadow of death light is sprung up" Matt. 4:16. Christ Himself was that Light. He said, "I am the light of the world: he that followeth me shall not walk in darkness, but shall have the light of life." Christ was not the light of one nation only, Israel, but the Light of "the world." Yes, He was the "salvation" which God "hast prepared before the face of all people; a light to lighten the Gentiles, and the glory of thy people Israel" (Luke 2:25-32). "For so hath the Lord commanded us, saying, I have set thee to be a light of the Gentiles, that thou shouldest be for salvation unto the ends of the earth" Acts 13:47.

Surely this was a glad morning to the inhabitants of earth, who for long centuries had sat enshrouded in the night of sin. Brilliant, transplendent light broke forth in the earth, salvation waters began to flow, and thousands were made to rejoice in a Redeemer's love. They could say, "The night is far spent, the day is at hand: let us therefore cast off the works of darkness, and let us put on the armour of light" Rom. 13:12. The gospel message was like "a light that shineth in a dark place"; and as people accepted it, Christ entered into their lives, like a beautiful "day-dawn" and "day-star" (2 Pet. 1:19). Oh, how beautiful, clear, and bright was the dawning of the gospel day!

The gospel of salvation that Christ preached penetrated the dark places of sin and idolatry, like sun-rays driving back the darkness of night. Wickedness in the hearts and lives of men gave way to grace and truth.

BIBLE PROPHECY FORETOLD JESUS

The Bible contains some 300+ prophecies (future predictions) about Jesus' birth, life, death, and resurrection. These prophecies were recorded (written down in Scripture) long before Christ was born – in some cases, many hundreds of years prior. And every single prophecy was fulfilled by Jesus of Nazareth. Jesus even said that "it is those *very Scriptures* [of the Old Testament] that testify about Me." A few of these prophecies are listed here:

A Coming Prince, on the Throne of David:

For a child [Jesus] will be born to us, a son will be given to us;
And the government will rest on His shoulders;
And His name will be called Wonderful Counselor, Mighty God,
Eternal Father, Prince of Peace.
There will be no end to the increase of *His* government or of peace,
On the throne of David and over his kingdom,
To establish it and to uphold it with justice and righteousness
From then on and forevermore.
The zeal of the LORD of hosts will accomplish this. – Isaiah 9:6-7

Born in Bethlehem:

"But as for you, Bethlehem Ephrathah,
Too little to be among the clans of Judah,
From you One will go forth for Me to be ruler in Israel.
His goings forth are from long ago,
From the days of eternity." – Micah 5:2

Born of a Virgin:

Therefore the Lord Himself will give you a sign: Behold, a virgin will be with child and bear a son, and she will call His name Immanuel. – Isaiah 7:14

Given an Eternal Kingdom:

"I kept looking in the night visions,
And behold, with the clouds of heaven
One like a Son of Man was coming,
And He came up to the Ancient of Days
And was presented before Him.
"And to Him was given dominion,
Glory and a kingdom,
That all the peoples, nations and *men of every* language
Might serve Him.
His dominion is an everlasting dominion
Which will not pass away;
And His kingdom is one
Which will not be destroyed." – Daniel 7:13-14

Pierced Through for our Transgressions (with details):

Who has believed our report?
And to whom has the arm of the LORD been revealed?
For He grew up before Him like a tender shoot,
And like a root out of parched ground;
He has no *stately* form or majesty
That we should look upon Him,

Nor appearance that we should be attracted to Him.
He was despised and forsaken of men,
A man of sorrows and acquainted with grief;
And like one from whom men hide their face
He was despised, and we did not esteem Him.

Surely our griefs He Himself bore,
And our sorrows He carried;
Yet we ourselves esteemed Him stricken,
Smitten of God, and afflicted.
But He was pierced through for our transgressions,
He was crushed for our iniquities;
The chastening for our well-being *fell* upon Him,
And by His scourging we are healed.
All of us like sheep have gone astray,
Each of us has turned to his own way;
But the LORD has caused the iniquity of us all
To fall on Him.

He was oppressed and He was afflicted,
Yet He did not open His mouth;
Like a lamb that is led to slaughter,
And like a sheep that is silent before its shearers,
So He did not open His mouth.
By oppression and judgment He was taken away;
And as for His generation, who considered
That He was cut off out of the land of the living
For the transgression of my people, to whom the stroke *was due*?
His grave was assigned with wicked men,
Yet He was with a rich man in His death,
Because He had done no violence,
Nor was there any deceit in His mouth.

But the LORD was pleased
To crush Him, putting *Him* to grief;
If He would render Himself *as* a guilt offering,
He will see *His* offspring,
He will prolong *His* days,
And the good pleasure of the LORD will prosper in His hand.
As a result of the anguish of His soul,
He will see *it and* be satisfied;
By His knowledge the Righteous One,
My Servant, will justify the many,
As He will bear their iniquities.
Therefore, I will allot Him a portion with the great,
And He will divide the booty with the strong;
Because He poured out Himself to death,
And was numbered with the transgressors;
Yet He Himself bore the sin of many,
And interceded for the transgressors. – Isaiah 53:1-12

He Would Heal the Broken and Sick:

The Spirit of the Lord GOD is upon me,
Because the LORD has anointed me
To bring good news to the afflicted;
He has sent me to bind up the brokenhearted,
To proclaim liberty to captives
And freedom to prisoners;
To proclaim the favorable year of the LORD
And the day of vengeance of our God;
To comfort all who mourn,
To grant those who mourn *in* Zion,
Giving them a garland instead of ashes,
The oil of gladness instead of mourning,
The mantle of praise instead of a spirit of fainting.
So they will be called oaks of righteousness,
The planting of the LORD, that He may be glorified. – Isaiah 61:1-3

"Then I Myself will gather the remnant of My flock out of all the countries where I have driven them and bring them back to their pasture, and they will be fruitful and multiply. I will also raise up shepherds over them and they will tend them; and they will not be afraid any longer, nor be terrified, nor will any be missing," declares the LORD.

"Behold, *the* days are coming," declares the LORD,
"When I will raise up for David a righteous Branch;
And He will reign as king and act wisely
And do justice and righteousness in the land.
"In His days Judah will be saved,
And Israel will dwell securely;
And this is His name by which He will be called,
'The LORD our righteousness.'" – Jeremiah 23:3-6

Riding on the Foal of a Donkey:

Rejoice greatly, O daughter of Zion!
Shout *in triumph*, O daughter of Jerusalem!
Behold, your king is coming to you;
He is just and endowed with salvation,
Humble, and mounted on a donkey,
Even on a colt, the foal of a donkey. – Zechariah 9:9

John the Baptist would precede Him (in the spirit and power of Elijah):

"Behold, I am going to send you Elijah the prophet before the coming of the great and terrible day of the LORD." – Malachi 4:5

He Would be Rejected:

The stone which the builders rejected
Has become the chief corner *stone*.

This is the LORD'S doing;
It is marvelous in our eyes.
This is the day which the LORD has made;
Let us rejoice and be glad in it.
O LORD, do save, we beseech You;
O LORD, we beseech You, do send prosperity!
Blessed is the one who comes in the name of the LORD;
We have blessed you from the house of the LORD.
The LORD is God, and He has given us light;
Bind the festival sacrifice with cords to the horns of the altar.
You are my God, and I give thanks to You;
You are my God, I extol You.
Give thanks to the LORD, for He is good;
For His lovingkindness is everlasting. – Psalm 118:22-29

He Would be Crucified (His Garments divided, etc.):

I am poured out like water,
And all my bones are out of joint;
My heart is like wax;
It is melted within me.
My strength is dried up like a potsherd,
And my tongue cleaves to my jaws;
And You lay me in the dust of death.
For dogs have surrounded me;
A band of evildoers has encompassed me;
They pierced my hands and my feet.
I can count all my bones.
They look, they stare at me;
They divide my garments among them,
And for my clothing they cast lots. – Psalm 22:14-18

He Would be Scourged:

I gave My back to those who strike *Me*,
And My cheeks to those who pluck out the beard;
I did not cover My face from humiliation and spitting. – Isaiah 50:6

None of His bones would be broken (on the cross):

He protects all his bones,
Not one of them is broken. – Psalm 34:20

It is by and through these fulfilled prophecies that we know:

1) The Bible is true and inspired of God, and that
2) Jesus is, in fact, the "Messiah," the "Savior," the "anointed one of God," the "Redeemer," and "the [spotless] Lamb of God, who takes away the sin of the world," and that
3) Jesus was "God manifest in the flesh" who "dwelled among us" (covered in an upcoming chapter)

The book *Science Speaks* by Peter Stoner lists many of these prophecies and calculates the odds that someone could have accidentally fulfilled just a subset of them is 1 in 5.76 x 10^{59}! When written out, we get a better realization of just how astronomically large that number is:

1 in 5,760,000,000,000,000,000,000,000,000,000,000,000,000,000,000,000,000,000,000! [27]

To further emphasize how enormous that number is, here are some comparisons. The number of grains of sand in the world is estimated to be 7.5 x 10^{18}. And the total number of stars in the entire universe is estimated to be 7 x 10^{22}. The total number of people who have ever lived on Earth is estimated to be about 100 billion (give or take a few billion). Let's be wildly and unrealistically conservative and error on the side of caution and multiply the number of people who have ever lived by a factor of 1,000 (to make sure we are not underestimating the odds), which gives us 100,000,000,000,000 or 1 x 10^{14} people that have lived on Earth over all time. So even if you had a million times a billion times a trillion planet Earths, the odds that in all of those that one person would have been randomly born by chance and fulfilled (even partially) the prophecies of Jesus are effectively zero. Jesus wasn't an accident.

The odds of an ant lifting up the Sun and putting it on its back are about the same as someone being born by chance matching and fulfilling the prophecies that are foretold concerning Jesus in the Bible: namely zero. So, His life was not by chance, or random, or a lucky set of coincidences; no, Scripture says that "He [Jesus] was foreknown before the foundation of the world, but has appeared in these last times for the sake of you who through Him are believers in God," appearing "when the fullness of time came" and "while we were still helpless [in sin], at *the* right time Christ died for the ungodly."

Furthermore, God is not asking us to "blindly believe" in Jesus without giving us overwhelming proof, evidence, and eyewitness testimony that He was, in fact, "the Son of God." God wants us to come to a fully rational, conscious, and informed decision to believe in Jesus based on hard evidence about his birth, life, death, and resurrection. The many miracles He performed were done to demonstrate and testify that He was indeed "the Son of God" – God in the flesh. If all of this evidence and eyewitness testimony presented today in an **unbiased** court of law as evidence in even the most severe of capital punishment cases, the preponderance of the evidence would support a verdict beyond a reasonable doubt that Jesus of Nazareth did, in fact, live, die and was resurrected as told in Scripture.

You simply have to look at the evidence without a preconceived bias against "religion" and against Jesus. Those who deny Jesus do so **against** the preponderance of the evidence – evidence that any jury in the world would say IS beyond a reasonable doubt! Even many reputable secular scholars (i.e., those who don't believe the Bible) concede and admit that Jesus, the man, did exist as the Bible claims.

[On a side note: The Bible itself is also the most highly documented, recorded, and confirmed book in history, many times more than other widely accepted books such as Homer's *Iliad,* for example, with more fragments and originals still present today than any other work ever written – and not just by a little bit, but by a wide margin. The accuracy and agreement/consistency among the widely found biblical fragments has

---

[27] Stoner, Peter and Newman, Robert C., *Science Speaks*, The Moody Bible Institute of Chicago, 1969/1976.

also been stunning. You can read up on this subject yourself, as much research is available on this topic.]

JESUS HAS THE AUTHORITY TO FORGIVE SIN

As will be explained more in the next chapter, Jesus did declare that He is God, the Second Person of the Holy Trinity (Father, Son, Holy Spirit) and that "all authority" was given Him by God the Father to forgive sins. It is therefore only through Jesus that forgiveness of sins must be obtained and how all men are saved:

> And Jesus came up and spoke to them, saying, "All authority has been given to Me in heaven and on earth." – Matthew 28:18

> "And there is salvation in no one else; for there is no other name under heaven that has been given among men by which we must be saved." – Acts 4:12

> Jesus said to him, "I am the way, and the truth, and the life; no one comes to the Father but through Me." – John 14:6

> For not even the Father judges anyone, but He has given all judgment to the Son. – John 5:22

> For there is one God, *and* one mediator also between God and men, *the* man Christ Jesus, who gave Himself as a ransom for all, the testimony *given* at the proper time. For this I was appointed a preacher and an apostle (I am telling the truth, I am not lying) as a teacher of the Gentiles in faith and truth. – 1 Timothy 2:5-7

Additionally, recall from the previous chapter that Jesus will be your judge on the great Day of Judgment, for "He [God] has given all judgment to the Son." Why? Because He became a man unto death, and He was tempted in all things as we are, so he knows what we have gone through here in this fallen world, and yet He remained without sin unto death. This makes Him the only "mediator" (between man and God) and also a fair and impartial judge. He was victorious over sin and death and the power of the Devil – He defeated sin, Satan, and death at the cross for us!

Jesus was born under the Old Testament's Mosaic Law and perfectly "fulfilled" that Law. He lived a perfect, sinless (morally pure) life in obedience to God, even "obedient to the point of death: death on a cross," being crucified as a substitutionary atonement (an atoning sacrifice, payment) for your sins.

THE IMAGE OF THE INVISIBLE GOD

Know that when you see (read about) Jesus, you are seeing (reading about) God:

> He [Jesus] is the image of the invisible God, the firstborn of all creation. For by Him all things were created, *both* in the heavens and on earth, visible and invisible, whether thrones or dominions or rulers or authorities—all things have been created through Him and for Him. – Colossians 1:15-16

What you see Jesus is like from reading Scripture is also exactly what God is like. The kindness, compassion, patience, healing, loving, caring, full of grace, slowness to anger, with extreme restraint and temperance person that Jesus was, and is, is also your God. God is not a God of evil, deception, trickery, lying, or deceit; in fact, no evil, sin, or deceit is found in Him. God is 100% holy, just, and pure.

Please also notice in Scripture how Jesus didn't use force or coerce anyone to follow Him, nor does God force anyone to follow Him. Sure, there are consequences for disobeying God, but the choice is yours. God doesn't want robots obeying out of rote command, for that is not love and "God is love." He wants those who come to Him to do so freely of their own choice, out of their own free will, and out of love for Him. True love cannot be commanded, nor coerced, from anyone.

IN SUMMARY

In summary:

- God became flesh in the man Jesus Christ who was fully God while also fully man,
- He was supernaturally born of "a virgin" (Mary) through the power of the Holy Spirit,
- He came humbly, born not in a palace but in "a manger,"
- He came not to the religious or political rulers/elites of the day but to people just like you and me: the sinners and the lost,
- He drew people not by His appearance (i.e., physical attraction) but by the message of His Word,
- He was "obedient to the point of death: death on a cross,"
- "He was pierced for our offenses [transgressions, sins],"
- He took our sins on Him ("He made Him who knew no sin *to be* sin in our behalf, so that we might become the righteousness of God in Him."),
- "He was buried, and that He was raised on the third day according to the Scriptures," and
- He is right now "seated at the right hand of God [the Father]" in heaven, ruling as King in His kingdom,
- He has existed from eternity past to eternity future, the "first and the last," the "alpha and omega," the great "I AM,"
- He walked among us and was "tempted in all things just as *we are*" so He can empathize/sympathize with us, so that He can mediate for us now in heaven before God (He is the "one [only] mediator between God and men"), and also so He can be (and will be) a completely fair and righteous Judge on the Day of Judgment, and that
- He will judge all mankind on the great Day of Judgment ("For not even the Father judges anyone, but He has given all judgment to the Son"). He is, in fact, both Judge and also your attorney if you choose Him to be! Your court victory can be certain even before trial begins – that is the "good news" of the gospel!

He was "declared [by God to be] the Son of God with power according to the Spirit of holiness" and also by supernatural miracles:

- He made wine from water,
- He healed the sick (blind, lame, deaf, lepers, etc.),
- He commanded nature (walked on water, calmed the storm, etc.),
- He fed thousands of people with only a small loaf of bread and fish (several times), and
- He raised people from the dead

The Message of Truth

I can only scratch the surface in this book about who Jesus the man was, but it is all written in the Bible. All I ask is that you evaluate the evidence with an unbiased and logical mind, free from any preconceived notions against Jesus. It is only a preconceived bias against God, and against religion, along with a willful rebellion and prideful refusal to submit to your Creator, that causes one not to see the logical verdict on this matter.

Now many today also claim: "Ok, I will grant you that Jesus existed as the man, but Jesus was simply a 'good moral person' or a 'good teacher.'" And others will say that He didn't really claim to be God. Such claims are in contradiction to Scripture, which is clear that He declared Himself to be "the Son of God" and also God Himself ("I AM"). Scripture also declares that Christ has "no beginning, and no end"; in other words, He is immortal – and only God is immortal. Scripture also says that "all things came into being through Him, and apart from Him not even one thing came into being that has come into being"; He was there "in the beginning." It is only through Christ that you can be saved from the judgment to come and be saved to eternal life, for only God can forgive sins, and He has told us how we must approach Him (through His Son).

Therefore, in the next chapter, we will look further at this most important question: Was (is) Jesus (the man) really God in the flesh?

FALSE TEACHING(S) YOU WILL ENCOUNTER:

- Jesus is just a mythical figure, not a real person
- Jesus was just a "good moral person," but not God
- Atheism (there is no God)
- The Bible is Simply fictional "myths, folklore, and poetry"

RELATED SCRIPTURE:

For He [Jesus] was foreknown before the foundation of the world, but has appeared in these last times for the sake of you who through Him are believers in God, who raised Him from the dead and gave Him glory, so that your faith and hope are in God. – 1 Peter 1:20-21

John answered and said to them all, "As for me, I baptize you with water; but One [Jesus] is coming who is mightier than I, and I am not fit to untie the thong of His sandals; He will baptize you with the Holy Spirit and fire." – Luke 3:16

Now the birth of Jesus Christ was as follows: when His mother Mary had been betrothed to Joseph, before they came together she was found to be with child by the Holy Spirit. And Joseph her husband, being a righteous man and not wanting to disgrace her, planned to send her away secretly. But when he had considered this, behold, an angel of the Lord appeared to him in a dream, saying, "Joseph, son of David, do not be afraid to take Mary as your wife; for the Child who has been conceived in her is of the Holy Spirit. She will bear a Son; and you shall call His name Jesus, for He will save His people from their sins." Now all this took place to fulfill what was spoken by the Lord through the prophet: "BEHOLD, THE VIRGIN SHALL BE WITH CHILD AND SHALL BEAR A SON, AND THEY SHALL CALL HIS NAME IMMANUEL," which translated means, "GOD WITH US." – Matthew 1:18-23

The next day he saw Jesus coming to him and said, "Behold, the Lamb of God who takes away the sin of the world!" – John 1:29

John testified saying, "I have seen the Spirit descending as a dove out of heaven, and He remained upon Him [Jesus]. I did not recognize Him, but He who sent me to baptize in water said to me, 'He upon whom you see the Spirit descending and remaining upon Him, this is the One who baptizes in the Holy Spirit.' I myself have seen, and have testified that this is the Son of God." – John 1:32-34

After being baptized, Jesus came up immediately from the water; and behold, the heavens were opened, and he saw the Spirit of God descending as a dove *and* lighting on Him [Jesus], and behold, a voice out of the heavens said, "This is My beloved Son, in whom I am well-pleased." – Matthew 3:16-17

In Him [Jesus] was life, and the life was the Light of men. The Light shines in the darkness, and the darkness did not comprehend it. – John 1:4-5

From that time Jesus began to preach and say, "Repent, for the kingdom of heaven is at hand." – Matthew 4:17

"My sheep hear My voice, and I know them, and they follow Me; and I give eternal life to them, and they will never perish; and no one will snatch them out of My hand. My Father, who has given *them* to Me, is greater than all; and no one is able to snatch *them* out of the Father's hand." – John 10:27-29

Therefore, since the children share in flesh and blood, He Himself likewise also partook of the same, that through death He might render powerless him who had the power of death, that is, the devil, and might free those who through fear of death were subject to slavery all their lives. – Hebrews 2:14-15

Now when Jesus was in Bethany, at the home of Simon the leper, a woman came to Him with an alabaster vial of very costly perfume, and she poured it on His head as He reclined *at the table*. But the disciples were indignant when they saw *this*, and said, "Why this waste? For this *perfume* might have been sold for a high price and *the money* given to the poor." But Jesus, aware of this, said to them, "Why do you bother the woman? For she has done a good deed to Me. For you always have the poor with you; but you do not always have Me. For when she poured this perfume on My body, she did it to prepare Me for burial. Truly I say to you, wherever this gospel is preached in the whole world, what this woman has done will also be spoken of in memory of her." – Matthew 26:6-13

Being found in appearance as a man, He humbled Himself by becoming obedient to the point of death, even death on a cross. For this reason also, God highly exalted Him, and bestowed on Him the name which is above every name, so that at the name of Jesus EVERY KNEE WILL BOW, of those who are in heaven and on earth and under the earth, and that every tongue will confess that Jesus Christ is Lord, to the glory of God the Father. – Philippians 2:8-11

Pilate then took Jesus and scourged Him [Jesus]. And the soldiers twisted together a crown of thorns and put it on His head, and put a purple robe on Him; and they *began* to come up to Him and say, "Hail, King of the Jews!" and to give Him slaps *in the face*. – John 19:1-3

They took Jesus, therefore, and He went out, bearing His own cross, to the place called the Place of a Skull, which is called in Hebrew, Golgotha. There they crucified Him, and with Him two other men, one on either side, and Jesus in between. Pilate also wrote an inscription and put it on the cross. It was written, "JESUS THE NAZARENE, THE KING OF THE JEWS." – John 19:17-19

For Christ also died for sins once for all, *the* just for *the* unjust, so that He might bring us to God, having been put to death in the flesh, but made alive in the spirit. – 1 Peter 3:18

For while we were still helpless, at the right time Christ died for the ungodly. For one will hardly die for a righteous man; though perhaps for the good man someone would dare even to die. But God demonstrates His own love toward us, in that while we were yet sinners, Christ died for us. – Romans 5:6-8

He [God] made Him [Jesus] who knew no sin *to be* sin on our behalf, so that we might become the righteousness of God in Him. – 2 Corinthians 5:21

For we do not have a high priest who cannot sympathize with our weaknesses, but One who has been tempted in all things as *we are, yet* without sin. – Hebrews 4:15

If you address as Father the One who impartially judges according to each one's work, conduct yourselves in fear during the time of your stay *on earth*; knowing that you were not redeemed with perishable things like silver or gold from your futile way of life inherited from your forefathers, but with precious blood, as of a lamb unblemished and spotless [without sin], *the blood* of Christ. – 1 Peter 1:17-19

My little children, I am writing these things to you so that you may not sin. And if anyone sins, we have an Advocate with the Father, Jesus Christ the righteous; and He Himself is the propitiation for our sins; and not for ours only, but also for *those of* the whole world. – 1 John 2:1-2

For I delivered to you as of first importance what I also received, that Christ died for our sins according to the Scriptures, and that He was buried, and that He was raised on the third day according to the Scriptures, and that He appeared to Cephas, then to the twelve. – 1 Corinthians 15:3-5

…"Why do you seek the living One among the dead? He is not here, but He [Jesus] has risen. Remember how He spoke to you while He was still in Galilee, saying that the Son of Man must be delivered into the hands of sinful men, and be crucified, and the third day rise again." – Luke 24:5b-7

…and if Christ has not been raised, then our preaching is vain, your faith also is vain. Moreover we are even found *to be* false witnesses of God, because we testified against God that He raised Christ, whom He did not raise, if in fact the dead are not raised. For if the dead are not raised, not even Christ has been raised; and if Christ has not been raised, your faith is worthless; you are still in your sins. – 1 Corinthians 15:14-17

"Do not let your heart be troubled; believe in God, believe also in Me. In My Father's house are many dwelling places; if it were not so, I would have told you; for I go to prepare a place for you. If I go and prepare a place for you, I will come again and receive you to Myself, that where I am, *there* you may be also." – John 14:1-3

And after He had said these things, He [Jesus] was lifted up while they were looking on, and a cloud received Him out of their sight. And as they were gazing intently into the sky while He was going, behold, two men in white clothing stood beside them. They also said, "Men of Galilee, why do you stand looking into the sky? This Jesus, who has been taken up from you into heaven, will come in just the same way as you have watched Him go into heaven." – Acts 1:9-11

But now Christ has been raised from the dead, the first fruits of those who are asleep. For since by a man *came* death, by a man also *came* the resurrection of the dead. For as in Adam all die, so also in Christ all will be made alive. But each in his own order: Christ the first fruits, after that those who are Christ's at His coming, then *comes* the end, when He hands over the kingdom to the God and Father, when He has abolished all rule and all authority and power. For He [Jesus] must reign until He has put all His enemies under His feet. The last enemy that will be abolished is death. For HE HAS PUT ALL THINGS IN SUBJECTION UNDER HIS FEET. But when He says, "All things are put in subjection," it is evident that He is excepted who put all things in subjection to Him. When all things are subjected to Him, then the Son Himself also will be subjected to the One who subjected all things to Him, so that God may be all in all. – 1 Corinthians 15:20-28

So also it is written, "The first MAN, Adam, BECAME A LIVING SOUL." The last Adam [Jesus] *became* a life-giving spirit. However, the spiritual is not first, but the natural; then the spiritual. The first man is from the earth, earthy; the second man is from heaven. As is the earthy, so also are those who are earthy; and as is the heavenly, so also are those who are heavenly. Just as we have borne the image of the earthy, we will also bear the image of the heavenly. – 1 Corinthians 15:45-49

Then Jesus again spoke to them, saying, "I am the Light of the world; he who follows Me will not walk in the darkness, but will have the Light of life." – John 8:12

Great indeed, we confess, is the mystery of godliness:

> He [Jesus] was manifested in the flesh,
> vindicated by the Spirit,
> seen by angels,
> proclaimed among the nations,
> believed on in the world,
> taken up in glory. – 1 Timothy 3:16 (ESV)

…through the resurrection of Jesus Christ, who is at the right hand of God, having gone into heaven, after angels and authorities and powers had been subjected to Him. – 1 Peter 3:21b-22

Every priest stands daily ministering and offering time after time the same sacrifices, which can never take away sins; but He [Jesus], having offered one sacrifice for sins for all time, SAT DOWN AT THE RIGHT HAND OF GOD, waiting from that time onward UNTIL HIS ENEMIES BE MADE A FOOTSTOOL FOR HIS FEET. – Hebrews 10:11-13

God, after He spoke long ago to the fathers in the prophets in many portions and in many ways, in these last days has spoken to us in His Son, whom He appointed heir of all things, through whom also He made the world. And He is the radiance of His glory and the exact representation of His nature, and upholds all things by the word of His power. When He had made purification of sins, He sat down at the right hand of the Majesty on high, having become as much better than the angels, as He has inherited a more excellent name than they. – Hebrews 1:1-4

2.1 IS JESUS REALLY GOD?

He is the image of the invisible God, the firstborn of all creation. For by Him all things were created, both in the heavens and on earth, visible and invisible, whether thrones or dominions or rulers or authorities—all things have been created through Him and for Him. – Colossians 1:15-16

The Son of God, The Son of Man, Immanuel. The previous chapter presented and described Jesus, the man – and that He was crucified in atoning payment (sacrifice) for your sins and that He rose again after three days. While many skeptics, agnostics, and atheists continue to deny that Jesus (the man) ever existed (despite overwhelming evidence that He did), others realize they cannot escape the force of that evidence, and so in a continued effort to discredit the gospel message, they resort to mockingly conceding: "Well, he never claimed to be God, he was just a good moral teacher"! Further compounding the matter, even some so-called (fake) "Christian" churches today (e.g., the Mormons, Jehovah Witnesses, etc.) make false claims such as: "Jesus was simply an angel, a created being," or even that "He is the brother of Satan." This is all blasphemy, and those are not true Christian churches; they are cults that deny Christ (see the Beware the Wolves chapter)!

Scripture clearly shows that Jesus of Nazareth was not just an ordinary man – for how many men (or women) were born to a virgin mother through the supernatural work of the Holy Spirit? Furthermore, the many miracles he performed along with His command over nature, witnessed by hundreds of people (thousands in some cases) and recorded in Scripture, served to confirm His claims and testify and prove that He was indeed God in the flesh. And lastly: did Jesus Himself actually claim to be God? This chapter shows you that yes, Jesus did, in fact, claim to be God, and He did so without any ambiguity whatsoever.

MIRACLES JESUS PERFORMED CONFIRMED HE WAS GOD

Jesus performed many miracles, which were witnessed by many (hundreds, thousands) of people. A partial list is given below:

- Cured the nobleman's son (John 4:46-47),
- Cast out demons/unclean spirits (Mark 1:23-28, Matthew 8:28-34, Matthew 12:22, Matthew 15:22-28, Matthew 17:14-21),
- Cured Peter's mother-in-law (Mark 1:30-31),
- Healed lepers (Mark 1:40-45, Luke 17:11-19),
- Healed the centurion's servant (Matthew 8:5-13),
- Raised people from the dead (Luke 7:11-18, Matthew 9:18-26, John 11:1-46),
- Cured a person with paralysis (Matthew 9:1-8),
- Healed a bleeding woman (Luke 8:43-48),
- Opened the eyes of the blind (Matthew 9:27-31, Mark 8:22-26, John 9:1-38, Matthew 20:30-34),
- Caused the mute to speak (Matthew 9:32-33),
- Healed the lame man at the pool Bethesda (John 5:1-9),
- Restored a withered hand (Matthew 12:10-13),
- Cured a deaf and mute man (Mark 7:31-37),
- Healed a crippled woman (Luke 13:10-17),

- Restored a cut-off ear (Luke 22:50-51),
- Rose from the dead Himself (Luke 24:5-6)

John, the beloved disciple of Jesus, writes:

> And there are also many other things [miracles] which Jesus did, which if they were written in detail, I suppose that even the world itself would not contain the books that would be written. – John 21:25

Additionally, the miracles (e.g., healing the sick and blind, raising people from the dead, etc.) served to demonstrate that He is able to reverse the curse that was placed on this world and all mankind (as a result of man's disobedience of God, see the earlier chapter on Humanity and Sin) and restore creation to a perfect state again – and this is part of the hope that a Christian has in Christ.

JESUS' COMMAND OVER NATURE CONFIRMED HE WAS GOD

Jesus repeatedly demonstrated His command over nature, something which only God can do. A partial list is given below:

- Changed water into wine (John 2:1-11),
- The disciple's great catches of fish (Luke 5:1-11, John 21:1-14),
- Calmed the storm (Matthew 8:23-27, Mark 4:36-41, Luke 8:22-25),
- Walked on water (Matthew 14:22-33),
- Fed at least 5,000 people (Matthew 14:15-21),
- Fed at least 4,000 people (Matthew 15:32-39),
- Caused a fig tree to wither (Matthew 21:18-22, Mark 11:20-24)

GOD (THE FATHER) DECLARED JESUS TO BE GOD

God (the Father) also unequivocally declares Jesus to be God:

> After being baptized, Jesus came up immediately from the water; and behold, the heavens were opened, and he saw the Spirit of God descending as a dove *and* lighting on Him [Jesus], and behold, a voice out of the heavens said, "This is My beloved Son, in whom I am well-pleased." – Matthew 3:16-17

Next, I want to call your attention to what is written in Hebrews 1:8, quoting from Psalm 45:6. Here you have in Scripture God (the Father) explicitly calling His Son Jesus God; this was written long before Jesus was even born:

> But of the Son *He [God] says*,
>
> "YOUR [JESUS] THRONE, O GOD, IS FOREVER AND EVER,
> AND THE RIGHTEOUS SCEPTER IS THE SCEPTER OF HIS KINGDOM." – Hebrews 1:8

Another remarkable occurrence was Jesus' transfiguration on the mountain (accompanied by Moses and Elijah) in front of Peter, James, and John:

> Six days later Jesus took with Him Peter and James and John his brother, and led them up on a high mountain by themselves. And He was transfigured before them; and His face shone like the sun, and His garments became as white as light. And behold, Moses and Elijah appeared to them, talking with Him. Peter said to Jesus,

"Lord, it is good for us to be here; if You wish, I will make three tabernacles here, one for You, and one for Moses, and one for Elijah." While he was still speaking, a bright cloud overshadowed them, and behold, a voice out of the cloud said, "This is My beloved Son, with whom I am well-pleased; listen to Him!" When the disciples heard *this*, they fell face down to the ground and were terrified. And Jesus came to *them* and touched them and said, "Get up, and do not be afraid." And lifting up their eyes, they saw no one except Jesus Himself alone. – Matthew 17:1-8

JESUS CLAIMED TO BE GOD

Jesus did, in fact, claim to be God. A couple of the verses where He did so are given here:

Again the high priest was questioning Him [Jesus], and saying to Him, "Are You the Christ, the Son of the Blessed *One*?" And Jesus said, "I am; and you shall see THE SON OF MAN SITTING AT THE RIGHT HAND OF POWER, and COMING WITH THE CLOUDS OF HEAVEN." Tearing his clothes, the high priest said, "What further need do we have of witnesses? You have heard the blasphemy; how does it seem to you?" And they all condemned Him to be deserving of death. – Mark 14:61-64

Jesus said to them, "Truly, truly, I say to you, before Abraham was born, I am." Therefore they picked up stones to throw at Him [to kill Him], but Jesus hid Himself and went out of the temple. – John 8:58-59

For this reason therefore the Jews were seeking all the more to kill Him [Jesus], because He not only was breaking the Sabbath, but also was calling God His own Father, making Himself equal with God. – John 5:18

[Jesus Said:] "I and the Father are one."

The Jews picked up stones again to stone Him. Jesus answered them, "I showed you many good works from the Father; for which of them are you stoning Me?" The Jews answered Him, "For a good work we do not stone You, but for blasphemy; and because You, being a man, make Yourself out to be God."– John 10:30-33

"If you had known Me, you would have known My Father also; from now on you know Him, and have seen Him." – John 14:7

"Do not be afraid; I am the first and the last, and the living One; and I was dead, and behold, I am alive forevermore, and I have the keys of death and of Hades." – Revelation 1:17b-18

It's worth noting that from some of the verses above, you can see that the Jews of Jesus' day had no doubt whatsoever that He was claiming to be God ("I AM") – for that is why they repeatedly tried to kill Him. Each time He made the claim, they rushed at Him again to try to stone Him to death!

JESUS' ATTRIBUTES DECLARE HIM TO BE GOD

There is another aspect that shows that Jesus is God. Several attributes are ascribed to Him which can only belong to deity: eternal being (having no beginning and no ending), holiness, and receiving of worship. Scripture assigns all of these attributes to Jesus.

Speaking of His eternal nature, Scripture is clear that Jesus has no beginning and no end – He is eternal. The Bible tells us that "He [Jesus] was foreknown before the foundation of the world." It declares that "He [Jesus] was in the beginning," and that "He [Jesus] was with God" and that "He [Jesus] was God." Scripture states that "all things came into being through Him [Jesus]." He has co-existed eternally with God the Father since eternity past and will continue to exist for eternity future.

Jesus Christ *is* the same yesterday and today and forever. – Hebrews 13:8

Jesus is not just "a created being," "a fallen angel," or "the brother of Satan," as some falsely teach. Any group (cult) teaching such things is denying the Jesus of the Bible! [28]

Jesus' voice can even be heard in the Old Testament. Even though the words aren't in red, you are actually hearing (by reading) Jesus' voice in many Old Testament passages. It was Jesus Who spoke all things into existence. Amazing! In God's infinite wisdom, Christ was veiled to mankind until just the right time in history when He was made "manifest in the flesh" as the man "Jesus of Nazareth," having "appeared in these last times for the sake of you" (i.e., when God decided it was time to reveal Him to the world as Savior and Redeemer). After His death and resurrection, He ascended again to heaven, and He will return to gather those who are His on the Last Day, which is the Day of Judgment

SCRIPTURE DECLARES JESUS TO BE GOD

And finally, Scripture declares Jesus is God:

> He [Jesus] is the image of the invisible God, the firstborn of all creation. For by Him all things were created, *both* in the heavens and on earth, visible and invisible, whether thrones or dominions or rulers or authorities—all things have been created through Him and for Him. – Colossians 1:15-16

> In the beginning was the Word [Jesus], and the Word was with God, and the Word was God. He was in the beginning with God. All things came into being through Him, and apart from Him nothing came into being that has come into being. – John 1:1-3

> For in Him [Jesus] all the fullness of Deity dwells in bodily form… – Colossians 2:9

> God, after He spoke long ago to the fathers in the prophets in many portions and in many ways, in these last days has spoken to us in His Son, whom He appointed heir of all things, through whom also He made the world. And He is the radiance of His glory and the exact representation of His nature, and upholds all things by the word of His power. When He had made purification of sins, He sat down at the right hand of the Majesty on high, having become as much better than the angels, as He has inherited a more excellent name than they.

---

[28] Jackson, Wayne. "Jehovah's Witnesses and the Doctrine of the Deity of Jesus Christ." *ChristianCourier.com*. Access date: July 28, 2019. https://christiancourier.com/articles/1604-jehovahs-witnesses-and-the-doctrine-of-the-deity-of-jesus-christ

For to which of the angels did He ever say,

> "YOU ARE MY SON,
> TODAY I HAVE BEGOTTEN YOU"?

And again,

> "I WILL BE A FATHER TO HIM
> AND HE SHALL BE A SON TO ME"?

And when He again brings the firstborn into the world, He says,

> "AND LET ALL THE ANGELS OF GOD WORSHIP HIM."

And of the angels He says,

> "WHO MAKES HIS ANGELS WINDS,
> AND HIS MINISTERS A FLAME OF FIRE."

But of the Son *He says*,

> "YOUR THRONE, O GOD, IS FOREVER AND EVER,
> AND THE RIGHTEOUS SCEPTER IS THE SCEPTER OF HIS KINGDOM."

– Hebrews 1:1-8

And we know that the Son of God has come, and has given us understanding so that we may know Him who is true; and we are in Him who is true, in His Son Jesus Christ. This is the true God and eternal life. – 1 John 5:20

The LORD says to my Lord [Jesus]:
"Sit at My right hand
Until I make Your enemies a footstool for Your feet."
The LORD will stretch forth Your strong scepter from Zion, *saying*,
"Rule in the midst of Your enemies."
Your people will volunteer freely in the day of Your power;
In holy array, from the womb of the dawn,
Your youth are to You *as* the dew.

The LORD has sworn and will not change His mind,
"You are a priest forever
According to the order of Melchizedek."
The Lord is at Your right hand;
He will shatter kings in the day of His wrath.
He will judge among the nations,
He will fill *them* with corpses,
He will shatter the chief men over a broad country.
He will drink from the brook by the wayside;
Therefore He will lift up *His* head. – Psalm 110

So, in summary:

1) Jesus unequivocally declared Himself to be, and is, God,
2) God declared Jesus to be God,
3) Scripture declares Jesus to be God,
4) Jesus' miracles demonstrated He was God,

5) Jesus' command over nature demonstrated He was God,
6) Jesus accepted and allowed worship without correcting those who did so; worship is reserved for God alone,
7) Jesus is of the same essence as God the Father and co-eternal with God the Father, having no beginning or end - He is not a created being,
8) And furthermore, He [Jesus] is ruling and reigning this very day in His Kingdom!

It is worth noting that the name He most often used when referring to Himself was "Son of Man" – reinforcing His love, affection, and bond with humanity and the value He places on His own humanity (despite also being God). Jesus will be identified with His (and our) humanity for all eternity.

In the next chapter, we discuss a matter of monumental and eternal importance: Was Jesus really raised from the dead? For without His resurrection, we have no "good news" and no hope.

FALSE TEACHING(S) YOU WILL ENCOUNTER:

- Jesus was just a "good moral" man (but not God) – even if the skeptics and atheists concede that Jesus did live as recorded in the Bible, they will still try to deny His deity
- Jesus is just "an angel" or "the brother of Satan" – i.e., He is a created being and not God. This false teaching is brought to you by some groups/churches which CLAIM to be "Christian" and even use the name of Jesus in their church name! Yes, the mind of man seems to have no limits when conjuring up bizarre interpretations and outright distortions of Scripture, and then others seem to be willing to believe and go along with them. Be not deceived!
- Cults that deny the deity of Christ, that He is God

RELATED SCRIPTURE:

"Do not let your heart be troubled; believe in God, believe also in Me [Jesus]. In My Father's house are many dwelling places; if it were not so, I would have told you; for I go to prepare a place for you. If I go and prepare a place for you, I will come again and receive you to Myself, that where I am, *there* you may be also." – John 14:1-3

Philip said to Him, "Lord, show us the Father, and it is enough for us." Jesus said to him, "Have I been so long with you, and *yet* you have not come to know Me, Philip? He who has seen Me has seen the Father; how *can* you say, 'Show us the Father'? Do you not believe that I am in the Father, and the Father is in Me? The words that I say to you I do not speak on My own initiative, but the Father abiding in Me does His works. Believe Me that I am in the Father and the Father is in Me; otherwise believe because of the works themselves." – John 14:8-11

"You search the Scriptures because you think that in them you have eternal life; it is these that testify about Me; and you are unwilling to come to Me so that you may have life. I do not receive glory from men; but I know you, that you do not have the love of God in yourselves. I have come in My Father's name, and you do not receive Me; if another comes in his own name, you will receive him. How can you believe, when you receive glory from one another and you do not seek the glory that is from the *one and only God*? Do not think that I will accuse you before the Father; the one who accuses you is Moses, in whom you have set your hope. For if you believed Moses, you would believe Me, for he wrote about Me. But if you do not believe his writings, how will you believe My words?" – John 5:39-47

And Jesus came up and spoke to them, saying, "All authority has been given to Me in heaven and on earth." – Matthew 28:18

Jesus said to her, "I am the resurrection and the life; he who believes in Me will live even if he dies, and everyone who lives and believes in Me will never die. Do you believe this?" – John 11:25-26

Simon Peter answered, "You are the Christ, the Son of the living God." And Jesus said to him, "Blessed are you, Simon Barjona, because flesh and blood did not reveal *this* to you, but My Father who is in heaven." – Matthew 16:16-17

...concerning His Son [Jesus], who was born of a descendant of David according to the flesh, who was declared the Son of God with power by the resurrection from the dead, according to the Spirit of holiness, Jesus Christ our Lord. – Romans 1:3-4

Now when John [the Baptist], while imprisoned, heard of the works of Christ, he sent *word* by his disciple, and said to Him, "Are You the Expected One, or shall we look for someone else?" Jesus answered and said to them, "Go and report to John what you hear and see: *the* BLIND RECEIVE SIGHT and *the* lame walk, *the* lepers are cleansed and *the* deaf hear, *the* dead are raised up, and *the* POOR HAVE THE GOSPEL PREACHED TO THEM. And blessed is he who does not take offense at Me." – Matthew 11:2-6

The angel answered and said to her, "The Holy Spirit will come upon you, and the power of the Most High will overshadow you; and for that reason the holy Child [Jesus] shall be called the Son of God." – Luke 1:35

The God of Abraham, Isaac and Jacob, the God of our fathers, has glorified His servant Jesus, *the one* whom you delivered and disowned in the presence of Pilate, when he had decided to release Him. But you disowned the Holy and Righteous One and asked for a murderer to be granted to you, but put to death the Prince of life, *the one* whom God raised from the dead, *a fact* to which we are witnesses. – Acts 3:13-15

Thomas answered and said to Him [Jesus], "My Lord and my God!" Jesus said to him, "Because you have seen Me, have you believed? Blessed *are* they who did not see, and *yet* believed." – John 20:28-29

No one has seen God at any time; the only begotten God [Jesus] who is in the bosom of the Father, He has explained *Him*. – John 1:18

For He [Jesus] was foreknown before the foundation of the world, but has appeared in these last times for the sake of you who through Him are believers in God, who raised Him from the dead and gave Him glory, so that your faith and hope are in God. – 1 Peter 1:20-21

2.2 WAS JESUS REALLY RAISED FROM THE DEAD?

Blessed be the God and Father of our Lord Jesus Christ, who according to His great mercy has caused us to be born again to a living hope through the resurrection of Jesus Christ from the dead. – 1 Peter 1:3

Jesus Lives! During His life and ministry, Jesus had claimed that He was:

- The Christ, the Son of God (Matt 16:16-20, Matt 26:63-63),
- The Son of Man (Matt 16:13; Mk 14:62),
- Sent by God (John 8:42),
- The Savior (John 3:14-16),
- The Messiah (John 4:26),
- The Light of the World (John 8:12),
- The Future Judge (John 5:22-23),
- One with the Father (John 10:30),
- Deserving honor (and worship) equal with the Father (John 5:23),
- The One with authority to forgive (your) sins, which is something only God has authority to do (Matthew 9:2-6, Mark 2:10),
- Able to give eternal life, and further, the ONLY way to truth and life (John 10:28, John 14:6),
- King and Lord (John 18:37, Luke 6:46),
- The Great "I AM" [i.e., God Himself] (John 8:58).

However, we have also read that Jesus died (was crucified) on a cross, so how could Jesus be the Savior, Redeemer, King, and future Judge if He was (and is) just a dead man? But Jesus lives! After being dead for three (3) days, Jesus rose again to life, as it is written:

> "Therefore having overlooked the times of ignorance, God is now declaring to men that all *people* everywhere should repent, because He has fixed a day in which He will judge the world in righteousness through a Man [Jesus] whom He has appointed, having furnished proof to all men by raising Him from the dead." – Acts 17:30-31

> *These are* in accordance with the working of the strength of His might which He brought about in Christ, when He [God] raised Him [Jesus] from the dead and seated Him at His right hand in the heavenly *places*, far above all rule and authority and power and dominion, and every name that is named, not only in this age but also in the one to come. – Ephesians 1:19b-21

> Blessed be the God and Father of our Lord Jesus Christ, who according to His great mercy has caused us to be born again to a living hope through the resurrection of Jesus Christ from the dead, to *obtain* an inheritance *which is* imperishable and undefiled and will not fade away, reserved in heaven for you, who are protected by the power of God through faith for a salvation ready to be revealed in the last time. – 1 Peter 1:3-5

> For He [Jesus] was foreknown before the foundation of the world, but has appeared in these last times for the sake of you who through Him are believers in

> God, who raised Him from the dead and gave Him glory, so that your faith and hope are in God. – 1 Peter 1:20-21

> For I delivered to you as of first importance what I also received, that Christ died for our sins according to the Scriptures, and that He was buried, and that He was raised on the third day according to the Scriptures, and that He appeared to Cephas, then to the twelve. After that He appeared to more than five hundred brethren at one time, most of whom remain until now, but some have fallen asleep; then He appeared to James, then to all the apostles; and last of all, as to one untimely born, He appeared to me [Paul] also. – 1 Corinthians 15:3-8

> …so that as Christ was raised from the dead through the glory of the Father, so we too might walk in newness of life. – Romans 6:4

During Jesus' life and ministry on earth, His miracles and command over nature testified about Him – that He was the Messiah, the anointed one of God, the Christ and also God incarnate (God in the flesh), fully man but also fully God. But it was His resurrection that proved beyond a shadow of a doubt that He was Who He said He was to the world: God. This is why Jesus is "the living and true God." In fact, Christianity is unique among all the religions of the world as it is <u>the only one to have a living God</u>! All other religions have a dead god or a god that is simply an impersonal "force" or feeling.

Without Jesus' resurrection from the dead, none of His claims would have meant anything – and there would be no Christianity, no hope, no victory over sin, Satan and death, and no future of eternal life. When Jesus was crucified on the cross, Satan and his evil forces thought they had won victory; the forces of evil thought they had defeated Him. In fact, if Jesus had remained dead, they would have been correct, and all of Jesus' promises and claims would have been nullified and proven false. That is why it is written that "if Christ has not been raised, then our preaching is vain, your faith also is vain":

> Now if Christ is preached, that He has been raised from the dead, how do some among you say that there is no resurrection of the dead? But if there is no resurrection of the dead, not even Christ has been raised; and if Christ has not been raised, then our preaching is vain, your faith also is vain. Moreover we are even found *to be* false witnesses of God, because we testified against God that He raised Christ, whom He did not raise, if in fact the dead are not raised. For if the dead are not raised, not even Christ has been raised; and if Christ has not been raised, your faith is worthless; you are still in your sins. Then those also who have fallen asleep in Christ have perished. If we have hoped in Christ in this life only, we are of all men most to be pitied. – 1 Corinthians 15:12-19

It was also Jesus' resurrection that broke the power of sin, Satan, and death over us:

> "Men of Israel, listen to these words: Jesus the Nazarene, a man attested to you by God with miracles and wonders and signs which God performed through Him in your midst, just as you yourselves know— this *Man*, delivered over by the predetermined plan and foreknowledge of God, you nailed to a cross by the hands of godless men and put *Him* to death. But God raised Him up again, putting an

end to the agony of death, since it was impossible for Him to be held in its power." – Acts 2:22-24

Wayne Jackson writes: [29]

> The resurrection of Jesus from the dead is the foundation of the Christian system (cf. 1 Corinthians 15:14ff). If there was no resurrection, Christianity is a hoax, and we are wasting our time. …
>
> First, the resurrection is one of the major evidences that Jesus Christ is **the Son of God**. Paul affirmed that Christ is "declared to be the Son of God with power…by the resurrection from the dead" (Romans 1:4).
>
> Second, Jesus' resurrection represents an assurance that we can have **forgiveness from our sins**. Paul contended: "[I]f Christ hath not been raised, our faith is vain; ye are yet in your sins" (1 Corinthians 15:17). The reverse of the apostle's affirmation would be this: if Jesus was raised, sins will be forgiven when we obey the gospel (Acts 2:38; 22:16).
>
> Third, the resurrection tells the world that **the kingdom of God is ruled by a living sovereign**. The founder of Islam is dead and his bones lie dormant in the earth. But the founder of Christianity—sixty years after his death—appeared to John on the island of Patmos and said: "I am the first and the last, and the Living one; and I was dead, and behold, I am alive for evermore" (Revelation 1:17-18).
>
> Fourth, Jesus' resurrection proves that **physical death is not the termination of human existence**. God, who is the giver of life (1 Timothy 6:13), has the power to reanimate the human body. Christ's triumph over the grave is Heaven's pledge to us that we too shall be raised. This is why Jesus is referred to as the "first fruits of them that are asleep" (1 Corinthians 15:20,23).
>
> Fifth, the Lord's resurrection previewed the **ultimate victory of Christianity over all its enemies**. In the book of Revelation, Jesus is depicted as a lamb that had been slain, but was standing again (5:6). This same Lord was "the lion of the tribe of Judah" that had overcome his foes (5:5). Christians too will overcome as a result of the Lamb's sacrifice and victory over death (cf. Revelation 12:11).

HIS DEATH & RESURRECTION WAS FORETOLD

His death on the cross and subsequent resurrection had been foretold (prophesied) way back in Genesis 3, written thousands of years before His birth, where it was written that Satan would "bruise his [Jesus'] heel," but that Jesus would "crush the serpent's [Satan's] head," delivering victory to us over sin, Satan and death. Furthermore, during his life and ministry, Jesus had repeatedly foretold (prophesied) both His own death and resurrection:

> Jesus answered them, "Destroy this temple, and in three days I will raise it up." The Jews then said, "It took forty-six years to build this temple, and will You raise it up in three days?" But He was speaking of the temple of His body. – John 2:19-21

---

[29] Jackson, Wayne. "The Significance of Christ's Resurrection." *ChristianCourier.com*. Access date: March 12, 2019. https://christiancourier.com/articles/64-significance-of-christs-resurrection-the

[Jesus speaking] "As Moses lifted up the serpent in the wilderness, even so must the Son of Man be lifted up [crucified]; so that whoever believes will in Him have eternal life." – John 3:14-15

And He began to teach them that the Son of Man must suffer many things and be rejected by the elders and the chief priests and the scribes, and be killed, and after three days rise again. And He was stating the matter plainly. – Mark 8:31-32a

"Why do you seek the living One among the dead? He is not here, but He has risen. Remember how He spoke to you while He was still in Galilee, saying that the Son of Man must be delivered into the hands of sinful men, and be crucified, and the third day rise again." And they remembered His words. – Luke 24:5b-8

From that time Jesus began to show His disciples that He must go to Jerusalem, and suffer many things from the elders and chief priests and scribes, and be killed, and be raised up on the third day. – Matthew 16:21

As they were coming down from the mountain, Jesus commanded them, saying, "Tell the vision to no one until the Son of Man has risen from the dead." – Matthew 17:9

And while they were gathering together in Galilee, Jesus said to them, "The Son of Man is going to be delivered into the hands of men; and they will kill Him, and He will be raised on the third day." And they were deeply grieved. – Matthew 17:22-23

As Jesus was about to go up to Jerusalem, He took the twelve *disciples* aside by themselves, and on the way He said to them, "Behold, we are going up to Jerusalem; and the Son of Man will be delivered to the chief priests and scribes, and they will condemn Him to death, and will hand Him over to the Gentiles to mock and scourge and crucify *Him*, and on the third day He will be raised up." – Matthew 20:17-19

"But after I [Jesus] have been raised, I will go ahead of you to Galilee." – Matthew 26:32

…saying, "The Son of Man must suffer many things and be rejected by the elders and chief priests and scribes, and be killed and be raised up on the third day." – Luke 9:22

"For this reason the Father loves Me, because I [Jesus] lay down My life so that I may take it again. No one has taken it away from Me, but I lay it down on My own initiative. I have authority to lay it down, and I have authority to take it up again. This commandment I received from My Father." – John 10:17-18

Now on the next day, the day after the preparation, the chief priests and the Pharisees gathered together with Pilate, and said, "Sir, we remember that when He [Jesus] was still alive that deceiver said, 'After three days I *am to* rise again.' Therefore, give orders for the grave to be made secure until the third day, otherwise His disciples may come and steal Him away and say to the people, 'He has risen from the dead,' and the last deception will be worse than the first." Pilate said to them, "You have a guard; go, make it *as* secure as you know how." And they went and made the grave secure, and along with the guard they set a seal on the stone. – Matthew 27:62-66

LITERAL BODILY RESURRECTION WITNESSED BY MANY

Scripture is clear that Jesus rose in a literal bodily resurrection, not just as a "vision" (spiritual) or a "ghost":

> While they were telling these things, He [Jesus] Himself stood in their midst and said to them, "Peace be to you." But they were startled and frightened and thought that they were seeing a spirit. And He said to them, "Why are you troubled, and why do doubts arise in your hearts? See My hands and My feet, that it is I Myself; touch Me and see, for a spirit does not have flesh and bones as you see that I have." And when He had said this, He showed them His hands and His feet. While they still could not believe *it* because of their joy and amazement, He said to them, "Have you anything here to eat?" They gave Him a piece of a broiled fish; and He took it and ate *it* before them. – Luke 24:36-43

> After eight days His disciples were again inside, and Thomas with them. Jesus came, the doors having been shut, and stood in their midst and said, "Peace *be* with you." Then He [Jesus] said to Thomas, "Reach here with your finger, and see My hands; and reach here your hand and put it into My side; and do not be unbelieving, but believing." Thomas answered and said to Him, "My Lord and my God!" Jesus said to him, "Because you have seen Me, have you believed? Blessed *are* they who did not see, and *yet* believed." – John 20:26-29

And that Jesus was seen by hundreds of people after His resurrection:

> To these [the disciples] He also presented Himself alive after His suffering, by many convincing proofs, appearing to them over *a period of* forty days and speaking of the things concerning the kingdom of God. – Acts 1:3

> For I delivered to you as of first importance what I also received, that Christ died for our sins according to the Scriptures, and that He was buried, and that He was raised on the third day according to the Scriptures, and that He appeared to Cephas, then to the twelve. After that He appeared to more than five hundred brethren at one time, most of whom remain until now, but some have fallen asleep; then He appeared to James, then to all the apostles; and last of all, as to one untimely born, He appeared to me also. – 1 Corinthians 15:3-8

> [Now after He had risen early on the first day of the week, He first appeared to Mary Magdalene, from whom He had cast out seven demons. She went and reported to those who had been with Him, while they were mourning and weeping. When they heard that He was alive and had been seen by her, they refused to believe it.] – Mark 16:9-11

> And behold, Jesus met them and greeted them. And they came up and took hold of His feet and worshiped Him. Then Jesus said to them, "Do not be afraid; go and take word to My brethren to leave for Galilee, and there they will see Me." – Matthew 28:9-10

God raised Him up on the third day and granted that He become visible, not to all the people, but to witnesses who were chosen beforehand by God, *that is*, to us who ate and drank with Him after He arose from the dead. – Acts 10:40-41

And behold, two of them were going that very day to a village named Emmaus, which was about seven miles from Jerusalem. And they were talking with each other about all these things which had taken place. While they were talking and discussing, Jesus Himself approached and *began* traveling with them. – Luke 24:13-15

And they approached the village where they were going, and He acted as though He were going farther. But they urged Him, saying, "Stay with us, for it is *getting* toward evening, and the day is now nearly over." So He went in to stay with them. When He had reclined *at the table* with them, He took the bread and blessed *it*, and breaking *it*, He *began* giving *it* to them. Then their eyes were opened and they recognized Him; and He vanished from their sight. They said to one another, "Were not our hearts burning within us while He was speaking to us on the road, while He was explaining the Scriptures to us?" And they got up that very hour and returned to Jerusalem, and found gathered together the eleven and those who were with them, saying, "The Lord has really risen and has appeared to Simon." They *began* to relate their experiences on the road and how He was recognized by them in the breaking of the bread. – Luke 24:28-35

To these [the apostles] He [Jesus] also presented Himself alive after His suffering [death on the cross], by many convincing proofs, appearing to them over *a period of* forty days and speaking of the things concerning the kingdom of God. Gathering them together, He commanded them not to leave Jerusalem, but to wait for what the Father had promised, "Which," *He said*, "you heard of from Me; for John baptized with water, but you will be baptized with the Holy Spirit not many days from now."

So when they had come together, they were asking Him, saying, "Lord, is it at this time You are restoring the kingdom to Israel?" He said to them, "It is not for you to know times or epochs which the Father has fixed by His own authority; but you will receive power when the Holy Spirit has come upon you; and you shall be My witnesses both in Jerusalem, and in all Judea and Samaria, and even to the remotest part of the earth."

And after He had said these things, He was lifted up while they were looking on, and a cloud received Him out of their sight. – Acts 1:3-9 [Note: He ascended into heaven to be seated at the right hand of God the Father. Jesus lives and reigns today!]

Matthew Henry writes on Acts 1:3: [30]

> The great evidence of his resurrection was that he showed himself alive to his apostles; being alive, he showed himself so, and he was seen of them. They were honest men, and one may depend upon their testimony; but the question is whether they were not imposed upon, as many a well-meaning man is. No, they were not; for,

---

[30] Henry, Matthew. Exposition *of the Old and New Testaments*, London. 1706-1710/1721.

1. The proofs were infallible, tekmēria - plain indications, both that he was alive (he walked and talked with them, he ate and drank with them) and that it was he himself, and not another; for he showed them again and again the marks of the wounds in his hands, and feet, and side, which was the utmost proof the thing was capable of or required.

2. They were many, and often repeated: He was seen by them forty days, not constantly residing with them, but frequently appearing to them, and bringing them by degrees to be fully satisfied concerning it, so that all their sorrow for his departure was done away by it. Christ's staying upon earth so long after he had entered upon his state of exaltation and glory, to confirm the faith of his disciples and comfort their hearts, was such an instance of condescension and compassion to believers as may fully assure us that we have a high priest that is touched with the feeling of our infirmities.

THE SKEPTICS

Since Jesus' resurrection is so vital to the Christian faith (i.e., Christianity is pointless without it), you will find skeptics abounding on all sides, with many liberals, atheists, agnostics, sects, and cults denying that Jesus was raised from the dead. They deny His resurrection in an attempt to defeat and discredit Him and to discourage others from following Him and declaring Him as their Lord and Savior. The most common claims made by skeptics trying to deny Jesus' bodily, literal resurrection are:

- Science can't prove it; therefore, it didn't happen. Many will claim that there was no physical, literal bodily resurrection on the basis of science, that it had to be a "spiritual" resurrection, if you will,
- The disciples came and stole His body so they could claim that He was resurrected and continue their popularity,
- Jesus' enemies (the Pharisees et al.) stole His body to quash all the resurrection talk and claims,
- Jesus was just a "vision" or a "ghost" and not really bodily raised from the dead. However, you have already read that the disciples didn't hallucinate in seeing Him – for they touched Him and also saw Him eat in their presence.

Regarding science can't prove it, this topic was already addressed in the chapter on Science vs. The Bible – science cannot explain many things about life and death, and furthermore, many of the works of God are simply supernatural. He is God, and we are the created beings (of immeasurably inferior and finite intellect); and yet because the science that our limited, finite minds have thought up can't measure the things of God, man feels justified in denying that there is a God or that He can work supernaturally. In effect, the clay pot (man) is telling the potter who created it (God) what the reality and truth actually is – how bizarre is that logic!

Regarding "the disciples stole the body" theory, all of the disciples except one died horrible, gruesome deaths for preaching Jesus resurrected. This is hardly something one (or all of them) would do if they were simply perpetuating a lie/hoax. One must also understand the times in which He was crucified. After death, His body was buried in a tomb by Joseph of Arimathea. The tomb was closed in with a huge stone, and the seal of the Roman governor was affixed to it, declaring it off-limits. Anyone tampering with the tomb would be subject to the penalty of death! Even further, Roman guards were stationed outside to make sure no one stole the body. Now the important part: if a prisoner (or a dead body in this case) escaped or were allowed to be carried away, the guards in charge would be put to death. So, you see, it was no light matter or a simple mistake that the guards would make in allowing Jesus' body to be taken/stolen from the tomb by the disciples – it would mean the guard's very own death! The guards would not succumb to a simple bribe from the disciples (or anyone else) to allow them to "steal the body" due to the severity of their punishment if they did so.

Regarding the "Jesus' enemies stole the body" theory (e.g., the Romans, the Jewish Pharisees, etc.), if they did, in fact, steal the body to quash the resurrection claims, why didn't they then just produce (show) the dead body to do just that? That would have ended Christianity right then and there – but they could produce no body, for Jesus Himself was raised from the dead, and He was seen by and interacted with hundreds of witnesses.

And now the part that I find absolutely astounding in all this: not only did the disciples die gruesome deaths for Christ, but even further, Scripture tells us that they were skeptical of Jesus' resurrection – even they didn't believe it at first! In fact, no one expected that He was going to be raised from the dead – not even His own disciples:

> And he said to them, "Do not be amazed; you are looking for Jesus the Nazarene, who has been crucified. He has risen; He is not here; behold, *here is* the place where they laid Him. But go, tell His disciples and Peter, 'He is going ahead of you to Galilee; there you will see Him, just as He told you.'" They went out and fled from the tomb, for trembling and astonishment had gripped them; and they said nothing to anyone, for they were afraid.
>
> [Now after He had risen early on the first day of the week, He first appeared to Mary Magdalene, from whom He had cast out seven demons. She went and reported to those who had been with Him, while they were mourning and weeping. When they heard that He was alive and had been seen by her, they refused to believe it.] – Mark 16:6-11
>
> While they were telling these things, He Himself stood in their midst and said to them, "Peace be to you." But they were startled and frightened and thought that they were seeing a spirit. And He said to them, "Why are you troubled, and why do doubts arise in your hearts? See My hands and My feet, that it is I Myself; touch Me and see, for a spirit does not have flesh and bones as you see that I have." And when He had said this, He showed them His hands and His feet. <u>While they still could not believe *it*</u> because of their joy and amazement, He said to them, "Have you anything here to eat?" They gave Him a piece of a broiled fish; and He took it and ate *it* before them. – Luke 24:36-43

Matthew Henry writes on Luke 24:41:[31]

> So far was it from truth that the disciples stole Jesus' body to fake his resurrection, nay, they at first didn't even believe his resurrection even when they saw him! ... It was their infirmity that they believed not, that yet they believed not, eti apistountōn autōn - they as yet being unbelievers.
>
> This very much corroborates the truth of Christ's resurrection that the disciples were so slow to believe it. Instead of stealing away his body, and saying, He is risen,

---

[31] Henry, Matthew. *Exposition of the Old and New Testaments*, London. 1706-1710/1721.

when he is not, as the chief priests suggested they would do, they are ready to say again and again, He is not risen, when he is.

Their being incredulous of it at first, and insisting upon the utmost proofs of it, show that when afterwards they did believe it, and venture their all upon it, it was not but upon the fullest demonstration of the thing that could be.

THE RESURRECTION IS VITAL

The resurrection of Christ is such a vital topic, and central to your future hope in Christ and eternal life (for what hope is there in a dead man?), that I've included what Wayne Jackson has written on it so you can hear what I've written expressed and reinforced by a different writer: [32]

What Does the Bible Say About Christ's Resurrection?

Unquestionably the Bible affirms the bodily resurrection of the Lord. Let us note three areas of information.

The Old Testament

The Old Testament by means of typology and prophecy announced the resurrection. When Abraham offered up "his only begotten son," he believed that God was able to raise him from the dead, "whence he did also in a figure receive him back" (Heb. 11:17-19). This was typical of the resurrection of God's only begotten Son.

Jonah's three days and nights in the belly of the great fish were typical of the Lord's entombment for the same period prior to his resurrection (Jon. 1:17; Mt. 12:40).

Also, David prophesied:

For thou wilt not leave my soul to Sheol; Neither wilt thou suffer thy holy one to see corruption (Psa. 16:10).

The inspired apostle Peter showed that this prophecy cannot refer to Israel's great king personally, for his body did experience decay and his tomb was testimony to that fact. Rather, the prophet spoke of the resurrection of Christ (cf. Acts 2:29-31; Acts 13:33ff.).

Christ's Predictions

On numerous occasions, Jesus foretold his coming resurrection from the dead. For instance, to the Jews Christ said: "Destroy this temple, and in three days I will raise it up." John adds, "he spake of the temple of his body" (Jn. 2:19-21).

See his other predictions:

- Matthew 16:21; 17:9, 22-23; 20:18-19; 26:32 27:63
- Mark 8:31-9:1; 9:10, 31; 14:28, 58; 10:32
- Luke 9:22-27
- John 10:17-18

Either Christ was raised from the dead, or else he was a false prophet!

---

[32] Jackson, Wayne. "Jesus Showed Himself Alive By Many Proofs." *ChristianCourier.com*. Access date: November 8, 2018. https://christiancourier.com/articles/1592-jesus-showed-himself-alive-by-many-proofs

Theme of the New Testament

The declaration of a **risen Lord** is the very heart and soul of apostolic preaching and writing. Everywhere the apostles went they shamelessly announced that the scandal of the cross was negated by the victory of the empty tomb.

The careful New Testament student will want to study the following passages:

- Acts 1:3; 2:2ff.; 3:15; 4:10, 33; 5:30; 10:40-41; 13:19-37; 17:23-31; 26:8;
- Romans 1:4; 4:25; 6:4-11; 7:4; 8:11, 23; 14:9;
- 1 Corinthians 15;
- 2 Corinthians 1:9-10; 4:14; 5:14-15;
- Ephesians 1:19-23;
- Philippians 3:10;
- Colossians 1:18; 2:12;
- 1 Thessalonians 1:10; 4:14; 5:10;
- 2 Timothy 1:10; 2:8;

The New Testament is saturated with confident declarations of Christ's resurrection.

Where Is the Lord's Body?

Since it is an unassailable fact that Jesus lived in first-century Palestine, and that he was crucified and buried (so asserts Christian, Jewish and pagan history), the intriguing question is this. What happened to the body of Jesus Christ? No honest historian can avoid this query.

Actually, there are but four possible explanations for the absence of the Savior's body:

1. It is still buried in some unknown Palestinian grave.
2. It was removed from the tomb by the Lord's enemies.
3. It was removed from the tomb by the Lord's friends.
4. It arose from the dead and is now in heaven.

Let us briefly consider each of these.

Still buried in Palestine?

It is simply not historically tenable that Christ's body is still interred somewhere near the city of Jerusalem. Why? For this reason.

When the apostles began to fill that city with the teaching of a risen Lord (Acts 5:28), the Jewish or Roman authorities could simply have produced the body and thus exploded the gospel "myth."

It will not do to suggest that the officials did not know where Jesus' body had been buried, because they had assigned soldiers to guard it.

Further, the tomb had been sealed (see Mt. 27:62-66), and records would have been available to document where the body of Christ had been lain.

Did Christ's enemies steal his body?

It is equally absurd to argue that the enemies of Christianity stole the body of Jesus.

On the day of Pentecost, Peter and the other apostles proclaimed the resurrection of Christ. Those enemies could have abruptly dumped the corpse of the Lord in the midst of that crowd and the Christian Way would have died with but a whimper ... right on the spot!

Did the apostles hide the body?

The common allegation of infidelity has been that the disciples of Christ confiscated his body and contrived the story of the resurrection.

This, in fact, was the tale fabricated by the chief priests who bribed the solders to claim that "His disciples came by night, and stole him away while we slept" (Mt. 28:13).

How brilliantly imaginative — sleeping witnesses!

And the apostle Matthew, writing at least two decades after the resurrection, observes that this ludicrous rumor "was spread abroad among the Jews, until this day" (Mt. 28:15).

In fact, the story continued many years beyond Matthew's time. Justin Martyr (c. A.D. 165) referred to it in his Dialogue with Trypho, and it is repeated in a document known as the Toledoth Jesu, thus proving that the Lord's body was **never found** (see Edersheim, 637). [33]

Besides, what possible motive could have possessed the disciples to steal the body and then claim a resurrection when **they had not even anticipated the resurrection** (cf. Mk. 16:11-13; Lk. 24:10ff; Jn. 20:25)?

And what did they gain by telling the resurrection story? They gained nothing **but torture and death**! While men may sacrifice their lives because they are deceived, they do not willingly go to their deaths **knowing they are perpetrating a hoax**!

Finally, there is that inexplicable problem of how the disciples breached that experienced guard of soldiers and made off with the body.

The notion that the Lord's body was stolen by his friends is at variance with the evidence.

He arose!

The honest student of history is, therefore, left with but one alternative — Jesus of Nazareth did actually rise from the dead!

Witnesses of the Resurrection

Luke, a physician (Col. 4:14) and first-rate historian, after having investigated the matter carefully, stated that Jesus "showed himself alive after his passion by many proofs" (Acts 1:3). He appeared on numerous occasions during the forty-day span between his death and ascension.

The word "proofs" translates a Greek term that was used by the classical writers to "denote the strongest proof of which a subject is susceptible" (Alexander, 5). [34]

The post-resurrection appearances of the Lord that are recorded are as follows.

---

[33] Edersheim, Alfred. 1947. *The Life and Times of Jesus the Messiah. Vol. 2*. Grand Rapids, MI: Eerdmans.

[34] Alexander, J. A. 1956. *Commentary on Acts*, Grand Rapids, MI: Zondervan.

Christ appeared to **Mary Magdalene** at the tomb after Peter and John had left (Jn. 20:11-17; cf. Mk. 16:9-11).

The Lord appeared to **a group of women disciples** who had visited his empty tomb (Mt. 28:9-10).

Jesus appeared to **Peter** on the afternoon of the resurrection day (Lk. 24:34; cf. 1 Cor. 15:5).

He appeared to **two disciples** on the road to Emmaus (Lk. 24:13-35; Mk. 16:12).

Christ appeared to **ten apostles** on the evening of the resurrection [Thomas being absent] (Mk. 16:14; Lk. 24:36-43; Jn. 20:19-23).

The Savior appeared to the **eleven disciples** on Sunday week following the resurrection [Thomas being present] (Jn. 20:26-29).

The Lord appeared to **seven of the disciples** beside the Sea of Tiberias, and thrice asked Peter if he loved him (Jn. 21:1-23).

He appeared on one occasion to more than **five hundred brethren**, most of whom were still alive when Paul wrote the letter called First Corinthians (1 Cor. 15:6), which demonstrates that the resurrection story could be checked.

Jesus appeared to **James** (1 Cor. 15:7) — probably the Lord's half-brother who formerly had disbelieved (Jn. 7:3-5).

Christ appeared to the **eleven disciples** on a mountain in Galilee where he gave what is called the "great commission" (Mt. 28:16-20).

The Lord appeared to his **disciples** on the Mount of Olives just prior to his ascension into heaven (Lk. 24:44-53; Acts 1:3-9).

The Living One (Rev. 1:18) appeared to **Stephen**, his first martyr (Acts 7:55-56). Christ appeared to the apostle **Paul** at least three times: on the Damascus road (Acts 9:3-6), later when Paul was praying in the temple (Acts 22:17-21), and while he was in prison in Caesarea (Acts 23:11). Also, the Lord appeared to the beloved apostle **John** on the isle of Patmos (Rev. 1:12-20).

Are the Witnesses Credible?

Clearly, the witnesses to the resurrection of Christ were manifold. The only remaining questions are these:

- Were the witnesses reasonably intelligent people — and not fools or wild hysterics?
- Were they honest individuals of worthy character?

One of the foremost authorities on legal evidence ever to live in this country was the renowned Simon Greenleaf (1783-1853). He served as Royall Professor of Law at Harvard and later as Dane Professor of Law at Harvard.

In 1852, he published his famous work, A Treatise on the Law of Evidence, which "is still considered the greatest single authority on evidence in the entire literature of legal procedure" (Smith, 423).[35]

In 1847, professor Greenleaf issued a significant work of more than 500 pages under the title of An Examination of the Testimony of the Four Evangelists by the Rules of Evidence Administered in Courts of Justice (Baker, 1965 reprint). In this remarkable work, Greenleaf concluded that it was:

---

[35] Smith, Wilbur M. 1974 reprint, Therefore Stand! Grand Rapids, MI: Baker.

> *"... impossible that they [the apostles] could have persisted in affirming the truths they have narrated, had not Jesus actually risen from the dead, and had they not known this fact as certainly as they knew any other fact" (Smith, 424).* [36]
>
> Numerous other highly-competent historical and legal authorities have testified in a similar fashion (see: Smith, 1974, chapter 8; McDowell, 1972, pp. 196ff). [37]

Many pages could be written on the subject of Jesus' resurrection, but this book is not meant to be an apologetics work as stated in the introduction. His resurrection has been extensively researched both by Christian advocates and skeptics. There is as much evidence that Jesus' resurrection was real (it wasn't faked, or a lie, etc.) as there is that Jesus Himself was actually born and lived as Scripture states – and this evidence exceeds the "beyond a reasonable doubt" standard any modern court of law would uphold, but only when the evidence is viewed with no preconceived bias against God, the Bible, and Jesus to begin with. No skeptic has been able to convincingly disprove Jesus' resurrection – none at all.

IN SUMMARY

In summary, Jesus was seen by and physically interacted with hundreds of people after His death and resurrection – after He had been very publicly crucified on the cross. They talked with Him, ate with Him, and walked with Him. These were real actions done by real men, and not just by one lone witness, but by hundreds. The testimony of many witnesses is in agreement. Old Testament Scripture prophesized not only Jesus' birth and death but also His resurrection – and all of those prophecies were fulfilled. The fact of His resurrection is (has been) established beyond a reasonable doubt. It is Jesus' resurrection that demonstrates His victory over sin, Satan, and death – His resurrection to life "destroyed the works of the devil" and also serve to demonstrate that Jesus is able to reverse the curse that was placed on this world and all mankind (as a result of man's disobedience of God, see the earlier chapter on Humanity and Sin).

Looking ahead in this book a bit further, know that Jesus is right now "seated at the right hand of God [the Father]" in heaven, ruling and reigning this very moment in His Kingdom, and interceding on behalf of those who call on His name with God the Father – for He is the "one [only] mediator between God and men." And just as Jesus' resurrection was a literal bodily one (not "symbolic" or "figurative"), His return on Judgment Day will be just as literal and real for everyone to see (even the dead).

In the next chapter, I bring this section of the book to a conclusion and explain the hope that we have in Jesus – the "good news" of the gospel.

FALSE TEACHING(S) YOU WILL ENCOUNTER:

- Christ didn't rise from the dead (the disciples stole the body, etc.)
- Christ's resurrection wasn't a literal bodily resurrection (it was just symbolic or spiritual, or he was a "ghost," etc.)
- Science can't prove it; therefore, it didn't happen

---

36 Greenleaf, Simon. 1965 reprint. An Examination of the Testimony of the Four Evangelists by the Rules of Evidence Administered in Courts of Justice. Grand Rapids, MI: Baker.

37 McDowell, Josh. 1972. Evidence that Demands a Verdict. San Bernardino, CA: Campus Crusade for Christ.

RELATED SCRIPTURE:

But Mary was standing outside the tomb weeping; and so, as she wept, she stooped and looked into the tomb; and she saw two angels in white sitting, one at the head and one at the feet, where the body of Jesus had been lying. And they said to her, "Woman, why are you weeping?" She said to them, "Because they have taken away my Lord, and I do not know where they have laid Him." When she had said this, she turned around and saw Jesus standing *there*, and did not know that it was Jesus. Jesus said to her, "Woman, why are you weeping? Whom are you seeking?" Supposing Him to be the gardener, she said to Him, "Sir, if you have carried Him away, tell me where you have laid Him, and I will take Him away." Jesus said to her, "Mary!" She turned and said to Him in Hebrew, "Rabboni!" (which means, Teacher). Jesus said to her, "Stop clinging to Me, for I have not yet ascended to the Father; but go to My brethren and say to them, 'I ascend to My Father and your Father, and My God and your God.'" – John 20:11-17

"The God of Abraham, Isaac and Jacob, the God of our fathers, has glorified His servant Jesus, *the one* whom you delivered and disowned in the presence of Pilate, when he had decided to release Him. But you disowned the Holy and Righteous One [Jesus] and asked for a murderer to be granted to you, but put to death the Prince of life [Jesus], *the one* whom God raised from the dead, *a fact* to which we are witnesses." – Acts 3:13-15

Then Peter, filled with the Holy Spirit, said to them, "Rulers and elders of the people, if we are on trial today for a benefit done to a sick man, as to how this man has been made well, let it be known to all of you and to all the people of Israel, that by the name of Jesus Christ the Nazarene, whom you crucified, whom God raised from the dead—by this *name* this man stands here before you in good health. He is the STONE WHICH WAS REJECTED by you, THE BUILDERS, *but* WHICH BECAME THE CHIEF CORNER *stone*. And there is salvation in no one else; for there is no other name under heaven that has been given among men by which we must be saved." – Acts 4:8-12

But on the first day of the week, at early dawn, they came to the tomb bringing the spices which they had prepared. And they found the stone rolled away from the tomb, but when they entered, they did not find the body of the Lord Jesus. While they were perplexed about this, behold, two men suddenly stood near them in dazzling clothing; and as *the women* were terrified and bowed their faces to the ground, *the men* said to them, "Why do you seek the living One among the dead? He is not here, but He has risen. Remember how He spoke to you while He was still in Galilee, saying that the Son of Man must be delivered into the hands of sinful men, and be crucified, and the third day rise again." And they remembered His words, and returned from the tomb and reported all these things to the eleven and to all the rest. Now they were Mary Magdalene and Joanna and Mary the *mother* of James; also the other women with them were telling these things to the apostles. But these words appeared to them as nonsense, and they would not believe them. But Peter got up and ran to the tomb; stooping and looking in, he saw the linen wrappings only; and he went away to his home, marveling at what had happened. – Luke 24:1-12

After these things Jesus manifested Himself again to the disciples at the Sea of Tiberias, and He manifested *Himself* in this way. Simon Peter, and Thomas called Didymus, and Nathanael of Cana in Galilee, and the *sons* of Zebedee, and two others of His disciples were together. Simon Peter said to them, "I am going fishing." They said to him, "We will also come with you." They went out and got into the boat; and that night they caught nothing.

But when the day was now breaking, Jesus stood on the beach; yet the disciples did not know that it was Jesus. So Jesus said to them, "Children, you do not have any fish, do you?" They answered Him, "No." And He said to them, "Cast the net on the right-hand side of the boat and you will find *a catch*." So they cast, and then they were not able to haul it in because of the great number of fish. Therefore that disciple whom Jesus loved said to Peter, "It is the Lord." So when Simon Peter heard that it was the Lord, he put his outer garment on (for he was stripped *for work*), and threw himself into the sea. But the other disciples came in the little boat, for they were not far from the land, but about one hundred yards away, dragging the net *full* of fish. – John 21:1-8

Paul, a bond-servant of Christ Jesus, called *as* an apostle, set apart for the gospel of God, which He promised beforehand through His prophets in the holy Scriptures, concerning His Son, who was born of a descendant of David according to the flesh, who was declared the Son of God with power by the resurrection from the dead, according to the Spirit of holiness, Jesus Christ our Lord… – Romans 1:1-4

But now Christ has been raised from the dead, the first fruits of those who are asleep. For since by a man *came* death, by a man also *came* the resurrection of the dead. For as in Adam all die, so also in Christ all will be made alive. But each in his own order: Christ the first fruits, after that those who are Christ's at His coming, then *comes* the end, when He hands over the kingdom to the God and Father, when He has abolished all rule and all authority and power. For He must reign until He has put all His enemies under His feet. The last enemy that will be abolished is death. – 1 Corinthians 15:20-26

2.3 THE "GOOD NEWS" OF THE GOSPEL

"For God so loved the world, that He gave His only begotten Son, that whoever believes in Him shall not perish, but have eternal life." – John 3:16

The Gospel of Jesus Christ. And so, we now come to the heart of the matter (pun intended). All of the prior chapters have been building up to this point; they have given you the elements and foundation of the gospel "message of truth," and this chapter brings it all together in review and summary form and then asks you to make a decision if you want to choose (accept) Christ, for while God "desires all people to be saved and to come to the knowledge of the truth" and "for all to come to repentance" so that none are lost (perish) in judgment, He doesn't force anyone – you must choose for yourself.

IN REVIEW

To recap, you have read so far in this book the truth that:

- There is a God: who created all things in heaven and on earth ("In the beginning God Created…," "all things were created, *both* in the heavens and on earth, visible and invisible, whether thrones, or dominions, or rulers, or authorities—all things have been created through Him and for Him"),
- We are God's creation: we were created "in the image of God" with an eternal spirit that lives on forever, even after the body dies ("So God created man in His own image, in the image of God He created him; male and female He created them."),
- Man disobeyed God: and sin entered the world, and we now live in a cursed, fallen world with sin, suffering, and death ("through one man sin entered into the world, and death through sin, and so death spread to all mankind, because all sinned"), and Satan as "ruler of this world,"
- We are all sinners: and the punishment for sin is eternal death, which is separation from God for all eternity ("as it is written: "THERE IS NO RIGHTEOUS PERSON, NOT EVEN ONE," "for all have sinned and fall short of the glory of God."),
- The great Day of Judgment is coming: in which we all will stand before God to give an account of ourselves, and when all sin is judged and eradicated forever by God ("For we must all appear before the judgment seat of Christ, so that each one may receive compensation for his deeds *done* through the body, in accordance with what he has done, whether good or bad," "So then each one of us will give an account of himself to God."),
- God desires that none perish in the coming judgment: He desires that all have eternal life with Him ("The Lord is not slow about His promise, as some count slowness, but is patient toward you, not willing for any to perish, but for all to come to repentance."),
- So God sent us a Savior: the "Christ of God," the "Messiah," the Anointed One of God, who was "Jesus of Nazareth," "Immanuel" (God with us), "God manifest in the flesh": God incarnate, the "Son of God," the "Son of Man," fully man and yet also fully God ("For God so loved the world, that He gave His only begotten Son, that whoever believes in Him shall not perish, but have eternal life," "He [Jesus] is the image of the invisible God"),

- Jesus was born of a virgin ("'BEHOLD, THE VIRGIN WILL CONCEIVE AND GIVE BIRTH TO A SON, AND THEY SHALL NAME HIM IMMANUEL,' which translated means, 'God with us.'"),
- He lived a perfect and sinless life ("*He* WHO COMMITTED NO SIN, NOR WAS ANY DECEIT FOUND IN HIS MOUTH," "He made Him who knew no sin *to be* sin in our behalf, so that we might become the righteousness of God in Him."),
- He died (was crucified) on the cross ("He humbled Himself by becoming obedient to the point of death, even death on a cross."), and
- He rose again after three (3) days to life ("Christ died for our sins according to the Scriptures, and that He was buried, and that He was raised on the third day according to the Scriptures.")

You have also read how Jesus' life, death, and resurrection were foretold hundreds of years in advance, with those prophecies being completely fulfilled and evidenced in history. These fulfilled prophecies give us complete confidence and confirm to us that:

1) The Bible is indeed true, and we can rely on what it tells us, and
2) Jesus is indeed the "Son of God," "God manifest in the flesh."

This chapter further explains that:

- His death on the cross was as an atoning sacrifice (full payment) for your sins ("although you were previously alienated and hostile in attitude, *engaged* in evil deeds, yet He has now reconciled you in His body of flesh through death, in order to present you before Him holy and blameless and beyond reproach," "He Himself is the propitiation for our sins; and not for ours only, but also for *the sins* of the whole world," "By this will, we have been sanctified through the offering of the body of Jesus Christ once for all *time*."), and
- It is only through Jesus' shed blood on the cross that you can stand before God on the Day of Judgment and declared righteous (your sins forgiven) and saved to eternal life as a child of God, and even more, a fellow heir with Christ ("There is salvation in no one else; for there is no other name under heaven that has been given among mankind by which we must be saved," "…if you confess with your mouth Jesus as Lord, and believe in your heart that God raised Him from the dead, you will be saved," "'EVERYONE WHO CALLS ON THE NAME OF THE LORD [through Christ in the manner specified in Scripture] WILL BE SAVED.'")

THE "GOOD NEWS" OF THE GOSPEL

Remember from the chapter on The Coming Great Day of Judgment that not only is God a God of love, but He is also a God of justice, and He will punish (judge) all sin (that has ever been committed) on that Day. He has further told us that "the wages [punishment] for sin is death" – eternal death, and that those who die in sin (the wicked) "will pay the penalty of eternal destruction [death], away from the presence of the Lord and from the glory of His power." This eternal death is separation from God for all eternity, for nothing sinful will be allowed to enter heaven – if you die in sin (i.e., without your sins being forgiven), you cannot enter heaven. It is sin that separates us from God. All things (and everyone) sinful will be cast into hell, "which has been prepared for the devil and his angels" who sinned for all eternity. Recall that hell was

The Message of Truth

created for "the devil and his angels" who sinned, but we will also go there if we choose to remain in sin (and disobedience of God).

But the "good news" (or "good message") of the gospel is that God in grace out of love and "not wishing for any to perish but for all to come to repentance" has provided a way for us to stand before Him on That Day with our sins forgiven, declared holy and blameless (righteous and justified), and receive the gift of eternal life with Him in heaven. That way is through His only begotten Son Jesus Christ, "Jesus of Nazareth," the Christ, the Messiah, your Redeemer, who was born of a virgin, who was both fully man and fully God, who lived a perfect and sinless life while being tempted in all things as we are, and who died (gave His life) on the cross. God tells us that He will accept His Son's death as an atoning sacrifice (full payment) for your sins (all of them) if you accept Christ as your Lord and Savior. [Note: I explain what accepting Christ means in the next section of this book and how Scripture tells us it must be done – for we must approach God on His terms, not however we feel like it].

God sent Jesus into the world to save sinners, those who are "in darkness" wandering through "the valley of the shadow of death" of this fallen world, to offer them forgiveness of sins and the hope of eternal life:

> "For God so loved the world, that He gave His only begotten Son, that whoever believes in Him shall not perish, but have eternal life. For God did not send the Son into the world to judge the world, but that the world might be saved through Him. He who believes in Him is not judged; he who does not believe has been judged already, because he has not believed in the name of the only begotten Son of God." – John 3:16-18

> And you were dead [spiritually] in your trespasses and sins, in which you formerly walked according to the course of this world, according to the prince of the power of the air, of the spirit that is now working in the sons of disobedience. Among them we too all formerly lived in the lusts of our flesh, indulging the desires of the flesh and of the mind, and were by nature children of wrath, even as the rest. But God, being rich in mercy, because of His great love with which He loved us, even when we were dead in our transgressions, made us alive together with Christ (by grace you have been saved), and raised us up with Him, and seated us with Him in the heavenly *places* in Christ Jesus, so that in the ages to come He might show the surpassing riches of His grace in kindness toward us in Christ Jesus. For by grace you have been saved through faith; and that not of yourselves, *it is* the gift of God; not as a result of works, so that no one may boast. For we are His workmanship, created in Christ Jesus for good works, which God prepared beforehand so that we would walk in them. – Ephesians 2:1-10

> For Christ also died for sins once for all, *the* just for *the* unjust, so that He might bring us to God, having been put to death in the flesh, but made alive in the spirit. – 1 Peter 3:18

> …and He Himself [Jesus] is the propitiation for our sins; and not for ours only, but also for *those of* the whole world. – 1 John 2:2

> Grace to you and peace from God our Father and the Lord Jesus Christ, who gave Himself for our sins so that He might rescue us from this present evil age, according to the will of our God and Father, to whom be the glory forevermore. Amen. – Galatians 1:3-5

> For He rescued us from the domain of darkness, and transferred us to the kingdom of His beloved Son, in whom we have redemption, the forgiveness of sins. – Colossians 1:13-14

Jesus was hung on a cross at a place called Calvary, a hill commonly used for executing thieves and criminals by crucifixion, located just outside of the city walls of Jerusalem. This is why the "cross of Calvary" is used as another expression of referring to the death of Christ. Christ offered Himself as a substitutionary sacrifice for you – for your sins. Jesus <u>willingly</u> surrendered His life for you; He didn't have to, nor was He forced to. While Jesus hung on the cross (or even before), He could have called on "twelve legions of angels" out of heaven to save Him, but He chose to die on the cross out of His love for you!

Furthermore, it is only through the death (shed blood) of Christ on the cross that one can obtain forgiveness of sins – it is not by the works of man or anything we do of or for ourselves, but by the grace of God alone. Grace means "undeserved favor." It is only the grace of God (out of love) that put Christ on the cross – so forgiveness of sins is not earned; it is a gift of God through the blood of Christ. Nor can forgiveness of sins or eternal life be bought through money, wealth, fame, or power.

God then raised Christ from the dead after three days to life so that all those who believe in and "call on the name of the Lord [Jesus]" can also have that same hope of eternal life:

> Now I make known to you, brethren, the gospel which I preached to you, which also you received, in which also you stand, by which also you are saved, if you hold fast the word which I preached to you, unless you believed in vain. For I delivered to you as of first importance what I also received, that Christ died for our sins according to the Scriptures, and that He was buried, and that He was raised on the third day according to the Scriptures. – 1 Corinthians 15:1-4

At the cross, Jesus was victorious over sin, Satan, and even death itself:

> …the one who practices sin is of the devil; for the devil has sinned from the beginning. The Son of God appeared for this purpose, to destroy the works of the devil. – 1 John 3:8

> Therefore, since the children share in flesh and blood, He Himself likewise also partook of the same, so that through death He might destroy the one who has the power of death, that is, the devil, and free those who through fear of death were subject to slavery all their lives. – Hebrews 2:14-15

> But when this perishable puts on the imperishable, and this mortal puts on immortality, then will come about the saying that is written: "DEATH HAS BEEN SWALLOWED UP in victory. WHERE, O DEATH, IS YOUR VICTORY? WHERE, O DEATH, IS YOUR STING?" The sting of death is sin, and the power of sin is the Law; but thanks be to God, who gives us the victory through our Lord Jesus Christ. – 1 Corinthians 15:54-57

> … but has now been revealed by the appearing of our Savior Christ Jesus, who abolished death and brought life and immortality to light through the gospel… – 2 Timothy 1:8-11

> "Do not be afraid; I am the first and the last, and the living One; and I was dead, and behold, I am alive forevermore, and I have the keys of death and of Hades." – Revelation 1:17b-18

> For the law of the Spirit of life in Christ Jesus has set you free from the law of sin and of death. – Romans 8:2

So, Christ can redeem you from death and bondage under sin and Satan to have new life in Him, for all who choose to accept that gift and to accept Him. To be redeemed means to be purchased – God actually had to buy you back from bondage under sin, Satan, and death by the blood (death) of His Son.

Adam Clarke writes on the gospel message: [38]

> *A message*, signifies good news, or glad tidings in general; and is evidently intended to point out, in this place, the good message or the glad tidings of great joy which God has sent to all mankind, preaching peace and reconciliation by Christ Jesus, who is Lord of all: proclaiming that he, as the promised Messiah, has, by the grace of God, tasted death for every man - for he has died for their offenses, and risen again for their justification; and that, through his grace, every sinner under the whole heaven, may turn to God, and find mercy. This is good news, glad tidings, a joyful message; and it is such to all mankind, as in it every human spirit is interested.

God "in these last days has spoken to us in [through] His Son" – through what Jesus spoke and taught as recorded in Scripture, His divinity being confirmed by the many miracles He performed, by His command over nature and by many witnesses and fulfilled prophecies. God asks you to place your complete faith, trust, and hope in Him by believing in His Son Jesus Christ and that if you do so, you will obtain eternal life. Jesus came the first time as a Savior and Suffering Servant to save those who are sick with sin but also sick of sin. He didn't come dressed in the fine purple linen attire of kings nor the business suit of commerce. He came as a shepherd to gather the lost and broken, and He died for those who are still sinners so that they could be saved:

> For while we were still helpless, at the right time Christ died for the ungodly [the lost, those who are in sin] … God demonstrates His own love toward us, in that while we were yet sinners, Christ died for us. Much more then, having now been justified by His blood, we shall be saved from the wrath *of God* through Him. For if while we were enemies we were reconciled to God through the death of His Son, much more, having been reconciled, we shall be saved by His life. And not only this, but we also exult in God through our Lord Jesus Christ, through whom we have now received the reconciliation. – Romans 5:6-11

The next time Jesus comes (when He returns) will be on the Great Day of Judgment when "Jesus is revealed with all His holy angels in skies of fire" in power and glory to judge the world.

Below is an excerpt from the book *The Pilgrim's Progress*; it is a book I highly recommend reading soon after you finish this one: [39]

---

[38] Clarke, Adam. (1810-1826), The New Testament of our Lord and Saviour Jesus Christ/Commentary on the Whole Bible, A Commentary and Critical Notes, New York.

[39] Bunyan, John. (1678/2018), The Pilgrim's Progress, (London/Holy Spirit Prints).

Then Christian began, and said, I will ask you a question. How came you to think at first of doing what you do now [becoming a Christian, following Christ]?

HOPEFUL: Do you mean, how came I at first to look after the good of my soul?

CHRISTIAN: Yes, that is my meaning.

HOPEFUL: I continued a great while in the delight of those things which were seen and sold at our fair [this world]; things which I believe now would have, had I continued in them still, drowned me in perdition and destruction.

CHRISTIAN: What things were they?

HOPEFUL: All the treasures and riches of the world. Also, I delighted much in rioting, reveling, drinking, swearing, lying, uncleanness, Sabbath-breaking, and what not, that tended to destroy the soul. But I found at last, by hearing and considering of things that are divine, which, indeed, I heard of you, as also of beloved Faithful, that was put to death for his faith and good living in Vanity Fair, that the end of these things is death, [Rom. 6:21-23]; and that for these things' sake, the wrath of God cometh upon the children of disobedience. [Eph. 5:6].

CHRISTIAN: And did you presently fall under the power of this conviction?

HOPEFUL: No, I was not willing presently to know the evil of sin, nor the damnation that follows upon the commission of it; but endeavored, when my mind at first began to be shaken with the word, to shut mine eyes against the light thereof.

CHRISTIAN: But what was the cause of your carrying of it thus to the first workings of God's blessed Spirit upon you?

HOPEFUL: The causes were, 1. I was ignorant that this was the work of God upon me. I never thought that by awakenings for sin, God at first begins the conversion of a sinner. 2. Sin was yet very sweet to my flesh, and I was loth to leave it. 3. I could not tell how to part with mine old companions, their presence and actions were so desirable unto me. 4. The hours in which convictions were upon me, were such troublesome and such heart-affrighting hours, that I could not bear, no not so much as the remembrance of them upon my heart.

CHRISTIAN: Then, as it seems, sometimes you got rid of your trouble?

HOPEFUL: Yes, verily, but it would come into my mind again; and then I should be as bad, nay, worse than I was before.

CHRISTIAN: Why, what was it that brought your sins to mind again?

HOPEFUL: Many things; as,
1. If I did but meet a good man in the streets; or,
2. If I have heard any read in the Bible; or,
3. If mine head did begin to ache; or,
4. If I were told that some of my neighbors were sick; or,
5. If I heard the bell toll for some that were dead; or,
6. If I thought of dying myself; or,
7. If I heard that sudden death happened to others.
8. But especially when I thought of myself, that I must quickly come to judgment.

CHRISTIAN: And could you at any time, with ease, get off the guilt of sin, when by any of these ways it came upon you? HOPEFUL: No, not I; for then they got faster hold of my conscience; and then, if I did but think of going back to sin, (though my mind was turned against it,) it would be double torment to me. CHRISTIAN: And how did you do then?

> HOPEFUL: I thought I must endeavor to mend my life; for else, thought I, I am sure to be damned.

WHY DID JESUS HAVE TO DIE?

I have explained that we must rely on what God says (as recorded in the Bible) about sin, life, and death, not on what man (or the science of man) thinks on such matters. What we think should be the punishment for sin is not what God says is the punishment for sin because our mortal, finite minds cannot fully comprehend, and grossly underestimates, the nature and severity of sin, particularly when compared to an absolutely holy God:

> "HOLY, HOLY, HOLY *IS* THE LORD GOD, THE ALMIGHTY, WHO WAS AND WHO IS AND WHO IS TO COME." – Revelation 4:8

God's justice can only be satisfied by a perfect, sinless, sacrificial offering as payment for your sins. There is nothing you can do to earn (e.g., through "meritorious works"), achieve through your own merits, purchase (God can't be bribed), "be good enough," "be religious enough," or "be spiritual enough" to be called blameless, sinless, righteous, and holy in God's eyes. You can only be saved from the coming judgment by having someone else (who is without sin) pay your penalty for sin. In order to do that, you would have to be without sin yourself (i.e., live a perfect and sinless life), and no man, not a single one in all of human history, has been able to do that – except Jesus. Prior chapters have explained that you simply cannot live a perfect and sinless life yourself – it is impossible, for we are all sinners! Someone else needs to make atonement for you to God; this someone must be perfect, without sin (holy and blameless) themselves before God.

Scripture tells us that God accepts Jesus' death as full payment for your sins – for He was "holy and blameless," and "without sin," "the [spotless] Lamb of God, who takes away the sin of the world." Jesus was born of a virgin, and He lived a perfect and sinless life while still being tempted in all things as we are, and He still willingly laid down His life. It is therefore only through Jesus' sacrificial death that our sins are forgiven, and we are redeemed (purchased) from (spiritual) death to life.

God allows you to be covered by Jesus' perfect righteousness, so you can stand blameless before God. In effect, you "put on" Jesus' own righteousness like a "white" garment by believing in Him – so you will be clothed in His righteousness on Judgment Day. Christ's righteousness is counted as your own! Jesus took your sins on Himself: "He has now reconciled you in His fleshly body through death, in order to present you before Him [God] holy and blameless and beyond reproach." What this all means is that your sins are erased and completely forgotten "as far as the east is from the west" (i.e., as if they never occurred), and you are declared "NOT GUILTY" of sin, and therefore not deserving of the punishment for sin, which is eternal death. Amazing and amen!

> "'But you have a few people in Sardis who have not soiled their garments; and they will walk with Me in white, for they are worthy. He who overcomes will thus be clothed in white garments; and I will not erase his name from the book of life, and I will confess his name before My Father and before His angels.'" – Revelation 3:4-5

> "Wash yourselves, make yourselves clean" …
> "Though your sins are as scarlet,
> They will be as white as snow." – Isaiah 1:16,18

> As far as the east is from the west,
> So far has He removed our transgressions from us. – Psalm 103:12

Even further, it is through Jesus that we become "children of God" – in fact, "fellow heirs" with Christ. We are actually adopted into the family of God:

> But as many as received Him, to them He gave the right to become children of God, *even* to those who believe in His name, who were born, not of blood nor of the will of the flesh nor of the will of man, but of God. – John 1:12-13

> For all who are being led by the Spirit of God, these are sons of God. For you have not received a spirit of slavery leading to fear again, but you have received a spirit of adoption as sons by which we cry out, "Abba! Father!" The Spirit Himself testifies with our spirit that we are children of God, and if children, heirs also, heirs of God and fellow heirs with Christ, if indeed we suffer with *Him* so that we may also be glorified with *Him*. – Romans 8:14-17

> Now I say, as long as the heir is a child, he does not differ at all from a slave although he is owner of everything, but he is under guardians and managers until the date set by the father. So also we, while we were children, were held in bondage under the elemental things of the world. But when the fullness of the time came, God sent forth His Son, born of a woman, born under the Law, so that He might redeem those who were under the Law, that we might receive the adoption as sons. Because you are sons, God has sent forth the Spirit of His Son into our hearts, crying, "Abba! Father!" Therefore you are no longer a slave, but a son; and if a son, then an heir through God. – Galatians 4:1-7

Yes, you choose (through free will) whether you want to be in either the family of God or the family of Satan. Scripture indicates that those who don't explicitly make a choice are by default a child of Satan ("you are of your father the devil") – so no action or choice on your part will in actuality turn out to have been a choice on Judgment Day. You must actively choose to disown Satan and accept Christ to become a child of God. And just like here on Earth, adoption is a costly process. In human terms, we must spend considerable amounts of time, effort, and money to complete the process of adopting a child. And for God to adopt us as sons, He had to redeem us from sin, and to do that, He had to sacrifice His own Son to death!

That paragraph goes by so quickly, but please take a moment to stop and reflect more deeply on what it means: The eternal, omniscient, omnipresent, all-powerful God and Creator of the entire universe, the One who simply spoke all creation into existence, the Source of all life itself, wants to adopt you as His son, so that you can live with Him forever in eternal life! And He wants that so much so that He died for you.

THE GOOD SHEPHERD

Jesus is also described as the "Good Shepherd" with us as His sheep who are "lost" and have "gone astray"; He willingly gave His life to rescue us:

> "I am the good shepherd; the good shepherd lays down His life for the sheep. He who is a hired hand, and not a shepherd, who is not the owner of the sheep, sees the wolf coming, and leaves the sheep and flees, and the wolf snatches them and scatters *them*. *He flees* because he is a hired hand and is not concerned about the sheep. I am the good shepherd, and I know My own and My own know Me, even as the Father knows Me and I know the Father; and I lay down My life for the sheep. I have other sheep, which are not of this fold; I must bring them also, and they will hear My voice; and they will become one flock *with* one shepherd. For this reason the Father loves Me, because I lay down My life so that I may take it again. No one has taken it away from Me, but I lay it down on My own initiative. I have authority to lay it down, and I have authority to take it up again. This commandment I received from My Father." – John 10:11-18

> All of us like sheep have gone astray,
> Each of us has turned to his own way;
> But the LORD has caused the iniquity of us all
> To fall on Him. – Isaiah 53:6

> For you have been called for this purpose, since Christ also suffered for you, leaving you an example for you to follow in His steps, WHO COMMITTED NO SIN, NOR WAS ANY DECEIT FOUND IN HIS MOUTH; and while being reviled, He did not revile in return; while suffering, He uttered no threats, but kept entrusting *Himself* to Him who judges righteously; and He Himself bore our sins in His body on the cross, so that we might die to sin and live to righteousness; for by His wounds you were healed. For you were continually straying like sheep, but now you have returned to the Shepherd and Guardian of your souls. – 1 Peter 2:21-25

> "My sheep hear My voice, and I know them, and they follow Me; and I give eternal life to them, and they will never perish; and no one will snatch them out of My hand." – John 10:27-28

Now, to be honest, when I first read that God calls us "sheep," I felt offended. He created us, so why is He calling us mere sheep? Sheep are pretty dumb in reality. But the older I get and the more I see how we humans act and behave, the more I see that the analogy is correct - for we are in the endless pursuit of lustful and fleshly desires, without regard for others in large measure, and completely oblivious to the fact that we lost in sin, wandering aimlessly in the "darkness" and "the valley of the shadow of death" of this fallen world under bondage to sin, Satan and death. What results is man's endless behavior of fraud, greed, corruption, lying, cheating, stealing, raping, pillaging, fornicating, never-ending wars, and the constant lust for power, fame, and fortune and the things of this world.

And have you ever watched sheep? They do, in fact, wander aimlessly without direction and are oblivious to any danger that might be around them - they are entirely helpless and without defense. We are also defenseless against the spiritual forces of darkness and evil which are arrayed against us under Satan; without God, you have no chance whatsoever of withstanding your enemy. That is written about in the book of Jude, where men "reject authority, and revile angelic majesties" out of ignorance and pride.

Friend, I urge you to stop being a "sheep," wandering aimlessly and lost in the "darkness" of this world and addicted to sin.

JESUS CAME TO SAVE SINNERS

Jesus came to save sinners (not the self-righteous), no matter what they have done:

"I have not come to call the righteous but sinners to repentance." – Luke 5:32

To approach God, you must admit you're a sinner and come to God in humility – right now, today – and receive His wonderful gift of eternal life in Christ offered through God's lovingkindness, mercy, and grace. It doesn't matter what sins you've committed, nor how long you've committed them. No sin is too great to be forgiven. God's lovingkindness, grace, and mercy are massive! Remember that God used:

- A murderer to lead the Jews out of Egypt (Moses),
- A prostitute to help protect the Jews (Rahab),
- Another murderer who became a great New Testament apostle (Paul), etc.

No matter what you have done, Jesus offers forgiveness to you, unlike men who keep a grudge and seek revenge for years (decades even). The apostle Paul had persecuted and even helped put to death those who believed in Christ, and yet Jesus forgave him, and then Paul went on to become one of the greatest saints of all time! He can do just the same for you. Don't decide for yourself that you cannot be forgiven for what you may have done – let Jesus decide.

Peter once asked Jesus how many times he should forgive those who sinned against him (see Matthew 18:21-22), probably expecting to hear the number three, or five and even suggested the number seven (i.e., a small number of times, a number that we humans think is reasonable). However, the Lord answered with the number "seventy times seven" (i.e., 490). Now the actual number given here isn't the important part (we are not to interpret that as a literal 490 times we are to forgive sins); what's important is the magnitude of the number – it's an ENORMOUS number which was far, far above anything that Peter might have even remotely imagined in his own mind! This again demonstrates that the depths of the love, kindness, mercy and grace of God are very great indeed – far greater than what the mind of man thinks or expects is reasonable!

ENTER THROUGH THE NARROW GATE

It is written:

> "Enter through the narrow gate; for the gate is wide and the way is broad that leads to destruction, and there are many who enter through it. For the gate is small and the way is narrow that leads to life, and there are few who find it." – Matthew 7:13-14

It is further written:

> Jesus said to him, "I am the way, and the truth, and the life; no one comes to the Father but through Me." – John 14:6

> "...let it be known to all of you and to all the people of Israel, that by the name of Jesus Christ the Nazarene, whom you crucified, whom God raised from the dead—by this *name* this man stands here before you in good health. He is the STONE WHICH WAS REJECTED by you, THE BUILDERS, *but* WHICH BECAME THE CHIEF CORNER *stone*. And there is salvation in no one else; for there is no other

> name under heaven that has been given among men by which we must be saved." – Acts 4:10-12

> For there is one God, *and* one mediator also between God and men, *the* man Christ Jesus, who gave Himself as a ransom for all, the testimony *given* at the proper time. For this I was appointed a preacher and an apostle (I am telling the truth, I am not lying) as a teacher of the Gentiles in faith and truth. – 1 Timothy 2:5-7

The gate to heaven and eternal life is called narrow (strait, difficult) because there is only one "door" through which you can enter (that door is Christ), and you will have to stop pursuing the things of this world, repent of your sins, and turn from your own selfish, lustful, sinful desires and instead pursue the things of God and His Christ. Jesus is that narrow gate – The Son of God, the Son of Man, our Savior, our Redeemer, our Hope, our Lord, our God, and our King!

> So Jesus said to them again, "Truly, truly, I say to you, I am the door of the sheep. All who came before Me are thieves and robbers, but the sheep did not hear them. I am the door; if anyone enters through Me, he will be saved, and will go in and out and find pasture." – John 10:7-9

Accepting Jesus Christ as your Lord and Savior is the **only way** designated by God for all men to obtain eternal life. There is no other way to heaven, despite the many false/popular teachings of man and the myriad of mysticism, religions, "traditions," and man-made schemes that abound in the world! The various man-made religions of this world offer no path to eternal life. Know also that simply going to church, being a "good person," doing "good deeds" (i.e., "meritorious works"), performing religious rituals, or "traditions" will not save you to eternal life.

The easy (wide) way is to simply go on in life as you always have in sin, without regard for God or others. That is also the worldly, popular way: "I'm gonna get what I can get now, by any means possible, for I only care about 'me and mine'…and when I die, so what…it's just all over, and I go into nothingness." But that broad way leads to eternal death, and as I have explained, you will not go into "nothingness" at death. Death is not an extinction event (our ending); it is the separation of the soul from the body. Your soul lives on forever; the only question is where – in heaven or in hell.

Please pay close attention to the fact that the verses above specifically say that Jesus is the only mediator between man and God – not Mary, or the Pope, or the dead, or angels, or false spirits, or idols, or men, or man-made religions. Also, we are not to pray to Mary; that is a false teaching of Roman Catholicism (see Beware the Wolves).

TODAY IS THE DAY OF SALVATION

The gospel message of hope is open to all who are "thirsty!" "Ask, and it will be given to you; seek, and you will find; knock, and it will be opened to you. For everyone who asks receives, and the one who seeks finds, and to the one who knocks it will be opened." God "desires all people to be saved and to come to the knowledge of the truth" so that none are lost in judgment. Do you want the "water of life" offered by Christ?

> The Spirit and the bride say, "Come." And let the one who hears say, "Come." And let the one who is thirsty come; let the one who wishes take the water of life without cost. – Revelation 22:17

> "Come to Me, all who are weary and heavy-laden, and I will give you rest. Take My yoke upon you and learn from Me, for I am gentle and humble in heart, and YOU WILL FIND REST FOR YOUR SOULS. For My yoke is easy and My burden is light." – Matthew 11:28-30

> This is good and acceptable in the sight of God our Savior, who desires all men to be saved and to come to the knowledge of the truth. – 1 Timothy 2:3-4

Today, if you find these words stirring your heart, please don't ignore them. That is a sign that God is calling out to you, right here and right now. For it is written:

> And working together *with Him*, we also urge you not to receive the grace of God in vain—for He says,
>
> > "AT THE ACCEPTABLE TIME I LISTENED TO YOU,
> > AND ON THE DAY OF SALVATION I HELPED YOU."
>
> Behold, now is "THE ACCEPTABLE TIME," behold, now is "THE DAY OF SALVATION." – 2 Corinthians 6:1-2

> "TODAY IF YOU HEAR HIS VOICE,
> DO NOT HARDEN YOUR HEARTS, AS WHEN THEY PROVOKED ME." – Hebrews 3:15

The verses above remind you that there may not be a tomorrow for you (or me or any of us). I urge you, therefore, to take it very seriously if you feel God calling you and moving in your heart. Don't harden your heart to that calling (like Pharaoh did); such hardening is the result of pride. We should also greatly heed the dire warning that is given to us in Scripture, for there comes a time when God will no longer strive to reach those who have hardened their hearts beyond the point of no return:

> Then the LORD said, "My Spirit shall not strive with man forever, because he also is flesh." – Genesis 6:3

YOU HAVE A CHOICE

So, friend, you now have some choices to make which will stand for all eternity. You must first decide whether God exists or not, for He is the author of all life. You will have to choose between God (and life) or sin, Satan, and death:

> The fool has said in his heart, "There is no God." – Psalm 14:1

> Without faith it is impossible to please *Him*, for he who comes to God must believe that He is and *that* He is a rewarder of those who seek Him. – Hebrews 11:6

> "If it is disagreeable in your sight to serve the LORD, choose for yourselves today whom you will serve: whether the gods which your fathers served which were beyond the River, or the gods of the Amorites in whose land you are living; but as for me and my house, we will serve the LORD." – Joshua 24:15

And will you choose to follow the ways of man and the ways of this world (which lead to eternal death) or the ways (and wisdom) of God which lead to eternal life?

> There is a way *which seems* right to a man,
> But its end is the way of death. – Proverbs 14:12

The Message of Truth

> The fear of the LORD is the beginning of knowledge;
> Fools despise wisdom and instruction. – Proverbs 1:7

> Trust in the LORD with all your heart
> And do not lean on your own understanding.
> In all your ways acknowledge Him,
> And He will make your paths straight.
> Do not be wise in your own eyes;
> Fear the LORD and turn away from evil. – Proverbs 3:5-7

> Let God be found true, though every man be found a liar. – Romans 3:4

> "Therefore, everyone who hears these words of Mine, and acts on them, will be like a wise man who built his house on the rock. And the rain fell and the floods came, and the winds blew and slammed against that house; and yet it did not fall, for it had been founded on the rock. And everyone who hears these words of Mine, and does not act on them, will be like a foolish man who built his house on the sand. And the rain fell and the floods came, and the winds blew and slammed against that house; and it fell—and its collapse was great." – Matthew 7:24-27

Will you continue to think yourself wise in your own eyes, or will you humble yourself and get down on your knees before God and acknowledge Him for Who He is and admit that you're a sinner in need of a Savior, repent of your sins, and ask for forgiveness with a contrite heart? It is human pride and arrogance that in large measure causes us to deny God and His Christ. Furthermore, do you want Jesus to be your Attorney on the great Day of Judgment, or do you want to go before God on that Day and try to plead your own case? Remember, Jesus is also going to be the Judge – and this Judge knows every single thing you have ever thought, said, and done! You can ensure yourself a verdict of "NOT GUILTY" of sin even before the trial starts by choosing life in Christ! Amazing!

Are you willing to become "as a child" again and realize that you don't know the truth and that you must start out again as a "child of God" instead of a child of Satan, learning God's truth instead of man's truth? And as a child trust's their parents, are you willing to trust in the Lord? We are told:

> At that time Jesus said, "I praise You, Father, Lord of heaven and earth, that You have hidden these things from *the* wise and intelligent and have revealed them to infants. Yes, Father, for this way was well-pleasing in Your sight. All things have been handed over to Me by My Father; and no one knows the Son except the Father; nor does anyone know the Father except the Son, and anyone to whom the Son wills to reveal *Him*." – Matthew 11:25-27

> ...and [Jesus] said, "Truly I say to you, unless you are converted and become like children, you will not enter the kingdom of heaven. Whoever then humbles himself as this child, he is the greatest in the kingdom of heaven." – Matthew 18:3-4

Or will you continue on as you always have, thinking that all this God, Bible, Jesus, and Judgment to come stuff is "foolishness"? Yes, it is written that many will, in fact, consider the gospel "message of truth" to be "foolishness":

> For the word of the cross is foolishness to those who are perishing, but to us who are being saved it is the power of God. For it is written,

> "I WILL DESTROY THE WISDOM OF THE WISE,
> AND THE CLEVERNESS OF THE CLEVER I WILL SET ASIDE."

Where is the wise man? Where is the scribe? Where is the debater of this age? Has not God made foolish the wisdom of the world? For since in the wisdom of God the world through its wisdom did not *come to* know God, God was well-pleased through the foolishness of the message preached to save those who believe. – 1 Corinthians 1:18-21

You must decide for yourself whether this gospel message is "foolishness" or "truth." You must pick one or the other, for there is no middle ground. You will have to decide whether you wish to continue in darkness or light. We are told that the "fear of the Lord" is the beginning of wisdom, for it is only from God's wisdom that you can obtain life, and we can only find God's wisdom in the Bible. Scripture also tells us that "men loved the darkness rather than the Light, for their deeds were evil."

You can continue your sinful behavior if you choose to, but God through Christ can bring you out of that darkness and into the light. When you accept Christ, He sets you free from bondage under sin and all those behaviors; this is what He means when He says His "burden is light."

> Therefore what benefit were you then deriving from the things of which you are now ashamed? For the outcome of those things is death. But now having been freed from sin and enslaved to God, you derive your benefit, resulting in sanctification, and the outcome, eternal life. For the wages of sin is death, but the free gift of God is eternal life in Christ Jesus our Lord. – Romans 6:21-23

> So Jesus was saying to those Jews who had believed Him, "If you continue in My word, *then* you are truly disciples of Mine; and <u>you will know the truth, and the truth will make you free</u>." They answered Him, "We are Abraham's descendants and have never yet been enslaved to anyone; how is it that You say, 'You will become free'?"

> Jesus answered them, "Truly, truly, I say to you, everyone who commits sin is the slave of sin. The slave does not remain in the house forever; the son does remain forever. So if the Son makes you free, you will be free indeed." – John 8:31-36

Truth be told, I also thought the "Word of God" was nonsense and "foolishness" for many (many) years, but I have come "out of darkness into His marvelous light," and I've learned that there is more wisdom, life, and power in a single syllable of Scripture than there is in all the atom bombs created by man and all the books written throughout history and stored up in the great libraries of the world. While mankind seems only intent on endless, nonstop destruction and killing, Jesus came to give life, and to give it "abundantly":

> "The thief comes only to steal and kill and destroy; I came that they may have life, and have *it* abundantly." – John 10:10

IT TAKES COURAGE

Friend, if you've read this far, it's right here, right now, at this very place in the book, that you face the greatest danger. The Bible tells us that the way forward to eternal life takes courage, strength, boldness, and perseverance! It's right here also that you can decide to reject all this "God and Jesus stuff" as "nonsense" and say: "the heck with it all," stop reading and turn back, thinking to yourself, "I'm just going to live my life how I want to – and when I die, that's it; it's all over to nothingness." I again remind you that that just isn't the case! All of us will stand before the Lord God on that great Day of Judgment! God's Word is truth, and nothing we think or do will alter that fact.

So, what do you do now? Do you still continue denying that God even exists? Do you continue in sin taking "the way [which] is broad that leads to destruction, and there are many who enter through it," or do you choose to "enter through the narrow gate" to eternal life, which is through Jesus Christ? It's also at this very point that you are most likely to make up excuses for not believing, for continuing in your own way, however you want, living as you always have. I've been there. I've told myself whatever lie or excuse I wanted to so I could continue to live how I wanted to. But you're only fooling yourself. You may even try to talk yourself out of believing this stuff – I've been there too. Maybe you are different than me, but I doubt it. Or maybe you're trapped in an addiction like I was. It doesn't matter what kind, for they are all the same at the core: lack of hope combined with chemical dependency. But Christ can take that from you also and give you hope in return!

It is also right here and right now where you will face doubts – as to how could all of this be true? Now it's natural to have questions and doubts about all this, for this is a very weighty matter we are discussing here. Even the great John the Baptist had to face his doubt at one time. Of John, we are told that "among those born of women there has not arisen *anyone* greater than John the Baptist." John was even "filled with the Holy Spirit while still in his mother's womb," a prophet of God, wholly set apart to be the forerunner for Christ. John had even seen Jesus confirmed by the voice of God Himself at Jesus' baptism (which John had administered personally): "…and the Holy Spirit descended upon Him [Jesus] in bodily form like a dove, and a voice came from heaven: 'You are My beloved Son, in You I am well pleased.'" And yet, even John had a moment of doubt, for we see it written:

> Now when John, while imprisoned, heard of the works of Christ, he sent *word* by his disciples and said to Him, "Are You the Expected One, or shall we look for someone else?" Jesus answered and said to them, "Go and report to John what you hear and see: *the* BLIND RECEIVE SIGHT and *the* lame walk, *the* lepers are cleansed and *the* deaf hear, *the* dead are raised up, and *the* POOR HAVE THE GOSPEL PREACHED TO THEM. And blessed is he who does not take offense at Me." – Matthew 11:2-6

While in prison, John inquired of Jesus again as to whether He was truly the Christ as foretold in Scripture. Jesus reminded John that the miracles He performed matched Old Testament Scripture and confirmed His deity claim. We are not told, but it is likely, that John went back through Old Testament Scriptures to re-confirm his belief that Jesus was, in fact, the Christ, the Messiah. But here is the important part: John addressed his doubt head-on; he didn't let it overcome and defeat him, or worse, cause him to not believe.

Please review the previous chapters of this book and even seek out other resources if needed to address any lingering questions or areas of doubt that you may still have. Maybe you still have questions on Science vs. the Bible, on Jesus and His life, death, and resurrection, or on His claim to be God. But, at some point, you will have to decide whether you believe the words of man (the "wisdom of this world") or the "Word of

God." You will find that in nearly all cases relating to the spiritual war we are engaged in with the forces of evil/darkness, it is the popular, trendy, and majority opinions of man that are actually the wrong way – following the herd will lead you to eternal death. Following God leads to life.

Know it is also at this time if you decide to keep going and accept Christ that you will almost certainly come under the most ferocious (spiritual) attack of your life. Others will try to talk you out of it. They will mock you and try to tell you this is all "garbage," "sheer nonsense," and taunt you saying, "Why are you dumb enough to believe all that religion stuff?" You will almost certainly face ridicule, taunting, insults, jokes against you, and maybe even persecution and tribulation(s) in going forward to eternal life. But forward in courage you must go – if you want eternal life with God and His Christ!

While it always seems to be "cool" for man to be part of the "rebels" (the resistance, if you will), in this particular (spiritual) war, it is eternally wiser to be one of the "saints"; for God and His Christ (and His saints) will prevail – indeed, He has already prevailed. Christ has already won final victory over sin and death at the cross ("it is finished"). There is nothing whatsoever that anyone or anything on, under, or above the earth can do to change that!

> But in all these things we overwhelmingly conquer through Him who loved us. For I am convinced that neither death, nor life, nor angels, nor principalities, nor things present, nor things to come, nor powers, nor height, nor depth, nor any other created thing, will be able to separate us from the love of God, which is in Christ Jesus our Lord. – Romans 8:37-39

To continue on further from this point, you must be fully convinced in your own mind that Jesus is, in fact, who He said He was: God in the flesh. We each have free will to choose Christ or not. If we don't want to be with Jesus in this life, we don't have to be. But also understand that if you don't want Him in this life, you won't be with Him in the next life either – which is eternal.

Hopefully, you are now asking: How do I accept Jesus Christ as my Lord and Savior? It's a huge step you are about to make. It is the biggest step you will ever take in your entire life, and it will change your life forever – in a good, even great, way! In the next section of this book, I show you how to accept Christ and be "born again" – the first step, and by far the most important step, on your path to eternal life.

FALSE TEACHING(S) YOU WILL ENCOUNTER:
- Atheism (there is no God)
- The Bible is simply fictional "myths, folklore, and poetry"
- Universalism (i.e., any name, or any religion, even one you make up, or even no belief at all, can save you to eternal life)
- Annihilation after death
- Cults that deny Christ

RELATED SCRIPTURE:
And when I came to you, brethren, I did not come with superiority of speech or of wisdom, proclaiming to you the testimony of God. For I determined to know nothing among you except Jesus Christ, and Him crucified. I was with you in weakness and in

fear and in much trembling, and my message and my preaching were not in persuasive words of wisdom, but in demonstration of the Spirit and of power, so that your faith would not rest on the wisdom of men, but on the power of God. – 1 Corinthians 2:1-5

The Lord is not slow about His promise, as some count slowness, but is patient toward you, not wishing for any to perish but for all to come to repentance. – 2 Peter 3:9

"I love those who love me;
And those who diligently seek me will find me." – Proverbs 8:17

Draw near to God and He will draw near to you. Cleanse your hands, you sinners; and purify your hearts, you double-minded. – James 4:8

"Blessed are those who hunger and thirst for righteousness, for they shall be satisfied." – Matthew 5:6

For the Scripture says, "WHOEVER BELIEVES IN HIM WILL NOT BE DISAPPOINTED." For there is no distinction between Jew and Greek; for the same *Lord* is Lord of all, abounding in riches for all who call on Him; for "WHOEVER WILL CALL ON THE NAME OF THE LORD WILL BE SAVED."

How then will they call on Him in whom they have not believed? How will they believe in Him whom they have not heard? And how will they hear without a preacher? How will they preach unless they are sent? Just as it is written, "HOW BEAUTIFUL ARE THE FEET OF THOSE WHO BRING GOOD NEWS OF GOOD THINGS!"

However, they did not all heed the good news; for Isaiah says, "LORD, WHO HAS BELIEVED OUR REPORT?" So faith *comes* from hearing, and hearing by the word of Christ. – Romans 10:11-17

"But an hour is coming, and now is, when the true worshipers will worship the Father in spirit and truth; for such people the Father seeks to be His worshipers. God is spirit, and those who worship Him must worship in spirit and truth." – John 4:23-24

"Truly, truly, I say to you, he who hears My [Jesus] word, and believes Him who sent Me, has eternal life, and does not come into judgment, but has passed out of death into life.

Truly, truly, I say to you, an hour is coming and now is, when the dead will hear the voice of the Son of God, and those who hear will live. For just as the Father has life in Himself, even so He gave to the Son also to have life in Himself; and He gave Him authority to execute judgment, because He is *the* Son of Man. Do not marvel at this; for an hour is coming, in which all who are in the tombs will hear His voice, and will come forth; those who did the good *deeds* to a resurrection of life, those who committed the evil *deeds* to a resurrection of judgment." – John 5:24-29

Jesus said to them, "I am the bread of life; he who comes to Me will not hunger, and he who believes in Me will never thirst. But I said to you that you have seen Me, and yet do not believe. All that the Father gives Me will come to Me, and the one who comes to Me I will certainly not cast out. For I have come down from heaven, not to do My own will, but the will of Him who sent Me. This is the will of Him who sent Me, that of all that He has given Me I lose nothing, but raise it up on the last day. For this is the will of My Father, that everyone who beholds the Son and believes in

Him will have eternal life, and I Myself will raise him [you] up on the last day." – John 6:35-40

"Men of Israel, listen to these words: Jesus the Nazarene, a man attested to you by God with miracles and wonders and signs which God performed through Him in your midst, just as you yourselves know— this *Man*, delivered over by the predetermined plan and foreknowledge of God, you nailed to a cross by the hands of godless men and put *Him* to death. But God raised Him up again, putting an end to the agony of death, since it was impossible for Him to be held in its power. For David says of Him,

> 'I SAW THE LORD ALWAYS IN MY PRESENCE;
> FOR HE IS AT MY RIGHT HAND, SO THAT I WILL NOT BE SHAKEN.
> 'THEREFORE MY HEART WAS GLAD AND MY TONGUE EXULTED;
> MOREOVER MY FLESH ALSO WILL LIVE IN HOPE;
> BECAUSE YOU WILL NOT ABANDON MY SOUL TO HADES,
> NOR ALLOW YOUR HOLY ONE TO UNDERGO DECAY.
> 'YOU HAVE MADE KNOWN TO ME THE WAYS OF LIFE;
> YOU WILL MAKE ME FULL OF GLADNESS WITH YOUR PRESENCE.'

"Brethren, I may confidently say to you regarding the patriarch David that he both died and was buried, and his tomb is with us to this day. And so, because he was a prophet and knew that GOD HAD SWORN TO HIM WITH AN OATH TO SEAT *one* OF HIS DESCENDANTS ON HIS THRONE, he looked ahead and spoke of the resurrection of the Christ, that HE WAS NEITHER ABANDONED TO HADES, NOR DID His flesh SUFFER DECAY. This Jesus God raised up again, to which we are all witnesses. Therefore having been exalted to the right hand of God, and having received from the Father the promise of the Holy Spirit, He has poured forth this which you both see and hear. For it was not David who ascended into heaven, but he himself says:

> 'THE LORD SAID TO MY LORD,
> "SIT AT MY RIGHT HAND,
> UNTIL I MAKE YOUR ENEMIES A FOOTSTOOL FOR YOUR FEET."'

Therefore let all the house of Israel know for certain that God has made Him both Lord and Christ—this Jesus whom you crucified."

Now when they heard *this*, they were pierced to the heart, and said to Peter and the rest of the apostles, "Brethren, what shall we do?" Peter *said* to them, "Repent, and each of you be baptized in the name of Jesus Christ for the forgiveness of your sins; and you will receive the gift of the Holy Spirit. For the promise is for you and your children and for all who are far off, as many as the Lord our God will call to Himself." And with many other words he solemnly testified and kept on exhorting them, saying, "Be saved from this perverse generation!" So then, those who had received his word were baptized; and that day there were added about three thousand souls. They were continually devoting themselves to the apostles' teaching and to fellowship, to the breaking of bread and to prayer. – Acts 2:22-42

…knowing that you were not redeemed with perishable things like silver or gold from your futile way of life inherited from your forefathers, but with precious blood, as of a lamb unblemished and spotless, *the blood* of Christ. For He [Jesus] was foreknown before the foundation of the world, but has appeared in these last times for the sake of you who through Him are believers in God, who raised Him from the dead and gave Him glory, so that your faith and hope are in God. – 1 Peter 1:18-21

But now apart from the Law *the* righteousness of God has been manifested, being witnessed by the Law and the Prophets, even *the* righteousness of God through faith in Jesus Christ for all those who believe; for there is no distinction; for all have sinned and fall short of the glory of God, being justified as a gift by His grace through the redemption which is in Christ Jesus; whom God displayed publicly as a propitiation in His blood through faith. *This was* to demonstrate His righteousness, because in the forbearance of God He passed over the sins previously committed; for the demonstration, *I say*, of His righteousness at the present time, so that He [God] would be just and the justifier of the one who has faith in Jesus. – Romans 3:21-26

Jesus answered and said to her, "Everyone who drinks of this water will thirst again; but whoever drinks of the water that I will give him shall never thirst; but the water that I will give him will become in him a well of water springing up to eternal life." – John 4:13-14

The LORD performs righteous deeds
And judgments for all who are oppressed.
He made known His ways to Moses,
His acts to the sons of Israel.
The LORD is compassionate and gracious,
Slow to anger and abounding in lovingkindness.
He will not always strive *with us*,
Nor will He keep *His anger* forever.
He has not dealt with us according to our sins,
Nor rewarded us according to our iniquities.
For as high as the heavens are above the earth,
So great is His lovingkindness toward those who fear Him.
As far as the east is from the west,
So far has He removed our transgressions from us.
Just as a father has compassion on *his* children,
So the LORD has compassion on those who fear Him.
For He Himself knows our frame;
He is mindful that we are *but* dust. – Psalm 103:6-14

Now on the last day, the great *day* of the feast, Jesus stood and cried out, saying, "If anyone is thirsty, let him come to Me and drink. He who believes in Me, as the Scripture said, 'From his innermost being will flow rivers of living water.'" – John 7:37-38

PART III:

THE NEW TESTAMENT PLAN OF SALVATION

3.0 THE PATH TO ETERNAL LIFE

Jesus answered and said to him, "Truly, truly, I say to you, unless one is born again he cannot see the kingdom of God." – John 3:3

In the previous chapter, you have read the good news of the gospel and seen that our hope is in Jesus of Nazareth – the Christ, the Son of God, the Son of Man, the Messiah, the Savior, your Redeemer, Immanuel (God with us) and God in the flesh. You read that God sent His only Son Jesus out of love for us to save us from bondage under sin, Satan, and death for God "desires all men to be saved and to come to the knowledge of the truth" so that no one is lost in judgment to eternal death. You read that He was born of a virgin, lived a perfect and sinless life and that He willingly gave His life for you being crucified on the cross as a substitutionary atoning sacrifice for your sins – the "spotless lamb," "the Lamb of God who takes away the sin of the world."

You read that it is only through the blood of Christ that you can be saved and stand holy and blameless and declared righteous (your sins forgiven) before the Lord on the great Day of Judgment and receive eternal life. You also read that He rose again to life after three days and is right now "seated at the right hand of God [the Father]" in heaven ruling and reigning in His kingdom – and interceding on our behalf with God the Father.

So, let us now start on the path towards eternal life. In this chapter, I give an outline of that path. I set a solid foundation on which to proceed and give you an overview of the way of a Christian. Each step will then be covered in greater detail in subsequent chapters of this book.

THE NEW TESTAMENT PLAN OF REDEMPTION/SALVATION

The path to eternal life starts with being "born again," as it is written:

> "Truly, truly, I [Jesus] say to you, unless one is born again he cannot see the kingdom of God." – John 3:3

This is commonly referred to by various terms:

- Accepting Christ,
- Believing in Christ or Becoming a Believer,
- Placing Your Faith in Christ,
- Being "Saved,"
- Being "Born Again," or
- Being Converted

Unfortunately, you will find that people mean different things when they say those words, for once again, there are many false teachings in this area (I address those shortly). So, I want to provide an overview of what Scripture gives as the plan of salvation (i.e., the path to eternal life), for unless you have the high-level map, you might be deceived and "come short of" eternal life. Scripture tells us that the road to eternal life involves <u>all</u> of the following:

1. **You Must Be Born Again** – This is the very first step in the path to eternal salvation. When you are born again of the Spirit, your sins are forgiven by the blood of Christ on the cross. No one can earn forgiveness of sins through "good works" or by simply being a "good and moral" person; forgiveness is only

found through the atoning sacrificial death of Christ by the grace of God. To be born again, one must:

- 1.1. **Hear the Gospel Message:** You hear the gospel message and the hope that is found in Jesus Christ correctly explained to you (what this book is doing), as it is written: "So faith *comes* from hearing, and hearing by the word of Christ,"
- 1.2. **Believe in Jesus:** You respond to that message by accepting Christ (believe in Him) and place your complete faith, trust, and hope in Jesus as your Lord and Savior,
- 1.3. **Repent of Your Sins:** You genuinely turn away from your sinful behaviors and turn towards Christ (repentance means a change of heart and attitude towards sin and God),
- 1.4. **Confess Christ:** You verbally confess Christ as your Lord and Savior (and King), and
- 1.5. **Be Baptized:** You get baptized by immersion in water "for the forgiveness of sins." It is at baptism that your old self is "buried with Him [Jesus] through baptism into death, so that, just as Christ was raised from the dead through the glory of the Father, so we too may walk in newness of life," and you are raised "a new creature [person]" in Christ.
2. **Obedience to Christ** – Once born again, you have been redeemed (purchased) by the blood of Christ; you are therefore a "bondservant" of Christ and must submit yourself to the will of Christ (and thereby the will of God). This is commonly referred to as turning your life over to Christ and also "picking up your cross." You must be obedient to the commands of Christ as given in the New Testament of the Bible. [Please also know that we are not under the Old Testament Mosaic Law/Ten Commandments given to the ancient Hebrews at Mt. Sinai – the Mosaic Law was "fulfilled" by Christ and "nailed to the cross" and is no longer in effect in this New Testament church age of grace. We are now under the New Testament Law of Grace.]
3. **The Role of Works (Bearing Fruit):** True Christianity is as much about action as it is about the profession of faith. Genuine saving faith will have as its natural result "good works," also called "bearing fruit" for the Lord (i.e., good works are the natural outpouring of genuine faith). We are following the examples set by Noah, Abraham, Moses, and others who not only proved that their faith is genuine (both before man and before God) by their works (actions), but they also "abounded in the work of the Lord." What the Bible calls an "idle" profession of faith is not pleasing to God and is not a saving faith – it is called a "dead" faith, for it is written: "faith without works is dead."
4. **Persevering in Faith** – And finally, you must persevere in faith (i.e., remain faithful) unto death no matter what, even in the face of trials, tribulations, and persecution. Those who persevere in faith until death will receive their "crown of life." Scripture is abundantly clear that one can still "fall away" from, turn back or quit the faith even after one has been born again!

This book uses the term "accepting Christ" to be synonymous with the entirety of step 1 when one is properly born again in accordance with Scripture, which includes all of the following: belief, repentance, confession, and baptism. Please know that the list above is not something that I just made up out of thin air! This is not "my opinion" on the matter – I am presenting to you what is plainly taught in New Testament Scripture, without the myriad of myths, fantasies, beliefs, "traditions," and false teachings of man.

WE MUST APPROACH GOD ON HIS TERMS

Now you will hear much disagreement among men (and even professing Christians) over what I have just written above. You have probably heard the saying: "a lie circles the world twice before the truth even puts its shoes on." In a similar fashion, false teachings are absolutely rampant today in the world of Christendom, and they are shouted from the rooftops and pulpits in ferocious volume seemingly everywhere you look (especially in America). These false teachings come from what appear to be "Christian" sources – from churches that claim to be "Christian" and even use the name of Jesus and/or Christ in their names. But be not deceived; they are what Scripture calls "ravenous wolves in sheep's clothing."

Scripture warns us that the way to eternal life is fraught with peril, with traps, landmines, dead-ends, false short-cuts, side paths to nowhere (death), dark alleys of man-made false teachings galore, and other snares and pitfalls. These are laid up in front of you at every step along the way like a giant obstacle course! Scripture refers to these as "snares" that are placed in front of you to keep you from reaching your goal: which is to be with Christ for eternity. Always remember, we are in a spiritual war. Your enemy, the devil, and his forces and followers are trying to stop you!

You should have noticed that whenever we are at a critical step on the path to God and eternal life, you will find that Satan (and those who follow him) has set up an array of false teachings to try to trick you, to stop you at that point, or steer you out of the "straight and narrow" path given in Scripture. When we first discussed God's Creation, you saw that many false teachings were posing as science (emanating from the secular God-denying world), which, in fact, are nothing more than the "theories" of man (i.e., fake science). The purpose of those false teachings was to try to stop you at the very first step: coming to a belief in God.

If they (Satan and the forces of evil) couldn't stop you at that first step, they fall back and regroup at the next step. So, when we discussed the coming Great Day of Judgment, you saw another avalanche of false teachings (this time coming from mainly within the so-called "Christian" church) which attempt to get you to procrastinate in taking all this "God, Jesus and judgment stuff" seriously, causing many to delay day after day after day in accepting Christ and preparing for eternal life. And if they weren't able to stop you at that step, they again fall back and regroup and will now try to stop you at this step. They will try to trick you into accepting Christ via the schemes and false teachings of man vs. being born again properly in accordance with Scripture. It is here, therefore, that you will also find another cluster of false teachings.

So not only must I teach you the truth as given in Scripture, but I must also prepare you to know what is not the truth, so you are not cheated, "tricked," or "deceived" out of eternal life, for you can be led astray by the false teachings of man (e.g., legalism, sabbath keeping, cults that deny Christ, etc.). That is why I am declaring the complete and accurate gospel "message of truth" to you herein, so you are fully informed as to what God expects, and so you do not "come short of" the goal of eternal life:

> Be on guard for yourselves and for all the flock, among which the Holy Spirit has made you overseers, to shepherd the church of God which He purchased with His own blood. I know that after my departure <u>savage wolves</u> will come in among you, not sparing the flock; and from among your own selves men will arise, speaking

perverse things, to draw away the disciples after them. Therefore be on the alert…
– Acts 20:28-31

But I am afraid that, as the serpent deceived Eve by his craftiness [trickery], your minds will be led astray from the simplicity and purity *of devotion* to Christ. For if one comes and preaches another Jesus whom we have not preached, or you receive a different spirit which you have not received, or a different gospel which you have not accepted, you bear *this* beautifully [i.e. you do not abandon the truth of Scripture for the false teachings of man]…For such men are false apostles, deceitful workers, disguising themselves as apostles of Christ. No wonder, for even Satan disguises himself as an angel of light. – 2 Corinthians 11:3-4,13-14

You therefore, beloved, knowing this beforehand, be on your guard so that you are not carried away by the error of unprincipled men and fall from your own steadfastness, but grow in the grace and knowledge [understanding] of our Lord and Savior Jesus Christ. – 2 Peter 3:17-18a

See to it that no one takes you captive through philosophy and empty deception, according to the tradition of men, according to the elementary principles of the world, rather than according to Christ. – Colossians 2:8

My people are destroyed for lack of knowledge. – Hosea 4:6

Brothers *and sisters*, my heart's desire and my prayer to God for them is for *their* salvation. For I testify about them that they have a zeal for God, but not in accordance with knowledge [i.e., having the correct knowledge and understanding of what is stated in Scripture for salvation]. – Romans 10:1-2

"'I am coming quickly; hold fast what you have, so that no one will take your crown.'" – Revelation 3:11

    Know also that these snares and false teachings do not stop even after you accept Christ and are born again; in fact, they seem to intensify. You will face a mind-boggling, bewildering array of false teachings from many so-called "Christian" churches, which try to turn you out of the straight and narrow way, back towards things like legalism (Old Testament Mosaic Law) and other ways of man, even after you are born again. Why? Because when you accept Christ, you have now moved to the front lines of the (spiritual) war where the battle is being fought. The forces of evil know that they may still be able to turn you back away again from the "straight and narrow" path to eternal life, and even if they cannot turn you back, they may be able to hinder you from helping others hear about and follow Christ.

    So, before we continue on in truth, I must call your attention to a few false teachings because they are widely taught and preached in nearly all denominations, churches, pulpits, and books. Please also be aware that these false teachings overlap and are interconnected with each other in many areas – and in nearly all cases, where you find one false teaching, you will surely find others lurking nearby within the same church, sect, or cult! Even further compounding the difficulty here is that when you hear someone today say that they are "saved," they often mean different things, and they almost always mean that they believe in some (or all) of these false teachings.

While these false teachings are covered in the Beware the Wolves chapter, I am also listing some of them here because you will, with nearly 100% certainty, encounter them:

A. **The Sinner's Prayer:** This false teaching proclaims that one is born-again (accepts Christ) simply by making a one-time profession of faith, often called the "sinner's prayer." This is usually performed as part of an "altar call" at the end of a church service or in a giant stadium evangelism or revival event. But contrary to popular belief, you are neither born again nor saved to eternal life by simply saying a magical set of words. This teaching is not in Scripture anywhere! At best, the "sinner's prayer" that you may be led to speak by your church or pastor is only a way to help you verbalize steps 1.2-4 listed above.

B. **Baptism Isn't an Essential Condition/Component of Salvation:** Some falsely teach that baptism isn't a necessary condition, component, or element of salvation (i.e., one does not need to be baptized to receive forgiveness of sins, to be born-again, or even to receive eternal life). They claim that baptism is simply performed out of obedience, and they almost always also claim that baptism is a "good work" of man (see the next false teaching) and therefore excluded from salvation. However, this book shows you that baptism is not a "good work" of man and that it is at baptism where one is both forgiven of sin (by the blood of Christ) and born-again (raised to new life in Christ).

C. **You Are Saved by Faith Alone (Faith Only):** This false teaching denies that obedience and works have any part whatsoever in the plan of salvation. However, Scripture is clear that "faith without works is dead" and that the life of a true child of God is marked by continued "obedience" to Christ, with "bearing fruit" for the Lord as the natural result of that obedience (the role of works) as a "bondservant" of Christ. True Christianity is as much about action and a life of service as it is about the profession of faith. A "dead" faith ("faith without works") will not save you to eternal life! To support this false teaching, Paul's writing in the letter to the Ephesians is widely distorted and taken out of context. Those who proclaim this false teaching almost always compound their error by also falsely teaching that baptism is a "good work" of man and therefore not a requirement for salvation. However, this book is showing you that these "wolves" are therefore triply wrong because: 1) baptism is not a "good work" of man, 2) it is required for salvation (to be born again), and 3) Scripture also teaches us that works do play an important role in the biblical plan of salvation.

D. **Once Saved Always Saved:** Another enormously popular false teaching today proclaims that once someone has accepted Christ, they can never lose their salvation regardless of how one subsequently lives the rest of their life (i.e., once saved, you are always saved to eternal life no matter what). In this false teaching, it is viewed that your (final eternal) salvation occurred at an instant of time when you first accepted Christ. This false teaching is also called "perseverance of the saints" by Calvinists. This teaching is not in agreement with Scripture, for the Bible clearly and repeatedly warns that one can "fall away" or "depart" from the faith (apostatize), "backslide," "turn back," quit the faith, or even be deceived and tricked out of your crown of life – even after you are born again! While it is true that God will never forsake or leave you, Scripture is abundantly clear that <u>you</u> can choose to leave/quit Him, and also that many will do just that even after being born again.

E. **Being Born Again is Sufficient for Eternal Life:** Right on the heels of the prior false teachings (this is a close cousin of them) comes another false teaching which claims that our ultimate and final goal is simply to be born again. This false teaching equates being born again with receiving eternal life – i.e., that there is no difference between initial salvation and forgiveness of sins (being born again) and eternal final salvation (when you receive your "crown of life"). Therefore, this false teaching is a sort of by-product of combining the "saved by faith alone/only" and "once saved always saved" false teachings together. However, Scripture is clear that our goal is eternal life (final salvation) with God and His Christ in heaven and that being born again is only the first step on the path to eternal life. Being born again represents your initial salvation and the moment when you receive forgiveness of sins at your baptism (by the blood of Christ). However, the way of a true Christian continues throughout the remainder of their life in continued obedience, repentance, works, and perseverance until death resulting in final eternal salvation. True Christianity isn't a one-time prayer…sure, it often starts that way, in an instant, when you see the light and decide to accept the truth of Christ…but true Christianity is a way of life until death.

F. **Predestination.** Many adherents to the Calvinistic (i.e., "Reformed Protestantism") set of false doctrines believe that God chose certain people to be saved and others to be damned before the world began, and therefore your destiny is completely out of your control (i.e., that man has no free-will choice to either accept or reject Christ). According to this false teaching, God apparently has pre-chosen people like one would program robots ahead of time. This is just one of the many false teachings of the man-made dogma known as Calvinism. Scripture teaches that each person is born sinless (not in "original sin," which is still yet another false teaching!), comes to an age of accountability where they understand right from wrong (and therefore become accountable for sin) and then must decide/choose for themselves to either accept or reject Christ. We will all be personally accountable for our own sins and sinful actions (and even our motives). God gave each person free will, and accepting or rejecting Christ is a free will choice each person will make. God, while ultimately sovereign, does not override your free will choice. Those who end up in hell will do so because of their own choice by rejecting God and life.

While I've done my best to untangle and explain these (and other) false teachings for you in this book, in reality, they are often interrelated and interwoven together in a giant tangled web or knot. Some "faith alone/only" advocates believe that a Christian must live a life in accord with Scripture (i.e., they believe in obedience), while others don't. Some deny the role of baptism in salvation, and some don't. Some "faith alone/only" people believe you can fall away from the faith, while others believe in "once saved always saved." So, there are many variations and permutations of these false teachings, where some groups believe in one false teaching and part of another false teaching, or vice versa.

Furthermore, to say one believes in one false teaching often implies another as an inescapable consequence. For example, can you really say that you were "saved" to eternal life by saying a "sinner's prayer" without also implying (whether you realize it or not) that you also believe in "once saved always saved" and even further that you are also saved by (a simple profession) of "faith alone/only"? By conceding that the

The Message of Truth

"sinner's prayer" saves you, aren't you therefore also implicitly denying the role of baptism, whether you admit to it or not? Similarly, can one really believe they are saved by "faith only/alone" without also (perhaps even unknowingly) believing that being born again is all one must do to receive eternal life? So, you see, they are all jumbled together in reality, spun into one giant web of deception.

Wow…what a mess man has made of the simple teachings of Scripture! I think a real-world example of how these false teachings show up in practice will go a long way in illustrating what I'm talking about here. And in my experience, whenever you see someone (a church, group, book, etc.) leading off with the "sinner's prayer" false teaching, you can rest assured that you will find many other false teachings in their materials as well (as a general rule). Jason Jackson writes about receiving a "Christian" tract that was being handed out. In examining the tract, he writes: [40]

> Two ladies walked up the driveway. They handed me a small, tri-folded brochure that contained the service times of their church group. It advertised the religious group as being "independent of any denomination, Bible-based in every part of ministry, soul-winning and missions minded, and distinctively Christian." The tract claimed that the religious body is "an old fashioned, independent, Baptist Church that believes, preaches, and practices the Bible."
>
> Their claims to being Bible-based, however, are negated in that section of the tract titled, "How to have a home in Heaven." Four points are designed that, supposedly, guide one to salvation. Unfortunately, the teaching is hardly "independent of any denomination ... and distinctively Christian."
>
> Some may object to this review, saying that it is neither friendly nor loving. But Paul asked on one occasion, "So then am I become your enemy because I tell you the truth?" (Gal. 4:16).
>
> The loving thing to do is to tell the truth. We must not judge people superficially or hypocritically (Mt. 7:1), but we are required by God to evaluate what we hear, "handling aright the word of truth" (2 Tim. 2:15). The truth will set us free; error will cause us to be lost (Jn. 8:32; 2 Tim. 2:18).
>
> So what does the tract say about "How to have a home in Heaven"? Here are the points and scriptures that are discussed — just as they appear in the tract.
>
> 1. All have sinned. "For all have sinned and come short of the glory of God" (Rom. 3:23).
> 2. The penalty for sin is death and hell. "For the wages of sin is death...." "And death and hell were cast into the lake of fire. This is the second death" (Rev. 20:14).
> 3. Jesus died to pay for our sins. "But God commendeth His love toward us in that while we were yet sinners, Christ died for us" (Rom. 5:8).
> 4. Trust Jesus as your Savior and your only hope for Heaven. "That if thou shalt confess with thy mouth the Lord Jesus, and shalt believe in thine heart that God hath raised Him from the dead, thou shalt be saved" (Rom. 10:9). "For whosoever shall call upon the name of the Lord shall be saved" (Rom. 10:13).
>
> After making these four points, the following conclusion was given:

---

[40] Jackson, Jason. "How to Go to Heaven – Sincere, but Wrong." ChristianCourier.*com*. Access date: May 31, 2018. https://christiancourier.com/articles/1183-how-to-go-to-heaven-sincere-but-wrong

"Pray a simple prayer to God, from your heart, such as the following: 'Dear Jesus, I know that I am a sinner. If I were to die today, I would deserve to go to hell to pay for my sins. I believe that you came to earth, lived a perfect life, and died on a cross to pay for my sins. I believe that you arose from the grave, and I ask you to forgive my sins. I am trusting only You to take me to heaven. Thank you for saving me, Jesus. Amen.'"

A Kindly Response

Like the Bereans of Acts 17:11, let us examine the Scriptures to see whether these things are so.

1. While allegedly pointing people to heaven, there is nothing said about repentance. But Jesus said, "Except you repent you shall all likewise perish" (Lk. 13:3). And Paul declared that God commands men everywhere to repent. (Acts 17:30). If God commands it, can we ignore it, and still be faithful teachers of his Word?
2. There is no mention of baptism in this section. But Paul was urged to arise, be baptized, and wash away his sins, "calling on his name" (Acts 22:16). Peter preached, "Repent ye, and be baptized, every one of you, in the name of Jesus Christ, unto [to obtain] the remission of your sins" (Acts 2:38). The apostles taught that baptism is essential for salvation because Jesus had said, "He who believes and is baptized shall be saved" (Mk. 16:16). Can we teach less than what Jesus taught?
3. There is not a single example in the New Testament where the non-Christian was instructed to pray for salvation. There are many examples, however, when believers were baptized for the forgiveness of sins.

Error is often mixed with truth. The devil himself quoted the Scriptures (cf. Mt. 4:6). There are a number of truths within this tract. Every verse is true, because they are quotations from the Bible. But one must consider all that the Bible says about salvation if he is going to obtain a home in heaven.

"The sum of thy word is truth; And every one of thy righteous ordinances endureth for ever" (Psalms 119:160).

As you see, the tract was full of false teachings despite being from a well-meaning "independent of any denomination, Bible-based in every part of ministry, soul-winning and missions minded, and distinctively Christian" church (their very own words). And unfortunately, false teachings won't be clearly labeled as such for you when you encounter them in the real world as in the example above – they are cleverly disguised by mixing in what appears to be biblically sounding language. Indeed, the tract appears to be very "biblical" on the surface, but, in fact, it is not in agreement with what is taught in Scripture.

I hope you are starting to see the daunting task you will be facing in seeking actual Scriptural truth as opposed to man-made opinions, schemes, and false teachings. This is one of the main reasons I decided to write this book, as I had to sort through all these false teachings myself, trying to find truth. Please don't just blindly believe whatever you hear being taught or preached as actual biblical truth without fully checking it against Scripture. It doesn't matter if you hear it from a man on the street corner or from someone in a position of authority with lots of important-sounding initials, abbreviations, and titles placed before and after their name dressed up in an expensive suit behind a fancy pulpit at a large and famous church. And this also goes for anything I write – check everything against Scripture for yourself, for the Bible is the final Word (pun intended).

By the time you have finished this book, I hope that you are able not only to recognize and defend the truth as given in Scripture but also able to recognize what is not truth. Remember though, false teachings won't be clearly labeled as such by those who are teaching them; they aren't always easy to spot. You must first know what Scripture actually teaches in aggregate as truth ("The sum of thy word is truth") in order to be able to recognize a false teaching when you encounter one.

THE ALLURE OF FALSE TEACHINGS

Why are these false teachings so widespread and popular? It is because they offer a feel-good, safe, easy and superficial form of "Christianity" that modern "itching ears" like to hear – but that is not what Scripture teaches, nor what history bears out as proof in the lives of the saints which have come before us. Scripture tells us that the path forward to eternal life isn't always easy and that it takes courage, the strength of character, discipline, and perseverance.

We are plainly told in Scripture to "count the cost" of following Jesus. When you decide to follow Christ, you may suffer the loss of friends, loved ones, and even family members who turn their back on you or ridicule you because of Jesus. You may face discrimination and setbacks or loss at work or business. In fact, many Christians who have gone before us were put to death for declaring (and sticking to) their faith in Christ! I highly recommend reading Foxe's *Book of Martyrs* (*The Actes and Monuments of the Christian Church*) and *The Church History* by Eusebius so you can get an idea of what followers of Christ in earlier days have had to suffer. Many had to seal their testimony with their gruesome deaths. Some of you who are reading this book and decide to follow Christ may also suffer severe persecution. It's easy for us to forget the reality of persecution, especially those of us who live in nations where freedom of religion and speech are allowed.

I'm not trying to scare you; I'm simply presenting to you the truth given in Scripture. We read in Scripture that when we look back from the other side of eternity, any time of persecution and suffering here on earth will seem to have been done and over with in an instant, a flash in time, quickly gone and behind you – it will pale in comparison to the glory of God and heaven for all eternity. The great apostle Paul, who suffered many things for preaching the gospel, wrote this:

> For I consider that the sufferings of this present time are not worthy to be compared with the glory that is to be revealed to us. – Romans 8:18

It is also written:

> Yet you do not know what your life will be like tomorrow. You are *just* a vapor that appears for a little while and then vanishes away. – James 4:14

> Man is like a mere breath;
> His days are like a passing shadow. – Psalm 144:4

> "Behold, You have made my days *as* handbreadths,
> And my lifetime as nothing in Your sight;
> Surely every man at his best is a mere breath." – Psalm 39:5

But know that you will be able to "stand firm" in your faith and persevere in all things by the power of Christ who now "abides (lives) in" you – this is called living in the Spirit ("walk by the Spirit") and is discussed more in an upcoming chapter.

SEEK THE THINGS ABOVE

Choosing to follow Christ also means sacrifice. You will need to give up seeking the things of this world (fame, fortune, lustful pursuits, power, etc.) and instead "seek the things which are from above," the things of God:

> Therefore, if you have been raised with Christ, keep seeking the things *that are* above, where Christ is, seated at the right hand of God. – Colossians 3:1

> You adulteresses, do you not know that friendship with the world is hostility toward God? Therefore whoever wishes to be a friend of the world makes himself an enemy of God. – James 4:4

The example recorded in Scripture about the rich young man at the time of Christ is instructive here:

> As He was setting out on a journey, a man ran up to Him and knelt before Him, and asked Him, "Good Teacher, what shall I do to inherit eternal life?" And Jesus said to him, "Why do you call Me good? No one is good except God alone. You know the commandments, 'DO NOT MURDER, DO NOT COMMIT ADULTERY, DO NOT STEAL, DO NOT BEAR FALSE WITNESS, Do not defraud, HONOR YOUR FATHER AND MOTHER.'" And he said to Him, "Teacher, I have kept all these things from my youth up." Looking at him, Jesus felt a love for him and said to him, "One thing you lack: go and sell all you possess and give to the poor, and you will have treasure in heaven; and come, follow Me." But at these words he was saddened, and he went away grieving, for he was one who owned much property.
>
> And Jesus, looking around, said to His disciples, "How hard it will be for those who are wealthy to enter the kingdom of God!" The disciples were amazed at His words. But Jesus answered again and said to them, "Children, how hard it is to enter the kingdom of God! It is easier for a camel to go through the eye of a needle than for a rich man to enter the kingdom of God." They were even more astonished and said to Him, "Then who can be saved?" Looking at them, Jesus said, "With people it is impossible, but not with God; for all things are possible with God." – Mark 10:17-27

We must be willing to sacrifice all things for Christ – worldly possessions, wealth, fame, and even life itself. The rich young man written about in Scripture wasn't willing to give up his worldly possessions for the treasure of Christ and eternal life in heaven! How sad, tragic even. And it was a decision of lasting, eternal consequences and duration. There are further warnings in Scripture about seeking worldly material possessions and wealth:

> And He told them a parable, saying, "The land of a rich man was very productive. And he began reasoning to himself, saying, 'What shall I do, since I have no place to store my crops?' Then he said, 'This is what I will do: I will tear down my barns and build larger ones, and there I will store all my grain and my goods. And I will say to my soul, "Soul, you have many goods laid up for many years *to come*; take

your ease, eat, drink *and* be merry.'" But God said to him, 'You fool! This *very* night your soul is required of you; and *now* who will own what you have prepared?' So is the man who stores up treasure for himself, and is not rich toward God." – Luke 12:16-21

"Do not store up for yourselves treasures on earth, where moth and rust destroy, and where thieves break in and steal. But store up for yourselves treasures in heaven, where neither moth nor rust destroys, and where thieves do not break in or steal; for where your treasure is, there your heart will be also." – Matthew 6:19-21

These topics are covered in more detail in later chapters.

INITIAL SALVATION VS. FINAL SALVATION

And finally, know that there is a difference between initial salvation/forgiveness of sins (which happens at baptism when you are born again) and final (eternal) salvation when you receive your "crown of life." You will find much emphasis on being born again (rightly so), but modern liberal "Christian" churches are simply not doing a good job of explaining the complete plan of salvation, much of which happens after one is born again. Scripture is abundantly clear that initial salvation/forgiveness of sins (i.e., being "born again") is not the same as final (eternal) salvation. Your ultimate goal is not being born again – it is having eternal life with God and His Christ in heaven.

Being born again is simply the first, but by far the most important, step on the path to eternal life. Said differently, being born again is a necessary but not sufficient requirement for eternal salvation. When you are "born again," you are a "new creature," "infants in Christ" – but never forget that it is only your first step on the rest of your Christian pilgrimage! You must "press on to maturity" through obedience, action ("good works"), and perseverance. Scripture is very clear that many who start out in faith (i.e., they are born again) will not finish their journey to eternal life. Let me give an analogy to help you understand. Suppose you want to be a doctor. Getting admitted to medical school is a very important (and necessary) first step, but unless you actually graduate so you can properly be called a doctor and practice medicine, it will have been meaningless.

Eternal salvation doesn't occur in an instant; it is a continually progressive process (called sanctification) that starts when one is born again (having been cleansed by the blood of Christ at baptism) and continues throughout the life of a Christian as they walk with the Lord until death. Wayne Jackson writes:[41]

> When many people hear the term "salvation," they immediately think of something that occurred in their past. Many Protestants believe that salvation was received the instant they expressed a genuine faith in Christ as their personal Savior, and that it never can be forfeited. As we shall notice, these ideas are not accurate.

The process of sanctification (and salvation) isn't completed until one receives their "crown of life" – which is awarded to you on the great Day of Judgment. Sanctification means being "set apart" for Christ, set apart from sin and this world ("I chose you out of the world"), and becoming dedicated to righteousness and the service

---

[41] Jackson, Wayne. "The Word-tenses of Salvation." *ChristianCourier.com*. Access date: May 22, 2019. https://christiancourier.com/articles/1344-word-tenses-of-salvation-the

of God. It conveys the sense of being made to conform more and more to the image of Christ.

And finally, Scripture warns us not to take our (eternal final) salvation for granted! We are called to be diligent and attentive to the Word of God, always "growing in the grace and knowledge [understanding]" of the Lord, being obedient to the commands of Christ as given in the New Testament and making sure we do not "come short of" our goal – which is eternal life. Scripture, therefore, exhorts us to:

- "Make your calling and election sure" (2 Peter 1:10 KJV),
- "Work out your salvation with fear and trembling" (Philippians 2:12),
- "Fight the good fight of faith; take hold of the eternal life to which you were called" (1 Timothy 6:12),
- "Finish the course…keep the faith" (2 Timothy 4:7), for
- "In the future there is laid up for me the crown of righteousness, which the Lord, the righteous Judge, will award to me on that day [the Great Day of Judgment]" (2 Timothy 4:8)

This vital topic is addressed in more detail in the upcoming chapters titled You are Born Again and Walking in the Way.

GOING FORWARD IN TRUTH

Now, having laid out the high-level roadmap for you, the following chapters in this section of the book show you how to be properly "born again" in accordance with New Testament Scripture. Remember that being "born again" is only the first, but by far the most important, step on the path towards eternal life. Then the next section of this book then picks up from there to discuss obedience, the role of works ("bearing fruit"), and persevering in faith, along with other important topics such as prayer.

FALSE TEACHING(S) YOU WILL ENCOUNTER:

- False teachings on baptism (it isn't required to be born again along with false teachings about how baptism is to be performed)
- Saying a "Sinner's Prayer" saves you
- You are saved by "Faith Alone/Only"
- "Once Saved Always Saved" (a.k.a. "Perseverance of the Saints")
- You get a "2nd Chance" after death
- Being "born again" is the only thing one must do to obtain eternal life (i.e., obedience, works, and perseverance are not required)
- Some are "predestined" to eternal life by God and others to eternal death – and no one has a choice in the matter
- Sabbath keeping/legalism
- Universalism (i.e., any name, or any religion, even one you make up, or even no belief at all, can save you to eternal life)
- Ecumenism
- Roman Catholicism masquerading as Christianity
- Mormonism masquerading as Christianity
- Calvinism
- Cults that deny Christ

The Message of Truth

<u>RELATED SCRIPTURE:</u>

This is good and acceptable in the sight of God our Savior, who desires all men to be saved and to come to the knowledge of the truth. – 1 Timothy 2:3-4

Now there was a man of the Pharisees, named Nicodemus, a ruler of the Jews; this man came to Jesus by night and said to Him, "Rabbi, we know that You have come from God *as* a teacher; for no one can do these signs that You do unless God is with him." Jesus answered and said to him, "Truly, truly, I say to you, unless one is born again he cannot see the kingdom of God."

Nicodemus said to Him, "How can a man be born when he is old? He cannot enter a second time into his mother's womb and be born, can he?" Jesus answered, "Truly, truly, I say to you, unless one is born of water [baptism, not birth] and the Spirit he cannot enter into the kingdom of God. That which is born of the flesh is flesh, and that which is born of the Spirit is spirit. Do not be amazed that I said to you, 'You must be born again.' The wind blows where it wishes and you hear the sound of it, but do not know where it comes from and where it is going; so is everyone who is born of the Spirit."

Nicodemus said to Him, "How can these things be?" Jesus answered and said to him, "Are you the teacher of Israel and do not understand these things? Truly, truly, I say to you, we speak of what we know and testify of what we have seen, and you do not accept our testimony. If I told you earthly things and you do not believe, how will you believe if I tell you heavenly things? No one has ascended into heaven, but He [Jesus] who descended from heaven: the Son of Man." – John 3:1-13

The first man is from the earth, earthy; the second man is from heaven. – 1 Corinthians 15:47

But what does it say? "THE WORD IS NEAR YOU, IN YOUR MOUTH AND IN YOUR HEART"—that is, the word of faith which we are preaching, that if you confess with your mouth Jesus *as* Lord, and believe in your heart that God raised Him from the dead, you will be saved; for with the heart a person believes, resulting in righteousness, and with the mouth he confesses, resulting in salvation. For the Scripture says, "WHOEVER BELIEVES IN HIM WILL NOT BE DISAPPOINTED." For there is no distinction between Jew and Greek; for the same *Lord* is Lord of all, abounding in riches for all who call on Him; for "WHOEVER WILL CALL ON THE NAME OF THE LORD WILL BE SAVED."

How then will they call on Him in whom they have not believed? How will they believe in Him whom they have not heard? And how will they hear without a preacher? How will they preach unless they are sent? Just as it is written, "HOW BEAUTIFUL ARE THE FEET OF THOSE WHO BRING GOOD NEWS OF GOOD THINGS!"

However, they did not all heed the good news; for Isaiah says, "LORD, WHO HAS BELIEVED OUR REPORT?" So faith *comes* from hearing, and hearing by the word of Christ. – Romans 10:8-17

3.1 BELIEVE IN JESUS
(By First Hearing the Gospel Message)

Jesus said to him, "I am the way, and the truth, and the life; no one comes to the Father but through Me." – John 14:6

Believe in Me. The central element of salvation is coming to a belief in Jesus Christ of Nazareth as your Lord and Savior. This is also called placing your faith in Jesus. You come to a belief in Christ by first hearing the gospel "message of truth," as it is written:

> For the Scripture says, "WHOEVER BELIEVES IN HIM WILL NOT BE DISAPPOINTED." For there is no distinction between Jew and Greek; for the same *Lord* is Lord of all, abounding in riches for all who call on Him; for "WHOEVER WILL CALL ON THE NAME OF THE LORD WILL BE SAVED."
>
> How then will they call on Him in whom they have not believed? How will they believe in Him whom they have not heard? And how will they hear without a preacher? How will they preach unless they are sent? Just as it is written, "HOW BEAUTIFUL ARE THE FEET OF THOSE WHO BRING GOOD NEWS OF GOOD THINGS!"
>
> However, they did not all heed the good news; for Isaiah says, "LORD, WHO HAS BELIEVED OUR REPORT?" So faith *comes* from hearing, and hearing by the word of Christ. – Romans 10:11-17

In another example, we see the apostle Philip explaining the gospel message of truth (and thereby Christ) to the Ethiopian eunuch:

> Philip ran up and heard him reading Isaiah the prophet, and said, "Do you understand what you are reading?" And he said, "Well, how could I, unless someone guides me?" And he invited Philip to come up and sit with him. Now the passage of Scripture which he was reading was this:
>
> "HE WAS LED AS A SHEEP TO SLAUGHTER;
> AND AS A LAMB BEFORE ITS SHEARER IS SILENT,
> SO HE DOES NOT OPEN HIS MOUTH.
> "IN HUMILIATION HIS JUDGMENT WAS TAKEN AWAY;
> WHO WILL RELATE HIS GENERATION?
> FOR HIS LIFE IS REMOVED FROM THE EARTH."
>
> The eunuch answered Philip and said, "Please *tell me*, of whom does the prophet say this? Of himself or of someone else?" Then Philip opened his mouth, and beginning from this Scripture he preached Jesus to him. – Acts 8:30-35

And that is what this book is all about – preaching the gospel "message of truth" to you completely and accurately, from start to finish, explaining to you the truth of God, explaining who Jesus was, showing you what His death and resurrection means, and that believing in Christ as your Lord and Savior is the first step on the path to eternal life, and the only way to stand before God on Judgment Day with your sins forgiven and inherit eternal life.

I have been preaching to you the gospel "message of truth" from the very beginning. I have explained to you that being a "good person," or being "religious," performing ceremonies, worshiping idols, or following after the "traditions" and schemes of man (e.g., praying to Mary, etc.) – none of these will get you into heaven. Only belief in Jesus and His sacrifice on the cross will. It is only through the shed blood of Jesus Christ on the cross that you can obtain forgiveness of sins. You cannot buy forgiveness or earn it through good works – you cannot buy the blood of Christ. Scripture also emphatically declares: "there is no other name under heaven that has been given among men by which we must be saved."

As discussed in a previous chapter, there is no way around the fact that Jesus did declare that He is God. Your (only) choices about Jesus are that:

1) He never existed (despite abundant historical evidence that proves beyond the shadow of a doubt that He did), or
2) He was simply a crazed, lying lunatic who then died a horrible death on the cross trying to keep His lies, or
3) He was indeed God, as He declared.

Do you believe that Jesus is God? That He was born of a virgin as it is written? That He lived a perfect and sinless life, fully man, but also fully God, being tempted in all things just like you are tempted, but never committing sin? That He was the Son of God and the Son of Man. That He willingly gave His life (He laid it down) for you on the cross by being crucified as payment in an atoning sacrifice for your sins? That He was raised up again to eternal life after the third day? And most amazingly, that He will raise you up to eternal life with Him when He comes back?

That is called putting your faith, trust, and hope in Jesus, and in Him alone, for "For there is one God, *and* one mediator also between God and men, *the* man Christ Jesus." Jesus said: "I am the way, and the truth, and the life; no one comes to the Father but through Me" and "I am the resurrection and the life; he who believes in Me will live even if he dies, and everyone who lives and believes in Me will never die. Do you believe this?"

Know that Jesus, God Himself in the flesh, willingly gave His own life on the cross, and He did that for you. He wasn't forced to; He chose to – because He loves you. To save Himself, Jesus could have called on 10,000 angels from heaven to come and instantly put a stop to His arrest and crucifixion (see Matthew 26:53), but He didn't. It is this Jesus who you are putting your faith, trust, and hope in. Matthew Henry eloquently writes:[42]

> Jesus Christ is the first and the last. It is but a little scantling of time that is allowed to us in this world, but our Redeemer is the first and the last. He is the first, for by him all things were made, and he was before all things with God and was God himself. He is the last, for all things are made for him, and he will be the Judge of all.
>
> This surely is the title of God, from everlasting and to everlasting, and it is the title of one that is an unchangeable Mediator between God and man, Jesus, the same yesterday, today, and forever. He was the first, for by him the foundation of the church was laid in the patriarchal state; and he is the last, for by him the top-stone will be brought forth and laid in the end of time.

---

[42] Henry, Matthew. *Exposition of the Old and New Testaments*, London. 1706-1710/1721.

He was dead and is alive. He was dead, and died for our sins; he is alive, for he rose again for our justification, and he ever lives to make intercession for us. He was dead, and by dying purchased salvation for us; he is alive, and by his life applies this salvation to us. And if, when we were enemies, we were reconciled by his death, much more, being reconciled, we shall be saved by his life.

It is written that Jesus "led captivity captive" (Ephesians 4:8 KJV); by this, it is meant that He has led you, who were slaves (i.e., captives) of sin, Satan and death, to now be His own captive/servant – i.e., He "captured" you from your prior captivity of bondage under sin into new life in Christ. And so, when you are "captured" by Christ, you have been redeemed from death to life. This was a state of spiritual death – "you were dead in your trespasses and sins," but are "made alive" in Christ.

And contrary to public opinion and the loud and relentless shilling of skeptics, agnostics, and atheists, coming to faith in Jesus doesn't mean you abandon your reason, intellect, and logical thinking. Becoming a Christian doesn't mean just "blindly believing" in Christ, without a lot of justification and proven historical facts and after evaluating the authenticity and accuracy of the Bible, the eyewitnesses, testimonies, fulfilled prophecies, recorded miracles, etc. God wants you to decide based on truth and understanding. You examine all the evidence and then make a rational, logical decision based on that evidence. Your step of faith is believing in the many things that we cannot directly measure (e.g., eternal life, God is Spirit, etc.). Documented miracles, fulfilled prophecies, His command over nature, and eyewitness testimonies all confirm that Jesus was indeed God. And those facts, testimonies, fulfilled prophecies, recorded miracles, etc., are all documented in Scripture.

Furthermore, new archeological finds continue to validate the Bible; in fact, not a single archeological or historical find nor scientific advancement has ever contradicted the Bible. Each new find has only strengthened and supported what is already written in the Bible – many things are recorded in Scripture hundreds or more years before they occurred.

If you are still unsure or have doubts and questions at this point, please face them head-on! You owe it to yourself to do that. It is your eternal life at stake here. Please don't let doubts and questions stand in your way; I did that for a very long time. Seek out material that addresses your questions. We today have access to a myriad of wonderful Christian resources, many from fully credentialed scientists who are experts in their fields. See the chapter on Science vs. the Bible again if needed to help you overcome any doubts.

FALSE TEACHING(S) YOU WILL ENCOUNTER:
- Atheism
- The Bible is simply fictional "myths, folklore, and poetry"
- Universalism (i.e., any name, or any religion, even one you make up, or even no belief at all, can save you to eternal life)
- Ecumenism
- Cults that deny Christ
- Jesus was just a "Good Moral Person" (but not God)
- You get a "2nd Chance" after death

The Message of Truth

RELATED SCRIPTURE:

"For God so loved the world, that He gave His only begotten Son, that whoever believes in Him shall not perish, but have eternal life. For God did not send the Son into the world to judge the world, but that the world might be saved through Him. He who believes in Him is not judged; he who does not believe has been judged already, because he has not believed in the name of the only begotten Son of God. This is the judgment, that the Light has come into the world, and men loved the darkness rather than the Light, for their deeds were evil. For everyone who does evil hates the Light, and does not come to the Light for fear that his deeds will be exposed. But he who practices the truth comes to the Light, so that his deeds may be manifested as having been wrought in God." – John 3:16-21

"Enter through the narrow gate [Jesus]; for the gate is wide and the way is broad that leads to destruction, and there are many who enter through it. For the gate is small and the way is narrow that leads to life, and there are few who find it." – Matthew 7:13-14

…"Sirs, what must I do to be saved?" They said, "Believe in the Lord Jesus, and you will be saved, you and your household." And they spoke the word of the Lord to him together with all who were in his house. And he took them that *very* hour of the night and washed their wounds, and immediately he was baptized, he and all his *household*. And he brought them into his house and set food before them, and rejoiced greatly, having believed in God with his whole household. – Acts 16:30-34

Then Peter, filled with the Holy Spirit, said to them, "Rulers and elders of the people, if we are on trial today for a benefit done to a sick man, as to how this man has been made well, let it be known to all of you and to all the people of Israel, that by the name of Jesus Christ the Nazarene, whom you crucified, whom God raised from the dead—by this *name* this man stands here before you in good health. He is the STONE WHICH WAS REJECTED by you, THE BUILDERS, *but* WHICH BECAME THE CHIEF CORNER *stone*. And there is salvation in no one else; for there is no other name under heaven that has been given among men by which we must be saved." – Acts 4:8-12

Being found in appearance as a man, He [Jesus] humbled Himself by becoming obedient to the point of death, even death on a cross. For this reason also, God highly exalted Him, and bestowed on Him the name which is above every name, so that at the name of Jesus EVERY KNEE WILL BOW, of those who are in heaven and on earth and under the earth, and that every tongue will confess that Jesus Christ is Lord, to the glory of God the Father. – Philippians 2:8-11

For He [Jesus] was foreknown before the foundation of the world, but has appeared in these last times for the sake of you who through Him are believers in God, who raised Him from the dead and gave Him glory, so that your faith and hope are in God. – 1 Peter 1:20-21

John testified saying, "I have seen the Spirit descending as a dove out of heaven, and He remained upon Him [Jesus]. I did not recognize Him, but He who sent me to baptize in water said to me, 'He upon whom you see the Spirit descending and remaining upon

Him, this is the One who baptizes in the Holy Spirit.' I myself have seen, and have testified that this is the Son of God." – John 1:32-34

…knowing that you were not redeemed with perishable things like silver or gold from your futile way of life inherited from your forefathers, but with precious blood, as of a lamb unblemished and spotless, *the blood* of Christ. – 1 Peter 1:18-19

Every priest stands daily ministering and offering time after time the same sacrifices, which can never take away sins; but He [Jesus], having offered one sacrifice for sins for all time, SAT DOWN AT THE RIGHT HAND OF GOD, waiting from that time onward UNTIL HIS ENEMIES BE MADE A FOOTSTOOL FOR HIS FEET. – Hebrews 10:11-13

But now Christ has been raised from the dead, the first fruits of those who are asleep. For since by a man *came* death, by a man also *came* the resurrection of the dead. For as in Adam all die, so also in Christ all will be made alive. – 1 Corinthians 15:20-22

For Christ also died for sins once for all, *the* just for *the* unjust, so that He might bring us to God, having been put to death in the flesh, but made alive in the spirit. – 1 Peter 3:18

Jesus said to him, "I am the way, and the truth, and the life; no one comes to the Father but through Me." – John 14:6

Jesus said to her, "I am the resurrection and the life; he who believes in Me will live even if he dies, and everyone who lives and believes in Me will never die. Do you believe this?" She said to Him, "Yes, Lord; I have believed that You are the Christ, the Son of God, *even* He who comes into the world." – John 11:25-27

Jesus said to them, "I am the bread of life; he who comes to Me will not hunger, and he who believes in Me will never thirst. But I said to you that you have seen Me, and yet do not believe. All that the Father gives Me will come to Me, and the one who comes to Me I will certainly not cast out. For I have come down from heaven, not to do My own will, but the will of Him who sent Me. This is the will of Him who sent Me, that of all that He has given Me I lose nothing, but raise it up on the last day. For this is the will of My Father, that everyone who beholds the Son and believes in Him will have eternal life, and I Myself will raise him [you!] up on the last day." – John 6:35-40

"Do not let your heart be troubled; believe in God, believe also in Me [Jesus]. In My Father's house are many dwelling places; if it were not so, I would have told you; for I go to prepare a place for you. If I go and prepare a place for you, I will come again and receive you to Myself, that where I am, *there* you may be also." – John 14:1-3

What was from the beginning, what we have heard, what we have seen with our eyes, what we have looked at and touched with our hands, concerning the Word of Life [Jesus]— and the life was manifested, and we have seen and testify and proclaim to you the eternal life, which was with the Father and was manifested to us— what we have seen and heard we proclaim to you also, so that you too may have fellowship with us; and indeed our fellowship is with the Father, and with His Son Jesus Christ. – 1 John 1:1-3

3.2 REPENT OF YOUR SINS

From that time Jesus began to preach and say,
"Repent, for the kingdom of heaven is at hand." – Matthew 4:17

Repent of your sins. Scripture is clear about the need for sinners to repent of their sins in order to be reconciled to God:

> From that time Jesus began to preach and say, "Repent, for the kingdom of heaven is at hand." – Matthew 4:17
>
> And Jesus answered and said to them, "*It is* not those who are well who need a physician, but those who are sick. I have not come to call the righteous but sinners to repentance." – Luke 5:31-32
>
> "Therefore repent and return, so that your sins may be wiped away, in order that times of refreshing may come from the presence of the Lord." – Acts 3:19
>
> "I tell you, no, but unless you repent, you will all likewise perish." – Luke 13:3
>
> Do not be wise in your own eyes;
> Fear the LORD and turn away from evil. – Proverbs 3:7
>
> "Therefore having overlooked the times of ignorance, God is now declaring to men that all *people* everywhere should repent, because He has fixed a day in which He will judge the world in righteousness through a Man whom He has appointed, having furnished proof to all men by raising Him from the dead." – Acts 17:30-31

Repentance means to genuinely and sincerely "turn away" from your sins – to stop doing deliberate, willful, and continued sinful behavior. The heart of the repentant sinner also feels guilt and remorse for the sins that have already been committed – by having a contrite heart. This implies that you now recognize that you are a sinner.

The need for repentance is not something newly added starting in the New Testament; Scripture is clear all the way back in Genesis and throughout the Old Testament dispensation (including the Jews under the Mosaic Law) about the need for man to repent of his sins in order to be reconciled with God. If you are turning to Christ, you must also turn away from sin; you cannot do one without the other. This is the step being performed here – initial repentance recognizing and acknowledging that you are a sinner and that you want to change your ways.

You have already read extensively in this book about how we are all sinners. Sins come in many forms, from the most obvious ones such as murder, theft, lying, and so forth, but also in less obvious forms such as gossiping, slander, idol worship, coveting, cheating in business dealings, and even failing to do something that you know you should have done (sins of omission). So, be honest with yourself, have you ever done any of these? Even just one single time? In your entire life? I think any honest person will admit that he or she has. Also, recognize that even the smallest sin is great in the sight of a holy and just God. God's holiness is not something to be trifled with; it is His character. We humans tend to horribly underestimate the holiness of God and rationalize that our sins must not be "that bad" and therefore not worthy of death and judgment. However, the Bible is clear that all sin is worthy of and punishable by death.

It is not what we think on the matter which is important – it is what Scripture tells us God thinks on the matter that counts.

At this point, do not worry or wonder how you will ever possibly be able to beat an addiction that you are trapped in (if you currently are) or worry that your sins are too great to be forgiven, for Jesus is The Great Physician and Healer. He offers life and forgiveness to all who come to Him, to all who call on His holy name. I know this firsthand from personal experience; I lived the addiction life. When I truly and finally turned my life over to Christ, things changed – the addiction was banished.

The Bible tells us that "all things are possible" with God. Or in other words, nothing is impossible with God. For He is not a small God, He is a big God – Creator of Heaven and Earth, yes, of all the universe, which He simply "spoke" into existence! Amazing! Imagine the unbelievable awesome power in such a Being! He knows what you've done and what you may be facing, and He wants you to come to Him now, today, just as you are! He already knows everything; nothing is hidden and kept secret from God. You will be amazed at what He can do in your life when you place your faith and trust in Him. The Bible is full of examples of men who were once murderers, who then gave their lives over to God and to Christ: people such as Moses, King David, and the apostle Paul. Scripture is full of amazing things that these people did subsequently in their lives – and they became men of solid character, courage, and strength all through the power of Christ living in them.

In this chapter, we are dealing specifically with the initial repentance you do as part of being born again. But also realize, once born again, a Christian continues in (ongoing daily) repentance over their lifetime with the avoidance of deliberate and continued sinful behavior and actions. None of us will be perfect and never commit sin; that is not what repentance is indicating. It's indicating a sincere desire and deliberate, willed choice to not participate in sinful actions and behavior. We are not to live under bondage to sin any longer, as a slave to sin and the flesh, carrying out its desires. We will still slip and stumble at times; that is normal. Just get back up, dust yourself off, confess and repent of the recent sin, learn from it and then continue walking towards Christ Jesus every single day, pressing even harder into Him if needed! If you confess your sins, the Bible says that "He is faithful and righteous to forgive us our sins and to cleanse us from all unrighteousness." Remember, you are not going to be doing this by your own "will-power"; you are doing it through His divine strength and might – by the power of Christ who "lives in you." No matter what you have done or struggle with at this very moment, the power of Christ will enable you to overcome it.

As your walk as a Christian deepens and matures, you will find that your old sinful actions and behaviors lessen over time as you become more "sanctified" (set apart for God and progressively conformed to the image of Christ). You no longer <u>want</u> to do those sins you used to do. Additionally, as you become a mature Christian, your awareness of sin becomes heightened. You start to realize how holy God really is, and you also start to see how your old sinful fleshly nature clashes with the new spirit in you. That is normal and to be expected. The Apostle Paul wrote about his own battles between his old and new natures. I talk more about this in the Living in the Spirit chapter.

You will also learn in subsequent chapters how to develop healthy God-fearing Christian habits and behaviors and learn how to fight off (spiritual) attacks of the enemy (Satan), who will try to turn you back into sin, the ways of this world, and back towards death. The spiritual forces of evil are very real; do not underestimate your enemy! He will try everything possible, even things you are not consciously aware of, to turn you away from Christ and eternal life. The path forward is not always easy, and sometimes victories are won after hard-fought battles, but it is possible to overcome any sin (or addiction) through the power of Christ living in you. Repent of your sins and place your trust in Jesus!

FALSE TEACHING(S) YOU WILL ENCOUNTER:

- The doctrine of "Original Sin"
- Saying a "Sinner's Prayer" saves you
- You get a "2nd Chance" after death
- A Christian no longer sins

RELATED SCRIPTURE:

Create in me a clean heart, O God,
And renew a steadfast spirit within me.
Do not cast me away from Your presence
And do not take Your Holy Spirit from me.
Restore to me the joy of Your salvation
And sustain me with a willing spirit.
Then I will teach transgressors Your ways,
And sinners will be converted to You.

Deliver me from bloodguiltiness, O God, the God of my salvation;
Then my tongue will joyfully sing of Your righteousness.
O Lord, open my lips,
That my mouth may declare Your praise.
For You do not delight in sacrifice, otherwise I would give it;
You are not pleased with burnt offering.
The sacrifices of God are a broken spirit;
A broken and a contrite heart, O God, You will not despise. – Psalm 51:10-17

Therefore if anyone is in Christ, *he is* a new creature; the old things passed away; behold, new things have come. Now all *these* things are from God, who reconciled us to Himself through Christ and gave us the ministry of reconciliation, namely, that God was in Christ reconciling the world to Himself, not counting their trespasses against them, and He has committed to us the word of reconciliation. – 2 Corinthians 5:17-19

…the Lord knows how to rescue the godly from temptation, and to keep the unrighteous under punishment for the day of judgment. – 2 Peter 2:9

As far as the east is from the west,
So far has He removed our transgressions from us. – Psalm 103:12

For if we go on sinning willfully after receiving the knowledge of the truth, there no longer remains a sacrifice for sins, but a terrifying expectation of judgment and THE FURY OF A FIRE WHICH WILL CONSUME THE ADVERSARIES. – Hebrews 10:26-27

3.3 CONFESS CHRIST

If you confess with your mouth Jesus as Lord, and believe in your heart that God raised Him from the dead, you will be saved; for with the heart a person believes resulting in righteousness, and with the mouth he confesses, resulting in salvation.
– Romans 10:9-10

Confess Jesus as Lord and Savior. We have seen that coming to faith (believing) in Jesus Christ and repentance from sins is necessary to be born again of the Spirit of God. Additionally, Scripture teaches that verbalizing (i.e., speaking, confessing) Christ publicly as your Lord and Savior is also necessary:

> If you confess with your mouth Jesus as Lord, and believe in your heart that God raised Him from the dead, you will be saved; for with the heart a person believes, resulting in righteousness, and with the mouth he confesses, resulting in salvation. – Romans 10:9-10
>
> He said to them, "But who do you say that I am?" Simon Peter answered, "You are the Christ, the Son of the living God." – Matthew 16:15-16
>
> "And I say to you, everyone who confesses Me before men, the Son of Man will confess him also before the angels of God." – Luke 12:8
>
> For I am not ashamed of the gospel, for it is the power of God for salvation to everyone who believes, to the Jew first and also to the Greek. For in it the righteousness of God is revealed from faith to faith; as it is written, "BUT THE RIGHTEOUS *man* SHALL LIVE BY FAITH." – Romans 1:16-17
>
> Whoever denies the Son does not have the Father; the one who confesses the Son has the Father also. – 1 John 2:23
>
> "Therefore everyone who confesses Me before men, I will also confess him before My Father who is in heaven. But whoever denies Me before men, I will also deny him before My Father who is in heaven." – Matthew 10:32-33

The steps of belief, repentance, and confession are intimately related and may be nearly simultaneous for you, but generally, you believe, repent and then confess in that order. Your confession of Christ should be genuine, real, from the heart, and publicly verbalized. Let's again review what it means to confess Christ. You are making a statement to the effect that you believe all of the following to be true:

1. He is the Christ, the Messiah, the anointed one of God, the Savior,
2. He is God in the flesh (i.e., the Son of God, the Son of Man, God's only begotten Son, fully man but also fully God),
3. He died for your sins on the cross as your Savior – i.e., that His death on the cross was a complete, final, and total substitutionary atonement (sacrifice, payment) for your sins,
4. He rose again (literally) from death to life after three days,
5. He is your Lord and King, to whom you are committing your allegiance and obedience,

6. You are stating a desire and willingness to repent of your sins and to turn your life over to Him in all areas, to trust in Him for all things at all times, and for His will to be done, not yours,
7. He is coming again (literally, physically, visibly in person) to judge all mankind for their deeds (sins) and to get you (literally and physically) to take you where He is, which is in heaven, where He has made a place for you,
8. He will raise you to eternal life

The Bible doesn't prescribe any particular set of words or prepared speech that you must use when confessing Christ. As you can see from the Scripture included in this chapter, the examples we see are actually fairly short, such as "You are the Christ" or "I believe that Jesus Christ is the Son of God." Let your heart guide you. While some may get nervous (stage fright) when speaking in public, a continued avoidance of confessing Jesus publicly and verbally may indicate that your faith and belief are not where they should be. If you are ashamed of Christ, He will be ashamed of you. If you are ashamed of Christ, He will be ashamed of you. If you confess Christ before men, He will confess you before the Father.

In confessing Christ, we are to do so with boldness, courage, honor, strength, and integrity; it is a victorious declaration that we now side with the "King of Kings" and "Lord of Lords," the One "living and true God," our "Rock" and "Our Redeemer," "The Chief Cornerstone," "The Alpha and the Omega," "The Beginning and The End," "The First and the Last," "The Bright and Morning Star," "The Sun of Righteousness," "The Firstborn from the Dead," our "High Priest," the "Spotless Lamb of God," our "Deliverer" from bondage under sin, Satan, and death which have held us captive, the "Son of David," the "Son of Man," and the "Son of God." Amen! We aren't supposed to sneak our way into the "Kingdom of God," we are to boldly proclaim our entrance with courage, confidence, assurance, and with a thankful and grateful heart.

We are proclaiming the Lord Jesus Christ for ourselves and for the whole world to see. We are now joined to the "Lion of the tribe of Judah," the "Almighty God," the "Prince of Peace," and the Creator and Sustainer of all things and all life, who simply "spoke" this universe into existence! We are declaring that sin, Satan, and even death itself have no power over us now or over how we live our lives any longer.

Like a massive tide sweeping over the shore, the gospel "message of truth" is going out across the earth until all nations and tongues have heard it, and there is nothing whatsoever that evil men or the powers of darkness under Satan can do to stop it! We are not afraid – victory has already been assured. We now live in victory with Christ, for He goes before us, comes after us, and surrounds us on all sides in complete support.

After you are born again (which happens at your baptism, see the next chapter!) and begin living as a Christian, you will (hopefully) have many occasions to continue to verbalize and confess your faith in front of others, as a public testimony to help them also come to belief in Christ.

FALSE TEACHING(S) YOU WILL ENCOUNTER:
- Atheism (there is no God)
- Saying a "Sinner's Prayer" saves you
- Universalism (i.e., any name, or any religion, even one you make up, or even no belief at all, can save you to eternal life)
- Ecumenism
- You get a "2nd Chance" after death

RELATED SCRIPTURE:

...sanctify Christ as Lord in your hearts, always *being* ready to make a defense to everyone who asks you to give an account for the hope that is in you, yet with gentleness and reverence. – 1 Peter 3:15

Whoever confesses that Jesus is the Son of God, God abides in him, and he in God. – 1 John 4:15

Jesus said to her, "I am the resurrection and the life; he who believes in Me will live even if he dies, and everyone who lives and believes in Me will never die. Do you believe this?" She said to Him, "Yes, Lord; I have believed that You are the Christ, the Son of God, *even* He who comes into the world." – John 11:25-27

The eunuch answered Philip and said, "Please *tell me*, of whom does the prophet say this? Of himself or of someone else?" Then Philip opened his mouth, and beginning from this Scripture he preached Jesus to him. As they went along the road they came to some water; and the eunuch said, "Look! Water! What prevents me from being baptized?" [And Philip said, "If you believe with all your heart, you may." And he answered and said, "I believe that Jesus Christ is the Son of God."] And he ordered the chariot to stop; and they both went down into the water, Philip as well as the eunuch, and he baptized him. – Acts 8:34-38

For this reason also, God highly exalted Him, and bestowed on Him the name which is above every name, so that at the name of Jesus EVERY KNEE WILL BOW, of those who are in heaven and on earth and under the earth, and that every tongue will confess that Jesus Christ is Lord, to the glory of God the Father. – Philippians 2:9-11

"But for you who fear My name, the sun of righteousness [Jesus] will rise with healing in its wings; and you will go forth and skip about like calves from the stall." – Malachi 4:2

With all prayer and petition pray at all times in the Spirit, and with this in view, be on the alert with all perseverance and petition for all the saints, and *pray* on my behalf, that utterance may be given to me in the opening of my mouth, to make known with boldness the mystery of the gospel, for which I am an ambassador in chains; that in *proclaiming* it I may speak boldly, as I ought to speak. – Ephesians 6:18-20

Therefore do not be ashamed of the testimony of our Lord or of me His prisoner, but join with *me* in suffering for the gospel according to the power of God, who has saved us and called us with a holy calling, not according to our works, but according to His own purpose and grace which was granted us in Christ Jesus from all eternity, but now has been revealed by the appearing of our Savior Christ Jesus, who abolished death and brought life and immortality to light through the gospel. – 2 Timothy 1:8-10

"I am the Alpha and the Omega," says the Lord God, "who is and who was and who is to come, the Almighty." – Revelation 1:8

When I saw Him, I fell at His feet like a dead man. And He placed His right hand on me, saying, "Do not be afraid; I am the first and the last, and the living One; and I was dead, and behold, I am alive forevermore, and I have the keys of death and of Hades." – Revelation 1:17-18

"The Son of God, who has eyes like a flame of fire, and His feet are like burnished bronze…" – Revelation 2:18b

"He who is holy, who is true, who has the key of David, who opens and no one will shut, and who shuts and no one opens…" – Revelation 3:7

"The Amen, the faithful and true Witness, the Beginning of the creation of God…" – Revelation 3:14

"Behold, I am coming quickly, and My reward *is* with Me, to render to every man according to what he has done. I am the Alpha and the Omega, the first and the last, the beginning and the end." – Revelation 22:12-13

3.4 BE BAPTIZED

"He who has believed and has been baptized shall be saved; but he who has disbelieved shall be condemned." – Mark 16:16

Be Baptized for the Forgiveness of Sins. Scripture teaches us that you receive "forgiveness of sins" by the blood of Christ (which cannot be bought or earned through works or any other means) when you are "buried with Him through baptism into death, so that, just as Christ was raised from the dead through the glory of the Father, so we too may walk in newness of life" and raised up "a new creature [person]" in Christ. The act of baptism unites one to Christ, for it is at baptism that one is "born again" and you "receive the Holy Spirit" – i.e., you "put on Christ" at baptism. Prior to baptism, one should have come to an understanding of the "message of truth," come to belief in Christ, repented of their sins, and confessed Christ as their Lord and Savior as discussed in the previous chapters.

The truth of Scripture is clear – the Bible calls for all believers to be baptized by immersion in water "for the forgiveness of sins." You cannot omit the step of baptism and be "born of the Spirit" (i.e., "born again") in accordance with New Testament Scripture. One cannot have "clothed yourself with Christ" without being baptized. You simply cannot negate the force of Scripture:

> For all of you who were baptized into Christ have clothed yourselves with Christ. – Galatians 3:27

> "He who has believed and has been baptized shall be saved; but he who has disbelieved shall be condemned." – Mark 16:16

> Corresponding to that, baptism now saves you—not the removal of dirt from the flesh, but an appeal to God for a good conscience—through the resurrection of Jesus Christ. – 1 Peter 3:21

> Peter *said* to them, "Repent, and each of you be baptized in the name of Jesus Christ for the forgiveness of your sins; and you will receive the gift of the Holy Spirit." – Acts 2:38

> Or do you not know that all of us who have been baptized into Christ Jesus have been baptized into His death? Therefore we have been buried with Him through baptism into death, so that as Christ was raised from the dead through the glory of the Father, so we too might walk in newness of life. For if we have become united with *Him* in the likeness of His death, certainly we shall also be *in the likeness* of His resurrection, knowing this, that our old self was crucified with *Him*, in order that our body of sin might be done away with, so that we would no longer be slaves to sin. – Romans 6:3-6

> "'<u>Now why do you delay</u>? Get up and <u>be baptized, and wash away your sins</u>, calling on His name.'" – Acts 22:16 (my underline)

It is at baptism where you die to your old self (you are "buried with Christ") and are raised up "a new creature [person]" (in Christ). If you were baptized as an infant or by "sprinkling," you should be re-baptized properly by immersion as an adult; such man-invented baptismal rites are not in agreement with Scripture. Wayne Jackson writes:[43]

> The baptismal candidate must be **immersed** in water. That is what the Greek term *baptizo* signifies. One is "buried" with Christ in baptism, and is raised from the water to walk in newness of life (Romans 6:3-4; Colossians 2:12). The practices of pouring water upon the candidate's head, or sprinkling him with water, are innovations that arose in post-apostolic times. There is not the slightest hint of these digressions in the New Testament.
>
> It was centuries before "sprinkling," as a substitute for immersion, became accepted in the community of "Christendom." We dealt with this issue in a recent article on our web site ("Does Archaeology Prove that Baptism May Be Administered by Sprinkling?"), and we recommend this discussion to those who are confused about the "mode" of baptism.

If you profess faith in Christ and have the opportunity and ability to be baptized but choose not to or find reasons (excuses) to keep putting it off and delaying it indefinitely, then you must realize that your faith is not in accord with the instructions given in Scripture. The Scripture passage about the Ethiopian is instructive:

> The [Ethiopian] eunuch answered Philip and said, "Please *tell me*, of whom does the prophet say this? Of himself or of someone else?" Then Philip opened his mouth, and beginning from this Scripture he preached Jesus to him. As they went along the road they came to some water; and the eunuch said, "Look! Water! What prevents me from being baptized?" [And Philip said, "If you believe with all your heart, you may." And he answered and said, "I believe that Jesus Christ is the Son of God."] And he ordered the chariot to stop; and they both went down into the water, Philip as well as the eunuch, and he baptized him. – Acts 8:34-38 (my underline)

> They said, "Believe in the Lord Jesus, and you will be saved, you and your household." And they spoke the word of the Lord to him together with all who were in his house. And he took them that *very* hour of the night and washed their wounds, and underline he was baptized, he and all his *household*. – Acts 16:31-33 (my underline)

Please take note of the immediate response and action of the Ethiopian new believer – getting baptized immediately at the very first site of water. As another example, the scene described above in the Acts 16 passage occurred at midnight – and at "that very hour," they were baptized. Contrast these verses to the widely followed modern-day practice of casually wandering in sometime later (days, weeks, months, or even years!) to get baptized after (supposedly) receiving (and accepting) Jesus as one's Savior.

I cannot think of a single reason why a healthy adult who professes faith in Jesus should decide not to be baptized; the Bible does not indicate that baptism is optional, and you should be baptized as soon as possible, as soon as you have found a worthy church that performs baptisms done in accord with Scripture. A true "Church of Christ" will perform the baptism on the very same day you believe, repent and confess Christ – not days, weeks, months, or even years later as many churches practice today.

---

[43] Jackson, Wayne. "Baptism: Essentials and Nonessentials." *ChristianCourier.com*. Access date: April 29, 2019. https://christiancourier.com/articles/928-baptism-essentials-and-nonessentials

Wayne Jackson writes on this important subject: [44]

"Baptism Is Just a Symbol of Salvation"

A common denominational declaration regarding the purpose of baptism is this: "Baptism is a mere symbol of salvation. It is an outward sign of an inward grace." Frequently 1 Peter 3:21 will be employed in an attempt to prove this assertion. Baptist writer B. H. Carroll, in his discussion of 1 Peter 3:21, declared that baptism "saves us in a figure, not reality" (218). [45]

But there is absolutely **no New Testament support** for this allegation. Consider the following:

First, the Bible plainly teaches that baptism is "for the remission of sins" (Acts 2:38), it is to "wash away your sins" (Acts 22:16), it puts one "into Christ" (Rom. 6:4, Gal. 3:27), etc.

Second, in every New Testament passage where baptism and salvation are mentioned together, baptism always comes **before salvation** (cf. Mk. 16:16; Acts 2:38; 1 Pet. 3:21).

Third, 1 Peter 3:21 does not say that baptism merely saves **figuratively**.

What it does teach is this. Noah and his family were saved **through water**. What does that mean? They were transported by means of water from a world of sin to a cleansed environment. Our salvation is the anti-type ("like-figure" — Greek: antitupos) of that. The anti-type refers to **the reality** that the figure represents. By baptism we are conveyed from the state of guilt to the state of redemption. Robert Stein, Baptist scholar, has recently acknowledged:

"At times salvation is said to come about through baptism. Here once again we can mention 1 Peter 3:21, where baptism is clearly said to save. The only way that we can separate baptism from salvation in this statement is by attributing to the word baptism a meaning different from which it usually bears" (335).

Elsewhere Dr. Stein declares that any attempt to spiritualize the water of 1 Peter 3:21 "drowns in the flood waters mentioned in verse 20!" (330). [46]

"Baptism Is a Work of Human Merit"

Another twist to the foregoing error is the charge that baptism is excluded from the plan of redemption because it is a "work." And since no one is saved by "works" (Eph. 2:9), baptism cannot be a part of our salvation.

Our response is as follows:

First, baptism is a divine command (Acts 10:48) given by the Lord. To classify it as a work of human merit disdained in Ephesians 2:9 is a gross form of wickedness.

Second, if baptism is a work of human merit, then those who receive it, believing that it is "for the remission of sins," have trusted in the wrong Savior and thus remain lost. No one can therefore patronizingly say: "We believe you are wrong on baptism, but we still accept you as brother in Christ." That is nonsense.

---

[44] Jackson, Wayne. "8 Mistaken Ideas About Baptism." *ChristianCourier.com*. Access date: March 17, 2019. https://christiancourier.com/articles/1598-8-mistaken-ideas-about-baptism

[45] Carroll, B. H. 1973. An Interpretation of the English Bible. Vol. 6. Grand Rapids: Baker.

[46] Stein, Robert H. 1990. Difficult Passages in the New Testament. Grand Rapids: Baker.

Third, the New Testament clearly denies that baptism is a work of human merit. Paul declared that we are not saved by **works of human righteousness**, but that we are saved by the **washing of regeneration** — or water baptism (Tit. 3:5). Even Baptist scholar A. T. Robertson admits that the expression "washing of regeneration" is probably a "reference to baptism," though he denies the plain language of the passage that connects the washing with salvation (607). [47]

Simply put, human works of merit and water baptism are not in the same category. When one is raised in baptism, it is a "working of God" (Col. 2:12), not a meritorious act of human effort. …

The Scriptures teach that both faith in Christ (Mk. 16:16) and repentance of sin (Acts 2:38) are conscious acts of obedience which must **precede** the reception of immersion. Baptism is not a **magical ritual** that automatically bestows redemption. It is simply the appointed means by which God cleanses the alien sinner through the blood of his Son. …

"It's Not Necessary to Understand the Purpose of Baptism"

It is becoming increasingly common for some to argue that one's baptism is valid as long as it was done "to obey God," regardless of whether the candidate understood its specific design or not. In other words, it really doesn't matter if someone wasn't baptized "for the remission of sins" (or some equivalent expression) as long as they had a good motive.

We believe this to be a mistaken viewpoint. The following questions put this issue in sharper focus.

If understanding the design of baptism is unnecessary, why is the purpose so frequently attached to the command in the New Testament?

If it is essential to understand that Jesus died "for the remission of sins" (Mt. 26:28), why isn't it necessary to understand that immersion is "for the remission of sins" (Acts 2:38)?

If "obeying God" is the sole intellectual criterion for validating one's baptism, would not virtually everyone who has been immersed be a Christian, since all who submit to baptism do so to obey (certainly not to disobey) the Lord?

Does not obeying "from the heart" (Rom. 6:17) imply that true obedience involves a correct understanding in the heart (cf. Mt. 13:15)?

Conclusion

Baptism is a very serious matter. Every person who truly wants to be well-pleasing to God should carefully consider whether they've been mistaken on this vital issue. The time to make correction is now.

Some, however, still object to baptism being a required component of salvation because it isn't mentioned in all verses related to salvation. Wayne Jackson also writes on this subject: [48]

---

[47] Robertson, A. T. 1931. Word Pictures in the New Testament. Vol. IV. (Nashville: Broadman, 1931).

[48] Jackson, Wayne. "A Dispute About the Purpose of Baptism." *ChristianCourier.com*. Access date: March 17, 2019. https://christiancourier.com/articles/234-dispute-about-the-purpose-of-baptism-a

Baptism Isn't Always Mentioned.

A gracious gentleman acknowledges that we have cited a number of passages which appear to connect baptism with salvation (e.g., Mt. 28:19-20; Mk. 16:16; Acts 2:38; 22:16; Rom. 6:3-4; 1 Cor. 12:13; Gal. 3:27; Eph. 5:26; Tit. 3:5; 1 Pet. 3:21). But he says:

"I'm also familiar with Ephesians 2:8, 'by grace are ye saved…,' and Romans 3:22-27. Nowhere in these passages is baptism mentioned as a requisite to salvation."

(1) While it is true that the passages referenced (Eph. 2:8; Rom. 3:22-27) do not explicitly mention baptism, neither do they contain any allusion to repentance. Are we to assume that repentance is not required for redemption? Surely not.

(2) It is rarely the case that a single context will totally exhaust the biblical material on a particular theme. It is the "sum" of the truth that counts (Psa. 119:160), not an isolated text, that may focus upon a limited point of emphasis.

Acts 2:38 contends for repentance and baptism as "requisites" for "forgiveness," with no specific mention of faith. However, by means of that interpretive rule known as "analogy of faith," belief in the Lord must be implied as well.[49]

And Jason Jackson writes further:

The third principle about New Testament baptism is this: baptism has a biblical purpose. It is to obtain the remission of sins. Peter said, "Repent and be baptized, every one of you, in the name of Jesus Christ, for the remission of your sins" (Acts 2:38).

Likewise, he wrote that baptism now saves you (1 Peter 3:21). He immediately qualified this truth by saying that baptism is not the putting away of the filth of the flesh. There is no scrubbing off of sins – no physical cleansing. There is no inherent power in the water. It is the "appeal to God for a clean conscience by the resurrection of Jesus Christ."

According to the teaching of the New Testament, a penitent believer is saved by the grace of God when he or she has the remission of sins. People have the remission of sins when they are buried with Christ, saved by his blood, having been united with him in his death by baptism (Romans 6:3-4).

Here then are three necessary elements of New Testament baptism:

a. the immersion
b. of a penitent believer
c. for the purpose of obtaining the forgiveness of sins by the grace of God.

Before I conclude, let me bring your attention to an interesting case. Paul met some men in Ephesus who had been baptized. They had been immersed. They had been immersed for the forgiveness of sins; they had been baptized with the baptism of John, which was for the remission of sins (Acts 19:3; cf. Luke 3:3). But they had not realized that the church of Christ had been established, the Holy Spirit having

---

[49] Jackson, Jason. "The Truth on Baptism Should Not Be 'Watered Down'", *ChristianCourier.com*. Access date: March 17, 2019. https://christiancourier.com/articles/1176-truth-on-baptism-should-not-be-watered-down-the

been sent and given. Although they formerly had been immersed for the forgiveness of sins, they were baptized again with the proper knowledge of the truth.

There are so many confusing things being taught on baptism today. I encourage you to read and study the Bible, letting it be your sole guide for what you believe and what you practice (see John 8:32).

You have just now read the truth about baptism as given in New Testament Scripture. Scripture is very clear, simple, and explicit on this, but there are some who teach and preach that one is saved by "faith alone/only" who are also of the opinion that baptism is not a required component of salvation – falsely claiming that it is a "good work" and done therefore solely out of obedience to Christ, not for the forgiveness of sins as Scripture states. Others teach "infant baptism" or "sprinkling" instead of immersion. Since this is such a critical component of salvation, I address false teachings about baptism in more detail in the Beware the Wolves chapter.

I stress in the Beware the Wolves chapter that the practice of taking one particular Bible verse and interpreting it in a way that contradicts other verses is all too common and the genesis of many false teachings. I want to remind you that we must approach God on His terms, not according to our own terms or beliefs about what we think "should" be the way. Scripture tells us that we are to worship the Lord "in spirit and in truth"; this book and chapter have explained to you the truth regarding baptism. One should therefore be baptized in accordance with the truth of Scripture, not the opinions of man.

FALSE TEACHING(S) YOU WILL ENCOUNTER:

- False teachings on baptism
- Saying a "Sinner's Prayer" saves you
- You are saved by "Faith Alone/Only"

RELATED SCRIPTURE:

But when they believed Philip preaching the good news about the kingdom of God and the name of Jesus Christ, they were being baptized, men and women alike. – Acts 8:12

Crispus, the leader of the synagogue, believed in the Lord with all his household, and many of the Corinthians when they heard were believing and being baptized. – Acts 18:8

And he ordered them to be baptized in the name of Jesus Christ. Then they asked him to stay on for a few days. – Acts 10:48

...having been buried with Him in baptism, in which you were also raised up with Him through faith in the working of God, who raised Him from the dead. – Colossians 2:12

Jesus answered and said to him, "Truly, truly, I say to you, unless one is born again he cannot see the kingdom of God."

Nicodemus said to Him, "How can a man be born when he is old? He cannot enter a second time into his mother's womb and be born, can he?" Jesus answered, "Truly, truly, I say to you, unless one is born of water [baptism] and the Spirit he cannot enter into the kingdom of God." – John 3:3-5

For you are all sons of God through faith in Christ Jesus. For all of you who were baptized into Christ have clothed yourselves with Christ. – Galatians 3:26-27

For by one Spirit we were all baptized into one body, whether Jews or Greeks, whether slaves or free, and we were all made to drink of one Spirit. – 1 Corinthians 12:13

"Go therefore and make disciples of all the nations, baptizing them in the name of the Father and the Son and the Holy Spirit, teaching them to observe all that I commanded you; and lo, I am with you always, even to the end of the age." – Matthew 28:19-20

3.5 YOU ARE BORN AGAIN
(You Are Now an Infant in Christ)

Therefore if anyone is in Christ, he is a new creature;
the old things passed away; behold, new things have come. – 2 Corinthians 5:17

WELCOME NEW BROTHER OR SISTER IN CHRIST! It is at this point (after belief, repentance, confession, and baptism) that you have been "born again" – you have "put on" Christ and been raised up "a new creature [person]" in Christ, being "born of the Spirit" in accordance with New Testament Scripture. While you were a captive to sin, Satan and death, you are now a captive to Christ in life, for Jesus has "led captivity captive" and "redeemed" you (purchased you back) from death to life; as the Psalmist says: "He restores my soul."

You have been redeemed from spiritual death to spiritual life and have had your sins forgiven by the blood of Christ; your sins have been removed "as far as the east is from the west." You have also "put on" Christ in righteousness and have been given spotless "clothes of white" to wear and are as a "virgin" again with regards to sin – "Though your sins are as scarlet, They will be as white as snow." So, rejoice greatly; for God Himself, the Creator of all the universe, the God of everything from eternity past to eternity future now has a personal relationship with you through the "one mediator between God and men, the *man* Christ Jesus." You are now reconciled to God by and through the "blood of Christ."

How awesome, staggering and stunning! And not only has God (your "heavenly Father") forgiven your sins, but He also now calls you His friend, and even more, He calls you His own son or daughter as you have been adopted into His very own family! You are now a brother or sister of Christ Jesus Himself, and indeed, you are also now a "fellow heir" with Jesus. Amen and amen!

Being born again, you were also translated into the "Kingdom of God" and are now part of the worldwide body of believers called simply the "Church of God" or the "Church of Christ," who are your brothers and sisters. There is only one worldwide "Church of Christ," founded by Jesus, which has local gatherings in each city (or locale). The many sects and denominations that you see today are not biblical. In fact, Jesus stressed and prayed for unity and not division among His followers. Please also see the chapter on Finding a Church.

YOU ARE AN INFANT IN CHRIST

Remember from an earlier chapter I explained that being born again is only the first step (but by far the most important step) on the path towards final salvation and eternal life with God and His Christ in heaven – it is at final salvation when you receive your "crown of life." Said another way, being "born again" is a necessary but not sufficient condition to receive the gift of eternal life! The way it is often taught and preached in modern, so-called "reformed," liberal (and apostate) "Christian" churches leads many to conclude wrongly that being born again is the only step they ever need to take to gain eternal life, but that is not what the Bible teaches.

As a new believer, you are just an "infant in Christ," a new baby Christian if you will, immature in the faith, and you must "press on to maturity," for it is written:

> My people are destroyed for lack of knowledge. – Hosea 4:6

Therefore My people go into exile [destruction] for their lack of knowledge. – Isaiah 5:13

Therefore leaving the elementary teaching about the Christ, let us press on to maturity, not laying again a foundation of repentance from dead works and of faith toward God, of instruction about washings and laying on of hands, and the resurrection of the dead and eternal judgment. And this we will do, if God permits. For in the case of those who have once been enlightened and have tasted of the heavenly gift and have been made partakers of the Holy Spirit, and have tasted the good word of God and the powers of the age to come, and *then* have fallen away… – Hebrews 6:1-6a

Scripture is very clear that Christ doesn't expect you to remain a baby Christian forever. You must "press on to maturity" by "growing in grace and knowledge [understanding] of the Lord," and you do that by reading and studying Scripture daily. Do not remain ignorant of the full teaching of Scripture; you must know all of what Scripture teaches, for it is written: "the sum of Your word is truth." Your "lack of knowledge" can enable the "ravenous wolves," "vipers," and modern-day "Pharisees" to "lead you astray" and "take you captive" (to their false theology) and still even now turn you out of the "straight and narrow path" to eternal life!

Yes, you must "contend earnestly for the faith that was once for all *time* handed down to the saints" and not be tricked into following "another gospel which is not another" (i.e., the many false teachings of man). If you fail to "press on to maturity," Scripture is clear you are at great risk of "falling away," backsliding, going apostate, or quitting the faith – i.e., turning back from following Christ to return again to your old sinful ways and the ways of this world "like a dog that returns to its vomit."

I hope you are sensing my urgent plea that you continue on, for you are only just starting to "fight the good fight of faith." You see, I also once started out here as you are now, and I fell away, so I know that the risk and the danger are very real. Please, brother or sister in Christ, "press on to maturity" in faith and towards your ultimate goal of eternal life! You have only just now started your Christian journey which actually lasts the rest of your lifetime…and you must not take your salvation for granted. Scripture exhorts us to "work out your salvation with fear and trembling," "be all the more diligent to make certain about His calling and choosing you," and "finish the course [race]." Always remember that we are just "pilgrims" ("sojourner," in "exile," "stranger," "foreigner") here in this world; for the Christian, "our citizenship is in heaven," not here on Earth.

In the next section of this book, we take a much deeper look at the Christian life, "the way" of a Christian (which lasts the rest of your lifetime), so you don't "come short of" your ultimate goal – which is "eternal life" with God and His Christ in heaven. I do not want you to "die in the wilderness" for lack of knowledge and understanding of the complete New Testament plan of salvation and knowing what God expects.

FALSE TEACHING(S) YOU WILL ENCOUNTER:
- Universalism (i.e., any name, or any religion, even one you make up, or even no belief at all, can save you to eternal life)
- False teachings on baptism
- Saying a "Sinner's Prayer" saves you

The Message of Truth

- You are saved by "Faith Alone/Only"
- Once saved always saved
- A Christian no longer sins

RELATED SCRIPTURE:

...for you have been born again not of seed which is perishable but imperishable, *that is*, through the living and enduring word of God. – 1 Peter 1:23

Blessed be the God and Father of our Lord Jesus Christ, who according to His great mercy has caused us to be born again to a living hope through the resurrection of Jesus Christ from the dead, to *obtain* an inheritance *which is* imperishable and undefiled and will not fade away, reserved in heaven for you, who are protected by the power of God through faith for a salvation ready to be revealed in the last time. In this you greatly rejoice, even though now for a little while, if necessary, you have been distressed by various trials, so that the proof of your faith, *being* more precious than gold which is perishable, even though tested by fire, may be found to result in praise and glory and honor at the revelation of Jesus Christ; and though you have not seen Him, you love Him, and though you do not see Him now, but believe in Him, you greatly rejoice with joy inexpressible and full of glory, obtaining as the outcome of your faith the salvation of your souls. – 1 Peter 1:3-9

"I have been crucified with Christ; and it is no longer I who live, but Christ lives in me; and the *life* which I now live in the flesh I live by faith in the Son of God, who loved me and gave Himself up for me." – Galatians 2:20

...knowing that you were not redeemed with perishable things like silver or gold from your futile way of life inherited from your forefathers, but with precious blood, as of a lamb unblemished and spotless, *the blood* of Christ. – 1 Peter 1:18-19

Therefore if anyone is in Christ, *he is* a new creature; the old things passed away; behold, new things have come. Now all *these* things are from God, who reconciled us to Himself through Christ and gave us the ministry of reconciliation, namely, that God was in Christ reconciling the world to Himself, not counting their trespasses against them, and He has committed to us the word of reconciliation. – 2 Corinthians 5:17-19

When you were dead in your transgressions and the uncircumcision of your flesh, He [Jesus] made you alive together with Him, having forgiven us all our transgressions, having canceled out the certificate of debt consisting of decrees against us, which was hostile to us; and He has taken it out of the way, having nailed it to the cross. When He had disarmed the rulers and authorities, He made a public display of them, having triumphed over them through Him. – Colossians 2:13-15

Grace to you and peace from God our Father and the Lord Jesus Christ, who gave Himself for our sins so that He might rescue us from this present evil age, according to the will of our God and Father, to whom be the glory forevermore. Amen. – Galatians 1:3-5

For this reason also, since the day we heard *of it*, we have not ceased to pray for you and to ask that you may be filled with the knowledge of His will in all spiritual wisdom and understanding, so that you will walk in a manner worthy of the Lord, to please *Him* in all respects, bearing fruit in every good work and increasing in the knowledge of God; strengthened with all power, according to His glorious might, for the attaining of all steadfastness and patience; joyously giving thanks to the Father, who has qualified us to share in the inheritance of the saints in Light.

For He rescued us from the domain of darkness, and transferred us to the kingdom of His beloved Son, in whom we have redemption, the forgiveness of sins. – Colossians 1:9-14

"I have wiped out your transgressions like a thick cloud,
And your sins like a heavy mist.
Return to Me, for I have redeemed you." – Isaiah 44:22

The LORD is compassionate and gracious,
Slow to anger and abounding in lovingkindness.
He will not always strive *with us*,
Nor will He keep *His anger* forever.
He has not dealt with us according to our sins,
Nor rewarded us according to our iniquities.
For as high as the heavens are above the earth,
So great is His lovingkindness toward those who fear Him.
As far as the east is from the west,
So far has He removed our transgressions [sins] from us. – Psalm 103:8-12

"FOR I WILL BE MERCIFUL TO THEIR INIQUITIES,
AND I WILL REMEMBER THEIR SINS NO MORE." – Hebrews 8:12

Blessed *be* the God and Father of our Lord Jesus Christ, who has blessed us with every spiritual blessing in the heavenly *places* in Christ, just as He chose us in Him before the foundation of the world, that we would be holy and blameless before Him. In love He predestined us to adoption as sons through Jesus Christ to Himself, according to the kind intention of His will, to the praise of the glory of His grace, which He freely bestowed on us in the Beloved. In Him we have redemption through His blood, the forgiveness of our trespasses, according to the riches of His grace which He lavished on us. In all wisdom and insight He made known to us the mystery of His will, according to His kind intention which He purposed in Him with a view to an administration suitable to the fullness of the times, *that is*, the summing up of all things in Christ, things in the heavens and things on the earth. In Him also we have obtained an inheritance, having been predestined according to His purpose who works all things after the counsel of His will, to the end that we who were the first to hope in Christ would be to the praise of His glory. In Him, you also, after listening to the message of truth, the gospel of your salvation—having also believed, you were sealed in Him with the Holy Spirit of promise, who is given as a pledge of our inheritance, with a view to the redemption of *God's own* possession, to the praise of His glory. – Ephesians 1:3-14

But thanks be to God that though you were slaves of sin, you became obedient from the heart to that form of teaching to which you were committed, and having been freed from sin, you became slaves of righteousness. – Romans 6:17-18

See how great a love the Father has bestowed on us, that we would be called children of God; and *such* we are. For this reason the world does not know us, because it did not know Him. Beloved, now we are children of God, and it has not appeared as yet what we will be. We know that when He appears, we will be like Him, because we will see

Him just as He is. And everyone who has this hope *fixed* on Him purifies himself, just as He is pure. – 1 John 3:1-3

But as many as received Him, to them He gave the right to become children of God, *even* to those who believe in His name, who were born, not of blood nor of the will of the flesh nor of the will of man, but of God. – John 1:12-13

But you are A CHOSEN RACE, A royal PRIESTHOOD, A HOLY NATION, A PEOPLE FOR *God's* OWN POSSESSION, so that you may proclaim the excellencies of Him who has called you out of darkness into His marvelous light; for you once were NOT A PEOPLE, but now you are THE PEOPLE OF GOD; you had NOT RECEIVED MERCY, but now you have RECEIVED MERCY. – 1 Peter 2:9-10

For even as the body is one and *yet* has many members, and all the members of the body, though they are many, are one body, so also is Christ. For by one Spirit we were all baptized into one body, whether Jews or Greeks, whether slaves or free, and we were all made to drink of one Spirit.

For the body is not one member, but many. If the foot says, "Because I am not a hand, I am not *a part* of the body," it is not for this reason any the less *a part* of the body. And if the ear says, "Because I am not an eye, I am not *a part* of the body," it is not for this reason any the less *a part* of the body. If the whole body were an eye, where would the hearing be? If the whole were hearing, where would the sense of smell be? But now God has placed the members, each one of them, in the body, just as He desired. If they were all one member, where would the body be? But now there are many members, but one body. And the eye cannot say to the hand, "I have no need of you"; or again the head to the feet, "I have no need of you." On the contrary, it is much truer that the members of the body which seem to be weaker are necessary; and those *members* of the body which we deem less honorable, on these we bestow more abundant honor, and our less presentable members become much more presentable, whereas our more presentable members have no need *of it*. But God has *so* composed the body, giving more abundant honor to that *member* which lacked, so that there may be no division in the body, but *that* the members may have the same care for one another. And if one member suffers, all the members suffer with it; if *one* member is honored, all the members rejoice with it.

Now you are Christ's body, and individually members of it. – 1 Corinthians 12:12-27

So then, my beloved, just as you have always obeyed, not as in my presence only, but now much more in my absence, work out your salvation with fear and trembling; for it is God who is at work in you, both to will and to work for *His* good pleasure. – Philippians 2:12-13

Simon Peter, a bond-servant and apostle of Jesus Christ,

To those who have received a faith of the same kind as ours, by the righteousness of our God and Savior, Jesus Christ: Grace and peace be multiplied to you in the knowledge of God and of Jesus our Lord; seeing that His divine power has granted to us everything pertaining to life and godliness, through the true knowledge of Him who called us by His own glory and excellence. For by these He has granted to us His precious and magnificent promises, so that by them you may become partakers of *the* divine nature, having escaped the corruption that is in the world by lust. Now for this very reason also, applying all diligence, in your faith supply moral excellence, and in *your* moral excellence, knowledge, and in *your* knowledge, self-control, and in *your* self-control, perseverance, and in *your* perseverance, godliness, and in *your* godliness, brotherly kindness, and in *your* brotherly kindness, love. For if these *qualities* are yours and are increasing, they render you neither useless nor unfruitful in the true knowledge of our Lord Jesus Christ. For he who lacks these *qualities* is blind *or* short-sighted, having forgotten *his* purification from his former sins. Therefore, brethren, be all the more diligent to make certain about His calling and choosing you; for as long as you practice these things, you will never stumble; for in this way the entrance into the eternal kingdom of our Lord and Savior Jesus Christ will be abundantly supplied to you. – 2 Peter 1:1-11

Concerning him we have much to say, and *it is* hard to explain, since you have become dull of hearing. For though by this time you ought to be teachers, you have need again for someone to teach you the elementary principles of the oracles of God, and you have come to need milk and not solid food. For everyone who partakes *only* of milk is not accustomed to the word of righteousness, for he is an infant. But solid food is for the mature, who because of practice have their senses trained to discern good and evil. – Hebrews 5:11-14

…be diligent to be found by Him in peace, spotless and blameless, and regard the patience of our Lord *as* salvation; just as also our beloved brother Paul, according to the wisdom given him, wrote to you, as also in all *his* letters, speaking in them of these things, in which are some things hard to understand, which the untaught and unstable distort, as *they do* also the rest of the Scriptures, to their own destruction. You therefore, beloved, knowing this beforehand, be on your guard so that you are not carried away by the error of unprincipled men and fall from your own steadfastness, but grow in the grace and knowledge of our Lord and Savior Jesus Christ. To Him *be* the glory, both now and to the day of eternity. Amen. – 2 Peter 3:14-18

"Abide in Me, and I in you. As the branch cannot bear fruit of itself unless it abides in the vine, so neither *can* you unless you abide in Me." – John 15:4

Therefore, being always of good courage, and knowing that while we are at home in the body we are absent from the Lord— for we walk by faith, not by sight. – 2 Corinthians 5:6-7

For our citizenship is in heaven, from which also we eagerly wait for a Savior, the Lord Jesus Christ; who will transform the body of our humble state into conformity with the body of His glory, by the exertion of the power that He has even to subject all things to Himself. – Philippians 3:20-21

Therefore, brethren, be all the more diligent to make certain about His calling and choosing you; for as long as you practice these things, you will never stumble; for in this way the entrance into the eternal kingdom of our Lord and Savior Jesus Christ will be abundantly supplied to you. – 2 Peter 1:10-11

I have fought the good fight, I have finished the course [race], I have kept the faith; in the future there is laid up for me the crown of righteousness, which the Lord, the righteous Judge, will award to me on that day; and not only to me, but also to all who have loved His appearing. – 2 Timothy 4:7-8

The Message of Truth

Blessed is a man who perseveres under trial; for once he has been approved, he will receive the crown of life which *the Lord* has promised to those who love Him. – James 1:12

But put on the Lord Jesus Christ, and make no provision for the flesh in regard to *its* lusts. – Romans 13:14

Therefore it says,

> "WHEN HE ASCENDED ON HIGH,
> HE LED CAPTIVE A HOST OF CAPTIVES,
> AND HE GAVE GIFTS TO MEN." – Ephesians 4:8

"Wash yourselves, make yourselves clean…
Though your sins are as scarlet,
They will be as white as snow." – Isaiah 1:16,18

Beloved, while I was making every effort to write you about our common salvation, I felt the necessity to write to you appealing that you contend earnestly for the faith that was once for all *time* handed down to the saints. For certain people have crept in unnoticed, those who were long beforehand marked out for this condemnation, ungodly persons who turn the grace of our God into indecent behavior and deny our only Master and Lord, Jesus Christ. – Jude 1:3-4

Fight the good fight of faith; take hold of the eternal life to which you were called, and you made the good confession in the presence of many witnesses. I charge you in the presence of God, who gives life to all things, and of Christ Jesus, who testified the good confession before Pontius Pilate, that you keep the commandment without stain or reproach until the appearing of our Lord Jesus Christ. – 1 Timothy 6:12-14

For our citizenship is in heaven, from which also we eagerly wait for a Savior, the Lord Jesus Christ; who will transform the body of our humble state into conformity with the body of His glory, by the exertion of the power that He has even to subject all things to Himself. – Philippians 3:20-21

…be diligent to be found by Him in peace, spotless and blameless, and regard the patience of our Lord *as* salvation; just as also our beloved brother Paul, according to the wisdom given him, wrote to you, as also in all *his* letters, speaking in them of these things, in which are some things hard to understand, which the untaught and unstable distort, as *they do* also the rest of the Scriptures, to their own destruction. You therefore, beloved, knowing this beforehand, be on your guard so that you are not carried away by the error of unprincipled men and fall from your own steadfastness, but grow in the grace and knowledge of our Lord and Savior Jesus Christ. To Him *be* the glory, both now and to the day of eternity. Amen. – 2 Peter 3:14-18

PART IV:

THE WAY OF A CHRISTIAN

(Living in the Spirit,
Obedience, The Role of Works,
Persevering in Faith)

4.0 WALKING IN THE WAY
(Taking Up Your Cross Daily)

And He was saying to them all, "If anyone wishes to come after Me, he must deny himself, and take up his cross daily and follow Me." – Luke 9:23

Taking Up Your Cross Daily. Again, I say welcome new brother or sister in Christ! You have been "born again" ("born of the Spirit"), and Christ now "abides in you," and you "in Him." You have been "redeemed" from death to life, "buried with Him through baptism" and "raised with Christ" to "new life"; your sins have been forgiven "as far as the east is from the west" through the blood of Christ on the cross. Amen!

But fully understand that your ultimate goal is not simply to be born again – it is eternal life with God and His Christ Jesus in heaven! You are just now starting your Christian journey, which will continue for the rest of your lifetime. This section of the book prepares you for that pilgrimage, so you do not "come short of" eternal life:

> Therefore, let us fear if, while a promise remains of entering His rest, any one of you may seem to have come short of it. – Hebrews 4:1

Much of the material in this chapter has been covered already, but it is summarized again here so you have it in one place. Like The Path to Eternal Life chapter provided a high-level map for the New Testament plan of salvation, this chapter provides a similar map for your Christian pilgrimage.

SALVATION IS A PROCESS, NOT A ONE-TIME EVENT

I first want to review the nature of salvation more fully to set a solid foundation on which to proceed. Eternal salvation doesn't occur in an instant, nor is it a one-time event or prayer; it is a continually progressive process (called sanctification) that starts at the moment you are born again (initial salvation, forgiveness of sins) but continues throughout the life of a Christian as they walk with the Lord, and doesn't complete until one receives their "crown of life" (final eternal salvation) – which is awarded to you on the great Day of Judgment by Jesus. The term sanctified means to be set apart for the Lord, being made to conform more and more to the image of Christ. God is still "at work in you" and will be for the rest of your life. True Christianity is a way of life until death.

Being "born again" is just the first, but by far the most important, step on the road to eternal (final) salvation; said differently, being born again is a necessary but not sufficient requirement for eternal salvation. Scripture is clear that "obedience," action (i.e., "good works," "bearing fruit" for the Lord), and "persevering" in faith are all required to obtain eternal salvation. Eternal salvation consists of all of these elements:

1. Being "born [again] of the Spirit": you have already taken this step,
2. Submission to the will of God through "obedience" to the "commandments" of Christ as given in the New Testament (not the Old Testament Mosaic Law): this is also called "dying to self" and "taking up your cross daily," for it is no longer you that lives, but Christ in you. You are now seeking God's "will be done," not your own will,
3. "Abounding in the work of the Lord" ("bearing fruit"): For if you do not act on your faith, it will neither justify you before God nor save you to eternal life.

Genuine saving faith will naturally result in "good works" for the Lord. Those who only profess faith have what the Bible calls a "dead" faith, for "faith without works is dead," and
4. "Finishing the race": "persevering" in faith unto death (remaining faithful)

You cannot omit any of those components and meet the Bible's criteria for being saved to eternal life. Please know that this list isn't something I made up – it is the truth of what is expressly stated in Scripture. Each of the above topics is covered in more detail in subsequent chapters.

Now you will hear many say they are "saved." However, recognize that people mean different things when they say that. Some mean that they said the "sinner's prayer" once and believe they are saved "by faith alone/only" (all the way to eternal life) regardless of how they live the rest of their life – in obedience to Christ or not. I have explained that both are false teachings. Wayne Jackson explains how the words "saved" and "salvation" are used in Scripture:[50]

> The verb "saved" is a perfect tense, suggesting the idea of a past act that results in a present state. Salvation from past sins occurs at the point of one's conversion, and that state abides as long as the child of God walks "in the light" (1 Jn. 1:7).

And further on the nature of salvation:[51]

> When many people hear the term "salvation," they immediately think of something that occurred in their past. Many Protestants believe that salvation was received the instant they expressed a genuine faith in Christ as their personal Savior, and that it never can be forfeited. As we shall notice, these ideas are not accurate.
>
> Let us consider several passages that speak of salvation — from varying "time" vantage points.

Future Salvation

> In the Great Commission, according to Mark's record, Jesus said: "He who believes and is immersed **shall be saved**..." (Mark 16:16). This passage speaks of the sinner who has never known Christ, but who learns of the Lord, believes his gospel, and, based upon penitent faith, is immersed in water.
>
> What is the result? He "shall be saved." The verb is a future tense form, the salvation being contingent upon the obedience specified. It is regrettable that so many repudiate this very clear declaration.
>
> First, the text negates the false notion of "universalism," i.e., the idea that all people will be saved ultimately. Second, it refutes the Calvinistic theory that "election" is "unconditional." Third, as noted already, it contradicts the erroneous idea that salvation is by "faith alone"; rather, "works" [obedience] also are involved in salvation (see James 2:24). [Note: J.H. Thayer described the "works"

---

[50] Jackson, Wayne. "Does the Grace in Ephesians 2:8-9 Exclude Baptism?" *ChristianCourier.com*. Access date: November 8, 2018. https://christiancourier.com/articles/1483-does-the-grace-in-ephesians-2-8-9-exclude-baptism

[51] Jackson, Wayne. "The Word-tenses of Salvation." *ChristianCourier.com*. Access date: November 8, 2018. https://christiancourier.com/articles/1344-word-tenses-of-salvation-the

in James 2 as having to do with "the conduct of men, measured by the standard of religion and righteousness" (Clark, p. 248).[52]]

Past Salvation

Writing from a different time perspective, Paul reminded Titus that as a result of his kindness and mercy, God "**saved us**, through the washing of regeneration and the renewing of the Holy Spirit" (Titus 3:4-5).

The verb here is a past tense form. It refers back to the salvation received when one submitted to the "washing" (baptism – cf. Acts 22:16) of "regeneration," (the new birth – John 3:3-5). This was a result of the "renewing" instruction of the Holy Spirit, operating through the gospel message (Ephesians 6:17). At the point of our baptism, all our past sins were pardoned forever.

Present Salvation

Contrary to the belief of many, the salvation process does not end with our conversion to Christ. One's redemption is not a "done deal" that never can be forfeited. That is the dogma of Calvin, not Christ.

In a letter to the church at Corinth, Paul wrote: "Now I make known unto you, brothers, the gospel which I preached unto you...by which also you **are saved**" (1 Corinthians 15:1-2). The Greek verb rendered "are saved" is a present tense form; literally, "are being saved" (see also 1:18, ASV footnote.). Salvation is a continuous process as we faithfully live the Christian life.

Future Final

Paul once stated that: "our salvation is nearer than when we first believed" (Romans 13:11). Later, he would tell Timothy, "The Lord will deliver me from every evil work, and **will save me** unto his heavenly kingdom" (2 Timothy 4:18). The apostle Peter would speak of Christians "receiving the end [goal] of your faith, even the salvation of your souls" (1 Peter 1:9).

Furthermore, we don't (can't) reach a state of perfect salvation while still in our earthly, fleshly bodies. Wayne Jackson writes:[53]

We are in the kingdom now (Col. 1:13), but there is a more glorious phase to yet be entered (2 Pet. 1:11). We enjoy salvation presently (Mk. 16:16), but there is a greater dimension, a heavenly salvation, to be received at death (2 Tim. 4:18). There is a sense in which we are with Christ now (Mt 18:20; 26:29; 28:20), but there is a more exalted state in which we will be with him ultimately (Phil. 1:23; 2 Cor. 5:8).

PRESS ON TO MATURITY

As a new believer, you are an "infant in Christ," a new baby Christian if you will, immature in the faith. You must continue to "grow in the grace and knowledge of our Lord and Savior Jesus Christ" and "press on to maturity" "like newborn babies, long for the pure milk of the word, so that by it you may grow in respect to salvation," for

---

[52] Thayer, J.J., *Greek-English Lexicon of the New Testament*, Edinburgh: T.&T. Clark, 1958

[53] Jackson, Wayne. "What Is the Morning Star of Revelation 2:28?" *ChristianCourier.com*. Access date: November 8, 2018. https://christiancourier.com/articles/1105-what-is-the-morning-star-of-revelation-2-28

you can still be "tricked" out of your "crown of life" by the "wolves," "vipers," and modern-day "Pharisees" who want to steal your crown by turning you out of the "straight and narrow path" to eternal life.

They will attempt to do so by deceiving you into following the "spirit of error" and the seemingly endless false teachings of man (yes, even after you are born again). And even further, beware that Scripture calls them "ravenous wolves" and "false prophets, who come to you in sheep's clothing," meaning they APPEAR to be true Christians and true Christian churches (they are all dressed up, if you will, to look like Christians, and even use the name of Jesus or Jesus Christ in their church names), but, in fact, they are not adhering to New Testament Scripture, and many even deny the deity of Christ if you look at their statement of faith. They mix some Bible verses together into something that sounds very "biblical" on the surface, but it is not what Scripture teaches.

Also, know that these "wolves" will try every trick "under the sun" to try to turn you away from the truth of Scripture and towards "another gospel which is not another" (i.e., their false teachings). This is why you see false teachings identified all the way throughout this book, from start to finish, and there is an entire section of the book called Beware the Wolves that lists some of the false teachings that are absolutely rampant today and believed by the vast majority of American Christendom. Amazing!

I am trying to warn you about the "snares" (and "doctrines of demons") that you will almost surely encounter. When starting out, a newly born-again Christian is extremely vulnerable to the forces of evil led by Satan and to the deceptions of man. I have explained that these false teachings are "snares" (traps, pitfalls) that are set up to try to stop you at each step along the way to eternal life, and they don't stop even after you are born again. These "snares" are laid out in front of and all around you like a minefield or a maze that you have to navigate; their goal is to try to cause you to stumble and fall, to turn you out of the "straight and narrow" path to eternal life, or to cause you to quit the faith altogether and turn back to this world and its sinful fleshly ways. I'm trying to help you from "falling away" from Christ and back towards the world or be "tricked" out of your "crown of life":

> But the Spirit explicitly says that in later times some will fall away from the faith, paying attention to deceitful spirits and doctrines of demons. – 1 Timothy 4:1

> Therefore, beloved, since you look for these things, be diligent to be found by Him in peace, spotless and blameless, and regard the patience of our Lord *as* salvation; just as also our beloved brother Paul, according to the wisdom given him, wrote to you, as also in all *his* letters, speaking in them of these things, in which are some things hard to understand, which the untaught and unstable distort, as *they do* also the rest of the Scriptures, to their own destruction. You therefore, beloved, knowing this beforehand, be on your guard so that you are not carried away by the error of unprincipled men and fall from your own steadfastness, but grow in the grace and knowledge of our Lord and Savior Jesus Christ. To Him *be* the glory, both now and to the day of eternity. Amen. – 2 Peter 3:14-18

> "Beware of the false prophets, who come to you in sheep's clothing, but inwardly are ravenous wolves. You will know them by their fruits. Grapes are not gathered from thorn *bushes* nor figs from thistles, are they? So every good tree bears good fruit, but the bad tree bears bad fruit. A good tree cannot produce bad fruit, nor can

a bad tree produce good fruit. Every tree that does not bear good fruit is cut down and thrown into the fire. So then, you will know them by their fruits." – Matthew 7:15-20

"Be on guard for yourselves and for all the flock, among which the Holy Spirit has made you overseers, to shepherd the church of God which He purchased with His own blood. I know that after my departure savage wolves will come in among you, not sparing the flock; and from among your own selves men will arise, speaking perverse things, to draw away the disciples after them." – Acts 20:28-30

For the time will come when they will not endure sound doctrine; but *wanting* to have their ears tickled, they will accumulate for themselves teachers in accordance to their own desires, and will turn away their ears from the truth and will turn aside to myths. – 2 Timothy 4:3-4

Beloved, while I was making every effort to write you about our common salvation, I felt the necessity to write to you appealing that you contend earnestly for the faith that was once for all *time* handed down to the saints. For certain people have crept in unnoticed, those who were long beforehand marked out for this condemnation, ungodly persons who turn the grace of our God into indecent behavior and deny our only Master and Lord, Jesus Christ. – Jude 1:3-4

To not be "deceived," you must "grow in the grace and knowledge of our Lord and Savior Jesus Christ" and "contend earnestly for the faith that was once for all *time* handed down to the saints," and to do that, you must know the sum of the truth of Scripture. I strongly recommend reading *The Pilgrim's Progress* by John Bunyan as soon as you can right after this book. It portrays the walk (pilgrimage) of "Christian" from the "City of Destruction" (this world) to that which is to come, the "Heavenly City" (The New Jerusalem, eternal life in heaven). While written as an allegory, the book is chock full of rock-solid biblical truth, and it is also free from the many false teachings that are common today. In particular, you will also note that the "once saved always saved" false teaching, which is of epidemic proportions today, had not infected Christian doctrine, teaching, and publications when the book was written. The book gives great insight into the "way" or "path" or "walk" of a Christian's life. "Christian," the main character in the book, runs across all manner of people (helpful and not so helpful), demons, worldly lures (snares), and false teachings by the "wolves" which try to trip him up, stop him from proceeding, turn him from the "straight and narrow" path to life or get him to quit and turn back towards things of the world. Scripture warns us to take great care "so that no one will take your crown [of life]"; yes, the Bible is clear that others will want to see you stumble and fall again!

You will also see that the esteemed writer of that day aligns with what I'm writing in this book also (or actually vice versa, given that I come after him), perhaps giving you some confidence that what I'm saying herein (on this matter, as well as others) is indeed truth and in accordance with Scripture. Below is a small snippet from *The Pilgrim's Progress* which describes where Christian finally arrives at the gates of the heavenly city itself, New Jerusalem, which is our eternal destination (heavenly, not earthly), and he sees that "that there was a way to hell, even from the gate of heaven":
[54]

---

[54] Bunyan, John. (1678/2018), *The Pilgrim's Progress*, (London/Holy Spirit Prints).

> Now, just as the gates [of the heavenly city] were opened to let in the men [Christian and Faithful at the end of their pilgrimage to the Holy City], I looked in after them, and behold the city shone like the sun; the streets also were paved with gold; and in them walked many men, with crowns on their heads, palms in their hands, and golden harps, to sing praises withal.
>
> There were also of them that had wings, and they answered one another without intermission, saying, Holy, holy, holy is the Lord.
>
> And after that they shut up the gates; which, when I had seen, I wished myself among them.
>
> Now, while I was gazing upon all these things, I turned my head to look back, and saw Ignorance come up to the river side; but he soon got over, and that without half the difficulty which the other two men met with. For it happened that there was then in that place one Vain-Hope, a ferryman, that with his boat helped him over; so he, as the other I saw, did ascend the hill, to come up to the gate; only he came alone, neither did any man meet him with the least encouragement. When he was come up to the gate, he looked up to the writing that was above, and then began to knock, supposing that entrance should have been quickly administered to him; but he was asked by the men that looked over the top of the gate, Whence come you? and what would you have? He answered, I have ate and drank in the presence of the King, and he has taught in our streets.
>
> Then they asked him for his certificate, that they might go in and show it to the King: so he fumbled in his bosom for one, and found none. Then said they, Have you none? but the man answered never a word. So they told the King, but he would not come down to see him, but commanded the two shining ones, that conducted Christian and Hopeful to the city, to go out and take Ignorance, and bind him hand and foot, and have him away. Then they took him up, and carried him through the air to the door that I saw in the side of the hill, and put him in there. Then I saw that there was a way to hell, even from the gate of heaven, as well as from the City of Destruction.

Yes, a Christian can lose his or her "crown of life" simply through ignorance of the Word of God and sheer neglect. If you fail to "press on to maturity," you are at great risk of "falling away," backsliding, going apostate, or quitting the faith – I know, for I fell away once. I was the "thorny soil," where the Word was choked out by the cares and concerns of this world, and because I had not pressed on into maturity of faith, I didn't even know that it was possible to "fall away" or realize that was happening to me at the time. That I am again walking with Christ now is only due to the unbelievable lovingkindness, mercy, grace, and patience of the Lord, who pursued me and drew me back again. I still don't quite know why He did that, but I've learned my lesson. Perhaps it was so I could help others by having gone through the experience of falling away after having once started out, or maybe it was so I could have the opportunity to write this book to help others avoid the same mistakes I made. Regardless, I'm eternally grateful!

You don't want to find yourself many years into your Christian walk and yet still need to be reminded of the very basics of the faith:

> And I, brethren, could not speak to you as to spiritual men, but as to men of flesh, as to infants in Christ. I gave you milk to drink, not solid food; for you were not yet

able *to receive it*. Indeed, even now you are not yet able, for you are still fleshly. – 1 Corinthians 3:1-3a

Concerning him we have much to say, and *it is* hard to explain, since you have become dull of hearing. For though by this time you ought to be teachers, you have need again for someone to teach you the elementary principles of the oracles of God, and you have come to need milk and not solid food. For everyone who partakes *only* of milk is not accustomed to the word of righteousness, for he is an infant. But solid food is for the mature, who because of practice have their senses trained to discern good and evil. – Hebrews 5:11-14

Therefore leaving the elementary teaching about the Christ, let us press on to maturity, not laying again a foundation of repentance from dead works and of faith toward God, of instruction about washings and laying on of hands, and the resurrection of the dead and eternal judgment. And this we will do, if God permits. For in the case of those who have once been enlightened and have tasted of the heavenly gift and have been made partakers of the Holy Spirit, and have tasted the good word of God and the powers of the age to come, and *then* have fallen away… – Hebrews 6:1-6a

If you don't press on studying and learning Scripture each and every day, you won't know what Christ expects from those who call on His name, and you won't be able to spot a false teaching when you encounter one. And further, if you don't know what Scripture says about what Christ has commanded, how can you be obedient? If you don't know His commandments, how can you do them? And so on…

We must not be ignorant of the complete plan of salvation as given to us by God in Scripture. The Bible does not condone ignorance (see Acts 17:22-32, Romans 4:15, Leviticus 5:17-18, 2 Peter 3:18, 2 Timothy 2:15). The chapters in this section of the book are, therefore, just as important as the prior chapters were on accepting Christ (i.e., being born again). We read:

> Therefore My people go into exile [destruction] for their lack of knowledge;
> And their honorable men are famished,
> And their multitude is parched with thirst.
> Therefore Sheol has enlarged its throat and opened its mouth without measure. – Isaiah 5:13-14a

> My people are destroyed for lack of knowledge. – Hosea 4:6

> Brothers *and sisters*, my heart's desire and my prayer to God for them is for *their* salvation. For I testify about them that they have a zeal for God, but not in accordance with knowledge [i.e., having the correct knowledge and understanding of what is stated in Scripture for salvation]. – Romans 10:1-2

I implore you, brother or sister in Christ, please do not be ignorant of the complete plan of salvation that Scripture actually teaches. We must approach God on His terms, not ours. We must seek and do His will, not ours. And we must "fight the good fight of faith" and "finish the [race] course"! The modern and liberal so-called "Christian" churches of today are not training up their members, or even their pastors, teachers, and elders, to know the complete plan of salvation. It seems to me that the Christian evangelical world spends 99% of its time, money, and effort in preaching on how one is to be born again and almost nothing thereafter on how to train you up properly in the way of a Christian. Wayne Jackson writes:[55]

> **Christianity: A Religion of Learning**
>
> Christianity is a religion of instruction. Where there is no solid biblical instruction, the Christian system can neither commence nor continue.
>
> One of the basic differences between the Mosaic regime (into which one was born physically) and the church of Jesus Christ, is the fact that knowledge is **prerequisite** to identifying with the faith of the gospel (Jer. 31:31-34). Jesus declared that favor with God must involve instruction, reception, comprehension, and commitment (Jn. 6:45).
>
> Anyone with a smattering of Bible knowledge, and any experience at all within our brotherhood, is aware of the fact that the church of today is facing a time of great crisis.
>
> We have those among us who have a pathetically low regard for the concept of Bible inspiration and authority. Not a few have made serious compromises with the dogma of evolution in an effort to mesh with society.
>
> Many of our people are very fuzzy on what constitutes a Christian. They think the church of Christ is but another denomination. A number of prominent personalities contend that there are few guidelines for regulating worship, and so the church must jazz-up its services to appeal to an entertainment-oriented culture. Basic truth has been thrown to the wind.
>
> Why are things in such a state of chaos? One of the reasons is ignorance. There probably has not been a time in this century when Bible knowledge among the Lord's people has sunk to such a base level. Let us be more specific.
>
> **A Crisis of Spiritual Ignorance**
>
> We are suffering a leadership crisis. Where are the **godly elders** who know the Bible from cover to cover? Where are the bishops who can, and will, stand and exhort in sound doctrine and convict the gainsayers (Tit. 1:9).
>
> There are still some great elders, but far too many who are serving in this capacity have been given the job because they were successful businessmen, had wealth, or possessed other traits that were wholly unrelated to **tending the flock of God**.
>
> The church has on its hands a new generation of preachers who have matriculated through some of our schools (or denominational seminaries), but who do not understand the most **elementary matters** about the role of the gospel preacher. They are experts in everything except the Word of God.
>
> These new princes are theological clones who can scarcely frame a sentence that the common man can understand. They know nothing, teach nothing, and stand for nothing—but, unfortunately, numerous people love it this way. It is no longer the case that the **average person** in the pew is a good Bible student. Everyone has probably heard the old story about the judge who couldn't find a

---

[55] Jackson, Wayne. "My People Are Destroyed for a Lack of Knowledge." *ChristianCourier.com*. Access date: June 1, 2019. https://christiancourier.com/articles/771-my-people-are-destroyed-for-a-lack-of-knowledge

Bible in his courtroom with which to swear in a witness. So he simply called for a Christian man and had the witness place his hand upon the brother's head.

The days are gone when God's people were known as a "Bible-toting, Bible-quoting, Bible-living" people. Many members of the church never carry a Bible to worship, and they could not cite scriptural references on the most basic doctrinal issues. Most of our schools are not the solid training centers they used to be. The time was when the presidents and faculty-members of our colleges were great gospel preachers and teachers who knew how to powerfully proclaim the truth and win souls. They were rich in **Bible knowledge**. Many of our current administrators have arrived in their positions because they are adept at fund-raising.

Too, we have become so "degree" oriented that we have allowed the secular accrediting systems to structure our teaching programs according to **their ideals**. Many labor under the illusion that one cannot be an effective herald of the gospel unless he has at least a Master's degree. Is it any wonder that some of our schools have become the Trojan horse by which corruption has wormed its way into the church?

MAKE OUR CALLING AND ELECTION SURE

Next, we are strongly and repeatedly exhorted not to take our eternal final salvation lightly or for granted:

- "Make your calling and election sure" (2 Peter 1:10 KJV),
- "Work out your salvation with fear and trembling" (Philippians 2:12),
- "Be all the more diligent to make certain about His calling and choosing you" (2 Peter 1:10),
- "Be diligent to be found by Him in peace, spotless and blameless," i.e., when you meet Christ – which happens either at our death or His return, whichever comes first (2 Peter 3:14),
- "Test yourselves to see if you are in the faith; examine yourselves!" (2 Corinthians 13:5),
- "Press on toward the goal for the prize of the upward call of God in Christ Jesus" (Philippians 3:14),
- "Fight the good fight of faith; take hold of the eternal life to which you were called" (1 Timothy 6:12),
- Make sure you "will not be disqualified" (1 Corinthians 9:27),
- "Finish the course…keep the faith" (2 Timothy 4:7), for
- "In the future there is laid up for me the crown of righteousness, which the Lord, the righteous Judge, will award to me on that day [the Great Day of Judgment]" (2 Timothy 4:8)

These verses involve several different aspects, but the central theme is that we must do our utmost to be serious, attentive, and determined to make sure that we are always on the path to eternal salvation! The great Apostle Paul wrote on this very topic where he indicates that even he had not yet obtained it [final salvation, eternal life], despite all the things he had already done (including hearing the gospel directly from Jesus!):

Not that I have already obtained *it* [salvation] or have already become perfect, but I press on so that I may lay hold of that for which also I was laid hold of by Christ

Jesus. Brethren, I do not regard myself as having laid hold of *it* yet; but one thing *I do*: forgetting what *lies* behind and reaching forward to what *lies* ahead, I press on toward the goal for the prize of the upward call of God in Christ Jesus. – Philippians 3:12-14

Paul then further writes about not being "disqualified" (even after having started out):

Everyone who competes in the games exercises self-control in all things. They then *do it* to receive a perishable wreath, but we an imperishable. Therefore I run in such a way, as not without aim; I box in such a way, as not beating the air; but I discipline my body and make it my slave, so that, after I have preached to others, I myself will not be disqualified. - 1 Corinthians 9:25-27

And if Paul could have been disqualified, how much more you and I! This is why Scripture warns us to:

So then, my beloved, just as you have always obeyed, not as in my presence only, but now much more in my absence, work out your salvation with fear and trembling; for it is God who is at work in you, both to will and to work for *His* good pleasure. – Philippians 2:12-13

Therefore, brethren, be all the more diligent to make certain about His calling and choosing you; for as long as you practice these things, you will never stumble. – 2 Peter 1:10

Matthew Henry writes on Philippians 2:12-13:[56]

I. He exhorts them to diligence and seriousness in the Christian course: *Work out your own salvation.* It is the salvation of our souls (1 Pet 1:9), and our eternal salvation (Heb 5:9), and contains deliverance from all the evils sin had brought upon us and exposed us to, and the possession of all good and whatsoever is necessary to our complete and final happiness. Observe, It concerns us above all things to secure the welfare of our souls: whatever becomes of other things, let us take care of our best interests. It is our own salvation, the salvation of our own souls. It is not for us to judge other people; we have enough to do to look to ourselves; and, though we must promote the common salvation (Jud 1:3) as much as we can, yet we must upon no account neglect our own.

We are required to *work out our salvation, katergazesthe.* The word signifies *working thoroughly* at a thing, and taking *true pains.* Observe, We must be diligent in the use of all the means which conduce to our salvation. We must not only work at our salvation, by doing something now and then about it; but we must work out our salvation, by doing all that is to be done, and persevering therein to the end. Salvation is the great thing we should mind, and set our hearts upon; and we cannot attain salvation without the utmost care and diligence. He adds, *With fear and trembling,* that is, with great care and circumspection: "Trembling for fear lest you miscarry and come short. Be careful to do every thing in religion in the best manner, and fear lest under all your advantages you should so much as *seem to come short,"* Heb 4:1. Fear is a great guard and preservative from evil.

---

[56] Henry, Matthew. *Exposition of the Old and New* Testaments, London. 1706-1710/1721.

II. He urges this from the consideration of their readiness always to obey the gospel: *"As you have always obeyed, not as in my presence only, but now much more in my absence"* Php 2:12. You have been always willing to comply with every discovery of the will of God; and that in my absence as well as presence. You make it to appear that regard to Christ, and care of your souls, sway more with you than any mode of showing respect whatsoever. They were not merely awed by the apostle's presence, but did it even *much more in his absence.* "And because *it is God who worketh in you,* do you work out your salvation. Work, for he worketh." It should encourage us to do our utmost, because our *labour shall not be in vain.* God is ready to concur with his grace, and assist our faithful endeavours. Observe, Though we must use our utmost endeavours in working out our salvation, yet still we must go forth, and go on, in a dependence upon the grace of God.

His grace works in us in a way suitable to our natures, and in concurrence with our endeavours; and the operations of God's grace in us are so far from excusing, that they are intended to quicken and engage our endeavours. "And work out our salvation *with fear and trembling,* for *he worketh in you.*" All our working depends upon his working in us. "Do not trifle with God by neglects and delays, lest you provoke him to withdraw his help, and all your endeavours prove in vain. Work with *fear,* for he works of his *good pleasure."* - *To will and to do:* he gives the whole ability. It is the grace of God which inclines the will to that which is good: and then enables us to perform it, and to act according to our principles. *Thou hast wrought all our works in us,* Isa 26:12. *Of his good pleasure.* As there is no strength in us, so there is no merit in us. As we cannot act without God's grace, so we cannot claim it, nor pretend to deserve it. God's good will to us is the cause of his good work in us; and he is under no engagements to his creatures, but those of his gracious promise.

As I have stressed, Christianity is a way of life unto death; it is not simply a one-time event or prayer that happens in an instant (i.e., the "sinner's prayer") and it's all done with and over with for the rest of your life, regardless of what you choose to do or not do thereafter. I have explained to you that salvation (present tense verb in the Bible) means all of these: you have been saved, you are being saved, and you will be saved (in the future). Salvation is an ongoing activity throughout the life of a Christian. The life of a Christian involves all of these:

a) Continued faithfulness,
b) Continued repentance (and avoidance of deliberate, willful sin),
c) Continued obedience (to the Word of God, and specifically to the commands of Christ),
d) Continual service ("good works"),
e) Continual reading and studying (eating) of the Word of God so that we "grow in the grace and knowledge" of the Lord,
f) Continual prayer,
g) Continual worship, and
h) Continual thanksgiving

The Bible refers to this as walking in "The Way" of Jesus, for Christ is "the way, and the truth and the life." You now live in ("abide in") Christ, and He lives in ("abides in") you. The way of a Christian only begins when one is born again, and the Christian is then called to "deny himself, and take up his cross daily and follow Me."

I also recommend reading *The Heavenly Footman* by John Bunyan, so you can get another author's perspective on the need to be extremely diligent about ensuring our eternal salvation – for we are not to casually stroll towards it, but run towards it with all attention and seriousness, for our eternal life is at stake. It must be noted that the Lord Jesus even condemned those who had just "lukewarm" faith:

> "To the angel of the church in Laodicea write:
>
> The Amen, the faithful and true Witness, the Beginning of the creation of God, says this:
>
> 'I know your deeds, that you are neither cold nor hot; I wish that you were cold or hot. So because you are lukewarm, and neither hot nor cold, I will spit you out of My mouth. Because you say, "I am rich, and have become wealthy, and have need of nothing," and you do not know that you are wretched and miserable and poor and blind and naked, I advise you to buy from Me gold refined by fire so that you may become rich, and white garments so that you may clothe yourself, and *that* the shame of your nakedness will not be revealed; and eye salve to anoint your eyes so that you may see. Those whom I love, I reprove and discipline; therefore be zealous and repent.'" – Revelation 3:14-19

OBEDIENCE (AND FAITH WITHOUT WORKS IS DEAD)

Additionally, Scripture is abundantly clear that it is not simply enough to profess Christ; you must also live for Him in obedience. Since many of the "commandments" of Christ involve taking action, you can't be an obedient "child of God" without also doing "good works" ("bearing fruit") for the Lord – "prove yourselves doers of the word, and not merely hearers who delude themselves," for "faith without works is dead." Works are evidence of your faith, and your actions (works) serve to prove your faith genuine – both before man and before God. Even further to the point, we are admonished to be found busy (not idle), always "abounding in the work of the Lord" until we die or He returns (whichever comes first).

Christianity is as much about action as it is about the profession of faith. For if you do not act on your faith, your faith will neither justify nor save you to eternal life; it will be what the Bible calls a "dead" faith – and how can a "dead" faith save you to "eternal life"? There are true believers, and there are "make believers" (the "hypocrites," who profess and do not do). But "God is not mocked"; He will sort those out on the Day of Judgment. We are called to "be steadfast, immovable, always abounding in the work of the Lord." It is prudent here to recall the words of Jesus on this subject:

> "If you love Me, you will keep My commandments." – John 14:15

> "Not everyone who says to Me, 'Lord, Lord,' will enter the kingdom of heaven, but he who does the will of My Father who is in heaven *will enter*. Many will say to Me on that day, 'Lord, Lord, did we not prophesy in Your name, and in Your name cast out demons, and in Your name perform many miracles?' And then I will declare to them, 'I never knew you; DEPART FROM ME, YOU WHO PRACTICE LAWLESSNESS.'

"Therefore everyone who hears these words of Mine and acts on them, may be compared to a wise man who built his house on the rock. And the rain fell, and the floods came, and the winds blew and slammed against that house; and *yet* it did not fall, for it had been founded on the rock. Everyone who hears these words of Mine and does not act on them, will be like a foolish man who built his house on the sand. The rain fell, and the floods came, and the winds blew and slammed against that house; and it fell—and great was its fall." – Matthew 7:21-27

And He spoke many things to them in parables, saying, "Behold, the sower went out to sow; and as he sowed, some *seeds* fell beside the road, and the birds came and ate them up. Others fell on the rocky places, where they did not have much soil; and immediately they sprang up, because they had no depth of soil. But when the sun had risen, they were scorched; and because they had no root, they withered away. Others fell among the thorns, and the thorns came up and choked them out. And others fell on the good soil and yielded a crop, some a hundredfold, some sixty, and some thirty. He who has ears, let him hear."… "Hear then the parable of the sower. When anyone hears the word of the kingdom and does not understand it, the evil *one* comes and snatches away what has been sown in his heart. This is the one on whom seed was sown beside the road. The one on whom seed was sown on the rocky places, this is the man who hears the word and immediately receives it with joy; yet he has no *firm* root in himself, but is *only* temporary, and when affliction or persecution arises because of the word, immediately he falls away. And the one on whom seed was sown among the thorns, this is the man who hears the word, and the worry of the world and the deceitfulness of wealth choke the word, and it becomes unfruitful. And the one on whom seed was sown on the good soil, this is the man who hears the word and understands it; who indeed bears fruit and brings forth, some a hundredfold, some sixty, and some thirty." – Matthew 13:3-9,18-23

Only you can determine whether you are "rocky," "thorny," or "good" soil! Only you can determine if you will "press on toward the goal for the prize of the upward call of God in Christ Jesus" and be able to say: "I have fought the good fight, I have finished the course, I have kept the faith; in the future there is laid up for me the crown of righteousness, which the Lord, the righteous Judge, will award to me on that day; and not only to me, but also to all who have loved His appearing." We must always strive to hear "well done, good and faithful servant." To be a servant means to be obedient (to the commands of Christ) and to be an active worker in the "Kingdom of the Lord" (the vineyard). We are not called to idleness or negligence in attending to (keeping, or more accurately, not losing) our salvation.

FIGHT THE GOOD FIGHT OF FAITH

And finally, we must also "persevere" in our faith (remain faithful) until death. Scripture contains repeated warnings that one must "persevere" in faith until death and that one can "fall away" from, "depart" from, turn back, go "apostate," "backslide," or simply quit the faith, even after having once started out (i.e., being born again). Contrary to the extremely widespread and popular false dogma today that a Christian is "once saved always saved" no matter what (see the Beware the Wolves chapter, a.k.a. Calvinism "Perseverance of the Saints"), Scripture is abundantly clear that many will not persevere in faith but will instead "fall-away from the faith." The "once saved always saved" false teaching is in clear contradiction with what is written in Scripture.

Scripture does inform us that the way of a Christian is not always easy. You may be severely tested at times; sadly, many of the saints that have come before us had to seal their faith and testimony in Christ with their own deaths in martyrdom for Christ. Jesus warns us about this:

> "If the world hates you, you know that it has hated Me before *it hated* you. If you were of the world, the world would love its own; but because you are not of the world, but I chose you out of the world, because of this the world hates you." – John 15:18-19

> "Then they will deliver you to tribulation, and will kill you, and you will be hated by all nations because of My name. At that time many will fall away and will betray one another and hate one another. Many false prophets will arise and will mislead many. Because lawlessness is increased, most people's love will grow cold. But the one who endures to the end, he will be saved." – Matthew 24:9-13

> And He was saying to *them* all, "If anyone wishes to come after Me, he must deny himself, and take up his cross daily and follow Me. For whoever wishes to save his life will lose it, but whoever loses his life for My sake, he is the one who will save it. For what is a man profited if he gains the whole world, and loses or forfeits himself? For whoever is ashamed of Me and My words, the Son of Man will be ashamed of him when He comes in His glory, and *the glory* of the Father and of the holy angels." – Luke 9:23-26

In fact, the way of a Christian ("take up his [your] cross and follow Me [Jesus]") has been one of extreme peril down throughout the centuries. Even today, in many parts of the world, a Christian's life is marked by trial, tribulation, and even persecution unto death. Even in the more "enlightened" parts of the world, a Christian can still face mocking, scorn, ridicule, discrimination, and economic sanctions. If you want to get a fuller appreciation of the atrocities committed against Christians over the years, I recommend reading *The Church History* by Eusebius and *Foxe's Book of Martyrs (The Actes and Monuments)*. Doing so will give you a much greater understanding of the persecution that the Christians who have gone before us have endured. Living as a Christian in a fallen world takes courage, strength of character, endurance, and above all, complete trust in the Lord in all things at all times.

When you come to Christ, you are giving Him your life to do with as He pleases; you are now a "bondservant" of Christ, for He bought and paid for you with His blood, having "redeemed" (purchased) you from slavery to sin. Do you think it worthy of sacrificing everything of this world, even your own life, for your eternal soul? Many Christians have had to sacrifice everything, including fame, jobs, power, possessions, friends, family, fortunes, and even their lives for their faith. The apostle Paul writes:

> "For I am ready not only to be bound, but even to die at Jerusalem for the name of the Lord Jesus." And since he would not be persuaded, we fell silent, remarking, "The will of the Lord be done!" – Acts 21:13b-14

> For not one of us lives for himself, and not one dies for himself; for if we live, we live for the Lord, or if we die, we die for the Lord; therefore whether we live or die, we are the Lord's. – Romans 14:7-8

Paul further writes that he had not yet obtained his Crown of Life, that he still presses on towards it, "counting all things to be loss" compared to what is found in Christ:

> But whatever things were gain to me, those things I have counted as loss for the sake of Christ. More than that, I count all things to be loss in view of the surpassing value of knowing Christ Jesus my Lord, for whom I have suffered the loss of all things, and count them but rubbish so that I may gain Christ, and may be found in Him, not having a righteousness of my own derived from *the* Law, but that which is through faith in Christ, the righteousness which *comes* from God on the basis of faith, that I may know Him and the power of His resurrection and the fellowship of His sufferings, being conformed to His death; in order that I may attain to the resurrection from the dead. – Philippians 3:7-11

> Fight the good fight of faith; take hold of the eternal life to which you were called, and you made the good confession in the presence of many witnesses. I charge you in the presence of God, who gives life to all things, and of Christ Jesus, who testified the good confession before Pontius Pilate, that you keep the commandment without stain or reproach until the appearing of our Lord Jesus Christ. – 1 Timothy 6:12-14

Yes, make no mistake, the way of a Christian is often filled with trials and tribulations here in this fallen world, for "through many tribulations we must enter the [future heavenly realm] kingdom of God," and Jesus directly warns us that "you will be hated by all because of My name, but it is the one who has endured to the end who will be saved." If our Lord Jesus was hated, you will also be hated by this world because of Him. But you must "stand firm" in your faith, persevering until death. While it is exceedingly and abundantly clear that Christ will never (ever) "fail you or forsake you," it is equally clear from Scripture that you can decide to quit the faith and quit Him. Scripture tells us to "put on the full armor" of God, so you can fend off the attacks of the enemy (Satan and his forces of evil, including the men who choose to follow him) and also "stand firm" in the faith; this subject is covered more in the upcoming chapters on Persevering in Faith and The Armor of God. You will notice that many of the verses used in this chapter apply to those chapters as well.

But also know that you will be able to persevere in faith through trials and tribulations by the power and strength of Christ "living [abiding] in you." You are not living on your own "will power" and strength any longer; you now "do all things through Him who strengthens me":

> "In the world you have tribulation, but take courage; I have overcome the world." – John 16:33

> Therefore, since we have so great a cloud of witnesses surrounding us, let us also lay aside every encumbrance and the sin which so easily entangles us, and let us run with endurance the race that is set before us, fixing our eyes on Jesus, the author and perfecter of faith, who for the joy set before Him endured the cross, despising

the shame, and has sat down at the right hand of the throne of God. – Hebrews 12:1-2

I have fought the good fight, I have finished the course, I have kept the faith; in the future there is laid up for me the crown of righteousness, which the Lord, the righteous Judge, will award to me on that day; and not only to me, but also to all who have loved His appearing. – 2 Timothy 4:7-8

I can do all things through Him who strengthens me. – Philippians 4:13

"'Not by might nor by power, but by My Spirit,' says the LORD of hosts." – Zechariah 4:6

So, therefore, let us now "press on to maturity," "grow in the grace and knowledge of our Lord and Savior Jesus Christ," "be diligent" about ensuring our final eternal salvation, "be obedient" to the commands of Christ, "always abounding in the work of the Lord," "fight the good fight of faith," and "finish the race"!

FALSE TEACHING(S) YOU WILL ENCOUNTER:
- Saying a "Sinner's Prayer" saves you
- You are saved by "Faith Alone/Only"
- Once saved always saved
- Being born again is the only required step one has to take for eternal life (i.e., obedience, works, and perseverance are not required)
- Roman Catholicism masquerading as Christianity (man can obtain salvation through observing the institutes of religion, i.e., performing ceremonies, sacraments, etc.)
- Universalism (i.e., any name, or any religion, even one you make up, or even no belief at all, can save you to eternal life)
- Calvinism
- Sabbath keeping/legalism (you must observe the "Sabbath" or OT Jewish laws, holidays, etc.)

RELATED SCRIPTURE:

Then Jesus said to His disciples, "If anyone wishes to come after Me, he must deny himself, and take up his cross and follow Me. For whoever wishes to save his life will lose it; but whoever loses his life for My sake will find it." – Matthew 16:24-25

How blessed is the man who does not walk in the counsel of the wicked,
Nor stand in the path of sinners,
Nor sit in the seat of scoffers!
But his delight is in the law of the LORD,
And in His law he meditates day and night.
He will be like a tree *firmly* planted by streams of water,
Which yields its fruit in its season
And its leaf does not wither;
And in whatever he does, he prospers. – Psalm 1:1-3

"If it is disagreeable in your sight to serve the LORD, choose for yourselves today whom you will serve: whether the gods which your fathers served which were beyond the

River, or the gods of the Amorites in whose land you are living; but as for me and my house, we will serve the LORD." – Joshua 24:15

We proclaim Him, admonishing every man and teaching every man with all wisdom, so that we may present every man complete in Christ. For this purpose also I labor, striving according to His power, which mightily works within me. – Colossians 1:28-29

But I am afraid that, as the serpent deceived Eve by his craftiness, your minds will be led astray from the simplicity and purity *of devotion* to Christ. – 2 Corinthians 11:3

"If you love Me, you will keep My commandments." – John 14:15 [Note: This verse is often distorted by those who falsely claim we are still under the Ten Commandments of the Mosaic Law because the word "commandments" is used here. The word commandments here refers to the commands of Christ as given in the New Testament.]

What use is it, my brethren, if someone says he has faith but he has no works? Can that faith save him? If a brother or sister is without clothing and in need of daily food, and one of you says to them, "Go in peace, be warmed and be filled," and yet you do not give them what is necessary for *their* body, what use is that? Even so faith, if it has no works, is dead, *being* by itself. – James 2:14-17

Therefore as you have received Christ Jesus the Lord, *so* walk in Him, having been firmly rooted *and now* being built up in Him and established in your faith, just as you were instructed, *and* overflowing with gratitude.

See to it that no one takes you captive through philosophy and empty deception, according to the tradition of men, according to the elementary principles of the world, rather than according to Christ. – Colossians 2:6-8

Therefore, being always of good courage, and knowing that while we are at home in the body we are absent from the Lord— or we walk by faith, not by sight— we are of good courage, I say, and prefer rather to be absent from the body and to be at home with the Lord. – 2 Corinthians 5:6-8

Blessed is a man who perseveres under trial; for once he has been approved, he will receive the crown of life which *the Lord* has promised to those who love Him. – James 1:12

"'Do not fear what you are about to suffer. Behold, the devil is about to cast some of you into prison, so that you will be tested, and you will have tribulation for ten days. Be faithful until death, and I will give you the crown of life. He who has an ear, let him hear what the Spirit says to the churches. He who overcomes will not be hurt by the second death.'" – Revelation 2:10-11

Be of sober *spirit*, be on the alert. Your adversary, the devil, prowls around like a roaring lion, seeking someone to devour. But resist him, firm in *your* faith, knowing that the same experiences of suffering are being accomplished by your brethren who are in the world. – 1 Peter 5:8-9

Be on the alert, stand firm in the faith, act like men, be strong. Let all that you do be done in love. – 1 Corinthians 16:13-14

"'I am coming quickly; hold fast what you have, so that no one will take your crown.'" – Revelation 3:11

"But I do not consider my life of any account as dear to myself, so that I may finish my course and the ministry which I received from the Lord Jesus, to testify solemnly of the gospel of the grace of God." – Acts 20:24

For as high as the heavens are above the earth,
So great is His lovingkindness toward those who fear Him. – Psalm 103:11

Trust in the LORD with all your heart
And do not lean on your own understanding.
In all your ways acknowledge Him,
And He will make your paths straight. – Proverbs 3:5-6

In the morning, O LORD, You will hear my voice;
In the morning I will order *my prayer* to You and *eagerly* watch. – Psalm 5:3

Rejoice always; pray without ceasing; in everything give thanks; for this is God's will for you in Christ Jesus. – 1 Thessalonians 5:16-18

Therefore we do not lose heart, but though our outer man is decaying, yet our inner man is being renewed day by day. – 2 Corinthians 4:16

The LORD is my shepherd,
I shall not want.
He makes me lie down in green pastures;
He leads me beside quiet waters.
He restores my soul;
He guides me in the paths of righteousness
For His name's sake. – Psalm 23:1-3

"He who loves his life loses it, and he who hates his life in this world will keep it to life eternal. If anyone serves Me, he must follow Me; and where I am, there My servant will be also; if anyone serves Me, the Father will honor him." – John 12:25-26

Finally, be strong in the Lord and in the strength of His might. Put on the full armor of God, so that you will be able to stand firm against the schemes of the devil. For our struggle is not against flesh and blood, but against the rulers, against the powers, against the world forces of this darkness, against the spiritual *forces* of wickedness in the heavenly *places*. Therefore, take up the full armor of God, so that you will be able to resist in the evil day, and having done everything, to stand firm. – Ephesians 6:10-13

The LORD'S lovingkindnesses indeed never cease,
For His compassions never fail.
They are new every morning;
Great is Your faithfulness. – Lamentations 3:22-23

"His master said to him, 'Well done, good and faithful servant. You have been faithful over a little; I will set you over much. Enter into the joy of your master.'" – Matthew 25:23 (ESV)

For I am confident of this very thing, that He who began a good work in you will perfect it until the day of Christ Jesus. – Philippians 1:6

4.1 LIVING IN THE SPIRIT
(The Fruit of the Spirit)

But the fruit of the Spirit is love, joy, peace, patience, kindness, goodness, faithfulness, gentleness, self-control; against such things there is no law.
– Galatians 5:22-23

A Christian is called to "walk by faith, not by sight," as opposed to "living in the lusts of our flesh." This is often referred to as "walking [living] by the Spirit." To walk means to live in, abide in, practice, progress, and advance daily in "the Way" of a Christian. You do this by continually "grow[ing] in the grace and knowledge [understanding] of our Lord and Savior Jesus Christ" and through the "Spirit of Christ" "dwelling in" you. This chapter only scratches the surface, for entire books have been written on just this subject. However, I want to highlight a few areas so you can start to understand what living in the spirit looks like.

BORN AGAIN OF THE SPIRIT OF GOD

Let us review what happened when you were "born again." At that time, you became a "child of God," as you were "born of the Spirit" of God instead of flesh. You received a new nature – you were "raised up" a "new creature" in Christ. It was also at that time that the "Spirit of God" began to "abide [live] in" you, and "you in Him" (through Christ):

> "That which is born of the flesh is flesh, and that which is born of the Spirit is spirit. Do not be amazed that I said to you, 'You must be born again.' The wind blows where it wishes and you hear the sound of it, but do not know where it comes from and where it is going; so is everyone who is born of the Spirit." – John 3:6-8

> "I have been crucified with Christ; and it is no longer I who live, but Christ lives in me; and the *life* which I now live in the flesh I live by faith in the Son of God, who loved me and gave Himself up for me." – Galatians 2:20

> The first man is from the earth, earthy; the second man is from heaven. – 1 Corinthians 15:47

> "Abide in Me, and I in you. As the branch cannot bear fruit of itself unless it abides in the vine, so neither *can* you unless you abide in Me." – John 15:4

> If you abide in Me, and My words abide in you… – John 15:7

> Therefore as you have received Christ Jesus the Lord, *so* walk in Him… – Colossians 2:6

> Therefore there is now no condemnation for those who are in Christ Jesus. For the law of the Spirit of life in Christ Jesus has set you free from the law of sin and of death. For what the Law could not do, weak as it was through the flesh, God *did*: sending His own Son in the likeness of sinful flesh and *as an offering* for sin, He condemned sin in the flesh, so that the requirement of the Law might be fulfilled in us, who do not walk according to the flesh but according to the Spirit. For those who are according to the flesh set their minds on the things of the flesh, but those who are according to the Spirit, the things of the Spirit. For the mind set on the flesh is death, but the mind set on the Spirit is life and peace, because the mind set on the

flesh is hostile toward God; for it does not subject itself to the law of God, for it is not even able *to do so*, and those who are in the flesh cannot please God.

However, you are not in the flesh but in the Spirit, if indeed the Spirit of God dwells in you. But if anyone does not have the Spirit of Christ, he does not belong to Him. If Christ is in you, though the body is dead because of sin, yet the spirit is alive because of righteousness. But if the Spirit of Him who raised Jesus from the dead dwells in you, He who raised Christ Jesus from the dead will also give life to your mortal bodies through His Spirit who dwells in you.

So then, brethren, we are under obligation, not to the flesh, to live according to the flesh— for if you are living according to the flesh, you must die; but if by the Spirit you are putting to death the deeds of the body, you will live. For all who are being led by the Spirit of God, these are sons of God. For you have not received a spirit of slavery leading to fear again, but you have received a spirit of adoption as sons by which we cry out, "Abba! Father!" The Spirit Himself testifies with our spirit that we are children of God, and if children, heirs also, heirs of God and fellow heirs with Christ, if indeed we suffer with *Him* so that we may also be glorified with *Him*. – Romans 8:1-17

Scripture also refers to this as being "sealed" with the Holy Spirit. This is symbolically described as having a "mark" placed on your "forehead," and this mark identifies you as now being a "child of God." King David writes about this in Psalm 23: "You have anointed my head with oil"; and Revelation 7:3 says: "sealed the bond-servants of our God on their foreheads." These verses speak symbolically of being marked as belonging to Christ, being "sealed" by the Holy Spirit, for those having accepted Christ by being born again of the Spirit and following Him in mind, body, and spirit. Note that this is not a literal mark placed on your forehead as some falsely teach.

We are to "walk by faith, not by sight," and not by our own power, might, or strength, but by the "Spirit of God" dwelling in us:

> Therefore, being always of good courage, and knowing that while we are at home in the body we are absent from the Lord— or we walk by faith, not by sight— we are of good courage, I say, and prefer rather to be absent from the body and to be at home with the Lord. – 2 Corinthians 5:6-8

> Jesus said to him, "Because you have seen Me, have you believed? Blessed *are* they who did not see, and *yet* believed." – John 20:29 [i.e., they believe by faith not sight]

> "'Not by might nor by power, but by My Spirit,' says the LORD of hosts." – Zechariah 4:6

The same Spirit of power that raised Jesus from the dead now lives in you. Always remember that! Much could be written about the Holy Spirit, enough to fill an entire book (or two). The Holy Spirit is the third Person of the Trinity – He is not a force or an "it." He feels, thinks, acts, and is fully God. The Holy Spirit is also described as:

- The Eternal Spirit,
- The Spirit of Christ,
- The Spirit of God,

- The Spirit of the Lord,
- The Spirit of Life,
- The Spirit of Promise,
- The Spirit of Truth,
- The Spirit of Wisdom and Understanding,
- The Spirit of Counsel and Strength,
- The Spirit of Judgment and Fire (Burning), and
- The Helper

THE FRUIT OF THE SPIRIT

Some expect to get a warm, fuzzy feeling when they are born again, but at least for me, there was no "feeling"; frankly, I didn't feel any different than I had before – it was just an intellectual and emotional decision to commit my life to Christ in response to hearing (and then believing) the gospel "message of truth." However, a born-again Christian should begin to notice changes in both their thoughts and behavior. It is by watching for these signs of a changed you that you know He is indeed working in, and through, you now with His Spirit. I do see such changes in my own life.

So, as you begin to walk with Christ, with Him abiding in you and you in He, your thoughts and behavior/actions should start to exhibit characteristics of the "fruit of the spirit," which include:

a. Meekness,
b. Love,
c. Joy,
d. Peace,
e. Patience,
f. Kindness (and compassion),
g. Goodness,
h. Faithfulness,
i. Gentleness,
j. Self-Control,
k. Forgiveness (forgiving others as you were also forgiven!),
l. Humility,
m. Not judging others,
n. Not gossiping, etc.

Contrast the above list with the things that God hates (fruit of the flesh):

> There are six things which the LORD hates,
> Yes, seven which are an abomination to Him:
> Haughty eyes, a lying tongue,
> And hands that shed innocent blood,
> A heart that devises wicked plans,
> Feet that run rapidly to evil,
> A false witness *who* utters lies,
> And one who spreads strife among brothers. – Proverbs 6:16-19

While you received a new nature when you were born again, you still have your old (fleshly) nature as well. The two now live together, in a constant struggle, a battle – the flesh actually wars against the spirit! You will see this constant struggle between the "natural man" (the old fleshly self) and the new "spiritual man" even after you are born again:

> "Keep watching and praying that you may not enter into temptation; the spirit is willing, but the flesh is weak." – Matthew 26:41
>
> But I say, walk by the Spirit, and you will not carry out the desire of the flesh. For the flesh sets its desire against the Spirit, and the Spirit against the flesh; for these are in opposition to one another, so that you may not do the things that you please. But if you are led by the Spirit, you are not under the Law. Now the deeds of the flesh are evident, which are: immorality, impurity, sensuality, idolatry, sorcery, enmities, strife, jealousy, outbursts of anger, disputes, dissensions, factions, envying, drunkenness, carousing, and things like these, of which I forewarn you, just as I have forewarned you, that those who practice such things will not inherit the kingdom of God. But the fruit of the Spirit is love, joy, peace, patience, kindness, goodness, faithfulness, gentleness, self-control; against such things there is no law. Now those who belong to Christ Jesus have crucified the flesh with its passions and desires. If we live by the Spirit, let us also walk by the Spirit. – Galatians 5:16-25
>
> For we know that the Law is spiritual, but I am of flesh, sold into bondage to sin. For what I am doing, I do not understand; for I am not practicing what I *would* like to *do*, but I am doing the very thing I hate. But if I do the very thing I do not want *to do*, I agree with the Law, *confessing* that the Law is good. So now, no longer am I the one doing it, but sin which dwells in me. For I know that nothing good dwells in me, that is, in my flesh; for the willing is present in me, but the doing of the good *is* not. For the good that I want, I do not do, but I practice the very evil that I do not want. But if I am doing the very thing I do not want, I am no longer the one doing it, but sin which dwells in me.
>
> I find then the principle that evil is present in me, the one who wants to do good. For I joyfully concur with the law of God in the inner man, but I see a different law in the members of my body, waging war against the law of my mind and making me a prisoner of the law of sin which is in my members. Wretched man that I am! Who will set me free from the body of this death? Thanks be to God through Jesus Christ our Lord! So then, on the one hand I myself with my mind am serving the law of God, but on the other, with my flesh the law of sin. – Romans 7:14-25

Now I confess to you that it is much easier to write this chapter than to change one's behavior – it is very hard at times to exhibit the "fruit of the Spirit," even after one is born again. But others around you should start to see visible changes in your behavior, attitude, moods, and actions now that you have been born again and the "Spirit of God" starts to work in you. I'm certainly not where I'd like to be in many areas, but I press forward each day waking towards Christ. It takes deliberate attention and discipline to be walking with Christ, combined with reading and meditating on His Word every single day (along with a solid prayer life). Make sure your new self is steering clear of the carnal and base behavior of the unsaved man. You are now living for (and in) Christ; you are not to continue living as a heathen does. This topic is discussed further in the Changing Your Worldly Habits chapter.

Know that it is by the strength of Christ and not your own willpower that you will be able to do this. Remember that Christ redeemed you, purchased you from the dead, and gave you "new life" in Him. You will soon see that you have new desires, not for the fame, fortune, and power of this world, but for the things of Christ. Christ promises to "give you the desires of your heart." It is an amazing transition to see happen in yourself; the Psalmist speaks to this very thing:

> Trust in the LORD and do good;
> Dwell in the land and cultivate faithfulness.
> Delight yourself in the LORD;
> And He will give you the desires of your heart.
> Commit your way to the LORD,
> Trust also in Him, and He will do it.
> He will bring forth your righteousness as the light
> And your judgment as the noonday. – Psalm 37:3-6

You won't always see changes happening all at once; they occur with hard work as you "press on to maturity" in your walk with Christ. However, others around you should start to see that you are indeed a changed person, now living for Christ. If there are no visible changes that others can clearly see, that is a huge red flag that your commitment to Christ may not where it needs to be. And know this – others around you are watching your newly born-again life very, *very* closely, and they will continue to do so, especially those who do not yet know Christ themselves. They are looking for any sign whatsoever of hypocrisy in you or that you are not genuine in your profession of faith. Be mindful that your life is now a living testimony to others, which either glorifies Christ or embarrasses Him. It is written that we are "ambassadors for Christ," members of "a royal PRIESTHOOD," and we are to be a witness to others, told to "let your light shine before men…and glorify your Father [God]":

> Therefore, we are ambassadors for Christ, as though God were making an appeal through us; we beg you on behalf of Christ, be reconciled to God. – 2 Corinthians 5:20

> But you are A CHOSEN RACE, A royal PRIESTHOOD, A HOLY NATION, A PEOPLE FOR *God's* OWN POSSESSION, so that you may proclaim the excellencies of Him who has called you out of darkness into His marvelous light; for you once were NOT A PEOPLE, but now you are THE PEOPLE OF GOD; you had NOT RECEIVED MERCY, but now you have RECEIVED MERCY. – 1 Peter 2:9-10

> "Let your light shine before men in such a way that they may see your good works, and glorify your Father who is in heaven." – Matthew 5:16

It is also written that let your "'Yes, [be] yes' or 'No, [be] no.'" So be true to your word, acting with integrity and being honest in all matters, dependable to do what you say you will do, just like God. Walk worthy of your God and King. Through your behavior and actions, your witness often speaks louder than anything else you do, even louder than things you say.

Speaking further to changes in personality and behavior that result from living in the Spirit, the biggest changes for me were that I became (gradually):

1. More tolerant and patient (although this has been an extreme test for me),
2. No longer vulgar in language (speech and writing),

3. No longer participating in "coarse jesting" (not repeating dirty/crude jokes nor laughing at them with others),
4. Without anxiety (calmer and more peaceful as I trusted in the Lord, instead of in other men or myself), and
5. Less judgmental of others (now having seen my own wretched sinful nature and behavior, but even further – seeing how unbelievably kind, compassionate, merciful, slow to anger and full of grace and lovingkindness the Lord has been with me). [A side note is warranted here: lovingly correcting and rebuking others for their false teachings and doctrine is not being "judgmental" – it's called telling the truth and instructing out of care, concern, and love for them. As a "watchman," I also have a duty to identify false teachings, for they are harming the glory of Christ and causing many to fall and stumble and "come short of" eternal life!]

In particular, I've seen item #2 above as a great indicator in myself as to how closely I'm walking in the Spirit with Christ and abiding in Him, for my speech gives me away – for good or bad. When I'm abiding closely in Christ, I find that all vulgarity is removed from both my thoughts and language. But if I'm slipping up in my walk or not spending time in the Word each day and I start to feel distant from God, I notice that my speech starts to slip back to my old habits, and this is one of the first warning signs that I see (as a heathen, my language was very crude and foul).

A person's language, therefore, is a huge tell as to where they are at in their walk with the Lord. I've noticed that many who claim to be Christians still frequently and repeatedly use vulgar language. But brother or sister in Christ, that just should not be, for it is written that "you will know them by their fruits" – and "fruit" includes both their actions/deeds but also their behavior and whether they are exhibiting the "fruit of the Spirit" or not. Remember it is written:

> Let no unwholesome word proceed from your mouth, but only such *a word* as is good for edification according to the need *of the moment*, so that it will give grace to those who hear. – Ephesians 4:29

Now don't get me wrong, I still mess up horribly at times in all of the above areas. But when I do, I just get back up and commit myself to do better next time and let His Spirit continue molding me for the better, for it is written: "His lovingkindness and compassions never fail, they are new every morning." So, no matter what – keep going, pressing into Christ even harder each day.

And lastly, the commonly held idea that some Christians are priests and the rest of us should follow those priests is not biblical. Every born-again believer is a priest and minister in and for Christ! That's why it's all the more important for you not to remain as a baby Christian but to "press on to maturity" so you can help and guide others and set a good example of what a Spirit-led life looks like.

KEEP SEEKING THE THINGS ABOVE

Also, as a child of God living in the Spirit, you are to "set your mind on the things above [heavenly things], not on the things that are on earth [this material world]." We are instructed: "do not be conformed to this world, but be transformed by the renewing of your mind," "seeking the things that are above, where Christ is, seated at the right hand of God," "for our citizenship is [now] in heaven," not on earth. This is also called being "filled with the Spirit." Don't worry if all of this doesn't make sense to you at this time; what's important is that you start emulating Christ through obedience to His commands as a "doer" of the word instead of merely a "hearer" of the word. As you continue along the path of obedience, you will find that things become clearer to you.

We are to be like Christ, emulating Him in all things, following in His examples. Following Christ takes committed selfless action ("obedience"), not just "idle" words of profession. Following Christ also means "denying oneself" (dying to self) daily and seeking God's will instead of your own will. The apostle Paul describes this as "put on your new self" (i.e., "put on the Lord Jesus Christ"):

> Therefore if you have been raised up with Christ, keep seeking the things above, where Christ is, seated at the right hand of God. Set your mind on the things above, not on the things that are on earth. For you have died and your life is hidden with Christ in God. When Christ, who is our life, is revealed, then you also will be revealed with Him in glory.
>
> Therefore consider the members of your earthly body as dead to immorality, impurity, passion, evil desire, and greed, which amounts to idolatry. For it is because of these things that the wrath of God will come upon the sons of disobedience, and in them you also once walked, when you were living in them. But now you also, put them all aside: anger, wrath, malice, slander, *and* abusive speech from your mouth. Do not lie to one another, since you laid aside the old self with its *evil* practices, and have put on the new self who is being renewed to a true knowledge according to the image of the One who created him— *a renewal* in which there is no *distinction between* Greek and Jew, circumcised and uncircumcised, barbarian, Scythian, slave and freeman, but Christ is all, and in all.
>
> So, as those who have been chosen of God, holy and beloved, put on a heart of compassion, kindness, humility, gentleness and patience; bearing with one another, and forgiving each other, whoever has a complaint against anyone; just as the Lord forgave you, so also should you. Beyond all these things *put on* love, which is the perfect bond of unity. Let the peace of Christ rule in your hearts, to which indeed you were called in one body; and be thankful. Let the word of Christ richly dwell within you, with all wisdom teaching and admonishing one another with psalms *and* hymns *and* spiritual songs, singing with thankfulness in your hearts to God. Whatever you do in word or deed, *do* all in the name of the Lord Jesus, giving thanks through Him to God the Father. – Colossians 3:1-17
>
> So this I say, and affirm together with the Lord, that you walk no longer just as the Gentiles also walk, in the futility of their mind, being darkened in their understanding, excluded from the life of God because of the ignorance that is in them, because of the hardness of their heart; and they, having become callous, have given themselves over to sensuality for the practice of every kind of impurity with greediness. But you did not learn Christ in this way, if indeed you have heard Him and have been taught in Him, just as truth is in Jesus, that, in reference to your former manner of life, you lay aside the old self, which is being corrupted in accordance with the lusts of deceit, and that you be renewed in the spirit of your mind, and put on the new self, which in *the likeness of* God has been created in righteousness and holiness of the truth.

> Therefore, laying aside falsehood, SPEAK TRUTH EACH ONE *of you* WITH HIS NEIGHBOR, for we are members of one another. BE ANGRY, AND *yet* DO NOT SIN; do not let the sun go down on your anger, and do not give the devil an opportunity. He who steals must steal no longer; but rather he must labor, performing with his own hands what is good, so that he will have *something* to share with one who has need. Let no unwholesome word proceed from your mouth, but only such *a word* as is good for edification according to the need *of the moment*, so that it will give grace to those who hear. Do not grieve the Holy Spirit of God, by whom you were sealed for the day of redemption. Let all bitterness and wrath and anger and clamor and slander be put away from you, along with all malice. Be kind to one another, tender-hearted, forgiving each other, just as God in Christ also has forgiven you. – Ephesians 4:17-32

> The night is almost gone, and the day is near. Therefore let us lay aside the deeds of darkness and put on the armor of light. Let us behave properly as in the day, not in carousing and drunkenness, not in sexual promiscuity and sensuality, not in strife and jealousy. But put on the Lord Jesus Christ, and make no provision for the flesh in regard to *its* lusts. – Romans 13:12-14

We are also called to be a "light to the world," pointing the way to Jesus and eternal salvation. We are to "let your light shine before others, so that they may see your good works and give glory to your Father who is in heaven" (ESV). We are not to be dominated any longer by the "lust [desires] of the flesh," the "lust of the eyes," and in continued pursuit of worldly fame, fortune and power, as it is written:

> But those who want to get rich fall into temptation and a snare and many foolish and harmful desires which plunge men into ruin and destruction. For the love of money is a root of all sorts of evil, and some by longing for it have wandered away from the faith and pierced themselves with many griefs. – 1 Timothy 6:9-10

> "No one can serve two masters; for either he will hate the one and love the other, or he will be devoted to one and despise the other. You cannot serve God and wealth." – Matthew 6:24

> And He told them a parable, saying, "The land of a rich man was very productive. And he began reasoning to himself, saying, 'What shall I do, since I have no place to store my crops?' Then he said, 'This is what I will do: I will tear down my barns and build larger ones, and there I will store all my grain and my goods. And I will say to my soul, "Soul, you have many goods laid up for many years *to come*; take your ease, eat, drink *and* be merry."' But God said to him, 'You fool! This *very* night your soul is required of you; and *now* who will own what you have prepared?' So is the man who stores up treasure for himself, and is not rich toward God." – Luke 12:16-21

> "Do not store up for yourselves treasures on earth, where moth and rust destroy, and where thieves break in and steal. But store up for yourselves treasures in heaven, where neither moth nor rust destroys, and where thieves do not break in or steal; for where your treasure is, there your heart will be also." – Matthew 6:19-21

Additionally, part of seeking the things above is also described as "taking every thought captive to the obedience of Christ." This means to start discarding sinful, fleshly, worldly, selfish thoughts and dismiss them through the power of Christ; banish them from your mind when they occur. Over time, this gets easier to do, although spiritual attacks will continue throughout your life; always remember we are in a spiritual war (see The Armor of God chapter).

In summary, you are moving from a life of worldly, selfish, and fleshly pursuits to a life of heavenly, unselfish, giving/loving pursuits and desiring to be more like Christ each day. You are now battling the forces of darkness, not walking under their command or power any longer. Even when you now see others partaking in worldly, fleshly, and carnal activities (or crude jokes, parties filled with lustful activities, etc.), you do not partake of them. You are called to a higher standard now:

> Therefore I urge you, brethren, by the mercies of God, to present your bodies a living and holy sacrifice, acceptable to God, *which is* your spiritual service of worship. And do not be conformed to this world, but be transformed by the renewing of your mind, so that you may prove what the will of God is, that which is good and acceptable and perfect. – Romans 12:1-2
>
> *Let* love *be* without hypocrisy. Abhor what is evil; cling to what is good. *Be* devoted to one another in brotherly love; give preference to one another in honor; not lagging behind in diligence, fervent in spirit, serving the Lord; rejoicing in hope, persevering in tribulation, devoted to prayer, contributing to the needs of the saints, practicing hospitality.
>
> Bless those who persecute you; bless and do not curse. Rejoice with those who rejoice, and weep with those who weep. Be of the same mind toward one another; do not be haughty in mind, but associate with the lowly. Do not be wise in your own estimation. Never pay back evil for evil to anyone. Respect what is right in the sight of all men. If possible, so far as it depends on you, be at peace with all men. Never take your own revenge, beloved, but leave room for the wrath *of God*, for it is written, "VENGEANCE IS MINE, I WILL REPAY," says the Lord. "BUT IF YOUR ENEMY IS HUNGRY, FEED HIM, AND IF HE IS THIRSTY, GIVE HIM A DRINK; FOR IN SO DOING YOU WILL HEAP BURNING COALS ON HIS HEAD." Do not be overcome by evil, but overcome evil with good. – Romans 12:9-21

This higher standard means that we emulate Christ ("be perfect") in all things, and we no longer utilize the ways of the world, which typically includes things such as lying, cheating, stealing, using false measures or "dishonest scales," weapons of war, violence, etc. We are to follow the example Christ set for us, even when doing so goes against the ways and wisdom of this world and even when it is difficult.

A CHRISTIAN TRUSTS THE LORD

Next, a Christian must completely trust in the Lord 100% at all times and in all things – in times of good and in times of peril, for the big things but also the small things. This is a vitally important subject. I explain further in The Peace of God chapter that a lack of trust in the Lord manifests itself as anxiety in the life of a Christian. Scripture tells us that He will never leave, forget or forsake you, that He promises to change you into His likeness. He sees and knows all things, and He has already been victorious over all things. We further read that "neither death, nor life, nor angels, nor principalities, nor things present, nor things to come, nor powers, nor height, nor depth, nor any other created thing will be able to separate us from the love of God that is in Christ Jesus our Lord." Scripture also tells us that His word will never fail:

> So will My word be which goes out of My mouth;
> It will not return to Me empty,
> Without accomplishing what I desire,
> And without succeeding *in the purpose* for which I sent it. – Isaiah 55:11

And so, we live in His assurance – the assurance of things to come that we read about in Scripture (i.e., His Promises).

Much can be learned about trusting in God by studying how the patriarchs of the faith behaved (e.g., Noah, Abraham, Daniel, Job, etc.) and how they trusted in God. Many of them never even lived to see the complete fulfillment of God's promises to them, yet they still trusted in Him completely! I encourage you to review their strength of faith and continued devotion to the Lord, even in (especially in) times of extreme trial or persecution (i.e., the flood, lion's den, bondage in Egypt, severe physical affliction, personal loss, loss of loved ones, etc.), and even when they knew they would be facing death for their faith. The book of Daniel shows how he (along with Shadrach, Meshach, and Abednego) handled himself in the face of certain death and is very inspiring to me.

A CHRISTIAN IS ALWAYS THANKFUL

And finally, a Christian should exhibit an attitude of true praise, gratefulness, and thanksgiving to the Lord (and should do so under all circumstances, good or bad), for you have been redeemed from death to life! What a wonderful gift to receive, wholly undeserved, and we should all be forever mindful and grateful, daily thanking the Lord, no matter what comes our way. A Christian is also a "cheerful giver," according to their own heart.

I hope that this chapter has given you a good jumpstart on living in the Spirit. Let us continue on the path to eternal salvation, realizing that it is only by "walking in the Spirit" and by "abiding in Christ" and "He in you" that you can be an obedient child of God, abounding in "good works," and also persevere in faith, which are the subjects of our next chapters.

FALSE TEACHING(S) YOU WILL ENCOUNTER:

- Once saved always saved
- A Christian no longer sins
- Bizarre interpretations of the "Mark of The Beast"

RELATED SCRIPTURE:

Or do you not know that your body is a temple of the Holy Spirit who is in you, whom you have from God, and that you are not your own? For you have been bought with a price: therefore glorify God in your body. – 1 Corinthians 6:19-20

Therefore we do not lose heart, but though our outer man is decaying, yet our inner man is being renewed day by day. – 2 Corinthians 4:16

My little children, I am writing these things to you so that you may not sin. And if anyone sins, we have an Advocate with the Father, Jesus Christ the righteous; and He

Himself is the propitiation for our sins; and not for ours only, but also for *those of* the whole world…but whoever keeps His word, in him the love of God has truly been perfected. By this we know that we are in Him: the one who says he abides in Him ought himself to walk in the same manner as He walked. – 1 John 2:1-2, 5-6

Do not love the world nor the things in the world. If anyone loves the world, the love of the Father is not in him. For all that is in the world, the lust of the flesh and the lust of the eyes and the boastful pride of life, is not from the Father, but is from the world. The world is passing away, and *also* its lusts; but the one who does the will of God lives forever. – 1 John 2:15-17

"Do not judge so that you will not be judged. For in the way you judge, you will be judged; and by your standard of measure, it will be measured to you. Why do you look at the speck that is in your brother's eye, but do not notice the log that is in your own eye?" – Matthew 7:1-3

But we request of you, brethren, that you appreciate those who diligently labor among you, and have charge over you in the Lord and give you instruction, and that you esteem them very highly in love because of their work. Live in peace with one another. We urge you, brethren, admonish the unruly, encourage the fainthearted, help the weak, be patient with everyone. See that no one repays another with evil for evil, but always seek after that which is good for one another and for all people. Rejoice always; pray without ceasing; in everything give thanks; for this is God's will for you in Christ Jesus. Do not quench the Spirit; do not despise prophetic utterances. But examine everything *carefully*; hold fast to that which is good; abstain from every form of evil.

Now may the God of peace Himself sanctify you entirely; and may your spirit and soul and body be preserved complete, without blame at the coming of our Lord Jesus Christ. Faithful is He who calls you, and He also will bring it to pass. – 1 Thessalonians 5:12-24

Therefore I, the prisoner of the Lord, implore you to walk in a manner worthy of the calling with which you have been called, with all humility and gentleness, with patience, showing tolerance for one another in love, being diligent to preserve the unity of the Spirit in the bond of peace. *There is* one body and one Spirit, just as also you were called in one hope of your calling; one Lord, one faith, one baptism, one God and Father of all who is over all and through all and in all. – Ephesians 4:1-6

Therefore be imitators of God, as beloved children; and walk in love, just as Christ also loved you and gave Himself up for us, an offering and a sacrifice to God as a fragrant aroma.

But immorality or any impurity or greed must not even be named among you, as is proper among saints; and *there must be no* filthiness and silly talk, or coarse jesting [dirty/crude/sexually suggestive joking, etc.], which are not fitting, but rather giving of thanks. For this you know with certainty, that no immoral or impure person or covetous man, who is an idolater, has an inheritance in the kingdom of Christ and God.

Let no one deceive you with empty words, for because of these things the wrath of God comes upon the sons of disobedience. Therefore do not be partakers with them; for you were formerly darkness, but now you are Light in the Lord; walk as children of Light (for the fruit of the Light *consists* in all goodness and righteousness and truth), trying to learn what is pleasing to the Lord. Do not participate in the unfruitful deeds of darkness, but instead even expose them. – Ephesians 5:1-11

Therefore be careful how you walk, not as unwise men but as wise, making the most of your time, because the days are evil. So then do not be foolish, but understand what the will of the Lord is. And do not get drunk with wine, for that is dissipation, but be filled with the Spirit, speaking to one another in psalms and hymns and spiritual songs, singing and making melody with your heart to the Lord; always giving thanks for all things in the name of our Lord Jesus Christ to God, even the Father; and be subject to one another in the fear of Christ. – Ephesians 5:15-21

Therefore do not let sin reign in your mortal body so that you obey its lusts, and do not go on presenting the members of your body to sin *as* instruments of unrighteousness; but present yourselves to God as those alive from the dead, and your members *as* instruments of righteousness to God. For sin shall not be master over you, for you are not under law but under grace.

What then? Shall we sin because we are not under law but under grace? May it never be! Do you not know that when you present yourselves to someone *as* slaves for obedience, you are slaves of the one whom you obey, either of sin resulting in death, or of obedience resulting in righteousness? But thanks be to God that though you were slaves of sin, you became obedient from the heart to that form of teaching to which you were committed, and having been freed from sin, you became slaves of righteousness. I am speaking in human terms because of the weakness of your flesh. For just as you presented your members as slaves to impurity and to lawlessness, resulting in *further* lawlessness, so now present your members as slaves to righteousness, resulting in sanctification. – Romans 6:12-19

Finally, brethren, whatever is true, whatever is honorable, whatever is right, whatever is pure, whatever is lovely, whatever is of good repute, if there is any excellence and if anything worthy of praise, dwell on these things. The things you have learned and received and heard and seen in me, practice these things, and the God of peace will be with you. – Philippians 4:8-9

Make sure that your character is free from the love of money, being content with what you have; for He Himself has said, "I WILL NEVER DESERT YOU, NOR WILL I EVER FORSAKE YOU." – Hebrews 13:5

Now this *I say*, he who sows sparingly will also reap sparingly, and he who sows bountifully will also reap bountifully. Each one *must do* just as he has purposed in his heart, not grudgingly or under compulsion, for God loves a cheerful giver. And God is able to make all grace abound to you, so that always having all sufficiency in everything, you may have an abundance for every good deed. – 2 Corinthians 9:6-8

Through Him then, let us continually offer up a sacrifice of praise to God, that is, the fruit of lips that give thanks to His name. And do not neglect doing good and sharing, for with such sacrifices God is pleased. – Hebrews 13:15-16

Simon Peter, a bond-servant and apostle of Jesus Christ,

To those who have received a faith of the same kind as ours, by the righteousness of our God and Savior, Jesus Christ: Grace and peace be multiplied to you in the knowledge of God and of Jesus our Lord; seeing that His divine power has granted to us everything pertaining to life and godliness, through the true knowledge of Him who called us by His own glory and excellence. For by these He has granted to us His precious and magnificent promises, so that by them you may become partakers of *the* divine nature, having escaped the corruption that is in the world by lust. Now for this very reason also, applying all diligence, in your faith supply moral excellence, and in *your* moral excellence, knowledge, and in *your* knowledge, self-control, and in *your* self-control, perseverance, and in *your* perseverance, godliness, and in *your* godliness, brotherly kindness, and in *your* brotherly kindness, love. For if these *qualities* are yours and are increasing, they render you neither useless nor unfruitful in the true knowledge of our Lord Jesus Christ. – 2 Peter 1:1-8

But being full of the Holy Spirit, he [Stephen] gazed intently into heaven and saw the glory of God, and Jesus standing at the right hand of God…They went on stoning Stephen as he called on *the Lord* and said, "Lord Jesus, receive my spirit!" Then falling on his knees, he cried out with a loud voice, "Lord, do not hold this sin against them!" Having said this, he fell asleep. – Acts 7:55, 59-60

For this reason also, since the day we heard *of it*, we have not ceased to pray for you and to ask that you may be filled with the knowledge of His will in all spiritual wisdom and understanding, so that you will walk in a manner worthy of the Lord, to please *Him* in all respects, bearing fruit in every good work and increasing in the knowledge of God; strengthened with all power, according to His glorious might, for the attaining of all steadfastness and patience; joyously giving thanks to the Father, who has qualified us to share in the inheritance of the saints in Light.

For He rescued us from the domain of darkness, and transferred us to the kingdom of His beloved Son, in whom we have redemption, the forgiveness of sins. – Colossians 1:9-14

The Lord's bond-servant must not be quarrelsome, but be kind to all, able to teach, patient when wronged, with gentleness correcting those who are in opposition, if perhaps God may grant them repentance leading to the knowledge of the truth, and they may come to their senses *and escape* from the snare of the devil, having been held captive by him to do his will. – 2 Timothy 2:24-26

Therefore, since Christ has suffered in the flesh, arm yourselves also with the same purpose, because he who has suffered in the flesh has ceased from sin, so as to live the rest of the time in the flesh no longer for the lusts of men, but for the will of God. For the time already past is sufficient *for you* to have carried out the desire of the Gentiles, having pursued a course of sensuality, lusts, drunkenness, carousing, drinking parties and abominable idolatries. In *all* this, they are surprised that you do not run with *them* into the same excesses of dissipation, and they malign *you*; but they will give account to Him who is ready to judge the living and the dead. For the gospel has for this purpose been preached even to those who are dead, that though they are judged in the flesh as men, they may live in the spirit according to *the will of* God.

The end of all things is near; therefore, be of sound judgment and sober *spirit* for the purpose of prayer. Above all, keep fervent in your love for one another, because love covers a multitude of sins. Be hospitable to one another without complaint. As each one has received a *special* gift, employ it in serving one another as good stewards of the manifold grace of God. Whoever speaks, *is to do so* as one who is speaking the utterances of God; whoever serves *is to do so* as one who is serving by the strength which God supplies; so that in all things God may be glorified through Jesus Christ, to whom belongs the glory and dominion forever and ever. Amen. – 1 Peter 4:1-11

Behold, now is "THE ACCEPTABLE TIME," behold, now is "THE DAY OF SALVATION"— giving no cause for offense in anything, so that the ministry will not be discredited, but in everything commending ourselves as servants of God, in much endurance, in afflictions, in hardships, in distresses, in beatings, in imprisonments, in tumults, in labors, in sleeplessness, in hunger, in purity, in knowledge, in patience, in kindness, in the Holy Spirit, in genuine love, in the word of truth, in the power of God; by the weapons of righteousness for the right hand and the left, by glory and dishonor, by evil report and good report; *regarded* as deceivers and yet true; as unknown yet well-known, as dying yet behold, we live; as punished yet not put to death, as sorrowful yet always rejoicing, as poor yet making many rich, as having nothing yet possessing all things. – 2 Corinthians 6:2b-10

Therefore, having these promises, beloved, let us cleanse ourselves from all defilement of flesh and spirit, perfecting holiness in the fear of God. – 2 Corinthians 7:1

Be anxious for nothing, but in everything by prayer and supplication with thanksgiving let your requests be made known to God. And the peace of God, which surpasses all comprehension, will guard your hearts and your minds in Christ Jesus. – Philippians 4:6-7

And the disciples were continually filled with joy and with the Holy Spirit. – Acts 13:52

The LORD is my strength and my shield;
My heart trusts in Him, and I am helped;
Therefore my heart exults,
And with my song I shall thank Him. – Psalm 28:7

I will say to the LORD, "My refuge and my fortress,
My God, in whom I trust!"
...
For He will give His angels charge concerning you,
To guard you in all your ways.
They will bear you up in their hands,
That you do not strike your foot against a stone. – Psalm 91:2, 11-12

The LORD'S lovingkindnesses indeed never cease,
For His compassions never fail.
They are new every morning;
Great is Your faithfulness. – Lamentations 3:22-23

This is the message we have heard from Him and announce to you, that God is Light, and in Him there is no darkness at all. If we say that we have fellowship with Him and *yet* walk in the darkness, we lie and do not practice the truth; but if we walk in the Light as He Himself is in the Light, we have fellowship with one another, and the blood of Jesus His Son cleanses us from all sin. If we say that we have no sin, we are deceiving ourselves and the truth is not in us. If we confess our sins, He is faithful and righteous to forgive us our sins and to cleanse us from all unrighteousness. If we say that we have not sinned, we make Him a liar and His word is not in us. – 1 John 1:5-10 [Note: These verses apply to those who are born again, as we have an advocate with the Father, Jesus Christ our Mediator, whereby if we sin (not willfully or deliberately in a continuing lifestyle choice), we can repent, and He is faithful and just to forgive us. I include the verse here for completeness, but this is something you will do on an ongoing basis in your Christian walk until death. See the "A Christian No Longer Sins" false teaching.]

We have come to know and have believed the love which God has for us. God is love, and the one who abides in love abides in God, and God abides in him. – 1 John 4:16

Love is patient, love is kind *and* is not jealous; love does not brag *and* is not arrogant, does not act unbecomingly; it does not seek its own, is not provoked, does not take into account a wrong *suffered*, does not rejoice in unrighteousness, but rejoices with the truth; bears all things, believes all things, hopes all things, endures all things. – 1 Corinthians 13:4-7

Now may the God of hope fill you with all joy and peace in believing, so that you will abound in hope by the power of the Holy Spirit. – Romans 15:13

With all prayer and petition pray at all times in the Spirit, and with this in view, be on the alert with all perseverance and petition for all the saints, and *pray* on my behalf, that utterance may be given to me in the opening of my mouth, to make known with boldness the mystery of the gospel, for which I am an ambassador in chains; that in *proclaiming* it I may speak boldly, as I ought to speak. – Ephesians 6:18-20

"But an hour is coming, and now is, when the true worshipers will worship the Father in spirit and truth; for such people the Father seeks to be His worshipers. God is spirit, and those who worship Him must worship in spirit and truth." – John 4:23-24

Now, little children, abide in Him, so that when He appears, we may have confidence and not shrink away from Him in shame at His coming. – 1 John 2:28

"Again, you have heard that the ancients were told, 'YOU SHALL NOT MAKE FALSE VOWS, BUT SHALL FULFILL YOUR VOWS TO THE LORD.' But I say to you, make no oath at all, either by heaven, for it is the throne of God, or by the earth, for it is the footstool of His feet, or by Jerusalem, for it is THE CITY OF THE GREAT KING. Nor shall you make an oath by your head, for you cannot make one hair white or black. But let your statement be, 'Yes, yes' *or* 'No, no'; anything beyond these is of evil." – Matthew 5:33-37

Therefore, prepare your minds for action, keep sober *in spirit*, fix your hope completely on the grace to be brought to you at the revelation of Jesus Christ. As obedient children, do not be conformed to the former lusts *which were yours* in your ignorance, but like the Holy One who called you, be holy yourselves also in all *your* behavior; because it is written, "YOU SHALL BE HOLY, FOR I AM HOLY." – 1 Peter 1:13-16

Therefore, putting aside all malice and all deceit and hypocrisy and envy and all slander, like newborn babies, long for the pure milk of the word, so that by it you may grow in respect to salvation, if you have tasted the kindness of the Lord.

And coming to Him as to a living stone which has been rejected by men, but is choice and precious in the sight of God, you also, as living stones, are being built up as a spiritual house for a holy priesthood, to offer up spiritual sacrifices acceptable to God through Jesus Christ. – 1 Peter 2:1-5

Beloved, I urge you as aliens and strangers to abstain from fleshly lusts which wage war against the soul. Keep your behavior excellent among the Gentiles, so that in the thing in which they slander you as evildoers, they may because of your good deeds, as they observe *them*, glorify God in the day of visitation.

Submit yourselves for the Lord's sake to every human institution, whether to a king as the one in authority, or to governors as sent by him for the punishment of evildoers and the praise of those who do right. For such is the will of God that by doing right you may silence the ignorance of foolish men. *Act* as free men, and do not use your freedom as a covering for evil, but *use it* as bondslaves of God. Honor all people, love the brotherhood, fear God, honor the king.

Servants, be submissive to your masters with all respect, not only to those who are good and gentle, but also to those who are unreasonable. For this *finds* favor, if for the sake of conscience toward God a person bears up under sorrows when suffering unjustly. For what credit is there if, when you sin and are harshly treated, you endure it with patience? But if when you do what is right and suffer *for it* you patiently endure it, this *finds* favor with God.

For you have been called for this purpose, since Christ also suffered for you, leaving you an example for you to follow in His steps, WHO COMMITTED NO SIN, NOR WAS ANY DECEIT FOUND IN HIS MOUTH; and while being reviled, He did not revile in return; while suffering, He uttered no threats, but kept entrusting *Himself* to Him who judges righteously; and He Himself bore our sins in His body on the cross, so that we might die to sin and live to righteousness; for by His wounds you were healed. For you were continually straying like sheep, but now you have returned to the Shepherd and Guardian of your souls. – 1 Peter 2:11-25

To sum up, all of you be harmonious, sympathetic, brotherly, kindhearted, and humble in spirit; not returning evil for evil or insult for insult, but giving a blessing instead; for you were called for the very purpose that you might inherit a blessing. – 1 Peter 3:8-9

For though we walk in the flesh, we do not war according to the flesh, for the weapons of our warfare are not of the flesh, but divinely powerful for the destruction of fortresses. *We are* destroying speculations and every lofty thing raised up against the knowledge of God, and *we are* taking every thought captive to the obedience of Christ. – 2 Corinthians 10:3-5

…however, let us keep living by that same *standard* to which we have attained.

Brethren, join in following my example, and observe those who walk according to the pattern you have in us. For many walk, of whom I often told you, and now tell you even weeping, *that they are* enemies of the cross of Christ, whose end is destruction, whose god is *their* appetite, and *whose* glory is in their shame, who set their minds on earthly things. For our citizenship is in heaven, from which also we eagerly wait for a Savior, the Lord Jesus Christ; who will transform the body of our humble state into conformity with the body of His glory, by the exertion of the power that He has even to subject all things to Himself. – Philippians 3:16-21

The Message of Truth

"I am the true vine, and My Father is the vinedresser. Every branch in Me that does not bear fruit, He takes away; and every *branch* that bears fruit, He prunes it so that it may bear more fruit. You are already clean because of the word which I have spoken to you. Abide in Me, and I in you. As the branch cannot bear fruit of itself unless it abides in the vine, so neither *can* you unless you abide in Me. I am the vine, you are the branches; he who abides in Me and I in him, he bears much fruit, for apart from Me you can do nothing." – John 15:1-5

Suffer hardship with *me*, as a good soldier of Christ Jesus. No soldier in active service entangles himself in the affairs of everyday life, so that he may please the one who enlisted him as a soldier. Also if anyone competes as an athlete, he does not win the prize unless he competes according to the rules. – 2 Timothy 2:3-5

This you know, my beloved brethren. But everyone must be quick to hear, slow to speak *and* slow to anger; for the anger of man does not achieve the righteousness of God. Therefore, putting aside all filthiness and *all* that remains of wickedness, in humility receive the word implanted, which is able to save your souls. – James 1:19-21

Your adornment must not be *merely* the external—braiding the hair, wearing gold *jewelry*, or putting on apparel; but *it should be* the hidden person of the heart, with the imperishable *quality* of a gentle and quiet spirit, which is precious in the sight of God. – 1 Peter 3:3-4

4.2 OBEDIENCE
(A Servant of Christ)

"If you love Me, you will keep My commandments [commands]." – John 14:15

Obedience to Christ's Commands. This chapter explains that obedience to the commands of Christ as given in the New Testament is a vital component of genuine saving faith. One cannot have true saving faith without the natural result of that faith being obedience to the commands of Christ. Christianity is as much about action as it is about the profession of faith, for a Christian is a servant of God. Furthermore, a professing Christian who is willfully and repeatedly disobedient to the commands of Christ is not following the plan of salvation as laid out in Scripture.

Additionally, since many of Christ's commands involve taking action, if one is obedient to them, one cannot help but to also "bear fruit" (do "good works") for the Lord – obedience and "good works" are therefore closely interrelated with each other, and this chapter is intimately tied to the next chapter on "bearing fruit" (the role of works). Both chapters could have been combined into one, but due to the length of material, and the fact that the role of works is grossly misunderstood today, I felt it best to spread the content across two chapters.

IF YOU LOVE ME, YOU WILL KEEP MY COMMANDMENTS

So, let us talk about obedience and what its true motivation is. A Christian's true motive for obedience is love:

> "If you love Me, you will keep My commandments." – John 14:15

> And this is love, that we walk according to His commandments. This is the commandment, just as you have heard from the beginning, that you should walk in it. – 2 John 1:6

> By this we know that we have come to know Him, if we keep His commandments. The one who says, "I have come to know Him," and does not keep His commandments, is a liar, and the truth is not in him; but whoever keeps His word, in him the love of God has truly been perfected. By this we know that we are in Him: the one who says he abides in Him ought himself to walk in the same manner as He walked. – 1 John 2:3-6

> "Just as the Father has loved Me, I have also loved you; abide in My love. If you keep My commandments, you will abide in My love; just as I have kept My Father's commandments and abide in His love." – John 15:9-10

> By this we know that we love the children of God, when we love God and observe His commandments. For this is the love of God, that we keep His commandments; and His commandments are not burdensome. – 1 John 5:2-3

> Jesus answered and said to him, "If anyone loves Me, he will keep My word; and My Father will love him, and We will come to him and make Our abode with him." – John 14:23

We should always look back on the cross and remember the love of God and His Christ Jesus, which They demonstrated to us "while we were still sinners," hostile to God, foreign to God, enemies of God, and separated from God in sin:

> But God demonstrates His own love toward us, in that while we were yet sinners, Christ died for us. – Romans 5:8

> "For God so loved the world, that He gave His only begotten Son, that whoever believes in Him shall not perish, but have eternal life." – John 3:16

> Greater love has no one than this, that one lay down his life for his friends. – John 15:13

We also see how Christ was obedient to the Father, and how it was through His obedience that we were saved:

> "I will not speak much more with you, for the ruler of the world is coming, and he has nothing in Me; but so that the world may know that I love the Father, I do exactly as the Father commanded Me." – John 14:30-31

> Although He was a Son, He learned obedience from the things which He suffered. And having been made perfect, He became to all those who obey Him the source of eternal salvation. – Hebrews 5:8-9

> … "Father, if You are willing, remove this cup from Me; yet not My will, but Yours be done." – Luke 22:42

> Have this attitude in yourselves which was also in Christ Jesus, who, although He existed in the form of God, did not regard equality with God a thing to be grasped, but emptied Himself, taking the form of a bond-servant, *and* being made in the likeness of men. Being found in appearance as a man, He humbled Himself by becoming obedient to the point of death, even death on a cross. – Philippians 2:5-8

> For as through the one man's disobedience the many were made sinners, even so through the obedience of the One [Jesus] the many will be made righteous. – Romans 5:19

And above all, as Christ loved the Father and was "obedient to the point of death, even death on a cross," we are obedient to Christ out of love for Him. Scripture tells us that it's not enough to simply profess to be a Christian – for what use is there to profess faith in Christ and then not do what Christ has commanded us to do? Can you claim to love Christ and then not do what He has asked (commanded) you to do? Such faith is "dead," worthless; Christ even condemns just "lukewarm" faith – typically characterized by a lack of obedience. Matthew Henry writes:[57]

> Of his obedience to his Father: "As the Father gave me commandment, even so I did – did the thing commanded me in the manner commanded."
> Note, the best evidence of our love to the Father is our doing as he hath given us commandment. As Christ loved the Father, and obeyed him, even to the death, so we must love Christ, and obey him. Christ's eye to the Father's commandment, obliging him to suffer and die, bore him up with cheerfulness, and overcame the reluctancies of nature; this took off the offence of the cross, that what he did was

---

[57] Henry, Matthew. *Exposition of the Old and New Testaments*, London. 1706-1710/1721.

by order from the Father. The command of God is sufficient to bear us out in that which is most disputed by others, and therefore should be sufficient to bear us up in that which is most difficult to ourselves: This is the will of him that made me, that sent me.

Note also that obedience is not something that is newly added in the New Testament. The need for obedience as a child of God has been there from the beginning. Remember that it was the *dis*obedience of man in the first place (back in the Garden of Eden, Genesis) that started the whole mess of sin, suffering, and death and this fallen world to begin with!

> Then the LORD God took the man and put him into the garden of Eden to cultivate it and keep it. The LORD God commanded the man, saying, "From any tree of the garden you may eat freely; but from the tree of the knowledge of good and evil you shall not eat, for in the day that you eat from it you will surely die." – Genesis 2:15-17

> "I will multiply your descendants as the stars of heaven, and will give your descendants all these lands; and by your descendants all the nations of the earth shall be blessed; because Abraham obeyed Me and kept My charge, My commandments, My statutes and My laws." – Genesis 26:4-5

> And He said to him, "'YOU SHALL LOVE THE LORD YOUR GOD WITH ALL YOUR HEART, AND WITH ALL YOUR SOUL, AND WITH ALL YOUR MIND.' This is the great and foremost commandment. The second is like it, 'YOU SHALL LOVE YOUR NEIGHBOR AS YOURSELF.' On these two commandments depend the whole Law and the Prophets." – Matthew 22:37-40

> You shall walk in all the way which the LORD your God has commanded you, that you may live and that it may be well with you, and that you may prolong *your* days in the land which you will possess. – Deuteronomy 5:33

> "Now it shall be, if you diligently obey the LORD your God, being careful to do all His commandments which I command you today, the LORD your God will set you high above all the nations of the earth." – Deuteronomy 28:1

> If you obey the LORD your God to keep His commandments and His statutes which are written in this book of the law, if you turn to the LORD your God with all your heart and soul. – Deuteronomy 30:10

GOD'S AUTHORITY

While we serve the Lord out of love with a glad heart and thanksgiving, we also equally recognize the authority of Christ as our Lord and King – for He created us, and He "redeemed" (bought and paid for) us from slavery to sin and death (and Satan) with His blood. When we come to Christ, we are giving Him our life to do with as He pleases – and we have a duty to God. We, therefore, willingly place ourselves under His command and His will; we choose to be obedient to Christ. We further read in Scripture that a Christian is described as a "bond-servant," "slave" or "servant" of Christ:

> Paul, a bond-servant [slave, servant] of Christ Jesus, called *as* an apostle, set apart for the gospel of God. – Romans 1:1

> Whatever you do, do your work heartily, as for the Lord rather than for men, knowing that from the Lord you will receive the reward of the inheritance. It is the Lord Christ whom you serve. – Colossians 3:23-24
>
> *Act* as free men, and do not use your freedom as a covering for evil, but *use it* as bondslaves of God. – 1 Peter 2:16
>
> Therefore, prepare your minds for action, keep sober *in spirit*, fix your hope completely on the grace to be brought to you at the revelation of Jesus Christ. As obedient children, do not be conformed to the former lusts *which were yours* in your ignorance, but like the Holy One who called you, be holy yourselves also in all *your* behavior; because it is written, "YOU SHALL BE HOLY, FOR I AM HOLY." – 1 Peter 1:13-16
>
> ...but in everything commending ourselves as servants of God... – 2 Corinthians 6:4
>
> But now having been freed from sin and enslaved to God... – Romans 6:22
>
> Following after Paul and us, she kept crying out, saying, "These men are bond-servants of the Most High God, who are proclaiming to you the way of salvation." – Acts 16:17

And Christ has elevated us from "bondservant" to "friend," and even further, a "child of God"! We read that we are now friends of God (and Christ), having been formerly His enemy in disobedience:

> "You are My friends if you do what I command you. No longer do I call you slaves, for the slave does not know what his master is doing; but I have called you friends, for all things that I have heard from My Father I have made known to you." – John 15:14-15
>
> And stretching out His hand toward His disciples, He said, "Behold My mother and My brothers! For whoever does the will of My Father who is in heaven, he is My brother and sister and mother." – Matthew 12:49-50

BLESSED IS THE SLAVE WHO THE MASTER FINDS DOING

The kind of faith that is pleasing to Christ is not one born out of a casual commitment, or one of convenience, nor foxhole faith, but a lifelong commitment to Christ – one that "denies himself" each day, one that "takes up the cross" of Christ and "follows Him" in obedience and action, one that "is willing to do His [God's] will" (not our own), one that "seeks the things above" (not the things of this world) and one that "endures [perseveres] to the [very] end." Foxhole faith is like foxhole prayers – it is fleeting in duration. It only appears for a moment, soon to vanish again into the darkness and nothingness once the immediate circumstances (usually danger) have passed. It seldom leads to a truly repentant and changed life.

Furthermore, Jesus exhorts us to be found by Him as obedient servants of His, actively doing His will and His work:

> "Who then is the faithful and sensible slave whom his master put in charge of his household to give them their food at the proper time? Blessed is that slave whom his master finds so doing when he comes. Truly I say to you that he will put him in charge of all his possessions. But if that evil slave says in his heart, 'My master is

not coming for a long time,' and begins to beat his fellow slaves and eat and drink with drunkards; the master of that slave will come on a day when he does not expect *him* and at an hour which he does not know, and will cut him in pieces and assign him a place with the hypocrites; in that place there will be weeping and gnashing of teeth." – Matthew 24:45-51

And as you just read, there are also the "hypocrites" who have heard the word of the Lord and profess faith, but then continue to do the selfish works of the flesh and not the will of God, who go on living just as they have always lived. The Lord will sort out mere "idle" professors and pretenders of faith in hypocrisy (make believers) on the great Day of Judgment:

"But as for you, son of man, your fellow citizens who talk about you by the walls and in the doorways of the houses, speak to one another, each to his brother, saying, 'Come now and hear what the message is which comes forth from the LORD.' They come to you as people come, and sit before you *as* My people and hear your words, but they do not do them, for they do the lustful desires *expressed* by their mouth, *and* their heart goes after their gain. Behold, you are to them like a sensual song by one who has a beautiful voice and plays well on an instrument; for they hear your words but they do not practice them. So when it comes to pass—as surely it will—then they will know that a prophet has been in their midst." – Ezekiel 33:30-33

"Not everyone who says to Me, 'Lord, Lord,' will enter the kingdom of heaven, but he who does the will of My Father who is in heaven *will enter*. Many will say to Me on that day, 'Lord, Lord, did we not prophesy in Your name, and in Your name cast out demons, and in Your name perform many miracles?' And then I will declare to them, 'I never knew you; DEPART FROM ME, YOU WHO PRACTICE LAWLESSNESS.'"

"Therefore everyone who hears these words of Mine and acts on them, may be compared to a wise man who built his house on the rock. And the rain fell, and the floods came, and the winds blew and slammed against that house; and *yet* it did not fall, for it had been founded on the rock. Everyone who hears these words of Mine and does not act on them, will be like a foolish man who built his house on the sand. The rain fell, and the floods came, and the winds blew and slammed against that house; and it fell—and great was its fall." – Matthew 7:21-27

In particular, note the word "many" in verses Matthew 7:21-27 above. Furthermore, realize that this scene will occur at the very gates of heaven itself on the great Day of Judgment. It is not just a "few" that will be turned away from entering heaven but "many" being seen for what they really are: mere professors ("hearers") of the word but not "doers" of the word! Be not deceived. All the fake/false Christians will be revealed on that day. Finally, also know that God reveals Himself more fully to those who are in obedience to Him:

"He who has My commandments and keeps them is the one who loves Me; and he who loves Me will be loved by My Father, and I will love him and will disclose Myself to him." – John 14:21

THE COMMANDS OF CHRIST

To be obedient, we must know the "commandments" (commands) of Christ as given in the New Testament. Just as in Old Testament times where the Mosaic Law had been given to the Jews, the New Testament also has a Law of Grace, which is expressed in the commandments of Christ. Most people (even non-Christians) can recite the two most important commandments given by Jesus:

- Love God, and
- Love others as yourself

> One of the scribes came and heard them arguing, and recognizing that He had answered them well, asked Him, "What commandment is the foremost of all?" Jesus answered, "The foremost is, 'HEAR, O ISRAEL! THE LORD OUR GOD IS ONE LORD; AND YOU SHALL LOVE THE LORD YOUR GOD WITH ALL YOUR HEART, AND WITH ALL YOUR SOUL, AND WITH ALL YOUR MIND, AND WITH ALL YOUR STRENGTH.' The second is this, 'YOU SHALL LOVE YOUR NEIGHBOR AS YOURSELF.' There is no other commandment greater than these." – Mark 12:28-31

However, Christ's commands go beyond those; a few are listed below:

- "Forgive others" as you were forgiven,
- "Do not judge" others,
- "Do not commit adultery,"
- "Let your light shine before others,"
- "Love" and "pray for your enemies,"
- "Render to Caesar what is Caesar's,"
- "Go into the all the world and preach the gospel to all creation,"
- "Do this in remembrance of me" (the Lord's Supper)

Therefore, to be obedient, you must learn and obey Jesus' commands/instructions as given in the New Testament. I'm not going to list them all here, and in fact, it's better if you study the Bible and seek them out for yourself. That way, they take on a deeper meaning. To know and therefore obey Christ's commands, one must read and diligently study the Bible – I hope you are starting to see that everything about the Christian life is connected together and ultimately linked back to reading and studying the Word of God – for it is our instruction manual, and the source of all Godly wisdom.

BE LIKE CHRIST (AN IMITATOR OF CHRIST)

And finally, we read in Scripture that we are to be "perfect":

> "Therefore you are to be perfect, as your heavenly Father is perfect." – Matthew 5:48

Now you are probably wondering what that verse has to do with a chapter on obedience. For the longest time, several years, in fact, I was confused by this verse even after becoming a Christian. I've heard it explained that this verse means that a Christian no longer sins; however, that is simply yet another false teaching of man (see again the Beware the Wolves chapter). Scripture is clear that the only Person who ever lived a sinless life was Jesus. So, how in the world could I be perfect? I didn't feel perfect, nor did (or do) I act perfect now, nor did I see a way to become perfect. If you ask anyone who knows me, you will certainly hear them confirm that I am indeed not perfect. In fact, the closer I got to Christ, the less perfect I felt, for I started to see my own wretched nature more clearly!

That verse didn't become clear to me until I wrote this book – and this very chapter. And now I see how that verse directly relates to obedience. It is through obedience to Christ that we press on towards perfection, being made to conform more and more each day to the image of Christ. We have been set "free from the law of sin and death" and "raised up" a "new creature [person]" in Christ, so we are "no longer slaves of sin." So, this verse is actually a beautiful exhortation to be obedient to Christ – to be "imitators of Christ [God]," and to follow His examples. This is also how Jesus was able to live a perfect and sinless life – He lived His life in 100% obedience to the Father. We see this written:

> "So that the world may know that I love the Father, I do exactly as the Father commanded Me." – John 14:31

> Therefore Jesus answered and was saying to them, "Truly, truly, I say to you, the Son can do nothing of Himself, unless *it is* something He sees the Father doing; for whatever the Father does, these things the Son also does in like manner." – John 5:19

> "For I did not speak on My own initiative, but the Father Himself who sent Me has given Me a commandment *as to* what to say and what to speak." – John 12:49

> Although He was a Son, He learned obedience from the things which He suffered. – Hebrews 5:8

> "For I have come down from heaven, not to do My own will, but the will of Him who sent Me." – John 6:38

> And He withdrew from them about a stone's throw, and He knelt down and *began* to pray, saying, "Father, if You are willing, remove this cup from Me; yet not My will, but Yours be done." – Luke 22:41-42

> Being found in appearance as a man, He humbled Himself by becoming obedient to the point of death, even death on a cross. – Philippians 2:8

> In the days of His flesh, He offered up both prayers and supplications with loud crying and tears to the One able to save Him from death, and He was heard because of His piety. Although He was a Son, He learned obedience from the things which He suffered. And having been made perfect, He became to all those who obey Him the source of eternal salvation, being designated by God as a high priest according to the order of Melchizedek. – Hebrews 5:7-10

And so imitating Christ (as best we can via obedience to His commands) is perfection for us, and this comes from being obedient:

> Therefore be imitators of God, as beloved children; and walk in love, just as Christ also loved you and gave Himself up for us, an offering and a sacrifice to God as a fragrant aroma. – Ephesians 5:1-2

> Be imitators of me, just as I also am of Christ. – 1 Corinthians 11:1

While we are still here in our mortal, fleshly, sinful bodies, we cannot attain the perfection of Christ, but we <u>can</u> strive to be more like Christ (to be conformed to Christ and to imitate Christ) each day. Therefore, perfection for us in this world means to "abide in Me [Christ]" daily, and He in you, and to strive to imitate Christ every day in obedience to His commands. To do this, we must also continue to "grow in the grace and knowledge of our Lord and Savior Jesus Christ," which we do by studying and reading His Word; this is also described as "continuing in the faith." When you do this, you are living under His power, His Spirit, His strength, His might, and His wisdom, and you will be triumphant in obedience. If you were to ever be completely obedient to all the commands of Christ, you would look just like Christ (not as a God, but in behavior). As with the changes to your thoughts and behavior which start to happen by living in the Spirit, the process of obedience doesn't happen instantly but is developed over a lifetime of conscious commitment to reading the Word and following Christ. As you continue to be obedient, you will find that you are moving towards perfection.

As you will read in later chapters, you will also need to change your worldly habits, entertainment choices, etc. If you fail to do those things, "sin is crouching right at your door" again, waiting to pull you back into it. In fact, the more obedient you are, the more that you will find that sinful, fleshly temptations of the world will come your way in an attempt by "the rulers…the powers…the world forces of this darkness…[and] the spiritual *forces* of wickedness in the heavenly *places*" to try to turn you back from following Christ; but we must "resist the devil [the tempter], and he will flee from you."

So, in summary: a truly saving faith is not simply a one-time profession of faith (in words only) followed by idleness – it is followed by obedience to the commands of Christ, as a thankful servant of Christ, as a friend of Christ, and a "child of God" in love. When "born again," God gives you a "new heart" and a "new Spirit," and He also gives you "the desires of your [new] heart" which actually makes you <u>want</u> to be "well pleasing" and obedient to your "Heavenly Father." Even further, the "Spirit of Christ" "dwelling in" you gives you the <u>ability and strength</u> to be obedient; we could not be obedient by our own strength, might, or willpower. Amazing and Amen!

And we are called to be "perfect" – to be "imitators of Christ," which we see by the example Christ Himself set for us comes through obedience. And since many of Christ's commands involve taking action, obedience cannot happen without "good works" also happening. Therefore, the discussion of obedience continues in the next chapter on the role of works in the plan of salvation (i.e., "bearing fruit" for the Lord). Works are the natural outpouring of genuine saving faith and obedience to Christ.

SPECIAL FALSE TEACHING WARNING – BEWARE:

I want to call your attention to the danger of the "sabbath keeping" false teaching (i.e., legalism). When Jesus said to keep His "commandments," He was referring to His commands as given in the New Testament, not the "Ten Commandments" (and thereby also the entire Mosaic Law) given to the ancient Jews. This false teaching is shouted loudly today from several leading cults and "ism's" masquerading as "Christian" churches. Following this false teaching puts you back under bondage to the entire Mosaic Law, which Christ nailed to the cross. Know that you are re-crucifying Christ again if you follow this false teaching! See the Beware the Wolves chapter.

FALSE TEACHING(S) YOU WILL ENCOUNTER:
- Saying a "Sinner's Prayer" saves you
- You are saved by "Faith Alone/Only"
- Once saved always saved
- Being born again is the only step required for eternal life (i.e., obedience, works, and perseverance are not required)
- Sabbath keeping/legalism

RELATED SCRIPTURE:

But Peter and the apostles answered, "We must obey God rather than men." – Acts 5:29

So Jesus was saying to those Jews who had believed Him, "If you continue in My word, *then* you are truly disciples of Mine; and you will know the truth, and the truth will make you free." – John 8:31-32

"Truly, truly, I say to you, if anyone keeps My word he will never see death." – John 8:51

Then Jesus said to His disciples, "If anyone wishes to come after Me, he must deny himself, and take up his cross and follow Me. For whoever wishes to save his life will lose it; but whoever loses his life for My sake will find it. For what will it profit a man if he gains the whole world and forfeits his soul? Or what will a man give in exchange for his soul? For the Son of Man is going to come in the glory of His Father with His angels, and WILL THEN REPAY EVERY MAN ACCORDING TO HIS DEEDS." – Matthew 16:24-27

Paul, a bond-servant of Christ Jesus, called *as* an apostle, set apart for the gospel of God, which He promised beforehand through His prophets in the holy Scriptures, concerning His Son, who was born of a descendant of David according to the flesh, who was declared the Son of God with power by the resurrection from the dead, according to the Spirit of holiness, Jesus Christ our Lord, through whom we have received grace and apostleship to bring about *the* obedience of faith among all the Gentiles for His name's sake, among whom you also are the called of Jesus Christ. – Romans 1:1-6

"Why do you call Me, 'Lord, Lord,' and do not do what I say? Everyone who comes to Me and hears My words and acts on them, I will show you whom he is like: he is like a man building a house, who dug deep and laid a foundation on the rock; and when a flood occurred, the torrent burst against that house and could not shake it, because it had been well built. But the one who has heard and has not acted *accordingly*, is like a man who built a house on the ground without any foundation; and the torrent burst against it and immediately it collapsed, and the ruin of that house was great." – Luke 6:46-49

Beloved, let us love one another, for love is from God; and everyone who loves is born of God and knows God. The one who does not love does not know God, for God is love. By this the love of God was manifested in us, that God has sent His only begotten Son into the world so that we might live through Him. In this is love, not that we loved God, but that He loved us and sent His Son *to be* the propitiation for our sins. Beloved, if God so loved us, we also ought to love one another. No one has seen God at any time; if we love one another, God abides in us, and His love is perfected in us. – 1 John 4:7-12

4.3 BEARING FRUIT
(The Role of Works)

For just as the body without the spirit is dead,
so also faith without works is dead. – James 2:26

Bearing Fruit for the Lord. This chapter explains the role of works (action on the part of the believer) in the plan of (eternal) salvation for a Christian. This is a very lengthy chapter, for we must once again confront and clear away the rampant and widespread false teachings of man on this subject, which have grossly distorted the truth of what is written in Scripture. Therefore, we must make our way through this chapter carefully so that we understand what Scripture actually teaches about this vital subject as opposed to relying on the opinions of man.

But before we begin, please turn to the book of James in your Bible....is it still there? Yes, it is? ... Whew, you can breathe a big sigh of relief, and we can therefore continue along on the path of truth.

FAITH WITHOUT WORKS IS DEAD

Scripture is abundantly clear that works play a role in the plan of salvation for a Christian. Let's make a list of what the Bible says about works:

- "Faith without works is dead" (James 2:26),
- "A man is justified by works and not by faith alone" (James 2:24),
- "Faith, if it has no works, is dead, being by itself" (James 2:17),
- "Prove yourselves doers of the word, and not merely hearers who delude themselves" (James 1:22),
- "...that you bear much fruit, and so prove to be My disciples" (John 15:8),
- "The harvest is plentiful but the workers are few" (Matthew 9:37),
- "If someone says he has faith but he has no works? Can that faith save him?" (James 2:14),
- "Was not Abraham our father justified by works?" (James 2:21),
- "...as a result of the works, faith was perfected" (James 2:22),
- "Let your light shine before men in such a way that they may see your good works" (Matthew 5:16),
- "Every tree that does not bear good fruit is cut down and thrown into the fire" (Matthew 7:19),
- "...that the man of God may be adequate, equipped for every good work" (2 Timothy 3:17),
- "...be steadfast, immovable, always abounding in the work of the Lord" (1 Corinthians 15:58),
- "'I know your deeds and your toil and perseverance...'" (Revelation 2:1),
- "'...for I have not found your deeds completed in the sight of My God.'" (Revelation 3:2),
- "'I know your deeds, that you are neither cold nor hot; I wish that you were cold or hot. So because you are lukewarm, and neither hot nor cold, I will spit you out of My mouth.'" (Revelation 3:15-16),

- "Write, 'Blessed are the dead who die in the Lord from now on!'" "Yes," says the Spirit, "so that they may rest from their labors, for their deeds follow with them." (Revelation 14:13)

As you can see for yourself, Scripture has <u>much</u> to say about the role of works in the plan of salvation and that truly genuine saving faith is manifest in action (works). Said another way, your works demonstrate the sincerity of your heart and profession of faith and are evidence of genuine faith. It is important to understand that good works come naturally from a heart that has given itself to God, in a changed life, not to earn forgiveness or diminish the grace of God one iota.

Wayne Jackson writes that faith is demonstrated to be an action term in Hebrews 11:[58]

> But it is important to note that "faith" in the biblical sense has never denoted a mere passive acceptance of certain facts. Rather it is a term of active obedience.
>
> Actually, faith consists of three elements:
> 1. An acknowledgement of historical facts;
> 2. A willingness to trust the Lord, and;
> 3. A wholehearted submission to the divine will.
>
> One cannot but notice how "faith is demonstrated to be an action term in Hebrews 11. "By faith" Abel offered; Noah prepared; Abraham obeyed; etc. The inspired James made it wonderfully clear that faith, divorced from obedience, is dead (James 2:26).

It's as if the entire book of James has been ripped out of the Bibles of many so-called "modern" or "reformed" Christians and their churches. Scripture is abundantly clear that true Christianity is as much about action as it about the profession of faith! Scripture explicitly states that "faith without works is dead" and that "a man is justified by works and not by faith alone." Those are very clear, literal, and direct verses that cannot be explained away or twisted into some other meaning; you simply cannot evade the force of those verses!

And even further, we read:

> "Beware of the false prophets, who come to you in sheep's clothing, but inwardly are ravenous wolves. You will know them by their fruits. Grapes are not gathered from thorn *bushes* nor figs from thistles, are they? So every good tree bears good fruit, but the bad tree bears bad fruit. A good tree cannot produce bad fruit, nor can a bad tree produce good fruit. Every tree that does not bear good fruit is cut down and thrown into the fire. So then, you will know them by their fruits.

> "Not everyone who says to Me, 'Lord, Lord,' will enter the kingdom of heaven, but he who does the will of My Father who is in heaven *will enter*. Many will say to Me on that day, 'Lord, Lord, did we not prophesy in Your name, and in Your name cast out demons, and in Your name perform many miracles?' And then I will declare to them, 'I never knew you; DEPART FROM ME, YOU WHO PRACTICE LAWLESSNESS.'" – Matthew 7:15-23

---

[58] Jackson, Wayne. "God's Great Plan Consummated." ChristianCourier.com. Access date: September 14, 2020. https://christiancourier.com/articles/1562-gods-great-plan-consummated

For we must all appear before the judgment seat of Christ, so that each one may be recompensed for his deeds in the body, according to what he has done, whether good or bad. – 2 Corinthians 5:10

"For the Son of Man is going to come in the glory of His Father with His angels, and WILL THEN REPAY EVERY MAN ACCORDING TO HIS DEEDS." – Matthew 16:27

But because of your stubbornness and unrepentant heart you are storing up wrath for yourself in the day of wrath and revelation of the righteous judgment of God, who WILL RENDER TO EACH PERSON ACCORDING TO HIS DEEDS. – Romans 2:5-6

Please note the prominence of the word "deeds" in the above verses. As you can see, the role of works is addressed in many New Testament passages.

ONCE AGAIN, BEWARE FALSE TEACHINGS

Despite, and in contradiction to, the very clear, direct, literal, compelling Scripture I have just shown you above, a couple of false teachings are absolutely rampant and widespread today. I point them out here, so you are not deceived. They are:

1) **You are Saved by "Faith alone/only":** Some falsely teach and preach that you are saved solely by a profession of faith ("faith alone/only"), i.e., that obedience and works have no place whatsoever in the plan of salvation or the justification of the believer. They teach this despite the clear and direct Scripture I have just shown you above! Note: Those who teach this usually teach the "sinner's prayer" false teaching as well.
2) **Baptism Related:** Some of the "faith alone/only" advocates will *additionally* claim that baptism is a "good work" of man, and therefore not required for salvation (since they exclude works from the plan of salvation). They arrive at this errant conclusion by a) ignoring Scripture, b) decreeing that baptism is a "good work" of man, and then c) because of their "faith alone/only" bias, they exclude it from salvation because they classify it as a "work." I hope you followed all that twisted logic.

This book is showing you that those who proclaim this "faith alone/only" false teaching are therefore triply wrong because:

1) Baptism is not a "good work" of man,
2) Baptism is required for salvation (to be born again, to receive forgiveness of sins), and
3) Works do play an important role in the biblical plan of salvation

The saved by "faith alone/only" false teaching comes primarily from those who call themselves "reformed protestants" (also Calvinists), and it is blaring out in ferocious volume 24/7/365 from so-called "Christian" pulpits, publications, radio stations, books, movies, and even seminary schools which train up new pastors in so-called "modern" and "reformed" Christianity. You see, I, too, was initially deceived by this false teaching because it was the only thing that I had ever heard taught and preached in any church that I attended! Wayne Jackson writes:[59]

> It is utterly incredible that some, professing an acquaintance with the New Testament, deny the role of works (obedience) in the sacred scheme of redemption. Jesus plainly taught that one must "work" for that spiritual sustenance which abides unto eternal life (Jn. 6:27), and that even faith itself is a divinely appointed "work" (Jn. 6:29).

I have further explained in a prior chapter that there is a difference between initial salvation ("forgiveness of sins," being "born again") and final eternal salvation ("crown of life"). A lack of understanding of that difference can lead one to believe both the "saved by faith alone/only" false teaching as well as the "once saved always saved" false teaching (see the upcoming chapter on Perseverance). False teachings are often interwoven and interconnected together – they usually travel as a pack of lies, all tangled together into a giant knot/web of deception. To support their "faith alone/only" false teaching, the "wolves" take Paul's writing in the letter to the Ephesians (Eph. 2:8-10) out of context and distort it; I explain that shortly.

SOME HISTORY

But first, it is helpful to understand where this "faith alone/only" false teaching originated. It didn't start until many centuries after Christ. It came about when Protestantism arose during the reformation movement to counter the blatantly unscriptural teachings of Roman Catholicism, which included concepts such as 1) the "selling of indulgences (sins)" (i.e., you can buy forgiveness), and 2) that "meritorious good works" justify man before God. This is what the "faith alone/only" advocates are usually referring to by a "works-based salvation": i.e., obtaining salvation (justification before God, forgiveness of sins) by doing meritorious works.

While opposition to the Roman Catholic Church's corrupt teachings was much needed, the Reformed Protestant movement (generally credited to Martin Luther in 1517) erred by pushing the pendulum too far in the opposite direction by negating the role of works altogether from the plan of salvation. In fact, Martin Luther objected to the book of James – he did not think it was part of the canon of Scripture (because he didn't agree with it!). He even further then rewrote Romans 3:28 by adding the word "only" to it! The word "only" is not found in the original Greek texts from which he was translating. Yes, Luther changed (added to) Scripture to make it conform to his own beliefs!

GETTING BACK ON TRACK (AND COMMON SENSE)

This chapter was by far the hardest for me to write because I felt the need to strongly counter this rampant "faith alone/only" false teaching. While most chapters in the book came pretty easily, I've had to rewrite this one several times in an attempt to find the best way to present the role of works to you. What I've decided to do is to list as many different ways as possible that I could think of to explain this subject to you, in the hope that one of them might resonate with you, so you get that "ah-ha" moment about it and shatter the brainwashing (i.e., false teachings) you've likely already been

---

[59] Jackson, Wayne. "JUSTIFICATION: By Faith or Works?" *ChristianCourier.com*. Access date: November 8, 2018. https://christiancourier.com/articles/294-justification-by-faith-or-works

exposed to on this subject. If you haven't been exposed to the "faith alone/only" false teaching yet, that's great, but please follow along closely anyway, as this topic is vital to eternal salvation. Also, know that you will almost surely encounter that false teaching as you go forward in your Christian walk.

I want to begin discussing the role of works with an example if you will, which allows us to use simple common sense to get started. Let me ask you: What if someone promised to give you a million dollars – but then days, weeks, months, and even years go by, and they never give you even so much as one single cent. Now I'm not talking about someone who said it jokingly, but someone who appeared to mean it, and they had the means to back it up and actually do it (e.g., maybe you even shook hands on it). Would you think their profession of giving was genuine? I don't think you would! In fact, if they keep on professing to give you the million dollars over and over again and never actually give you anything, you will soon realize that they are a liar, a fake, and a fraud. In the same way, without works, your profession of faith is not genuine; that is why Scripture says that we will "know them by their fruits." A true Christian will produce fruit for the Lord ("some a hundredfold, some sixty, and some thirty") – and fruit can only come from works.

And to drive the point home even further, let's list a few things which the secular world says on this subject:

- "Talk is cheap,"
- "This is where the rubber meets the road,"
- "Actions speak louder than words,"
- "Put up or shut up,"
- Giving "lip service" to something (but not doing it),
- "Putting your money where your mouth is,"
- "You've got to walk the walk and not just talk the talk"

Now don't get me wrong, I'm not suggesting that you get your Christian doctrine from the secular world, but I think you can see that even the secular world understands that it is actions which demonstrate and prove professions to be genuine. In the same way, God expects you, and Scripture commands you, to prove your faith is real by backing it up with action: this is called doing "good works" or "producing fruit" for the Lord after you have been born again. Scripture is abundantly clear that you must act on your faith to be saved (justified before God) and for your faith to be pleasing to God.

What if Noah, Abraham, and Moses didn't ever "do anything" after they proclaimed faith in God? – i.e., Noah never actually built an ark and Abraham never offered up Isaac. Would you believe that their professions of faith were real and genuine? I don't think you would. And let's take this up to the very top, the absolute highest pinnacle of authority: God Himself. What if God constantly talked about how He wants humanity to be saved from sin to eternal life with Him in heaven, but He never actually <u>did</u> anything about it? What if He never actually gave His Son Jesus Christ to die on the cross for you? What if Jesus made a lot of claims that He could heal people, but He never actually did heal anyone? And finally, what if Jesus said He would die on the cross for your sins, but He never actually did it? Would you take God seriously? You can see that even God backs up His professions and words with action!

Make no mistake, faith and works aren't mutually exclusive, nor are they in opposition to each other – they both work together for a Christian. Christ expects your faith to be an active faith, not passive or idle (or even lukewarm). When God says He will do something, He always does; in contrast, what man says he seldom does. Hence it is written: "be doers of the word, not hearers only" – it is not the hearers and idle professors ("make believers") of the Word which will be saved, but "doers" of the Word. I hope you can see that it is by actual deeds and works that you prove your faith is a real, live, saving faith – both before men and before God.

It is my works that testify (demonstrate, prove) that I am a Christian, and it is your works that testify (demonstrate, prove) that you are a Christian. Your works actually complete (perfect) your faith as it is written:

> You see that faith was working with his works, and as a result of the works, faith was perfected. – James 2:22

Faith and works are like two sides of the same hand, both working together, with one important exception: faith comes first, and it is by and through your faith in Christ that you can do any works. "Good works" will come about as a natural result of truly genuine saving faith, as one is obedient to the commands of Christ, as a bondservant of God doing the will of God, loving and serving others. As God's grace was made manifest in Jesus, true genuine saving Christian faith is made manifest by your works/deeds. While it is the grace (and love) of God that put Jesus on the cross for us (so that we could be saved, have our sins forgiven), it is never written that you are saved by "faith only" in Scripture. True genuine saving Christian faith manifests itself in producing good works for the Lord, for it is written: "Faith without works is dead"! Do you think that a "<u>dead</u>" faith will save you to eternal <u>life</u>? Will a "dead" faith please God?

So now I ask you straight away: Do you want "dead" faith? Does the Bible state that God accepts "dead" faith? Does the Bible state that God even accepts "lukewarm" faith? The answer is unequivocally no to all those questions. It is further written that Christ expects to find you "doing" when He returns (at His Second Coming to judge the world). In fact, Scripture condemns those who profess to be in Christ in faith but who are found idle.

In the previous chapter, we learned that the life of a true Christian is marked by continued, willful obedience to the commands of Christ as given in the New Testament. Since many of Christ's commands involve taking action of some kind, you cannot be obedient to Christ and obey His commandments and yet not "do" anything! Following those commands will result in us doing work for the Lord – "bearing fruit" for the Lord, helping to build the Kingdom of God, in which you are now a "fellow partaker" of as a born-again Christian. Therefore, if you are a servant of God in Christ, active in your faith, you cannot help but "bear fruit" for the Lord. Also, note that Scripture describes us as members of the "body" of Christ; a body is designed and needed to do work – otherwise, there is no need for a body.

RECONCILING WHAT PAUL AND JAMES WROTE

Much of the confusion about the role of works comes from trying to reconcile the following verses written by Paul and James, both inspired writers:

> For by grace you have been saved through faith; and that not of yourselves, *it is* the gift of God; not as a result of works, so that no one may boast. For we are His workmanship, created in Christ Jesus for good works, which God prepared beforehand so that we would walk in them. – Ephesians 2:8-10 (written by Paul)

For we maintain that a man is justified by faith apart from works of the Law. – Romans 3:28 (also written by Paul)

Even so faith, if it has no works, is dead, *being* by itself. – James 2:17 (written by James)

You see that a man is justified by works and not by faith alone. – James 2:24 (written by James)

So why does one verse say that salvation is not the result of works, and the other writes that faith without works is dead? How are these verses to be reconciled? Keep in mind that both writers were inspired, and Scripture is 100% truth, and it never contradicts itself – so both have to be true statements when correctly interpreted. No correct interpretation or understanding of one part or verse of Scripture can result in contradicting any other part or verse of Scripture! If your interpretation of one verse causes it to conflict with another verse, then your interpretation is wrong, not Scripture! Additionally, you cannot interpret verses of Scripture that may be more difficult to understand (which are more obscure) in a way that contradicts other simple, clear, direct, and easily understood verses of Scripture.

Wayne Jackson summarizes this well:[60]

> First, one cannot take one passage that appears to contain a difficulty and array it against an almost encyclopedic collection of information that leads to an opposite conclusion. That is not a legitimate approach to biblical interpretation, and it reveals more about those who argue in this vein than is complimentary to them.
>
> It is rather analogous to the procedure of the skeptic who ignores the vast conglomerate of data that argue for the unity of the Bible (hence its divine origin) by the appeal to a single text that superficially appears to imply a contradiction.
>
> It also is similar to the Protestant who disregards all the texts that require immersion in water as an act of faith in obtaining the remission of sins, and focusing only on such passages as mention "faith" as a condition of salvation.
>
> …
>
> It is a regrettable circumstance that far too many Christian people have their **minds made up** on a variety of biblical themes before ever carefully studying the matter.
>
> Such individuals are easily disposed to sweep under the carpet much evidence pertaining to a subject, and then almost frantically search for a single text that will justify them in what they already want to believe. This is a common though sad situation.

Yet, this is precisely what people do. They pick one verse they like and disregard the other, even when the verse they have "decided on" for their interpretation (and subsequent belief) is less direct than the other(s). That, however, is faulty exposition, and it leads to faulty teaching! In applying this to the subject at hand, the role of faith <u>and</u> works in the process of salvation, those who proclaim the "faith alone/only" false teaching are taking Paul's verse in Ephesians completely out of context, as I will explain below. Neither inspired writer contradicts the other.

---

[60] Jackson, Wayne. "Buy a Sword?" *ChristianCourier.com*. Access date: November 8, 2018. https://christiancourier.com/articles/1458-buy-a-sword

But first, let's read James 2 in fuller context as it will be crucial in arriving at the correct understanding:

> What use is it, my brethren, if someone says he has faith but he has no works? Can that faith save him? If a brother or sister is without clothing and in need of daily food, and one of you says to them, "Go in peace, be warmed and be filled," and yet you do not give them what is necessary for *their* body, what use is that? Even so faith, if it has no works, is dead, *being* by itself.
>
> But someone may *well* say, "You have faith and I have works; show me your faith without the works, and I will show you my faith by my works." You believe that God is one. You do well; the demons also believe, and shudder. But are you willing to recognize, you foolish fellow, that faith without works is useless? Was not Abraham our father justified by works when he offered up Isaac his son on the altar? You see that faith was working with his works, and as a result of the works, faith was perfected; and the Scripture was fulfilled which says, "AND ABRAHAM BELIEVED GOD, AND IT WAS RECKONED TO HIM AS RIGHTEOUSNESS," and he was called the friend of God. You see that a man is justified by works and not by faith alone. In the same way, was not Rahab the harlot also justified by works when she received the messengers and sent them out by another way? For just as the body without *the* spirit is dead, so also faith without works is dead. – James 2:14-26

So then, how are these verses (Paul's and James') reconciled when they appear to contradict each other? Since Scripture can't contradict itself, we must go beyond just a simple reading of the words and carefully consider the context of the verses. Simply put, Paul is talking about trying to "earn" salvation through doing works under the Mosaic Law, while James is talking about the works that result from obedience to Christ. There is no contradiction. They have different contexts.

Remember, the Jewish religion under the Mosaic Law was one based in large part on works; this is why Paul is correcting them sternly in the books of Galatians and Ephesians – that salvation is not of those works done under the Mosaic Law. The early Christians, many of whom were Jews, kept wanting to return to that old system, which was done away with (abolished and fulfilled) on the cross, and they also were turning others (gentiles) back into doing works of the law to obtain salvation, and hence they were placing themselves once again under the curse of the law, instead of grace under Christ.

ISAIAH'S "FILTHY RAGS"

Next, what about this verse where Isaiah says our "deeds" are as "filthy rags [garment]":

> For all of us have become like one who is unclean,
> And all our righteous deeds are like a filthy garment;
> And all of us wither like a leaf,
> And our iniquities, like the wind, take us away. – Isaiah 64:6

As usual, the false teachers of the "faith alone/only" crowd engage in their most common magic trick: they take a verse completely out of context and distort and generalize it to mean whatever they wish. In the verse above, Isaiah is lamenting how wretched and pitiful (disgusting) the ancient Jews had become in their worship of the Lord. Even when they occasionally did "righteous deeds" according to the Mosaic Law, they did them half-heartedly, without sincerity, in rote mechanical observation without any hint of true reverence for the Lord.

Furthermore, a couple of additional comments are warranted on this verse as it's widely used to support denial of the works component of salvation. First, compared to the unimaginable holiness of God, all things about us and anything we might do (including our works) will indeed appear as "filthy rags" when compared to the glory of God beheld. Secondly, it is an abuse of interpretation and disrespect to God to apply this to the specific commandments of Christ, to which we are to be obedient – in other words, the Isaiah verse is not to be generalized and applied to the works that a born-again Christian does in obedience to the explicit commands of Christ. Why would actions done in obedience to Christ's commands be interpreted as "filthy rags"? By way of illustration, surely God would not consider the act (work) of preaching the Gospel to all creation (which is an act of obedience to one of Christ's commands) to be viewed as a "filthy rag," now would He? Such an interpretation does great violence to the Gospel and even to Christ Himself! "May it never be!" On the contrary, God would view such acts of obedience as being "well done" by a "good and faithful servant"!

However, we must always keep in mind that the works themselves do nothing whatsoever to enhance or make us righteous (forgiven of sin) before God – our righteousness before God is solely and wholly derived from Christ alone, and His blood sacrificed on the cross.

ON BOASTING ABOUT WORKS

When discussing works, we must also talk about boasting. Always remember that we are only sinners before God, and very frankly, we have nothing that God needs – and we have no righteousness of our own, it all comes from Christ, and no man can stand justified and righteous before God without being covered by the blood and righteousness of Christ. We can only offer our worship, love, and service to God, and our service is manifest through our works done for others. Therefore, nothing in this chapter should be misconstrued to mean you can or should boast about your good works - not before men and most certainly not before God, for:

1. "There is no righteous person, not even one" – all righteousness comes from Christ, not from ourselves (for we have none),
2. You were saved from your sins and death (born again with your sins forgiven) by the grace of God through the blood of Christ, for it is that grace of God out of love (not your works) that put Christ on the cross so that your sins can be forgiven,
3. You are obedient by the power of Christ living (abiding) in you,
4. You are only able to do good works through Christ living (abiding) in you, and
5. You also persevere in faith by the strength of Christ living (abiding) in you.

We must always remember that we have no righteousness of our own – for all righteousness is derived from the blood of Christ, but oh how that covers us like a white garment! As the apostle Paul writes, if we boast, let us boast of Christ and not of ourselves:

> But may it never be that I would boast, except in the cross of our Lord Jesus Christ, through which the world has been crucified to me, and I to the world. – Galatians 6:14

> Most gladly, therefore, I will rather boast about my weaknesses, so that the power of Christ may dwell in me. Therefore I am well content with weaknesses, with insults, with distresses, with persecutions, with difficulties, for Christ's sake; for when I am weak, then I am strong. – 2 Corinthians 12:9-10

> For consider your calling, brethren, that there were not many wise according to the flesh, not many mighty, not many noble; but God has chosen the foolish things of the world to shame the wise, and God has chosen the weak things of the world to shame the things which are strong, and the base things of the world and the despised God has chosen, the things that are not, so that He may nullify the things that are, so that no man may boast before God. But by His doing you are in Christ Jesus, who became to us wisdom from God, and righteousness and sanctification, and redemption, so that, just as it is written, "LET HIM WHO BOASTS, BOAST IN THE LORD." – 1 Corinthians 1:26-31

> Do nothing from selfishness or empty conceit, but with humility consider one another as more important than yourselves. – Philippians 2:3

And further:

> "I am the vine, you are the branches; he who abides in Me and I in him, he bears much fruit, for apart from Me you can do nothing." – John 15:5

> I said to the LORD, "You are my Lord;
> I have no good besides You." – Psalm 16:2

Always remember that "every good thing given and every perfect gift is from above," and it is also written, "I can do all things through Him [Christ] who strengthens me." So, boasting of any kind is wholly excluded from the behavior of the true Christian. Never forget that you were redeemed, wholly bought and paid for, from death to life by the blood of Christ, and it is only through your faith in Christ and Christ abiding in you that you are able to do any good work. Remembering this keeps us properly humble.

Additionally, remember that grace is undeserved favor ["gratuitous lovingkindness of the Lord"[61]], wholly undeserved by anyone, for as Matthew Henry writes, we have forfeited it (and the right to eternal life) a thousand times already by our own actions:[62]

> His conclusion concerning both these we have, Rom 9:18. He hath mercy on whom he will have mercy, and whom he will he hardeneth. The various dealings of God, by which he makes some to differ from others, must be resolved into his absolute sovereignty. He is debtor to no man, his grace is his own, and he may give it or withhold it as it pleaseth him; we have none of us deserved it, nay, we have all justly forfeited it a thousand times, so that herein the work of our salvation is admirably well ordered that those who are saved must thank God only, and those

---

[61] Moule, H. C. G. 1977. Studies in Ephesians. Grand Rapids, MI: Kregel.
[62] Henry, Matthew. Exposition of the Old and New Testaments, London. 1706-1710/1721.

who perish must thank themselves only, Hos 13:9. We are bound, as God hath bound us, to do our utmost for the salvation of all we have to do with; but God is bound no further than he has been pleased to bind himself by his own covenant and promise, which is his revealed will; and that is that he will receive, and not cast out, those that come to Christ; but the drawing of souls in order to that coming is a preventing distinguishing favour to whom he will.

So, remember that in our standing before God, it is Christ's righteousness that counts, not ours – for we have none. God is no respecter of abilities; the wisest, strongest, smartest, richest, most powerful man is but like a mere puff of wind, soon passing away again, back to dust. Pride is still a formidable enemy of the Christian, and it's helpful to keep the words of John the Baptist in mind:

"He [Jesus] must increase, but I must decrease." – John 3:30

WHAT OTHER SAINTS HAVE WRITTEN

If you are still struggling to reconcile the role of works, it may also help you to read what has been written about the subject of faith vs. works by other saints who have come before us. First, here is what Wayne Jackson has written; I think it is very well said:[63]

> Most Protestants, reacting adversely to the "works system" of Roman Catholicism, have adopted the extreme (and unscriptural) view that works play no role whatever in human salvation. Some allege that salvation is on the basis of "faith alone," while others (e.g., radical Calvinists) argue that God chose the redeemed before the world began, and that redemption, therefore, is entirely unconditional.
>
> "But is it not true" someone is bound to argue, "that the Scriptures state that we are not saved by works (Eph. 2:9)?" Yes, that is correct. But it is also the case that the New Testament asserts that we are saved, i.e., justified, by works (Jas. 2:14,24). Since the Bible, being the word of God, does not contradict itself, there must be a sensible solution to this seeming difficulty. How is the problem to be resolved?
>
> Well, it is not (as Luther suggested) that one is at liberty to repudiate the book of James as an inspired document! Rather, the careful student must recognize that there are different kinds of works addressed in the divine record. Let us give brief consideration to this matter with a spirit of genuine investigation.
>
> ### Works of the Law
>
> In his letter to the Romans, Paul makes it clear that no one can be saved by keeping the works of Moses' law. The apostle argued that "a man is justified by faith apart from the works of the law" (3:28). The term "law" in this passage is broader than the Mosaic system, though it certainly includes that law.
>
> This certainly does not suggest, however, that obedience to Christ may be ignored with impunity. In the same epistle, Paul affirmed that these saints in Rome had embraced freedom from the penalty of sin as a result of having been "obedient

---

[63] Jackson, Wayne. "The Role of "Works" in God's Plan of Redemption." *ChristianCourier.com*. Access date: November 8, 2018. https://christiancourier.com/articles/729-role-of-works-in-gods-plan-of-redemption-the

from the heart" to the "pattern of teaching" whereby they were delivered (6:17; cf. 3-4).

The works of the Mosaic law could not save because they required perfect compliance (Gal. 3:10b), which no person could achieve. Moreover, the regime of Moses had only the blood of animals, which could not atone for sin in the absolute sense (Heb. 10:4). The primary focus of the Hebrew system was to direct attention to the coming Messiah (Gal. 3:24-25); it was never designed to provide the ultimate phase of God's plan of salvation. Had the Mosaic law that kind of power, Christ need never have died as the sin-offering (Gal. 2:21).

Works of Human Merit

In his Ephesian letter, Paul wrote: "[F]or by grace have you been saved through faith; and that not of yourselves, it is the gift of God; not of works that no man should glory" (2:8-9).

The works here excluded are charitable works which men pile up, imagining that such will justify them, while they, with a smug self-sufficiency, ignore the sacrifice of Christ and his redemptive system.

The Red Cross is famous for its benevolent efforts, but there is no justification to be found therein, because its "works" are mere human benevolent efforts, wholly divorced from the mission of the Son of God. The man who boasts: "I am a good person; I do not need Jesus Christ," is guilty of the same mistake.

Works of Obedience

There are works mentioned in the Bible that are designated as "works of God." By this expression it is not implied that these are works which God himself performs. Rather, they are works ordained of God, to be obeyed by men, that are indispensable to salvation.

Consider a text in John, chapter 6. The disciples inquired of the Lord: "What must we do, that we may work the works of God?"

Jesus responded: "This is the work of God that you believe on him who he has sent" (vv. 28-29). Observe that this "work of [from] God" required a human response — that of believing. Regarding the term "work," as here used, J.H. Thayer commented: "... the works required and approved by God" (Clark, p. 248).[64]

The term "works" is sometimes the equivalent of "obedience." Elsewhere Jesus promised victory to those who "keep my works," i.e., the works (commands) prescribed by him (Rev. 2:26). If, therefore, all "works" are excluded from the plan of salvation, faith itself would be eliminated, for it is identified as a work.

It must be noted as well that "repentance" is a component in God's scheme of redemption (Acts 2:38; 3:19). And yet, repentance is classified as a "work." Jesus once said that the people of ancient Nineveh "repented" when Jonah preached to them (Mt. 12:41). The book of Jonah explains the meaning of this. God saw their "works, that they turned from their evil way" (3:10). There is no question about it, works — of a certain sort — are a part of the salvation process.

Next, I present commentary written by Matthew Henry on the role of faith and works. He correctly states that "faith alone/only" is not what saves, but it is faith with your works. He also reinforces that we have no reason to boast before God, even for

---

[64] Clark, T. & T., Greek-English Lexicon of the New Testament, Edinburgh, 1958.

the works we do out of obedience to God, for we are all fallen sinners undeserving of God's grace, and we had no part in what Christ did on the cross – that was all God's doing:[65]

> In this latter part of the chapter (James 2), the apostle shows the error of those who rested in a bare profession of the Christian faith, as if that would save them, while the temper of their minds and the tenor of their lives were altogether disagreeable to that holy religion which they professed. To let them see, therefore, what a wretched foundation they built their hopes upon, it is here proved at large that a man is justified, not by faith only, but by works. Now,
>
> I. Upon this arises a very great question, namely, how to reconcile Paul and James… *Amicae scripturarum lites, utinam et nostrae – There is a very happy agreement between one part of scripture and another, notwithstanding seeming differences: it were well if the differences among Christians were as easily reconciled.* "Nothing," says Mr. Baxter, "but men's misunderstanding the plain drift and sense of Paul's epistles, could make so many take it for a matter of great difficulty to reconcile Paul and James." …
>
> 1. When Paul says that *a man is justified by faith, without the deeds of the law* (Rom 3:28), he plainly speaks of another sort of work than James does, but not of another sort of faith. Paul speaks of works wrought in obedience to the law of Moses, and before men's embracing the faith of the gospel; and he had to deal with those who valued themselves so highly upon those works that they rejected the gospel (as Rom. 10, at the beginning most expressly declares); but James speaks of works done in obedience to the gospel, and as the proper and necessary effects and fruits of sound believing in Christ Jesus. Both are concerned to magnify the faith of the gospel, as that which alone could save us and justify us; but Paul magnifies it by showing the insufficiency of any works of the law before faith, or in opposition to the doctrine of justification by Jesus Christ; James magnifies the same faith, by showing what are the genuine and necessary products and operations of it.
>
> 2. Paul not only speaks of different works from those insisted on by James, but he speaks of a quite different use that was made of good works from what is here urged and intended. Paul had to do with those who depended on the merit of their works in the sight of God, and thus he might well make them of no manner of account. James had to do with those who cried up faith, but would not allow works to be used even as evidence; they depended upon a bare profession, as sufficient to justify them; and with these he might well urge the necessity and vast importance of good works. As we must not break one table of the law, by dashing it against the other, so neither must we break in pieces the law and the gospel, by making them clash with one another: those who cry up the gospel so as to set aside the law, and those who cry up the law so as to set aside the gospel, are both in the wrong; for we must take our work before us; there must be both faith in Jesus Christ and good works the fruit of faith.
>
> 3. The justification of which Paul speaks is different from that spoken of by James; the one speaks of our persons being justified before God, the other speaks of our faith being justified before men: "*Show me thy faith by thy works,*" says James, "let thy faith be justified in the eyes of those that behold thee by thy works";

---

[65] Henry, Matthew. Exposition of the Old and New Testaments, London. 1706-1710/1721.

but Paul speaks of justification in the sight of God, who justifies those only that believe in Jesus, and purely on account of the redemption that is in him. Thus we see that our persons are justified before God by faith, but our faith is justified before men by works. This is so plainly the scope and design of the apostle James that he is but confirming what Paul, in other places, says of his faith, that it is a laborious faith, and a faith working by love, Gal 5:6; 1Th 1:3; Tit 3:8; and many other places.

Paul may be understood as speaking of that justification which is inchoate, James of that which is complete; it is by *faith* only that we are put into a justified state, but then good works come in for the completing of our justification at the last great day; then, *Come you children of my Father – for I was hungry, and you gave me meat,* etc.

II. Having thus cleared this part of scripture from everything of a contradiction to other parts of it, let us see what is more particularly to be learnt from this excellent passage of James; we are taught,

1. That faith without works will not profit and cannot save us. *What doth it profit, my brethren, if a man say he hath faith, and have not works? Can faith save him?* Observe here,

(1.) That faith which does not save will not really profit us; a bare profession may sometimes seem to be profitable, to gain the good opinion of those who are truly good, and it may procure in some cases worldly good things; but what profit will this be, for any to gain the world and to lose their souls? *What doth it profit? – Can faith save him?* All things should be accounted profitable or unprofitable to us as they tend to forward or hinder the salvation of our souls. And, above all other things, we should take care thus to make account of faith, as that which does not profit, if it does not save, but will aggravate our condemnation and destruction at last.

(2.) For a man to have faith, and to say he has faith, are two different things; the apostle does not say, *If a man have faith without works,* for that is not a supposable case; the drift of this place of scripture is plainly to show that an opinion, or speculation, or assent, without works, is not faith; but the case is put thus, *If a man say he hath faith,* etc. Men may boast of that to others, and be conceited of that in themselves, of which they are really destitute.

2. We are taught that, as love or charity is an operative principle, so is faith, and that neither of them would otherwise be good for anything; and, by trying how it looks for a person to pretend he is very charitable who yet never does any works of charity, you may judge what sense there is in pretending to have faith without the proper and necessary fruits of it: *"If a brother or a sister be naked, and destitute of daily food, and one of you say unto them, Depart in peace, be you warmed and filled, notwithstanding you give them not those things which are needful to the body, what doth it profit"?* Jas 2:15-17. What will such a charity as this, that consists in bare words, avail either you or the poor? Will you come before God with such empty shows of charity as these? You might as well pretend that your love and charity will stand the test without acts of mercy as think that a profession of faith will bear you out before God without works of piety and obedience. *"Even so faith, if it hath not works, is dead, being along,"* Jas 2:17. We are too apt to rest in a bare profession of faith, and to think that this will save us; it is a cheap and easy religion to say, "We believe the articles of the Christian faith"; but it is a great delusion to imagine that this is enough to bring us to heaven. Those who argue thus

wrong God and put a cheat upon their own souls; a mock-faith is as hateful as mock-charity, and both show a heart dead to all real godliness. You may as soon take pleasure in a dead body, void of soul, or sense, or action, as God take pleasure in a dead faith, where there are no works.

3. We are taught to compare a faith boasting of itself without works and a faith evidenced by works, by looking on both together, to try how this comparison will work upon our minds. Yea, a man may say, Thou hast faith, and I have works. Show me thy faith without thy works, and I will show thee my faith by my works, v. 18. Suppose a true believer thus pleading with a boasting hypocrite, "Thou makest a profession, and sayest thou hast faith; I make no such boasts, but leave my works to speak for me. Now give any evidence of having the faith thou professest without works if thou canst, and I will soon let thee see how my works flow from faith and are the undoubted evidences of its existence." This is the evidence by which the scriptures all along teach men to judge both of themselves and others. And this is the evidence according to which Christ will proceed at the day of judgment. The dead were judged according to their works, Rev. 20:12. How will those be exposed then who boast of that which they cannot evidence, or who go about to evidence their faith by anything but works of piety and mercy!

4. We are taught to look upon a faith of bare speculation and knowledge as the faith of devils: Thou believest that there is one God; thou doest well; the devils also believe, and tremble, v. 19. That instance of faith which the apostle here chooses to mention is the first principle of all religion. "Thou believest that there is a God, against the atheists; and that there is but one God, against the idolaters; thou doest well: so far all is right. But to rest here, and take up a good opinion of thyself, or of thy state towards God, merely on account of thy believing in him, this will render thee miserable: The devils also believe, and tremble. If thou contentest thyself with a bare assent to articles of faith, and some speculations upon them, thus far the devils go. And as their faith and knowledge only serve to excite horror, so in a little time will thine." The word tremble is commonly looked upon as denoting a good effect of faith; but here it may rather be taken as a bad effect, when applied to the faith of devils. They tremble, not out of reverence, but hatred and opposition to that one God on whom they believe. To rehearse that article of our creed, therefore, I believe in God the Father Almighty, will not distinguish us from devils at last, unless we now give up ourselves to God as the gospel directs, and love him, and delight ourselves in him, and serve him, which the devils do not, cannot do.

5. We are taught that he who boasts of faith without works is to be looked upon at present as a foolish condemned person. But wilt thou know, O vain man, that faith without works is dead? v. 20. The words translated vain man —anthrope kene, are observed to have the same signification with the word Raca, which must never be used to private persons, or as an effect of anger (Mt. 5:22), but may be used as here, to denote a just detestation of such a sort of men as are empty of good works, and yet boasters of their faith. And it plainly declares them fools and abjects in the sight of God. Faith without works is said to be dead, not only as void of all those operations which are the proofs of spiritual life, but as unavailable to eternal life: such believers as rest in a bare profession of faith are dead while they live.

6. We are taught that a justifying faith cannot be without works, from two examples, Abraham and Rahab.

(1.) The first instance is that of Abraham, the father of the faithful, and the prime example of justification, to whom the Jews had a special regard (Jas 2:21): *Was not Abraham our father justified by works, when he had offered Isaac his son upon the altar?* Paul, on the other hand, says (in ch. 4 of the epistle to the Romans) that Abraham *believed, and it was counted to him for righteousness.* But these are well reconciled, by observing what is said in Heb. 11, which shows that the faith both of Abraham and Rahab was such as to produce those good works of which James speaks, and which are not to be separated from faith as justifying and saving. By what Abraham did, it appeared that he truly believed. Upon this footing, the words of God himself plainly put this matter. Gen 22:16, Gen 22:17, *Because thou hast done this thing, and hast not withheld thy son, thine only son; therefore in blessing I will bless thee.* Thus the faith of Abraham was a working faith (Jas 2:22), *it wrought with his works, and by works was made perfect.* And by this means you come to the true sense of that scripture which saith, Abraham believed God, *and it was imputed unto him for righteousness,* Jas 2:23. And thus he became the *friend of God.* Faith, producing such works, endeared him to the divine Being, and advanced him to very peculiar favours and intimacies with God. It is a great honour done to Abraham that he is called and counted the friend of God. You see then (Jas 2:24) how that *by works a man is justified* (comes into such a state of favour and friendship with God), *and not by faith only;* not by a bare opinion, or profession, or believing without obeying, but by having such a faith as is productive of good works. Now besides the explication of this passage and example, as thus illustrating and supporting the argument James is upon, many other useful lessons may be learned by us from what is here said concerning Abraham.

[1.] Those who would have Abraham's blessings must be careful to copy after his faith: to boast of being Abraham's seed will not avail any, if they do not believe as he did.

[2.] Those works which evidence true faith must to works of self-denial, and such as God himself commands (as Abraham's offering up his son, his only son, was), and not such works as are pleasing to flesh and blood and may serve our interest, or are the mere fruits of our own imagination and devising.

[3.] What we piously purpose and sincerely resolve to do for God is accepted as if actually performed. Thus Abraham is regarded as offering up his son, though he did not actually proceed to make a sacrifice of him. It was a done thing in the mind, and spirit, and resolution of Abraham, and God accepts it as if fully performed and accomplished.

[4.] The actings of faith make it grow perfect, as the truth of faith makes it act.

[5.] Such an acting faith will make others, as well as Abraham, friends of God. Thus Christ says to his disciples, *I have called you friends,* Joh 15:15. All transactions between God and the truly believing soul are easy, pleasant, and delightful. There is one will and one heart, and there is a mutual complacency. *God rejoiceth over those* who truly believe, to do them good; and they delight themselves in him.

(2.) The second example of faith's justifying itself and us with and by works is Rahab: *Likewise also was not Rahab the harlot justified by works, when she had received the messengers, and had sent them out another way?* Jas 2:25. The former instance was of one renowned for his faith all his life long, This is of one noted for sin, whose faith was meaner and of a much lower degree; so that the strongest faith will not do, nor the meanest be allowed to go without works. Some say that the word here rendered *harlot* was the proper name of Rahab. Others tell us that it signifies no more than a *hostess,* or one who keeps a public house, with whom therefore the spies lodged. But it is very probable that her character was infamous; and such an instance is mentioned to show that faith will save the worst, when evidenced by proper works; and it will not save the best without such works as God requires. This Rahab believed the report she had heard of God's powerful presence with Israel; but that which proved her faith sincere was, that, to the hazard of her life, she *received the messengers, and sent them out another way.* Observe here,

[1.] The wonderful power of faith in transforming and changing sinners.

[2.] The regard which an operative faith meets with from God, to obtain his mercy and favour.

[3.] Where great sins are pardoned, there must prefer the honour of God and the good of his people before the preservation of her own country. Her former acquaintance must be discarded, her former course of life entirely abandoned, and she must give signal proof and evidence of this before she can be in a justified state; and even after she is justified, yet her former character must be remembered; not so much to her dishonour as to glorify the rich grace and mercy of God. Though justified, she is called *Rahab the harlot.*

7. And now, upon the whole matter, the apostle draws this conclusion, *As the body without the spirit is dead, so faith without works is dead also,* Jas 2:26. These words are read differently; some reading them, *As the body without the breath is dead, so is faith without works:* and then they show that works are the companions of faith, as breathing is of life. Others read them, *As the body without the soul is dead, so faith without works is dead also:* and then they show that as the body has no action, nor beauty, but becomes a loathsome carcass, when the soul is gone, so a bare profession without works is useless, yea, loathsome and offensive. Let us then take head of running into extremes in this case. For,

(1.) The best works, without faith, are dead; they want their root and principle. It is by faith that any thing we do is really good, as done with an eye to God, in obedience to him, and so as to aim principally at his acceptance.

(2.) The most plausible profession of faith, without works, is dead: as the root is dead when it produces nothing green, nothing of fruit. Faith is the root, good works are the fruits, and we must see to it that we have both. We must not think that either, without the other, will justify and save us. This is the grace of God wherein we stand, and we should stand to it.

GOD SAW THEIR DEEDS

And finally, to close up this chapter, Scripture is abundantly clear that the Lord notices what a man does as much as what he says. This can be seen in the case of Nineveh, in the book of Jonah. At the preaching of Jonah (when he finally went to Nineveh after his three-day detour in the belly of a fish), the city of Nineveh repented of their sinful ways. However, note what Scripture says about how God viewed this situation:

> When God saw their deeds, that they turned from their wicked way, then God relented concerning the calamity which He had declared He would bring upon them. And He did not do *it.* – Jonah 3:10

It was their deeds that God noticed as proof of their repentance, so He relented on the judgment that He had pronounced on them. God needed to see their profession of faith borne out by their actions. They proved their repentance was genuine and sincere by their works! This is a great example of how your profession of faith and repentance are to be backed up by actions that demonstrate your sincerity of heart. In a further example from the book of Revelation, we see again that God takes notice of your deeds:

> "He who has the seven Spirits of God and the seven stars, says this: 'I know your deeds, that you have a name that you are alive, but you are dead.'" – Revelation 3:1

> "And to the angel of the church in Philadelphia write: He who is holy, who is true, who has the key of David, who opens and no one will shut, and who shuts and no one opens, says this: 'I know your deeds....'" – Revelation 3:7-8

We also read that Christ will condemn those who profess faith (only) but are found idle when He comes:

> "Who then is the faithful and wise servant, whom his master has set over his household, to give them their food at the proper time? Blessed is that servant whom his master will find so doing when he comes. Truly, I say to you, he will set him over all his possessions. But if that wicked servant says to himself, 'My master is delayed,' and begins to beat his fellow servants and eats and drinks with drunkards, the master of that servant will come on a day when he does not expect him and at an hour he does not know and will cut him in pieces and put him with the hypocrites. In that place there will be weeping and gnashing of teeth." – Matthew 24:45-51 (ESV)

> Therefore, beloved, since you look for these things, be diligent to be found by Him in peace, spotless and blameless. – 2 Peter 3:14

The writings of Matthew Henry are again instructive (on 2 Peter 3:14):[66]

> "That you be *found of Christ without spot, and blameless.*" Follow after *holiness* as well as peace: and even spotless and perfect; we must not only take heed of all spots which are not the spots of God's children (this only prevents our being found of men without spot), we must be pressing towards spotless purity, absolute perfection. Christians must be *perfecting holiness,* that they may be not only blameless before men, but also in the sight of God; and all this deserves and needs the greatest diligence; he who does this work negligently can never do it successfully. "Never expect to be found at that day of God in peace, if you are lazy and idle in this your day, in which we must finish the work that is given us to do. It is only the diligent Christian who will be the happy Christian in the day of the Lord. Our Lord will suddenly come to us, or shortly call us to him; and would you have him find you idle?" Remember there is a curse denounced against him *who does the work of the Lord negligently,* Marg. Jeremiah 48:10. Heaven will be a sufficient recompense for all our diligence and industry; therefore, let us labor and take pains in the work of the Lord; he will certainly reward us if we be diligent in the work he has allotted us; now, that you may be diligent, *account the long-suffering of our Lord to be salvation.*

---

[66] Henry, Matthew. *Exposition of the Old and New Testaments,* London. 1706-1710/1721.

SUMMARY

It was the grace of God that brought Christ down from heaven for us; this is what offers us the gift of salvation. We have been forgiven of sins and redeemed to new life only by and through the blood of Christ and faith in Christ. This happened when we were born again in accordance with New Testament Scripture, specifically at one's baptism, where "having been buried with Him through baptism into death, so that, just as Christ was raised from the dead through the glory of the Father, so we too may walk in newness of life," "raised up" "a new creation [person]" "in Christ." Forgiveness of sins (the blood of Christ) cannot be bought with money or earned through works – it is the gift of God through grace.

However, once born again, Scripture teaches us that genuine Christian faith, which is pleasing to God (i.e., not a "dead" faith), has as its natural result "good works" for the Lord, which result from obedience to Christ, out of love for Christ, as a "servant" of Christ, as a "friend" of Christ, as a true "child of God," as we love and serve others and we love and serve God. Such obedience and resulting works do not diminish anything about what Christ did on the cross; on the contrary, it glorifies Christ and brings glory to the Father. Your works show your faith to be genuine both before men and before God. For if you do not act on your faith, your faith will neither justify you nor save you to eternal salvation; it is what the Bible calls a "dead faith."

The false teaching that you are saved by "faith alone/only" has no factual basis in Scripture. God says that He will reward the one who is faithful to Him, and Scripture then goes on to clearly define what faithful means: it is one who actually <u>does</u> the Word of God, not the one who just hears (and professes) the Word of God. Idle professions of faith are not pleasing to God; in fact, such a "faith without works" is a "dead" faith. And I again ask you: Can a "<u>dead</u>" faith save you to eternal <u>life</u>?

God expects those who are saved to "work" in His vineyard (Matt 20:1-16), which is His Kingdom. God does not condone nor tolerate idleness; on the contrary, idleness is condemned, and those who bear no fruit will be cut off. Scripture tells us that we will know false prophets by their fruit and that we (Christians) will also be known by our fruit…and even further, that "Every tree that does not bear good fruit is cut down and thrown into the fire."

This isn't to imply that you are being placed again under a great burden to produce good works continually (i.e., nonstop) or you lose your salvation. In fact, it is written: "Come to Me, all who are weary and heavy-laden, and I will give you rest. Take My yoke upon you and learn from Me, for I am gentle and humble in heart, and you will find rest for your souls. For My yoke is easy and My burden is light." Compared to being in bondage under sin with Satan as your master or trying to fulfill 100% of the requirements of the Mosaic Law yourself (which no man can do), you are under the amazing Law of Grace in Christ! Furthermore, Christ Himself now abiding in you gives you the necessary wisdom, strength, power, and perseverance to produce fruit (through good works) for the Lord. Amazing! I hope you see how easy and light that is?

If you are waking up each day seeking to do God's will instead of your own, loving God and loving and serving others, good works will be the natural result. If you love God, you will do what pleases Him. What pleases Him is that you love and serve others. How do you show love? You support, help, instruct, provide for, care for, and serve others as if they were yourself. You place other people's needs first. We are also

The Message of Truth

told to share the gospel far and wide, to the very ends of the earth; I don't believe that there is any dispute over this "good work" that is commanded.

These actions (works) are what produce fruit for the Lord. Please realize that we are not all called to do the same works. Some examples of good works might include:

- Helping those who are needy, widows, homeless, sick, in prison, etc.,
- Leading someone to Christ by sharing the gospel with them,
- Raising your children to know and love the Lord,
- Looking after the needs of your family,
- Being kind and considerate to others so that your "light shines before men,"
- Doing your job well, with integrity and honesty, and with an attitude of: "whatever you do, do your work heartily, as for the Lord and not for people,"
- Loving others as yourself

Some will be called to great works and others to more routine works – but all works done in obedience to Christ are good works. Remember, it is written: "For we are His workmanship, created in Christ Jesus for good works, which God prepared beforehand so that we would walk in them." We are following the examples set before us of the giants in the faith that have preceded us – Noah, Abraham, Moses, Paul, and even Jesus Himself. Writing this book was an attempt to do a good work for the Lord by sharing the gospel "message of truth" with others. There is no ulterior motive, and hopefully, it will be counted as a "good work," but I won't know until the great Day of Judgment when all works are tested as if by fire, to see if any of them stand as being worthy. I'd like to see some of my works survive as having produced fruit for the Lord.

I hope that this chapter has now helped the following verses become clear to you:

> But someone may *well* say, "You have faith and I have works; show me your faith without the works, and I will show you my faith by my works." – James 2:18

> You see that faith was working with his works, and as a result of the works, faith was perfected. – James 2:22

You may choose to stand before the Lord without any works, but I want to be able to stand before the Lord on Judgment Day, both covered by the righteousness of the blood of Christ for the forgiveness of sins and also justified by being able to say: "Lord, I show you my faith by my works," and by doing so, stand in the blessed company of Noah, Abraham and countless others who will be able to do the same. And I hope to hear "well done good and faithful servant." Let's close this chapter with a verse:

> Then He [Jesus] said to His disciples, "The harvest is plentiful, but the <u>workers</u> are few. Therefore beseech the Lord of the harvest to send out <u>workers</u> into His harvest." – Matthew 9:37-38

In the next chapter, we discuss the final component of the Christian plan of redemption/salvation: persevering in faith unto death.

<u>FALSE TEACHING(S) YOU WILL ENCOUNTER:</u>

- Saying a "Sinner's Prayer" saves you
- You are saved by "Faith Alone/Only"
- Being born again is the only required step one has to take for eternal life (i.e., obedience, works, and perseverance are not required)
- Sabbath keeping/legalism

RELATED SCRIPTURE:

"Therefore bear fruit in keeping with repentance; and do not suppose that you can say to yourselves, 'We have Abraham for our father'; for I say to you that from these stones God is able to raise up children to Abraham. The axe is already laid at the root of the trees; therefore every tree that does not bear good fruit is cut down and thrown into the fire." – Matthew 3:8-10

But prove yourselves doers of the word, and not merely hearers who delude themselves. – James 1:22

And He said to them, "What things?" And they said to Him, "The things about Jesus the Nazarene, who was a prophet mighty in deed and word in the sight of God and all the people, and how the chief priests and our rulers delivered Him to the sentence of death, and crucified Him." – Luke 24:19-20

So then, my beloved, just as you have always obeyed, not as in my presence only, but now much more in my absence, work out your salvation with fear and trembling. – Philippians 2:12

For in Christ Jesus neither circumcision nor uncircumcision means anything, but faith working through love. – Galatians 5:6

"Beware of false prophets, who come to you in sheep's clothing, but inwardly they are ravenous wolves. You will know them by their fruits. Do men gather grapes from thornbushes or figs from thistles? Even so, every good tree bears good fruit, but a bad tree bears bad fruit. A good tree cannot bear bad fruit, nor *can* a bad tree bear good fruit. Every tree that does not bear good fruit is cut down and thrown into the fire. Therefore by their fruits you will know them.

"I am the true vine, and My Father is the vinedresser. Every branch in Me that does not bear fruit, He takes away; and every *branch* that bears fruit, He prunes it so that it may bear more fruit. You are already clean because of the word which I have spoken to you. Abide in Me, and I in you. As the branch cannot bear fruit of itself unless it abides in the vine, so neither *can* you unless you abide in Me. I am the vine, you are the branches; he who abides in Me and I in him, he bears much fruit, for apart from Me you can do nothing. If anyone does not abide in Me, he is thrown away as a branch and dries up; and they gather them, and cast them into the fire and they are burned. If you abide in Me, and My words abide in you, ask whatever you wish, and it will be done for you. My Father is glorified by this, that you bear much fruit, and *so* prove to be My disciples." – John 15:1-8

"You are the light of the world. A city set on a hill cannot be hidden; nor does *anyone* light a lamp and put it under a basket, but on the lampstand, and it gives light to all who are in the house. Let your light shine before men in such a way that they may see your good works, and glorify your Father who is in heaven." – Matthew 5:14-16

If you address as Father the One who impartially judges according to each one's work, conduct yourselves in fear during the time of your stay *on earth*. – 1 Peter 1:17

Watch yourselves, that you do not lose what we have accomplished, but that you may receive a full reward. – 2 John 1:8

The Message of Truth

...so that the man of God may be adequate, equipped for every good work. – 2 Timothy 3:17

Whatever you do, do your work heartily, as for the Lord rather than for men, knowing that from the Lord you will receive the reward of the inheritance. It is the Lord Christ whom you serve. – Colossians 3:23-24

And do not neglect doing good and sharing, for with such sacrifices God is pleased. – Hebrews 13:16

Let us not lose heart in doing good, for in due time we will reap if we do not grow weary. – Galatians 6:9

"'I know your deeds [works], that you are neither cold nor hot; I wish that you were cold or hot. So because you are lukewarm, and neither hot nor cold, I will spit you out of My mouth. Because you say, "I am rich, and have become wealthy, and have need of nothing," and you do not know that you are wretched and miserable and poor and blind and naked, I advise you to buy from Me gold refined by fire so that you may become rich, and white garments so that you may clothe yourself, and *that* the shame of your nakedness will not be revealed; and eye salve to anoint your eyes so that you may see.'" – Revelation 3:15-18

Therefore, to one who knows *the* right thing to do and does not do it, to him it is sin. – James 4:17

Do not withhold good from those to whom it is due,
When it is in your power to do *it*.
Do not say to your neighbor, "Go, and come back,
And tomorrow I will give *it*,"
When you have it with you. – Proverbs 3:27-28

They profess to know God, but by *their* deeds they deny *Him*, being detestable and disobedient and worthless for any good deed. – Titus 1:16

Instruct them to do good, to be rich in good works, to be generous and ready to share, storing up for themselves the treasure of a good foundation for the future, so that they may take hold of that which is life indeed. – 1 Timothy 6:18-19

For the grace of God has appeared, bringing salvation to all men, instructing us to deny ungodliness and worldly desires and to live sensibly, righteously and godly in the present age, looking for the blessed hope and the appearing of the glory of our great God and Savior, Christ Jesus, who gave Himself for us to redeem us from every lawless deed, and to purify for Himself a people for His own possession, zealous for good deeds. – Titus 2:11-14

For God is not unjust so as to forget your work and the love which you have shown toward His name, in having ministered and in still ministering to the saints. – Hebrews 6:10

...and let us consider how to stimulate one another to love and good deeds. – Hebrews 10:24

This is a trustworthy statement; and concerning these things I want you to speak confidently, so that those who have believed God will be careful to engage in good deeds. These things are good and profitable for men. – Titus 3:8

Likewise urge the young men to be sensible; in all things show yourself to be an example of good deeds, *with* purity in doctrine, dignified, sound *in* speech which is beyond reproach, so that the opponent will be put to shame, having nothing bad to say about us. – Titus 2:6-8

Therefore, my beloved brethren, be steadfast, immovable, always abounding in the work of the Lord, knowing that your toil is not *in* vain in the Lord. – 1 Corinthians 15:58

According to the grace of God which was given to me, like a wise master builder I laid a foundation, and another is building on it. But each man must be careful how he builds on it. For no man can lay a foundation other than the one which is laid, which is Jesus Christ. – 1 Corinthians 3:10-11

And God is able to make all grace abound to you, so that always having all sufficiency in everything, you may have an abundance for every good deed. – 2 Corinthians 9:8

For this reason also, since the day we heard *of it*, we have not ceased to pray for you and to ask that you may be filled with the knowledge of His will in all spiritual wisdom and understanding, so that you will walk in a manner worthy of the Lord, to please *Him* in all respects, bearing fruit in every good work and increasing in the knowledge of God; strengthened with all power, according to His glorious might, for the attaining of all steadfastness and patience; joyously giving thanks to the Father, who has qualified us to share in the inheritance of the saints in Light.

For He rescued us from the domain of darkness, and transferred us to the kingdom of His beloved Son, in whom we have redemption, the forgiveness of sins. – Colossians 1:9-14

Now the word of the LORD came to Jonah the second time, saying, "Arise, go to Nineveh the great city and proclaim to it the proclamation which I am going to tell you." So Jonah arose and went to Nineveh according to the word of the LORD. Now Nineveh was an exceedingly great city, a three days' walk. Then Jonah began to go through the city one day's walk; and he cried out and said, "Yet forty days and Nineveh will be overthrown."

Then the people of Nineveh believed in God; and they called a fast and put on sackcloth from the greatest to the least of them. When the word reached the king of Nineveh, he arose from his throne, laid aside his robe from him, covered *himself* with sackcloth and sat on the ashes. He issued a proclamation and it said, "In Nineveh by the decree of the king and his nobles: Do not let man, beast, herd, or flock taste a thing. Do not let them eat or drink water. But both man and beast must be covered with sackcloth; and let men call on God earnestly that each may turn from his wicked way and from the violence which is in his hands. Who knows, God may turn and relent and withdraw His burning anger so that we will not perish."

When God saw their deeds, that they turned from their wicked way, then God relented concerning the calamity which He had declared He would bring upon them. And He did not do *it*. – Jonah 3

"'I know your deeds, and your love and faith and service and perseverance, and that your deeds of late are greater than at first.'" – Revelation 2:19

By faith Noah, being warned *by God* about things not yet seen, in reverence prepared an ark for the salvation of his household, by which he condemned the world, and became an heir of the righteousness which is according to faith. – Hebrews 11:7

By faith Abraham, when he was tested, offered up Isaac, and he who had received the promises was offering up his only begotten *son*; *it was he* to whom it was said, "IN ISAAC YOUR DESCENDANTS SHALL BE CALLED." – Hebrews 11:17-18

We give thanks to God always for all of you, making mention *of you* in our prayers; constantly bearing in mind your work of faith and labor of love and steadfastness of hope in our Lord Jesus Christ in the presence of our God and Father. – 1 Thessalonians 1:2-3

…that they are to repent and turn to God, performing deeds [works] consistent with repentance. – Acts 26:20

4.4 PERSEVERING IN FAITH
(Yes, You Can "Fall Away" From the Faith!)

I have fought the good fight, I have finished the race, I have kept the faith. Henceforth there is laid up for me the crown of righteousness, which the Lord, the righteous judge, will award to me on that day, and not only to me but also to all who have loved his appearing. – 2 Timothy 4:7-8 (ESV)

Finish the Race. Prior chapters have touched on the need to persevere in faith (i.e., "remains faithful") unto death, but we now go into much more detail. The Bible is abundantly clear and replete with warnings that you can "fall away from the faith" and that it is only those who "persevere" in faith unto death ("be faithful until death," "keeps My deeds until the end") that will receive their "crown of [eternal] life."

Persevering in faith is a matter of utmost importance. You have already read that final salvation (when you receive your "crown of life") is not the same as initial salvation ("forgiveness of sins," when you are "born again"). Modern liberal churches are doing a poor job explaining the difference, thereby putting many at risk of losing their "crown of life." From the sheer number of verses given in Scripture that admonish one to persevere in faith, you will see it is a vitally important topic. Please also note that the need to persevere in faith didn't just surface as a new requirement in the New Testament, for the Old Testament also discusses this subject (see Zephaniah 1:6, Jude 1:5).

And as you might guess by now, false teachings by the "wolves" and "vipers" also abound on this subject – particularly the "once saved always saved" false teaching (also known as "perseverance of the saints" under Calvinism), which is shilled endlessly in absolutely blaring volume 24/7/365.25 from nearly all so-called "reformed" Christian churches, media outlets, books, and even seminaries! This false teaching claims that a Christian can never lose their salvation, for any reason whatsoever – even if one is blatantly disobedient to the commands of Christ, doesn't lead a repentant life, doesn't bear any fruit for the Lord, and even if one turns back from Christ and abandons their faith altogether! This is in clear contradiction with many verses of Scripture, one of which is:

> But the Spirit explicitly says that in later times <u>some will fall away from the faith</u>, paying attention to deceitful spirits and doctrines of demons, by means of the hypocrisy of liars seared in their own conscience as with a branding iron, *men* who forbid marriage *and advocate* abstaining from foods which God has created to be gratefully shared in by those who believe and know the truth. – 1 Timothy 4:1-3

Please understand that to "fall away" from something or to leave it (go apostate), you must have once first had it to begin with, or you could not "fall away" from it! There are several terms used to describe this:

- "No longer walk" (John 6:66),
- "Shrink back," "turn back," "turn away" (Hebrews 10:39),
- Going "apostate" (2 Thessalonians 2:3, 2 Peter 2:20-22),
- "Falling away" from (i.e., quit) the faith (Matthew 24:10, Luke 8:13, Hebrews 3:12, 1 Timothy 4:1, Hebrews 6:4-6),
- "Depart from the faith" (1 Timothy 4:1 ESV),
- "Abandon the faith" (1 Timothy 4:1 NIV),
- Backsliding (Proverbs 14:14 ESV, Jeremiah 2:19, Jeremiah 3:22),
- "Looking back" (Genesis 19:26, Luke 9:62)
- Going prodigal (Luke 15:11-32),
- Becoming "neither hot nor cold," i.e., "lukewarm" (Revelation 3:15-16),
- "Abandoning the love you had at first," which is Christ (Revelation 2:4),
- "Being alive, but you are dead" (Revelation 3:1),
- Being "led astray," "deceived" or misled by others such as the false teachers, i.e., the "wolves" and "vipers" (2 Corinthians 11:3, 2 Peter 2:1, 2 Peter 3:17, 1 Timothy 4:1-3, Luke 21:8, Revelation 2:4, Revelation 2:20, Acts 20:28-30, Hebrews 13:9, 2 Timothy 4:4, Revelation 3:11, Matthew 24:10-13), and even
- Having your "crown of life" stolen/seized (Revelation 3:11)!

Now I ask you, if it were impossible to lose your salvation, why is Scripture so full of warnings about this very thing? I hope you can see that those who proclaim the "once saved always saved" false teaching are doing so in the face of overwhelming Scripture to the contrary! It should be noted that false teachings almost always travel in packs, and the "once saved always saved" false teaching is almost always accompanied by the "sinner's prayer" and the "saved by faith only/alone" false teachings.

CAUSES OF FALLING AWAY

There are several prominent reasons why a Christian falls away from or quits (abandons) their faith:

1. **Ignorance (and Indifference)**: They don't take the warnings given in Scripture seriously – that one must "work out your salvation with fear and trembling" and to "be all the more diligent to make certain about His calling and choice of you," so they fail to "grow in the grace and knowledge [understanding]" of Christ. They often stop reading the Bible, stop praying, stop going to church, etc. I've also heard it said that it's "boring" to read the Bible. May I kindly suggest that if you find it boring to read the Bible, then you are not really living in the Spirit. Something to consider. If you are not feeding your new Spirit with the Word of God, it will die.
2. **Cares of This World**: They let the cares and concerns of this world along with a continued lustful desire for fame, fortune, power, and wealth reassert itself as the controlling force in their lives, and they stop pursuing the "things above" and once again "set their minds on things of this world" (i.e., they are "thorny soil," see Matthew 13).
3. **The Threat of Persecution**: They wish to preserve their own life (or income) instead of "standing firm" in their faith when severe trials and tribulations come their way, and they "count the cost" of following Christ to high and therefore return to the ways of this world and obey men instead of God.

4. **They Follow "Another Gospel Which is Not Another"**: They are led astray ("tricked," "deceived") by the false teachings of man (e.g., legalism, sabbath keeping, cults that deny Christ, etc.). This results in large measure from item #1, failing to "grow in the grace and knowledge [understanding]" of Christ and failing to be diligent in reading, studying, and meditating on the Word of God. Yes, you can be tricked out of your "crown of life." "Be not deceived!"

WE MUST FINISH THE RACE

Scripture admonishes us not to take our eternal salvation lightly or with carelessness. We are exhorted to "work out your salvation with fear and trembling" and to "test yourselves [examine yourselves!] to see if you are in the faith":

> So then, my beloved, just as you have always obeyed, not as in my presence only, but now much more in my absence, work out your salvation with fear and trembling; for it is God who is at work in you, both to will and to work for *His* good pleasure. – Philippians 2:12-13

> Test yourselves *to see* if you are in the faith; examine yourselves! Or do you not recognize this about yourselves, that Jesus Christ is in you—unless indeed you fail the test? – 2 Corinthians 13:5

You "work out" your salvation by serving the Lord each and every day, by seeking His will instead of your own, and always "grow[ing] in the grace and knowledge [understanding] of our Lord and Savior Jesus Christ." A Christian must "take up his cross," "deny himself," and "put off your old self" each day. Also, remember that "fear of the Lord" doesn't mean to be literally afraid of Him – it means to live in humility, awe, honor, and respect to God, knowing who He is (His holy and righteous nature), and doing so with worship, thankfulness, trust, and obedience. The verse also conveys the sense that the closer you get to God in your walk as a Christian (by "abiding in" Christ and "He in you"), the more you realize how far away from His holiness and righteousness you really are – but that is actually a good thing, for it keeps us humble and aware of our shortcomings and weaknesses and reminds us of the need to persevere in faith through the power of Christ living in us.

It is also written:

> Simon Peter, a bond-servant and apostle of Jesus Christ,
>
> To those who have received a faith of the same kind as ours, by the righteousness of our God and Savior, Jesus Christ: Grace and peace be multiplied to you in the knowledge of God and of Jesus our Lord; seeing that His divine power has granted to us everything pertaining to life and godliness, through the true knowledge of Him who called us by His own glory and excellence. For by these He has granted to us His precious and magnificent promises, so that by them you may become partakers of *the* divine nature, having escaped the corruption that is in the world by lust. Now for this very reason also, applying all diligence, in your faith supply moral excellence, and in *your* moral excellence, knowledge, and in *your* knowledge, self-control, and in *your* self-control, perseverance, and in *your* perseverance, godliness, and in *your* godliness, brotherly kindness, and in *your* brotherly kindness, love. For if these *qualities* are yours and are increasing, they render you neither useless nor unfruitful in the true knowledge of our Lord Jesus

> Christ. For he who lacks these *qualities* is blind *or* short-sighted, having forgotten *his* purification from his former sins. Therefore, brethren, <u>be all the more diligent to make certain about His calling and choosing you</u>; for as long as you practice these things, you will never stumble; for in this way the entrance into the eternal kingdom of our Lord and Savior Jesus Christ will be abundantly supplied to you. – 2 Peter 1:1-11

    The verses above exhort us to "be diligent" (daily) about our faith and not take God, or our salvation, for granted. As long as you are walking towards Christ, you know that you are not "stumbling" or "falling away" from Him and back into sin and eternal death. "We must obey God rather than men," and we must seek and want to please God, not man. We must seek Godly wisdom ("the wisdom from above"), not the wisdom of man and this world. We must value "the things above [heavenly, eternal things]" over material things. We must "Worship God" and not "idols." We must "*do* everything in the name of the Lord Jesus, giving thanks through Him to God the Father," and "whatever you do, do your work heartily, as for the Lord and not for people" – with reverence, careful and sustained attention, persevering unto the very end to make sure we don't "come short of" eternal life.

    The apostle Paul wrote that he had not yet "finished the race" nor had he yet "received the crown of life." And if even the great apostle Paul tells us that he had not yet obtained the prize of eternal life in Christ, how much less should we think that we have!

> Not that I have already obtained *it* or have already become perfect, but I press on so that I may lay hold of that for which also I was laid hold of by Christ Jesus. Brethren, I do not regard myself as having laid hold of *it* yet; but one thing *I do*: forgetting what *lies* behind and reaching forward to what *lies* ahead, I press on toward the goal for the prize of the upward call of God in Christ Jesus. – Philippians 3:12-14

> For I am already being poured out as a drink offering, and the time of my departure has come. I have fought the good fight, I have finished the course, I have kept the faith; in the future there is laid up for me the crown of righteousness, which the Lord, the righteous Judge, will award to me on that day; and not only to me, but also to all who have loved His appearing. – 2 Timothy 4:6-8

    And even further, Paul writes about being "disqualified"; and if Paul could be disqualified, how much more could you and I be disqualified:

> Do you not know that those who run in a race all run, but *only* one receives the prize? Run in such a way that you may win. Everyone who competes in the games exercises self-control in all things. They then *do it* to receive a perishable wreath, but we an imperishable. Therefore I run in such a way, as not without aim; I box in such a way, as not beating the air; but I discipline my body and make it my slave, so that, after I have preached to others, I myself will not be disqualified. – 1 Corinthians 9:24-27

    To borrow a real-world analogy, you are not said to have "run" (i.e., completed) a marathon race by simply starting out from the starting line – you must also cross the finish line for it to count and be recorded as officially completed. Is the marathon runner awarded a prize for starting the race or for finishing the race? Being born again, you have only started the race – you must also finish! Scripture is abundantly clear that even after one is born again and starts out in faith, one can still "come short of" the glory of heaven:

> Therefore, we must fear if, while a promise remains of entering His rest, any one of you may seem to have come short *of it*. – Hebrews 4:1

YOU CAN BE TRICKED OUT OF YOUR CROWN OF LIFE!

Not only must you "stand firm" in the face of trials, tribulation, and persecution to the very end, but you must also withstand the false teachings of man (the "wolves," "vipers," and modern-day "Pharisees") that you will encounter all along the way. Scripture tells us that you can be "tricked" out of your "crown of life" by false teachings ("carried away by the error of unprincipled men," "deceived," "led astray," "taken captive"):

> We are no longer to be children [gullible, infants in Christ], tossed here and there by waves and carried about by every wind of doctrine, by the trickery of men, by craftiness in deceitful scheming. – Ephesians 4:14

> But the Spirit explicitly says that in later times some will fall away from the faith, paying attention to deceitful spirits and doctrines of demons, by means of the hypocrisy of liars seared in their own conscience as with a branding iron, *men* who forbid marriage *and advocate* abstaining from foods which God has created to be gratefully shared in by those who believe and know the truth. – 1 Timothy 4:1-3

> For the time will come when they will not endure sound doctrine; but *wanting* to have their ears tickled, they will accumulate for themselves teachers in accordance to their own desires, and will turn away their ears from the truth and will turn aside to myths. – 2 Timothy 4:3-4

> But I am afraid that, as the serpent deceived [tricked] Eve by his craftiness [cunning, trickery], your minds will be led astray from the simplicity and purity of *devotion* to Christ. – 2 Corinthians 11:3

> "'Because you have kept the word of My perseverance, I also will keep you from the hour of testing, that *hour* which is about to come upon the whole world, to test those who dwell on the earth. I am coming quickly; hold fast what you have, so that no one will take your crown.'" – Revelation 3:10-11

This happens primarily through ignorance, but also through laziness in not reading and diligently studying (meditating on) God's Word – by not knowing Scripture well enough yourself. This is partly how Satan deceived ("tricked") Eve (and then Adam) in the Garden of Eden. This is also why we are strongly admonished to always be "growing in the grace and knowledge [understanding]" of Christ, which we do through daily reading and studying Scripture. We must know what the Word of God actually says ourselves:

> You therefore, beloved, knowing this beforehand, be on your guard so that you are not carried away by the error of unprincipled men and fall from your own steadfastness, but grow in the grace and knowledge of our Lord and Savior Jesus Christ. – 2 Peter 3:17-18a

So yes, you <u>can</u> be led off of the "straight and narrow" path to eternal life by the false teachings of man – false teachings which lead away from Christ and back into bondage under sin and death. The "wolves" do this by convincing you through clever distortions of Scripture where they mix a little truth in with a bunch of man-made conjurings (by subtly adding to, distorting, or subtracting from Scripture) and devise what APPEAR to be biblically sounding doctrines, but which are really the false teachings of man which lead away from Christ. These false teachings abound in many directions and many different areas. Many of the false teachings "crucify once again" Christ on the cross! This is why the Bible contains numerous and explicit warnings about these false teachers (the "wolves"). This is also why I have devoted an entire section of this book to identify false teachings so you will not be led astray (see Beware the Wolves). You will almost surely encounter the false teachings identified in that section of the book as they are rampant today.

You see, I started out once begin born again, but I fell away from Christ and back into this world of sin and addiction. I fell away through neglect of the Word of God and also through undo concern again for the cares of this world. I fell away for reasons #1 and #2 listed above in this chapter. This is why I provide a 30-day head-start list of things that I recommend you do to get off on the right foot later in this book – so you won't make the same mistakes I did as you begin your walk as a Christian.

In fact, there is an entire parable taught by Christ Himself on this very subject: the parable of the sower (Matthew 13:1-23). You see, I was the "thorny soil!" I started out in faith, but I fell away – back into selfish, worldly, fleshly, lustful, sinful pursuits and addiction. I still don't know why the Lord pursued me and brought me back to Him again (it wasn't through anything I did or deserved). He reached out for me and snatched me back to Him again – through His relentless lovingkindness, patience, mercy, and grace. It has been truly staggering for me to see how He has pursued me.

And contrary to even more false teachings (e.g., the "prosperity gospel," etc.), you don't get rich, famous, or live "happily ever after" just because you are a Christian. Not all of your prayers, desires, and wishes will be answered to your liking. However, know that God's will is being done, and as a Christian, you will now be a part of that. Seek His will, not your own, and you will never go wrong.

PERSEVERANCE (AND OBEDIENCE) IN THE OLD TESTAMENT

The need for perseverance (and obedience) is also clearly demonstrated throughout the Old Testament. As an example, we have the Jews whom God led out of bondage in Egypt towards the Promised Land. Many of the Jews fell away because they didn't persevere in faith. They grumbled, wanted the things of the world again, looked back towards Egypt and idolatry, and fell back into disbelief and sin. These verses are helpful on this matter (with my comments added in brackets to assist with understanding only):

> Now I desire to remind you, though you know all things once for all, that the Lord, after saving a people out of the land of Egypt, subsequently destroyed those who did not believe. – Jude 1:5

> For who provoked *Him* when they had heard? Indeed, did not all those who came out of Egypt *led* by Moses? And with whom was He angry for forty years? Was it not with those who sinned, whose bodies fell in the wilderness? And to whom did

He swear that they would not enter His rest, but to those who were disobedient? *So we see that they were not able to enter because of unbelief.* – Hebrews 3:16-19

For I do not want you to be unaware, brethren, that our fathers [the Jews lead out of bondage in Egypt] were all under the cloud and all passed through the sea; and all were baptized into Moses in the cloud and in the sea; and all ate the same spiritual food; and all drank the same spiritual drink, for they were drinking from a spiritual rock which followed them; and the rock was Christ. Nevertheless, with most of them God was not well-pleased; for they were laid low [died in sin] in the wilderness.

Now these things happened as examples for us, so that we would not crave evil things as they also craved. Do not be idolaters, as some of them were; as it is written, "THE PEOPLE SAT DOWN TO EAT AND DRINK, AND STOOD UP TO PLAY." Nor let us act immorally, as some of them did [even after in effect being "born again"], and twenty-three thousand fell in one day. Nor let us try the Lord, as some of them did, and were destroyed by the serpents. Nor grumble, as some of them did, and were destroyed by the destroyer. Now these things happened to them as an example [for us today], and they were written for our instruction [which is what I'm giving you in this chapter], upon whom the ends of the ages have come. Therefore let him who thinks he stands take heed that he does not fall. – 1 Corinthians 10:1-12

As you can see, God required one to persevere in faith even in the Old Testament, and He rewards eternally those who do so – those who "fight the good fight" and "finish the race," not those who "quit the faith."

GOD IS NOT MOCKED

Be not deceived – "God is not mocked." Christ will sort out all the imposters, the "make-believers," the "hypocrites," and the pretenders of faith at the end of time on the great Day of Judgment. And this leads us to one of the most terrifying verses in all of Scripture:

"Not everyone who says to Me, 'Lord, Lord,' will enter the kingdom of heaven, but he who does the will of My Father who is in heaven *will enter*. Many will say to Me on that day, 'Lord, Lord, did we not prophesy in Your name, and in Your name cast out demons, and in Your name perform many miracles?' And then I will declare to them, 'I never knew you; DEPART FROM ME, YOU WHO PRACTICE LAWLESSNESS.'"
– Matthew 7:21-23

Imagine the shock and (eternal) horror of those professing "Christians" who were Christians in name only – but not in truth, obedience, action (deed/works), and perseverance because they didn't know the truth of what is written in Scripture. They will realize too late that they "came short of" eternal life, that they didn't "work out their salvation with fear and trembling" and make "their calling and election sure." So please do not take your salvation for granted, or you too might "fall away" from or depart from the faith and then hear Jesus say on that great Day of Judgment: "Depart from me…" I personally want to hear: "Well done, good and faithful servant! Enter into My rest." It is up to each of us individually to ensure that we hear that.

The Message of Truth

PERSECUTION

Scripture does tell us very plainly that a Christian may be called to face trials, tribulation, and even persecution unto death in the name of Christ:

> Beloved, do not be surprised at the fiery ordeal among you, which comes upon you for your testing, as though some strange thing were happening to you; but to the degree that you share the sufferings of Christ, keep on rejoicing, so that also at the revelation of His glory you may rejoice with exultation. If you are reviled for the name of Christ, you are blessed, because the Spirit of glory and of God rests on you. Make sure that none of you suffers as a murderer, or thief, or evildoer, or a troublesome meddler; but if *anyone suffers* as a Christian, he is not to be ashamed, but is to glorify God in this name. For *it is* time for judgment to begin with the household of God; and if *it begins* with us first, what *will be* the outcome for those who do not obey the gospel of God? AND IF IT IS WITH DIFFICULTY THAT THE RIGHTEOUS IS SAVED, WHAT WILL BECOME OF THE GODLESS MAN AND THE SINNER? Therefore, those also who suffer according to the will of God shall entrust their souls to a faithful Creator in doing what is right. – 1 Peter 4:12-19

> Blessed is a man who perseveres under trial; for once he has been approved, he will receive the crown of life which *the Lord* has promised to those who love Him. – James 1:12

> But we are not of those who shrink back to destruction, but of those who have faith to the preserving of the soul. – Hebrews 10:39

> "These things I have spoken to you, so that in Me you may have peace. In the world you have tribulation, but take courage; I have overcome the world." – John 16:33

> "'I know your tribulation and your poverty (but you are rich), and the blasphemy by those who say they are Jews and are not, but are a synagogue of Satan. Do not fear what you are about to suffer. Behold, the devil is about to cast some of you into prison, so that you will be tested, and you will have tribulation for ten days. Be faithful until death, and I will give you the crown of life.'" – Revelation 2:9-10

And even further, it is written that all who follow Christ "will" suffer persecution:

> Indeed, all who desire to live godly in Christ Jesus will be persecuted. – 2 Timothy 3:12

So, brother or sister in Christ (and I'm also addressing this question to myself): Are you suffering for Christ? If not, maybe you are not serving or walking with Christ as you should be? This suffering and persecution may manifest in various forms, from minor ridicule and mocking for telling others about Christ to economic sanctions or disenfranchisement for not agreeing to do business in a dishonest or fraudulent manner, all the way up to threats of violence and actual martyrdom in death. The attitude and perspective of the early disciples should be very inspiring to us when we do face persecution for the sake of Christ:

> So they [the disciples] went on their way from the presence of the Council, rejoicing that they had been considered worthy to suffer shame for *His* name. – Acts 5:41

For anyone who doubts that trials and tribulations may come to a Christian, I suggest reading the books *The Church History* by Eusebius, *The Pilgrim's Progress*, and the *Acts and Monuments* (known as *The Book of Martyrs*). The latter details the torture and horrible/gruesome deaths that many early Christians had to endure, all in the name of Christ, as they persevered in their faith to the very end (death in martyrdom).

WE PERSEVERE BY THE POWER OF CHRIST

The life of a Christian may certainly require courage, grit, determination, sacrifice, struggles, danger, trials, tribulations, and even persecution unto death. For it is written: "you will be hated because of my name." But know that you will be able to "stand firm" in your faith not on your own strength or willpower but by the power of Christ who lives in you. If you trust in Him and seek Him diligently each day, He will hold you in His power through His lovingkindness. He will never leave or forsake you! It is written:

> "'Not by might nor by power, but by My Spirit,' says the LORD of hosts." – Zechariah 4:6

Know also that it is through your trials and tribulations that your faith is tested, strengthened, and purified, just like a refiner purifies gold through fire:

> Blessed be the God and Father of our Lord Jesus Christ, who according to His great mercy has caused us to be born again to a living hope through the resurrection of Jesus Christ from the dead, to *obtain* an inheritance *which is* imperishable and undefiled and will not fade away, reserved in heaven for you, who are protected by the power of God through faith for a salvation ready to be revealed in the last time. In this you greatly rejoice, even though now for a little while, if necessary, you have been distressed by various trials, so that the proof of your faith, *being* more precious than gold which is perishable, even though tested by fire, may be found to result in praise and glory and honor at the revelation of Jesus Christ; and though you have not seen Him, you love Him, and though you do not see Him now, but believe in Him, you greatly rejoice with joy inexpressible and full of glory, obtaining as the outcome of your faith the salvation of your souls. – 1 Peter 1:3-9

> Consider it all joy, my brethren, when you encounter various trials, knowing that the testing of your faith produces endurance. And let endurance have *its* perfect result, so that you may be perfect and complete, lacking in nothing. – James 1:2-4

In fact, it is written that you should rejoice when you face trials as a Christian; when the early apostles faced persecution, they went away "rejoicing that they had been considered worthy to suffer shame for His name." And for every temptation, trial, or tribulation that you face, God will also provide you with a way out/forward.

Also, it is crucial to remember that we are at the front lines in a war between the spiritual forces of darkness and evil (led by Satan) vs. those of God (led by God and His Christ); in effect, we actually live behind enemy lines here in this fallen world:

> Finally, be strong in the Lord and in the strength of His might. Put on the full armor of God, so that you will be able to stand firm against the schemes of the devil. <u>For our struggle is not against flesh and blood, but against the rulers, against the powers, against the world forces of this darkness, against the spiritual *forces* of wickedness in the heavenly *places*</u>. Therefore, take up the full armor of God, so

> that you will be able to resist in the evil day, and having done everything, to stand firm. Stand firm therefore, HAVING GIRDED YOUR LOINS WITH TRUTH, and HAVING PUT ON THE BREASTPLATE OF RIGHTEOUSNESS, and having shod YOUR FEET WITH THE PREPARATION OF THE GOSPEL OF PEACE; in addition to all, taking up the shield of faith with which you will be able to extinguish all the flaming arrows of the evil *one [Satan]*. And take THE HELMET OF SALVATION, and the sword of the Spirit, which is the word of God. – Ephesians 6:10-17

We are therefore instructed to put on the "full armor of God" (see The Armor of God Chapter) and to "stand firm" in the faith; notice that we are not attackers – we are simply to "stand firm." We are to let God win all advances, to gain ground on the enemy, and then we fill that ground with new believers who also "stand firm" in the faith. This is how the Kingdom of God expands and grows.

While Christ victoriously defeated Satan on the cross and he (Satan) is "bound" today from many things he would like to do, he still can, and will, attack Christians to try to turn them away from the faith! This is why you must constantly be "growing in grace and knowledge of the Lord," daily eating the Word of life, to fend off the attacks and "fiery darts" of the devil. You may even find that his attacks after you are born again are even more vigorous than before! Do not underestimate the spiritual forces of darkness with which you are engaged – make no mistake; this is a war for eternal life and death! Matthew Henry writes on 2 Peter 1:5-11:[67]

> In these words, the apostle comes to the chief thing intended in this epistle – to excite and engage them to advance in grace and holiness, they having already obtained precious faith, and been made partakers of the divine nature [being born again]. This is a very good beginning, but it is not to be rested in, as if we were already perfect. The apostle had prayed that grace and peace might be multiplied to them, and now he exhorts them to press forward for the obtaining of more grace. We should, as we have opportunity, exhort those we pray for, and excite them to the use of all proper means to obtain what we desire God to bestow upon them; and those who will make any progress in religion must be very diligent and industrious in their endeavors. Without giving all diligence, there is no gaining any ground in the work of holiness; those who are slothful in the business of religion will make nothing of it; we must strive if we will enter in at the strait gate, Luke 13:24.
>
> I. Here we cannot but observe how the believer's way is marked out step by step.
>
> 1. He must get virtue, by which some understand justice; and then the knowledge, temperance, and patience that follow, being joined with it, the apostle may be supposed to put them upon pressing after the four cardinal virtues, or the four elements that go to the making up of every virtue or virtuous action. But seeing it is a faithful saying, and constantly to be asserted, that those who have faith be careful to maintain good works (Titus 3:8), by virtue here we may understand strength and courage, without which the believer cannot stand up for good works, by abounding and excelling in them. The righteous must be bold as a lion (Proverbs 28:1); a cowardly Christian, who is afraid to profess the doctrines or practice the duties of the gospel, must expect that Christ will be ashamed of him

---

[67] Henry, Matthew. *Exposition of the Old and New Testaments*, London. 1706-1710/1721.

another day. "Let not your hearts fail you in the evil day, but show yourselves valiant in standing against all opposition, and resisting every enemy, world, flesh, devil, yea, and death too." We have need of virtue while we live, and it will be of excellent use when we come to die.

2. The believer must add knowledge to his virtue, prudence to his courage; there is a knowledge of God's name which must go before our faith (Psalm 9:10), and we cannot approve of the good, and acceptable, and perfect will of God, till we know it; but there are proper circumstances for duty, which must be known and observed; we must use the appointed means and observe the accepted time. Christian prudence regards the persons we have to do with and the place and company we are in. Every believer must labor after the knowledge and wisdom that are profitable to direct, both as to the proper method and order wherein all Christian duties are to be performed and as to the way and manner of performing them.

3. We must add temperance to our knowledge. We must be sober and moderate in our love to, and use of, the good things of this life; and, if we have a right understanding and knowledge of outward comforts, we shall see that their worth and usefulness are vastly inferior to those of spiritual mercies. Bodily exercises and bodily privileges profit but little, and therefore are to be esteemed and used accordingly; the gospel teaches sobriety as well as honesty, Titus 2:12. We must be moderate in desiring and using the good things of natural life, such as meat, drink, clothes, sleep, recreations, and credit; an inordinate desire after these is inconsistent with an earnest desire after God and Christ; and those who take more of these than is due can render to neither God nor man what is due to them.

4. Add to temperance patience, which must have its perfect work, or we cannot be perfect and entire, wanting nothing (James 1:4), for we are born to trouble, and must through many tribulations enter into the kingdom of heaven; and it is this tribulation (Romans 5:3) which worketh patience, that is, requires the exercise and occasions the increase of this grace, whereby we bear all calamities and crosses with silence and submission, without murmuring against God or complaining of him, but justifying him who lays all affliction upon us, owning that our sufferings are less than our sins deserve, and believing they are no more than we ourselves need.

5. To patience we must add godliness, and this is the very thing which is produced by patience, for that works experience, Romans 5:4. When Christians bear afflictions patiently, they get an experimental knowledge of the loving-kindness of their heavenly Father, which he will not take from his children, even when he visits their iniquity with the rod and their transgression with stripes (Psalm 89:32, Psalm 89:33), and hereby they are brought to the child-like fear and reverential love wherein true godliness consists: to this,

6. We must add brotherly-kindness, a tender affection to all our fellow-Christians, who are children of the same Father, servants of the same Master, members of the same family, travelers to the same country, and heirs of the same inheritance, and therefore are to be loved with a pure heart fervently, with a love of complacency, as those who are peculiarly near and dear to us, in whom we take particular delight, Psalm 16:3.

7. Charity, or a love of good-will to all mankind, must be added to the love of delight which we have for those who are the children of God. God has made of one blood all nations, and all the children of men are partakers of the same human nature, are all capable of the same mercies, and liable to the same afflictions, and therefore, though upon a spiritual account Christians are distinguished and dignified above those who are without Christ, yet are they to sympathize with others in their calamities, and relieve their necessities, and promote their welfare both in body and soul, as they have opportunity: thus must all believers in Christ evidence that they are the children of God, who is good to all, but is especially good to Israel.

II. All the aforementioned graces must be had, or we shall not be thoroughly furnished for all good works – for the duties of the first and second table, for active and passive obedience, and for those services wherein we are to imitate God as well as for those wherein we only obey him – and therefore to engage us to an industrious and unwearied pursuit of them, the apostle sets forth the advantages that redound to all who successfully labor so as to get these things to be and abound in them, 2 Peter 1:8-11. These are proposed,

1. More generally, 2 Peter 1:8. The having these things make not barren (or slothful) nor unfruitful, where, according to the style of the Holy Ghost, we must understand a great deal more than is expressed; for when it is said concerning Ahaz, the vilest and most provoking of all the kings of Judah, that he did not right in the sight of the Lord (2 Kings 16:2), we are to understand as much as if it had been said, He did what was most offensive and abominable, as the following account of his life shows; so, when it is here said that the being and abounding of all Christian graces in us will make us neither inactive nor unfruitful, we are thereby to understand that it will make us very zealous and lively, vigorous and active, in all practical Christianity, and eminently fruitful in the works of righteousness. these will bring much glory to God, by bringing forth much fruit among men, being fruitful in knowledge, or the acknowledging of our Lord Jesus Christ, owning him to be their Lord, and evidencing themselves to be his servants by their abounding in the work that he has given them to do.

This is the necessary consequence of adding one grace to another; for, where all Christian graces are in the heart, they improve and strengthen, encourage and cherish, one another; so they all thrive and grow (as the apostle intimates in the beginning of 2 Peter 1:8), and wherever grace abounds there will be an abounding in good works. How desirable it is to be in such a case the apostle evidences, 2 Peter 1:9. There he sets forth how miserable it is to be without those quickening fructifying graces; for he who has not the aforementioned graces, or, though he pretends or seems to have them, does not exercise and improve them, is blind, that is, as to spiritual and heavenly things, as the next words explain it: He cannot see far off. This present evil world he can see, and dotes upon, but has no discerning at all of the world to come, so as to be affected with the spiritual privileges and heavenly blessings thereof.

He who sees the excellences of Christianity must needs be diligent in endeavors after all those graces that are absolutely necessary for obtaining glory, honor, and immortality; but, where these graces are not obtained nor endeavored after, men are not able to look forward to the things that are but a very little way off in reality, though in appearance, or in their apprehension, they are at a great distance, because they put them far away from them; and how wretched is their condition who are thus blind as to the awfully great things of the other world, who cannot see anything of the reality and certainty, the greatness and nearness, of the glorious rewards God will bestow on the righteous, and the dreadful punishment he will inflict on the ungodly! But this is not all the misery of those who do not add to their faith virtue, knowledge, etc. They are as unable to look backward as forward, their memories are slippery and unable to retain what is past, as their sight is short and unable to discern what is future; they forget that they have been baptized, and had the means, and been laid under the obligations to holiness of heart and life. By baptism we are engaged in a holy war against sin, and are solemnly bound to fight against the flesh, the world, and the devil. Often call to mind, and seriously meditate on, your solemn engagement to be the Lord's, and your peculiar advantages and encouragements to lay aside all filthiness of flesh and spirit.

2. The apostle proposes two particular advantages that will attend or follow upon diligence in the work of a Christian: stability in grace, and a triumphant entrance into glory. These he brings in by resuming his former exhortation and laying it down in other words; for what in 2 Peter 1:5 is expressed by giving diligence to add to faith virtue, etc., is expressed in 2 Peter 1:10 by giving diligence to make our calling and election sure. Here we may observe,

(1.) It is the duty of believers to make their election sure, to clear it up to themselves that they are the chosen of God.

(2.) The way to make sure their eternal election is to make out their effectual calling: none can look into the book of God's eternal counsels and decrees; but, inasmuch as whom God did predestinate those he also called, if we can find we are effectually called, we may conclude we are chosen to salvation.

(3.) It requires a great deal of diligence and labor to make sure our calling and election; there must be a very close examination of ourselves, a very narrow search and strict enquiry, whether we are thoroughly converted, our minds enlightened, our wills renewed, and our whole souls changed as to the bent and inclination thereof; and to come to a fixed certainty in this requires the utmost diligence, and cannot be attained and kept without divine assistance, as we may learn from Psalm 139:23; Romans 8:16. "But, how great so ever the labor is, do not think much of it, for great is the advantage you gain by it; for,"

[1.] "By this you will be kept from falling, and that at all times and seasons, even in those hours of temptation that shall be on the earth." When others shall fall into heinous and scandalous sin, those who are thus diligent shall be enabled to walk circumspectly and keep on in the way of their duty; and, when many fall into errors, they shall be preserved sound in the faith, and stand perfect and complete in all the will of God.

[2.] Those who are diligent in the work of religion shall have a triumphant entrance into glory; while of those few who get to heaven some are scarcely saved (1 Peter 4:18), with a great deal of difficulty, even as by fire (1 Corinthians 3:15), those who are growing in grace, and abounding in the work of the Lord, shall have an abundant entrance into the joy of their Lord, even that everlasting kingdom where Christ reigns, and they shall reign with him for ever and ever.

The Message of Truth

FIX YOUR EYES ON CHRIST

While those all around you who deny Christ will continue their endless lustful chase and pursuit of the fleeting lures and temptations of this world, being turned every which way by the forces of darkness and tossing and turning in every direction like the waves of the sea in a great commotion, a Christian must remain steadfast on the "straight and narrow" path towards eternal life, constantly "fixing our eyes on Jesus, the author and perfecter of faith" every single day:

> Now large crowds were going along with Him; and He turned and said to them, "If anyone comes to Me, and does not hate his own father and mother and wife and children and brothers and sisters, yes, and even his own life, he cannot be My disciple. Whoever does not carry his own cross and come after Me cannot be My disciple." – Luke 14:25-27

> Therefore, since we have so great a cloud of witnesses surrounding us, let us also lay aside every encumbrance and the sin which so easily entangles us, and let us run with endurance the race that is set before us, fixing our eyes on Jesus, the author and perfecter of faith, who for the joy set before Him endured the cross, despising the shame, and has sat down at the right hand of the throne of God. – Hebrews 12:1-2

Note that the word "hate" here is used to mean that we must value, cherish and choose Christ above all others, at all costs, at all times, even above our own family members if necessary. It does not mean to literally hate your family as some falsely teach in a gross distortion of Scripture. Matthew Henry writes on the above verses: [68]

> If we must either deny Christ or be banished from our families and relations (as many of the primitive Christians were), we must rather lose their society than his favour. Every man loves his own life, no man ever yet hated it; and we cannot be Christ's disciples if we do not love him better than our own lives, so as rather to have our lives embittered by cruel bondage, nay, and taken away by cruel deaths, than to dishonour Christ, or depart from any of his truths and ways. The experience of the pleasures of the spiritual life, and the believing hopes and prospects of eternal life, will make this hard saying easy. When tribulation and persecution arise because of the word, then chiefly the trial is, whether we love better, Christ or our relations and lives; yet even in the days of peace this matter is sometimes brought to the trial. Those that decline the service of Christ, and opportunities of converse with him, and are ashamed to confess him, for fear of disobliging a relation or friend, or losing a customer, give cause to suspect that they love him better than Christ.

Press on to the goal of eternal life when you receive your Crown of life and trust in the Lord Jesus Christ for all things, for He says: "These things I have spoken to you, so that in Me you may have peace. In the world you have tribulation, but take courage; I have overcome the world."

---

[68] Henry, Matthew. *Exposition of the Old and New Testaments*, London. 1706-1710/1721.

FALSE TEACHING(S) YOU WILL ENCOUNTER:
- Saying a "Sinner's Prayer" saves you
- You are saved by "Faith Alone/Only"
- Once saved always saved
- Predestination
- Calvinism

RELATED SCRIPTURE:

For if, after they have escaped the defilements of the world by the knowledge of the Lord and Savior Jesus Christ, they are again entangled in them and are overcome, the last state has become worse for them than the first. For it would be better for them not to have known the way of righteousness, than having known it, to turn away from the holy commandment handed on to them. It has happened to them according to the true proverb, "A DOG RETURNS TO ITS OWN VOMIT," and, "A sow, after washing, *returns* to wallowing in the mire." – 2 Peter 2:20-22

Now Moses was faithful in all His house as a servant, for a testimony of those things which were to be spoken later; but Christ *was faithful* as a Son over His house—whose house we are, if we hold fast our confidence and the boast of our hope firm until the end. – Hebrews 3:5-6

Take care, brethren, that there not be in any one of you an evil, unbelieving heart that falls away from the living God. But encourage one another day after day, as long as it is *still* called "Today," so that none of you will be hardened by the deceitfulness of sin. For we have become partakers of Christ, if we hold fast the beginning of our assurance firm until the end, while it is said,

> "TODAY IF YOU HEAR HIS VOICE,
> DO NOT HARDEN YOUR HEARTS, AS WHEN THEY PROVOKED ME." – Hebrews 3:12-15

For in the case of those who have once been enlightened and have tasted of the heavenly gift and have been made partakers of the Holy Spirit, and have tasted the good word of God and the powers of the age to come, and *then* have fallen away, it is impossible to renew them again to repentance, since they again crucify to themselves the Son of God and put Him to open shame. – Hebrews 6:4-6

You will say then, "Branches were broken off so that I might be grafted in." Quite right, they were broken off for their unbelief, but you stand by your faith. Do not be conceited, but fear; for if God did not spare the natural branches, He will not spare you, either. Behold then the kindness and severity of God; to those who fell, severity, but to you, God's kindness, if you continue in His kindness; otherwise you also will be cut off. – Romans 11:19-22

"At that time many will fall away and will betray one another and hate one another. Many false prophets will arise and will mislead many. Because lawlessness is increased, most people's love will grow cold. But the one who endures to the end, he will be saved." – Matthew 24:10-13

Be on the alert, stand firm in the faith, act like men, be strong. – 1 Corinthians 16:13

The Message of Truth

Be of sober *spirit*, be on the alert. Your adversary, the devil, prowls around like a roaring lion, seeking someone to devour. – 1 Peter 5:8

"By your endurance you will gain your lives." – Luke 21:19

"His master said to him, 'Well done, good and faithful servant. You have been faithful over a little; I will set you over much. Enter into the joy of your master.'" – Matthew 25:23 (ESV)

"And they overcame him because of the blood of the Lamb and because of the word of their testimony, and they did not love their life even when faced with death." – Revelation 12:11

When the Lamb broke the fifth seal, I saw underneath the altar the souls of those who had been slain because of the word of God, and because of the testimony which they had maintained. – Revelation 6:9

Pay close attention to yourself and to your teaching; persevere in these things, for as you do this you will ensure salvation both for yourself and for those who hear you. – 1 Timothy 4:16

But whatever things were gain to me, those things I have counted as loss for the sake of Christ. More than that, I count all things to be loss in view of the surpassing value of knowing Christ Jesus my Lord, for whom I have suffered the loss of all things, and count them but rubbish so that I may gain Christ, and may be found in Him, not having a righteousness of my own derived from *the* Law, but that which is through faith in Christ, the righteousness which *comes* from God on the basis of faith, that I may know Him and the power of His resurrection and the fellowship of His sufferings, being conformed to His death; in order that I may attain to the resurrection from the dead.

Not that I have already obtained *it* or have already become perfect, but I press on so that I may lay hold of that for which also I was laid hold of by Christ Jesus. Brethren, I do not regard myself as having laid hold of *it* yet; but one thing *I do*: forgetting what *lies* behind and reaching forward to what *lies* ahead, I press on toward the goal for the prize of the upward call of God in Christ Jesus. – Philippians 3:7-14

But remember the former days, when, after being enlightened, you endured a great conflict of sufferings, partly by being made a public spectacle through reproaches and tribulations, and partly by becoming sharers with those who were so treated. For you showed sympathy to the prisoners and accepted joyfully the seizure of your property, knowing that you have for yourselves a better possession and a lasting one. Therefore, do not throw away your confidence, which has a great reward. For you have need of endurance, so that when you have done the will of God, you may receive what was promised.

> FOR YET IN A VERY LITTLE WHILE,
> HE WHO IS COMING WILL COME, AND WILL NOT DELAY.
> BUT MY RIGHTEOUS ONE SHALL LIVE BY FAITH;
> AND IF HE SHRINKS BACK, MY SOUL HAS NO PLEASURE IN HIM.

But we are not of those who shrink back to destruction, but of those who have faith to the preserving of the soul. – Hebrews 10:32-39

…for now we *really* live, if you stand firm in the Lord. – 1 Thessalonians 3:8

…but in everything commending ourselves as servants of God, in much endurance, in afflictions, in hardships, in distresses, in beatings, in imprisonments, in tumults, in labors, in sleeplessness, in hunger, in purity, in knowledge, in patience, in kindness, in the Holy Spirit, in genuine love, in the word of truth, in the power of God; by the weapons of righteousness for the right hand and the left, by glory and dishonor, by evil report and good report; *regarded* as deceivers and yet true; as unknown yet well-known, as dying yet behold, we live; as punished yet not put to death, as sorrowful yet always rejoicing, as poor yet making many rich, as having nothing yet possessing all things. – 2 Corinthians 6:4-10

They took his advice; and after calling the apostles in, they flogged them and ordered them not to speak in the name of Jesus, and *then* released them. So they went on their way from the presence of the Council, rejoicing that they had been considered worthy to suffer shame for *His* name. And every day, in the temple and from house to house, they kept right on teaching and preaching Jesus *as* the Christ. – Acts 5:40-42

"I have been crucified with Christ; and it is no longer I who live, but Christ lives in me; and the *life* which I now live in the flesh I live by faith in the Son of God, who loved me and gave Himself up for me." – Galatians 2:20

Then Jesus said to His disciples, "If anyone wishes to come after Me, he must deny himself, and take up his cross and follow Me. For whoever wishes to save his life will lose it; but whoever loses his life for My sake will find it. For what will it profit a man if he gains the whole world and forfeits his soul? Or what will a man give in exchange for his soul?" – Matthew 16:24-26

"Have I not commanded you? Be strong and courageous! Do not tremble or be dismayed, for the LORD your God is with you wherever you go." – Joshua 1:9

The wicked flee when no one is pursuing,
But the righteous are bold as a lion. – Proverbs 28:1

This was in accordance with the eternal purpose which He carried out in Christ Jesus our Lord, in whom we have boldness and confident access through faith in Him. – Ephesians 3:11-12

Such confidence we have through Christ toward God. Not that we are adequate in ourselves to consider anything as *coming* from ourselves, but our adequacy is from God, who also made us adequate *as* servants of a new covenant, not of the letter but of the Spirit; for the letter kills, but the Spirit gives life. – 2 Corinthians 3:4-6

But Peter and the apostles answered, "We must obey God rather than men." – Acts 5:29

No temptation has overtaken you but such as is common to man; and God is faithful, who will not allow you to be tempted beyond what you are able, but with the temptation will provide the way of escape also, so that you will be able to endure it. – 1 Corinthians 10:13

So that we confidently say,

"THE LORD IS MY HELPER, I WILL NOT BE AFRAID.
WHAT WILL MAN DO TO ME?" – Hebrews 13:6

The Message of Truth

"And those who have turned back from following the LORD." – Zephaniah 1:6

"But I do not consider my life of any account as dear to myself, so that I may finish my course and the ministry which I received from the Lord Jesus, to testify solemnly of the gospel of the grace of God." – Acts 20:24

"In a similar way these are the ones on whom seed was sown on the rocky *places*, who, when they hear the word, immediately receive it with joy; and they have no *firm* root in themselves, but are *only* temporary; then, when affliction or persecution arises because of the word, immediately they fall away." – Mark 4:16-17

That day Jesus went out of the house and was sitting by the sea. And large crowds gathered to Him, so He got into a boat and sat down, and the whole crowd was standing on the beach.

And He spoke many things to them in parables, saying, "Behold, the sower went out to sow; and as he sowed, some *seeds* fell beside the road, and the birds came and ate them up. Others fell on the rocky places, where they did not have much soil; and immediately they sprang up, because they had no depth of soil. But when the sun had risen, they were scorched; and because they had no root, they withered away. Others fell among the thorns, and the thorns came up and choked them out. And others fell on the good soil and yielded a crop, some a hundredfold, some sixty, and some thirty. He who has ears, let him hear." ...

"Hear then the parable of the sower. When anyone hears the word of the kingdom and does not understand it, the evil *one* comes and snatches away what has been sown in his heart. This is the one on whom seed was sown beside the road. The one on whom seed was sown on the rocky places, this is the man who hears the word and immediately receives it with joy; yet he has no *firm* root in himself, but is *only* temporary, and when affliction or persecution arises because of the word, immediately he falls away. And the one on whom seed was sown among the thorns, this is the man who hears the word, and the worry of the world and the deceitfulness of wealth choke the word, and it becomes unfruitful. And the one on whom seed was sown on the good soil, this is the man who hears the word and understands it; who indeed bears fruit and brings forth, some a hundredfold, some sixty, and some thirty." – Matthew 13:1-9, 18-23 [the parable of the sower]

For not one of us lives for himself, and not one dies for himself; for if we live, we live for the Lord, or if we die, we die for the Lord; therefore whether we live or die, we are the Lord's. – Romans 14:7-8

I charge you in the presence of God and of Christ Jesus, who is to judge the living and the dead, and by his appearing and his kingdom: preach the word; be ready in season and out of season; reprove, rebuke, and exhort, with complete patience and teaching. For the time is coming when people will not endure sound teaching, but having itching ears they will accumulate for themselves teachers to suit their own passions, and will turn away from listening to the truth and wander off into myths. As for you, always be sober-minded, endure suffering, do the work of an evangelist, fulfill your ministry.

For I am already being poured out as a drink offering, and the time of my departure has come. I have fought the good fight, I have finished the race, I have kept the faith. Henceforth there is laid up for me the crown of righteousness, which the Lord, the righteous judge, will award to me on that day, and not only to me but also to all who have loved his appearing. – 2 Timothy 4:1-8 (ESV)

"If the world hates you, you know that it has hated Me before *it hated* you. If you were of the world, the world would love its own; but because you are not of the world, but I chose you out of the world, because of this the world hates you." – John 15:18-19

Let us hold fast the confession of our hope without wavering, for He who promised is faithful; and let us consider how to stimulate one another to love and good deeds, not forsaking our own assembling together, as is the habit of some, but encouraging *one another*; and all the more as you see the day drawing near. – Hebrews 10:23-25

And although you were formerly alienated and hostile in mind, *engaged* in evil deeds, yet He has now reconciled you in His fleshly body through death, in order to present you before Him holy and blameless and beyond reproach— if indeed you continue in the faith firmly established and steadfast, and not moved away from the hope of the gospel that you have heard, which was proclaimed in all creation under heaven, and of which I, Paul, was made a minister. – Colossians 1:21-23

You were bought with a price; do not become slaves of men. – 1 Corinthians 7:23

And not only this, but we also exult in our tribulations, knowing that tribulation brings about perseverance; and perseverance, proven character; and proven character, hope; and hope does not disappoint, because the love of God has been poured out within our hearts through the Holy Spirit who was given to us. – Romans 5:3-5

Know this first of all, that in the last days mockers will come with *their* mocking, following after their own lusts, and saying, "Where is the promise of His coming? For *ever* since the fathers fell asleep, all continues just as it was from the beginning of creation." For when they maintain this, it escapes their notice that by the word of God *the* heavens existed long ago and *the* earth was formed out of water and by water, through which the world at that time was destroyed, being flooded with water. But by His word the present heavens and earth are being reserved for fire, kept for the day of judgment and destruction of ungodly men.

But do not let this one *fact* escape your notice, beloved, that with the Lord one day is like a thousand years, and a thousand years like one day. The Lord is not slow about His promise, as some count slowness, but is patient toward you, not wishing for any to perish but for all to come to repentance.

But the day of the Lord will come like a thief, in which the heavens will pass away with a roar and the elements will be destroyed with intense heat, and the earth and its works will be burned up.

Since all these things are to be destroyed in this way, what sort of people ought you to be in holy conduct and godliness, looking for and hastening the coming of the day of God, because of which the heavens will be destroyed by burning, and the elements will melt with intense heat! But according to His promise we are looking for new heavens and a new earth, in which righteousness dwells.

Therefore, beloved, since you look for these things, be diligent to be found by Him in peace, spotless and blameless, and regard the patience of our Lord *as* salvation; just as also our beloved brother Paul, according to the wisdom given him, wrote to you, as also in all *his* letters, speaking in them of these things, in which are some things hard to understand, which the untaught and unstable distort, as *they do* also the rest of the Scriptures, to their own destruction. – 2 Peter 3:3-16

"But the *seed* in the good soil, these are the ones who have heard the word in an honest and good heart, and hold it fast, and bear fruit with perseverance." – Luke 8:15

Let us not lose heart in doing good, for in due time we will reap if we do not grow weary. – Galatians 6:9

For whatever was written in earlier times was written for our instruction, so that through perseverance and the encouragement of the Scriptures we might have hope. – Romans 15:4

"Brother will betray brother to death, and a father *his* child; and children will rise up against parents and cause them to be put to death. You will be hated by all because of My name, but it is the one who has endured to the end who will be saved." – Matthew 10:21-22

"'I know your deeds and your toil and perseverance, and that you cannot tolerate evil men, and you put to the test those who call themselves apostles, and they are not, and you found them *to be* false; and you have perseverance and have endured for My name's sake, and have not grown weary.'" – Revelation 2:2-3

"'I know your deeds, and your love and faith and service and perseverance, and that your deeds of late are greater than at first.'" – Revelation 2:19

Now you followed my teaching, conduct, purpose, faith, patience, love, perseverance, persecutions, *and* sufferings, such as happened to me at Antioch, at Iconium *and* at Lystra; what persecutions I endured, and out of them all the Lord rescued me! Indeed, all who desire to live godly in Christ Jesus will be persecuted. – 2 Timothy 3:10-12

Do not fret because of evildoers,
Be not envious toward wrongdoers.
For they will wither quickly like the grass
And fade like the green herb.
Trust in the LORD and do good;
Dwell in the land and cultivate faithfulness.
Delight yourself in the LORD;
And He will give you the desires of your heart.
Commit your way to the LORD,
Trust also in Him, and He will do it.
He will bring forth your righteousness as the light
And your judgment as the noonday. – Psalm 37:1-6

Now, little children, abide in Him, so that when He appears, we may have confidence and not shrink away from Him in shame at His coming. – 1 John 2:28

4.5 SOME ENCOURAGEMENT

I can do all things through Him who strengthens me. – Philippians 4:13

The previous chapters have been fairly lengthy and heavy chapters. Perhaps you are feeling a bit down or somewhat overwhelmed after reading the chapter on perseverance in particular, and you may be wondering how you will be able to "stand firm in the faith," "fight the good fight of faith," and "finish the race." But know this, not only has God redeemed you from bondage under sin, Satan, and death and given you new life, He also gives you everything that you will need in order to persevere in faith until the very end. Amazing, yes?

As surely as trials and tribulations will come your way, you will also see that the Word of God and the power of His Spirit stand firm to hold you up. Even further, God actually equips you with the tools, power, wisdom, and strength that you will need. We discuss these further in upcoming chapters:

- **The Peace of God:** God will give you His supernatural peace as you walk with Him; a Christian is called to be a warrior for Christ, not a worrier for Christ! Constant anxiety has no part in the life of a Christian.
- **The Wisdom of God:** God will guide you through His wisdom. A Christian should seek "the wisdom from above [which] is first pure, then peaceable, gentle, reasonable, full of mercy and good fruits, unwavering, without hypocrisy," which is the wisdom of God, not the wisdom of man. The wisdom of man only leads to myths, wild speculation, mystical conjurings, opinions, "traditions," schemes, false teachings, and the continued endless wars, violence, suffering, destruction, and death we see all around us in this fallen world.
- **The Armor of God:** A Christian is to put on what is called "the full armor of God" so they can "stand firm" in the faith and persevere in all things. Remember that we are in a spiritual war with the forces of darkness and evil, and as a Christian, you have now moved to the front lines of the battle!
- **The Power of Prayer:** Prayer is how we talk with God, and it is a vital part of the life of every Christian. It is also through prayer that you do battle with the (spiritual) forces of evil. A Christian is not called to pick up the carnal weapons of war and destruction created by man, for they are not effective whatsoever in the battle we are fighting (see also 2 Corinthians 10:3-5, Isaiah 2:1-4).
- **The Kingdom of God:** You are now part of the "Kingdom of God," which is not at some future time on earth; it is right now! Jesus is right now ruling and reigning as Lord and King in His Kingdom, and you are also in the kingdom as a "child of God." You are called to be about the business of the Lord, being a Kingdom Builder if you will, and not to be entangled with the political or nationalistic affairs of this world and man.

Know that you will be able to do "all things" now by the power of Christ who "abides [lives] in you." Always remember, Jesus has already won and assured us of victory:

> "These things I have spoken to you, so that in Me you may have peace. In the world you have tribulation, but take courage; I have overcome the world." – John 16:33

> I can do all things through Him who strengthens me. – Philippians 4:13

We further read, in what I think is among the loftiest passages in all of Scripture as they soar to unimaginable heights, that nothing whatsoever can separate us from the love of God:

> And we know that God causes all things to work together for good to those who love God, to those who are called according to *His* purpose. For those whom He foreknew, He also predestined *to become* conformed to the image of His Son, so that He would be the firstborn among many brethren; and these whom He predestined, He also called; and these whom He called, He also justified; and these whom He justified, He also glorified.
>
> What then shall we say to these things? If God *is* for us, who *is* against us? He who did not spare His own Son, but delivered Him over for us all, how will He not also with Him freely give us all things? Who will bring a charge against God's elect? God is the one who justifies; who is the one who condemns? Christ Jesus is He who died, yes, rather who was raised, who is at the right hand of God, who also intercedes for us. Who will separate us from the love of Christ? Will tribulation, or distress, or persecution, or famine, or nakedness, or peril, or sword? Just as it is written,
>
> > "FOR YOUR SAKE WE ARE BEING PUT TO DEATH ALL DAY LONG;
> > WE WERE CONSIDERED AS SHEEP TO BE SLAUGHTERED."
>
> But in all these things we overwhelmingly conquer through Him who loved us. For I am convinced that neither death, nor life, nor angels, nor principalities, nor things present, nor things to come, nor powers, nor height, nor depth, nor any other created thing, will be able to separate us from the love of God, which is in Christ Jesus our Lord. – Romans 8:28-39

Those verses are truly awesome in their power, hope, conviction, and assurance! Below is a note of encouragement from one of the verse cards in our *Rays of Hope* booklet on Romans 8:28-29:

> *God sees you, and He sees everything that happens to you. He sees everything that happens, past, present, and future; He knows all. Nothing surprises Him; nothing sneaks past Him. He promises that all things work together for your good and the good of all those together with you who love Him, whether it is easy to understand the "why" right now or not. You are in His loving care! He will never forget or forsake you. His nature is perfect holiness, love, mercy, and grace. Trust in His nature with confidence, joy, and hope.*

So, we live in His assurance – "the assurance of *things* hoped for" that we read about in Scripture, and Scripture tells us that God's word will never fail ("return void"):

> Now faith is the assurance of *things* hoped for, the conviction of things not seen. – Hebrews 11:1

> So will My word be which goes forth from My mouth;
> It will not return to Me empty [return void],
> Without accomplishing what I desire,
> And without succeeding *in the matter* for which I sent it. – Isaiah 55:11

Understand that everything that happens to you as a Christian is now under the watch, care, and protection of Christ – there is no such thing as being "lucky" or "a coincidence" for a Christian. Matthew Henry writes: [69]

> Providence must be acknowledged when things happen thus opportunely, and we are favoured by some little circumstances that contribute to the expediting of our affairs; and we must say, it is God that maketh our way perfect

Matthew Henry further writes these notes of encouragement:

> Another instance of favor that Christ promises to this church is persevering grace in the most trying times (Rev 3:10), and this as the reward of their past fidelity. To him that hath shall be given. Here observe,
> [1.] The gospel of Christ is the word of his patience. It is the fruit of the patience of God to a sinful world; it sets before men the exemplary patience of Christ in all his sufferings for men; it calls those that receive it to the exercise of patience in conformity to Christ.
> [2.] This gospel should be carefully kept by all that enjoy it; they must keep up to the faith, and practice, and worship prescribed in the gospel.
> [3.] After a day of patience, we must expect an hour of temptation; a day of gospel peace and liberty is a day of God's patience, and it is seldom so well improved as it should be and therefore it is often followed by an hour of trial and temptation.
> [4.] Sometimes the trial is more general and universal; it comes upon all the world, and, when it is so general, it is usually the shorter.
> [5.] Those who keep the gospel in a time of peace shall be kept by Christ in an hour of temptation. By keeping the gospel, they are prepared for the trial; and the same divine grace that has made them fruitful in times of peace will make them faithful in times of persecution. ...
> After his usual manner, our Savior promises a glorious reward to the victorious believer, in two things:
> (1.) He shall be a monumental pillar in the temple of God; not a pillar to support the temple (heaven needs no such props), but a monument of the free and powerful grace of God, a monument that shall never be defaced nor removed, as many stately pillars erected in honor to the Roman emperors and generals have been.
> (2.) On this monumental pillar there shall be an honorable inscription, as in those cases is usual.
> [1.] The name of God, in whose cause he engaged, whom he served, and for whom he suffered in this warfare; and the name of the city of God, the church of God, the new Jerusalem, which came down from heaven. On this pillar shall be recorded all the services the believer did to the church of God, how he asserted her

---

[69] Henry, Matthew. *Exposition of the Old and New Testaments*, London. 1706-1710/1721.

> rights, enlarged her borders, maintained her purity and honor; this will be a greater name than Asiaticus, or Africanus; a soldier under God in the wars of the church. And then another part of the inscription is,
>
> [2.] The new name of Christ, the Mediator, the Redeemer, the captain of our salvation; by this it will appear under whose banner this conquering believer had enlisted, under whose conduct he acted, by whose example he was encouraged, and under whose influence he fought the good fight, and came off victorious.

Furthermore, God doesn't change His mind, break His promises, or speak lies. He cannot; His nature is perfect, holy, pure, righteous, and true. Remember His words as a stronghold in times of distress and look forward to the joy of heaven with Christ. God promises to "make all things new," and as a believer in Christ, you will be there to see it with Him. Look past the trials and tribulations of this present world to the future time of unspeakable glory, joy, peace, and happiness with Christ in heaven.

You start each day new in Christ. Learn from yesterday's mistakes (and successes) but press on today towards Christ, no matter what happened yesterday. Pick yourself up, go forward toward Christ (lean into Him) and persevere in your faith. Trust in His perfect will and in His commandments. Trust in your faith, strengthened by Him. He will never forget or forsake you. Pray to Him daily, constantly, with boldness and with full honesty; let Him walk with you today. If you sinned yesterday, confess it and repent (1 John 1:9) and let His peace guard your heart. Stay focused only on Jesus each day. Remember we have these powerful verses to help remind us that:

> The LORD'S lovingkindnesses indeed never cease,
> For His compassions never fail.
> *They* are new every morning;
> Great is Your faithfulness.
> "The LORD is my portion," says my soul,
> "Therefore I have hope in Him."
> The LORD is good to those who wait for Him,
> To the person who seeks Him.
> *It is* good that he waits silently
> For the salvation of the LORD. – Lamentations 3:22-26

The Bible is so full of hope, inspiration, and victory that it's hard to know which verses to include in this chapter. I've included some that helped me greatly when I was starting out on pilgrimage as a Christian; I'm sure you will find your own favorites over time as well. It's good to have verses memorized so that you can recall them in times of need or distress and to have them handy to encourage and teach others. See also the inspirational Psalms at the end of this book.

FALSE TEACHING(S) YOU WILL ENCOUNTER:

- How about we have one chapter without false teachings getting in the way

RELATED SCRIPTURE:

And not only this, but we also exult in our tribulations, knowing that tribulation brings about perseverance; and perseverance, proven character; and proven character, hope; and hope does not disappoint, because the love of God has been poured out within our hearts through the Holy Spirit who was given to us. – Romans 5:3-5

Consider it all joy, my brethren, when you encounter various trials, knowing that the testing of your faith produces endurance. And let endurance have *its* perfect result, so that you may be perfect and complete, lacking in nothing. – James 1:2-4

So they went on their way from the presence of the Council, rejoicing that they had been considered worthy to suffer shame for *His* name. – Acts 5:41

"Do not fear those who kill the body but are unable to kill the soul; but rather fear Him who is able to destroy both soul and body in hell." – Matthew 10:28

For whatever was written in earlier times was written for our instruction, so that through perseverance and the encouragement of the Scriptures we might have hope. – Romans 15:4

For I am confident of this very thing, that He who began a good work in you will perfect it until the day of Christ Jesus. – Philippians 1:6

"Are not two sparrows sold for a cent? And *yet* not one of them will fall to the ground apart from your Father. But the very hairs of your head are all numbered. So do not fear; you are more valuable than many sparrows." – Matthew 10:29-31

Jesus said to them, "I am the bread of life; he who comes to Me will not hunger, and he who believes in Me will never thirst. But I said to you that you have seen Me, and yet do not believe. All that the Father gives Me will come to Me, and the one who comes to Me I will certainly not cast out. For I have come down from heaven, not to do My own will, but the will of Him who sent Me. This is the will of Him who sent Me, that of all that He has given Me I lose nothing, but raise it up on the last day. For this is the will of My Father, that everyone who beholds the Son and believes in Him will have eternal life, and I Myself will raise him up on the last day." – John 6:35-40

"Now judgment is upon this world; now the ruler of this world will be cast out. And I, if I am lifted up from the earth, will draw all men to Myself." – John 12:31-32

"Do not let your heart be troubled; believe in God, believe also in Me. In My Father's house are many dwelling places; if it were not so, I would have told you; for I go to prepare a place for you. If I go and prepare a place for you, I will come again and receive you to Myself, that where I am, *there* you may be also." – John 14:1-3

You are from God, little children, and have overcome them; because greater is He who is in you than he who is in the world. – 1 John 4:4

I have fought the good fight, I have finished the race, I have kept the faith. Henceforth there is laid up for me the crown of righteousness, which the Lord, the righteous judge, will award to me on that day, and not only to me but also to all who have loved his appearing. – 2 Timothy 4:7-8 (ESV)

And I heard a loud voice from the throne, saying, "Behold, the tabernacle of God is among men, and He will dwell among them, and they shall be His people, and God Himself will be among them, and He will wipe away every tear from their eyes; and there will no longer be *any* death; there will no longer be *any* mourning, or crying, or pain; the first things have passed away." – Revelation 21:3-4

The Message of Truth

Then He said to me, "It is done. I am the Alpha and the Omega, the beginning and the end. I will give to the one who thirsts from the spring of the water of life without cost. He who overcomes will inherit these things, and I will be his God and he will be My son. But for the cowardly and unbelieving and abominable and murderers and immoral persons and sorcerers and idolaters and all liars, their part *will be* in the lake that burns with fire and brimstone, which is the second death." – Revelation 21:6-8

And He has said to me, "My grace is sufficient for you, for power is perfected in weakness." Most gladly, therefore, I will rather boast about my weaknesses, so that the power of Christ may dwell in me. Therefore I am well content with weaknesses, with insults, with distresses, with persecutions, with difficulties, for Christ's sake; for when I am weak, then I am strong. – 2 Corinthians 12:9-10

But we have this treasure in earthen vessels, so that the surpassing greatness of the power will be of God and not from ourselves; *we are* afflicted in every way, but not crushed; perplexed, but not despairing; persecuted, but not forsaken; struck down, but not destroyed; always carrying about in the body the dying of Jesus, so that the life of Jesus also may be manifested in our body. For we who live are constantly being delivered over to death for Jesus' sake, so that the life of Jesus also may be manifested in our mortal flesh. So death works in us, but life in you. – 2 Corinthians 4:7-12

Therefore we do not lose heart, but though our outer man is decaying, yet our inner man is being renewed day by day. For momentary, light affliction is producing for us an eternal weight of glory far beyond all comparison, while we look not at the things which are seen, but at the things which are not seen; for the things which are seen are temporal, but the things which are not seen are eternal. – 2 Corinthians 4:16-18

Therefore, my beloved brethren, be steadfast, immovable, always abounding in the work of the Lord, knowing that your toil is not *in* vain in the Lord. – 1 Corinthians 15:58

"As for me, I know that my Redeemer lives,
And at the last He will take His stand on the earth.
"Even after my skin is destroyed,
Yet from my flesh I shall see God;
Whom I myself shall behold,
And whom my eyes will see and not another.
My heart faints within me!" – Job 19:25-27

"If it is disagreeable in your sight to serve the LORD, choose for yourselves today whom you will serve: whether the gods which your fathers served which were beyond the River, or the gods of the Amorites in whose land you are living; but as for me and my house, we will serve the LORD." – Joshua 24:15

As for God, His way is blameless;
The word of the LORD is tried;
He is a shield to all who take refuge in Him. – Psalm 18:30

For I consider that the sufferings of this present time are not worthy to be compared with the glory that is to be revealed to us. – Romans 8:18

But You are a God of forgiveness,
Gracious and compassionate,
Slow to anger and abounding in lovingkindness. – Nehemiah 9:17

"For I know the plans that I have for you,' declares the LORD, 'plans for welfare and not for calamity to give you a future and a hope. Then you will call upon Me and come and pray to Me, and I will listen to you. You will seek Me and find *Me* when you search for Me with all your heart." – Jeremiah 29:11-13

The LORD is my light and my salvation;
Whom shall I fear?
The LORD is the defense of my life;
Whom shall I dread? – Psalm 27:1

"I love You, O LORD, my strength."
The LORD is my rock and my fortress and my deliverer,
My God, my rock, in whom I take refuge;
My shield and the horn of my salvation, my stronghold.
I call upon the LORD, who is worthy to be praised,
And I am saved from my enemies. – Psalm 18:1-3

Do you not know? Have you not heard?
The Everlasting God, the LORD, the Creator of the ends of the earth
Does not become weary or tired.
His understanding is inscrutable.
He gives strength to the weary,
And to *him who* lacks might He increases power.
Though youths grow weary and tired,
And vigorous young men stumble badly,
Yet those who wait for the LORD
Will gain new strength;
They will mount up *with* wings like eagles,
They will run and not get tired,
They will walk and not become weary. – Isaiah 40:28-31

But the LORD abides forever;
He has established His throne for judgment,
And He will judge the world in righteousness;
He will execute judgment for the peoples with equity.
The LORD also will be a stronghold for the oppressed,
A stronghold in times of trouble;
And those who know Your name will put their trust in You,
For You, O LORD, have not forsaken those who seek You. – Psalm 9:7-10

The end of all things is near; therefore, be of sound judgment and sober *spirit* for the purpose of prayer. Above all, keep fervent in your love for one another, because love covers a multitude of sins. Be hospitable to one another without complaint. As each one has received a *special* gift, employ it in serving one another as good stewards of the manifold grace of God. Whoever speaks, *is to do so* as one who is speaking the utterances of God; whoever serves *is to do so* as one who is serving by the strength which God supplies; so that in all things God may be glorified through Jesus Christ, to whom belongs the glory and dominion forever and ever. Amen.

The Message of Truth

Beloved, do not be surprised at the fiery ordeal among you, which comes upon you for your testing, as though some strange thing were happening to you; but to the degree that you share the sufferings of Christ, keep on rejoicing, so that also at the revelation of His glory you may rejoice with exultation. If you are reviled for the name of Christ, you are blessed, because the Spirit of glory and of God rests on you. – 1 Peter 4:7-14

In this you greatly rejoice, even though now for a little while, if necessary, you have been distressed by various trials, so that the proof of your faith, *being* more precious than gold which is perishable, even though tested by fire, may be found to result in praise and glory and honor at the revelation of Jesus Christ. – 1 Peter 1:6-7

When you were dead in your transgressions and the uncircumcision of your flesh, He made you alive together with Him, having forgiven us all our transgressions, having canceled out the certificate of debt consisting of decrees against us, which was hostile to us; and He has taken it out of the way, having nailed it to the cross. When He had disarmed the rulers and authorities, He made a public display of them, having triumphed over them through Him. – Colossians 2:13-15

"Heaven and earth will pass away, but My words will not pass away." – Matthew 24:35

"As for me, I know that my Redeemer lives,
And at the last He will take His stand on the earth.
"Even after my skin is destroyed,
Yet from my flesh I shall see God;
Whom I myself shall behold,
And whom my eyes will see and not another." – Job 19:25-27

"Have I not commanded you? Be strong and courageous! Do not tremble or be dismayed, for the LORD your God is with you wherever you go." – Joshua 1:9

Even though I walk through the valley of the shadow of death,
I fear no evil, for You are with me. – Psalm 23:4

"Blessed are you when *people* insult you and persecute you, and falsely say all kinds of evil against you because of Me. Rejoice and be glad, for your reward in heaven is great; for in the same way they persecuted the prophets who were before you." – Matthew 5:11-12

My soul *waits* in silence for God only;
From Him is my salvation.
He only is my rock and my salvation,
My stronghold; I shall not be greatly shaken.
…
My soul, wait in silence for God only,
For my hope is from Him.
He only is my rock and my salvation,
My stronghold; I shall not be shaken.
On God my salvation and my glory *rest*;
The rock of my strength, my refuge is in God.
Trust in Him at all times, O people;
Pour out your heart before Him;
God is a refuge for us. *Selah.* – Psalm 62:1-2,5-8

Therefore, since we have so great a cloud of witnesses surrounding us, let us also lay aside every encumbrance and the sin which so easily entangles us, and let us run with endurance the race that is set before us, fixing our eyes on Jesus, the author and perfecter of faith, who for the joy set before Him endured the cross, despising the shame, and has sat down at the right hand of the throne of God. – Hebrews 12:1-2

For this reason I also suffer these things, but I am not ashamed; for I know whom I have believed and I am convinced that He is able to guard what I have entrusted to Him until that day [the great Day of Judgment]. – 2 Timothy 1:12

The Lord will rescue me from every evil deed, and will bring me safely to His heavenly kingdom; to Him *be* the glory forever and ever. Amen. – 2 Timothy 4:18

Finally, be strong in the Lord and in the strength of His might. Put on the full armor of God, so that you will be able to stand firm against the schemes of the devil. For our struggle is not against flesh and blood, but against the rulers, against the powers, against the world forces of this darkness, against the spiritual *forces* of wickedness in the heavenly *places*. Therefore, take up the full armor of God, so that you will be able to resist in the evil day, and having done everything, to stand firm. – Ephesians 6:10-13

Trust in the LORD with all your heart
And do not lean on your own understanding.
In all your ways acknowledge Him,
And He will make your paths straight. – Proverbs 3:5-6

I will lift up my eyes to the mountains;
From where shall my help come?
My help *comes* from the LORD,
Who made heaven and earth. – Psalm 121:1-2

…so that we confidently say,

> "THE LORD IS MY HELPER, I WILL NOT BE AFRAID.
> WHAT WILL MAN DO TO ME?" – Hebrews 13:6

"Lo, I [Jesus] am with you always, even to the end of the age." – Matthew 28:20

Jesus said to him, "Because you have seen Me, have you believed? Blessed *are* they who did not see, and *yet* believed." – John 20:29

The Lord GOD has given Me the tongue of disciples,
That I may know how to sustain the weary one with a word.
He awakens *Me* morning by morning,
He awakens My ear to listen as a disciple.
The Lord GOD has opened My ear;
And I was not disobedient
Nor did I turn back.
I gave My back to those who strike *Me*,
And My cheeks to those who pluck out the beard;
I did not cover My face from humiliation and spitting.
For the Lord GOD helps Me,
Therefore, I am not disgraced;

The Message of Truth

Therefore, I have set My face like flint,
And I know that I will not be ashamed. – Isaiah 50:4-7

Blessed *be* the God and Father of our Lord Jesus Christ, the Father of mercies and God of all comfort, who comforts us in all our affliction so that we will be able to comfort those who are in any affliction with the comfort with which we ourselves are comforted by God. – 2 Corinthians 1:3-4

More than that, I count all things to be loss in view of the surpassing value of knowing Christ Jesus my Lord, for whom I have suffered the loss of all things, and count them *mere* rubbish, so that I may gain Christ. – Philippians 3:8

For not one of us lives for himself, and not one dies for himself; for if we live, we live for the Lord, or if we die, we die for the Lord; therefore whether we live or die, we are the Lord's. – Romans 14:7-8

For to me, to live is Christ, and to die is gain. – Philippians 1:21

"Speak to Aaron and to his sons, saying, 'In this way you shall bless the sons of Israel. You are to say to them:

> The LORD bless you, and keep you;

> The LORD cause His face to shine on you,
> And be gracious to you;

> The LORD lift up His face to you,
> And give you peace.'" – Numbers 6:23-26

When you pass through the waters, I will be with you;
And through the rivers, they will not overflow you.
When you walk through the fire, you will not be scorched,
Nor will the flame burn you. – Isaiah 43:2

4.6 THE PEACE OF GOD

> *Be anxious for nothing, but in everything by prayer and supplication with thanksgiving let your requests be made known to God. And the peace of God, which surpasses all comprehension, will guard your hearts and your minds in Christ Jesus.*
> *– Philippians 4:6-7*

Is your life marked by a state of peace or one of constant uneasiness, worry, and anxiety over nearly all things? No matter where you find yourself, as a "child of God," know that Christ is right there with you. He knows your situation, your circumstances, and your heart, and He promises never to forget or forsake you. Remember, your hope and peace are in Christ, not in man or the things of this world!

Now the anxiety I'm talking about here is not the same as real physical fear, nor behavior caused or induced by a chemical imbalance or medical issues. I'm talking about the terrible anxiety that nearly everyone seems to have in today's world. It's more than just constant worrying; it's actually a debilitating state that one can enter into. Anxiety today is of epidemic proportions, even among Christians. This is a very important subject, for I constantly see Christians as anxious and worried as those who do not even know God, and some even more so! But that just should not be – anxiety has no part in the life of a Christian. Simply put, anxiety for a Christian is due to a lack of faith and trust in the Lord. Said another way, a Christian banishes anxiety through faith and unconditional trust in the Lord. We are called to be warriors for Christ, not worriers for Christ!

Trusting in the Lord means: do you believe He will do all the things He has said He will do? If you are anxious, you are consciously (or subconsciously) thinking (and implying) that God doesn't know what you need, or that He doesn't know your circumstances and situation, or that maybe He can't handle whatever is happening. We are to trust in the Lord for "all things" – not just some things, not only on Wednesdays, not only when things are going well, not only when it's convenient, etc. Furthermore, not trusting in God is making the omniscient, omnipresent, omnipotent Lord God Almighty small, and we must not do that. Remember, He is the God who simply "spoke" the entire universe (and all life) into existence! He is not a small God! Remember in Whom you have placed your faith: the most holy Lord God who created all things, heaven and earth, and who rules and reigns supreme over all matters.

We read:

> Be anxious for nothing, but in everything by prayer and supplication with thanksgiving let your requests be made known to God. And the peace of God, which surpasses all comprehension, will guard your hearts and your minds in Christ Jesus. – Philippians 4:6-7

> "Peace I leave with you; My peace I give to you; not as the world gives do I give to you. Do not let your heart be troubled, nor let it be fearful." – John 14:27

Those verses tell you both how to get the peace of God and also what the source of that peace is – it is of God Himself. Included below is a study note on Philippians 4:6-7 from *The Peace of God* booklet that we publish:

> *Do you trust completely in the Lord Jesus Christ? I mean for all things, great and small? For health, wealth, happiness, and also in persecution, trials, and tribulations? When you fully trust in the Lord, you will find that anxiety disappears, and this "peace of God," which does, in fact, surpass all understanding, will come over you, and you can definitely feel it. It is a distinct feeling that you get – a sense of complete calmness. You are not the source of this peace – it is of God Himself, which He is giving to you. But this only happens when you fully and completely trust in the Lord for all things. Peace and trust are closely linked. Nothing happens to a Christian by luck or chance – God is in full control of all things in the life of a Christian. In fact, anxiety for a Christian stems largely from a lack of faith. So, when you are facing something tough, offer up your prayers and petitions (requests) to God, and then let Him be in control – trust in the Lord completely. And He will give you His peace, which is amazing!*

There are some great examples of peace and trust in the Bible, especially when faced with the most difficult situations and the harshest of trials. A few of my favorites are:

- Daniel, as he was about to be thrown into the lion's den (Daniel 6),
- Shadrach, Meshach, and Abednego, as they were about to be thrown into the fiery furnace (Daniel 3),
- Peter in prison (Acts 12:5-7)

Regarding Peter in prison, at first, this might seem like a strange verse to include in a chapter about peace but think about what was happening. Peter was arrested and in jail, facing serious charges, possibly even the death penalty. And yet, on the very night before he was to appear before the judge for his hearing and sentencing, he was sleeping soundly and peacefully! He was resting in the supernatural "peace of God." He was confident in his faith, and he was trusting completely in the Lord, no matter what happens. Peter had done all he could do for the Lord, and now things rested in God's hands – "Your will be done"!

You see, I also suffered from terrible anxiety all my life. It wasn't until I finally realized what was causing it (a lack of faith/trust in the Lord) that it went away. Now don't get me wrong, it may rise up occasionally from time to time, but I now recognize it for what it is, and it soon passes. And here is the important part – it doesn't take control over me any longer. If anything, I use such occasions now to remind me to trust in the Lord even more! Understand that everything that happens to a Christian is known to God.

Anxiety commonly manifests itself primarily as a result of either a) worrying about losing something you have (health, money, spouse, girlfriend, boyfriend, job, etc.), or b) worrying about not getting something you want (new job, car, more money, fame, fortune, power, boyfriend, girlfriend, etc.). You will note that these are all material things of this world! Yet a Christian is called to "seek the things above," not the things of this world. Notice also that we tend to worry endlessly about things we want, which are not always the things we need.

The "peace of God" can only be found while a Christian is "living in [by] the Spirit" according to the will of God and "seeking the things above." The chapter on Living in the Spirit has explained that in more detail. Scripture also tells us that a Christian is not even supposed to worry or obsess about where their food, clothing, or shelter will come from, nor even about tomorrow itself. (Please note that I said worry and obsess, not take proper and prudent steps in planning or preparing for tomorrow, which all Christians are supposed to do; see the book of Proverbs, ants, bees, etc.). The apostle Luke writes:

> And He [Jesus] said to His disciples, "For this reason I say to you, do not worry about *your* life, *as to* what you will eat; nor for your body, *as to* what you will put on. For life is more than food, and the body more than clothing. Consider the ravens, for they neither sow nor reap; they have no storeroom nor barn, and *yet* God feeds them; how much more valuable you are than the birds! And which of you by worrying can add a *single* hour to his life's span? If then you cannot do even a very little thing, why do you worry about other matters? Consider the lilies, how they grow: they neither toil nor spin; but I tell you, not even Solomon in all his glory clothed himself like one of these. But if God so clothes the grass in the field, which is *alive* today and tomorrow is thrown into the furnace, how much more *will He clothe* you? You men of little faith! And do not seek what you will eat and what you will drink, and do not keep worrying. For all these things the nations of the world eagerly seek; but your Father knows that you need these things. But seek His kingdom, and these things will be added to you. Do not be afraid, little flock, for your Father has chosen gladly to give you the kingdom." – Luke 12:22-32

Matthew Henry discusses this further in his commentary on Matthew 6:25-34. It's a bit lengthy, but I think it's worth including here in total, for one can draw many lessons from this as it also helps you better understand what "living in [by] the Spirit" should look like, and more specifically, relying on and trusting in God completely at all times for all things: [70]

> There is scarcely any one sin against which our Lord Jesus more largely and earnestly warns his disciples, or against which he arms them with more variety of arguments, than the sin of disquieting, distracting, distrustful cares about the things of life, which are a bad sign that both the *treasure* and the heart are *on the earth;* and therefore he thus largely insists upon it. Here is,
>
> I. The prohibition laid down. It is the counsel and command of the Lord Jesus, that we *take no thought* about the things of this world; *I say unto you.* He says it as our Lawgiver, and the Sovereign of our hearts; he says it as our Comforter, and the Helper of our joy. What is it that he says? It is this, and *he that hath ears to hear, let him hear it. Take no thought for your life, nor yet for your body* (Mat 6:25). *Take no thought, saying, What shall we eat?* (Mat 6:31) and again (Mat 6:34), *Take no thought,* mē merimnate - *Be not in care.* As against hypocrisy, so against worldly cares, the caution is thrice repeated, and yet no vain repetition: *precept* must be *upon precept, and line upon line,* to the same purport, and all little enough; it is a *sin which doth so easily beset us.* It intimates how pleasing it is to Christ, and of how much concern it is to ourselves, that we should live without carefulness. It is the repeated command of the Lord Jesus to his disciples, that they should not divide and pull in pieces their own minds with care about the world. There is a *thought* concerning the things of this life, which is not only lawful, but duty, such as is commended in the virtuous woman. See Pro 27:23. The word is

---

[70] Henry, Matthew. Exposition *of the Old and New Testaments*, London. 1706-1710/1721.

used concerning Paul's care of the churches, and Timothy's care for the state of souls, 2 Co 11:28; Php 2:20.

But the *thought* here forbidden is,

1. A disquieting, tormenting *thought,* which hurries the mind hither and thither, and hangs it in suspense; which disturbs our joy in God, and is a damp upon our hope in him; which breaks the sleep, and hinders our enjoyment of ourselves, of our friends, and of what God has given us.

2. A distrustful, unbelieving *thought.* God has promised to provide for those that are his all things needful for life as well as godliness, *the life that now is,* food and a covering: not dainties, but necessaries. He never said, "They shall be feasted," but, "*Verily, they shall be fed."* Now an inordinate care for time to come, and fear of wanting those supplies, spring from a disbelief of these promises, and of the wisdom and goodness of Divine Providence; and that is the evil of it. As to present sustenance, we may and must use lawful means to get it, else we tempt God; we must be diligent in our callings, and prudent in proportioning our expenses to what we have, and we must pray for *daily bread;* and if all other means fail, we may and must ask relief of those that are able to give it. He was none of the best of men that said, *To beg I am ashamed* (Luk 16:3); as he was, who (Luk 16:21) *desired to be fed with the crumbs;* but for the future, we must *cast our care upon God,* and *take no thought,* because it looks like a jealousy of God, who knows how to give what we want when we know not now to get it. Let our souls dwell at ease in him! This gracious carelessness is the same with that sleep which God gives to his beloved, in opposition to the worldling's toil, Psa 127:2. Observe the cautions here,

(1.) *Take no thought for your life.* Life is our greatest concern for this world; *All that a man has will he give for his life;* yet take no thought about it. [1.] Not about the *continuance* of it; refer it to God to *lengthen* or *shorten* it as he pleases; *my times are in thy hand,* and they are in a good hand. [2.] Not about the *comforts* of this life; refer it to God to embitter or sweeten it as he pleases. We must not be solicitous, no not about the necessary support of this life, *food* and *raiment;* these God has promised, and therefore we may more confidently expect; say not, *What shall we eat?* It is the language of one at a loss, and almost despairing; whereas, though many good people have the prospect of little, yet there are few but have present support.

(2.) *Take no thought for the morrow,* for the time to come. Be not solicitous for the future, how you shall live next year, or when you are old, or what you shall leave behind you. As we must not *boast* of tomorrow, so we must not *care for* tomorrow, or the events of it.

II. The reasons and arguments to enforce this prohibition. One would think the command of Christ was enough to restrain us from this foolish sin of disquieting, distrustful care, independently of the comfort of our own souls, which is so nearly concerned; but to show how much the heart of Christ is upon it, and what *pleasures he takes* in those that *hope in his mercy,* the command is backed with the most powerful arguments. If reason may but rule us, surely we shall ease ourselves of these thorns. To free us from anxious thoughts, and to expel them, Christ here suggests to us *comforting* thoughts, that we may be filled with them. It will be worth while to take pains with our own hearts, to argue them out of their disquieting cares, and to make ourselves ashamed of them. They may be weakened by right reason, but it is by an active faith only that they can be overcome. Consider then,

1. *Is not the life more than meat, and the body than raiment?* Mat 6:25. Yes, no doubt it is; so he says who had reason to understand the true value of present things, for he made them, he supports them, and supports us by them; and the thing speaks for itself. Note,

(1.) Our *life* is a greater blessing than our *livelihood.* It is true, life cannot subsist without a livelihood; but the meat and raiment which are here represented as inferior to the life and body are such as are for ornament and delight; for about such as are for ornament ad delight; for about such we are apt to be solicitous. Meat and raiment are in order to life, and the *end* is more noble and excellent than the *means.* The daintiest food and finest raiment are from the *earth,* but life from the *breath of God.* Life is the *light of men;* meat is but the *oil* that feeds that light: so that the difference between rich and poor is very inconsiderable, since, in the greatest things, they stand on the same level, and differ only in the less.

(2.) This is an encouragement to us to trust God for *food* and *raiment,* and so to ease ourselves of all perplexing cares about them. God has given us life, and given us the body; it was an act of power, it was an act of favour, it was done without our care: what cannot he do for us, who did that? - what will he not? If we take care about our souls and eternity, which are more than the body, and its life, we may leave it to God to provide for us food and raiment, which are less. God has maintained our lives hitherto; if sometimes with pulse and water, that has answered the end; he has protected us and kept us alive. He that guards us against the evils we are exposed to, will supply us with the *good things* we are in need of. If he had been pleased to kill us, to starve us, he would not so often have *given his angels a charge concerning us* to keep us.

2. *Behold the fowls of the air,* and *consider the lilies of the field.* Here is an argument taken from God's common providence toward the inferior creatures, and their dependence, according to their capacities, upon that providence. A fine pass fallen man has come to, that he must be sent to school to the *fowls of the air,* and that they must *teach him!* Job 12:7, Job 12:8.

(1.) Look upon the *fowls,* and learn to trust God *for food* (Mat 6:26), and disquiet not yourselves with thoughts *what you shall eat.*

[1.] Observe the providence of God concerning them. Look upon them, and receive instruction. There are various sorts of fowls; they are numerous, some of them ravenous, but they are all fed, and fed with food convenient for them; it is rare that any of them perish for want of food, even in winter, and there goes no little to feed them all the year round. The fowls, as they are least serviceable to man, so they are least within his care; men often feed upon them, but seldom feed them; yet they are fed, we know not how, and some of them fed best in the hardest weather; and it is *your heavenly Father that feeds them;* he *knows all the wild fowls of the mountains,* better than you know the tame ones at your own barn-door, Psa 50:11. Not a sparrow lights to the ground, to pick up a grain of corn, but by the providence of God, which extends itself to the meanest creatures. But that which is especially observed here is, that they are fed without any care or project of their own; *they sow not, neither do they reap, nor gather into barns.* The ant indeed does, and the bee, and they are set before us as examples of prudence and industry; but the fowls of the air do not; they make no provision for the future themselves, and yet every day, as duly as the day comes, provision is made for them, and their *eyes wait on God,* that great and good Housekeeper, who *provides food for all flesh.*

[2.] Improve this for your encouragement to trust in God. *Are ye not much better than they?* Yes, certainly you are. Note, The *heirs* of heaven are much better than the *fowls* of heaven; nobler and more excellent beings, and, by faith, they soar higher; they are of a better nature and nurture, *wiser than the fowls of heaven* (Job 35:11): though the children of this world, that *know not the judgment of the Lord,* are not so wise as *the stork, and the crane, and the swallow* (Jer 8:7), you are dearer to God, and nearer, though they fly in the open firmament of heaven. He is their Master and Lord, their Owner and Master; but besides all this, he is your Father, and in his account *ye are of more value than many sparrows;* you are his children, his first-born; now he that feeds his birds surely will not starve his babes. They trust your Father's providence, and will not you trust it? In dependence upon that, they are careless for the morrow; and being so, they live the merriest lives of all creatures; they *sing among the branches* (Psa 104:12), and, to the best of their power, they praise their Creator. If we were, by faith, as unconcerned about the morrow as they are, we should sing as cheerfully as they do; for it is worldly care that mars our mirth and damps our joy, and silences our praise, as much as any thing.

(2.) Look upon the *lilies,* and learn to trust God for *raiment.* That is another part of our care, *what we shall put on;* for decency, to cover us; for defense, to keep us warm; yea, and, with many, for dignity and ornament, to make them look great and fine; and so much concerned are they for gaiety and variety in their clothing, that this care returns almost as often as that for their daily bread. Now to ease us of this care, let us *consider the lilies of the field;* not only *look upon* them (every eyes does that with pleasure), but *consider* them. Note, There is a great deal of good to be learned from what we see every day, if we would but consider it, Pro 6:6; Pro 24:32.

[1.] Consider how *frail* the lilies are; they are the *grass of the field.* Lilies, though distinguished by their colours, are still but *grass.* Thus *all flesh is grass:* though some in the endowments of body and mind are as lilies, much admired, still they are grass; the grass of the field in nature and constitution; they stand upon the same level with others. Man's days, at best, are *as grass,* as the *flower of the grass* 1 Pe 1:24. This grass *today is,* and *tomorrow is cast into the oven;* in a little while the place that *knows us* will *know us no more.* The grave is the oven into which we shall be cast, and in which we shall be consumed as grass in the fire, Psa 49:14. This intimates a reason why we should not take thought for the morrow, what we shall put on, because perhaps, by tomorrow, we may have occasion for our grave-clothes.

[2.] Consider how *free from care* the lilies are: they *toil not* as men do, to earn clothing; as servants, to earn their liveries; *neither do they spin,* as women do, to make clothing. It does not follow that we must therefore neglect, or do carelessly, the proper business of this life; it is the praise of the virtuous woman, that *she lays her hand to the spindle, makes fine linen and sells it,* Pro 31:19, Pro 31:24. Idleness *tempts* God, instead of *trusting* him; but he that provides for inferior creatures, without their labour, will much more provide for us, by blessing our labour, which he has made our duty. And if we should, through sickness, be unable to *toil* and *spin,* God can furnish us with what is necessary for us.

[3.] Consider how *fair,* how *fine* the lilies are; *how they grow;* what they *grow from.* The root of the lily or tulip, as other bulbous roots, is, in winter, lost and buried under ground, yet, when spring returns, it appears, and starts up in a little time; hence it is promised to God's Israel, that they should grow *as the lily,* Hos 14:5. Consider what they *grow to.* Out of that obscurity in a few weeks they come to be so very gay, that even *Solomon, in all his glory, was not arrayed like one of these.* The array of Solomon was very splendid and magnificent: he that had the peculiar treasure of kings and provinces, and studiously affected pomp and gallantry, doubtless had the richest clothing, and the best made up, that could be got; especially when he appeared in his glory on high days. And yet, let him dress himself as fine as he could, he comes far short of the beauty of the lilies, and a bed of tulips outshines him. Let us, therefore, be ambitious of the *wisdom* of Solomon, in which he was outdone by none (wisdom to do our duty in our places), rather than the *glory* of Solomon, in which he was outdone by the lilies. Knowledge and grace are the perfection of man, not beauty, much less fine clothes. Now God is here said thus to *clothe the grass of the field.* Note, All the excellences of the creature flow from God, the Fountain and spring of them. It was he that gave the horse his strength, and the lily its beauty; every creature is in itself, as well as to us, what he makes it to be.

[4.] Consider how instructive all this is to us, Mat 6:30.

First, As to *fine* clothing, this teaches us not to care for it at all, not to covet it, nor to be proud of it, not to make the *putting on of apparel* our *adorning,* for after all our care in this the lilies will far outdo us; we cannot dress so fine as they do, why then should we attempt to vie with them? Their adorning will soon perish, and so will ours; they fade - *are today,* and *tomorrow are cast,* as other rubbish, *into the oven;* and the clothes we are proud of are wearing out, the gloss is soon gone, the color fades, the shape goes out of fashion, or in awhile the garment itself is worn out; such is man in all his pomp (Isa 40:6, Isa 40:7), especially rich men (Jas 1:10); they *fade away in their ways.*

Secondly, As to *necessary* clothing; this teaches us to cast the care of it upon God - Jehovah-jireh; trust him that clothes the lilies, to provide for you what you shall *put on.* If he give such fine clothes to the grass, much more will he give fitting clothes to his own children; clothes that shall be warm upon them, not only *when he quieteth the earth with the south wind,* but when he disquiets it with the *north wind,* Job 37:17. He shall much more clothe you: for you are nobler creatures, of a more excellent being; if so he clothe the short-lived grass, much more will he clothe you that are made for immortality. Even the children of Nineveh are preferred before the gourd (Jon 4:10, Jon 4:11), much more the sons of Zion, that are in covenant with God. Observe the title he gives them (Mat 6:30), *O ye of little faith.* This may be taken,

1. As an encouragement to truth faith, though it be but weak; it entitles us to the divine care, and a promise of suitable supply. Great faith shall be commended, and shall procure great things, but little faith shall not be rejected, even that shall procure food and raiment. *Sound* believers shall be provided for, though they be not *strong* believers. The babes in the family are fed and clothed, as well as those

that are grown up, and with a special care and tenderness; say not, I am but a child, but a dry tree (Isa 56:3, Isa 56:5), for though *poor and needy* yet *the Lord thinketh on thee.* Or,

2. It is rather a rebuke to weak faith, though it be true, Mat 14:31. It intimates what is at the bottom of all our inordinate care and thoughtfulness; it is owing to the weakness of our faith, and the remains of unbelief in us. If we had but more faith, we should have less care.

3. *Which of you,* the wisest, the strongest of you, *by taking thought, can add one cubit to his stature?* (Mat 6:27) to *his age,* so some; but the measure of a cubit denotes it to be meant of the stature, and the age at longest is but a span, Psa 39:5. Let us consider,

(1.) We did not arrive at the stature we are of by our own care and thought, but by the providence of God. An infant of a span long has grown up to be a man of six feet, and how was one cubit after another added to his stature? not by his own forecast or contrivance; he grew he knew not how, by the power and goodness of God. Now he that made our bodies, and made them of such size, surely will take care to provide for them. Note, God is to be acknowledged in the increase of our bodily strength and stature, and to be trusted for all needful supplies, because he has made it to appear, that he is mindful for the body. The growing age is the thoughtless, careless age, yet we grow; and shall not he who reared us to this, provide for us now we are reared?

(2.) We cannot alter the stature we are of, if we would: what a foolish and ridiculous thing would it be for a man of low stature to perplex himself, to break his sleep, and beat his brains, about it, and to be continually taking thought how he might be a cubit higher; when, after all, he knows he cannot effect it, and therefore he had better be content and take it as it is! We are not all of a size, yet the difference in stature between one and another is not material, nor of any great account; a little man is ready to wish he were as tall as such a one, but he knows it is to no purpose, and therefore does as well as he can with it. Now as we do in reference to our bodily stature, so we should do in reference to our worldly estate.

[1.] We should not covet an abundance of the wealth of this world, any more than we would covet the addition of a cubit to one's stature, which is a great deal in a man's height; it is enough to grow by inches; such an addition would but make one unwieldy, and a burden to one's self.

[2.] We must reconcile ourselves to our state, as we do to our stature; we must set the conveniences against the inconveniences, and so make a virtue of necessity: what cannot be remedied must be made the best of. We cannot alter the disposals of Providence, and therefore must acquiesce in them, accommodate ourselves to them, and relieve ourselves, as well as we can, against inconveniences, as Zaccheus against the inconvenience of his stature, by climbing into the tree.

4. *After all these things do the Gentiles seek,* Mat 6:32. Thoughtfulness about the world is a *heathenish* sin, and unbecoming *Christians.* The *Gentiles* seek *these things,* because they know not *better things;* they are eager for this world, because they are strangers to a better; they seek these things with care and anxiety, because they are *without God in the world,* and understand not his providence. They fear and worship their idols, but know not how to trust them for deliverance and supply, and, therefore, are themselves full of care; but it is a shame for Christians,

who build upon nobler principles, and profess a religion which teaches them not only that there is a Providence, but that there are promises made to the good of the life that now is, which teaches them a confidence in God and a contempt of the world, and gives such reasons for both; it is a shame for them to walk as Gentiles walk, and to fill their heads and hearts with these things.

5. *Your heavenly Father knows ye have need of all these things;* these necessary things, food and raiment; he knows our wants better than we do ourselves; though he be in heaven, and his children on earth, he observes what the least and poorest of them has occasion for (Rev 2:9), *I know thy poverty.* You think, if such a good friend did not but know your wants and straits, you would soon have relief: your God knows them; and he is your Father that loves you and pities you, and is ready to help you; your heavenly Father, who has wherewithal to supply all your needs: away, therefore, with all disquieting thoughts and cares; go to thy Father; tell him, *he knows that thou has need of such and such things;* he asks you, Children, have *you any meat?* Joh 21:5. Tell him whether you have or have not. Though he knows our wants, he will know them from us; and when we have opened them to him, let us cheerfully refer ourselves to his wisdom, power, and goodness, for our supply. Therefore, we should ease ourselves of the burthen of care, by casting it upon God, because it is he *that careth for us* (1 Pe 5:7), and what needs all this ado? If he care, why should be care?

6. *Seek first the kingdom of God, and his righteousness, and all these things shall be added unto you.* Mat 6:33. Here is a double argument against the sin of *thoughtfulness; take no thought* for your life, the life of the body; for,

(1.) You have greater and better things to take thought about, the life of your soul, your eternal happiness; that is the *one thing needful* (Luk 10:42), about which you should employ your thoughts, and which is commonly neglected in those hearts wherein worldly cares have the ascendant. If we were but more careful to please God, and to work out our own salvation, we should be less solicitous to please ourselves, and work out an estate in the world. Thoughtfulness for our souls in the most effectual cure of thoughtfulness for the world.

(2.) You have a surer and easier, a safer and more compendious way to obtain the necessaries of this life, than by carking, and caring, and fretting about them; and that is, by *seeking first the kingdom of God,* and making religion your business: say not that this is the way to starve, no, it is the way to be well provided for, even in this world. Observe here,

[1.] The great duty required: it is the sum and substance of our whole duty: "*Seek first the kingdom of God,* mind religion as your great and principle concern." Our duty is to seek; to desire, pursue, and aim at these things; it is a word that has in it much of the constitution of the new covenant in favour of us; *though we have not attained,* but in many things fail and come short, sincere seeking (a careful concern and an earnest endeavor) is accepted.

Now here observe, *First,* The object of this seeking; *The kingdom of God, and his righteousness;* we must mind heaven as our end, and holiness as our way. "Seek the comforts of the kingdom of grace and glory as your felicity. Aim at the *kingdom of heaven;* press towards it; give diligence to make it sure; resolve not to take up short of it; seek for this glory, honour, and immortality; prefer heaven and heavenly blessings far before earth and earthly delights." We make nothing of our religion, if we do not make heaven of it. And with the *happiness* of this kingdom, seek the *righteousness* of it; *God's righteousness,* the righteousness which he requires to be wrought *in* us, and wrought *by* us, such as exceeds that of the scribes and Pharisees; we must *follow peace and holiness,* Heb 12:14.

Secondly, The order of it. *Seek first the kingdom of God.* Let your care for your souls and another world take the place of all other cares: and let all the concerns of this life be made subordinate to those of the life to come: we must seek the things of Christ more than our own things; and if every they come in competition, we must remember to which we are to give the preference. "Seek these things *first;* first in thy days: let the morning of thy youth be dedicated to God. Wisdom must be sought early; it is good beginning betimes to be religious. Seek the first every day; let waking thoughts be of God." Let this be our principle, to do that first which is most needful, and let him that is the First, have the first.

[2.] The gracious promise annexed; *all these things,* the necessary supports of life, *shall be added unto you;* shall be *given over and above;* so it is in the margin. You shall have what you seek, the *kingdom of God and his righteousness,* for never any sought *in vain,* that sought *in earnest;* and besides that, you shall have food and raiment, by way of overplus; as he that buys goods has paper and packthread given him in the bargain. *Godliness has the promise of the life that now is,* 1 Ti 4:8. Solomon asked wisdom, and had that and other things added to him, 2 Ch 1:11, 2 Ch 1:12. O what a blessed change would it make in our hearts and lives, did we but firmly believe this truth, that the best way to be comfortably provided for in this world, is to be most intent upon another world! We then begin at the right end of our work, when we begin with God. If we give diligence to make sure to ourselves the kingdom of God and the righteousness thereof, as to all the things of this life, Jehovah-jireh - the Lord will provide as much of them as he sees good for us, and more we would not wish for.

Have we trusted in him for the *portion of our inheritance* at our end, and shall we not trust him for the *portion of our cup,* in the way to it? God's Israel were not only brought to Canaan at last, but had their charges borne through the wilderness. O that we were more thoughtful about the things that are not seen, that are eternal, and then the less thoughtful we should be, and the less thoughtful we should need to be, about the things that are seen, that are temporal! *Also regard not your stuff,* Gen 45:20, Gen 45:23.

7. *The morrow shall take thought for the things of itself: sufficient unto the day is the evil thereof,* Mat 6:34. We must not perplex ourselves inordinately about future events, because every day brings along with it its own burthen of cares and grievances, as, if we look about us, and suffer not our fears to betray the succours which grace and reason offer, it brings along with it its own strength and supply too. So that we are here told,

(1.) That *thoughtfulness* for the morrow is *needless; Let the morrow take thought for the things of itself.* If wants and troubles be renewed with the day, there are aids and provisions renewed likewise; *compassions,* that are *new every morning,* Lam 3:22, Lam 3:23. The saints have a Friend that is *their arm every morning,* and gives out fresh supplies daily (Isa 33:2), according *as the business of every day requires* (Ezr 3:4), and so he keeps his people in constant dependence upon him. Let us refer it therefore to the morrow's strength, to do the morrow's work, and bear the morrow's burthen. Tomorrow, and the things of it, will be provided for without us; why need we anxiously care for that which is so wisely cared for already? This does not forbid a prudent foresight, and preparation accordingly, but a perplexing solicitude, and a prepossession of difficulties and calamities, which may perhaps never come, or if they do, may be easily borne, and the evil of them guarded against. The meaning is, let us *mind present duty,* and then *leave events to God;* do the *work of the day in its day,* and then let *tomorrow bring its work along with it.*

(2.) That thoughtfulness for the morrow is one of those *foolish and hurtful lusts,* which those that will be rich fall into, and one of the *many sorrows,* wherewith they *pierce themselves through. Sufficient unto the day is the evil thereof.* This present day has trouble enough attending it, we need not *accumulate* burthens by *anticipating* our trouble, nor borrow perplexities from tomorrow's evils to add to those of this day. It is uncertain what tomorrow's evils may be, but whatever they be, it is time enough to take thought about them when they come. What a folly it is to take that trouble upon ourselves this day by care and fear, which belongs to another day, and will be never the lighter when it comes? Let us not pull that upon ourselves all together at once, which Providence has wisely ordered to be borne by parcels.

The conclusion of this whole matter then is, that it is the will and command of the Lord Jesus, that his disciples should not be their own tormentors, nor make their passage through this world more dark and unpleasant, by their apprehension of troubles, than God has made it by the troubles themselves. By our daily prayers we may procure strength to bear us up under our daily troubles, and to arm us against the temptations that attend them, and then let none of these things move us.

IN SUMMARY

In summary, we won't have "the peace of God" when:

- We don't trust God,
- We don't think He can handle things (this is making God small),
- We don't think He knows what we're facing/going through (making God small),
- We are quarrelsome with others,
- We take vengeance into our own hands,
- We try to solve all things through our own willpower and might, instead of by the Spirit and the strength of the Lord,
- We are focused on things of this material world, which we either want or need, or fear we may lose,
- We continue to focus on things of this material world (fame, fortune, power, etc.),
- We are not abiding in Christ each day,
- We are not reading God's Word regularly (hint: every day),
- We are not in constant and continued prayer with God,
- We are not thankful for all things at all times

In contrast, we can have "the peace of God" when:

- We let God be the judge of others,
- We let God handle all vengeance ("not repaying evil with evil"),
- We live at peace with all men (to the greatest extent possible),

- We trust God completely in all things great or small at all times (even in matters of life and death itself),
- We rely on God's strength instead of our own strength,
- We've laid our cares, concerns, worries, doubts, etc. before Him through prayer, <u>with thanksgiving</u>, and know that He has heard us (we are to "cast all our anxiety on Him"),
- We remember that He knows all things, everywhere, at all times, and that nothing whatsoever catches Him off guard, surprises Him, or is something He cannot handle, for He is a BIG God,
- We "seek the things above," not the material things of this world with their attendant endless worries and anxiety,
- We've been diligent in preparing the best we possibly can under the guidance of Godly wisdom, and then let the outcome (victory) be up to the Lord,
- We read Scripture daily and are refreshed by the examples of the saints who have gone before us and are reminded of how they handled difficult situations, even when faced with imminent death,
- We are in prayer with God daily,
- We remember that He is with us each and every moment of every day, "to the very end of the age,"
- We remember that He will never lead us into temptation or give us more than we can handle,
- We remember that "God is not a man, that He should lie, Or has He spoken, and will He not make it good?," and that "He is not a man that He should change His mind," and that every single one of His promises in Scripture will come true ("So will My word be which goes out of My mouth; It will not return to Me empty, Without accomplishing what I desire, And without succeeding in the purpose for which I sent it."),
- We remember that God has <u>already</u> won complete and total victory for us over sin, Satan, and death ("it is finished"),
- We remember He promises to "make all things new,"
- We are thankful to God for all things,
- We take time to stop and reflect on the unimaginable and awesome holiness, power, might, and majesty of the Lord God Almighty

I wrote in the list above that peace comes when we have been diligent in preparing properly. You might be wondering what this has to do with the peace of God. Let me explain. This is related to the proverb:

> The horse is prepared for the day of battle,
> But victory belongs to the LORD. – Proverbs 21:31

A Christian is not called to laziness, idleness, or sloppy workmanship. Remember that we are doing all things as if we were doing them to please God, not to please man. This includes minor tasks as well as great works that we may be called to do. This applies to every area of our life, including our jobs. If you need more training, new tools, or new skills to do your job better, then go get them. A good example is my photography. It is my responsibility to make sure I have the right equipment (which the Lord has also graciously provided me, for all things come from the Lord) and also learn, know, practice, and utilize the very best technique that I can. I plan and prepare for the shoot as best I can, and when all that is done, I let the results be up to the will of the Lord.

Note that preparing also includes diligently and carefully studying the Word of God, thoughtful prayer, seeking Godly wisdom, and worshiping the Lord with a thankful heart — regardless of the outcome. God deserves and demands our very best. And when you have done everything you possibly can to prepare for the task, job, or situation at hand (this may also include making sure others are trained and properly prepared), you trust in the Lord – for the final outcome (victory) now rests with Him according to His will. When you've done this, you will find that "the peace of God" will come over you, knowing you've done your very best to prepare as a wise "child of God."

Always remember that Christ is right now this very minute ruling large and in charge in His kingdom, "seated at the right hand of God [the Father]" in heaven. He sees you and He sees everything that happens to you. In fact, He sees everything that happens, past, present, and future. He knows all. Nothing surprises Him. Nothing sneaks past Him. He promises that all things work together for your good and the collective good of all those who love Him and call on His name.

> And we know that God causes all things to work together for good to those who love God, to those who are called according to *His* purpose. For those whom He foreknew, He also predestined *to become* conformed to the image of His Son, so that He would be the firstborn among many brethren; and these whom He predestined, He also called; and these whom He called, He also justified; and these whom He justified, He also glorified. – Romans 8:28-30

He will never forget you or forsake you. Nothing happens to a Christian that He doesn't fully know about. Ever. For a Christian, there is no such thing as luck (good or bad), coincidences, or "good (or bad) fortune." Now I'm the first to admit that it's not always easy to understand the "why" of many things that happen in this fallen world, but always remember that you are in His loving care! His nature is perfect holiness, love, mercy, and grace. Trust in His nature with confidence, joy, and hope.

I want to mention another aspect of this that maybe you haven't considered yet. Have you ever prayed to the Lord, asking Him not to give you something? There are some things, that if we actually got them, might cause us to stumble and fall and "come short of" eternal life? It's human nature that we always focus on what we don't have and what we want, but God knows what is best for us. This is why we must trust God, who knows all things. This is also why some prayers are not answered – for God knows it is not best for us. Remember He says: "My ways are not your ways, and My thoughts are not your thoughts"; He sees the big picture, even when we cannot!

And finally, the ultimate peace for a Christian is firmly believing that Jesus will once again come and get all who call on His name to be with Him in heaven forevermore, where there is no more sin, suffering, or death – that He will raise all of His own up to eternal life on the last Day. He is with us to "the very end of this [gospel/church] age"! Do you trust fully in what the Bible (and Jesus) has said? He went ahead to make a place for you, as He says, "so that where I am, *there* you also will be"! When He returns, He will "raise them [you, all who are in Christ] up at the last day."

Leave all judgment, vengeance, "payback," and retribution to the Lord. He will bring all things to light and all men and deeds into righteous and true judgment on the

Great Day of Judgment; trust Him to do that. Grant to others the same forgiveness God has granted to you. For He alone "WILL RENDER TO EACH PERSON ACCORDING TO HIS DEEDS." Jesus Christ is the one "living and true God," the Lord God Almighty Himself. He has conquered all; He is already victorious. Rest in Him and His great name. I pray that you let "the peace of God" rule in your heart.

RELATED SCRIPTURE:

Rejoice in the Lord always; again I will say, rejoice! – Philippians 4:4

And He said to them, "Because of the littleness of your faith; for truly I say to you, if you have faith the size of a mustard seed, you will say to this mountain, 'Move from here to there,' and it will move; and nothing will be impossible to you." – Matthew 17:20

So Peter was kept in the prison, but prayer for him was being made fervently by the church to God. On the very night when Herod was about to bring him forward, Peter was sleeping between two soldiers, bound with two chains, and guards in front of the door were watching over the prison. And behold, an angel of the Lord suddenly appeared and a light shone in the cell; and he struck Peter's side and woke him up, saying, "Get up quickly." And his chains fell off his hands. – Acts 12:5-7

When He got into the boat, His disciples followed Him. And behold, there arose a great storm on the sea, so that the boat was being covered with the waves; but Jesus Himself was asleep. And they came to *Him* and woke Him, saying, "Save *us*, Lord; we are perishing!" He said to them, "Why are you afraid, you men of little faith?" Then He got up and rebuked the winds and the sea, and it became perfectly calm. – Matthew 8:23-26

For not one of us lives for himself, and not one dies for himself; for if we live, we live for the Lord, or if we die, we die for the Lord; therefore whether we live or die, we are the Lord's. – Romans 14:7-8

I said to myself, "God will judge both the righteous man and the wicked man," for a time for every matter and for every deed is there. – Ecclesiastes 3:17

I will say to the LORD, "My refuge and my fortress,
My God, in whom I trust!" …
For He will give His angels charge concerning you,
To guard you in all your ways.
They will bear you up in their hands,
That you do not strike your foot against a stone. – Psalm 91:2,11-12

If possible, so far as it depends on you, be at peace with all men. Never take your own revenge, beloved, but leave room for the wrath *of God*, for it is written, "VENGEANCE IS MINE, I WILL REPAY," says the Lord. "BUT IF YOUR ENEMY IS HUNGRY, FEED HIM, AND IF HE IS THIRSTY, GIVE HIM A DRINK; FOR IN SO DOING YOU WILL HEAP BURNING COALS ON HIS HEAD." Do not be overcome by evil, but overcome evil with good. – Romans 12:18-21

"Behold, I am coming quickly, and My reward *is* with Me, to render to every man according to what he has done. I am the Alpha and the Omega, the first and the last, the beginning and the end." – Revelation 22:12-13

The LORD is my shepherd,
I shall not want.
He makes me lie down in green pastures;
He leads me beside quiet waters.
He restores my soul;
He guides me in the paths of righteousness
For His name's sake.

Even though I walk through the valley of the shadow of death,
I fear no evil, for You are with me. – Psalm 23:1-4

Therefore if you have been raised up with Christ, keep seeking the things above, where Christ is, seated at the right hand of God. Set your mind on the things above, not on the things that are on earth. For you have died and your life is hidden with Christ in God. …

Let the peace of Christ rule in your hearts, to which indeed you were called in one body; and be thankful. – Colossians 3:1-3,15

Therefore humble yourselves under the mighty hand of God, that He may exalt you at the proper time, casting all your anxiety on Him, because He cares for you. – 1 Peter 5:6-7

But the wisdom from above is first pure, then peaceable, gentle, reasonable, full of mercy and good fruits, unwavering, without hypocrisy. And the seed whose fruit is righteousness is sown in peace by those who make peace. – James 3:17-18

The LORD sat *as King* at the flood;
Yes, the LORD sits as King forever.
The LORD will give strength to His people;
The LORD will bless His people with peace. – Psalm 29:10-11

"These things I have spoken to you, so that in Me you may have peace. In the world you have tribulation, but take courage; I have overcome the world." – John 16:33

"Lo, I [Jesus] am with you always, even to the end of the age." – Matthew 28:20

4.7 THE KINGDOM OF GOD
(Your Citizenship is in Heaven Above)

Jesus answered, "My kingdom is not of this world." – John 18:36

The Bible tells us of a "Kingdom of God" and His Christ. The expressions "Kingdom of Heaven" and "Kingdom of God" are synonymous, and in many ways, the Bible equates the Kingdom with the Church. Brother or sister in Christ, be not deceived; you are in the "Kingdom of Heaven" right now, today, this very day; it is not some "future earthly millennial reign" yet to come! The "Kingdom of God" coincides with this age of grace, this gospel period, and the church age, and will continue until Jesus returns from heaven "in the same way as you have watched Him go into heaven": literally, visibly and also "in His glory" "with His mighty angels in flaming fire" for all to see on the great Day of Judgment.

The Kingdom is referred to by several names:

- The Kingdom of God (62 times)
- The Kingdom of Heaven (32 times)
- My Father's Kingdom (Matthew 26:29),
- My Kingdom (Luke 22:30),
- The Kingdom of the Son of Man (Matthew 13:41),
- The Kingdom of Jesus (Revelation 1:9),
- The Kingdom of Christ Jesus (2 Timothy 4:1),
- The Kingdom of Christ and God (Ephesians 5:5),
- The Kingdom of Our Lord and His Christ (Revelation 11:15),
- The Kingdom of Our God and the Authority of His Christ (Revelation 12:10),
- The Kingdom of His Beloved Son (Colossians 1:13)

ONCE AGAIN, MANY FALSE TEACHINGS

I realize it's very tiring (exhausting actually) to have to constantly confront false teachings, but we must continue to do so as we "contend earnestly for the faith that was once for all *time* handed down to the saints." So, once again, you will find rampant and widespread false teachings today about the "Kingdom of God." These false teachings come under the names "dispensational premillennialism" or "pre-tribulation rapture" (and its related permutations and false teachings such as the "3rd Temple"), which make the claim that Jesus will return to reign on earth in a "1000-year earthly millennial reign" from the literal city of Jerusalem and that all of this is still sometime yet in the future. These false teachings deny that your very own Lord and King is ruling and reigning right now in His Kingdom, today, this very day from heaven, seated on the "throne of His father David." These false teachings seek only after the nationalistic, political, and economic agendas and schemes of man, not the things of Christ. These false teachings also contradict the very statements of Jesus.

A SPIRITUAL KINGDOM

The Kingdom is much more spiritual than physical; it is spiritually understood (like the book of Revelation), and unless one is born again, he cannot see (or understand) or enter the Kingdom of God. Jesus is in our midst, and therefore the Kingdom is "in your midst" – for wherever Jesus is, there also is the Kingdom. Where the King is, there also is the Kingdom. With Christ dwelling in our hearts, there again is the Kingdom among (and within) us and within the Church – the Kingdom is in the heart of every believer.

The Jews of Jesus' day were looking for and expecting that He was going to establish a literal, earthly, physical kingdom where Israel would break free from Roman occupation and rule with Jesus as king. Jesus tried to correct their misconception when He clearly and unambiguously declared that His kingdom is not an earthly kingdom ("my kingdom is not of this world") and that it is not coming with "signs to be observed" (i.e., that it is a spiritual kingdom, that it is not "of this realm"), and that it is "in your midst" (i.e., among us, the body of believers in Christ):

> Jesus answered, "My kingdom is not of this world. If My kingdom were of this world, then My servants would be fighting so that I would not be handed over to the Jews; but as it is, My kingdom is not of this realm." – John 18:36

> Now having been questioned by the Pharisees as to when the kingdom of God was coming, He answered them and said, "The kingdom of God is not coming with signs to be observed; nor will they say, 'Look, here *it is*!' or, 'There *it is*!' For behold, the kingdom of God is in your midst." – Luke 17:20-21

Those clear and direct statements of Christ cannot be twisted to mean anything but what they say.

We also see above that Christ said that the Kingdom is among those who follow Him (i.e., comprised of, within, among you, "in your midst," the Church). If you will, the "Kingdom of God" can be described as a Spiritual Monarchy with Christ as King. The Kingdom has two realms, or natures: 1) it is heavenly and above where Christ is ruling and reigning, and 2) it is also among us, the worldwide body of believers, the body of Christ, which is also the "Church of Christ" and "wherein Christ also dwells" as He reigns in the hearts of believers.

Furthermore, the "Kingdom of Heaven" is to endure for eternity, so we are not to look for still yet another future so-called "millennial kingdom," and it will be fully manifest when all things are made new:

> Your kingdom is an everlasting kingdom,
> And Your dominion *endures* throughout all generations. – Psalm 145:13

> …for in this way the entrance into the eternal kingdom of our Lord and Savior Jesus Christ will be abundantly supplied to you. – 2 Peter 1:11

> "I kept looking in the night visions,
> And behold, with the clouds of heaven
> One like a Son of Man was coming,
> And He came up to the Ancient of Days
> And was presented before Him.
> "And to Him was given dominion,
> Glory and a kingdom,
> That all the peoples, nations and *men of every* language
> Might serve Him.
> His dominion is an everlasting dominion
> Which will not pass away;

> And His kingdom is one
> Which will not be destroyed." – Daniel 7:13-14

THE KINGDOM IS NOW (Jesus is Already Ruling and Reigning!)

You have already read in the chapter on the coming great Day of Judgment that when Jesus returns, it will not be for an additional "1000-year millennial" reign here on earth; no, the great Day of Judgment will have arrived, for it is written:

> But now Christ has been raised from the dead, the first fruits of those who are asleep. For since by a man *came* death, by a man also *came* the resurrection of the dead. For as in Adam all die, so also in Christ all will be made alive. But each in his own order: Christ the first fruits, after that those who are Christ's <u>at His coming, then *comes* the end</u>, when He hands over the kingdom to the God and Father, when He has abolished all rule and all authority and power. For He must reign until He has put all His enemies under His feet. The last enemy that will be abolished is death. – 1 Corinthians 15:20-26

John the Baptist had foretold the arrival of the kingdom at the start of Jesus' ministry (i.e., the kingdom was already "at hand" – near), and Jesus repeated that same message:

> Now in those days John the Baptist came, preaching in the wilderness of Judea, saying, "Repent, for the kingdom of heaven is at hand." – Matthew 3:1-2

> From that time Jesus began to preach and say, "Repent, for the kingdom of heaven is at hand." – Matthew 4:17

Scripture also tells us that Christ would receive His kingdom (and thereby begin His rule and reign) after He ascended to the Father:

> "In the days of those kings the God of heaven will set up a kingdom which will never be destroyed, and *that* kingdom will not be left for another people; it will crush and put an end to all these kingdoms, but it will itself endure forever." – Daniel 2:44

"In the days of those kings" refers to the fourth kingdom of Daniel's dream, which is identified with the Roman Empire, which also corresponds to when Jesus lived on earth. He ascended to the Father from the Mount of Olives forty days after He was resurrected from death:

> And after He had said these things, He was lifted up while they were looking on, and a cloud received Him out of their sight. And as they were gazing intently into the sky while He was going, behold, two men in white clothing stood beside them. They also said, "Men of Galilee, why do you stand looking into the sky? This Jesus, who has been taken up from you into heaven, will come in just the same way as you have watched Him go into heaven." – Acts 1:9-11

After His ascension, Jesus was "seated at the right hand of God" the Father in heaven, and He is ruling and reigning right now (and "who also intercedes for us" with the Father – for He is the "one [only] mediator between God and men"):

> When He [God] raised Him [Jesus] from the dead and seated Him at His right hand in the heavenly *places*, far above all rule and authority and power and

dominion, and every name that is named, not only in this age but also in the one to come. – Ephesians 1:20-21

Christ Jesus is He who died, yes, rather who was raised, who is at the right hand of God, who also intercedes for us. – Romans 8:34

Therefore He is able also to save forever those who draw near to God through Him, since He always lives to make intercession for them. – Hebrews 7:25

For there is one God, *and* one mediator also between God and men, *the* man Christ Jesus. – 1 Timothy 2:5

Jesus said that some of His disciples would see Him "coming in His kingdom" before they died and that the Kingdom was to arrive visibly and "with power":

"Truly I say to you, there are some of those who are standing here who will not taste death until they see the Son of Man coming in His kingdom." – Matthew 16:28

Jesus was saying to them, "Truly I say to you, there are some of those who are standing here who will not taste death until they see the kingdom of God after it has come with power." – Mark 9:1

This coming in power (and hence seeing Him in His Kingdom) was fulfilled at Pentecost when the Holy Spirit was poured out:

"…for John baptized with water, but you will be baptized with the Holy Spirit not many days from now." – Acts 1:5

"…you will receive power when the Holy Spirit has come upon you; and you shall be My witnesses both in Jerusalem, and in all Judea and Samaria, and even to the remotest part of the earth." – Acts 1:8

When the day of Pentecost had come, they were all together in one place. And suddenly there came from heaven a noise like a violent rushing wind, and it filled the whole house where they were sitting. And there appeared to them tongues as of fire distributing themselves, and they rested on each one of them. And they were all filled with the Holy Spirit and began to speak with other tongues, as the Spirit was giving them utterance. – Acts 2:1-4

We further read other inspired writers (Paul and John) stating that they were already "fellow partakers" and priests in the Kingdom. This was written before A.D. 81-90, so if the Kingdom was already in effect then, it surely is in effect now (not at some future "earthly millennial reign" time):

…and from Jesus Christ, the faithful witness, the firstborn of the dead, and the ruler of the kings of the earth. To Him who loves us and released us from our sins by His blood— and He has made us *to be* a kingdom, priests to His God and Father—to Him *be* the glory and the dominion forever and ever. Amen. – Revelation 1:5-6

I, John, your brother and fellow partaker in the tribulation and kingdom and perseverance *which are* in Jesus, was on the island called Patmos because of the word of God and the testimony of Jesus. – Revelation 1:9

> For He rescued us from the domain of darkness, and transferred us to the kingdom of His beloved Son, in whom we have redemption, the forgiveness of sins. – Colossians 1:13-14

THE KINGDOM – CURRENT AND FUTURE

Many are unsure if the "Kingdom of God" is here now or still in the future and whether it's on earth or in heaven. It actually encompasses all of those, for the "Kingdom of God" has several aspects or realms:

1. Here and now: The current state of the Kingdom is the people of God on earth, which is the church under the gospel dispensation (which is also described as "the bride of Christ") and under the leadership and headship of Christ for Christ is reigning right now, and
2. Future heavenly: The future state after Jesus' return will be a heavenly kingdom, when "He will wipe away every tear" and there will be no more sin, suffering, or death. This is wonderfully described (using symbolism) in the ending chapters of the book of Revelation (see the chapter All Things Made New).

It should also be noted that the "New Jerusalem" city described in Revelation is not some literal city on earth but is a symbolic depiction of the heavenly "Kingdom of God" (i.e., the "Kingdom of Heaven") and the church (referred to again as the "bride of Christ") where the people of God dwell together with Him. "New Jerusalem" is also equated to "the bride of Christ" (i.e., the church).

THE WOLF WILL DWELL WITH THE LAMB

The verses of Isaiah 11:6-9 are perhaps some of the most widely misunderstood verses in the entire Bible:

> And the wolf will dwell with the lamb,
> And the leopard will lie down with the young goat,
> And the calf and the young lion and the fatling together;
> And a little boy will lead them.
> Also the cow and the bear will graze,
> Their young will lie down together,
> And the lion will eat straw like the ox.
> The nursing child will play by the hole of the cobra,
> And the weaned child will put his hand on the viper's den.
> They will not hurt or destroy in all My holy mountain,
> For the earth will be full of the knowledge of the LORD
> As the waters cover the sea. – Isaiah 11:6-9

These verses are used to support false teachings about the kingdom (i.e., that it is still yet future and earthly). The error made is in forcing a literal interpretation of the verses. The Bible often refers to the various types (characters, natures) of man using the symbolism of animals. Jesus Himself was described as a "lamb." Paul, when he was persecuting the early church, was described as a "wolf," and false teachers are also described as "wolves" – for they devour the "sheep" of the Lord (true Christians). The hypocritical religious rulers of Jesus' day were described as a "den of vipers."

These verses mean that under the New Testament gospel age of grace (this church age right now), those who accept and abide in Christ will all dwell together peacefully as brothers and sisters. Those who by nature were "wolves," after conversion in accepting Christ, will become as "lambs"; just like the Apostle Paul after he was converted on the road to Damascus – he went from persecuting (and even killing) Christians to then peacefully dwelling with them. These verses do not mean that there will be a literal "millennial reign of Christ" on Earth where literal wolves will lie alongside literal lambs. The same goes for the rest of the Isaiah passage.

WE ARE FELLOW PARTAKERS AND PRIESTS IN HIS KINGDOM (i.e., BE A KINGDOM BUILDER)

Prophecy from the book of Daniel is also abused, distorted, and twisted to support the earthly political agendas of man, but be not deceived. The "seventy weeks" of Daniel prophecies were completely fulfilled in Christ's time – for Christ died (He was "cut off," i.e., crucified) for your sins in the middle of the 70th week as stated in the book of Daniel and fulfilling the prophecy. There is no "missing" week of years left (the so-called "7-year great tribulation of the Antichrist") before Christ's kingdom is set up.

When Jesus had won victory over sin, Satan and death (which He did at the cross through His own death and resurrection), He ascended back into heaven (from whence He came) to begin His rule and reign in the Kingdom of God, which began on the day of Pentecost when the Holy Spirit was poured out "with power" as a visible manifestation of the arrival of the kingdom. The prophecy of the Old Testament book of Daniel 2 states that a series of earthly kingdoms were to arise (Babylon, Media/Persia, Greece, and the Roman Empire) and that the kingdom of heaven and our Lord Jesus Christ will be set up during the days of "those kings." It was indeed during the time of the Roman Empire that Christ was born, lived, died, and was resurrected. It was at this time that Christ ascended to be "[seated] at the right hand God" in heaven, "far above all rule and authority and power and dominion." It was also at this time that Satan, the "prince [ruler] of this world," was "cast down [out]" and Christ began His eternal rule and reign as "King" and "High Priest" for all eternity in His Kingdom, which "will never be destroyed, and *that* kingdom will not be left for another people; it will crush and put an end to all these kingdoms, but it will itself endure forever."

Contrary to how it may appear to many in this fallen world, Satan is no longer in charge; Christ is. Satan was "cast out" as "ruler of this world" by Christ when He was victorious over sin and death at the cross. However, Christ has not returned yet, and judgment has not occurred yet, solely because Jesus is allowing more time for the lost to come to Him and receive the gift of eternal life.

So, brother or sister in Christ, know that all true believers in the Lord Jesus Christ are fellow "priests" with Him in His kingdom this very day – and yes, even more, we are "ambassadors for Christ"! It's not just the job of your "Pastor" to lead others to Christ; it is your job. You are a priest also! In fact, the modern Church leader titles that have arisen in various denominations of so-called "Christianity" (e.g., a single "Pastor," "Cardinal," "Bishop," "Pope," "Father," "Reverend," etc.) have so deformed the true, basic, and simple nature of the gospel message that it's no wonder many Christians today are lost and confused. So be about the work of your Lord and King and share the gospel message with someone today.

You are a kingdom builder, a fellow priest in the kingdom, so step out in confidence and boldness, sharing Christ with the lost. We are called to always be about the business of our Lord and King, which is to help build His kingdom. We do this as we obey one of the commandments of Christ which, is to "preach [share] the gospel with all of creation (everyone)." A Christian is not called to worry about, nor participate and get entangled in, worldly affairs and matters such as politics and the agendas of man. We are to focus on what Christ has commanded us to do, which is to reach the lost. By wasting our time and energy worrying about, participating in, and endlessly arguing about worldly or political matters, we are not giving our best to what is most important. Also, note that we cannot be kingdom builders unless there is already a kingdom. Let us, therefore, look to our Lord and King in confidence, knowing He is righteous and true, "always abounding in the work of the Lord."

THE KINGDOM GROWS TO FILL THE EARTH

The kingdom of heaven will grow from a tiny "mustard seed" to fill the entire earth, as the gospel is preached to all of creation (everyone):

> He presented another parable to them, saying, "The kingdom of heaven is like a mustard seed, which a man took and sowed in his field; and this is smaller than all *other* seeds, but when it is full grown, it is larger than the garden plants and becomes a tree, so that THE BIRDS OF THE AIR come and NEST IN ITS BRANCHES." – Matthew 13:31-32

> "…it will crush and put an end to all these kingdoms, but it will itself endure forever." – Daniel 2:44

> Now it will come about that
> In the last days
> The mountain of the house of the LORD
> Will be established as the chief of the mountains,
> And will be raised above the hills;
> And all the nations will stream to it.
> And many peoples will come and say,
> "Come, let us go up to the mountain of the LORD,
> To the house of the God of Jacob;
> That He may teach us concerning His ways
> And that we may walk in His paths."
> For the law will go forth from Zion
> And the word of the LORD from Jerusalem.
> And He will judge between the nations,
> And will render decisions for many peoples;
> And they will hammer their swords into plowshares and their spears into pruning hooks.
> Nation will not lift up sword against nation,
> And never again will they learn war. – Isaiah 2:2-4

This Kingdom is also referred to as Mount Zion, the holy mountain of the Lord, which will be set up in "the last days" (which is this church age and this age of grace under Christ in which we now live) and which grows to fill the whole earth:

> And it will come about in the last days
> That the mountain of the house of the LORD
> Will be established as the chief of the mountains.

It will be raised above the hills,
And the peoples will stream to it.
Many nations will come and say,
"Come and let us go up to the mountain of the LORD
And to the house of the God of Jacob,
That He may teach us about His ways
And that we may walk in His paths."
For from Zion will go forth the law,
Even the word of the LORD from Jerusalem.
And He will judge between many peoples
And render decisions for mighty, distant nations.
Then they will hammer their swords into plowshares
And their spears into pruning hooks;
Nation will not lift up sword against nation,
And never again will they train for war.
Each of them will sit under his vine
And under his fig tree,
With no one to make *them* afraid,
For the mouth of the LORD of hosts has spoken.
Though all the peoples walk
Each in the name of his god,
As for us, we will walk
In the name of the LORD our God forever and ever.

"In that day," declares the LORD,
"I will assemble the lame
And gather the outcasts,
Even those whom I have afflicted.
"I will make the lame a remnant
And the outcasts a strong nation,
And the LORD will reign over them in Mount Zion
From now on and forever.
"As for you, tower of the flock,
Hill of the daughter of Zion,
To you it will come—
Even the former dominion will come,
The kingdom of the daughter of Jerusalem." – Micah 4:1-8

The Kingdom grows as we press forward in confidence, boldness, and perseverance, continuing to share the gospel "message of truth" with those who are lost. Know without any doubt that the Kingdom of our Lord and Savior is advancing every single day, and nothing whatsoever under the sun, on Earth, under the earth, in the heavens, nor the schemes of man or Satan can stop it. Victory has already been assured (past tense).

Note: This by no means indicates that there will be widespread "peace on earth" before Christ returns, a so-called "golden age" of Christianity – that is still yet another false teaching of the "ravenous wolves" called "dispensational postmillennialism."

KINGDOM OF GLORY REVEALED

The Kingdom will be fully revealed in glory on Judgment Day at Christ's return:

> "But when the Son of Man comes in His glory, and all the angels with Him, then He will sit on His glorious throne. All the nations will be gathered before Him; and He will separate them from one another, as the shepherd separates the sheep from the goats; and He will put the sheep on His right, and the goats on the left.
>
> "Then the King will say to those on His right, 'Come, you who are blessed of My Father, inherit the kingdom prepared for you from the foundation of the world.'" – Matthew 25:31-34

Only Old Testament saints and those who have been born again of the Spirit according to the instructions given in the New Testament (and as explained correctly in this book) who have remained faithful until death, been obedient to the commandments of God and His Christ, and not found idle will be allowed entry to the eternal Kingdom. It is written that "many" will be turned away right from the very gates of heaven and eternity itself:

> "Not everyone who says to Me, 'Lord, Lord,' will enter the kingdom of heaven, but he who does the will of My Father who is in heaven *will enter*. Many will say to Me on that day, 'Lord, Lord, did we not prophesy in Your name, and in Your name cast out demons, and in Your name perform many miracles?' And then I will declare to them, 'I never knew you; DEPART FROM ME, YOU WHO PRACTICE LAWLESSNESS.'
>
> "Therefore everyone who hears these words of Mine and acts on them, may be compared to a wise man who built his house on the rock. And the rain fell, and the floods came, and the winds blew and slammed against that house; and *yet* it did not fall, for it had been founded on the rock. Everyone who hears these words of Mine and does not act on them, will be like a foolish man who built his house on the sand. The rain fell, and the floods came, and the winds blew and slammed against that house; and it fell—and great was its fall." – Matthew 7:21-27

This is why this book has constantly reinforced the need for the believer in Christ to understand that being born again is only the first step in their Christian pilgrimage. A Christian must also be obedient to the commands of Christ, be active and working in the Kingdom of God (i.e., not being a mere professor of the word, but a "doer" of the word – "bearing fruit," "good works"), and also persevere in faith until death. We must pay heed to the strong warning in Scripture to NOT take our salvation lightly or for granted. It is up to each of us individually to ensure our own salvation and not "come short of" eternal life!

> So then, my beloved, just as you have always obeyed, not as in my presence only, but now much more in my absence, work out your salvation with fear and trembling; for it is God who is at work in you, both to will and to work for *His* good pleasure. – Philippians 2:12-13

> Test yourselves *to see* if you are in the faith; examine yourselves! Or do you not recognize this about yourselves, that Jesus Christ is in you—unless indeed you fail the test? – 2 Corinthians 13:5

Therefore, we must fear if, while a promise remains of entering His rest, any one of you may seem to have come short *of it*. – Hebrews 4:1

I hope to see you in the heavenly Kingdom of Glory when Christ returns on Judgment Day. Amen.

FALSE TEACHING(S) YOU WILL ENCOUNTER:

- Distortions of Matthew 24 (the Olivet Discourse)
- Setting dates for Jesus' return
- Dispensational Premillennialism
- Dispensational Postmillennialism
- Modern/popular eschatology (we are waiting for a "Third Temple" to be built, or the "Battle of Armageddon" to occur first, or "the Antichrist" person to arise, or Gog and Magog, or "signs and wonders" in the skies, or the "Secret Rapture," or the "7-Year Great Tribulation" period, and other bizarre interpretations of the book of Revelation, the "Mark of the Beast" as a chip implant or tattoo, etc. ad infinitum it seems…and all false)
- Jesus already returned in A.D. 70 (i.e., Preterism)

RELATED SCRIPTURE:

These are in accordance with the working of the strength of His might which He brought about in Christ, when He raised Him from the dead and seated Him at His right hand in the heavenly *places*, far above all rule and authority and power and dominion, and every name that is named, not only in this age but also in the one to come. – Ephesians 1:19b-21

For a child will be born to us, a son will be given to us;
And the government will rest on His shoulders;
And His name will be called Wonderful Counselor, Mighty God,
Eternal Father, Prince of Peace.
There will be no end to the increase of *His* government or of peace,
On the throne of David and over his kingdom,
To establish it and to uphold it with justice and righteousness
From then on and forevermore.
The zeal of the LORD of hosts will accomplish this. – Isaiah 9:6-7

"Now judgment is upon this world; now the ruler of this world will be cast out. And I, if I am lifted up from the earth, will draw all men to Myself." – John 12:31-32

For He rescued us from the domain of darkness, and transferred us to the kingdom of His beloved Son, in whom we have redemption, the forgiveness of sins. – Colossians 1:13-14

For our citizenship is in heaven, from which also we eagerly wait for a Savior, the Lord Jesus Christ; who will transform the body of our humble state into conformity with the body of His glory, by the exertion of the power that He has even to subject all things to Himself. – Philippians 3:20-21

Jesus presented another parable to them, saying, "The kingdom of heaven may be compared to a man who sowed good seed in his field. But while his men were sleeping, his enemy came and sowed tares among the wheat, and went away. But when the wheat sprouted and bore grain, then the tares became evident also." – Matthew 13:24-26

Therefore, since we receive a kingdom which cannot be shaken, let us show gratitude, by which we may offer to God an acceptable service with reverence and awe. – Hebrews 12:28

Then I saw an angel coming down from heaven, holding the key of the abyss and a great chain in his hand. And he laid hold of the dragon, the serpent of old, who is the devil and Satan, and bound him for a thousand years; and he threw him into the abyss, and shut *it* and sealed *it* over him, so that he would not deceive the nations any longer, until the thousand years were completed; after these things he must be released for a short time. – Revelation 20:1-3

"Then the kingdom of heaven will be comparable to ten virgins, who took their lamps and went out to meet the bridegroom. Five of them were foolish, and five were prudent. For when the foolish took their lamps, they took no oil with them, but the prudent took oil in flasks along with their lamps. Now while the bridegroom was delaying, they all got drowsy and *began* to sleep. But at midnight there was a shout, 'Behold, the bridegroom! Come out to meet *him*.' Then all those virgins rose and trimmed their lamps. The foolish said to the prudent, 'Give us some of your oil, for our lamps are going out.' But the prudent answered, 'No, there will not be enough for us and you *too*; go instead to the dealers and buy *some* for yourselves.' And while they were going away to make the purchase, the bridegroom came, and those who were ready went in with him to the wedding feast; and the door was shut. Later the other virgins also came, saying, 'Lord, lord, open up for us.' But he answered, 'Truly I say to you, I do not know you.' Be on the alert then, for you do not know the day nor the hour. – Matthew 25:1-13

Then I heard a loud voice in heaven, saying,

"Now the salvation, and the power, and the kingdom of our God and the authority of His Christ have come, for the accuser of our brethren has been thrown down, he who accuses them before our God day and night." – Revelation 12:10

Then I saw a new heaven and a new earth; for the first heaven and the first earth passed away, and there is no longer *any* sea. And I saw the holy city, new Jerusalem, coming down out of heaven from God, made ready as a bride adorned for her husband. And I heard a loud voice from the throne, saying, "Behold, the tabernacle of God is among men, and He will dwell among them, and they shall be His people, and God Himself will be among them, and He will wipe away every tear from their eyes; and there will no longer be *any* death; there will no longer be *any* mourning, or crying, or pain; the first things have passed away." – Revelation 21:1-4

4.8 THE WISDOM OF GOD

But if any of you lacks wisdom, let him ask of God, who gives to all generously and without reproach, and it will be given to him. – James 1:5

The Wisdom from Above. To serve God, one must have Godly wisdom. And Godly wisdom only comes "from above," from God, not from man. The foolish man's heart directs him to serve the gods of this world (idols, pride, lust, wealth, fame, power, material possessions, etc.) and worship what the minds of man create (i.e., false teachings, etc.). The wise Christian's heart directs him to seek the "wisdom from above" and to serve God and God alone:

> The fool has said in his heart, "There is no God." – Psalm 14:1

A Christian must therefore realize the following:

1) All Godly wisdom comes from above, from God – it only comes from reading, studying, and meditating on His Holy Word (the Bible),
2) One must desire it; one must earnestly want to get it (acquire wisdom, "get understanding"), and
3) One simply needs to "ask" of God to get it through prayer (Amazing!)

Scripture gives the above sequence as:

1. The fear of the LORD is the beginning of wisdom,
   And the knowledge of the Holy One is understanding. – Proverbs 9:10
2. "The beginning of wisdom *is*: Acquire wisdom; And with all your acquiring, get understanding." – Proverbs 4:7, and "His delight is in the law of the LORD, And in His law he meditates day and night." – Psalm 1:2
3. But if any of you lacks wisdom, let him ask of God, who gives to all generously and without reproach, and it will be given to him. – James 1:5

The three steps above then culminate with the admonition to always be "growing in the grace and knowledge [understanding]" of the Lord:

4. You therefore, beloved, knowing this beforehand, be on your guard so that you are not carried away by the error of unprincipled men and fall from your own steadfastness, but grow in the grace and knowledge of our Lord and Savior Jesus Christ. – 2 Peter 3:17-18

The ways and wisdom of man and this world (the crowd of "popular opinion") say: "might makes right," "I'm going to get mine first!," "you're going to pay for this," and "I'm going to get even!" In contrast, the "wisdom from above" says:

> "You have heard that it was said, 'YOU SHALL LOVE YOUR NEIGHBOR and hate your enemy.' But I say to you, love your enemies and pray for those who persecute you." – Matthew 5:43-44

How blessed is he who considers the helpless. – Psalm 41:1

> Who among you is wise and understanding? Let him show by his good behavior his deeds in the gentleness of wisdom. But if you have bitter jealousy and selfish ambition in your heart, do not be arrogant and *so* lie against the truth. This wisdom

is not that which comes down from above, but is earthly, natural, demonic. For where jealousy and selfish ambition exist, there is disorder and every evil thing. But the wisdom from above is first pure, then peaceable, gentle, reasonable, full of mercy and good fruits, unwavering, without hypocrisy. And the seed whose fruit is righteousness is sown in peace by those who make peace. – James 3:13-18

Beloved, do not avenge yourselves, but *rather* give place to wrath; for it is written, "Vengeance *is* Mine, I will repay," says the Lord. – Romans 12:19

Make no mistake, it is much easier to simply follow the crowd; in contrast, following the "wisdom from above" takes boldness, courage, confidence, and strength of character! It is not easy to stand against the crowd, against popular opinion, and against the ways of this world, and there may be dire consequences for doing so. But the way of a Christian is clear: we are to please God, not man, as it is written:

"If it is disagreeable in your sight to serve the LORD, choose for yourselves today whom you will serve: whether the gods which your fathers served which were beyond the River, or the gods of the Amorites in whose land you are living; but as for me and my house, we will serve the LORD." – Joshua 24:15

But Peter and the apostles answered, "We must obey God rather than men." – Acts 5:29

For am I now seeking the favor of men, or of God? Or am I striving to please men? If I were still trying to please men, I would not be a bond-servant of Christ. – Galatians 1:10

I have shown you in this book that the wisdom of this world leads to false teachings, fake science, and the seemingly endless "traditions," myths, superstitions, opinions, and schemes of man. These lies and deceptions are then constantly shouted at us in staggering volume. Those, we are told by the secular world and the secular media, represent modern, educated, and enlightened man's wisdom. What they really represent is the foolishness and folly of man and this fallen world. The wisdom of this world is described as "foolishness before God":

Let no man deceive himself. If any man among you thinks that he is wise in this age, he must become foolish, so that he may become wise. For the wisdom of this world is foolishness before God. For it is written, "*He is* THE ONE WHO CATCHES THE WISE IN THEIR CRAFTINESS"; and again, "THE LORD KNOWS THE REASONINGS of the wise, THAT THEY ARE USELESS." – 1 Corinthians 3:18-20

This planet has seen firsthand the wisdom of man for thousands of years, and what has it gotten us? War after war, killing, stealing, raping, pillaging, looting, lying, cheating, greed, fraud, corruption, oppression, and many other evils, all stemming from selfish ambitions, pride and lust, and the endless ravenous pursuit of fame, money, and power, which is what the wisdom of this world values. Furthermore, the wisdom of the world has led to rebellion against God, denial of God, worshipping of idols, and moral depravity at every turn.

Yes, one must discard the wisdom of man (the wisdom of this world) to see God, and furthermore, only God, through His Spirit, can reveal the things of God to us:

Now we have received, not the spirit of the world, but the Spirit who is from God, so that we may know the things freely given to us by God, which things we also speak, not in words taught by human wisdom, but in those taught by the Spirit, combining spiritual *thoughts* with spiritual *words*.

But a natural man does not accept the things of the Spirit of God, for they are foolishness to him; and he cannot understand them, because they are spiritually appraised. – 1 Corinthians 2:12-14

So good Christian, do you follow the foolish ways of man and this sinful, fallen world or the ways of God? Do you seek the things of this world or the things from above? The ways of man are all dressed up to make them appear as "wisdom" and to be good and profitable for a man, but it is written:

> There is a way *which seems* right to a man,
> But its end is the way of death. – Proverbs 14:12

> Therefore if you have been raised up with Christ, keep seeking the things above, where Christ is, seated at the right hand of God. Set your mind on the things above, not on the things that are on earth. – Colossians 3:1-2

Or expressed differently: Do you "follow the crowd," or do you follow God? They almost always lead in opposite directions, and you must deliberately and consciously choose to follow one or the other, even after you are born again. A Christian must constantly be "grow[ing] in the grace and knowledge [understanding] of our Lord and Savior Jesus Christ," or they risk falling back into the ways of this world and back under bondage to sin, Satan, and death. If you are not "pressing on to maturity" in your faith by growing in an understanding of the truth, you can be led astray by the "wolves," "vipers," and modern-day "Pharisees" (false and hypocritical teachers) as explained throughout this book. The wisdom of this world <u>always</u> leads away from Christ and back to sin, suffering, and death; it is the blind leading the blind:

> And He also spoke a parable to them: "A blind man cannot guide a blind man, can he? Will they not both fall into a pit?" – Luke 6:39

> "Leave them alone; they are blind guides of blind people. And if a person who is blind guides another who is blind, both will fall into a pit." – Matthew 15:14

And just because you hear something repeated loudly and often doesn't make it true or even wise, and furthermore, as stated in Scripture:

> Let God be found true, though every man be found a liar. – Romans 3:4

> The brethren immediately sent Paul and Silas away by night to Berea [the Bereans], and when they arrived, they went into the synagogue of the Jews. Now these were more noble-minded than those in Thessalonica, for they received the word with great eagerness, examining the Scriptures daily *to see* whether these things were so. – Acts 17:10-11

Yes, the wisdom of this world will expire completely worthless at the Second Advent of our Lord and Savior Jesus Christ. God will have been "found true" in all things, and the "wisdom from above" will have been vindicated, while the wisdom of this world will be judged and found that it amounts to nothing at all except "foolishness."

You will also hear some claim that the Bible is outdated or "out of touch" with the culture and societal norms of today and that the Bible needs to be more "progressive" or "liberal" and "updated" to match current trends and fashions. However, once again, nothing could be further from the truth, for the Bible tells us that:

> That which has been is that which will be,
> And that which has been done is that which will be done.
> So there is nothing new under the sun. – Ecclesiastes 1:9

In contrast to the wisdom of this world, the "wisdom from above" gives man an understanding of God, His Son Jesus Christ, and the ways of righteousness and peace which lead to eternal life. The "wisdom from above" is like a solid rock, enduring, unchanging, a sure foundation – outlasting the folly of man. It is written:

> Remember those who led you, who spoke the word of God to you; and considering the result of their conduct, imitate their faith. Jesus Christ *is* the same yesterday and today and forever. Do not be carried away by varied and strange teachings. – Hebrews 13:7-9a

> "Therefore, everyone who hears these words of Mine, and acts on them, will be like a wise man who built his house on the rock. And the rain fell and the floods came, and the winds blew and slammed against that house; and yet it did not fall, for it had been founded on the rock. And everyone who hears these words of Mine, and does not act on them, will be like a foolish man who built his house on the sand. And the rain fell and the floods came, and the winds blew and slammed against that house; and it fell—and its collapse was great." – Matthew 7:24-27

The "wisdom from above" comes from God alone to those who believe in Him, humble themselves before Him, and call on His name. There is no admission fee for obtaining it, as God offers it freely to those who simply ask Him for it:

> But if any of you lacks wisdom, let him ask of God, who gives to all generously and without reproach, and it will be given to him. But he must ask in faith without any doubting, for the one who doubts is like the surf of the sea, driven and tossed by the wind. For that man ought not to expect that he will receive anything from the Lord, *being* a double-minded man, unstable in all his ways. – James 1:5-8

And finally, the Christian only gets the "wisdom from above" from God's Holy Word. You won't find Godly wisdom in the materials produced by man.

> "It is written, 'MAN SHALL NOT LIVE ON BREAD ALONE, BUT ON EVERY WORD THAT PROCEEDS OUT OF THE MOUTH OF GOD.'" – Matthew 4:4

> How blessed is the man who does not walk in the counsel of the wicked,
> Nor stand in the path of sinners,
> Nor sit in the seat of scoffers!
> But his delight is in the law of the LORD,
> And in His law he meditates day and night.
> He will be like a tree *firmly* planted by streams of water,
> Which yields its fruit in its season
> And its leaf does not wither;
> And in whatever he does, he prospers. – Psalm 1:1-3

> Teach me Your way, O LORD;
> I will walk in Your truth;
> Unite my heart to fear Your name. – Psalm 86:11

See also the chapters on Choosing a Bible and Reading and Studying the Bible for more information.

RELATED SCRIPTURE:

The LORD by wisdom founded the earth,
By understanding He established the heavens. – Proverbs 3:19

"For My thoughts are not your thoughts,
Nor are your ways My ways," declares the LORD.
"For *as* the heavens are higher than the earth,
So are My ways higher than your ways
And My thoughts than your thoughts." – Isaiah 55:8-9

For the LORD gives wisdom;
From His mouth *come* knowledge and understanding.
He stores up sound wisdom for the upright;
He is a shield to those who walk in integrity,
Guarding the paths of justice,
And He preserves the way of His godly ones. – Proverbs 2:6-8

Then the mystery was revealed to Daniel in a night vision. Then Daniel blessed the God of heaven; Daniel said,

> "Let the name of God be blessed forever and ever,
> For wisdom and power belong to Him.
> "It is He who changes the times and the epochs;
> He removes kings and establishes kings;
> He gives wisdom to wise men
> And knowledge to men of understanding.
> "It is He who reveals the profound and hidden things;
> He knows what is in the darkness,
> And the light dwells with Him.
> "To You, O God of my fathers, I give thanks and praise,
> For You have given me wisdom and power;
> Even now You have made known to me what we requested of You,
> For You have made known to us the king's matter." – Daniel 2:19-23

How blessed is the man who finds wisdom
And the man who gains understanding.
For her profit is better than the profit of silver
And her gain better than fine gold.
She is more precious than jewels;
And nothing you desire compares with her.
Long life is in her right hand;
In her left hand are riches and honor.

Her ways are pleasant ways
And all her paths are peace. – Proverbs 3:13-17

Acquire wisdom! Acquire understanding!
Do not forget nor turn away from the words of my mouth.
"Do not forsake her, and she will guard you;
Love her, and she will watch over you.
"The beginning of wisdom *is*: Acquire wisdom;
And with all your acquiring, get understanding.
"Prize her, and she will exalt you;
She will honor you if you embrace her.
"She will place on your head a garland of grace;
She will present you with a crown of beauty." – Proverbs 4:5-9

How much better it is to get wisdom than gold!
And to get understanding is to be chosen above silver. – Proverbs 16:16

"With Him [God] are wisdom and might;
To Him belong counsel and understanding." – Job 12:13

For wisdom is protection *just as* money is protection,
But the advantage of knowledge is that wisdom preserves the lives of its possessors. – Ecclesiastes 7:12

…that their hearts may be encouraged, having been knit together in love, and *attaining* to all the wealth that comes from the full assurance of understanding, *resulting* in a true knowledge of God's mystery, *that is*, Christ *Himself*, in whom are hidden all the treasures of wisdom and knowledge. – Colossians 2:2-3

For this reason also, since the day we heard *of it*, we have not ceased to pray for you and to ask that you may be filled with the knowledge of His will in all spiritual wisdom and understanding, so that you will walk in a manner worthy of the Lord, to please *Him* in all respects, bearing fruit in every good work and increasing in the knowledge of God; strengthened with all power, according to His glorious might, for the attaining of all steadfastness and patience; joyously giving thanks to the Father, who has qualified us to share in the inheritance of the saints in Light. – Colossians 1:9-12

Oh, the depth of the riches both of the wisdom and knowledge of God! How unsearchable are His judgments and unfathomable His ways! For WHO HAS KNOWN THE MIND OF THE LORD, OR WHO BECAME HIS COUNSELOR? Or WHO HAS FIRST GIVEN TO HIM THAT IT MIGHT BE PAID BACK TO HIM AGAIN? For from Him and through Him and to Him are all things. To Him *be* the glory forever. Amen. – Romans 11:33-36

"But where can wisdom be found?
And where is the place of understanding?
"Man does not know its value,
Nor is it found in the land of the living.
"The deep says, 'It is not in me';
And the sea says, 'It is not with me.'
"Pure gold cannot be given in exchange for it,
Nor can silver be weighed as its price.
"It cannot be valued in the gold of Ophir,

In precious onyx, or sapphire.
"Gold or glass cannot equal it,
Nor can it be exchanged for articles of fine gold.
"Coral and crystal are not to be mentioned;
And the acquisition of wisdom is above *that of* pearls.
"The topaz of Ethiopia cannot equal it,
Nor can it be valued in pure gold.
"Where then does wisdom come from?
And where is the place of understanding?
"Thus it is hidden from the eyes of all living
And concealed from the birds of the sky.
"Abaddon and Death say,
'With our ears we have heard a report of it.'

"God understands its way,
And He knows its place.
"For He looks to the ends of the earth
And sees everything under the heavens.
"When He imparted weight to the wind
And meted out the waters by measure,
When He set a limit for the rain
And a course for the thunderbolt,
Then He saw it and declared it;
He established it and also searched it out.
"And to man He said, 'Behold, the fear of the Lord, that is wisdom;
And to depart from evil is understanding.'" – Job 28:12-28

In that night God appeared to Solomon and said to him, "Ask what I shall give you." And Solomon said to God, "You have dealt with my father David with great faithfulness, and have made me king in his place. Now, LORD God, Your promise to my father David is fulfilled, for You have made me king over a people as numerous as the dust of the earth. Now give me wisdom and knowledge, so that I may go out and come in before this people, for who can rule this great people of Yours?" Then God said to Solomon, "Because this was in your heart, and you did not ask for riches, wealth, or honor, or the life of those who hate you, nor did you even ask for long life, but you asked for yourself wisdom and knowledge so that you may rule My people over whom I have made you king, wisdom and knowledge have been granted to you. I will also give you riches, wealth, and honor, such as none of the kings who were before you has possessed, nor *will* those who will come after you." So Solomon went from the high place which was at Gibeon, from the tent of meeting, to Jerusalem, and he reigned over Israel. – 2 Chronicles 1:7-13

4.9 THE ARMOR OF GOD

Put on the full armor of God, so that you will be able to stand firm against the schemes of the devil. For our struggle is not against flesh and blood, but against the rulers, against the powers, against the world forces of this darkness, against the spiritual forces of wickedness in the heavenly places. – Ephesians 6:11-12

Scripture tells us that this fallen world is a war zone – a great spiritual war is raging in this material universe. This is a spiritual war going on for your soul. On one side are God and His holy angels, along with His saints (all those who have been born-again, who have "put on Christ" in baptism) here on Earth. On the other side are the very real spiritual forces of darkness and evil led by Satan (the Devil) and his angels and demons who followed him in sin, and it is they who oppose everything that is good and of God – and they oppose you. Satan is not a myth; he is your "accuser" before God. The forces of evil are working tirelessly in an attempt to lead you to eternal death.

We further read that "our struggle is not against flesh and blood, but against the rulers, against the powers, against the world forces of this darkness, against the spiritual forces of wickedness in the heavenly places." Be not deceived, this is a very real war, and it is raging right now all around you. As a Christian here in this fallen world, we live right on (and behind) enemy lines! In fact, a Christian must "stand firm" against all of the following:

1. Satan – "the devil," "the ruler/prince of this world," "the prince of the power of the air," "the ruler of the demons," "Beelzebul" (literally means the lord of the flies/dung), the "tempter," who "prowls around like a roaring lion, seeking someone to devour" and your "accuser" before God,
2. "The rulers, against the powers, against the world forces of this darkness, against the spiritual forces of wickedness in the heavenly places,"
3. Evil men – who seek to destroy you or turn you out of the way to eternal life, and even
4. Our old sinful nature – "the lust of the flesh," "the lust of the eyes," "pride," etc.

However, you must not dare to try to "stand firm" on your own power, but only by the power of Christ who "abides in" you. If you try to "stand firm" on your own power, the forces of evil will eat you up and spit you out, and you'll be left standing there wondering what just happened to you. You would have no chance, none whatsoever, trying to prevail by your own power, might, and strength – it is only by the power of Christ in you that you can overcome. Do not take this warning lightly. Do not underestimate the very real spiritual forces of darkness with which we are at war – this is a war to the death, eternal death.

We are therefore instructed to "put on the full armor of God":

> Finally, be strong in the Lord and in the strength of His might. Put on the full armor of God, so that you will be able to stand firm against the schemes of the devil. <u>For our struggle is not against flesh and blood, but against the rulers, against the powers, against the world forces of this darkness, against the spiritual *forces* of wickedness in the heavenly *places*</u>. Therefore, take up the full armor of God, so that you will be able to resist in the evil day, and having done everything, to stand firm. Stand firm therefore, HAVING GIRDED YOUR LOINS WITH TRUTH, and

HAVING PUT ON THE BREASTPLATE OF RIGHTEOUSNESS, and having shod YOUR FEET WITH THE PREPARATION OF THE GOSPEL OF PEACE; in addition to all, taking up the shield of faith with which you will be able to extinguish all the flaming arrows of the evil *one*. And take THE HELMET OF SALVATION, and the sword of the Spirit, which is the word of God. – Ephesians 6:10-17

Those are amazing verses of Scripture. Note the tools which comprise the armor of God:

- **Knowing the truth:** we read and study Scripture so that we are always "grow[ing] in the grace and knowledge [understanding] of our Lord and Savior Jesus Christ,"
- **Wearing righteousness (love):** walking in the Spirit, "abiding in Him [Christ]" and "He in you," loving and serving others,
- **Prepared with the gospel of peace:** this "message of truth," by which you have been born again,
- **Using a shield of faith:** for "without faith it is impossible to please God" or "stand firm" and resist the attacks of the enemy,
- **Putting on a helmet of salvation:** which is your hope, and it is this hope which keeps you always looking forward and "press[ing] on toward the goal for the prize of the upward call of God in Christ Jesus" in all things at all times, and
- **The Sword of the Spirit:** "which is the Word of God!"

From the above list, it is abundantly clear that if we are to "stand firm" in this war between good and evil, we must prepare ourselves for battle. We do this by always "working out" our own salvation, by intimately knowing the Word of God (part of which involves memorizing Scripture), and by always "grow[ing] in the grace and knowledge [understanding] of our Lord and Savior Jesus Christ." It is through those actions along with prayer that our faith matures, and we are able to "stand firm."

ON WIELDING CARNAL AND WORLDLY WEAPONS

It is vitally important that you understand we are not called to pick up and wield (use) the material and carnal worldly weapons of war created by man and this world – for our battle is spiritual:

> For though we walk in the flesh, we do not war according to the flesh, for the weapons of our warfare are not of the flesh, but divinely powerful for the destruction of fortresses. – 2 Corinthians 10:3-4

Some may object to what I'm teaching here, thinking (having their minds already made up) that Christians are told by Jesus to "get a sword" (Luke 22:36) which allows and justifies their use of worldly weapons for self-defense (or even war). But brother or sister in Christ, that simply is not the case. Wayne Jackson writes on this verse, adding much-needed clarity of thought and logic: [71]

> Question from Reader: "Would you discuss Luke 22:36 — '[L]et him sell his cloak and buy a sword'? Some claim this passage is in conflict with Matthew

---

[71] Jackson, Wayne. "Buy a Sword?" ChristianCourier.com. Access date: April 26, 2020. https://christiancourier.com/articles/1458-buy-a-sword

5:39, which prohibits a disciple of Christ from exercising physical retaliation, while others allege that Luke's statement authorizes the Christian's use of carnal weapons in defense of the cause of Christ."

Several observations regarding this matter are in order.

First, one cannot take one passage that appears to contain a difficulty and array it against an almost encyclopedic collection of information that leads to an opposite conclusion. That is not a legitimate approach to biblical interpretation, and it reveals more about those who argue in this vein than is complimentary to them.

It is rather analogous to the procedure of the skeptic who ignores the vast conglomerate of data that argue for the unity of the Bible (hence its divine origin) by the appeal to a single text that superficially **appears** to imply a contradiction.

It also is similar to the Protestant who disregards all the texts that require immersion in water as an act of faith in obtaining the remission of sins, and focusing only on such passages as mention "faith" as a condition of salvation.

Second, the immediate context (Luke 22:35-38) pertains to the instructions concerning how the disciples would be treated as they would embark upon their dangerous mission of proclaiming his gospel. They were to go forth trusting in God to care for them.

The Lord reminds them of the providential care that surrounded them in their previous evangelistic labors. As they initially went forth, were they abundantly provisioned? No. God took care of them day by day. Did they lack anything? They conceded that they did not.

Christ then quoted from Isaiah 53:12, where the prophet foretold that he, Christ himself, would be "reckoned with transgressors," i.e., treated as a common sinner. The larger context of Isaiah 53 reveals that in implementing Heaven's gracious plan of redemption, the lamb of God would do "no violence" (Is. 53:9). His example in dealing with hostility was to be their model.

Third, when the authorities came to arrest Jesus, Peter attempted to defend his Master with his sword, and the Savior sternly rebuked his apostle for the effort (Mt. 26:51-52).

Fourth, with reference to Luke 22:36, I introduce the testimony of the late William Arndt, professor of New Testament exegesis and hermeneutics at Concordia Seminary in St. Louis. Incidentally, he was one of the esteemed editors of the world famous *Greek-English Lexicon of the New Testament*, in collaboration with Gingrich and Danker.

In his book, *Does The Bible Contradict Itself?*, he wrote regarding Luke 22:36: [72]

"It is a warning to the disciples that troublous times, days of suffering and persecution, are coming for them and that they will have to arm themselves to withstand the onslaughts that are impending. The connection makes it clear that our Lord is not speaking of swords of iron or steel in this admonition. The disciples thought that He was referring to such physical weapons, and they said, v. 38: 'Lord, here are two swords.' Jesus, seeing that they are still very dull in their understanding of the spiritual teaching He has been giving them, says: 'It is

---

[72] Arndt, William. 1955. Does the Bible Contradict Itself? St. Louis, MO: Concordia.

enough.' He does not pursue the instruction any further, leaving it to the Holy Spirit to open up the full meaning of this matter to them later on. To put it briefly, the words of Jesus, Luke 22:36, are a figurative way of saying: Perilous times are coming; prepare for them. The swords He has in mind are the spiritual weapons of strong faith, fervent love of the Savior, fortitude, patience, and hope. This text, then, treats an altogether different subject from the one touched on in Matt. 5:39, and a collision of the two passages is out of the question (1955, 147-148)."

It is a regrettable circumstance that far too many Christian people have their minds made up on a variety of biblical themes before ever carefully studying the matter.

Such individuals are easily disposed to sweep under the carpet much evidence pertaining to a subject, and then almost frantically search for a single text that will justify them in what they already want to believe. This is a common though sad situation.

The weapons of man have absolutely no impact whatsoever in this war. Also, note that our only offensive weapon is the "Sword of the Spirit, which is the word of God." Brother or sister in Christ, I ask you: Is your sword a polished, "sharp two-edged sword" worthy of battle or a tarnished, dull kitchen butter knife?

> For the word of God is living and active and sharper than any two-edged sword, and piercing as far as the division of soul and spirit, of both joints and marrow, and able to judge the thoughts and intentions of the heart. – Hebrews 4:12

We wield the Word of God by becoming a prayer warrior for God – we pray the Word, and we then trust in God for all victories. We win spiritual battles not by relying on our own strength and power, but on the Spirit of God, for it is written:

> "'Not by might nor by power, but by My Spirit,' says the LORD of hosts." – Zechariah 4:6

JESUS LED BY EXAMPLE

We have the perfect example of spiritual warfare shown to us by Jesus when He was in the wilderness facing the attacks (temptations) of Satan:

> Then Jesus was led up by the Spirit into the wilderness to be tempted by the devil. And after He had fasted forty days and forty nights, He then became hungry. And the tempter [Satan] came and said to Him, "If You are the Son of God, command that these stones become bread." But He answered and said, "It is written,
>
> > 'MAN SHALL NOT LIVE ON BREAD ALONE, BUT ON EVERY WORD THAT PROCEEDS OUT OF THE MOUTH OF GOD.'"
>
> Then the devil took Him into the holy city and had Him stand on the pinnacle of the temple, and said to Him, "If You are the Son of God, throw Yourself down; for it is written,
>
> > 'HE WILL COMMAND HIS ANGELS CONCERNING YOU';
>
> and

> 'ON *their* HANDS THEY WILL BEAR YOU UP,
> SO THAT YOU WILL NOT STRIKE YOUR FOOT AGAINST A STONE.'"
>
> Jesus said to him, "On the other hand, it is written, 'YOU SHALL NOT PUT THE LORD YOUR GOD TO THE TEST.'"
>
> Again, the devil took Him to a very high mountain and showed Him all the kingdoms of the world and their glory; and he said to Him, "All these things I will give You, if You fall down and worship me." Then Jesus said to him, "Go, Satan! For it is written, 'YOU SHALL WORSHIP THE LORD YOUR GOD, AND SERVE HIM ONLY.'" Then the devil left Him; and behold, angels came and *began* to minister to Him. – Matthew 4:1-11

Notice that Jesus didn't pick up sticks and stones (or knives, guns, and bombs – the material weapons of war of man and this world) in His fight with the devil, nor did He get into a physical altercation with Satan. He wielded the "sword of the Spirit which is the word of God." We are to do the same. It was even prophesied in the Old Testament that in the age of grace, the Christian would no longer wield worldly weapons of war:

> Now it will come about that
> In the last days [this gospel age of grace]
> The mountain of the house of the LORD
> Will be established as the chief of the mountains,
> And will be raised above the hills;
> And all the nations will stream to it.
> And many peoples will come and say,
> "Come, let us go up to the mountain of the LORD,
> To the house of the God of Jacob;
> That He may teach us concerning His ways
> And that we may walk in His paths."
> For the law will go forth from Zion
> And the word of the LORD from Jerusalem.
> And He will judge between the nations,
> And will render decisions for many peoples;
> And they will hammer their swords into plowshares and their spears into pruning hooks.
> Nation will not lift up sword against nation,
> And never again will they learn war. – Isaiah 2:1-4

Jesus always used the Word of God as His only weapon; and He will once again do so at the end of time, on the great Day of Judgment:

> Then that lawless one will be revealed whom the Lord will slay with the breath of His mouth and bring to an end by the appearance of His coming. – 2 Thessalonians 2:8

> In His right hand He held seven stars, and out of His mouth came a sharp two-edged sword; and His face was like the sun shining in its strength. – Revelation 1:16

> From His mouth comes a sharp sword, so that with it He may strike down the nations, and He will rule them with a rod of iron; and He treads the wine press of the fierce wrath of God, the Almighty...And the rest were killed with the sword which came from the mouth of Him who sat on the horse, and all the birds were filled with their flesh. – Revelation 19:15, 21

While Christ was victorious over Satan at the cross, it is written:

> Be of sober *spirit*, be on the alert. Your adversary, the devil, prowls around like a roaring lion, seeking someone to devour. But resist him, [standing] firm in *your* faith, knowing that the same experiences of suffering are being accomplished by your brethren who are in the world. – 1 Peter 5:8-9

So, if you are actively engaged in this battle for eternal souls as a kingdom builder for Christ, you will face spiritual attacks all along your path (pilgrimage) to eternal life. In fact, the more "good works" you are doing for God, the more attacks you will likely face. If you are not being attacked, it may be because Satan has no reason to fear you: maybe you are not even in the battle, for you may be doing nothing at all to win souls for the Lord. When attacks do occur, you will find that they often happen right before or after you have a major spiritual breakthrough in your walk with God, or when you are about to or have just accomplished some "good work" for the Lord and feel good about things. Satan often attacks when your guard is down, and we are often most vulnerable right after we have had a personal victory or advance of some kind in our walk with Christ.

So do not underestimate your adversary – Satan still can, and does, attack Christians and try to turn them away from the faith and away from Christ and back towards this world and sin and death! Before you came to Christ, he attacked you with doubts about God and creation. After you are born again, he still tries to put doubts into your mind, or wicked evil thoughts (these are called "fiery darts") which show up out of nowhere; these evil thoughts appear to be your own (they appear to come from within your own mind), but they are actually coming from outside, from Satan. The first few times this happens, it can be very confusing, but if you "stand firm" in your faith, resisting them by the Word of God, they will once again vanish into nothingness:

> Submit therefore to God. Resist the devil and he will flee from you. – James 4:7

Some of these attacks can be quite ferocious. Early in my walk with Christ, one attack was so relentless, continuing for hours, and nothing I did would stop it. This one blasphemous thought kept bombarding me. It was only after some time that the Spirit showed me which verse(s) to use; He did this by recalling to my mind several verses of Scripture (Matthew 4:4 in particular). I re-read the verse, studied on it, meditated on it (thinking about it), and then wielded it by speaking it directly against the attack. You don't have to speak these verses out loud; you can simply do so in your mind. The attack instantly ceased. That was my best lesson and training that I have received in this area. The "Sword of the Spirit" is the only offensive weapon we have and how we must repel such attacks, and that is why having Scripture memorized is extremely important. As you "press on to maturity" as a Christian, you will be better able to spot these attacks and realize what is happening. I know now what to do when these "fiery darts" show up; I may not always know which Scripture to use, but the Spirit will lead you into all truth.

The Message of Truth

STAND FIRM

A Christian is called to "stand firm" and "hold fast" in the faith:

> Be on the alert, stand firm in the faith, act like men, be strong. – 1 Corinthians 16:13

> Now I make known to you, brethren, the gospel which I preached to you, which also you received, in which also you stand, by which also you are saved, if you hold fast the word which I preached to you, unless you believed in vain. – 1 Corinthians 15:1-2

> Therefore, my beloved brethren whom I long *to see*, my joy and crown, in this way stand firm in the Lord, my beloved. – Philippians 4:1

> …for this reason, brethren, in all our distress and affliction we were comforted about you through your faith; for now we *really* live, if you stand firm in the Lord. – 1 Thessalonians 3:7-8

Notice that we are not attackers – we are simply to "stand firm." We are to let God win all advances, to gain ground on the enemy, and then we help fill that ground with new believers who also "stand firm" in the faith. This is how the Kingdom of God expands to fill the entire Earth (but don't again mistake that to mean the false teaching of Dispensational Postmillennialism).

Finally, know that even though this is a spiritual war, Satan often works by and through evil men here on Earth; but our response is no different – it is still a spiritual attack. We are never to "pay back evil for evil to anyone," but are admonished to "overcome evil with good," leaving all revenge, retribution, payback, and vengeance to the Lord. We are to "love your enemies and pray for those who persecute you," and "if possible, so far as it depends on you, be at peace with all men" – in fact, it is through these very acts of love and prayer by which a Christian fights the battle of spiritual warfare. Satan and the forces of evil have no defense whatsoever against that. We must follow the example of Jesus: a Christian is fighting a spiritual battle and never has occasion to harm others physically!

It is also wise for a Christian to periodically re-check their armor from time to time and perhaps give it a tune-up. See also the chapters on Choosing a Bible and Start Memorizing Verses.

FALSE TEACHING(S) YOU WILL ENCOUNTER:

- Satan (The Devil) is just a myth

RELATED SCRIPTURE:

Then Jesus said to him, "Put your sword back into its place; for all those who take up the sword shall perish by the sword. Or do you think that I cannot appeal to My Father, and He will at once put at My disposal more than twelve legions of angels?" – Matthew 26:52-53

…the one who practices sin is of the devil; for the devil has sinned from the beginning. The Son of God appeared for this purpose, to destroy the works of the devil. – 1 John 3:8

"…thus says the LORD to you, 'Do not fear or be dismayed because of this great multitude, for the battle is not yours but God's.'" – 2 Chronicles 20:15

"Have I not commanded you? Be strong and courageous! Do not tremble or be dismayed, for the LORD your God is with you wherever you go." – Joshua 1:9

What then shall we say to these things? If God *is* for us, who *is* against us? – Romans 8:31

You are my King, O God;
Command victories for Jacob.
Through You we will push back our adversaries;
Through Your name we will trample down those who rise up against us.
For I will not trust in my bow,
Nor will my sword save me.
But You have saved us from our adversaries,
And You have put to shame those who hate us.
In God we have boasted all day long,
And we will give thanks to Your name forever. *Selah.* – Psalm 44:4-8

But since we are of *the* day, let us be sober, having put on the breastplate of faith and love, and as a helmet, the hope of salvation. For God has not destined us for wrath, but for obtaining salvation through our Lord Jesus Christ, who died for us, so that whether we are awake or asleep, we will live together with Him. Therefore encourage one another and build up one another, just as you also are doing. – 1 Thessalonians 5:8-11

Never pay back evil for evil to anyone. Respect what is right in the sight of all men. If possible, so far as it depends on you, be at peace with all men. Never take your own revenge, beloved, but leave room for the wrath *of God*, for it is written, "VENGEANCE IS MINE, I WILL REPAY," says the Lord. "BUT IF YOUR ENEMY IS HUNGRY, FEED HIM, AND IF HE IS THIRSTY, GIVE HIM A DRINK; FOR IN SO DOING YOU WILL HEAP BURNING COALS ON HIS HEAD." Do not be overcome by evil, but overcome evil with good. – Romans 12:17-21

"You have heard that it was said, 'YOU SHALL LOVE YOUR NEIGHBOR and hate your enemy.' But I say to you, love your enemies and pray for those who persecute you." – Matthew 5:43-44

Then I turned to see the voice that was speaking with me. And having turned I saw seven golden lampstands; and in the middle of the lampstands *I saw* one like a son of man, clothed in a robe reaching to the feet, and girded across His chest with a golden sash. His head and His hair were white like white wool, like snow; and His eyes were like a flame of fire. His feet *were* like burnished bronze, when it has been made to glow in a furnace, and His voice *was* like the sound of many waters. In His right hand He held seven stars, and out of His mouth came a sharp two-edged sword; and His face was like the sun shining in its strength. – Revelation 1:12-16

And I saw heaven opened, and behold, a white horse, and He who sat on it *is* called Faithful and True, and in righteousness He judges and wages war. His eyes *are* a flame of fire, and on His head *are* many diadems; and He has a name written *on Him* which no one knows except Himself. *He is* clothed with a robe dipped in blood, and His name is called The Word of God. And the armies which are in heaven, clothed in fine linen, white *and* clean, were following Him on white horses. From His mouth comes a sharp sword, so that with it He may strike down the nations, and He will rule them with a rod of iron; and He treads the wine press of the fierce wrath of God, the Almighty. And on His robe and on His thigh He has a name written, "KING OF KINGS, AND LORD OF LORDS."

Then I saw an angel standing in the sun, and he cried out with a loud voice, saying to all the birds which fly in midheaven, "Come, assemble for the great supper of God, so that you may eat the flesh of kings and the flesh of commanders and the flesh of mighty men and the flesh of horses and of those who sit on them and the flesh of all men, both free men and slaves, and small and great."

And I saw the beast and the kings of the earth and their armies assembled to make war against Him who sat on the horse and against His army.

And the beast was seized, and with him the false prophet who performed the signs in his presence, by which he deceived those who had received the mark of the beast and those who worshiped his image; these two were thrown alive into the lake of fire which burns with brimstone. And the rest were killed with the sword which came from the mouth of Him who sat on the horse, and all the birds were filled with their flesh. – Revelation 19:11-21

He who dwells in the shelter of the Most High
Will abide in the shadow of the Almighty.
I will say to the LORD, "My refuge and my fortress,
My God, in whom I trust!"
For it is He who delivers you from the snare of the trapper
And from the deadly pestilence.
He will cover you with His pinions,
And under His wings you may seek refuge;
His faithfulness is a shield and bulwark. – Psalm 91:1-4

4.10 THE POWER OF PRAYER
(Understanding Prayer)

Rejoice always; pray without ceasing; in everything give thanks; for this is God's will for you in Christ Jesus. – 1 Thessalonians 5:16-18

While God speaks to us through His word, prayer is how a Christian talks with their "Heavenly Father." Remember, God is not a material being (i.e., flesh) like we are – for "God is Spirit," and prayer is how He asks that we communicate with Him. Please also remember that God is not some "magic genie lantern in the sky" that you make wishes upon and expect/hope to get them granted. Much could be said on prayer; it's hard to know what to include in this book. We're going to cover a lot of ground quickly; I hope to just get you started doing it and not worry about too many details at first. While there are many right ways to pray, there are also some wrong ways to pray that Scripture warns of. Those warnings should be heeded, of course.

PRAYER BASICS

Prayer is something a Christian does constantly, all day, every day, not just in times of duress. We see it written:

> Rejoice always; pray without ceasing; in everything give thanks; for this is God's will for you in Christ Jesus. – 1 Thessalonians 5:16-18

> Be anxious for nothing, but in everything by prayer and supplication with thanksgiving let your requests be made known to God. And the peace of God, which surpasses all comprehension, will guard your hearts and your minds in Christ Jesus. – Philippians 4:6-7

> These all [the disciples] with one mind were continually devoting themselves to prayer, along with *the* women, and Mary the mother of Jesus, and with His brothers. – Acts 1:14

Prayer is the central element in the life of a Christian, the glue, if you will, which ties together and connects the various aspects of Christian life you have been reading about:

- **Living in the Spirit:** It is through prayer that one is able to "live in the Spirit" and also offer thanksgiving to God,
- **The Peace of God:** Prayer is how you "let your requests be made known to God" and one finds "the peace of God,"
- **Godly Wisdom:** It is through the study of God's Word combined with prayer, "asking of God," that one finds and receives the "wisdom from above," and
- **The Armor of God:** It is through prayer by which a Christian engages the spiritual forces of evil and does battle with them. Always remember we are in a spiritual war, battling for the lives of eternal human souls.

Prayer today seems to have been needlessly made both mysterious and also superficial (of rite and repetition) when it is really quite simple as defined in the Bible. So, it is first instructive to say what prayer is not, since there are many preconceived notions in this area that one has learned or been taught from childhood. Christian prayer is not some mystical chanting or new age mantra involving rituals, "babbling," incantations, repetition of "Hail Mary's," talking in weird "tongues," rambling on endlessly, and other such nonsense. We see it written:

> "And when you are praying, do not use meaningless repetition [babble] as the Gentiles do, for they suppose that they will be heard for their many words. So do not be like them; for your Father knows what you need before you ask Him." – Matthew 6:7-8

> Do not be hasty in word or impulsive in thought to bring up a matter in the presence of God. For God is in heaven and you are on the earth; therefore let your words be few. – Ecclesiastes 5:2

As you just read, Scripture exhorts us to be direct and to the point in our prayers, concise if you will, not rambling and droning on forever and ever (I surely have seen prayers like that!). This "babbling" doesn't indicate that you are more pious or have a more devout prayer life; it just indicates that you are babbling. Christian prayer is supposed to be simple, open, and honest communication with God, much like a child talking with his or her father. In fact, such a relationship conveys a lot of understanding in how we are to view ourselves with respect to the Lord. This sets up a proper humble and contrite heart and a proper mentality of respect in our approaching God.

There are no specifically prescribed sets of words that you must say when you pray. You simply let Him know your feelings, desires, needs, wishes, and anything else on your mind. Remember that there is "nothing hidden" from God. Remember also that He says:

> "For My thoughts are not your thoughts,
> Nor are your ways My ways," declares the LORD.
> "For *as* the heavens are higher than the earth,
> So are My ways higher than your ways
> And My thoughts than your thoughts." – Isaiah 55:8-9

So, while God sees and knows all things at all times, He still asks us to let Him know what we need, to "make our requests known" before Him. We are doing so not for God's benefit but for ours. It is also okay (and good) to express any hurt, anger, frustration, etc. that you are feeling; indeed, we see great examples of doing just that in the Psalms of David – but remember to do so in a respectful way.

PRAYER POSTURE

Where possible and practical, a posture of humility before God is the most common example set before us in Scripture, which repeatedly shows prayer being done while kneeling or even prone (face down to the ground), out of respect to the Lord. However, God searches the heart, not the postures. It also doesn't matter if your eyes are open or closed, hands clasped or not, head bowed or not, etc. You can pray kneeling, prone, standing, sitting down, in the morning, at night, during the day, while in the car at a stoplight, etc. Vain attempts to make one appear more pious before others during prayer are not valued before the Lord.

Matthew Henry writes: [73]

---

[73] Henry, Matthew. Exposition of the Old and New Testaments, London. 1706-1710/1721.

III. A direction how to pray, 1Ti 2:8. 1. Now, under the gospel, prayer is not to be confined to any one particular house of prayer, but men must pray every where: no place is amiss for prayer, no place more acceptable to God than another, Joh 4:21. Pray every where. We must pray in our closets, pray in our families, pray at our meals, pray when we are on journeys, and pray in the solemn assemblies, whether more public or private. 2. It is the will of God that in prayer we should lift up holy hands: Lifting up holy hands, or pure hands, pure from the pollution of sin, washed in the fountain opened for sin and uncleanness. I will wash my hands, etc., Psa 26:6. 3. We must pray in charity: Without wrath, or malice, or anger at any person. 4. We must pray in faith without doubting (Jas 1:6), or, as some read it, without disputing, and then it falls under the head of charity.

Remember that you are having a heartfelt talk with the Creator of heaven and earth, the Lord God Almighty Himself; you should therefore approach prayer with utmost reverence, honor, respect, humility, and contriteness of heart. Even Jesus humbled Himself in front of God the Father, despite being fully God Himself; how much more then should we do likewise!

Then Jesus came with them to a place called Gethsemane, and said to His disciples, "Sit here while I go over there and pray." And He took with Him Peter and the two sons of Zebedee, and began to be grieved and distressed. Then He said to them, "My soul is deeply grieved, to the point of death; remain here and keep watch with Me."

And He went a little beyond *them*, and fell on His face and prayed, saying, "My Father, if it is possible, let this cup pass from Me; yet not as I will, but as You will." And He came to the disciples and found them sleeping, and said to Peter, "So, you *men* could not keep watch with Me for one hour? Keep watching and praying that you may not enter into temptation; the spirit is willing, but the flesh is weak."

He went away again a second time and prayed, saying, "My Father, if this cannot pass away unless I drink it, Your will be done." Again He came and found them sleeping, for their eyes were heavy. And He left them again, and went away and prayed a third time, saying the same thing once more. Then He came to the disciples and said to them, "Are you still sleeping and resting? Behold, the hour is at hand and the Son of Man is being betrayed into the hands of sinners. Get up, let us be going; behold, the one who betrays Me is at hand!" – Matthew 26:36-46

Now when Daniel knew that the document was signed, he entered his house (now in his roof chamber he had windows open toward Jerusalem); and he continued kneeling on his knees three times a day, praying and giving thanks before his God, as he had been doing previously. – Daniel 6:10 [Note: Notice also that Daniel kept praying to God even when it very likely doing so would lead to his imminent death!]

PRAY WITHOUT CEASING

A Christian should "pray without ceasing" (i.e., constantly). It is also prudent for a Christian to begin and end each day in prayer with the Lord (see the chapter on Essential First 30-Days Activities for a new Christian). The revered Old Testament

Daniel prayed three times per day, even if it wasn't convenient for him, or worse, even when it would put him in mortal danger for his life. Nothing whatsoever interfered with his prayer life. This sets an outstanding example for us to follow.

Scripture shows us that even Jesus needed to pray and that He prayed often. And if Jesus, being fully God, needed to pray, how much more should we be doing the same! Now I also confess that my prayer life, even today, is nowhere near where I'd like it to be. It really takes perseverance and desire to set aside the things and activities of this world in order to spend time alone with the Lord. It is a constant struggle to do that.

THE NOISE OF THIS WORLD

It is truly staggering how much noise this world gives off; we can grow used to it and therefore barely notice it, but it is constantly there, always vying for our attention. I have also found the early morning to be a great time for prayer, the best time, in fact, before the cares, concerns, and duties of this world start to demand your attention. It is written that God communicates in a "still, small voice," a "gentle whisper," a "soft whisper," or a "gentle breeze":

> And he said, Go forth, and stand upon the mount before the LORD. And, behold, the LORD passed by, and a great and strong wind rent the mountains, and brake in pieces the rocks before the LORD; but the LORD was not in the wind: and after the wind an earthquake; but the LORD was not in the earthquake: And after the earthquake a fire; but the LORD was not in the fire: and after the fire a still small voice. And it was so, when Elijah heard it, that he wrapped his face in his mantle, and went out, and stood in the entering in of the cave. When Elijah heard *it*, he wrapped his face in his mantle and went out and stood in the entrance of the cave. And behold, a voice *came* to him and said, "What are you doing here, Elijah?" – 1 Kings 19:11-13 (KJV)

We see that Jesus often prayed either early in the morning, in the stillness of the early hours of the day before the noise, clamor, and distractions of the world begin to take hold of us, or late at night when the noise of this world has died down again. It is very easy for the loud noise of this world (which is deafening at times) to drown out the voice of the Lord:

> In the early morning, while it was still dark, Jesus got up, left *the house*, and went away to a secluded place, and was praying there. – Mark 1:35

> And it happened that while He was praying alone, the disciples were with Him, and He questioned them, saying, "Who do the people say that I am?" – Luke 9:18

> After He had sent the crowds away, He went up on the mountain by Himself to pray; and when it was evening, He was there alone. – Matthew 14:23

> It was at this time that He went off to the mountain to pray, and He spent the whole night in prayer to God. – Luke 6:12

> Give ear to my words, O LORD,
> Consider my groaning.
> Heed the sound of my cry for help, my King and my God,
> For to You I pray.
> In the morning, O LORD, You will hear my voice;
> In the morning I will order *my prayer* to You and *eagerly* watch. – Psalm 5:1-3

IN PRIVATE

And when we pray, we are to do so in private, not as a public spectacle to show how pious we are in front of others. Prayer is our alone time with our "Heavenly Father." Jesus would often withdraw to an inner room or remote location (mountaintop, wilderness, etc.) to pray:

> "When you pray, you are not to be like the hypocrites; for they love to stand and pray in the synagogues and on the street corners so that they may be seen by men. Truly I say to you, they have their reward in full. But you, when you pray, go into your inner room, close your door and pray to your Father who is in secret, and your Father who sees *what is done* in secret will reward you." – Matthew 6:5-6

> But Jesus Himself would *often* slip away to the wilderness and pray. – Luke 5:16

> After bidding them farewell, He left for the mountain to pray. – Mark 6:46

The Bible tells us to pray in the "inner room" of our house, i.e., a place of quiet and stillness without distraction. This again helps us shut out the noise of this world and quiet our minds. But also realize that you can pray at other times and places where you find yourself alone. In fact, I've found that prayer spots are available all day long, nearly all the time. You can even pray while waiting in an elevator or while waiting in line somewhere.

It can also be profitable to come before God without trying to tell Him things; simply make yourself available for Him by quieting your mind. Prayer is a time of stillness and meditation. I fully realize how hard it is to take my own advice on this; truth be told, I also need to do a much better job in this area. Writing this book has been a blessing, as it has helped me realize some of the things I need to do better myself.

WE APPROACH GOD THROUGH CHRIST

While adding the words "In Jesus Name" or "In the Name of Jesus" at the end of the prayer can be used to express (and remind us) that we are approaching our Heavenly Father through His Son (the Mediator) and that we are calling on the authority of Christ, they are not required, and in fact, those who habitually and without thinking tack-on these three words at the end of each and every prayer as if they are some magical mantra are showing a superficial understanding of Christ's instructions in this area.

In ancient times, a person's name also conveyed an indication of their character, their nature. Praying "in the name" of someone means according to their character and also by (through) their authority; so, Scripture is telling us to pray according to Jesus' character, which is selfless, humble, pure, noble, kind, merciful, gentle, gracious, giving, loving, etc., and by His authority as the "one [only] mediator also between God and men." We are not to pray to Mary, the dead, or the Saints, etc.

As a reminder to you on this matter and to help break any unconscious habits, may I suggest that you try to mix in some other prayer endings at times. Here are some suggestions:

- "Through Jesus I pray,"
- "It is through Christ I/we pray,"
- "Through Christ as mediator I pray,"
- "By the blood of Christ I pray,"

- "Through Jesus alone I approach the throne,"
- "We pray everything through your Son Jesus"

SIMPLE, DIRECT, AND HONEST

Just be yourself and talk with God, your Heavenly Father, as if He were right there in front of you, knowing that nothing whatsoever can be hidden from Him; your deepest darkest fears, desires, failures, ill thoughts, etc....they are all wide open to God. Do not try to hide them; in fact, confess them, and ask Him to take that burden from you! That is when prayer really becomes wonderful, knowing you can fully trust in the Lord and give your burdens to Him. We are able to come directly into His presence through the blood of Christ; we are in effect coming right into His throne room in prayer, into the equivalent today of the "holy of holies":

> Therefore let us draw near with confidence [and boldness] to the throne of grace, so that we may receive mercy and find grace to help in time of need. – Hebrews 4:16

If you don't know what to pray, may I suggest this simple prayer to help you get started:

> *"God, thank you for the gift of today and for your Son Jesus Christ. Thank you for everything. Father, create a clean heart in me, O God, and renew a right spirit in me! Amen!"*

That is a very simple but effective prayer; also, do not underestimate the power of such a simple prayer. We should remember to keep our words few and that prayer doesn't have to "babble" and drone on forever! That simple prayer above was one that I prayed daily for months until I started to "press on to maturity" in the faith. At the time, it is what I felt I needed most, a clean (and humble) heart and a right spirit (the Holy Spirit) to help me through the day.

It's good to stop and reflect in awe and amazement that God, the Creator of heaven and earth and all the universe, takes time out of His busy schedule to spend time with you anytime you want! You don't have to schedule an appointment with Him or try to fit into His schedule. He's always there, ready and waiting for you. Imagine trying to do that with an important politician, V.I.P., or powerful CEO here in the world. And yet, God allows us to do just that through Jesus Christ. Amazing!

PERSISTENCE

It is also taught in Scripture that we are to be persistent in our prayers and petitions before the Lord. This is taught in the Parable of the Lady and the Unjust Judge in the book of Luke:

> Now He was telling them a parable to show that at all times they ought to pray and not to lose heart, saying, "In a certain city there was a judge who did not fear God and did not respect man. There was a widow in that city, and she kept coming to him, saying, 'Give me legal protection from my opponent.' For a while he was unwilling; but afterward he said to himself, 'Even though I do not fear God nor respect man, yet because this widow bothers me, I will give her legal protection, otherwise by continually coming she will wear me out.'" – Luke 18:1-5

> Then He said to them, "Suppose one of you has a friend, and goes to him at midnight and says to him, 'Friend, lend me three loaves; for a friend of mine has

come to me from a journey, and I have nothing to set before him'; and from inside he answers and says, 'Do not bother me; the door has already been shut and my children and I are in bed; I cannot get up and give you *anything*.' I tell you, even though he will not get up and give him *anything* because he is his friend, yet because of his persistence he will get up and give him as much as he needs.

"So I say to you, ask, and it will be given to you; seek, and you will find; knock, and it will be opened to you. For everyone who asks, receives; and he who seeks, finds; and to him who knocks, it will be opened. Now suppose one of you fathers is asked by his son for a fish; he will not give him a snake instead of a fish, will he? Or *if* he is asked for an egg, he will not give him a scorpion, will he? If you then, being evil, know how to give good gifts to your children, how much more will *your* heavenly Father give the Holy Spirit to those who ask Him?" – Luke 11:5-13

PRAYING FOR OTHERS

We are to offer prayers not only for ourselves but also for others. There are many examples in Scripture of the disciples and apostles praying for others. So, brother or sister in Christ (and myself also), have you prayed for others today? Have you even prayed for your enemies today?

> But I say to you, love your enemies and pray for those who persecute you, so that you may prove yourselves to be sons of your Father who is in heaven. – Matthew 5:44-45

> And He will yet deliver us, *if* you also join in helping us through your prayers, so that thanks may be given by many persons in our behalf for the favor *granted* to us through *the prayers of* many. – 2 Corinthians 1:10-11

> Devote yourselves to prayer, keeping alert in it with *an attitude of* thanksgiving; praying at the same time for us as well, that God will open up to us a door for the word, so that we may proclaim the mystery of Christ, for which I have also been imprisoned; that I may make it clear in the way that I ought to proclaim *it*. – Colossians 4:2-4

> First of all, then, I urge that entreaties *and* prayers, petitions *and* thanksgivings, be made on behalf of all men, for kings and all who are in authority, so that we may lead a tranquil and quiet life in all godliness and dignity. This is good and acceptable in the sight of God our Savior, who desires all men to be saved and to come to the knowledge of the truth. – 1 Timothy 2:1-4

> Therefore, confess your sins to one another, and pray for one another so that you may be healed. The effective prayer of a righteous man can accomplish much. – James 5:16

> We always give thanks to God for all of you, making mention *of you* in our prayers; constantly keeping in mind your work of faith and labor of love and perseverance of hope in our Lord Jesus Christ in the presence of our God and Father. – 1 Thessalonians 1:2-3

It's also good to note how the Lord "restored the fortunes of Job" after he prayed for others:

> The LORD restored the fortunes of Job when he prayed for his friends, and the LORD increased all that Job had twofold. – Job 24:10

DANIEL'S EXAMPLE

Below is a prayer by Daniel, who was highly esteemed by the Lord:

> So I gave my attention to the Lord God to seek *Him by* prayer and supplications, with fasting, sackcloth and ashes. I prayed to the LORD my God and confessed and said, "Alas, O Lord, the great and awesome God, who keeps His covenant and lovingkindness for those who love Him and keep His commandments, we have sinned, committed iniquity, acted wickedly and rebelled, even turning aside from Your commandments and ordinances. Moreover, we have not listened to Your servants the prophets, who spoke in Your name to our kings, our princes, our fathers and all the people of the land.
>
> "Righteousness belongs to You, O Lord, but to us open shame, as it is this day— to the men of Judah, the inhabitants of Jerusalem and all Israel, those who are nearby and those who are far away in all the countries to which You have driven them, because of their unfaithful deeds which they have committed against You. Open shame belongs to us, O Lord, to our kings, our princes and our fathers, because we have sinned against You. To the Lord our God *belong* compassion and forgiveness, for we have rebelled against Him; nor have we obeyed the voice of the LORD our God, to walk in His teachings which He set before us through His servants the prophets. Indeed all Israel has transgressed Your law and turned aside, not obeying Your voice; so the curse has been poured out on us, along with the oath which is written in the law of Moses the servant of God, for we have sinned against Him. Thus He has confirmed His words which He had spoken against us and against our rulers who ruled us, to bring on us great calamity; for under the whole heaven there has not been done *anything* like what was done to Jerusalem. As it is written in the law of Moses, all this calamity has come on us; yet we have not sought the favor of the LORD our God by turning from our iniquity and giving attention to Your truth. Therefore the LORD has kept the calamity in store and brought it on us; for the LORD our God is righteous with respect to all His deeds which He has done, but we have not obeyed His voice.
>
> "And now, O Lord our God, who have brought Your people out of the land of Egypt with a mighty hand and have made a name for Yourself, as it is this day— we have sinned, we have been wicked. O Lord, in accordance with all Your righteous acts, let now Your anger and Your wrath turn away from Your city Jerusalem, Your holy mountain; for because of our sins and the iniquities of our fathers, Jerusalem and Your people *have become* a reproach to all those around us. So now, our God, listen to the prayer of Your servant and to his supplications, and for Your sake, O Lord, let Your face shine on Your desolate sanctuary. O my God, incline Your ear and hear! Open Your eyes and see our desolations and the city which is called by Your name; for we are not presenting our supplications before You on account of any merits of our own, but on account of Your great compassion. O Lord, hear! O Lord, forgive! O Lord, listen and take action! For

Your own sake, O my God, do not delay, because Your city and Your people are called by Your name."

Now while I was speaking and praying, and confessing my sin and the sin of my people Israel, and presenting my supplication before the LORD my God in behalf of the holy mountain of my God, while I was still speaking in prayer, then the man Gabriel, whom I had seen in the vision previously, came to me in *my* extreme weariness about the time of the evening offering. He gave *me* instruction and talked with me and said, "O Daniel, I have now come forth to give you insight with understanding. At the beginning of your supplications the command was issued, and I have come to tell *you*, for you are highly esteemed; so give heed to the message and gain understanding of the vision." – Daniel 9:3-23

That is a fantastic example of prayer; in fact, Daniel's prayer was heard immediately, and a messenger (the angel Gabriel) was dispatched to him from the time he started praying. Now that's one powerful prayer! Sometimes I receive an answer to a prayer almost immediately, but at other times, the answer takes quite a while, maybe even years.

Also, remember that God knows more than we do, and He sees a much bigger picture than we do, so as a result, He may not give us things we ask for; but we need to always "trust in the Lord." Know that God hears you, and He also knows what you need (which is not always that same as what you want), and He has promised lovingkindness to those who call on His great name:

> The LORD is near to all who call upon Him,
> To all who call upon Him in truth. – Psalm 145:18

> In my distress I called upon the LORD,
> And cried to my God for help;
> He heard my voice out of His temple,
> And my cry for help before Him came into His ears. – Psalm 18:6

> "For the eyes of the LORD move to and fro throughout the earth that He may strongly support those whose heart is completely His." – 2 Chronicles 16:9

Daniel's prayer also shows us the elements that comprise a good prayer:

- Acknowledging God as sovereign Lord and showing respect,
- Approaching the throne with boldness, but also with humility,
- Confession of sins (even for others), along with sincere repentance,
- Petitions and supplications, and
- Thankfulness and gratitude

In another powerful example of prayer, we see how the apostles prayed when they were being persecuted by the Jews:

> And when they heard *this*, they lifted their voices to God with one accord and said, "O Lord, it is You who MADE THE HEAVEN AND THE EARTH AND THE SEA, AND ALL THAT IS IN THEM, who by the Holy Spirit, *through* the mouth of our father David Your servant, said,

The Message of Truth

> 'WHY DID THE GENTILES RAGE,
> AND THE PEOPLES DEVISE FUTILE THINGS?
> 'THE KINGS OF THE EARTH TOOK THEIR STAND,
> AND THE RULERS WERE GATHERED TOGETHER
> AGAINST THE LORD AND AGAINST HIS CHRIST.'
>
> For truly in this city there were gathered together against Your holy servant Jesus, whom You anointed, both Herod and Pontius Pilate, along with the Gentiles and the peoples of Israel, to do whatever Your hand and Your purpose predestined to occur. And now, Lord, take note of their threats, and grant that Your bond-servants may speak Your word with all confidence, while You extend Your hand to heal, and signs and wonders take place through the name of Your holy servant Jesus." And when they had prayed, the place where they had gathered together was shaken, and they were all filled with the Holy Spirit and *began* to speak the word of God with boldness. – Acts 4:24-31

CONFESS OUR SINS, ETC.

Remember that a Christian's life this side of heaven, while we are still in our mortal, sinful bodies, is one of continued struggle against the flesh (and sin) and one of continued repentance. While a true Christian does not live in continued willful habitual sin once born again, you will still find that you sin at times (see the "A Christian No Longer Sins" false teaching). If a new realization or conviction of your sins (current or past) comes to you, be honest with God and confess them in prayer before Him, and "He is faithful and righteous [just] to forgive us our sins and to cleanse us from all unrighteousness":

> If we walk in the Light as He Himself is in the Light, we have fellowship with one another, and the blood of Jesus His Son cleanses us from all sin. If we say that we have no sin, we are deceiving ourselves and the truth is not in us. If we confess our sins, He is faithful and righteous to forgive us our sins and to cleanse us from all unrighteousness. – 1 John 1:7-9

You use prayer to confess your sins before God, and Christ as mediator intercedes for you with forgiveness. How amazing is that! However, don't use God's grace and mercy as justification for continuing to go on willfully sinning, as that is not abiding in Christ, nor being obedient to Him and does harm to Christ's name instead of glorifying Him.

Also, contrary to the popular teaching out there, the "where two or three have gathered together in My name, I am there in their midst" (Matthew 18:20) and "if two of you agree on earth about anything that they may ask, it shall be done for them" (Matthew 18:19) verses do not even relate to prayer, as if by magic, if two or three Christians got together and prayed for a Ferrari sports car that they would magically get one. Those verses are about Church discipline, not prayer.

And finally, quoting Scripture in your prayers is fine and, in fact, strongly encouraged. God's Word was given to us to use, not just read. Reminding God of what He has promised in His Word is not being disrespectful; King David did that often in his psalms. Doing that serves to remind us of God's promises, for it is we who are weak and need constant reassurance. Also, a good prayer often includes any heartfelt cries of emotion that you have. It's fine to cry out to God in pain and anguish during trials and tribulations here on earth. The more you lean on Him in times of distress, the more He can help you.

HE HEARS US

And lastly, a Christian who prays well also has an attitude and expectation of the prayer being heard and answered. This is not presumption on our part; Scripture tells us this is proper. It demonstrates trust in the Lord and that you understand that He always does what He says He will do as recorded in His Word. We may not always get the answer we like, and the answer may come in God's time (not our time), but our prayers are heard.

> The LORD is far from the wicked,
> But He hears the prayer of the righteous. – Proverbs 15:29
>
> I have called upon You, for You will answer me, O God;
> Incline Your ear to me, hear my speech. – Psalm 17:6
>
> Answer me when I call, God of my righteousness!
> You have relieved me in my distress;
> Be gracious to me and hear my prayer. – Psalm 4:1
> [Note: This is also an example of boldly approaching the throne of God, but doing so with reverence and humility.]
>
> This is the confidence which we have before Him, that, if we ask anything according to His will, He hears us. And if we know that He hears us *in* whatever we ask, we know that we have the requests which we have asked from Him. – 1 John 5:14-15
>
> "Therefore I say to you, all things for which you pray and ask, believe that you have received them, and they will be *granted* you. Whenever you stand praying, forgive, if you have anything against anyone, so that your Father who is in heaven will also forgive you your transgressions." – Mark 11:24-25
>
> When He had taken the book, the four living creatures and the twenty-four elders fell down before the Lamb, each one holding a harp and golden bowls full of incense, which are the prayers of the saints. – Revelation 5:8

I hope this chapter has given you a brief, but solid head start on the vitally important topic of prayer.

RELATED SCRIPTURE:

After this manner therefore pray ye: Our Father which art in heaven, Hallowed be thy name. Thy kingdom come, Thy will be done in earth, as it is in heaven. Give us this day our daily bread. And forgive us our debts, as we forgive our debtors. And lead us not into temptation, but deliver us from evil: For thine is the kingdom, and the power, and the glory, for ever. Amen. – Matthew 6:9-13 (KJV)

[Side note: The verses above are often called the "Lord's Prayer," but in actuality, it's not really the Lord's Prayer, it is a prayer given to us. See John 17 for the actual Lord's Prayer. Noting how the prayer is constructed can help us: 1) Addressed to the Father, 2) Approached with humility and respect, 3) Acknowledging Him for who He is, 4) Asking for His will to be done instead of ours, 5) Requesting that we have the right heart, and 6) Acknowledging His ultimate authority and power. Also, these verses are a sample prayer, a template if you will, that can help show you the structure for a proper prayer. They are not some magical incantation in and of themselves that we are to just blindly repeat without thinking. At the time this prayer was given to the disciples, Christ's kingdom had not yet come in its power and glory (which happened at Pentecost), hence they were to pray for it to come. Today, we are already in Christ's kingdom, so we aren't to still blindly pray/repeat for "your kingdom come." Christ is right now, this very instant, "seated at the right hand of God" the Father, ruling and reigning over His Kingdom (see the Dispensational Premillennialism false teaching). It is of course however still profitable and good to pray for God's eternal heavenly Kingdom of Glory to be fully established and realized, which will be on the great Day of Judgment; the same words "Your kingdom come" can apply to this if your intent is clear.]

Is anyone among you suffering? *Then* he must pray. Is anyone cheerful? He is to sing praises. – James 5:13

You do not have because you do not ask. You ask and do not receive, because you ask with wrong motives, so that you may spend *it* on your pleasures. – James 4:3

With all prayer and petition pray at all times in the Spirit, and with this in view, be on the alert with all perseverance and petition for all the saints, and *pray* on my behalf, that utterance may be given to me in the opening of my mouth, to make known with boldness the mystery of the gospel, for which I am an ambassador in chains; that in *proclaiming* it I may speak boldly, as I ought to speak. – Ephesians 6:18-20

For this reason I too, having heard of the faith in the Lord Jesus which *exists* among you and your love for all the saints, do not cease giving thanks for you, while making mention *of you* in my prayers; that the God of our Lord Jesus Christ, the Father of glory, may give to you a spirit of wisdom and of revelation in the knowledge of Him. *I pray that* the eyes of your heart may be enlightened, so that you will know what is the hope of His calling, what are the riches of the glory of His inheritance in the saints, and what is the surpassing greatness of His power toward us who believe. – Ephesians 1:15-19a

For this reason I bow my knees before the Father, from whom every family in heaven and on earth derives its name, that He would grant you, according to the riches of His glory, to be strengthened with power through His Spirit in the inner man, so that Christ may dwell in your hearts through faith; *and* that you, being rooted and grounded in love, may be able to comprehend with all the saints what is the breadth and length and height and depth, and to know the love of Christ which surpasses knowledge, that you may be filled up to all the fullness of God. – Ephesians 3:14-19

But about midnight Paul and Silas were praying and singing hymns of praise to God, and the prisoners were listening to them. – Acts 16:25

Create in me a clean heart, O God,
And renew a steadfast spirit within me.
Do not cast me away from Your presence
And do not take Your Holy Spirit from me.
Restore to me the joy of Your salvation
And sustain me with a willing spirit.

Then I will teach transgressors Your ways,
And sinners will be converted to You. – Psalm 51:10-13

"You have heard that it was said, 'YOU SHALL LOVE YOUR NEIGHBOR and hate your enemy.' But I say to you, love your enemies and pray for those who persecute you, so that you may be sons of your Father who is in heaven; for He causes His sun to rise on *the* evil and *the* good, and sends rain on *the* righteous and *the* unrighteous." – Matthew 5:43-45

The sacrifice of the wicked is an abomination to the LORD,
But the prayer of the upright is His delight. – Proverbs 15:8

Let love *be* without hypocrisy. Abhor what is evil; cling to what is good. *Be* devoted to one another in brotherly love; give preference to one another in honor; not lagging behind in diligence, fervent in spirit, serving the Lord; rejoicing in hope, persevering in tribulation, devoted to prayer, contributing to the needs of the saints, practicing hospitality. – Romans 12:9-13

But if any of you lacks wisdom, let him ask of God [through prayer], who gives to all generously and without reproach, and it will be given to him. But he must ask in faith without any doubting, for the one who doubts is like the surf of the sea, driven and tossed by the wind. – James 1:5-6

"Ask, and it will be given to you; seek, and you will find; knock, and it will be opened to you. For everyone who asks receives, and he who seeks finds, and to him who knocks it will be opened. Or what man is there among you who, when his son asks for a loaf, will give him a stone? Or if he asks for a fish, he will not give him a snake, will he? If you then, being evil, know how to give good gifts to your children, how much more will your Father who is in heaven give what is good to those who ask Him!" – Matthew 7:7-11

In the same way the Spirit also helps our weakness; for we do not know how to pray as we should, but the Spirit Himself intercedes for *us* with groanings too deep for words; and He who searches the hearts knows what the mind of the Spirit is, because He intercedes for the saints according to *the will of* God. – Romans 8:26-27

For nothing is hidden that will not become evident, nor *anything* secret that will not be known and come to light. – Luke 8:17 [Note: This also speaks to confessing your sins before the Lord in prayer.]

If I shut up the heavens so that there is no rain, or if I command the locust to devour the land, or if I send pestilence among My people, and My people who are called by My name humble themselves and pray and seek My face and turn from their wicked ways, then I will hear from heaven, will forgive their sin and will heal their land. – 2 Chronicles 7:13-14

"It will also come to pass that before they call, I will answer; and while they are still speaking, I will hear." – Isaiah 65:24

4.11 HOLY, HOLY, HOLY

"HOLY, HOLY, HOLY is THE LORD GOD, THE ALMIGHTY, WHO WAS AND WHO IS AND WHO IS TO COME." – Revelation 4:8

For God is Love. We, in large measure, greatly underestimate the holiness of God, while we simultaneously underestimate the severity of our sins in relation to His holiness. God is morally pure, perfect, without any flaw or defect whatsoever; that is what holy means. Do not make the same mistake I did for many years of judging God based on what you see all around us in this fallen, sinful world (or by the actions of sinful man), for this is not what He created. What we see today is what man created by being disobedient to God.

In the fullness of time, we will see sin for what it really is and how bad it really is (and that it deserves the penalty of death), and we will see God for who He truly is. "God is love" – in fact, a love so pure that we have a very hard time understanding it, for "as the heavens are higher than the earth, are His ways higher than our ways." Even further, there is not (cannot be) even the merest, tiniest, most infinitesimal amount of anything but love in God! For if any moral impurity whatsoever (i.e., hate, pride, malice, dishonesty, deception, lying, unrighteous anger, etc.) were to be found in God, it would be magnified by His omnipotence and perfected by His eternality to fill His entire being instantly, leading to self-extinction (see 1 Corinthians 5:6). God "dwells" in light. He appears in the brightest, purest white light you've ever seen or can ever imagine. It is not an impure light like the sun, but imagine something a million times brighter, whiter and purer. It's not like any light we see in this material world.

The true nature of His love is so far beyond our level of comprehension that we struggle to find words to adequately describe it. We often hear the words "holy" and "love," but we seldom pause or stop to think very deeply about Who God really is, to contemplate His nature and His holiness. When you do, it leaves you in a state of complete and total awe and wonder (amazement), with a healthy respect and righteous "fear of the Lord." I am limited to using finite imperfect vocabulary here to convey the nature of an infinitely holy God; any words, therefore, fail to do adequate justice to the subject.

And finally, always remember that when we see Jesus, we are seeing Holy God Himself, for they are One and the Same, as it is written:

> He [Jesus] is the image of the invisible God, the firstborn of all creation. For by Him all things were created, *both* in the heavens and on earth, visible and invisible, whether thrones or dominions or rulers or authorities—all things have been created through Him and for Him. – Colossians 1:15-16

When Christ returns on the Great Day of Judgment and everyone who has ever lived (both the saved and the lost) sees for themselves the unimaginable holiness and glory of the Lord fully revealed before their very eyes, they will be in such utter awe, shock, and amazement that it will almost certainly be a moment without words of any kind. It is written:

> For we will all stand before the judgment seat of God. For it is written,
>
> "AS I LIVE, SAYS THE LORD, EVERY KNEE SHALL BOW TO ME,
> AND EVERY TONGUE SHALL GIVE PRAISE TO GOD."

So then each one of us will give an account of himself to God. – Romans 14:10b-12

Jesus said to him, "Because you have seen Me, have you believed? Blessed *are* they who did not see, and *yet* believed." – John 20:29

The glory of the Lord will so far surpass anything they ever even remotely imagined that it will be almost beyond comprehension. And then to think, after seeing such glory and holiness of the Lord fully revealed, the lost will be banished to the "place of outer darkness" forever, "away from the presence" of the Lord. That is truly gut-wrenching to think about. I really wish more people would stop and seriously contemplate the Lord's holiness, as I think it would help them come to see God for Who He really is and want to know more about Him and His Christ Jesus.

RELATED SCRIPTURE:

The one who does not love does not know God, for God is love. – 1 John 4:8

[God]…who alone possesses immortality and dwells in unapproachable light, whom no man has seen or can see. To Him *be* honor and eternal dominion! Amen. – 1 Timothy 6:16

Do you not know that a little leaven leavens the whole lump *of dough*? – 1 Corinthians 5:6

This is the message we have heard from Him and announce to you, that God is Light, and in Him there is no darkness at all. – 1 John 1:5

"For My thoughts are not your thoughts,
Nor are your ways My ways," declares the LORD.
"For *as* the heavens are higher than the earth,
So are My ways higher than your ways
And My thoughts than your thoughts." – Isaiah 55:8-9

Your way, O God, is holy;
What god is great like our God? – Psalm 77:13

Be glad in the LORD, you righteous ones,
And give thanks to His holy name. – Psalm 97:12

But the LORD of hosts will be exalted in judgment,
And the holy God will show Himself holy in righteousness. – Isaiah 5:16

And they sang the song of Moses, the bond-servant of God, and the song of the Lamb, saying,

> "Great and marvelous are Your works,
> O Lord God, the Almighty;
> Righteous and true are Your ways,
> King of the nations!
> "Who will not fear, O Lord, and glorify Your name?
> For You alone are holy;
> For ALL THE NATIONS WILL COME AND WORSHIP BEFORE YOU,
> FOR YOUR RIGHTEOUS ACTS HAVE BEEN REVEALED." – Revelation 15:3b-4

"I kept looking
Until thrones were set up,
And the Ancient of Days took *His* seat;
His vesture *was* like white snow
And the hair of His head like pure wool.
His throne *was* ablaze with flames,
Its wheels *were* a burning fire.
"A river of fire was flowing
And coming out from before Him;
Thousands upon thousands were attending Him,
And myriads upon myriads were standing before Him;
The court sat,
And the books were opened." – Daniel 7:9-10

In the year of King Uzziah's death I saw the Lord sitting on a throne, lofty and exalted, with the train of His robe filling the temple. Seraphim stood above Him, each having six wings: with two he covered his face, and with two he covered his feet, and with two he flew. And one called out to another and said,

"Holy, Holy, Holy, is the LORD of hosts,
The whole earth is full of His glory."

And the foundations of the thresholds trembled at the voice of him who called out, while the temple was filling with smoke. Then I said,

"Woe is me, for I am ruined!
Because I am a man of unclean lips,
And I live among a people of unclean lips;
For my eyes have seen the King, the LORD of hosts." – Isaiah 6:1-5

Then I turned to see the voice that was speaking with me. And having turned I saw seven golden lampstands; and in the middle of the lampstands *I saw* one like a son of man, clothed in a robe reaching to the feet, and girded across His chest with a golden sash. His head and His hair were white like white wool, like snow; and His eyes were like a flame of fire. His feet *were* like burnished bronze, when it has been made to glow in a furnace, and His voice *was* like the sound of many waters. In His right hand He held seven stars, and out of His mouth came a sharp two-edged sword; and His face was like the sun shining in its strength.

When I saw Him, I fell at His feet like a dead man. And He placed His right hand on me, saying, "Do not be afraid; I am the first and the last, and the living One; and I was dead, and behold, I am alive forevermore, and I have the keys of death and of Hades. – Revelation 1:12-18

Out from the throne come flashes of lightning and sounds and peals of thunder. And *there were* seven lamps of fire burning before the throne, which are the seven Spirits of God; and before the throne *there was something* like a sea of glass, like crystal; and in the center and around the throne, four living creatures full of eyes in front and behind. The first creature *was* like a lion, and the second creature like a calf, and the third creature had a face like that of a man, and the fourth creature *was* like a flying eagle. And the four living creatures, each one of them having six wings, are full of eyes around and within; and day and night they do not cease to say,

"Holy, holy, holy *is* the Lord God, the Almighty, who was and who is and who is to come."

And when the living creatures give glory and honor and thanks to Him who sits on the throne, to Him who lives forever and ever, the twenty-four elders will fall down before Him who sits on the throne, and will worship Him who lives forever and ever, and will cast their crowns before the throne, saying,

"Worthy are You, our Lord and our God, to receive glory and honor and power; for You created all things, and because of Your will they existed, and were created."

I saw in the right hand of Him who sat on the throne a book written inside and on the back, sealed up with seven seals. And I saw a strong angel proclaiming with a loud voice, "Who is worthy to open the book and to break its seals?" And no one in heaven or on the earth or under the earth was able to open the book or to look into it. Then I *began* to weep greatly because no one was found worthy to open the book or to look into it; and one of the elders said to me, "Stop weeping; behold, the Lion that is from the tribe of Judah, the Root of David, has overcome so as to open the book and its seven seals."

And I saw between the throne (with the four living creatures) and the elders a Lamb standing, as if slain, having seven horns and seven eyes, which are the seven Spirits of God, sent out into all the earth. And He came and took the book out of the right hand of Him who sat on the throne. When He had taken the book, the four living creatures and the twenty-four elders fell down before the Lamb, each one holding a harp and golden bowls full of incense, which are the prayers of the saints. And they sang a new song, saying,

"Worthy are You to take the book and to break its seals; for You were slain, and purchased for God with Your blood *men* from every tribe and tongue and people and nation.

"You have made them *to be* a kingdom and priests to our God; and they will reign upon the earth."

Then I looked, and I heard the voice of many angels around the throne and the living creatures and the elders; and the number of them was myriads of myriads, and thousands of thousands, saying with a loud voice,

"Worthy is the Lamb that was slain to receive power and riches and wisdom and might and honor and glory and blessing."

And every created thing which is in heaven and on the earth and under the earth and on the sea, and all things in them, I heard saying,

"To Him who sits on the throne, and to the Lamb, *be* blessing and honor and glory and dominion forever and ever." – Revelation 4:5-5:13

4.12 ALL THINGS MADE NEW

And He who sits on the throne said, "Behold, I am making all things new." And He said, "Write, for these words are faithful and true." – Revelation 21:5

To wrap up the good news of the gospel, let's get a glimpse of the future that waits for all those who "call on the name of our Lord Jesus Christ" and take hold of eternal life. What we see around us in this world today is not what we as Christians have to look forward to in the future for all eternity. God has promised to make "all things new." Looking back, we have seen how God's initial creation was without sin, suffering, disease, and death; it was "very good" (i.e., perfect). Then man (Eve and then Adam) disobeyed God, and mankind fell into sin under bondage to Satan and death. God's creation was also "cursed" at that same time; remember that this was done out of love by God, for our own good, so we would not live forever in a state of sin and spiritual separation from God. It is that cursed creation that we see all around us today, and it is still "groaning" under the curse:

> For I consider that the sufferings of this present time are not worthy to be compared with the glory that is to be revealed to us. For the anxious longing of the creation waits eagerly for the revealing of the sons of God. For the creation was subjected to futility, not willingly, but because of Him who subjected it, in hope that the creation itself also will be set free from its slavery to corruption into the freedom of the glory of the children of God. For we know that the whole creation groans and suffers the pains of childbirth together until now. And not only this, but also we ourselves, having the first fruits of the Spirit, even we ourselves groan within ourselves, waiting eagerly for *our* adoption as sons, the redemption of our body. – Romans 8:18-23

So, God sent His Son Jesus Christ to die on the cross to redeem mankind from bondage under sin, Satan and death – and all who choose to accept Jesus as Lord and Savior via His sacrificial death as atonement for their sins are restored to life. First, we are restored to spiritual life ("He restores my soul," "blessed and holy is the one who has a part in the first resurrection"), being "born again" ("born of the Spirit"). When Jesus rose from the dead, He ascended into heaven and was "seated at the right hand of God" the Father, ruling in reigning in His kingdom (which you are in today as a "fellow participant in the tribulation and kingdom and perseverance in Jesus").

Before He ascended, He left us with these promises:

> "Do not let your heart be troubled; believe in God, believe also in Me. In My Father's house are many dwelling places; if it were not so, I would have told you; for I go to prepare a place for you. If I go and prepare a place for you, I will come again and receive you to Myself, that where I am, *there* you may be also." – John 14:1-3

CHRIST'S RETURN

Scripture tells us that Jesus will come back one final time visibly, literally, bodily, in power and glory for all to see (not in some fake "secret rapture" event as some falsely teach) to gather His elect, and to begin the Great Day of Judgment:

And just as it is destined for people to die once, and after this *comes* judgment, so Christ also, having been offered once to bear the sins of many, will appear a second time for salvation without *reference to* sin, to those who eagerly await Him. – Hebrews 9:27-28

And after He had said these things, He [Jesus] was lifted up while they were watching, and a cloud took Him up, out of their sight. And as they were gazing intently into the sky while He was going, then behold, two men in white clothing stood beside them, and they said, "Men of Galilee, why do you stand looking into the sky? This Jesus, who has been taken up from you into heaven, will come in the same way as you have watched Him go into heaven." – Acts 1:9-11

For after all it is *only* just for God to repay with affliction those who afflict you, and *to give* relief to you who are afflicted and to us as well when the Lord Jesus will be revealed from heaven with His mighty angels in flaming fire, dealing out retribution to those who do not know God and to those who do not obey the gospel of our Lord Jesus. These will pay the penalty of eternal destruction, away from the presence of the Lord and from the glory of His power, when He comes to be glorified in His saints on that day, and to be marveled at among all who have believed—for our testimony to you was believed. – 2 Thessalonians 1:6-10

BEHOLD, HE IS COMING WITH THE CLOUDS, and every eye will see Him, even those who pierced Him; and all the tribes of the earth will mourn over Him. So it is to be. Amen. – Revelation 1:7

At the end of time ("the end of the [gospel/church] age"), God has promised to "wipe away every tear," and that "there will be no more death," and we will be "raised to eternal life" in our new "immortal bodies" with Christ:

> Now I say this, brethren, that flesh and blood cannot inherit the kingdom of God; nor does the perishable inherit the imperishable. Behold, I tell you a mystery; we will not all sleep, but we will all be changed, in a moment, in the twinkling of an eye, at the last trumpet; for the trumpet will sound, and the dead will be raised imperishable, and we will be changed. For this perishable must put on the imperishable, and this mortal must put on immortality. But when this perishable will have put on the imperishable, and this mortal will have put on immortality, then will come about the saying that is written, "DEATH IS SWALLOWED UP in victory. O DEATH, WHERE IS YOUR VICTORY? O DEATH, WHERE IS YOUR STING?" The sting of death is sin, and the power of sin is the law; but thanks be to God, who gives us the victory through our Lord Jesus Christ. – 1 Corinthians 15:50-57

Remember that to the Christian, death is not an awful event to be feared and dreaded; instead, it ushers in the hope and reality of eternal life with God and Jesus in heaven. A Christian doesn't have the same perspective as the unsaved man or woman does when facing death. While there is sadness at the loss of a friend or loved one, death is the doorway to eternal life for the child of God. We will be given new heavenly immortal bodies, free from the issues and corruption (decay) we have today in our mortal fleshly bodies. When you are "raised up" on the last day with Christ to "meet the Lord [Jesus] in the air" (this is the actual true and correct "rapture"), your immortal spirit will be united with your new immortal body:

The Message of Truth

> But we do not want you to be uninformed, brothers *and sisters*, about those who are asleep, so that you will not grieve as indeed the rest *of mankind do*, who have no hope. For if we believe that Jesus died and rose *from the dead*, so also God will bring with Him those who have fallen asleep through Jesus. For we say this to you by the word of the Lord, that we who are alive and remain until the coming of the Lord will not precede those who have fallen asleep. For the Lord Himself will descend from heaven with a shout, with the voice of *the* archangel and with the trumpet of God, and the dead in Christ will rise first. Then we who are alive, who remain, will be caught up together with them in the clouds to meet the Lord in the air, and so we will always be with the Lord. – 1 Thessalonians 4:13-17

How amazing that will be! We will see God and His Christ face to face as they really are – in the fullness of their awesome splendor, holiness, and glory, and God will dwell among us, and He will be our Lord and our Light ("the Lord God will illumine them [us]"). Amazing wonders await us in heaven with Jesus for all eternity.

The Bible describes this new heaven and new earth (as well as the Church) as "New Jerusalem," wherein God and righteousness dwells. Scripture gives us this wonderful and highly symbolic description of what it will be like:

> Then I saw a new heaven and a new earth; for the first heaven and the first earth passed away, and there is no longer *any* sea. And I saw the holy city, new Jerusalem, coming down out of heaven from God, made ready as a bride adorned for her husband. And I heard a loud voice from the throne, saying, "Behold, the tabernacle of God is among men, and He will dwell among them, and they shall be His people, and God Himself will be among them, and He will wipe away every tear from their eyes; and there will no longer be *any* death; there will no longer be *any* mourning, or crying, or pain; the first things have passed away."
>
> And He who sits on the throne said, "Behold, I am making all things new." And He said, "Write, for these words are faithful and true." Then He said to me, "It is done. I am the Alpha and the Omega, the beginning and the end. I will give to the one who thirsts from the spring of the water of life without cost. He who overcomes will inherit these things, and I will be his God and he will be My son. But for the cowardly and unbelieving and abominable and murderers and immoral persons and sorcerers and idolaters and all liars, their part *will be* in the lake that burns with fire and brimstone, which is the second death."
>
> Then one of the seven angels who had the seven bowls full of the seven last plagues came and spoke with me, saying, "Come here, I will show you the bride, the wife of the Lamb."
>
> And he carried me away in the Spirit to a great and high mountain, and showed me the holy city, Jerusalem, coming down out of heaven from God, having the glory of God. Her brilliance was like a very costly stone, as a stone of crystal-clear jasper. It had a great and high wall, with twelve gates, and at the gates twelve angels; and names *were* written on them, which are *the names* of the twelve tribes of the sons of Israel. *There were* three gates on the east and three gates on the north and three gates on the south and three gates on the west. And the wall of the city had twelve foundation stones, and on them *were* the twelve names of the twelve apostles of the Lamb.

The one who spoke with me had a gold measuring rod to measure the city, and its gates and its wall. The city is laid out as a square, and its length is as great as the width; and he measured the city with the rod, fifteen hundred miles; its length and width and height are equal. And he measured its wall, seventy-two yards, *according to* human measurements, which are *also* angelic *measurements*. The material of the wall was jasper; and the city was pure gold, like clear glass. The foundation stones of the city wall were adorned with every kind of precious stone. The first foundation stone was jasper; the second, sapphire; the third, chalcedony; the fourth, emerald; the fifth, sardonyx; the sixth, sardius; the seventh, chrysolite; the eighth, beryl; the ninth, topaz; the tenth, chrysoprase; the eleventh, jacinth; the twelfth, amethyst. And the twelve gates were twelve pearls; each one of the gates was a single pearl. And the street of the city was pure gold, like transparent glass.

I saw no temple in it, for the Lord God the Almighty and the Lamb are its temple. And the city has no need of the sun or of the moon to shine on it, for the glory of God has illumined it, and its lamp *is* the Lamb. The nations will walk by its light, and the kings of the earth will bring their glory into it. In the daytime (for there will be no night there) its gates will never be closed; and they will bring the glory and the honor of the nations into it; and nothing unclean, and no one who practices abomination and lying, shall ever come into it, but only those whose names are written in the Lamb's book of life. – Revelation 21:1-27

Then he showed me a river of the water of life, clear as crystal, coming from the throne of God and of the Lamb, in the middle of its street. On either side of the river was the tree of life, bearing twelve *kinds of* fruit, yielding its fruit every month; and the leaves of the tree were for the healing of the nations. There will no longer be any curse; and the throne of God and of the Lamb will be in it, and His bond-servants will serve Him; they will see His face, and His name *will be* on their foreheads. And there will no longer be *any* night; and they will not have need of the light of a lamp nor the light of the sun, because the Lord God will illumine them; and they will reign forever and ever. – Revelation 22:1-5

Again, this passage of Scripture is highly symbolic; it is using the best and noblest of materials we know of today here in this physical world (gold, jasper, sapphire, clear crystal, etc.), to convey to us the almost unimaginable beauty, grandeur, splendor, majesty, and purity of heaven, where nothing unclean (i.e., sinful) enters. Contrast the symbolism and appearance of that pure city of gleaming crystal and gold vs. the appearance of this fallen earthly world that we now inhabit.

It's truly a sad state of affairs, and a disgrace to the mind of man, that even on this final grand and glorious culmination of God's creation and restoration to glory, we must still yet once again fend off the false teachings of man! Some falsely teach that "New Jerusalem" will be a literal city with literal streets of gold with literal mansions we dwell in, etc.; they teach that this earth will simply be "renovated" and that it will be our home for eternity. But we must confront such discouraging nonsense. Wayne Jackson writes on this subject:[74]

---

[74] Jackson, Jason. "What Are the New Heavens and New Earth?" *ChristianCourier.com.* Access date: April 2, 2019. https://christiancourier.com/articles/1159-what-are-the-new-heavens-and-new-earth

The Message of Truth

What Are the New Heavens and New Earth?

"What does the phrase 'new heavens and new earth' (2 Pet. 3:13) mean?"

There are two views concerning the meaning of the phrase, "new heavens and new earth." Since they represent opposing viewpoints, one of them obviously is false. The phrase means either a "renewed earth," or it is a figurative expression for "heaven" itself.

The Premillennial View

Many religious groups advocate the doctrine of premillennialism. There are, however, different forms of premillennialism. For instance, The Watchtower Society, the Seventh-day Adventists, and many Protestant denominations, hold to some form of millennialism. Yet they have significant differences between them.

Although it is not our intent to deal with the theory of premillennialism extensively, we note that those who believe in that dogma envision the "new heavens and new earth" as a **literal** earth, cleansed by fire.

Consider what Peter wrote.

First, the "heavens and earth" of the present are reserved for fire against the "day of judgment" (2 Pet. 3:7).

Second, the Judgment will come unexpectedly and suddenly. The heavens and earth will **pass away** with a great noise, the elements will dissolve with fervent heat, and the earth and its works shall be consumed (2 Pet. 3:10,12).

Third, after the Judgment, there will be the "new heavens and new earth."

Notice what Peter did **not say**. He did not say that the earth would be refurbished to be an earthly paradise. He did not say that the Lord would reign upon the earth. He did not say that anyone would inhabit earth after the Second Coming. No biblical writer affirms any of these ideas.

The "Heavenly" View

Consistent with New Testament teaching concerning "final things," the phrase "new heavens and new earth" stands for the saved environment, following the Judgment Day; this **environment** is more commonly called "heaven" (Mt. 6:19-20).

John wrote, "And I saw a new heaven and a new earth: for the first heaven and the first earth are passed away; and the sea is no more" (Rev. 21:1). The expression "heaven and earth" stands for a place of existence — our familiar environment, i.e., land and sky. But what John saw was not the **first** heaven and earth. It was gone. So, he describes, in symbolic fashion, the place of the realm of the saved, where they shall reign "for ever and ever" — not a mere 1,000 years.

This environment of the saved is simply heaven. Paul wrote that our citizenship is in heaven (Phil. 3:20). The apostle also said that we have **one hope**, and that our hope is in **heaven** (Eph. 4:4; Col. 1:5).

In every respect, heaven will be characterized by newness. It is a place never before inhabited by Christians. It is the first time the saved, in a glorified state, will be in the very presence of God — face to face (cf. 1 Jn. 3:2; Rev. 22:4). This new state, where sin and death are no more, will be the eternal abode of the saved when the Lord returns, and the living are caught up with the redeemed of all ages to be with the Lord forever (cf. 1 Thes. 4:13-18).

So, know that heaven will be glorious – imagine the glory of God beheld face to face, when we will see Him in all His glory for Who, What and how He really is, a place so pure and clean, ahh…now that's what we have to look forward to! Creation will have been restored to righteousness, wherein God's Law, which is the Law of Love, again rules everywhere and where sin, and all things sinful including Satan (the Devil), the angels that sinned and those humans who have chosen to remain in their sins will be banished from heaven forever "away from the presence of the Lord." Those who claimed eternal life in Jesus Christ will then dwell with Him in heaven for all eternity. Amen.

FALSE TEACHING(S) YOU WILL ENCOUNTER:
- Dispensational Premillennialism
- Dispensational Postmillennialism
- Distortions of Matthew 24
- Modern/Popular eschatology (a "Third Temple," etc.)
- This present Earth will simply be "renovated"

RELATED SCRIPTURE:

And the devil who deceived them [all those who followed him instead of Christ] was thrown into the lake of fire and brimstone, where the beast and the false prophet are also; and they will be tormented day and night forever and ever.

Then I saw a great white throne [on the great Day of Judgment] and Him who sat upon it, from whose presence earth and heaven fled away, and no place was found for them. And I saw the dead, the great and the small, standing before the throne, and books were opened; and another book was opened, which is *the book* of life; and the dead were judged from the things which were written in the books, according to their deeds. And the sea gave up the dead which were in it, and death and Hades gave up the dead which were in them; and they were judged, every one *of them* according to their deeds. Then death and Hades were thrown into the lake of fire. This is the second death, the lake of fire. And if anyone's name was not found written in the book of life, he was thrown into the lake of fire. – Revelation 20:10-15

"But when the Son of Man comes in His glory, and all the angels with Him, then He will sit on His glorious throne. And all the nations will be gathered before Him; and He will separate them from one another, just as the shepherd separates the sheep from the goats; and He will put the sheep on His right, but the goats on the left.

"Then the King will say to those on His right, 'Come, you who are blessed of My Father, inherit the kingdom prepared for you from the foundation of the world. For I was hungry, and you gave Me *something* to eat; I was thirsty, and you gave Me *something* to drink; I was a stranger, and you invited Me in; naked, and you clothed Me; I was sick, and you visited Me; I was in prison, and you came to Me.' Then the righteous will answer Him, 'Lord, when did we see You hungry, and feed You, or thirsty, and give You *something* to drink? And when did we see You *as* a stranger, and invite You in, or naked, and clothe You? And when did we see You sick, or in prison, and come to You?' And the King will answer and say to them, 'Truly I say to you, to the extent that you did *it* for one of the least of these brothers *or sisters* of Mine, you did *it* for Me.'

"Then He will also say to those on His left, 'Depart from Me, accursed ones, into the eternal fire which has been prepared for the devil and his angels; for I was hungry, and you gave Me *nothing* to eat; I was thirsty, and you gave Me nothing to drink; I was a stranger, and you did not invite Me in; naked, and you did not clothe Me; sick, and in prison, and you did not visit Me.' Then they themselves also will answer, 'Lord, when did we see You hungry, or thirsty, or a stranger, or naked, or sick, or in prison, and did not take care of You?' Then He will answer them, 'Truly I say to you, to the extent that you did not do it to one of the least of these, you did not do it to Me.' These will go away into eternal punishment, but the righteous into eternal life." – Matthew 25:31-46

Since all these things are to be destroyed in this way, what sort of people ought you to be in holy conduct and godliness, looking for and hastening the coming of the day of God, because of which the heavens will be destroyed by burning, and the elements will melt with intense heat! But according to His promise we are looking for new heavens and a new earth, in which righteousness dwells. – 2 Peter 3:11-13

"His master said to him, 'Well done, good and faithful servant. You have been faithful over a little; I will set you over much. Enter into the joy of your master.'" – Matthew 25:23 (ESV)

"They will hunger no longer, nor thirst anymore; nor will the sun beat down on them, nor any heat; for the Lamb in the center of the throne will be their shepherd, and will guide them to springs of the water of life; and God will wipe every tear from their eyes." – Revelation 7:16-17

"Behold, I am coming quickly, and My reward *is* with Me, to render to every man according to what he has done. I am the Alpha and the Omega, the first and the last, the beginning and the end."

Blessed are those who wash their robes, so that they may have the right to the tree of life, and may enter by the gates into the city. ...

The Spirit and the bride say, "Come." And let the one who hears say, "Come." And let the one who is thirsty come; let the one who wishes take the water of life without cost. – Revelation 22:12-14, 17

He who testifies to these things says, "Yes, I am coming quickly." Amen. Come, Lord Jesus.

The grace of the Lord Jesus be with all. Amen. – Revelation 22:20-21

Beloved, now we are children of God, and it has not appeared as yet what we will be. We know that when He appears, we will be like Him, because we will see Him just as He is. – 1 John 3:2

4.13 NOW GO AND TELL OTHERS

*And He said to them, "Go into all the world
and preach the gospel to all creation." – Mark 16:15*

Ambassadors for Christ. As commanded by Christ, go and share "the message of truth" with another who is still lost, for it is written, "faith *comes* from hearing, and hearing by the word of Christ." We are surrounded by a sea of the lost, and it is written that "the harvest is plentiful, but the workers are few." In an exceedingly dark and sinful world, the little light we can shine can greatly help the lost find their way. It is entirely possible that you might be the only one to share Jesus with someone in their entire lifetime, and it will be beyond horrible to be standing there on Judgment day among the saved (the "sheep," arranged "on His [Jesus] right") and look over and see someone that we knew who is lost forever (the "goats," arranged "on His [Jesus] left") – and realize that we had a chance to reach out and share the gospel with them but never did. Oh, what a tragedy!

Also, remember you are an "ambassador" for Christ, a member of the "royal priesthood" with Christ as your "High Priest" (and "King") – so go forth boldly proclaiming "the message of truth" and be a kingdom builder for Christ as a "fisher of men":

> "Go therefore and make disciples of all the nations, baptizing them in the name of the Father and the Son and the Holy Spirit, teaching them to observe all that I commanded you; and lo, I am with you always, even to the end of the age." – Matthew 28:19-20

> But you are A CHOSEN RACE, A royal PRIESTHOOD, A HOLY NATION, A PEOPLE FOR *God's* OWN POSSESSION, so that you may proclaim the excellencies of Him who has called you out of darkness into His marvelous light; for you once were NOT A PEOPLE, but now you are THE PEOPLE OF GOD; you had NOT RECEIVED MERCY, but now you have RECEIVED MERCY. – 1 Peter 2:9-10

> And he said to them, "Follow me, and I will make you fishers of men." – Matthew 4:19 (ESV)

It is true that you might be ridiculed, mocked, ignored, laughed at, scorned, and even persecuted for sharing the truth, but don't let that stop you, for you are helping others hear about the gift of eternal life. Jesus was treated likewise, and we are not better than our Master. And even further, we are to be joyful if we have been found "worthy to suffer" for His name. We are to not be ashamed, but to proclaim the good news of the gospel "message of truth" with boldness:

> For God has not given us a spirit of timidity, but of power and love and discipline.

> Therefore do not be ashamed of the testimony of our Lord or of me His prisoner, but join with *me* in suffering for the gospel according to the power of God, who has saved us and called us with a holy calling, not according to our works, but according to His own purpose and grace which was granted us in Christ Jesus from all eternity, but now has been revealed by the appearing of our Savior Christ Jesus, who abolished death and brought life and immortality to light through the

gospel, or which I was appointed a preacher and an apostle and a teacher. For this reason I also suffer these things, but I am not ashamed; for I know whom I have believed and I am convinced that He is able to guard what I have entrusted to Him until that day. Retain the standard of sound words which you have heard from me, in the faith and love which are in Christ Jesus. Guard, through the Holy Spirit who dwells in us, the treasure which has been entrusted to *you*. – 2 Timothy 1:7-14

For I am not ashamed of the gospel, for it is the power of God for salvation to everyone who believes, to the Jew first and also to the Greek [Gentiles]. – Romans 1:16

"You are the light of the world. A city set on a hill cannot be hidden; nor does *anyone* light a lamp and put it under a basket, but on the lampstand, and it gives light to all who are in the house. Let your light shine before men in such a way that they may see your good works, and glorify your Father who is in heaven." – Matthew 5:14-16

And when they had prayed, the place where they had gathered together was shaken, and they were all filled with the Holy Spirit and *began* to speak the word of God with boldness. – Acts 4:31

And remember, sharing the gospel message applies to those closest to you as well. For parents who raise their children in the way of the Lord (and the way of truth) do a great honor and service both to themselves and their children; and the husband who leads (guides) his wife into truth and eternal life is showing great leadership in accordance with the commands of God.

THE PARABLE OF THE SOWER

It's instructive at this point to again share the Parable of the Sower:

And He spoke many things to them in parables, saying, "Behold, the sower went out to sow; and as he sowed, some *seeds* fell beside the road, and the birds came and ate them up. Others fell on the rocky places, where they did not have much soil; and immediately they sprang up, because they had no depth of soil. But when the sun had risen, they were scorched; and because they had no root, they withered away. Others fell among the thorns, and the thorns came up and choked them out. And others fell on the good soil and yielded a crop, some a hundredfold, some sixty, and some thirty. He who has ears, let him hear." ... "Hear then the parable of the sower. When anyone hears the word of the kingdom and does not understand it, the evil *one* comes and snatches away what has been sown in his heart. This is the one on whom seed was sown beside the road. The one on whom seed was sown on the rocky places, this is the man who hears the word and immediately receives it with joy; yet he has no *firm* root in himself, but is *only* temporary, and when affliction or persecution arises because of the word, immediately he falls away. And the one on whom seed was sown among the thorns, this is the man who hears the word, and the worry of the world and the deceitfulness of wealth choke the word, and it becomes unfruitful. And the one on whom seed was sown on the good soil, this is the man who hears the word and understands it; who indeed bears fruit and brings forth, some a hundredfold, some sixty, and some thirty." – Matthew 13:3-9,18-23

"You are the light of the world. A city set on a hill cannot be hidden." – Matthew 5:14

From the parable, Christ is the sower who spreads the seed (as well as His evangelists, i.e., you), which is "the message [word] of truth" – by boldly proclaiming the gospel message as the "light of the world" and as a "city set on a hill." The type of ground represents the type of person who has heard "the message of truth":

- Hard Packed: The roadside soil where the seed falls on the hardened ground and is not understood or believed and therefore snatched away again with no effect by Satan, leaving no impact on the one who heard it who had no interest in it, or
- Rocky: The rocky soil where the seed is received eagerly at first and for a time, but then discarded through neglect or when trial and tribulation or persecution arise, or
- Thorny: The thorny soil is where the cares and desires for the pleasures of this world win out over perseverance in faith, which therefore chokes out the seed from growing, or
- Good: The good soil which receives the Word in truth and fullness, growing and maturing in Christ and always abounding in the work of the Lord, producing a crop 30x, 60x, or 100x for the Lord, and persevering in faith unto death.

Matthew Henry writes on the parable: [75]

1) While the good soil brings forth plentifully: so it is with the hearts of men, whose different characters are here represented by four sorts of ground, of which three are bad, and but one good. Note, the number of fruitless hearers is very great, even of those who heard Christ himself. Who has believed our report?
2) The sower that scatters the seed is our Lord Jesus Christ, either by himself, or by his ministers. The people are God's husbandry, his tillage, so the word is; and ministers are laborer's together with God (1 Corinthians 3:9). Preaching to a multitude is sowing the corn; we know not where it must light; only see that it be good, that it be clean, [that it be pure] and be sure to give it seed enough. The sowing of the word is the sowing of a people for God's field [Christ's Kingdom], the corn of his floor (Isaiah 21:10).

Now that this book has sown the seed of "the message of truth" in you, what type of soil will you be?

THOSE WHO LEAD THE MANY TO RIGHTEOUSNESS

It is written that "those who lead the many to righteousness, [will shine] like the stars forever and ever." When I was writing this book, a thought crossed my mind that if I had died today, I would shine in heaven like a lump of coal! Yes, if you took my entire life and added it up to see what I had done to grow the "Kingdom of God," it would add up to a big fat nothing, zilch, nada – not a single thing that I could think of! Yes, my entire life added up to nothing. All my works would have been burned up to

---

[75] Henry, Matthew. *Exposition of the Old and New Testaments*, London. 1706-1710/1721.

nothing on the great Day of Judgment; I hope to change that. There are three things I hope to hear from the Lord on the Last Day:

1) Well done good and faithful servant, enter into My rest,
2) You have correctly divided (handled) the Word of Truth, and
3) Receive your crown of life

> For,
>
> > "ALL FLESH IS LIKE GRASS,
> > AND ALL ITS GLORY LIKE THE FLOWER OF GRASS.
> > THE GRASS WITHERS,
> > AND THE FLOWER FALLS OFF,
> > BUT THE WORD OF THE LORD ENDURES FOREVER."
>
> And this is the word which was preached to you. – 1 Peter 1:24-25

Therefore, I testify to you this day that I am innocent of the blood of all men. For I did not shrink from declaring to you the whole purpose of God. – Acts 20:26-27

For if I preach the gospel, I have nothing to boast of, for I am under compulsion; for woe is me if I do not preach the gospel. – 1 Corinthians 9:16

In Him, you also, after listening to the message of truth, the gospel of your salvation—having also believed, you were sealed in Him with the Holy Spirit of promise, who is given as a pledge of our inheritance, with a view to the redemption of *God's own* possession, to the praise of His glory. – Ephesians 1:13-14

H. M. Riggle writes in *The Christian Church, Its Rise and Progress*: [76]

> He [Jesus] testified, saying, "The words that I speak unto you I speak not of myself: but the Father that dwelleth in me, he doeth the works" John 14:10. Therefore "God, who at sundry times and in divers manners spake in time past unto the fathers by the prophets, hath in these last days spoken unto us by his Son" Heb. 1:1-2. This adorable Christ came into the world and delivered the perfect laws of His kingdom, and when about to finish His mission on earth He said, "I have given unto them the words which thou gavest me; and they have received them." John 17:8.
>
> And when He sent forth His ministers to preach His gospel to every creature, He commissioned them to make disciples in all nations, "baptizing them in the name of the Father, and of the Son, and of the Holy Ghost: teaching them to observe all things whatsoever I have commanded you" (Matt. 28:19-20). Thus we see that Christ Jesus spoke all the words that the Father "put into his mouth," and all that He had commanded Him to speak; and the Son likewise commissioned His apostles to publish all that, and only that, which He gave them.

IT IS FINISHED

And so now friend (and hopefully new brother or sister in Christ), I have declared to you, and you have read and heard the whole gospel "message [word] of truth" and the hope that can be found in Jesus Christ, from start to finish, free from the distortions,

---

[76] Riggle, H.M. (1912), The Christian Church, Its Rise and Progress, (The Gospel Trumpet Company).

myths, mystical beliefs, superstitions, "traditions" and myriads of modern and liberal false teachings and schemes of man which abound today. The eternal question is: What will you do with it? Will you act on it and be wise or ignore it? Will you seek the wisdom of God or the wisdom of man?

Will you discard it like "hard packed" soil, or will you believe it? Will you start out enthusiastically and then grow tired and stop (quit the faith, "fall away") when trials and tribulations come your way ("rocky soil"). Will you let it get choked out by the continued pursuit of the things of this world and the cares of this world ("thorny soil")? I pray you receive "the message of truth" with gladness, sincerity of heart, and now go forth abundantly in Christ, always "abounding in the work of the Lord," working in His Kingdom to "go into all the world and preach the gospel to all creation," producing a crop ("bearing fruit") of "thirty," "sixty" or a "hundredfold" for the Lord. If I were to ask you next year how many have you led to the Lord, would the answer be: 30? 60? Or a hundredfold? Or would it be zero? Only you can honestly answer that.

The Bible is full of characters that we can read and learn from, great men and women of faith who have come before us. Which one will you be like: A Pharaoh of Egypt, a Saul (the first King of Israel), a David, a Judas (Iscariot), a Demas, an Ananias, a Peter, a Paul, a Daniel, a Samaritan woman at the well, a Noah, a Cain or an Abel? …the choice is yours (and mine) to make. And, as this book has shown you, there are only two great families of people on Earth: those who stand with and for the Lord through faith in Jesus Christ and those who are against Him (and with Satan).

> Fight the good fight of faith; take hold of the eternal life to which you were called, and you made the good confession in the presence of many witnesses. I charge you in the presence of God, who gives life to all things, and of Christ Jesus, who testified the good confession before Pontius Pilate, that you keep the commandment without stain or reproach until the appearing of our Lord Jesus Christ, which He will bring about at the proper time—He who is the blessed and only Sovereign, the King of kings and Lord of lords, who alone possesses immortality and dwells in unapproachable light, whom no man has seen or can see. To Him *be* honor and eternal dominion! Amen. – 1 Timothy 6:12-16

The remaining sections of the book provide some helpful advice on what I have found to be effective in beginning my walk as a Christian (Next Steps) and also on avoiding the false teachings of man (Beware the Wolves). For while you have now read and heard the gospel "message of truth," you have also seen that we have had to relentlessly fight off the false teachings of man and the "spirit of error" at every single step along the way – from the very beginning in Genesis all the way to the end in Revelation. "Be on guard" and "be on the alert," both for Christ's return and because you can still yet be "tricked" out of your "crown of life"! I therefore strongly encourage you to continue reading the remainder of this book, and to continue "grow[ing] in the grace and knowledge [understanding] of our Lord and Savior Jesus Christ" so you can "stand firm," "fight the good fight of faith," "finish the race" and not "come short of" eternal life with God and His Christ Jesus in heaven.

Now may you have life, joy, rest, and peace in Christ, and may He raise you up to eternal life with Him on the Last Day. Amen.

> Jesus said to them, "I am the bread of life; he who comes to Me will not hunger, and he who believes in Me will never thirst. But I said to you that you have seen

Me, and yet do not believe. All that the Father gives Me will come to Me, and the one who comes to Me I will certainly not cast out. For I have come down from heaven, not to do My own will, but the will of Him who sent Me. This is the will of Him who sent Me, that of all that He has given Me I lose nothing, but raise it up on the last day. For this is the will of My Father, that everyone who beholds the Son and believes in Him will have eternal life, and I Myself will raise him up on the last day." – John 6:35-40

And Jesus said "It is finished" – John 19:30

***

RELATED SCRIPTURE:

And He said to them, "Go into all the world and preach the gospel to all creation. He who has believed and has been baptized shall be saved; but he who has disbelieved shall be condemned." – Mark 16:15-16

Finally, brethren, pray for us that the word of the Lord will spread rapidly and be glorified, just as it did also with you. – 2 Thessalonians 3:1

Now if any man builds on the foundation with gold, silver, precious stones, wood, hay, straw, each man's work will become evident; for the day [the great Day of Judgment] will show it because it is *to be* revealed with fire, and the fire itself will test the quality of each man's work. If any man's work which he has built on it remains, he will receive a reward. If any man's work is burned up, he will suffer loss; but he himself will be saved, yet so as through fire. – 1 Corinthians 3:12-15

Now as they observed the confidence [boldness] of Peter and John and understood that they were uneducated and untrained men, they were amazed, and *began* to recognize them as having been with Jesus. – Acts 4:13

They laid hands on the apostles and put them in a public jail. But during the night an angel of the Lord opened the gates of the prison, and taking them out he said, "Go, stand and speak to the people in the temple the whole message of this Life." Upon hearing *this*, they entered into the temple about daybreak and *began* to teach. – Acts 5:18-21

And He ordered us to preach to the people, and solemnly to testify that this is the One who has been appointed by God as Judge of the living and the dead. – Acts 10:42

And when I came to you, brethren, I did not come with superiority of speech or of wisdom, proclaiming to you the testimony of God. For I determined to know nothing among you except Jesus Christ, and Him crucified. I was with you in weakness and in fear and in much trembling, and my message and my preaching were not in persuasive words of wisdom, but in demonstration of the Spirit and of power, so that your faith would not rest on the wisdom of men, but on the power of God. – 1 Corinthians 2:1-5

"When I say to the wicked, 'You will surely die,' and you do not warn him or speak out to warn the wicked from his wicked way that he may live, that wicked man shall die in his iniquity, but his blood I will require at your hand. Yet if you have warned the wicked and he does not turn from his wickedness or from his wicked way, he shall die in his iniquity; but you have delivered yourself." – Ezekiel 3:18-19

The third time he said to him, "Simon son of John, do you love me?"

Peter was hurt because Jesus asked him the third time, "Do you love me?" He said, "Lord, you know all things; you know that I love you."

Jesus said, "Feed my sheep." – John 21:17 [Note: We do this "feeding" by preaching and teaching the Word of God, see Matthew 4:4.]

Then He said to His disciples, "The harvest is plentiful, but the workers are few. Therefore beseech the Lord of the harvest to send out workers into His harvest." – Matthew 9:37-38

Preach the word; be ready in season *and* out of season. – 2 Timothy 4:2

And the word of the LORD came to me, saying, "Son of man, speak to the sons of your people and say to them, 'If I bring a sword upon a land, and the people of the land take one man from among them and make him their watchman, and he sees the sword coming upon the land and blows on the trumpet and warns the people, then he who hears the sound of the trumpet and does not take warning, and a sword comes and takes him away, his blood will be on his *own* head. He heard the sound of the trumpet but did not take warning; his blood will be on himself. But had he taken warning, he would have delivered his life. But if the watchman sees the sword coming and does not blow the trumpet and the people are not warned, and a sword comes and takes a person from them, he is taken away in his iniquity; but his blood I will require from the watchman's hand.'" – Ezekiel 33:1-6

How then will they call on Him in whom they have not believed? How will they believe in Him whom they have not heard? And how will they hear without a preacher? How will they preach unless they are sent? Just as it is written, "HOW BEAUTIFUL ARE THE FEET OF THOSE WHO BRING GOOD NEWS OF GOOD THINGS!"

However, they did not all heed the good news; for Isaiah says, "LORD, WHO HAS BELIEVED OUR REPORT?" So faith *comes* from hearing, and hearing by the word of Christ. – Romans 10:14-17

And I am not writing these things so that it will be done so in my case; for it would be better for me to die than have any man make my boast an empty one. For if I preach the gospel, I have nothing to boast of, for I am under compulsion; for woe is me if I do not preach the gospel. For if I do this voluntarily, I have a reward; but if against my will, I have a stewardship entrusted to me. What then is my reward? That, when I preach the gospel, I may offer the gospel without charge, so as not to make full use of my right in the gospel. – 1 Corinthians 9:15b-18

The Spirit of the Lord GOD is upon me,
Because the LORD has anointed me
To bring good news to the afflicted;
He has sent me to bind up the brokenhearted,
To proclaim liberty to captives
And freedom to prisoners;
To proclaim the favorable year of the LORD
And the day of vengeance of our God;

The Message of Truth

To comfort all who mourn,
To grant those who mourn *in* Zion,
Giving them a garland instead of ashes,
The oil of gladness instead of mourning,
The mantle of praise instead of a spirit of fainting.
So they will be called oaks of righteousness,
The planting of the LORD, that He may be glorified. – Isaiah 61:1-3

First of all, then, I urge that entreaties *and* prayers, petitions *and* thanksgivings, be made on behalf of all men, for kings and all who are in authority, so that we may lead a tranquil and quiet life in all godliness and dignity. This is good and acceptable in the sight of God our Savior, who desires all men to be saved and to come to the knowledge of the truth. – 1 Timothy 2:1-4

With all prayer and petition pray at all times in the Spirit, and with this in view, be on the alert with all perseverance and petition for all the saints, and *pray* on my behalf, that utterance may be given to me in the opening of my mouth, to make known with boldness the mystery of the gospel, for which I am an ambassador in chains; that in *proclaiming* it I may speak boldly, as I ought to speak. – Ephesians 6:18-20

Those who have insight will shine brightly like the brightness of the expanse of heaven, and those who lead the many to righteousness, like the stars forever and ever. – Daniel 12:3

Let us not lose heart in doing good, for in due time we will reap if we do not grow weary. – Galatians 6:9

Then I heard the voice of the Lord, saying, "Whom shall I send, and who will go for Us?" Then I said, "Here am I. Send me!" – Isaiah 6:8

"His master said to him, 'Well done, good and faithful servant. You have been faithful over a little; I will set you over much. Enter into the joy of your master.'" – Matthew 25:23 (ESV)

And Jesus said to them, "Follow Me, and I will have you become fishers of people." – Mark 1:17

…sanctify Christ as Lord in your hearts, always *being* ready to make a defense to everyone who asks you to give an account for the hope that is in you, yet with gentleness and reverence. – 1 Peter 3:15

PART V:

NEXT STEPS

5.0 THE STRAIT AND NARROW PATH

*"Enter through the narrow gate;
for the gate is wide and the way is broad that leads to destruction,
and there are many who enter through it." – Matthew 7:13*

This section is written for new believers in Christ who have been "born again" in accordance with Scripture. You may be wondering, great, what do I do now? I don't feel any different! What do I do next? How do I live as a true Christian? Looking back, I didn't do the basic things that any/all Christians should be doing. I didn't know any better; perhaps others tried to tell me, and I just didn't listen or hear them. Regardless, I have learned from my experience, and now I hope to help you avoid the same mistakes I made.

Becoming a Christian doesn't mean you accept Christ ("get saved"), and then that's all there is to it, that you can simply continue to live your life just like you always have. Christianity is a way of life until death, not something that is done and over with in an instant. It means to truly dedicate your life to the Lord Jesus Christ and to pick up the cross each and every day of your life and follow Him, no matter what. It means seeking the will of God through Christ, denying oneself for Him, learning and obeying His teachings (commandments), growing and abounding in His grace and knowledge each day, and remaining faithful (persevering in faith) unto death.

I wrote this section of the book because after I was born again, I traveled way off the narrow road to Christ in the years after that, and I never really knew why (I figured that out later). Yes, I was a believer in Christ, but I didn't feel any different. I didn't get any warm fuzzy feeling all over when I confessed Christ. I didn't see a vision, or bright lights, or angels, or speak in tongues (which isn't biblical today anyway), or see heaven, etc. I didn't really feel anything. It was just a conscious decision to accept Jesus.

No one ever sat me down and helped me understand the basics of being a Christian, or the next steps going forward, or anything. I was a baby Christian, but I still didn't know anything or how I should live now. I continued to live life pretty much as I always had before I accepted Christ, and my life, therefore, continued to be a pretty big mess (see my testimony). In fact, it actually got much worse after I accepted Christ. That's not His fault; it's mine. It is a very dangerous world, and it is a long and dangerous journey that the Christian travels, with many traps, snares, pits, worldly temptations still present, false teachings, false prophets, "wolves in sheep's clothing," and other fatal lures which can trip you up and cause you to "come short of" your goal, which is eternal life with God and His Christ in heaven for eternity. We are told:

> "Behold, I send you out as sheep in the midst of wolves; so be shrewd as serpents and innocent as doves." – Matthew 10:16

> Little children, guard yourselves from idols. – 1 John 5:19-21

> Therefore, we must fear if, while a promise remains of entering His rest, any one of you may seem to have come short *of it*. – Hebrews 4:1

Matthew Henry reinforces the inspired apostle's admonition to keep ourselves spotless and pure, undefiled by the idols of this world, lest you find yourself standing before God once again naked and ashamed/disgraced on the great Day of Judgment: [77]

> The apostle's concluding monition: "Little children" (dear children, as it has been interpreted), "keep yourselves from idols," 1Jn 5:21. Since you know the true God, and are in him, let your light and love guard you against all that is advanced in opposition to him, or competition with him. Flee from the false gods of the heathen world [i.e., idol worship, false religions, fame, power, wealth, money, lust, etc.]
>
> They are not comparable to the God whose you are and whom you serve. Adore not your God by statues and images, which share in his worship. Your God is an incomprehensible Spirit and is disgraced by such sordid representations. Hold no communion with your heathen neighbors in their idolatrous worship. Your God is jealous, and would have you come out, and be separated from among them; mortify the flesh, and be crucified to the world, that they may not usurp the throne of dominion in the heart, which is due only to God.
>
> The God whom you have known is he who made you, who redeemed you by his Son, who has sent his gospel to you, who has pardoned your sins, begotten you unto himself by his Spirit, and given you eternal life. Cleave to him in faith, and love, and constant obedience, in opposition to all things that would alienate your mind and heart from God. To this living and true God be glory and dominion for ever and ever. Amen.

So, to help you out, I've outlined a few steps in this section of the book that you should take as a new Christian. Although I've arranged them in the sequence that I think works best, the steps aren't necessarily given in chronological order. Some of the steps are quite simple (changing your radio habits), while others can be unbelievably difficult (e.g., finding a church, changing your worldly habits) – at least they were for me. While the prior sections of this book laid out doctrine as given in Scripture, this section is more subjective as it contains my opinions on some things. In effect, I'm describing and showing you what has worked best for me as a Christian. But know that what worked best for me may not work best for you.

Above all, remember to continually ask God for wisdom (James 1:5) as you now live in and for Him and walk with Christ. He will guide you; He will never leave or forsake you. Ask, and you shall receive.

NEXT STEPS:
1. Choosing a Bible
2. Reading & Studying the Bible
3. Start Memorizing Verses
4. Finding a Church
5. Utilizing Technology (Apps, etc.)
6. Changing Your Worldly Habits
7. Changing Your Entertainment Habits
8. Attending a New Believer/Believer 101 Starter Class

---

[77] Henry, Matthew. *Exposition of the Old and New Testaments*, London. 1706-1710/1721.

9. Finding Your First Bible Study
10. Being a Berean
11. Essential First 30-Days Activities

5.1 CHOOSING A BIBLE

All Scripture is inspired by God and profitable for teaching, for reproof, for correction, for training in righteousness; so that the man of God may be adequate, equipped for every good work. – 2 Timothy 3:16-17

It is through His Word, the Holy Bible (i.e., Scripture), that God has revealed Himself to us (as well as through His Son Jesus Christ). We are therefore called to read and study Scripture daily as a child of God:

> All Scripture is inspired by God and profitable for teaching, for reproof, for correction, for training in righteousness; so that the man of God may be adequate, equipped for every good work. – 2 Timothy 3:16-17

> But He [Jesus] answered and said, "It is written, 'MAN SHALL NOT LIVE ON BREAD ALONE, BUT ON EVERY WORD THAT PROCEEDS OUT OF THE MOUTH OF GOD.'" – Matthew 4:4

> The brethren immediately sent Paul and Silas away by night to Berea [the Bereans], and when they arrived, they went into the synagogue of the Jews. Now these were more noble-minded than those in Thessalonica, for they received the word with great eagerness, examining the Scriptures daily *to see* whether these things were so. – Acts 17:10-11

Those are powerful verses, and Matthew 4:4, in particular, is a staggering statement: when you are born again, your new spirit actually feeds on the Word of God! Amazing! Because of this, reading the Bible is among the most important things you can do, perhaps the most important thing (along with prayer). Just as your fleshly body needs food to live, your new spirit needs to be fed the Word of God. If you do not read, study, and meditate on the Word, you will drift away from Christ and back towards this world and sin – towards spiritual death again. Make no mistake, this risk is very real, for it happened to me. As I've explained in this book, you can "fall away" even after being born again. In my own experience, I've found that skipping just a few days of Bible reading can lead to a feeling of separation from God – almost like He is hiding from you. But of course, it is not God who is hiding; it is your new spirit starving for His Word.

So, to begin, you must get a Bible to read and study. There are many different kinds of Bibles, along with a myriad of translations available. It's like navigating a maze. This chapter, therefore, outlines some things to consider when choosing a Bible. I once again focus on what has worked best for me.

ORIGIN OF THE BIBLE (AND THE CANON OF SCRIPTURE)

First, a little background – what exactly is the Bible, and where did it come from? The completed canon of Scripture (the set of 66 books we now have in the Bible) was written by human authors over a period of several thousand years; these human writers were inspired by God (via the Holy Spirit, the Third Person of the Trinity). A common question is: Who determined which books to include in the Bible. Wayne Jackson writes:[78]

> ### The Canon of Sacred Scripture
>
> Bible scholars refer to the "canon" of the Scriptures. What is meant by that expression? The term "canon" is an anglicized form of the Greek *kanon*. Originally, the word had to do with a straight rod or rule, to which a builder would compare his work for trueness.
>
> Gradually, the term came to be employed figuratively of a "norm or standard." In his letter to the Galatians, Paul referred to the "rule" (*kanon*) by which Christians are expected to live (6:16). Eventually, the expression came to signify that which has "passed the test."
>
> When, therefore, the word is applied to the books of the Bible, it denotes those documents which, over a period of time, have passed the test of critical examination, hence, warrant the designation "sacred scripture." In his **Commentary on Matthew**, Origen (c. A.D. 185-254), one of the Greek "church fathers," alluded to the "canonized Scriptures" (Sec. 28). Today, the "Canon" refers to those 66 books which constitute the common Bible.
>
> But this introduces several questions. Who determined which books were to go into the Bible? Exactly when did that occur? And what are the Apocryphal books?
>
> ### The Standard of Determination
>
> The question of: "which books belong in the Bible?" was determined gradually and on the basis of *evidence*. By "gradually" we mean that there was not a definite historical date when a synod or council made a determination — "these are the true biblical books!" Rather, over a period of years, by the application of reasonable tests, the documents truly inspired were separated from those works that are spurious. The evidence leading to this decision is classified as *external* and *internal*.
>
> External evidence has to do with the testimony of those who had access to the documents originally. How did they view them, and why?
>
> Internal evidence relates to the nature of the material itself. Does it claim to be from God? Is it internally consistent? Does it harmonize with other documents that are perceived to be inspired? Is it characterized by a lofty tone, i.e., that "essence" which one would expect in a narrative that claims inspiration? Does it bear the marks of factual accuracy?
>
> These sorts of things, as applied by reasonable minds, ultimately separated the genuinely sacred books from those unworthy of that recognition.
>
> ### Old Testament Books
>
> Jewish tradition traces the collection of the Old Testament books to the time of Ezra (mid-5th century B.C.). It may have been a while later before the entire "canon" was actually recognized. By the time Christ was born, there were two versions of the Old Testament.

---

[78] Jackson, Wayne. "The Canon of Sacred Scripture." *ChristianCourier.com*. Access date: March 7, 2019. https://christiancourier.com/articles/757-canon-of-sacred-scripture-the

The Hebrew canon consisted of the 39 books that currently make up our Old Testament — though in the Palestinian version they numbered only 24 (due to a different arrangement — some books being combined).

The Septuagint version (a Greek translation from the 3rd/2nd centuries B.C.) contained various other documents which were "bound up" with the regular 39 books of the Hebrew Bible (the number of these extra books varying in different editions). While these additional books, called the Apocrypha, reflected some historical matters, they were not perceived as "inspired" by God, and, significantly, were never sanctioned by Christ nor any New Testament writer. Some of them, though, are incorporated into Roman Catholic editions of the Bible. For a review of this, see "The Apocrypha: Inspired of God?" elsewhere on this web site.

One of the most significant evidences for the sacred nature of the Old Testament books is the manner in which they are quoted, or alluded to, in the New Testament, having the sanction of Christ and his sacred penmen.

According to one computation (Horn, p. 173), the New Testament contains 433 direct quotations from the Old Testament.[79] No less than 30 of the 39 books are definitely quoted, with numerous additional allusions.

Moreover, it is not just the fact that the Old Testament is quoted, it is the *way* in which it is quoted that is significant. The technical phrase, "It is written" (used of an *inspired* work — cf. Thayer, p. 121) is employed in 73 New Testament passages.[80] In some 21 New Testament passages, the Old Testament documents are referred to as "scripture."

Quotations from at least 11 of the Old Testament books are attributed to God or the Holy Spirit. For example, Peter, quoting from Psalm 69, says that "it was needful that the scripture should be fulfilled, which the *Holy Spirit spake* before by the mouth of David" (Acts 1:1 6ff). In some 46 New Testament passages, the names of 10 Old Testament books (or authors) are mentioned.

Again, let us emphasize that no Apocryphal book from the LXX is given endorsement, even though the New Testament writers were familiar with these books.

New Testament Books

The New Testament authors considered their writings to be as authoritative as those of the Old Testament scriptures. For example, Paul quotes from the book of Deuteronomy (25:4), and the Gospel of Luke (10:7) and classifies both of these as "scripture" (1 Tim. 5:18).

Peter places "all" of Paul's "epistles" in the same category as "the other scriptures" (2 Pet. 3:16). The word "other" translates the Greek *loipos* which denotes "the *rest of any number* or *class* under consideration" (Thayer, p. 382). Too, note how Peter puts the "apostles" in the same category as the "holy prophets" of Old Testament fame (2 Pet. 3:2).

The ancient church was unanimous in its acceptance of most of the New Testament books; for a while there was some dispute over James, 2nd & 3rd John, Jude, Hebrews and Revelation. Too, during this time period (2nd/3rd centuries), other books, which had generated some interest (e.g., the "Epistle of Barnabas," the

---

[79] Horn, S. H. 1960. *SDA Bible Dictionary*. Washington: Review & Herald.

[80] Thayer, J. H. 1958. *Greek-English Lexicon*. Edinburgh: T. & T. Clark.

"Shepherd of Hermas") were being eliminated. By the 4th century, it was a settled issue that the currently accepted 27 books of our New Testament, and only these, are canonical.

It was not a matter of any official council "deciding" which books would be acknowledged as "inspired"; it was a matter of critically examining, sorting, sifting, and identifying what had become perfectly obvious.

The writings of the New Testament were so profusely quoted by the antenicene "fathers" (AD. 325 and back), that it is said that if the whole New Testament were destroyed, it could be reproduced entirely from their citations — with the exception of about a dozen verses (Hastings, p. 12).[81]

Conclusion

We may have every confidence, therefore, that the sixty-six books which compose our present Bible are the true embodiment of the Word of God.

Let us now learn about the different types of Bibles available and how best to read (and study) them.

BIBLE TYPES

There are many different types of Bibles:

- Compact (easy to carry) Bibles,
- Regular (for lack of a better word) Bibles,
- Study Bibles,
- Life Application Study Bibles,
- Journaling Bibles,
- Specialty Bibles (e.g., women's, men's, teen, prophecy, recovery, etc., etc.)

For your first and main Bible, it is best to get a study Bible that has commentary/notes in it to help you understand it. The notes may also help you understand how it can be applied in your life. I've found that the Life Application Study Bible has been the best choice for me when starting out as a new baby Christian. While it's a bit bigger to carry around than some of the others, the study notes with each verse helped me figure out how the verse(s) apply in my life.

The difference between a "Life Application" study Bible vs. a regular study Bible is that the life application notes help you see how the Bible can be applied in your daily life, while study Bibles help you understand Scripture to Scripture references at a deeper level. For me, I needed to know how to apply the Scripture in my own life to start with.

If you want, also get a second compact or regular Bible to take with you while traveling, etc.…but for the first year or two, it would be highly profitable to spend your time mainly using your study Bible. Don't be afraid to get it all marked up and worn…Bibles like that kind of treatment!

I'm making these suggestions based on adults, with reasonable reading skills, not for kids, teens, those with learning disabilities, etc., …as I don't have any experience with those areas personally. I should also point out that the further you get into the specialty Bibles, the more chance you have of editors and publishers introducing their own theology, doctrines, and false teachings, so be very, very careful.

---

[81] Hastings, H. L. 1890. *The Inspiration of the Bible*. Elgin, IL: Brethren Publishing House.

Bibles are available today in both print and electronic versions that you can take along with you on your phone or tablet. I use both; in fact, I have about ten different translations on my phone and tablet, all easily accessible wherever I go!

BIBLE TRANSLATIONS/VERSIONS

The books of the Bible were originally written in Hebrew, Aramaic, and Greek, typically on animal skin or parchment scrolls. Scribes over the years were meticulous in preserving the Word of God, and the accuracy across all of the earliest known versions of the Bible is stunning. In these original languages, the Bible is inerrant – without error.

But very few of us today can read those original languages; so, instead, we must find a translation that has been done into a modern language that we can read and understand. And as these translations are done by men (or committees), there is the possibility of introducing errors. To perform any translation, choices must be made about how to best render the original words in the new language; and sometimes, there is no exact modern counterpart for the original language words. So, we'll tackle next the hardest part of picking a Bible: which translation to read.

Below is a list of the English translations that are commonly available today (in alphabetical order):

- 21st Century King James Version (KJ21)
- American Standard Version (ASV)
- Amplified Bible (AMP)
- Bible in Basic English (BBE)
- Bishops' Bible
- Common English Bible (CEB)
- Complete Jewish Bible (CJB)
- Contemporary English Version (CEV)
- Douay-Rheims Version (DRV)
- Easy-To-Read Version (ERV)
- English Standard Version (ESV)
- Geneva Bible
- God's Word Translation (GW)
- Good News Bible (GNB) / Today's English Version (TEV)
- Green's Literal Translation (LITV)
- Holman Christian Standard Bible (HCSB)
- Jerusalem Bible (JB)
- King James Version (KJV), 1611
- Modern English Version (MEV)
- Modern King James Version (MKJV)
- New American Bible (NAB)
- New American Standard Bible (NASB)
- New Century Version (NCV)
- New English Bible (NEB)
- New English Translation (NET)
- New International Readers Version (NIRV)
- New International Version (NIV)
- New King James Version (NKJV)

- New Living Translation (NLT)
- New Revised Standard Version (NRSV)
- Open Bible
- Revised English Bible (REB)
- Revised Standard Version (RSV)
- The Living Bible (TLB)
- The Message (MSG)
- Today's English Version (TEV)/ Good News Bible (GNB)
- Today's New International Version (TNIV)
- Tyndale Bible
- World English Bible (WEB)
- Young's Literal Translation (YLT)

Wow, that's quite a list! As you can see, there are many translations to choose from, with new ones seemingly being added every year. There are many heated opinions about why one translation is better than another. Once again, I'm simply going to suggest what has worked best for me. I have therefore underlined the ones which I think are worthy of serious consideration to be your main Bible. My first (and still current) main Bible is the NASB translation. I have also found the not as widely known LITV and YLT translations to be helpful at times when comparing word choices.

Note that some "KJV Only" zealots claim that the 1611 KJV translation is the only correct English language Bible ever published. This "KJV Only" false teaching is covered in more detail in the Beware the Wolves chapter, but I mention it here again because it is proclaimed in ferocious volume to scare you. The "KJV Only" zealots are even so bold as to claim that if you use any other translation, you will go to hell! This is complete rubbish and utter nonsense. Furthermore, even the KJV translation has well-documented issues where the translators made unfortunate word choices. All translations involve choices by the translators, and the 1611 KJV is no different. While the KJV Bible is certainly a good and regal one (one of the better ones, in fact), it is just one of several that you should be reading and comparing.

It's a further point of note that the various translations started from different sets of original manuscripts (in Greek, Aramaic, and Hebrew); that is a fascinating topic in itself to learn more about, but it is beyond the scope of this book.

TRANSLATION METHODS

There are also three methods used when making translations:

1. **Literal (Formal Equivalence) Translations**: This type of translation aims to perform a word-for-word translation from the original manuscripts (e.g., the KJV, NKJV, NASB),
2. **Dynamic Equivalence Translations**: This type of translation uses a thought-for-thought method of translating the original manuscripts (e.g., the NIV, TEV/GNB), and
3. **Paraphrase Translations**: This type of translation involves the translator rewriting/rewording in the new language what they think the original manuscript stated (e.g., the NLT, MSG, TLB). Anytime you are dealing with a paraphrase translation, you are not reading the original words – you are instead reading what the interpreters thought the verses were saying! Therefore, this method of translation is wide open to abuse (even

unintentionally) and allows the translator/editor/publisher to insert their own opinions and theology. Because of this issue, I do not recommend this type of translation for your main Bible. In fact, be very wary of these types of Bibles.

The majority opinion, and I agree with it, is that literal translations produce the most accurate results. I have already factored this advice in when underlining the prior translations.

MY RECOMMENDATION

So, what is one to make of all this, with so many types of Bibles and different translations to choose from? Here's my advice, which I follow myself: I recommend that you use one of the literal translations as your main reading/study Bible and that you also compare at least five (5) different translations side-by-side whenever you read and study Scripture. Comparing multiple translations helps to weed out any particular idiosyncrasies or poor translation/word choices made by any one translation. By comparing multiple translations at the same time, you can also sometimes see the original intent of the verse more clearly. You can also check to see if the divinity of God, the Trinity, or Jesus, or the blood of Christ has been diminished in any of the translations, which is by far the greatest concern.

Wayne Jackson also eloquently notes: [82]

> The renowned scholar D. J. Wiseman has observed that no single English translation is adequate to reflect the depth or richness of the text of the Old Testament. [Note: I also extend this comment to the New Testament]

Reading and comparing multiple translations today is made easy with the help of technology and digital Bibles, where multiple translations can be displayed and read side by side quickly and easily. I've found that I come away with a much better and fuller understanding of God's Word when I study in this manner. There are also parallel Bibles that list translations side-by-side. So instead of sticking exclusively to one translation, being fluent and capable of using several reputable ones is far and away the wisest choice.

COMMENTARIES, DICTIONARIES, CONCORDANCE, ETC.

It is very helpful to have additional resources when studying the Bible:

1) Commentaries. It is prudent for the student of the Bible today to learn from the wise and learned saints that have gone before us, some of whom gave their lives to seal their testimony. Therefore, having a couple of commentaries from trusted writers goes a long way towards understanding Scripture. I've found the Matthew Henry exposition and the Christian Courier commentaries by Wayne Jackson to be the ones I consult most frequently. Others are also available (e.g., the J.W. McGarvey Commentary on Acts, Adam Clarke's commentary, etc.).
2) Dictionaries: An English language (or whatever language you speak) dictionary and a Bible dictionary (which explains biblical terms) can help with understanding unfamiliar words.
3) Concordance: A cross-reference index of words and verses.

---

[82] Jackson, Wayne. *The Book of Job*, Christian Courier Publications, 1983

4) Biblical Maps: Helpful in understanding the ancient geography and land of Jesus' time and the missionary journeys of the apostles.

These resources are often available today in electronic format, making them easy to always carry with you, and also enabling easy word lookup and cross-referencing. Obviously, one must use caution, discretion, and discernment when reading any resource, for they are the non-inspired words of man.

NOTES AND CAUTIONS

And lastly, when reading <u>any</u> Bible, be wary of any words that have been added by man. While such notes can be helpful at times (e.g., see the notes added to 1 Thessalonians 5:12-22 in the AMP Bible), they are not inspired or inerrant, and they must be examined carefully. These include things such as section/chapter headings, study notes, and words added inline to verses (e.g., AMP Bible). These words only represent the opinions of the men/publishers that have added them. This warning also applies to any pictures or illustrations added, for they also convey the artist's interpretation and can be very misleading. Even the verse numbers themselves, while helpful, were added by man – the original Hebrew and Greek divinely inspired manuscripts did not have them in there. This warning strongly applies to any notes or headlines related to Bible prophecy (and eschatology/end-times matters), as those areas are highly corrupted today. Again, I repeat, it is through these added words that the opinions, false teachings, and doctrines of men and publishers can and do sneak into the Bible unawares! See the chapters on Beware the Wolves chapter and Being a Berean.

FALSE TEACHING(S) YOU WILL ENCOUNTER:
- The Bible is simply fictional "myths, folklore, and poetry"
- The "KJV Only" Bible movement

RELATED SCRIPTURE:

Your righteousness is an everlasting righteousness,
And Your law is truth. – Psalm 119:142

How blessed is the man who does not walk in the counsel of the wicked,
Nor stand in the path of sinners,
Nor sit in the seat of scoffers!
But his delight is in the law of the LORD,
And in His law he meditates day and night. – Psalm 1:1-2

The sum of Your word is truth,
And every one of Your righteous ordinances is everlasting. – Psalm 119:160

Sanctify them in the truth; Your word is truth. – John 17:17

However, they did not all heed the good news; for Isaiah says, "LORD, WHO HAS BELIEVED OUR REPORT?" So faith *comes* from hearing, and hearing by the word of Christ. – Romans 10:16-17

So Jesus was saying to those Jews who had believed Him, "If you continue in My word, *then* you are truly disciples of Mine; and you will know the truth, and the truth will make you free." – John 8:31-32

For whatever was written in earlier times was written for our instruction, so that through perseverance and the encouragement of the Scriptures we might have hope. – Romans 15:4

5.2 READING AND STUDYING THE BIBLE
(Bible Reading Plan, Get Wisdom)

"It is written, 'MAN SHALL NOT LIVE ON BREAD ALONE, BUT ON EVERY WORD THAT PROCEEDS OUT OF THE MOUTH OF GOD.'" – Matthew 4:4

Many new believers fret needlessly over finding just the right Bible "reading plan." In fact, entire books, apps, and websites are written and created to help with this, and even further, whole Bibles are cut up and reprinted in some special order that they want you to follow. But most books, including the Bible, tend to have a built-in reading plan, and it's not very hard to find or remember. So, to cut to the chase, for a new believer, here is the best "reading plan":

1. Start in Genesis 1:1
2. Continue reading until Revelation 22:21
3. Repeat from step 1

There, I've just saved you countless hours and days of frustration in searching through a lot of nonsense trying to find the perfect Bible reading plan! You could also add the reading of one Psalm and Proverb each day if you want – I've found those to be very helpful to my soul and to reinforce the assurance of God's perfect and holy hope as you begin to trust the Lord and His Word in all things at all times.

START AT THE BEGINNING

To emphasize this point: Would you buy a new and exciting romance novel or thriller and then pick it up and start reading it randomly in the middle? I didn't think so. And yet, some think that it is okay to do just that with the Bible. I confess in truth that I was also under that belief when I was first saved, and I thought that God would (through the Holy Spirit) open the Bible to just the right page I needed. I now see that as nonsense. While the Spirit certainly guides us in all things, it is not how one should regularly approach reading and studying the Bible. The reason you don't just start reading in the middle (or randomly wherever you happen to open it) is that the beginning of the book introduces the main character (God in our case) and the main plotline for the book's story (humanity and sin in our case).

Others believe that they can ignore the Old Testament (OT) because it is "obsolete." I originally did that also, and now realize that is also wrong. Without reading the OT, you won't understand why we are where we are today or the need for Jesus, or the nature of God Himself, etc. The OT gives context and understanding to the New Testament (NT). You cannot ignore either one; some churches teach that you should only read the NT – that is yet another false teaching! You won't understand the NT and Jesus Christ very well if you don't first understand the OT (God)...for God "is the same yesterday, today and forever" – He never changes. We also see the example of Christ using OT Scripture to explain "all things concerning Himself" to the disciples:

> Then beginning with Moses and with all the prophets, He [Jesus] explained to them the things concerning Himself in all the [OT] Scriptures. – Luke 24:27

Matthew Henry writes: [83]

---

[83] Henry, Matthew. *Exposition of the Old and New Testaments*, London. 1706-1710/1721.

Beginning at Moses, the first inspired writer of the Old Testament, he went in order through all the prophets, and expounded to them the things concerning himself, showing that the sufferings he had now gone through were so far from defeating the prophecies of the scripture concerning him that they were the accomplishment of them.

He expounded to them the scriptures of the Old Testament, which spoke of the Messiah, and showed them how they were fulfilled in Jesus of Nazareth, and now can tell them more concerning him than they could before tell him (Luke 24:27): Beginning at Moses, the first inspired writer of the Old Testament, he went in order through all the prophets, and expounded to them the things concerning himself, showing that the sufferings he had now gone through were so far from defeating the prophecies of the scripture concerning him that they were the accomplishment of them.

He began at Moses, who recorded the first promise, in which it was plainly foretold that the Messiah should have his heel bruised, but that by it the serpent's head should be incurably broken. Note,

First: There are things dispersed throughout all the scriptures concerning Christ, which it is of great advantage to have collected and put together. You cannot go far in any part of Scripture, but you meet with something that has reference to Christ, some prophecy, some promise, some prayer, some type or other; for he is the true treasure his in the field of the Old Testament. A golden thread of gospel grace runs through the whole web of the Old Testament. There is an eye of that white to be discerned in every place.

Secondly: The things concerning Christ need to be expounded. The eunuch, though a scholar, would not pretend to understand them, except some man should guide him (Act 8:31); for they were delivered darkly, according to that dispensation: but now that the veil is taken away the New Testament expounds the Old.

Thirdly: Jesus Christ is himself the best expositor of scripture, particularly the scriptures concerning himself; and even after his resurrection it was in this way that he led people into the knowledge of the mystery concerning himself; not by advancing new notions independent upon the scripture, but by showing how the scripture was fulfilled, and turning them over to the study of it. Even the Apocalypse itself is but a second part of the Old Testament prophecies and has continually an eye to them. If men believe not Moses and the prophets, they are incurable.

Fourthly: In studying the scriptures, it is good to be methodical, and to take them in order; for the Old Testament light shone gradually to the perfect day, and it is good to observe how at sundry times, and in divers manners (subsequent predictions improving and giving light to the preceding ones), God spoke to the fathers concerning his Son, by whom he has now spoken to us.

Some begin their bible at the wrong end, who study the Revelation first; but Christ has here taught us to begin at Moses.

It should be noted that the NT quotes from the OT nearly 900 times, further enhancing the need for modern-day gospel saints to read and understand what is in the OT. [Side note: However, beware today as many "wolves" push this OT emphasis way too far and resurrect legalism (Sabbath Keeping, etc.) – teaching that we are still (back) under the OT Mosaic Law, and specifically the Ten Commandments, which were given to the ancient Jews. The Mosaic Law (all of it) was done away with ("fulfilled"), nailed to the cross with (and by) Christ. In fact, the entire book of Galatians addresses this very issue. So, the modern practice of honoring the Jewish Sabbath is not supported by Scripture – and if you put yourself back under the bondage/yoke of the Mosaic Law, you must keep all of it perfectly from your birth. No man has ever been able to do that except Christ! So please don't succumb to the false teachings of those "wolves" who try to place you back under the Mosaic Law of the OT. We are under the law of grace as defined by the NT. See the Sabbath Keeping false teaching in the Beware the Wolves chapter.]

As a bonus, the reading plan I advocate takes no special effort to remember either. And whatever you do, keep going. If you come to some verses or chapters that are tedious to read or hard to understand, do the best you can reading through them, but do not stop. Keep going! The most important thing is to read daily. Your new born again spirit actually needs to be fed God's Holy Word to survive; it literally starves a bit each day you skip reading God's word. Yes, it is the Word of God that actually feeds your new born again spirit! Amazing!

Please do not worry that you are not getting enough exposure to the NT right away because you are starting "all the way back" in Genesis. If you follow the other steps that I'm giving you in this section of the book, you will also be reading the NT as a result of those activities.

IT TAKES WORK!

It is often said that "the Bible is just too hard to understand!" I agree that Scripture can be hard to understand in places (e.g., see 2 Peter 3:14-18) – and it was meant to be that way, for you must really want to dig into it and understand the Bible with "ALL YOUR HEART, AND WITH ALL YOUR SOUL, AND WITH ALL YOUR STRENGTH, AND WITH ALL YOUR MIND"! You must want to understand it as if your very life depends on it – and it does, eternally so! You must read it with an open mind and an open heart. You must seek out and love the truth, which is revealed only through God's Word by God's wisdom; you must diligently and tirelessly seek it out as if it were more valuable than silver or even gold (Proverbs 2:1-4). You must humbly ask God for His wisdom, and you must ask Him to reveal His Holy Word to you. This is typically done through prayer, often at the start of each study session. Remember, the Bible is God revealing Himself to us.

At first, you almost certainly will not understand all of what is written, but if you continue to diligently and consistently seek, study and meditate on His Word, you will see that He will lead you into all truth, perhaps quickly or perhaps slowly over time – all according to His timing. God often reveals His Word progressively. Ask that He open your eyes and your ears to hear His truth and that He grant you His wisdom. Then press forward in full assurance of His promises (e.g., James 1:5). And if at first you do not receive wisdom, pray again in persistence – keep asking reverently of God! This lesson is given to us in the parable of the Unjust Judge (Luke 18:1-8). We are to be persistent in prayer and our requests, not in a rude or demanding attitude, but pressing our requests, presenting them before Him in persistence. If you're like me, one day you may read a portion of Scripture and not really get much out of it, and then at a later time, it's as if your eyes and ears have been opened, and it just really comes alive to you in understanding and meaning. As you unlock (correctly understand) some truth in one area, that then gives you the ability and understanding to unlock more truth in another area. I want to also point out that it wasn't until I stopped trying to always seek out and find errors and contradictions in the Bible (to trap it in a contradiction, if you will) that I really started to grow in understanding it.

Lastly, do you find your time of Bible study and prayer to be a "chore" that you have to force yourself to do each day or a time you relish and look forward to with joy as you spend time with the Lord? People tend to find (make) the time to do the things they really want to do and that they feel are important – are you finding time for reading the Word, or does other stuff always come along and push it off? Reflection on this matter can reveal a lot about your priorities, your heart, and your desire to seek and serve Christ each day.

LEARN PROPER BIBLE INTERPRETATION

In this book, I've tried to list as many relevant verses in each chapter as possible, not just to multiply verses, but to show you that correct doctrine can only be attained by considering in aggregate <u>all</u> of what Scripture has to say on any particular topic, for it is written:

> "The <u>sum</u> of thy word is truth;
> And every one of thy righteous ordinances endureth for ever." – Psalms 119:160

You build biblical truth by having interpretations that are in agreement with all Scripture, not just some specific verses you've chosen or happen to favor. Nearly all false teachings arise when some verses are picked and interpretations made of those specific verses in isolation, while others are conveniently ignored, which don't fit with one's preferred interpretation. One of the most basic principles of Bible study is that if your interpretation and understanding of a verse cause a conflict/disagreement with other simple, clear, literal, and well-understood verses, then it's your understanding and interpretation that is wrong – for Scripture never contradicts itself. Said another way, if your belief, theology, dogma, or doctrine causes Scripture to contradict itself, it is not Scripture that is wrong; it is your own belief, theology, doctrine, or dogma which is wrong. One must also be a careful reader of Scripture, not reading into it things (or words) that are not there.

Wayne Jackson writes about selective interpretation:[84]

> First, it must be recognized that virtually no single passage contains the full complement of information that may be associated with a biblical theme. A failure to recognize this is a common fallacy committed by both secular and sectarian writers in a variety of issues. For example, skeptics will select a text which mentions a judgment from God inflicted upon a disobedient rebel (e.g., Num. 15:32ff) and then generalize that the Lord must be a harsh, hateful being. In this procedure, they neglect the scores of passages that reveal the love and mercy of the Creator and his acts of benevolence, along with reasons for those divine judgments of which the skeptic is critical. Similarly, the faith-only advocate will single out texts that mention only one component of the plan of salvation (e.g., faith; Jn. 3:16; Rom. 5:1) and conclude that salvation is by faith alone, wholly ignoring other complimentary passages (e.g., Acts 2:38). This is an egregious interpretive flaw.

---

[84] Jackson, Wayne. "Did Jesus Exclude Repentance from Forgiveness?" *ChristianCourier.com*. Access date: May 16, 2019. https://christiancourier.com/articles/1537-did-jesus-exclude-repentance-from-forgiveness

In closing, remember that it is the daily reading of the Word which enables you to be "growing in the grace and knowledge" of the Lord and that feeds your born-again Spirit in Christ. Just as your body will die without eating food, your new spirit will die without eating spiritual food – the Word of God.

RELATED SCRIPTURE:

"It is written, 'MAN SHALL NOT LIVE ON BREAD ALONE, BUT ON EVERY WORD THAT PROCEEDS OUT OF THE MOUTH OF GOD.'" – Matthew 4:4

For the word of God is living and active and sharper than any two-edged sword, and piercing as far as the division of soul and spirit, of both joints and marrow, and able to judge the thoughts and intentions of the heart. – Hebrews 4:12

For whatever was written in earlier times was written for our instruction, so that through perseverance and the encouragement of the Scriptures we might have hope. – Romans 15:4

How blessed is the man who does not walk in the counsel of the wicked,
Nor stand in the path of sinners,
Nor sit in the seat of scoffers!
But his delight is in the law of the LORD,
And in His law he meditates day and night.
He will be like a tree *firmly* planted by streams of water,
Which yields its fruit in its season
And its leaf does not wither;
And in whatever he does, he prospers. – Psalm 1:1-3

For the LORD gives wisdom;
From His mouth *come* knowledge and understanding.
He stores up sound wisdom for the upright;
He is a shield to those who walk in integrity,
Guarding the paths of justice,
And He preserves the way of His godly ones. – Proverbs 2:6-8

But if any of you lacks wisdom, let him ask of God, who gives to all generously and without reproach, and it will be given to him. But he must ask in faith without any doubting, for the one who doubts is like the surf of the sea, driven and tossed by the wind. For that man ought not to expect that he will receive anything from the Lord, *being* a double-minded man, unstable in all his ways. – James 1:5-8

Acquire wisdom! Acquire understanding!
Do not forget nor turn away from the words of my mouth.
"Do not forsake her, and she will guard you;
Love her, and she will watch over you.
"The beginning of wisdom *is*: Acquire wisdom;
And with all your acquiring, get understanding.
"Prize her, and she will exalt you;
She will honor you if you embrace her.
"She will place on your head a garland of grace;
She will present you with a crown of beauty." – Proverbs 4:5-9

5.3 START MEMORIZING VERSES
(Wielding the Sword of the Spirit)

Finally, be strong in the Lord and in the strength of His might. Put on the full armor of God, so that you will be able to stand firm against the schemes of the devil.
– Ephesians 6:10-11

You read and study the Bible in good times so that you have the verses stored up and ready "in you" when the bad (hard, trying) times come. Furthermore, you may not always have the Bible handy, especially at a critical time of trial or tribulation.

The Word is described as the "Sword of the Spirit," which is "sharper than any two-edged sword, and piercing as far as the division of soul and spirit." It is also part of the "Armor of God" that you need to "put on" as a Christian to fend off the attacks and "fiery darts" of the enemy (led by Satan). For it is by (and in) the Word of God that one finds life, and it is also this very same Word which will condemn sinners on Judgment Day. The Word cuts both ways.

Never forget that we are in the middle of a war – a raging spiritual war. And, as a born-again Christian, you are now on the front lines of the battle. It is also this sword, the Word of God, by which a Christian fights battles of the spiritual war. The enemy (Satan and his forces of darkness and evil) will attack you as often as they can. The attacks seem to be specially timed to occur when a) you might be feeling weak, anxious, tired, or doubtful about something, b) right before you are about to do a good work for the Lord, and also c) right after you just did a good work for the Lord and are feeling particularly close to Him. The enemy hates that. And to be prepared for battle (which can happen any time), you must have the "Sword of the Spirit" already committed to your mind, memorized, and ready to use at a moment's notice. You do not know when the forces of evil will attack, and they will always try to do so when you are off guard and unprepared.

It's a sad fact today that many Christians are badly outclassed, outgunned, outmanned, outstudied, and overmatched by Satan, who knows Scripture better than they do. Notice also that the "Sword of the Spirit" is your only offensive weapon which you have to confront the spiritual forces of evil! It is written that the Word is "sharper than any two-edged sword," but that's only true if you actually know it and have it memorized well enough to be able to use it.

You will be attacked spiritually, and you will need to use the Word to repel those attacks. One time I was under a ferocious spiritual attack that just wouldn't stop. The "fiery darts" of the enemy (Satan) just kept attacking me. These "fiery darts" are thoughts you get that genuinely appear to be your own thoughts, and in nearly all cases, they are blasphemous and stir up doubt or fear in your mind about God. This is the enemy trying to turn you back or turn you away from some good work you are about to do. This particular attack was so ferocious it lasted for over an hour, and I just couldn't make the blasphemous thoughts stop. It was then that Matthew 4:4 came to my mind. I confess that I hadn't really meant to memorize that verse before that point, but apparently, I had read it often enough that I was, therefore, able to recall it. When I used that verse against the attack, it stopped immediately. I've found that particular verse to be one of the most powerful verses in the entire Bible, especially for me, whenever there is a spiritual attack. Others I've found especially helpful are: "Satan, get behind me" and "the LORD rebuke you." We also have the example of how Jesus confronted Satan in the wilderness in a similar fashion. See the Armor of God chapter for more information.

And lastly, you need the Word memorized so you can help, correct, admonish, and encourage other brothers and sisters in Christ. I must call attention here to the fact that you are using a "two-edged" sword: so, beware that it cuts both ways, in that whatever Scripture you wield at others (in admonishing them) also often cuts right back at you! Whenever I am about to admonish anyone using Scripture, I first try to determine how I am also convicted by that very same verse and make sure I'm not guilty of the same thing. I've found this to be very helpful in finding my own sinful behavior/heart, or the "plank [log] in my own eye" (Matthew 7:1-3).

RELATED SCRIPTURE:

"It is written, 'MAN SHALL NOT LIVE ON BREAD ALONE, BUT ON EVERY WORD THAT PROCEEDS OUT OF THE MOUTH OF GOD.'" – Matthew 4:4

For the word of God is living and active and sharper than any two-edged sword, and piercing as far as the division of soul and spirit, of both joints and marrow, and able to judge the thoughts and intentions of the heart. – Hebrews 4:12

How blessed is the man who does not walk in the counsel of the wicked,
Nor stand in the path of sinners,
Nor sit in the seat of scoffers!
But his delight is in the law of the LORD,
And in His law he meditates day and night. – Psalm 1:1-2

My son, observe the commandment of your father
And do not forsake the teaching of your mother;
Bind them continually on your heart. – Proverbs 6:20-21

Let the word of Christ richly dwell within you, with all wisdom teaching and admonishing one another with psalms *and* hymns *and* spiritual songs, singing with thankfulness in your hearts to God. – Colossians 3:16

Finally, be strong in the Lord and in the strength of His might. Put on the full armor of God, so that you will be able to stand firm against the schemes of the devil. For our struggle is not against flesh and blood, but against the rulers, against the powers, against the world forces of this darkness, against the spiritual *forces* of wickedness in the heavenly *places*. Therefore, take up the full armor of God, so that you will be able to resist in the evil day, and having done everything, to stand firm. Stand firm therefore, HAVING GIRDED YOUR LOINS WITH TRUTH, and HAVING PUT ON THE BREASTPLATE OF RIGHTEOUSNESS, and having shod YOUR FEET WITH THE PREPARATION OF THE GOSPEL OF PEACE; in addition to all, taking up the shield of faith with which you will be able to extinguish all the flaming arrows [fiery darts] of the evil *one*. And take THE HELMET OF SALVATION, and the sword of the Spirit, which is the word of God. – Ephesians 6:10-17

But He turned and said to Peter, "Get behind Me, Satan! You are a stumbling block to Me; for you are not setting your mind on God's interests, but man's." – Matthew 16:23

The Message of Truth

"This book of the law shall not depart from your mouth, but you shall meditate on it day and night, so that you may be careful to do according to all that is written in it; for then you will make your way prosperous, and then you will have success."– Joshua 1:8

"Behold, I send you out as sheep in the midst of wolves; so be shrewd as serpents and innocent as doves." – Matthew 10:16

Be on the alert, stand firm in the faith, act like men, be strong. – 1 Corinthians 16:13

Now I make known to you, brethren, the gospel which I preached to you, which also you received, in which also you stand, by which also you are saved, if you hold fast the word which I preached to you, unless you believed in vain. – 1 Corinthians 15:1-2

Therefore, my beloved brethren whom I long *to see*, my joy and crown, in this way stand firm in the Lord, my beloved. – Philippians 4:1

…for now we *really* live, if you stand firm in the Lord. – 1 Thessalonians 3:8

For though we walk in the flesh, we do not war according to the flesh, for the weapons of our warfare are not of the flesh, but divinely powerful for the destruction of fortresses. – 2 Corinthians 10:3-4

For whatever was written in earlier times was written for our instruction, so through perseverance and the encouragement of the Scriptures we might have hope. – Romans 15:4

All Scripture is inspired by God and profitable for teaching, for reproof, for correction, for training in righteousness; so that the man of God may be adequate, equipped for every good work. – 2 Timothy 3:16-17

"Do not judge so that you will not be judged. For in the way you judge, you will be judged; and by your standard of measure, it will be measured to you. Why do you look at the speck that is in your brother's eye, but do not notice the log that is in your own eye?" – Matthew 7:1-3

5.4 FINDING A CHURCH

Let us consider how to stimulate one another to love and good deeds, not forsaking our own assembling together, as is the habit of some, but encouraging one another; and all the more as you see the day drawing near. – Hebrews 10:24-25

The Church Which Christ Founded. First, the title for this chapter isn't technically correct, although I'm using it here because that is the terminology most people are familiar with. This chapter should be more accurately titled "Finding a Local Congregation." As Bruce Eubank says [85]: "We don't go to church, for we are the Church (the people of God) – we go to worship," and we go for Bible study. Additionally, the building where the local congregation gathers is just that: a building; it has no significance in and of itself before God. In fact, the early Church often met in their homes, which is still the case in some places of the world even today. So now, let us focus on the true Christian Church which Jesus founded.

There is only one worldwide non-denominational body of believers in Christ named in Scripture as the "Church of God" or the "Church of Christ," and it was established by Christ, not by men. The church is also referred to as the "bride of Christ." The church began on the day of Pentecost when the Spirit was poured out on the apostles and the believers with them. The "Church of Christ" has local gatherings/meeting places in each city, town, or locale as appropriate and warranted. The sectarian and denominational divisions we see in churches today are not biblical! The book by H. M. Riggle called *The Christian Church, Its Rise and Progress* is well worth reading.

Jesus prayed expressly for unity among believers, and yet, the myriad beliefs, "traditions," and false teachings of man have only led to endless division:

> "I am no longer in the world; and *yet* they themselves are in the world, and I come to You. Holy Father, keep them in Your name, *the name* which You have given Me, that they may be one even as We *are*…
>
> "For their sakes I sanctify Myself, that they themselves also may be sanctified in truth…
>
> "I do not ask on behalf of these alone, but for those also who believe in Me through their word; that they may all be one; even as You, Father, *are* in Me and I in You, that they also may be in Us, so that the world may believe that You sent Me." – John 17:11,19-21

A true "Church of Christ" will have the following characteristics:

- They will simply be called by the name given in Scripture, which is the "Church of God" or the "Church of Christ," usually prefixed with the town or locale name (which is fine) – although beware, see the notes later about the "Church of God" name that has been co-opted today). If you're in one of the "modern" so-called "Christian" churches which go by any other name, or in one of the endless flavors of denominations today (e.g., Baptist, Methodist, Lutheran, Presbyterian, Roman Catholic, etc.), you are not in the church that

---

[85] Bruce Eubank, Preacher, South Valley Church of Christ, Las Vegas.

Jesus founded, but you are in an imposter church, a fake Christian church, and you are not worshipping the Lord "in spirit and in truth,"
- They will be free from every single false teaching identified in this book (amazing!),
- They will meet on the Lord's Day, the first day of the week, which is Sunday (so beware the "Sabbath Keeping" false teaching),
- They will hold services in the manner prescribed in the New Testament, with only a cappella singing by members in worship – they will not consider worship as performance entertainment or an "experience," nor include musical instruments, singing groups, or solos performed for an audience, dancing around as the heathens do, yelling, shouting, etc.
- The church (and its elders, preachers, and teachers) should sincerely love God. You can usually tell whether this is so by simply watching how they act, their behavior and demeanor, etc. The "fruit of the Spirit," which is "love, joy, peace, patience, kindness, goodness, faithfulness, gentleness, self-control," should be evident,
- They should have elder(s) which are in accord with Scriptural qualifications and instructions (Note: I'm noticing that many Church of Christ locations today simply don't have any elders, as they are unable to find any qualified men. This, I think, probably reflects on the state of Christianity in recent times.),
- They should read, teach and preach the Word of God in an expositional manner at every service and not just use Jesus and the Bible as a prop behind them on stage while they tell cutesy stories of how good your life will be and how rich and successful Jesus will make you (and them),
- They should get the Gospel message correct "that was once for all *time* handed down to the saints" in Scripture, free from the false teachings of man,
- They will be active in faith and service to the Lord,
- They will conduct baptisms, done by immersion in accordance with New Testament Scripture, on the very same day someone comes to faith in Christ by hearing the gospel "message of truth" (not days, weeks, months, or even years later),
- They will train up their members to be growing and maturing in faith, for we are admonished to always be "growing in the grace and knowledge of the Lord,"
- They should be exercising biblical discipline with their members, and they will also lovingly admonish, teach and correct members who are going astray,
- They will show no personal favoritism due to appearances, status in the community, wealth, etc.,
- They are solely focused on building the Kingdom of God, not on the politics of this world,
- They may take up a free-will offering from members according to the heart of the individual believer – constant church "begging" for money is not in the Bible. To a Christian, the Spirit of God should move you to contribute financially as you are led to of a glad, cheerful, and thankful heart,
- They should conduct regular prayer meetings,
- They should practice communion (Breaking of Bread, the Lord's Supper) each Lord's day (Sunday) in remembrance of Christ,

- They should conduct services in an orderly and organized manner, not with wild yelling, shouting, dancing around hysterically or with emotional audio-visual stimulations, etc. (see 1 Corinthians 14:40),
- They should not have women in positions of leadership or teaching over men, but in all other aspects, women are fully equal with men,
- They will have a heart for the lost and be a light to the community around them (if your church is surrounded by a sea of the lost but you are not seeing frequent baptisms, it may be a sign that their evangelism and outreach is not where it should be),
- They should welcome and love all who come, no matter what sins those people are (or have been) involved in,
- They do not establish man-made positions and titles nor elevate men in a hierarchy of leadership which is not in agreement with New Testament Scripture (see Matthew 23:5-12). [86]

Generally, if you are new to an area, you can search the Internet for the name of your town/city along with the words "Church of Christ" (e.g., "Medford Church of Christ"). That can help you find ones that are nearby but be sure to do proper diligence on any church, whether it has those words in the title or not. Be very aware that many so-called "Christian" churches, which even use the name of Jesus or Christ in their names, are not true Christian churches! Also, beware that those who now go by the name "Church of God" may not be the true church, as that name (while biblical) has been co-opted and corrupted.

If you desire to worship the Lord "in spirit and truth" (John 4:24), you will need to come out of the fake "Christian" churches which teach any of the false teachings outlined in this book (Revelation 18:4); see the Beware the Wolves chapter on how far and wide false teachings pervade the so-called "reformed," modern, or liberal churches today. Oftentimes (but not always), their false teachings will be documented as part of their foundational statement of faith – but you have to make sure you find and read it. Many of the cults and sects go to great lengths to actually hide their foundational beliefs from you! Furthermore, churches that place man's writings on equal footing with Scripture or rely on "false prophets" with new "special revelations from God" are to be avoided. Also, if your church describes its service as an "experience," run away as fast as you can.

Additionally, nearly all Christian churches today fail to conduct services in accordance with New Testament instructions. Wayne Jackson writes: [87]

Is Your Worship Becoming Disney Church?

There was a time in most churches when the services were focused upon worship that glorified God, and the preaching consisted of reverent instruction from the Scriptures. In some places, it's still that way.

On the other hand, drastic changes are underway in hundreds of churches across the land…

---

[86] Jackson, Wayne. "Are Preachers To Be Called 'Reverend'?" ChristianCourier.com. Access date: April 26, 2020. https://christiancourier.com/articles/579-are-preachers-to-be-called-reverend

[87] Jackson, Wayne. "Is Your Worship Becoming Disney Church?" ChristianCourier.com. Access date: February 22, 2021. https://christiancourier.com/articles/92-is-your-worship-becoming-disney-church

In a word, "worship" services have become "**us**-centered," rather than "**God**-centered."

Would you rather have your Sundays free to camp, play golf, or visit with family? Fine, we'll implement a "quickie," convenience-service for you at some other time so your conscience will be mollified, and you can enjoy your weekends. A news program featured one group that offers a Sunday drive-through communion to accommodate those who prefer not to get out of the car on their way to the beach, etc.!

Do you find the Lord's supper too musty with tradition? Hey, that can be fixed. How about some Coke? One minister has written that he has no problem with Coca-Cola on the Lord's table. Why not make it a bit more sophisticated and have Dr. Pepper? Many feel we need not be manacled to a beverage that was voguish in Palestine twenty centuries ago!

Are the old songs boring? Are you sick of "Rock of Ages" and "Amazing Grace"? We understand. We'll jazz it up for you. How about: "Me and Jesus – Got Our Own Thing Going"? Let's get rhythm—with some hand-clapping, foot-stomping, swaying, get-with-it gospel boogie. Fan those emotions!

Tired of being "preached to"? How would you like some "sharing" sessions where everyone can relate their personal experiences, air their frustrations, and share their "opinions" on a variety of topics? We could talk about unsafe conditions on the job, how to control your weight, dysfunctional sexual problems, how to take advantage of tax laws, etc.

After all, this is the practical side of life. Great therapy!

Do references to "sin" and "repentance" turn you off? Okay, we can restrict ourselves to sessions on self-esteem, how to have healing in your life for emotional distress, skills in effective conversation, and so on.

The Christian Chronicle (1999) tells of an Alabama church that uses videos of the "Andy Griffith Show" as a part of their Sunday school curriculum. They spend the first portion of the class watching Andy and Barney, and then talk about moral lessons learned from the episodes.

Have we totally forgotten there is a book called the Bible that is the most exciting volume in the world? It is from Heaven—not Hollywood.

The "new church" for the coming millennium in many cases may well be a "Disney Church," (i.e., entertainment-oriented). Snap, crackle, and pop. Feel good, laid back, play it cool. A church in Amarillo, Texas has what they call a "casual" dress, "high energy" Sunday morning service, with lots of "testimonies." Do you dig it, dude? They claim eight hundred members—three hundred of whom have been baptized! (Can you do math?)

Is this what God intended? Such "worship" ideology is as far from the New Testament pattern as it could be. It is what an inspired apostle called "will-worship" (Col. 2:23), and it's carnal to the core.

Spiritual people will make **God and his Word** the center of their worship life.

Furthermore, the modern practice of having one person acting as the church leader with the title of "Pastor," also isn't Biblical. Wayne Jackson writes on this: [88]

> The modern-day "pastor" system is as much a departure from the New Testament pattern of church organization as is an ecclesiastical hierarchy. No one man can assume the role of "the pastor," whether by title or by practice, for a congregation. Neither can a congregation delegate one man to be the sole church manager, regardless of the unanimity of vote or the crises at hand.

Whew…I hope you are starting to see the difficulty in finding a true church! You may have noticed that I didn't list finding a church as the first step you should take as a new Christian. The most important thing you must do when you are born again is to start reading, understanding, and memorizing Scripture. If you do not know (extremely well) the gospel "that was once for all *time* handed down to the saints" in New Testament Scripture, you won't be able to recognize the churches and false teachings which can lead you astray, and you will very likely end up in an apostate, "lukewarm," "dead" church and not even realize it. "Wolves in sheep's clothing" abound in all directions as far as the eye can see!

You will also find that if you start to eliminate churches one by one if they contain the false teachings identified in this book, you will soon end up with only <u>one</u> church left to choose from: which is the true "Church of Christ"! Amazing! Now some may accuse me of writing this book (and the false teachings) to lead directly to that result because I (now) belong to that church. But nothing could be further from the truth. In actuality, I didn't even have a church for many years, and all the way up until the 2nd draft of this book was completed, and I left this chapter blank the whole time because I didn't even know what to put in it! I had given up trying to find a church because no matter where I looked or which church I tried, I found that it was full of false teachings, and I would therefore not become a member of it. I knew that Scripture exhorted me to "not forsake assembling together," but I couldn't find a single church without false teachings.

I tried to force myself to keep going to some of the churches, but I just couldn't sit there while they preached nonsense. It wasn't until I was nearly finished with this book that I found the local "Church of Christ" – and I was then able to write this chapter to finish the book. Frankly, I was astonished that I had finally found <u>a church that didn't have even one single false teaching</u>! I didn't think such a church existed anywhere – and I had pretty much given up trying to find one! I don't know why it worked this way with me, but it is written that God "works in mysterious ways" (Isaiah 45:15) and that "as the heavens are higher than the earth, so are my ways higher than your ways and my thoughts than your thoughts" (Isaiah 55:8-9) So, amen and amen!

I've included the instructions (praise and admonitions) to the churches from the book of Revelation at the end of this chapter. These instructions were written to real literal churches that existed when John wrote the book of Revelation; they are not prophecies mapped to "historical periods" of church history as many falsely teach/claim. These verses contain a wealth of information for the born-again Christian on exactly what Christ expects from the churches (and believers) who call on His name.

---

[88] Jackson, Jason. "What Is a Pastor?" ChristianCourier.com. Access date: March 27, 2021. https://christiancourier.com/articles/1178-what-is-a-pastor

These instructions apply equally to churches (and believers) in every age – including today. We can learn much from what Christ says to each of the churches and take great heed, for there is a little (or a lot) of each church in each one of us individually. If you find that any of Christ's admonitions to the churches apply to your church or to yourself, pay close attention and strive to correct that. We must be constantly watchful and wary of straying out of the path to eternal life.

FALSE TEACHING(S) YOU WILL ENCOUNTER:

- Myriads of "Entertainment" and "Experience" so-called churches of today, along with modern and liberal churches, all trying to masquerade as Christian
- Denominationalism (Methodists, Baptists, Pentecostal, Adventism, Lutheran, Calvinism, Arminianism, Roman Catholicism, etc., etc., ad-nauseum…)
- Sabbath keeping/legalism
- Abstaining from certain foods
- False teachings on baptism
- Saying a "Sinner's Prayer" saves you
- You are saved by "Faith Alone/Only"
- Once saved always saved
- Predestination
- The "One True End-Times Church"
- Universalism (i.e., any name, or any religion, even one you make up, or even no belief at all, can save you to eternal life)
- Ecumenism
- The "Prosperity Gospel"
- Mormonism masquerading as Christianity
- Cults that deny Christ

RELATED SCRIPTURE:

…and let us consider how to stimulate one another to love and good deeds, not forsaking our own assembling together, as is the habit of some, but encouraging *one another*; and all the more as you see the day drawing near. – Hebrews 10:24-25

Let love *be* without hypocrisy. Abhor what is evil; cling to what is good. *Be* devoted to one another in brotherly love; give preference to one another in honor; not lagging behind in diligence, fervent in spirit, serving the Lord; rejoicing in hope, persevering in tribulation, devoted to prayer, contributing to the needs of the saints, practicing hospitality. – Romans 12:9-13

Therefore encourage one another and build up one another, just as you also are doing. – 1 Thessalonians 5:11

Iron sharpens iron,
So one man sharpens another. – Proverbs 27:17

And He gave some *as* apostles, and some *as* prophets, and some *as* evangelists, and some *as* pastors and teachers, for the equipping of the saints for the work of service, to the building up of the body of Christ. – Ephesians 4:11-12

Let the word of Christ richly dwell within you, with all wisdom teaching and admonishing one another with psalms *and* hymns *and* spiritual songs, singing with thankfulness in your hearts to God. – Colossians 3:16

Love is patient, love is kind *and* is not jealous; love does not brag *and* is not arrogant, does not act unbecomingly; it does not seek its own, is not provoked, does not take into account a wrong *suffered*, does not rejoice in unrighteousness, but rejoices with the truth; bears all things, believes all things, hopes all things, endures all things. – 1 Corinthians 13:4-7

But encourage one another day after day, as long as it is *still* called "Today," so that none of you will be hardened by the deceitfulness of sin. – Hebrews 3:13

Without consultation, plans are frustrated,
But with many counselors they succeed. – Proverbs 15:22

And He summoned the twelve and began to send them out in pairs… – Mark 6:7

Now we who are strong ought to bear the weaknesses of those without strength and not *just* please ourselves. – Romans 15:1

For I received from the Lord that which I also delivered to you, that the Lord Jesus in the night in which He was betrayed took bread; and when He had given thanks, He broke it and said, "This is My body, which is for you; do this in remembrance of Me." In the same way *He took* the cup also after supper, saying, "This cup is the new covenant in My blood; do this, as often as you drink *it*, in remembrance of Me." For as often as you eat this bread and drink the cup, you proclaim the Lord's death until He comes. – 1 Corinthians 11:23-26 [Note: Communion, Breaking of Bread, or the Lord's supper]

Day by day continuing with one mind in the temple, and breaking bread [communion, or the Lord's supper] from house to house, they were taking their meals together with gladness and sincerity of heart, praising God and having favor with all the people. – Acts 2:46-47a

Now this *I say*, he who sows sparingly will also reap sparingly, and he who sows bountifully will also reap bountifully. Each one *must do* just as he has purposed in his heart, not grudgingly or under compulsion, for God loves a cheerful giver. And God is able to make all grace abound to you, so that always having all sufficiency in everything, you may have an abundance for every good deed. – 2 Corinthians 9:6-8 [Note: relates to church giving]

But they do all their deeds to be noticed by men; for they broaden their phylacteries and lengthen the tassels *of their garments*. They love the place of honor at banquets and the chief seats in the synagogues, and respectful greetings in the market places, and being called Rabbi by men. But do not be called Rabbi; for One is your Teacher, and you are all brothers. Do not call *anyone* on earth your father; for One is your Father, He who is in heaven. Do not be called leaders; for One is your Leader, *that is*, Christ. But the greatest among you shall be your servant. Whoever exalts himself shall be humbled; and whoever humbles himself shall be exalted. – Matthew 23:5-12 [Note: this speaks to establishing titles, such as "Father," "Reverend", etc. in the church.]

"To the angel of the church in Ephesus write:

The One who holds the seven stars in His right hand, the One who walks among the seven golden lampstands, says this:

'I know your deeds and your toil and perseverance, and that you cannot tolerate evil men, and you put to the test those who call themselves apostles, and they are not, and you found them *to be* false; and you have perseverance and have endured for My name's sake, and have not grown weary. But I have *this* against you, that you have left your first love. Therefore remember from where you have fallen, and repent and do the deeds you did at first; or else I am coming to you and will remove your lampstand out of its place—unless you repent. Yet this you do have, that you hate the deeds of the Nicolaitans, which I also hate. He who has an ear, let him hear what the Spirit says to the churches. To him who overcomes, I will grant to eat of the tree of life which is in the Paradise of God.'" – Revelation 2:1-7

"And to the angel of the church in Smyrna write:

The first and the last, who was dead, and has come to life, says this:

'I know your tribulation and your poverty (but you are rich), and the blasphemy by those who say they are Jews and are not, but are a synagogue of Satan. Do not fear what you are about to suffer. Behold, the devil is about to cast some of you into prison, so that you will be tested, and you will have tribulation for ten days. Be faithful until death, and I will give you the crown of life. He who has an ear, let him hear what the Spirit says to the churches. He who overcomes will not be hurt by the second death.'" – Revelation 2:8-11

"And to the angel of the church in Pergamum write:

The One who has the sharp two-edged sword says this:

'I know where you dwell, where Satan's throne is; and you hold fast My name, and did not deny My faith even in the days of Antipas, My witness, My faithful one, who was killed among you, where Satan dwells. But I have a few things against you, because you have there some who hold the teaching of Balaam, who kept teaching Balak to put a stumbling block before the sons of Israel, to eat things sacrificed to idols and to commit *acts of* immorality. So you also have some who in the same way hold the teaching of the Nicolaitans. Therefore repent; or else I am coming to you quickly, and I will make war against them with the sword of My mouth. He who has an ear, let him hear what the Spirit says to the churches. To him who overcomes, to him I will give *some* of the hidden manna, and I will give him a white stone, and a new name written on the stone which no one knows but he who receives it.'" – Revelation 2:12-17

"And to the angel of the church in Thyatira write:

The Son of God, who has eyes like a flame of fire, and His feet are like burnished bronze, says this:

'I know your deeds, and your love and faith and service and perseverance, and that your deeds of late are greater than at first. But I have *this* against you, that you tolerate the woman Jezebel, who calls herself a prophetess, and she teaches and leads My bond-servants astray so that they commit *acts of* immorality and eat things sacrificed to idols. I gave her time to repent, and she does not want to repent of her immorality. Behold, I will throw her on a bed *of sickness*, and those who commit adultery with her into great tribulation, unless they repent of her deeds. And I will kill her children with pestilence, and all the churches will know that I am He who searches the minds and hearts; and I will give to each one of you according to your deeds. But I say to you, the rest who are in Thyatira, who do not hold this teaching, who have not known the deep things of Satan, as they call them—I place no other burden on you. Nevertheless what you have, hold fast until I come. He who overcomes, and he who keeps My deeds until the end, TO HIM I WILL GIVE AUTHORITY OVER THE NATIONS; AND HE SHALL RULE THEM WITH A ROD OF IRON, AS THE VESSELS OF THE POTTER ARE BROKEN TO PIECES, as I also have received *authority* from My Father; and I will give him the morning star. He who has an ear, let him hear what the Spirit says to the churches.'" – Revelation 2:18-29

"To the angel of the church in Sardis write:

He who has the seven Spirits of God and the seven stars, says this:

'I know your deeds, that you have a name that you are alive, but you are dead. Wake up, and strengthen the things that remain, which were about to die; for I have not found your deeds completed in the sight of My God. So remember what you have received and heard; and keep *it*, and repent. Therefore if you do not wake up, I will come like a thief, and you will not know at what hour I will come to you. But you have a few people in Sardis who have not soiled their garments; and they will walk with Me in white, for they are worthy. He who overcomes will thus be clothed in white garments; and I will not erase his name from the book of life, and I will confess his name before My Father and before His angels. He who has an ear, let him hear what the Spirit says to the churches.'" – Revelation 3:1-6

"And to the angel of the church in Philadelphia write:

He who is holy, who is true, who has the key of David, who opens and no one will shut, and who shuts and no one opens, says this:

'I know your deeds. Behold, I have put before you an open door which no one can shut, because you have a little power, and have kept My word, and have not denied My name. Behold, I will cause *those* of the synagogue of Satan, who say that they are Jews and are not, but lie—I will make them come and bow down at your feet, and *make them* know that I have loved you. Because you have kept the word of My perseverance, I also will keep you from the hour of testing, that *hour* which is about to come upon the whole world, to test those who dwell on the earth. I am coming quickly; hold fast what you have, so that no one will take your crown. He who overcomes, I will make him a pillar in the temple of My God, and he will not go out from it anymore; and I will write on him the name of My God, and the name of the city of My God, the new Jerusalem, which comes down out of heaven from My God, and My new name. He who has an ear, let him hear what the Spirit says to the churches.'" – Revelation 3:7-13

"To the angel of the church in Laodicea write:

The Amen, the faithful and true Witness, the Beginning of the creation of God, says this:

'I know your deeds, that you are neither cold nor hot; I wish that you were cold or hot. So because you are lukewarm, and neither hot nor cold, I will spit you out of My mouth. Because you say, "I am rich, and have become wealthy, and have need of nothing," and you do not know that you are wretched and miserable and poor and blind and naked, I advise you to buy from Me gold refined by fire so that you may become rich, and white garments so that you may clothe yourself, and *that* the shame of your nakedness will not be revealed; and eye salve to anoint your eyes so that you may see. Those whom I love, I reprove and discipline; therefore be zealous and repent. Behold, I stand at the door and knock; if anyone hears My voice and opens the door, I will come in to him and will dine with him, and he with Me. He who overcomes, I will grant to him to sit down with Me on My throne, as I also overcame and sat down with My Father on His throne. He who has an ear, let him hear what the Spirit says to the churches.'" – Revelation 3:14-22

5.5 UTILIZING TECHNOLOGY

"But as for you, Daniel, conceal these words and seal up the book until the end of time; many will go back and forth, and knowledge will increase." – Daniel 12:4

We have access today to many excellent resources through the wonders of modern technology. Some prominent Christian pastors proclaim loudly that you should avoid all technology, that it is "of the devil," etc....I say that proclamation is nonsense. Technology by itself is just a tool to be used for good or bad, like anything else. Prudent use of technology can be of great benefit to believers and help us quickly learn, search and explore the Word of God. We can also read and search through many wonderful writings by the worthy saints who have gone before us.

Technology allows one to "go to and fro" in God's Word quickly and allows one to look up verses easily, find study notes, and do research. I can carry ten or more Bible translations with me everywhere I go on my phone – complete with study notes, dictionaries, lexicons, maps, etc....amazing! Why not use technology to your advantage? You can gain access to many resources that would otherwise be impossible or difficult to reach, for instance, radio stations from other geographical areas or even countries.

I recommend that you get at least one Bible app for your phone and tablet – and use them. They allow you to carry several Bible translations in your pocket or purse anywhere you go. Here are some apps I have used:

- E-Sword App (my primary tool)
- YouVersion Bible App
- Apologetics Press App
- GBN (Gospel Broadcasting Network) App
- Audio Bible (to listen to the Bible while driving, traveling, sitting on an airplane, etc.)

There are also many wonderful Internet sites with correct teachings and the true Gospel message. I list some trustworthy websites at the end of this book. However, just because you see or read something on the Internet (or anywhere else) doesn't make it true, factual, let alone solid biblical advice for a Christian. So, as with any information you come across, extreme discernment and discretion are required when reading anything, for there is also an abundance of false teachings on the Internet. Pray boldly for the Holy Spirit to guide you (and keep this book close!).

One of the best things I've done (utilizing modern technology) is to get an audio version of my preferred Bible and put it on my phone. This way, I can listen to the Word of God whenever I'm driving, which sometimes is several hours a day; I often listen to a single chapter repeatedly, as you may hear different things in the chapter each time you listen to it. It's an amazing way to hear the Word of God and make use of what would otherwise be idle and wasted time.

In closing, I need to mention that technology can also consume, overwhelm and take over your life if you let it; it can be addictive and isolating to one who seeks immersion in it. So, please be aware of this potential risk of abuse which can lead to isolation.

The Message of Truth

FALSE TEACHING(S) YOU WILL ENCOUNTER:
- Technology is evil (no, it is just a tool to be used)

RELATED SCRIPTURE:

"But as for you, Daniel, conceal these words and seal up the book until the end of time; many will go back and forth [in Scripture and in the world], and knowledge will increase." – Daniel 12:4

Whether, then, you eat or drink or whatever you do, do all to the glory of God. – 1 Corinthians 10:31

I told them how the hand of my God had been favorable to me and also about the king's words which he had spoken to me. Then they said, "Let us arise and build." So they put their hands to the good *work*. – Nehemiah 2:18

Now the God of peace, who brought up from the dead the great Shepherd of the sheep through the blood of the eternal covenant, *even* Jesus our Lord, equip you in every good thing to do His will, working in us that which is pleasing in His sight, through Jesus Christ, to whom *be* the glory forever and ever. Amen. – Hebrews 13:20-21

For whatever was written in earlier times was written for our instruction, so that through perseverance and the encouragement of the Scriptures we might have hope. – Romans 15:4

5.6 CHANGING YOUR WORLDLY HABITS

You adulteresses, do you not know that friendship with the world is hostility toward God? Therefore whoever wishes to be a friend of the world makes himself an enemy of God. – James 4:4

"And if you do not do well, sin is crouching at the door; and its desire is for you, but you must master it." – Genesis 4:7

When you were born again with your sins forgiven, you were covered by the blood of Christ and clothed with the righteousness of Christ. We are to be a holy people set apart for God, not entangled again in the world. Scripture reads, "the LORD is my shepherd," not "the world is my shepherd." We should heed the words of the apostle Paul:

> Do you not know that those who run in a race all run, but *only* one receives the prize? Run in such a way that you may win. Everyone who competes in the games exercises self-control in all things. They then *do it* to receive a perishable wreath, but we an imperishable. Therefore I run in such a way, as not without aim; I box in such a way, as not beating the air; but I discipline my body and make it my slave, so that, after I have preached to others, I myself will not be disqualified. – 1 Corinthians 9:24-27

In effect, you were given spotless and pure clothes of "white" to wear when you were born again, for you have become as a "virgin" again to sin:

> For all of you who were baptized into Christ have clothed yourselves with Christ. – Galatians 3:27

> "Wash yourselves, make yourselves clean" …
>
> "Though your sins are as scarlet,
> They will be as white as snow." – Isaiah 1:16,18

> After these things I looked, and behold, a great multitude which no one could count, from every nation and *all* tribes and peoples and tongues, standing before the throne and before the Lamb, clothed in white robes, and palm branches *were* in their hands. – Revelation 7:9

> "Let us rejoice and be glad and give the glory to Him, for the marriage of the Lamb has come and His bride has made herself ready. It was given to her to clothe herself in fine linen, bright *and* clean; for the fine linen is the righteous acts of the saints." – Revelation 19:7-8

> It is these who have not defiled themselves with women, for they are virgins. It is these who follow the Lamb wherever he goes. These have been redeemed from mankind as firstfruits for God and the Lamb, and in their mouth no lie was found, for they are blameless. – Revelation 14:4-5 (ESV)

However, even after we are born again, we must still confront sin on a daily basis and prevail over it, for if you return once again to the ways of this world, you will again be tarnished by sin. While we remain in this fallen world, we must contend with this awful, sinful pull every single day of our lives, for it is written:

> "Keep watching and praying that you may not enter into temptation; the spirit is willing, but the flesh is weak." – Matthew 26:41

> Submit therefore to God. Resist the devil and he will flee from you. – James 4:7

Just because you are born again doesn't make this pull go away, for we are still in our mortal fleshly bodies until death. The teaching that a born-again Christian no longer sins is a false teaching (see Beware the Wolves). Luke 9:23 says, "if anyone wants to come after Me, he must deny himself, take up his cross daily, and follow Me," and we read that "sin is crouching right at the door," ready and waiting to devour us:

> "If you do well, will not *your countenance* be lifted up? And if you do not do well, sin is crouching at the door; and its desire is for you, but you must master it." – Genesis 4:7

Now I fully confess right here that it's <u>much</u> easier to write (and read) this chapter than it is to actually change one's worldly habits. Truth be told, I have found this to be one of the hardest things to do – but you must do it. Also, notice that this is the only chapter in the entire book which starts with two Scripture verses at its head! This fallen world (and the schemes of man) call out to your flesh every moment of every day, bombarding you with "lust of the flesh" and "lust of the eyes" temptations (entertainment, media, books, internet, movies, etc.), which are blaring out in staggering volume and frequency from this fallen world and fallen man.

> Do not love the world nor the things in the world. If anyone loves the world, the love of the Father is not in him. For all that is in the world, the lust of the flesh and the lust of the eyes and the boastful pride of life, is not from the Father, but is from the world. The world is passing away, and *also* its lusts; but the one who does the will of God lives forever. – 1 John 2:15-17

Scripture also warns that excessive cares and concerns for this material world can be a significant risk for your eternal salvation. They can hinder your ability to focus on God, and they can also steer you back into sinful behavior and idol worship. We are not to idolize the things of this world (money, fame, power, possessions, etc.), for they are snares that can draw you away from following Christ. Anything that we put above God is an "idol" to us. Riches ("the love of money"), in particular, is called out as a specific snare to be very wary of (i.e., idolizing money and the relentless pursuit of it and trusting in it instead of God).

Also, do not fall victim to the deceptions of the "once saved always saved" false teaching. One who is born again can later "fall away," go apostate, backslide, turn back, or quit the faith. Please re-read the chapter on persevering in faith, where that subject was covered in much more detail. The great apostle Paul wrote that he strived to remain pure and undefiled. Now, if even the great apostle and inspired writer could have "disqualified" himself, how much more should we also "be diligent to be found by him [Christ] without spot or blemish," lest we "be found naked" once again (i.e., not covered by and clothed in the righteousness of Christ) on the great Day of Judgment:

> Not that I have already obtained this or am already perfect, but I press on to make it my own, because Christ Jesus has made me his own. Brothers, I do not consider

that I have made it my own. But one thing I do: forgetting what lies behind and straining forward to what lies ahead, I press on toward the goal for the prize of the upward call of God in Christ Jesus. Let those of us who are mature think this way, and if in anything you think otherwise, God will reveal that also to you. Only let us hold true to what we have attained.

Brethren, join in following my example, and observe those who walk according to the pattern you have in us. For many walk, of whom I often told you, and now tell you even weeping, *that they are* enemies of the cross of Christ, whose end is destruction, whose god is *their* appetite, and *whose* glory is in their shame, who set their minds on earthly things. For our citizenship is in heaven, from which also we eagerly wait for a Savior, the Lord Jesus Christ; who will transform the body of our humble state into conformity with the body of His glory, by the exertion of the power that He has even to subject all things to Himself. – Philippians 3:12-21

Do you not know that those who run in a race all run, but *only* one receives the prize? Run in such a way that you may win. Everyone who competes in the games exercises self-control in all things. They then *do it* to receive a perishable wreath, but we an imperishable. Therefore I run in such a way, as not without aim; I box in such a way, as not beating the air; but I discipline my body and make it my slave, so that, after I have preached to others, I myself will not be disqualified. – 1 Corinthians 9:24-27

"'But you have a few people in Sardis who have not soiled their garments; and they will walk with Me in white, for they are worthy. He who overcomes will thus be clothed in white garments; and I will not erase his name from the book of life, and I will confess his name before My Father and before His angels. He who has an ear, let him hear what the Spirit says to the churches.'" – Revelation 3:4-6

However, we are able to prevail by the power of Christ who lives in us, but must keep our eyes fixed above and not on the things of this world:

Therefore if you have been raised up with Christ, keep seeking the things above, where Christ is, seated at the right hand of God. Set your mind on the things above, not on the things that are on earth. For you have died and your life is hidden with Christ in God. When Christ, who is our life, is revealed, then you also will be revealed with Him in glory.

Therefore consider the members of your earthly body as dead to immorality, impurity, passion, evil desire, and greed, which amounts to idolatry. For it is because of these things that the wrath of God will come upon the sons of disobedience, and in them you also once walked, when you were living in them. But now you also, rid yourselves of all of them: anger, wrath, malice, slander, and obscene speech from your mouth. Do not lie to one another, since you stripped off the old self with its *evil* practices. – Colossians 3:1-9

Finally, brethren, whatever is true, whatever is honorable, whatever is right, whatever is pure, whatever is lovely, whatever is of good repute, if there is any excellence and if anything worthy of praise, dwell on these things. – Philippians 4:8

> Do not be deceived, God is not mocked; for whatever a man sows, this he will also reap. For the one who sows to his own flesh will from the flesh reap corruption, but the one who sows to the Spirit will from the Spirit reap eternal life. – Galatians 6:7-8

SET APART

And while it's true we are to share the gospel message with the lost, it is not true that we are to socialize with them, partaking in their worldly activities continually. We are to be "set apart" for Christ:

> Herefore I urge you, brethren, by the mercies of God, to present your bodies a living and holy sacrifice, acceptable to God, *which is* your spiritual service of worship. And do not be conformed to this world, but be transformed by the renewing of your mind, so that you may prove what the will of God is, that which is good and acceptable and perfect. – Romans 12:1-2

> Do not be bound together with unbelievers; for what partnership have righteousness and lawlessness, or what fellowship has light with darkness? Or what harmony has Christ with Belial, or what has a believer in common with an unbeliever? Or what agreement has the temple of God with idols? For we are the temple of the living God; just as God said,
>
> "I WILL DWELL IN THEM AND WALK AMONG THEM;
> AND I WILL BE THEIR GOD, AND THEY SHALL BE MY PEOPLE."
> "Therefore, COME OUT FROM THEIR MIDST AND BE SEPARATE,"
> says the Lord.
> "AND DO NOT TOUCH WHAT IS UNCLEAN;
> And I will welcome you.
> "And I will be a father to you,
> And you shall be sons and daughters to Me,"
> Says the Lord Almighty. – 2 Corinthians 6:14-18

> Therefore, if anyone cleanses himself from these *things*, he will be a vessel for honor, sanctified [set apart], useful to the Master, prepared for every good work. Now flee from youthful lusts and pursue righteousness, faith, love *and* peace, with those who call on the Lord from a pure heart. – 2 Timothy 2:21-22

> You adulteresses, do you not know that friendship with the world is hostility toward God? Therefore whoever wishes to be a friend of the world makes himself an enemy of God. – James 4:4

> Do not quench the Spirit; do not despise prophetic utterances. But examine everything *carefully*; hold fast to that which is good; abstain from every form of evil. – 1 Thessalonians 5:19-22

The more you are around immorality, sensuality, and the things of this world, and the more you watch, listen and participate in such things, the further from God you will again drift. Socializing with those who still live in the flesh will infect you; in fact, it's much more likely that they will influence you to sin than you will influence them to Christ, as it is written:

> A little leaven [sin] leavens the whole lump *of dough*. – Galatians 5:9

We must be ever so mindful to remain as a "virgin" bride of Christ (see 2 Cor 11:2, Rev. 14 – undefiled by sin as much as humanly possible) and strive not to dirty (pollute) our "white garments" again with sin (see Rev. 3:18, Rev. 7, Rev. 19 – white clothes indicating purity), so we will not be ashamed when we stand before Him on Judgment Day (Rev. 7). So, I'm simply going to state the obvious here:

- It's best to fellowship with those who love and serve the Lord,
- It's best not to go to bars, social clubs, nightclubs, and other such places (and no, this is not where you go to share Christ, as a general habit),
- You will find many old "friends" are no longer "friends" due to your change in activities, and they fall away from you (and probably mock you) as you decline to participate in their worldly/fleshly gratifying activities. So be it.

In distilling this chapter down to a simple question, I would phrase it as: Are you striving to understand and partake of the ways of man or the ways of God? It is by that distinction you can discern the difference between living in the Spirit vs. living in the flesh (world). By understanding the ways of man, you may be able to manipulate them for your own fame and fortune, but you will not be able to manipulate God on the great Day of Judgment – for all the ways of man lead to death. On the other hand, if you understand the ways of God, they lead to eternal life. This choice is yours to make. Each day, you must choose to move towards Christ or back towards this world.

THE PARABLE OF THE SOWER

The Parable of the Sower given in Matthew 17:3-8, 18-23 is relevant here, symbolizing someone who hears and accepts the word of God (believes, is born again), but then the cares of the world (thorns) choke it out. Make no mistake about it – seeking again the things of this world after you have been born again will drown out God. This also completely contradicts any "once saved always saved" false teaching you may hear! "For the one who sows to his own flesh will from the flesh reap corruption, but the one who sows to the Spirit will from the Spirit reap eternal life."

Perspective is key. Remember, for a Christian, "friendship with the world is hostility toward God." You are also commanded not to entangle yourself in worldly affairs, for "our Christian citizenship is in heaven," not this fallen world. A parable from *The Pilgrim's Progress* is helpful here: [89]

> INTERPRETER: I saw moreover in my dream, that the Interpreter took him by the hand, and had him into a little room, where sat two little children, each one in his chair. The name of the eldest was Passion, and the name of the other Patience. Passion seemed to be much discontented, but Patience was very quiet. Then Christian asked, "What is the reason of the discontent of Passion?" The Interpreter answered, "The governor of them would have him stay for his best things till the beginning of the next year, but he will have all now; but Patience is willing to wait."
>
> Then I saw that one came to Passion, and brought him a bag of treasure, and poured it down at his feet: the which he took up, and rejoiced therein, and withal laughed Patience to scorn. But I beheld but a while, and he had lavished all away, and had nothing left him but rags.

---

[89] Bunyan, John. (1678/2018), *The Pilgrim's Progress*, (London/Holy Spirit Prints).

> CHRISTIAN: Then said Christian to the Interpreter, Expound this matter more fully to me.
>
> INTERPRETER: So he said, These two lads are figures; Passion of the men of this world, and Patience of the men of that which is to come; for, as here thou seest, passion will have all now, this year, that is to say, in this world; so are the men of this world: They must have all their good things now; they cannot stay till the next year, that is, until the next world, for their portion of good. That proverb, "A bird in the hand is worth two in the bush," is of more authority with them than are all the divine testimonies of the good of the world to come. But as thou sawest that he had quickly lavished all away, and had presently left him nothing but rags, so will it be with all such men at the end of this world.
>
> CHRISTIAN: Then said Christian, Now I see that Patience has the best wisdom, and that upon many accounts. 1. Because he stays for the best things. 2. And also because he will have the glory of his, when the other has nothing but rags.
>
> INTERPRETER: Nay, you may add another, to wit, the glory of the next world will never wear out; but these are suddenly gone. Therefore Passion had not so much reason to laugh at Patience because he had his good things first, as Patience will have to laugh at Passion because he had his best things last; for first must give place to last, because last must have his time to come: but last gives place to nothing, for there is not another to succeed. He, therefore, that hath his portion first, must needs have a time to spend it; but he that hath his portion last, must have it lastingly: therefore it is said of Dives, "In thy lifetime thou receivedst thy good things, and likewise Lazarus evil things; but now he is comforted, and thou art tormented." [Luke 16:25].
>
> CHRISTIAN: Then I perceive it is not best to covet things that are now, but to wait for things to come.
>
> INTERPRETER: You say truth: for the things that are seen are temporal, but the things that are not seen are eternal. [2 Cor. 4:18]. But though this be so, yet since things present and our fleshly appetite are such near neighbors one to another; and again, because things to come and carnal sense are such strangers one to another; therefore it is, that the first of these so suddenly fall into amity, and that distance is so continued between the second.

ON TURNING BACK INTO THE WORLD (AND SIN)

John Bunyan writes this warning in *The Heavenly Footman* about returning to (towards) the world after once starting out in the way of a Christian: [90]

> If this will not provoke thee [to run towards heaven and Christ], consider thus: What then will become of them that some time since were running post-haste to heaven, (insomuch that they seemed to outstrip many,) but now are running as fast back again? Do you think those will ever come thither? What! To run back again—back again to sin, to the world, to the devil—back again to the lust of the flesh! Oh, "it had been better for them not to have known the way of righteousness, than after they have known it to turn (to turn back again) from the holy commandment." Those men shall not only be damned for sin, but for professing to all the world that sin is better than Christ; for the man that runs back again, he doth as good as say, I have tried Christ, and I have tried sin, and I do not find so

---

[90] The Heavenly Footman, by John Bunyan, 1698

much profit in Christ as in sin. I say, this man declareth this, even by his running back again. Oh sad! What a doom they will have who were almost at heaven-gates and then run back again! "If any draweth back," saith Christ, "my soul shall have no pleasure in him." Again, "No man having put his hand to the plough, (that is, set forward in the ways of God,) and looking back, (turning back again,) is fit for the kingdom of heaven." And if not fit for the kingdom of heaven, then for certain he must needs be fit for the fire of hell. And therefore (saith the apostle) those that bring forth these apostatizing fruits, as "briers and thorns, are rejected, being nigh unto cursing, whose end is to be burned."

And further:

> Now, that you may be provoked to run [towards heaven and Christ] with the foremost [urgency and attention], take notice of this. When Lot and his wife were running from cursed Sodom to the mountains to save their lives, it is said that his wife looked back from behind him, and she became a pillar of salt; and yet you see that neither her practice, nor the judgment of God that fell upon her for the same, would cause Lot to look behind him. I have sometimes wondered at Lot in this particular; his wife looked behind her and died immediately, but let what would become of her. Lot would not so much as look behind him to see her. We do not read that he did so much as once look where she was or what was become of her; his heart was indeed upon his journey, and well it might; there was the mountain before him and the fire and brimstone behind him; his life lay at stake, and he had lost it if he had but looked behind him. Do thou so run; and in thy race remember Lot's wife and remember her doom, and remember for what that doom did overtake her, and remember that God made her an example for all lazy runners to the end of the world; and take heed thou fall not after the same example.

Consider also the Jews leaving Egypt and then longing to return to bondage (see Numbers 14) – they all perished in the wilderness. Please take heed of yourself.

DO NOT UNDERESTIMATE THE PULL OF THE WORLD

I can't warn you strongly enough not to underestimate how hard the world tries to draw you back into it, with nonstop, glitzy, flashy, sexy, seemingly glamorous allures and temptations, shouted from the rooftops and all secular media sources 24/7/365 at full volume. It is truly staggering how much noise the world makes in an attempt to drown out the simple message of the gospel and also to allure the newly born-again baby Christian back into the clutches of sin and eternal death.

This excerpt from *The Pilgrim's Progress* about the "Vanity Fair" of the world offers an excellent synopsis of this subject:[91]

> INTERPRETER: Then I saw in my dream, that when they were got out of the wilderness, they presently saw a town before them, and the name of that town is Vanity; and at the town there is a fair kept, called Vanity Fair. It is kept all the year long. It beareth the name of Vanity Fair, because the town where it is kept is lighter than vanity, [Psa. 62:9]; and also because all that is there sold, or that cometh thither,

---

[91] Bunyan, John. (1678/2018), *The Pilgrim's Progress*, (London/Holy Spirit Prints).

is vanity; as is the saying of the wise, "All that cometh is vanity." [Eccl. 11:8; see also 1:2-14; 2:11-17; Isa. 40:17].

This fair is no new-erected business but a thing of ancient standing. I will show you the original of it.

Almost five thousand years ago there were pilgrims walking to the Celestial City, as these two honest persons are: and Beelzebub, Apollyon, and Legion, with their companions, perceiving by the path that the pilgrims made, that their way to the city lay through this town of Vanity, they contrived here to set up a fair; a fair wherein should be sold all sorts of vanity, and that it should last all the year long. Therefore, at this fair are all such merchandise sold as houses, lands, trades, places, honors, preferments, titles, countries, kingdoms, lusts, pleasures; and delights of all sorts, as harlots, wives, husbands, children, masters, servants, lives, blood, bodies, souls, silver, gold, pearls, precious stones, and what not.

And moreover, at this fair there is at all times to be seen jugglings, cheats, games, plays, fools, apes, knaves, and rogues, and that of every kind.

Here are to be seen, too, and that for nothing, thefts, murders, adulteries, false-swearers, and that of a blood-red color.

And, as in other fairs of less moment, there are the several rows and streets under their proper names, where such and such wares are vended; so here, likewise, you have the proper places, rows, streets, (namely, countries and kingdoms,) where the wares of this fair are soonest to be found. Here is the Britain Row, the French Row, the Italian Row, the Spanish Row, the German Row, where several sorts of vanities are to be sold. But, as in other fairs, some one commodity is as the chief of all the fair; so the ware of Rome and her merchandise is greatly promoted in this fair; only our English nation, with some others, have taken a dislike thereat.

Now, as I said, the way to the Celestial City lies just through this town, where this lusty fair is kept; and he that will go to the city, and yet not go through this town, "must needs go out of the world." [1 Cor. 4:10]. The Prince of princes himself, when here, went through this town to his own country, and that upon a fair-day too; yea, and, as I think, it was Beelzebub, the chief lord of this fair, that invited him to buy of his vanities, yea, would have made him lord of the fair, would he but have done him reverence as he went through the town. Yea, because he was such a person of honor, Beelzebub had him from street to street, and showed him all the kingdoms of the world in a little time, that he might, if possible, allure that blessed One to cheapen and buy some of his vanities; but he had no mind to the merchandise, and therefore left the town, without laying out so much as one farthing upon these vanities. [Matt. 4:8,9; Luke 4:5-7]. This fair, therefore, is an ancient thing, of long standing, and a very great fair.

Now, these pilgrims, as I said, must needs go through this fair. Well, so they did; but behold, even as they entered into the fair, all the people in the fair were moved; and the town itself, as it were, in a hubbub about them, and that for several reasons: for,

First, The Pilgrims were clothed with such kind of raiment as was diverse from the raiment of any that traded in that fair. The people, therefore, of the fair made a great gazing upon them: some said they were fools; [1 Cor. 4:9,10]; some, they were bedlams; and some, they were outlandish men.

Secondly, And as they wondered at their apparel, so they did likewise at their speech; for few could understand what they said. They naturally spoke the language of Canaan; but they that kept the fair were the men of this world: so that from one end of the fair to the other, they seemed barbarians each to the other. [1 Cor. 2:7,8].

Thirdly, But that which did not a little amuse the merchandisers was, that these pilgrims set very light by all their wares. They cared not so much as to look upon them; and if they called upon them to buy, they would put their fingers in their ears, and cry, "Turn away mine eyes from beholding vanity," [Psa. 119:37], and look upward, signifying that their trade and traffic was in heaven. [Phil. 3: 20,21].

One chanced, mockingly, beholding the carriage of the men, to say unto them, "What will ye buy?" But they, looking gravely upon him, said, "We buy the truth." [Prov. 23:23]. At that there was an occasion taken to despise the men the more; some mocking, some taunting, some speaking reproachfully, and some calling upon others to smite them. At last, things came to an hubbub and great stir in the fair, insomuch that all order was confounded. Now was word presently brought to the great one of the fair, who quickly came down, and deputed some of his most trusty friends to take those men into examination about whom the fair was almost overturned. So the men were brought to examination; and they that sat upon them asked them whence they came, whither they went, and what they did there in such an unusual garb. The men told them they were pilgrims and strangers in the world, and that they were going to their own country, which was the heavenly Jerusalem, [Heb. 11:13-16]; and that they had given no occasion to the men of the town, nor yet to the merchandisers, thus to abuse them, and to let them in their journey, except it was for that, when one asked them what they would buy, they said they would buy the truth.

So be on guard, for many will quit the faith, even after starting out as you now have, and many will turn back to the ways of this world – longing again for their old sinful ways, habits, behaviors, and friends. We should heed the strong warning given to us by the example of Lot's wife, who longed again (looked back to) for the ways of sin after leaving Sodom and was therefore turned into a "pillar of salt" (see Genesis 19). Always remember that Satan, the devil, "prowls around like a roaring lion," seeking to turn you back any way that he can!

ON CONTINUED SINS

I want to add one important teaching note to this chapter, so you do not get discouraged, and that is about the continued fight with sin even after one is born again (see the false teaching: A Christian No Longer Sins).

Even after one is born-again, you still retain your old fleshly nature as well as your new spirit nature in Christ. They will wage war with each other (Matthew 26:41, Romans 7:14-25, 2 Corinthians 4:16, 1 Peter 2:11). But if you do fall down and sin, confess your sins before Christ, who is "faithful and just to forgive" you (1 John 1:9). His mercy, compassion, lovingkindness, and grace are absolutely massive. Just pick yourself up, again walk in the Spirit, ask the Lord for wisdom to deal with whatever weakness you have, as well as for His strength and guidance going forward (Psalm 23:1). A Christian's life is one of continued repentance. One of my favorite verses helps a lot here:

> The LORD'S lovingkindnesses indeed never cease,
> For His compassions never fail.

> *They* are new every morning;
> Great is Your faithfulness. – Lamentations 3:22-23

Remember the teaching of Christ also. Peter once asked Jesus how many times he should forgive those who sinned against him (see Matthew 18:21-22), probably expecting to hear the number three or five and even suggested the number seven (i.e., a small number of times). However, the Lord answered with the number "seventy times seven" (i.e., 490). Now the actual number given here isn't the important part (we are not to interpret that as a literal 490 times we are to forgive sins); what's important is the magnitude of the number – it's an ENORMOUS number which was far, far above anything that Peter might have even remotely imagined in his own mind! This again demonstrates that the depths of the love, kindness, mercy, and grace of God are very great indeed!

One last matter for this chapter: A conscientious Christian, a son of God, a "new creature" in Christ, should evaluate their lifestyle and re-examine any habits or behaviors that may have carried over from before their conversion (when they were born again) – things such as smoking, drinking alcohol, etc. Scripture tells us that "we are no longer our own" and that we are "living stones" in the temple of God. We should strive to "do all things to the glory of God." Harmful habits and behavior may need to be addressed; let your conscience be your guide. I'm speaking here to behaviors that are not expressly forbidden by Scripture.

The subject at hand continues in the next chapter, which discusses changing your entertainment habits, for they are very much related.

FALSE TEACHING(S) YOU WILL ENCOUNTER:

- Once saved always saved
- A Christian no longer sins

RELATED SCRIPTURE:

And He was saying to *them* all, "If anyone wishes to come after Me, he must deny himself, and take up his cross daily and follow Me." – Luke 9:23

For the grace of God has appeared, bringing salvation to all men, instructing us to deny ungodliness and worldly desires and to live sensibly, righteously and godly in the present age. – Titus 2:11-12

Therefore, prepare your minds for action, keep sober *in spirit*, fix your hope completely on the grace to be brought to you at the revelation of Jesus Christ. As obedient children, do not be conformed to the former lusts *which were yours* in your ignorance, but like the Holy One who called you, be holy yourselves also in all *your* behavior; because it is written, "YOU SHALL BE HOLY, FOR I AM HOLY." – 1 Peter 1:13-16

For if we have become united with *Him* in the likeness of His death, certainly we shall also be *in the likeness* of His resurrection, knowing this, that our old self was crucified with *Him*, in order that our body of sin might be done away with, so that we would no longer be slaves to sin; for he who has died is freed from sin. – Romans 6:5-7

Therefore do not let sin reign in your mortal body so that you obey its lusts, and do not go on presenting the members of your body to sin *as* instruments of unrighteousness; but present yourselves to God as those alive from the dead, and your members *as* instruments of righteousness to God. For sin shall not be master over you, for you are not under law but under grace.

What then? Shall we sin because we are not under law but under grace? May it never be! Do you not know that when you present yourselves to someone *as* slaves for obedience, you are slaves of the one whom you obey, either of sin resulting in death, or of obedience resulting in righteousness? But thanks be to God that though you were slaves of sin, you became obedient from the heart to that form of teaching to which you were committed, and having been freed from sin, you became slaves of righteousness. I am speaking in human terms because of the weakness of your flesh. For just as you presented your members as slaves to impurity and to lawlessness, resulting in *further* lawlessness, so now present your members as slaves to righteousness, resulting in sanctification. – Romans 6:12-19

My son, if sinners entice you,
Do not consent. – Proverbs 1:10

Do not be deceived: "Bad company corrupts good morals." Become sober-minded as you ought, and stop sinning; for some have no knowledge of God. I speak *this* to your shame. – 1 Corinthians 15:33-34

Do not let your heart envy sinners,
But *live* in the fear of the LORD always.
Surely there is a future,
And your hope will not be cut off.
Listen, my son, and be wise,
And direct your heart in the way.
Do not be with heavy drinkers of wine,
Or with gluttonous eaters of meat;
For the heavy drinker and the glutton will come to poverty,
And drowsiness will clothe *one* with rags. – Proverbs 23:17-21

Beloved, I urge you as aliens and strangers [pilgrims] to abstain from fleshly lusts which wage war against the soul. Keep your behavior excellent among the Gentiles, so that in the thing in which they slander you as evildoers, they may because of your good deeds, as they observe *them*, glorify God in the day of visitation. – 1 Peter 2:11-12

…in us who do not walk according to the flesh but according to the Spirit. For those who are according to the flesh set their minds on the things of the flesh, but those who are according to the Spirit, the things of the Spirit. For the mind set on the flesh is death, but the mind set on the Spirit is life and peace, because the mind set on the flesh is hostile toward God; for it does not subject itself to the law of God, for it is not even able *to do so*, and those who are in the flesh cannot please God. – Romans 8:4b-8

So then, brethren, we are under obligation, not to the flesh, to live according to the flesh— for if you are living according to the flesh, you must die; but if by the Spirit you are putting to death the deeds of the body, you will live. For all who are being led by the Spirit of God, these are sons of God. – Romans 8:12-14

Therefore be imitators of God, as beloved children; and walk in love, just as Christ also loved you and gave Himself up for us, an offering and a sacrifice to God as a fragrant aroma.

But immorality or any impurity or greed must not even be named among you, as is proper among saints; and *there must be no* filthiness and silly talk, or coarse jesting, which are not fitting, but rather giving of thanks. For this you know with certainty, that no immoral or impure person or covetous man, who is an idolater, has an inheritance in the kingdom of Christ and God.

Let no one deceive you with empty words, for because of these things the wrath of God comes upon the sons of disobedience. Therefore do not be partakers with them; for you were formerly darkness, but now you are Light in the Lord; walk as children of Light (for the fruit of the Light *consists* in all goodness and righteousness and truth), trying to learn what is pleasing to the Lord. Do not participate in the unfruitful deeds of darkness, but instead even expose them; for it is disgraceful even to speak of the things which are done by them in secret. But all things become visible when they are exposed by the light, for everything that becomes visible is light. For this reason it says,

"Awake, sleeper,
And arise from the dead,
And Christ will shine on you."

Therefore be careful how you walk, not as unwise men but as wise, making the most of your time, because the days are evil. So then do not be foolish, but understand what the will of the Lord is. And do not get drunk with wine, for that is dissipation, but be filled with the Spirit, speaking to one another in psalms and hymns and spiritual songs, singing and making melody with your heart to the Lord; always giving thanks for all things in the name of our Lord Jesus Christ to God, even the Father; and be subject to one another in the fear of Christ. – Ephesians 5:1-21

Grace to you and peace from God our Father and the Lord Jesus Christ, who gave Himself for our sins so that He might rescue us from this present evil age, according to the will of our God and Father, to whom be the glory forevermore. Amen. – Galatians 1:3-5

"If the world hates you, you know that it has hated Me before *it hated* you. If you were of the world, the world would love its own; but because you are not of the world, but I chose you out of the world, because of this the world hates you." – John 15:18-19

I heard another voice from heaven, saying, "Come out of her [Babylon], my people, so that you will not participate in her sins and receive of her plagues." – Revelation 18:4

Then Jesus said to His disciples, "If anyone wishes to come after Me, he must deny himself, and take up his cross and follow Me. For whoever wishes to save his life will lose it; but whoever loses his life for My sake will find it. For what will it profit a man if he gains the whole world and forfeits his soul? Or what will a man give in exchange for his soul? For the Son of Man is going to come in the glory of His Father with His angels, and WILL THEN REPAY EVERY MAN ACCORDING TO HIS DEEDS." – Matthew 16:24-27

"I have been crucified with Christ; and it is no longer I who live, but Christ lives in me; and the *life* which I now live in the flesh I live by faith in the Son of God, who loved me and gave Himself up for me." – Galatians 2:20

Do you not know that you are a temple of God and *that* the Spirit of God dwells in you? If any man destroys the temple of God, God will destroy him, for the temple of God is holy, and that is what you are. – 1 Corinthians 3:16-17

So this I say, and affirm together with the Lord, that you walk no longer just as the Gentiles also walk, in the futility of their mind, being darkened in their understanding, excluded from the life of God because of the ignorance that is in them, because of the hardness of their heart; and they, having become callous, have given themselves over to sensuality for the practice of every kind of impurity with greediness. But you did not learn Christ in this way, if indeed you have heard Him and have been taught in Him, just as truth is in Jesus, that, in reference to your former manner of life, you lay aside the old self, which is being corrupted in accordance with the lusts of deceit, and that you be renewed in the spirit of your mind, and put on the new self, which in *the likeness of* God has been created in righteousness and holiness of the truth. – Ephesians 4:17-24

Let no unwholesome word proceed from your mouth, but only such *a word* as is good for edification according to the need *of the moment*, so that it will give grace to those who hear. Do not grieve the Holy Spirit of God, by whom you were sealed for the day of redemption. Let all bitterness and wrath and anger and clamor and slander be put away from you, along with all malice. – Ephesians 4:29-31

Therefore, having these promises, beloved, let us cleanse ourselves from all defilement of flesh and spirit, perfecting holiness in the fear of God. – 2 Corinthians 7:1

But those who want to get rich fall into temptation and a snare and many foolish and harmful desires which plunge men into ruin and destruction. For the love of money is a root of all sorts of evil, and some by longing for it have wandered away from the faith and pierced themselves with many griefs. – 1 Timothy 6:9-10

You therefore, my son, be strong in the grace that is in Christ Jesus. The things which you have heard from me in the presence of many witnesses, entrust these to faithful men who will be able to teach others also. Suffer hardship with *me*, as a good soldier of Christ Jesus. No soldier in active service entangles himself in the affairs of everyday life, so that he may please the one who enlisted him as a soldier. Also if anyone competes as an athlete, he does not win the prize unless he competes according to the rules. The hard-working farmer ought to be the first to receive his share of the crops. Consider what I say, for the Lord will give you understanding in everything. – 2 Timothy 2:1-7 [Note: You are a soldier for Christ now!]

By faith Moses, when he was born, was hidden for three months by his parents, because they saw he was a beautiful child; and they were not afraid of the king's edict. By faith Moses, when he had grown up, refused to be called the son of Pharaoh's daughter, choosing rather to endure ill-treatment with the people of God than to enjoy the passing pleasures of sin, considering the reproach of Christ greater riches than the treasures of Egypt. – Hebrews 11:23-26

For if, after they have escaped the defilements of the world by the knowledge of the Lord and Savior Jesus Christ, they are again entangled in them and are overcome, the last state has become worse for them than the first. For it would be better for them not to have known the way of righteousness, than having known it, to turn away from the holy commandment handed on to them. It has happened to them according to the true proverb, "A DOG RETURNS TO ITS OWN VOMIT," and, "A sow, after washing, *returns* to wallowing in the mire." – 2 Peter 2:20-22

Therefore, beloved, since you look for these things, be diligent to be found spotless and blameless by Him. – 2 Peter 3:14

The Lord's bond-servant must not be quarrelsome, but be kind to all, able to teach, patient when wronged, with gentleness correcting those who are in opposition, if perhaps God may grant them repentance leading to the knowledge of the truth, and they may come to their senses *and escape* from the snare of the devil, having been held captive by him to do his will. – 2 Timothy 2:24-26

But I say, walk by the Spirit, and you will not carry out the desire of the flesh. For the flesh sets its desire against the Spirit, and the Spirit against the flesh; for these are in opposition to one another, so that you may not do the things that you please. But if you are led by the Spirit, you are not under the Law. Now the deeds of the flesh are evident, which are: immorality, impurity, sensuality, idolatry, sorcery, enmities, strife, jealousy, outbursts of anger, disputes, dissensions, factions, envying, drunkenness, carousing, and things like these, of which I forewarn you, just as I have forewarned you, that those who practice such things will not inherit the kingdom of God. But the fruit of the Spirit is love, joy, peace, patience, kindness, goodness, faithfulness, gentleness, self-control; against such things there is no law. Now those who belong to Christ Jesus have crucified the flesh with its passions and desires. If we live by the Spirit, let us also walk by the Spirit. – Galatians 5:16-25

Therefore, since Christ has suffered in the flesh, arm yourselves also with the same purpose, because he who has suffered in the flesh has ceased from sin, so as to live the rest of the time in the flesh no longer for the lusts of men, but for the will of God. For the time already past is sufficient *for you* to have carried out the desire of the Gentiles, having pursued a course of sensuality, lusts, drunkenness, carousing, drinking parties and abominable idolatries. In *all* this, they are surprised that you do not run with *them* into the same excesses of dissipation, and they malign *you*; but they will give account to Him who is ready to judge the living and the dead. For the gospel has for this purpose been preached even to those who are dead, that though they are judged in the flesh as men, they may live in the spirit according to *the will of* God. – 1 Peter 4:1-6

And He spoke many things to them in parables, saying, "Behold, the sower went out to sow; and as he sowed, some *seeds* fell beside the road, and the birds came and ate them up. Others fell on the rocky places, where they did not have much soil; and immediately they sprang up, because they had no depth of soil. But when the sun had risen, they were scorched; and because they had no root, they withered away. Others fell among the thorns, and the thorns came up and choked them out. And others fell on the good soil and yielded a crop, some a hundredfold, some sixty, and some thirty.

"Hear then the parable of the sower. When anyone hears the word of the kingdom and does not understand it, the evil *one* comes and snatches away what has been sown in his heart. This is the one on whom seed was sown beside the road. The one on whom seed was sown on the rocky places, this is the man who hears the word and immediately receives it with joy; yet he has no *firm* root in himself, but is *only* temporary, and when affliction or persecution arises because of the word, immediately he falls away. And the one on whom seed was sown among the thorns, this is the man who hears the word, and the worry of the world and the deceitfulness of wealth choke the word, and it becomes unfruitful. And the one on whom seed was sown on the good soil, this is the man who hears the word and understands it; who indeed bears fruit and brings forth, some a hundredfold, some sixty, and some thirty." – Matthew 13:3-8, 18-23

For though we walk in the flesh, we do not war according to the flesh, for the weapons of our warfare are not of the flesh, but divinely powerful for the destruction of fortresses. *We are* destroying speculations and every lofty thing raised up against the knowledge of God, and *we are* taking every thought captive to the obedience of Christ. – 2 Corinthians 10:3-5

Leave the presence of a fool,
Or you will not discern words of knowledge. – Proverbs 14:7

A wise man is cautious and turns away from evil,
But a fool is arrogant and careless. – Proverbs 14:16

A wise man's heart *directs him* toward the right, but the foolish man's heart *directs him* toward the left. Even when the fool walks along the road, his sense is lacking and he demonstrates to everyone *that* he is a fool. – Ecclesiastes 10:2-3

The night is almost gone, and the day is near. Therefore let us lay aside the deeds of darkness and put on the armor of light. Let us behave properly as in the day, not in carousing and drunkenness, not in sexual promiscuity and sensuality, not in strife and jealousy. But put on the Lord Jesus Christ, and make no provision for the flesh in regard to *its* lusts. – Romans 13:12-14

"They are not of the world, just as I am not of the world." – John 17:16

Therefore I urge you, brothers *and sisters*, by the mercies of God, to present your bodies as a living and holy sacrifice, acceptable to God, *which is* your spiritual service of worship. And do not be conformed to this world, but be transformed by the renewing of your mind, so that you may prove what the will of God is, that which is good and acceptable and perfect. – Romans 12:1-2

And you were dead in your offenses and sins, in which you previously walked according to the course of this world, according to the prince of the power of the air, of the spirit that is now working in the sons of disobedience. Among them we too all previously lived in the lusts of our flesh, indulging the desires of the flesh and of the mind, and were by nature children of wrath, just as the rest. – Ephesians 2:1-3

This is the message we have heard from Him and announce to you, that God is Light, and in Him there is no darkness at all. If we say that we have fellowship with Him and *yet* walk in the darkness, we lie and do not practice the truth; but if we walk in the Light as He Himself is in the Light, we have fellowship with one another, and the blood of Jesus His Son cleanses us from all sin. If we say that we have no sin, we are deceiving ourselves and the truth is not in us. If we confess our sins, He is faithful and righteous to forgive us our sins and to cleanse us from all unrighteousness. If we say that we have not sinned, we make Him a liar and His word is not in us. – 1 John 1:5-10

5.7 CHANGING YOUR ENTERTAINMENT HABITS
(Radio, Television, Movies, etc.)

Finally, brethren, whatever is true, whatever is honorable, whatever is right, whatever is pure, whatever is lovely, whatever is of good repute, if there is any excellence and if anything worthy of praise, dwell on these things. – Philippians 4:8

This chapter is effectively a continuation of the previous chapter (Changing Your Worldly Habits). Like the last chapter, the advice in this one can be unbelievably hard to follow through with in daily life. It is only through the grace and strength of God that you can overcome. With that introduction, let me state the recommendation upfront and then talk through it.

I strongly recommend that you abstain from watching 99.99% of what is on TV (and Netflix, YouTube, or whatever your favorite sources are) and the movies (so-called entertainment) produced by the entertainment industry. In summary, there is nothing whatsoever morally pure about anything that is produced by the worldly entertainment industry at large. Their "entertainment" simply appeals to the "lust of the eyes," "lust of the flesh," greed, idolatry, and other corrupt fleshly desires. Furthermore, nearly all of the so-called "Christian" movies are based on the false teachings outlined in this book, so beware. This "entertainment" is at worst completely corrupted, fallen, sin-laden productions from start to finish, and at best, they are a means to deceive you when they appear to be promoted as "Christian" films (and books, etc.), but they are replete with false teachings.

The entertainment of the world is only designed to appeal to the carnal, fleshly, lustful, sinful, prideful, selfish man, and it is the primary means by which you are brainwashed, dumbed-down, and made to take your eyes and focus off of Christ. It is simply staggering how blatantly corrupt, immoral, sexually explicit, sexually innuendo containing, demeaning, and blaspheming of God the things that are produced for TV and movies have become, in nearly all instances, on all channels, all genres, at all times. I suppose you might find a wholesome cooking show, but I think you get the point. Yes, this sinful, fallen, fleshly world with its lustful pursuits generates a staggering amount of noise each and every day, desperately trying to drown out the goodness of God and of His Christ, and the good news of the gospel, and God's Word in total. If you let it, even as a Christian, you run a great risk of backsliding, apostasy, or worse.

The same recommendation applies to other forms of entertainment as well, such as your music choices. Without getting into a debate about musical styles and tastes, it must be said that discretion is required even when listening to modern so-called "Christian" music (yes, there's the word again in quotes), because it seems to focus more on self-justification, self-worth, happiness, the "feel good" gospel and glorification of self than anything else, and it is also not always performed in a reverent (respectful) manner to a Holy God.

You might argue: hey, it's still okay to watch nature shows, documentaries, etc., right? Such material might be educational and informative but be especially alert and aware that even this content is created to intentionally deny God as Creator and to implement the constant and endless bombardment/brainwashing of the "theory of evolution" and "millions of years" false teachings on which they almost always base their so-called "science." God is not to be found among these shows.

The hardest area of all for me has been sporting events. I'm pretty active in sports and have found them to be healthy and good in large part. But today, I find that even when I watch sporting events, particularly football which is my favorite, the advertisements are so sexual nowadays that as a Christian, I cannot simply sit there and watch them any longer. It seems to be just an endless parade of advertising for beer, trucks, the latest Hollywood entertainment flick, and a whole host of other items which only appeal to sinful, lustful fleshly desires.

I pray that the Spirit will be with you and guide you in this area. If you are not careful, your entertainment choices can lure you back into the world very quickly, and it will do so in a very silent and insidious manner; and before you even realize it, you will find yourself walking in, partaking of, and wandering among the fleshly carnal world again. It is prudent to remember what God told Cain: "sin is crouching at the door; and its desire is for you."

FALSE TEACHING(S) YOU WILL ENCOUNTER:
- Once saved always saved
- A Christian no longer sins

RELATED SCRIPTURE: (see prior chapter verses also)

Do not love the world nor the things in the world. If anyone loves the world, the love of the Father is not in him. For all that is in the world, the lust of the flesh and the lust of the eyes and the boastful pride of life, is not from the Father, but is from the world. The world is passing away, and *also* its lusts; but the one who does the will of God lives forever. – 1 John 2:15-17

Therefore if you have been raised up with Christ, keep seeking the things above, where Christ is, seated at the right hand of God. Set your mind on the things above, not on the things that are on earth. For you have died and your life is hidden with Christ in God. When Christ, who is our life, is revealed, then you also will be revealed with Him in glory.

Therefore consider the members of your earthly body as dead to immorality, impurity, passion, evil desire, and greed, which amounts to idolatry. For it is because of these things that the wrath of God will come upon the sons of disobedience, and in them you also once walked, when you were living in them. But now you also, rid yourselves of all of them: anger, wrath, malice, slander, and obscene speech from your mouth. Do not lie to one another, since you stripped off the old self with its *evil* practices. – Colossians 3:1-9

Finally, brethren, whatever is true, whatever is honorable, whatever is right, whatever is pure, whatever is lovely, whatever is of good repute, if there is any excellence and if anything worthy of praise, dwell on these things. – Philippians 4:8 [Note: There is very little of anything that meets this criterion in modern Hollywood entertainment!]

And do not be conformed to this world, but be transformed by the renewing of your mind, so that you may prove what the will of God is, that which is good and acceptable and perfect. – Romans 12:2

You adulteresses, do you not know that friendship with the world is hostility toward God? Therefore whoever wishes to be a friend of the world makes himself an enemy of God. – James 4:4

Then Jesus said to His disciples, "If anyone wishes to come after Me, he must deny himself, and take up his cross and follow Me." – Matthew 16:24

"I have been crucified with Christ; and it is no longer I who live, but Christ lives in me; and the *life* which I now live in the flesh I live by faith in the Son of God, who loved me and gave Himself up for me." – Galatians 2:20

"If you do well, will not *your countenance* be lifted up? And if you do not do well, sin is crouching at the door; and its desire is for you, but you must master it." – Genesis 4:7

5.8 ATTENDING A NEW BELIEVER CLASS

You therefore, beloved, knowing this beforehand, be on your guard
so that you are not carried away by the error of unprincipled men
and fall from your own steadfastness, but grow in the grace and knowledge
of our Lord and Savior Jesus Christ. – 2 Peter 3:17-18

If you do not grow and mature as a Christian, you face a very high risk of falling away or being led astray! I know – I did fall away once myself! Please see my testimony at the end of this book. Therefore, if your church (assuming you have found one) offers a "believer 101" or "new believer" class, I recommend you take it and do so as soon as you possibly can!

These classes usually cover many common questions, thoughts, doubts, and concerns that a new believer can have, and this can also help you get involved in other areas (e.g., a Bible study). If your church doesn't offer one of these classes, there are some available online, or you can purchase workbooks and go through one yourself (although I don't recommend those except as a last resort if nothing else is available to you).

The goal of doing this is to allow mature Christians to help you get started on the right path and guide you. Please also beware that when you use any online Bible study or workbook, you are subject to the beliefs, opinions, and doctrines of the group that published it, so you must use extreme care and discernment. Newly born-again Christians can be very gullible and easy prey for false teachings – once again, I know, for I was one!

RELATED SCRIPTURE:

My people are destroyed for lack of knowledge. – Hosea 4:6

And I, brethren, could not speak to you as to spiritual men, but as to men of flesh, as to infants in Christ. I gave you milk to drink, not solid food; for you were not yet able *to receive it*. Indeed, even now you are not yet able, for you are still fleshly. For since there is jealousy and strife among you, are you not fleshly, and are you not walking like mere men? – 1 Corinthians 3:1-3

When I was a child, I used to speak like a child, think like a child, reason like a child; when I became a man, I did away with childish things. – 1 Corinthians 13:11

For this reason also, since the day we heard *of it*, we have not ceased to pray for you and to ask that you may be filled with the knowledge of His will in all spiritual wisdom and understanding, so that you will walk in a manner worthy of the Lord, to please *Him* in all respects, bearing fruit in every good work and increasing in the knowledge of God. – Colossians 1:9-10

Therefore, beloved, since you look for these things, be diligent to be found by Him in peace, spotless and blameless, and regard the patience of our Lord *as* salvation; just as also our beloved brother Paul, according to the wisdom given him, wrote to you, as also in all *his* letters, speaking in them of these things, in which are some things hard to understand, which the untaught and unstable distort, as *they do* also the rest of the Scriptures, to their own destruction. You therefore, beloved, knowing this beforehand, be on your guard so that you are not carried away by the error of unprincipled men and fall from your own steadfastness, but grow in the grace and knowledge of our Lord and Savior Jesus Christ. To Him *be* the glory, both now and to the day of eternity. Amen. – 2 Peter 3:14-18

And He gave some *as* apostles, and some *as* prophets, and some *as* evangelists, and some *as* pastors and teachers, for the equipping of the saints for the work of service, to the building up of the body of Christ; until we all attain to the unity of the faith, and of the knowledge of the Son of God, to a mature man, to the measure of the stature which belongs to the fullness of Christ. As a result, we are no longer to be children, tossed here and there by waves and carried about by every wind of doctrine, by the trickery of men, by craftiness in deceitful scheming; but speaking the truth in love, we are to grow up in all *aspects* into Him who is the head, *even* Christ, from whom the whole body, being fitted and held together by what every joint supplies, according to the proper working of each individual part, causes the growth of the body for the building up of itself in love. – Ephesians 4:11-16

Iron sharpens iron,
So one man sharpens another. – Proverbs 27:17

5.9 FINDING YOUR FIRST BIBLE STUDY

Be diligent [study] to present yourself approved to God as a workman who does not need to be ashamed, accurately handling the word of truth. – 2 Timothy 2:15

I recommend enrolling in the next Bible study class that starts at your church (assuming you have found one), regardless of what book they are currently studying. Take the very next one that is starting, which fits your schedule. If you are at a smaller church and only one is offered, or there is only one available which fits your schedule, take it – don't worry about its book/topic/subject. Trust in the Lord to guide you to the right one. If one isn't starting for a long time, it's fine to join one already in progress. Just realize you won't know very much at first, but that is perfectly fine and normal. Just getting started is the most important consideration!

If you can choose from several different classes, just pick the one you think sounds the most interesting. The goal here is to get you into <u>any</u> Bible study so you start to learn and study God's Word. Besides, you should have already started on your own Bible reading plan at home, right? If women or men only classes are available, and the topic suits you, those are fine also. Single or mixed-gender doesn't really matter that much – what matters the most is that you just get started.

RELATED SCRIPTURE:

"Behold, I send you out as sheep in the midst of wolves; so be shrewd as serpents and innocent as doves." – Matthew 10:16

How blessed is the man who does not walk in the counsel of the wicked,
Nor stand in the path of sinners,
Nor sit in the seat of scoffers!
But his delight is in the law of the LORD,
And in His law he meditates day and night. – Psalm 1:1-2

But He answered and said, "It is written, 'MAN SHALL NOT LIVE ON BREAD ALONE, BUT ON EVERY WORD THAT PROCEEDS OUT OF THE MOUTH OF GOD.'" – Matthew 4:4

Where there is no guidance the people fall,
But in abundance of counselors there is victory. – Proverbs 11:14

Be diligent [study] to present yourself approved to God as a workman who does not need to be ashamed, accurately handling [rightly dividing, interpreting] the word of truth. – 2 Timothy 2:15

5.10 BEING A BEREAN

Now these were more noble-minded than those in Thessalonica [the Bereans], for they received the word with great eagerness, examining the Scriptures daily to see whether these things were so. – Acts 17:11

As you have read in previous chapters, a Christian is called to use the "Sword of the Spirit," which is the Word of God. This is an essential part of your (spiritual) "Armor of God." Do not trust what anyone says (not me, not friends, not even your pastor or preacher) without first checking it against what is written in Scripture! "Being a Berean" is a phrase taken from Acts 17:11, which means to study the Scriptures daily to see what they say and to diligently compare and check everything you read and hear against Scripture!

In this book, you have seen that the false teachings and false doctrines of man abound in all directions, as far as the eye can see. The only way you will not be deceived is if you know Scripture better than the "wolves" do. Even Satan and his demons know Scripture! We see examples in the Bible where Satan quotes Scripture, but he always does so by subtly altering or twisting it with the intention to deceive. He does this by adding to, misquoting, distorting, or taking away from the words of Scripture, mixing in some actual biblical truth with lies so that it all sounds very convincing and "biblical" to you. You must be able to detect half-truths, lies-of-omissions, etc., which the forces of evil love to use to trick, trap and ensnare us. Do not underestimate the danger of those tricks – for this is how Satan tricked Eve and Adam!

I want to be called "noble-minded" by God, don't you? In particular, notice the exhortation given to us in 1 John 4:1-3 to "test the spirits." This also applies to testing preachers, pastors, authors, me, this book, and everything else you hear or read related to the Bible. But how do you test them? You do so by checking that what they are speaking (or writing) matches the truth of Scripture, the written Word of God. Scripture is the final authority. It is, therefore, essential that you know what the Bible actually says; it is also essential to be able to read and utilize multiple Bible translations for this very reason! This is what "being a Berean" is all about. That is what I strive for myself.

I have explained throughout this book that you must not only know the Word of God, but you must also know what is <u>not</u> the Word of God! See also the chapters on Choosing a Bible and Beware the Wolves.

RELATED SCRIPTURE:

The brethren immediately sent Paul and Silas away by night to Berea [the Bereans], and when they arrived, they went into the synagogue of the Jews. Now these were more noble-minded than those in Thessalonica, for they received the word with great eagerness, examining the Scriptures daily *to see* whether these things were so. – Acts 17:10-11

Finally, be strong in the Lord and in the strength of His might. Put on the full armor of God, so that you will be able to stand firm against the schemes of the devil. For our struggle is not against flesh and blood, but against the rulers, against the powers, against the world forces of this darkness, against the spiritual *forces* of wickedness in the heavenly *places*. Therefore, take up the full armor of God, so that you will be able to resist in the evil day, and having done everything, to stand firm. Stand firm therefore, HAVING GIRDED YOUR LOINS WITH TRUTH, and HAVING PUT ON THE BREASTPLATE OF

RIGHTEOUSNESS, and having shod YOUR FEET WITH THE PREPARATION OF THE GOSPEL OF PEACE; in addition to all, taking up the shield of faith with which you will be able to extinguish all the flaming arrows of the evil *one*. And take THE HELMET OF SALVATION, and the sword of the Spirit, which is the word of God. – Ephesians 6:10-17

But He answered and said, "It is written, 'MAN SHALL NOT LIVE ON BREAD ALONE, BUT ON EVERY WORD THAT PROCEEDS OUT OF THE MOUTH OF GOD.'" – Matthew 4:4

All Scripture is inspired by God and profitable for teaching, for reproof, for correction, for training in righteousness; so that the man of God may be adequate, equipped for every good work. – 2 Timothy 3:16-17

From everyone who has been given much, much will be required; and to whom they entrusted much, of him they will ask all the more. – Luke 12:48b

Be diligent [study] to present yourself approved to God as a workman who does not need to be ashamed, accurately handling [rightly dividing] the word of truth. – 2 Timothy 2:15

Beloved, do not believe every spirit, but test the spirits to see whether they are from God, because many false prophets have gone out into the world. By this you know the Spirit of God: every spirit that confesses that Jesus Christ has come in the flesh is from God; and every spirit that does not confess Jesus is not from God; this is the *spirit* of the antichrist, of which you have heard that it is coming, and now it is already in the world. – 1 John 4:1-3

But I am afraid that, as the serpent deceived Eve by his craftiness, your minds will be led astray from the simplicity and purity *of devotion* to Christ. For if one comes and preaches another Jesus whom we have not preached, or you receive a different spirit which you have not received, or a different gospel which you have not accepted, you bear *this* beautifully. – 2 Corinthians 11:3-4

I am amazed that you are so quickly deserting Him who called you by the grace of Christ, for a different gospel; which is *really* not another; only there are some who are disturbing you and want to distort the gospel of Christ. But even if we, or an angel from heaven, should preach to you a gospel contrary to what we have preached to you, he is to be accursed! As we have said before, so I say again now, if any man is preaching to you a gospel contrary to what you received, he is to be accursed! – Galatians 1:6-9

I solemnly charge *you* in the presence of God and of Christ Jesus, who is to judge the living and the dead, and by His appearing and His kingdom: preach the word; be ready in season *and* out of season; reprove, rebuke, exhort, with great patience and instruction. For the time will come when they will not endure sound doctrine; but *wanting* to have their ears tickled, they will accumulate for themselves teachers in accordance to their own desires, and will turn away their ears from the truth and will turn aside to myths. – 2 Timothy 4:1-4

5.11 ESSENTIAL FIRST 30-DAYS ACTIVITIES

He restores my soul;
He guides me in the paths of righteousness
For His name's sake. – Psalm 23:3

As a newly born-again Christian, it is vitally important to begin to develop a <u>daily</u> routine as you walk as a Christian. I offer a starting point in this chapter. These are only suggestions. You can build on this as you see fit, but this is what I recommend as the very minimum you do each day. Once again, I'm just listing what has worked for me in an attempt to help you get started. For the first 30-days, every single day, without fail:

MORNING:
- Get down on your knees and thank God for giving you the gift of today and for the gift of Jesus on the cross and the forgiveness of your sins. You can add other things also. As new sins come up or are revealed, you should confess them before God.
- The important thing isn't really what you pray about or exactly how you pray, it's the act of doing it; by doing this, you are learning to humble yourself before God and be thankful above all.
- As you pray in the morning, watch your heart; God may reveal things to you that you need to confess, work on, or realize about your own heart.
- Read 1-2 chapters from your Bible reading plan. If you cannot do this in the morning (which I strongly recommend), try to do it during the day. However, I've found that if you don't do this first thing in the morning, you will find many reasons (excuses) to put it off the rest of the day also, and pretty soon, you will realize that the whole day is over and you didn't even read a single word of Scripture (remember, it is the Word which feeds your spirit, see Matthew 4:4). Satan loves it when this happens.
- If you like, a daily devotional can serve as inspiration also. Just beware that some devotionals are designed to appeal to your emotions (and your wallet) instead of adhering to sound doctrine and biblical truth. They may also contain false teachings.

DURING THE DAY:
- Pray and talk to God as often as you can remember to do so. Don't worry about formalities, technique, body position (sitting, standing, kneeling, etc.), words, language, semantics, topics, etc.…just talk to God as if He were right with you as your Heavenly Father. You don't need to (and can't) hide things from God – for He knows all. Be 100% candid and open with Him.
- Remember that prayer is not just talking to God; it's talking with God.
- If you find that you do not remember to pray during the day, make some simple reminders to help you.

EVENING:
- Get down on your knees again and thank God for giving you the gift of that day, for the gift of Jesus on the cross, and His forgiveness of your sins. You can add other things you feel you want to confess before God also.
- The important thing isn't really the specifics of what you pray about; it is the act of doing it and learning to do it regularly, humbling yourself before God, and being thankful above all.

BEFORE ALL MEALS:
- Thank God for His provisions (Psalm 24:1)

WHAT TO PRAY:

If you are unsure what to pray each morning and evening (or at any time), I offer the following as a suggestion. This same prayer could be used every morning and evening for all 30 days if you want. Over time, you will adapt it, and it will then change each time you pray, but this gives you a starting point:

> *"Father in heaven, hallowed be Thy great name. Thank You for the gift of today and for the gift of Your Son Jesus Christ on the cross. Thank You for the forgiveness of my sins. Father, please forgive me for {_____insert anything here you want to confess, maybe something the Spirit is bringing to your attention today____}. Father, help me to walk worthy of You today and to seek and do Your will, not mine. Help me to seek the things above, the things of Your Kingdom, and not the things of this world. Help me to read and understand your Word and to dwell on good things which come from above. Father grant me Your wisdom, teach me Your ways, and keep me safe from selfish, worldly, and fleshly pursuits. Create in me a clean heart, O God, and renew a right and humble spirit within me. Thank you so much. It is through Jesus I pray. Amen."*

RELATED SCRIPTURE:

Give ear to my words, O LORD,
Consider my groaning.
Heed the sound of my cry for help, my King and my God,
For to You I pray.
In the morning, O LORD, You will hear my voice;
In the morning I will order *my prayer* to You and *eagerly* watch. – Psalm 5:1-3

The LORD'S lovingkindnesses indeed never cease,
For His compassions never fail.
They are new every morning;
Great is Your faithfulness. – Lamentations 3:22-23

How blessed is the man who does not walk in the counsel of the wicked,
Nor stand in the path of sinners,
Nor sit in the seat of scoffers!
But his delight is in the law of the LORD,
And in His law he meditates day and night. – Psalm 1:1-2

The earth is the LORD'S, and all it contains,
The world, and those who dwell in it. – Psalm 24:1

The Message of Truth

Be anxious for nothing, but in everything by prayer and supplication with thanksgiving let your requests be made known to God. And the peace of God, which surpasses all comprehension, will guard your hearts and your minds in Christ Jesus. – Philippians 4:6-7

And we know that God causes all things to work together for good to those who love God, to those who are called according to *His* purpose. For those whom He foreknew, He also predestined *to become* conformed to the image of His Son, so that He would be the firstborn among many brethren. – Romans 8:28-29

For I am confident of this very thing, that He who began a good work in you will perfect it until the day of Christ Jesus. – Philippians 1:6

For I am convinced that neither death, nor life, nor angels, nor principalities, nor things present, nor things to come, nor powers, nor height, nor depth, nor any other created thing, will be able to separate us from the love of God, which is in Christ Jesus our Lord. – Romans 8:38-39

But we request of you, brethren, that you appreciate those who diligently labor among you, and have charge over you in the Lord and give you instruction, and that you esteem them very highly in love because of their work. Live in peace with one another. We urge you, brethren, admonish the unruly, encourage the fainthearted, help the weak, be patient with everyone. See that no one repays another with evil for evil, but always seek after that which is good for one another and for all people. Rejoice always; pray without ceasing; in everything give thanks; for this is God's will for you in Christ Jesus. Do not quench the Spirit; do not despise prophetic utterances. But examine everything *carefully*; hold fast to that which is good; abstain from every form of evil.

Now may the God of peace Himself sanctify you entirely; and may your spirit and soul and body be preserved complete, without blame at the coming of our Lord Jesus Christ. Faithful is He who calls you, and He also will bring it to pass. – Ephesians 5:12-24

Finally, be strong in the Lord and in the strength of His might. Put on the full armor of God, so that you will be able to stand firm against the schemes of the devil. For our struggle is not against flesh and blood, but against the rulers, against the powers, against the world forces of this darkness, against the spiritual *forces* of wickedness in the heavenly *places*. Therefore, take up the full armor of God, so that you will be able to resist in the evil day, and having done everything, to stand firm. Stand firm therefore, HAVING GIRDED YOUR LOINS WITH TRUTH, and HAVING PUT ON THE BREASTPLATE OF RIGHTEOUSNESS, and having shod YOUR FEET WITH THE PREPARATION OF THE GOSPEL OF PEACE; in addition to all, taking up the shield of faith with which you will be able to extinguish all the flaming arrows of the evil *one*. And take THE HELMET OF SALVATION, and the sword of the Spirit, which is the word of God. – Ephesians 6:10-17

I press on toward the goal for the prize of the upward call of God in Christ Jesus. – Philippians 3:14

PART VI:

BEWARE THE WOLVES

6.0 BE NOT DECEIVED
(Avoid False Teachings and False Prophets)

"Beware of the false prophets, who come to you in sheep's clothing, but inwardly are ravenous wolves." – Matthew 7:15

Beware the Wolves. As much as I wish this section of the book weren't required, it is needed badly, perhaps today more than ever. In fact, this book has shown you that we have had to confront (and overcome) the false teachings, distortions, and perversions of Scripture by man at every single step along the way, literally from the very first sentence of Genesis right up until the very last chapter of Revelation! And at each and every step along the way, you have had to choose whether to believe in the wisdom of man and Satan or believe in the wisdom of God, which is given in Scripture.

We are called to worship the Lord "in spirit <u>and in truth,</u>" not in spirit and the opinions, theories, schemes, conjurings, fake prophecies, false religions, theological systems and frameworks, fanciful interpretations, catechisms, rites, rules, rituals, ceremonies, "traditions," myths, wild-speculation, superstition, mysticism and seemingly endless made-up rubbish and nonsense of man, committees and institutions. So, I urge you brother or sister in Christ, to not be ignorant of the truth as given in Scripture and thereby gullible and misled by the "wolves," "vipers," and modern-day "Pharisees." Be on guard, so that no-one takes or deceives you out of your "crown of life" – yes, Scripture warns that you can be "tricked" out of your "crown of life" by the false teachings of man ("carried away by the error of unprincipled men," "deceived," "led astray," "taken captive"):

> See to it that <u>no one takes you captive</u> through philosophy and empty deception, according to the tradition of men, according to the elementary principles of the world, rather than according to Christ. – Colossians 2:8

> My <u>people are destroyed</u> for lack of knowledge. – Hosea 4:6

> "'I am coming quickly; hold fast what you have, <u>so that no one will take your crown</u>.'" – Revelation 3:11

> But the Spirit explicitly says that in later times <u>some will fall away</u> from the faith, paying attention to deceitful spirits and doctrines of demons, by means of the hypocrisy of liars seared in their own conscience as with a branding iron, *men* who forbid marriage *and advocate* abstaining from foods which God has created to be gratefully shared in by those who believe and know the truth. – 1 Timothy 4:1-3

> For the time will come when they will not endure sound doctrine; but *wanting* to have their ears tickled [itching ears], they will accumulate for themselves teachers in accordance to their own desires, and <u>will turn away their ears from the truth and will turn aside to myths [false teachings]</u>. – 2 Timothy 4:3-4

> But I am afraid that, as the serpent deceived [tricked] Eve by his craftiness, your minds <u>will be led astray</u> from the simplicity and purity *of devotion* to Christ. For if one comes and preaches another Jesus whom we have not preached, or you receive a different spirit which you have not received, or a different gospel which you have not accepted, you bear *this* beautifully [i.e., you do not abandon the truth for the false teaching]. – 2 Corinthians 11:3-4

Yes, the way of a Christian is fraught with all kinds of perils, traps, pitfalls, and snares of man and Satan, which are laid up for you at each step of the way. You are literally surrounded by a pack of "wolves" (false teachers) trying to trick and deceive you. As explained in the introduction of this book, we've had nearly 2000 years now of man-made false teachings and a myriad of sectarian and denominational divisions all being taught, preached, published, and masquerading as so-called "Christianity." The fact that this section of the book even exists is both an abomination to the Lord and a complete disgrace to man, for the minds of man have twisted and distorted the gospel almost beyond recognition. We will have to cover some difficult ground here. Not only must I teach you what the true Word of God is, but I must also show you what is not the Word of God – so you are not "deceived" and "come short of" eternal life! The false teachings of man lead many to have a false sense of security; in reality, many will therefore be led to destruction. That is why these false teachings are not just a simple matter of "minor doctrinal differences." The false teachings will actually cause many to be eternally lost!

Compounding all this are the "itching ears" of modern American Christendom which gravitate towards "easy faith," trying to take the easy way to heaven, using "feel-good" religion with a (very) large number of professing "Christians" today believing that simply saying a little prayer (the so-called "sinner's prayer") at one instant of their life saves them for all eternity, with nothing else whatsoever required of them! I challenge those who teach, preach, and believe that to go resurrect one of the martyrs from *The Acts & Monuments of the Christian Faith* (i.e., *Foxe's Book of Martyrs*) and ask them what they believe – after having sacrificed their lives for Christ, often being beheaded, torn in pieces, sawn in half, tortured and mutilated or burned in flames at the stake for their faith. Those true saints of Christ were not looking for the easy way or a feel-good form of Christianity – they were truly devoted Christians willing to sacrifice anything and everything, even their own lives, for Christ. Many do not even realize today that one could be burned at the stake simply for having a copy of the Bible in English at various times and places throughout history!

THE SWORD OF THE SPIRIT

It's time to wield the sharp "sword of the Spirit which is the word of God" (in truth) to cut through the absolute rubbish and nonsense that passes for "Christianity" today in modern, liberal, and even so-called "reformed" churches! I trust you will understand and respect that I am trying to prepare you to stand firm in the "faith that was once for all *time* handed down to the saints" in Scripture. I must prepare you to confront any and all teachings which lead away from Christ and eternal life.

Scripture says that Satan is the originator of lies, for he is described as the "deceiver," "our adversary," and a "liar" (Genesis 3:1-5, 1 Peter 5:8-9, 1 John 3:8, 2 Corinthians 11:3, John 8:44, John 10:10, Revelation 12:9). He deceives many who therefore teach falsely (the "false prophets," "wolves," and "vipers") in an attempt to deceive you.

> "Beware of the false prophets, who come to you in sheep's clothing, but inwardly are ravenous wolves. You will know them by their fruits. Grapes are not gathered from thorn *bushes* nor figs from thistles, are they? So every good tree bears good fruit, but the bad tree bears bad fruit. A good tree cannot produce bad fruit, nor can a bad tree produce good fruit. Every tree that does not bear good fruit is cut down

and thrown into the fire. So then, you will know them by their fruits." – Matthew 7:15-20

"Be on guard for yourselves and for all the flock, among which the Holy Spirit has made you overseers, to shepherd the church of God which He purchased with His own blood. I know that after my departure savage wolves will come in among you, not sparing the flock; and from among your own selves men will arise, speaking perverse things, to draw away the disciples after them." – Acts 20:28-30

For the time will come when they will not endure sound doctrine; but *wanting* to have their ears tickled, they will accumulate for themselves teachers in accordance to their own desires, and will turn away their ears from the truth and will turn aside to myths. – 2 Timothy 4:3-4

Jesus warned us not to be naïve and gullible:

"Behold, I send you out as sheep in the midst of wolves; so be shrewd as serpents and innocent as doves." – Matthew 10:16

But evil men and impostors will proceed *from bad* to worse, deceiving and being deceived. You, however, continue in the things you have learned and become convinced of, knowing from whom you have learned *them*, and that from childhood you have known the sacred writings which are able to give you the wisdom that leads to salvation through faith which is in Christ Jesus. – 2 Timothy 3:13-15

This warning is true especially for "infants in Christ" (i.e., a newly born-again Christian) and those who are what might be termed gullible Christians who have not "pressed on to maturity" and continued to "grow in the grace and knowledge [understanding]" of the Lord. We are further admonished not to succumb to the "spirit of error":

Beloved, do not believe every spirit, but test the spirits to see whether they are from God, because many false prophets have gone out into the world. By this you know the Spirit of God: every spirit that confesses that Jesus Christ has come in the flesh is from God; and every spirit that does not confess Jesus is not from God; this is the *spirit* of the antichrist, of which you have heard that it is coming, and now it is already in the world. You are from God, little children, and have overcome them; because greater is He who is in you than he who is in the world. They are from the world; therefore they speak *as* from the world, and the world listens to them. We are from God; he who knows God listens to us; he who is not from God does not listen to us. By this we know the spirit of truth and the spirit of error. – 1 John 4:1-6

It is also written that we must "contend earnestly" (actually fight) for the "faith that was once for all *time* handed down to the saints" in Scripture. You must really, **really**, REALLY want and desire God's truth (not man's truth) with all your heart, all your mind, all your soul, and your entire being:

Beloved, while I was making every effort to write you about our common salvation, I felt the necessity to write to you appealing that you contend earnestly for the faith that was once for all *time* handed down to the saints. For certain people have crept in unnoticed, those who were long beforehand marked out for this condemnation, ungodly persons who turn the grace of our God into indecent behavior and deny our only Master and Lord, Jesus Christ. – Jude 1:3-4

HOW FALSE TEACHINGS ARISE

Most false teachings arise when some verses are picked (which one personally favors), and interpretations are then made and beliefs constructed upon those verses in isolation, while other verses that may contradict that interpretation/belief are conveniently ignored. One of the most basic principles of Bible study is that if your interpretation and understanding of a verse cause either: 1) a conflict/disagreement with other verses (especially clear literal, obvious, unambiguous ones), or 2) gives God the slightest appearance of being unloving, unmerciful, hateful, mean or having any moral flaw whatsoever – then your understanding and interpretation is wrong.

You must harmonize all of what Scripture says on any given topic in order to "rightly divide the word of truth" and arrive at correct doctrine. You build solid biblical truth by having interpretations and doctrine that are in agreement with all of Scripture, not just some specific verses that can be misconstrued to support whatever personal interpretation and doctrine you fancy:

> Be diligent [study] to present yourself approved to God as a workman who does not need to be ashamed, accurately handling [rightly dividing, correctly interpreting] the word of truth. – 2 Timothy 2:15

> "The sum of thy word is truth; And every one of thy righteous ordinances endureth for ever." – Psalms 119:160

That is why I list as many relevant verses in each chapter of this book as possible, not simply to multiply verses, but because correct doctrine can only be attained by considering in aggregate all of what Scripture has to say on any particular subject. We even have the example set before us of Jesus countering the Devil's false teachings and distortions of Scripture in this exact manner by reinforcing that it is the sum of all Scripture which is truth. Satan tried to pick one verse in isolation and use that as truth, when in fact, it contradicted other Scripture:

> Then the devil took Him into the holy city and had Him stand on the pinnacle of the temple, and said to Him, "If You are the Son of God, throw Yourself down; for it is written,
>
> 'HE WILL COMMAND HIS ANGELS CONCERNING YOU';
>
> and
>
> 'ON *their* HANDS THEY WILL BEAR YOU UP,
> SO THAT YOU WILL NOT STRIKE YOUR FOOT AGAINST A STONE.'"
>
> Jesus said to him, "On the other hand, it is written, 'YOU SHALL NOT PUT THE LORD YOUR GOD TO THE TEST.'" – Matthew 4:5-7

This selective interpretation often consists of taking one verse (which may be harder to understand) completely out of context and then finding other verses (also taken out of context) to support that interpretation, thereby building up a whole theology and doctrine behind it. The wolves favor their fanciful interpretations of difficult or more obscure verses (which often use symbolic or figurative language) even when they are in direct opposition to other easily understood, clear and direct literal plain-spoken verses. Wayne Jackson summarizes: [92]

> First, the Bible student needs to remind himself of this premise. The Scriptures are the inspired word of God (1 Thes. 2:13; 2 Tim. 3:16-17). Coming, then, from Jehovah as the ultimate source, they do not contradict themselves; instead, they are perfectly harmonious (Dt. 32:4; 1 Cor. 14:33a). When one encounters a passage, therefore, that may appear to conflict with plain-spoken texts contained elsewhere in Scripture, he must look carefully at the more obscure text and determine if there is a reasonable way to bring it into harmony with the other.

False teachings also arise when:

1) We just don't like what Scripture says, so we twist it to conform to our own preferred liking (but remember "let God be found true, though every man be found a liar"),
2) We apply human rationalization to Scripture because we simply don't think God meant what He actually said,
3) Scripture is interpreted (forced) to match the so-called "traditions" of man,
4) People simply repeat whatever they have heard others say without "being a Berean" and checking it against Scripture. An example of this is the belief that three (3) wise men came to Jerusalem at Jesus' birth. But Scripture doesn't say that it was only "three," and further, a careful study of Scripture reveals that they came after His birth, not while He was in the manger. While this is a harmless and trivial error, it again shows how "traditions" can absolutely overwhelm and blind you to the actual truth of what is written in Scripture – and you may not even be aware that the deception is occurring! And lastly, of course,
5) Scripture is distorted intentionally with the intent to mislead and deceive (for various reasons).

Many groups (e.g., 7th Day Adventists, Mormons, etc.) go even further, claiming to have their own special prophets who have received new revelation or inspiration directly from God. Scripture also warns against this:

> Beloved, do not believe every spirit, but test the spirits to see whether they are from God, because many false prophets have gone out into the world. – 1 John 4:1

Scripture Further states:

> "Beware of the false prophets, who come to you in sheep's clothing, but inwardly are ravenous wolves." – Matthew 7:15

> God, after He spoke long ago to the fathers in the prophets in many portions and in many ways, in these last days has spoken to us in His Son, whom He appointed heir of all things, through whom also He made the world. – Hebrews 1:1-2

> But false prophets also arose among the people, just as there will also be false teachers among you, who will secretly introduce destructive heresies, even denying the Master who bought them, bringing swift destruction upon themselves. Many

---

[92] Jackson, Wayne. "Does John 6:37 Teach Calvinist 'Predestination'?" ChristianCourier.com. Access date: September 14, 2020. https://christiancourier.com/articles/778-does-john-6-37-teach-calvinist-predestination

> will follow their sensuality, and because of them the way of the truth will be maligned; and in *their* greed they will exploit you with false words; their judgment from long ago is not idle, and their destruction is not asleep. – 2 Peter 2:1-3

The canon of Scripture was closed up and sealed with the Book of Revelation, complete and final for all time. Therefore, every group or person who claims to be a prophet of God having received special revelations or inspiration directly from God (but not given in Scripture) is a false prophet, a liar, and a deceiver! There are no exceptions.

REMEMBER, THIS IS SPIRITUAL WARFARE

For the reader who may not have encountered this avalanche of false teachings yet, count yourself fortunate, but also be advised that you will with almost 100% certainty encounter them at some point in your life, either before you accept Christ or after (or both). In fact, even after you have been born again, you will be continually bombarded by lies, half-truths, blatant distortions, and misinterpretations of Scripture which are cleverly designed to turn you away from Christ again! These false teachings all have the appearance of truth and sound very "biblical" on the surface, but when you know Scripture better, you will see that they are all just deceptions hiding behind a very thin veil/veneer of distorted verses masquerading as Christianity.

Always remember that we are in the middle of a raging spiritual war. Do not make the mistake of ignoring this fact (truth):

> For our struggle is not against flesh and blood, but against the rulers, against the powers, against the world forces of this darkness, against the spiritual *forces* of wickedness in the heavenly *places*. – Ephesians 6:12

While we are blessed to be living in these last days (this gospel/church age of grace) where Satan's activities have been largely bound (by Christ's victory on the cross), we are still strongly admonished to: "Be of sober *spirit*, be on the alert. Your adversary, the devil, prowls around like a roaring lion, seeking someone to devour." Therefore, please do not make the mistake of underestimating him. Although unlike in times past where he has had the power to harm humans directly (see the book of Job, for example), today he is largely limited to using the method of deception – but wow, does he work overtime in doing just that!

It is important to understand what is going on here. Satan and his forces of evil are trying to lay as many obstacles as possible in front of you and all around you, working through men who do not know God or His Christ and also those who actually desire to serve Satan. These obstacles are also called "snares," "traps," and "pitfalls" designed to:

a) Turn you or "trick" you out of the "straight and narrow" path which leads towards Christ and eternal life,
b) Cause you to quit the faith altogether, "fall away," and turn back, or
c) Lure you into some man-made "religious" system that leads away from Christ

You have already read in the chapter on Science vs. the Bible that the "Theory of Evolution" false teaching (fake science) aims to stop you at the very first sentence(s) of the Bible – knowing that if you doubt or disbelieve those, then you almost surely won't read or believe the rest of the Bible either. However, many other false teachings are laid up for you after you are born again. In fact, by now, I hope you have noticed in the course of reading this book that these snares are laid up for you at every step along the way – you have encountered them in nearly every single chapter! These snares, traps, and pitfalls are thrown down in front of and all around you, on all sides, nearly as far as the eye can see – it's as if you are in a minefield or a maze trying to make your way through to eternal life, running the gauntlet, if you will, through these deceptions. Once you are aware of them, you will notice that these false teachings are shouted with extreme ferocity and volume today; in fact, they are shouted nearly 24/7/365.25 (i.e., all day, every day, all year, every year) from both secular as well as so-called "Christian" sources, publications, radio, movies, media, and even pulpits! I'm using "Christian" in quotes here for a reason, as the teachings are anything but Christian.

You have already been exposed to many of these lies, propaganda, and conditioning, starting all the way back to the time you were a small child! The basis for many of the false teachings have their origins in the secular God-denying world, and they infect nearly every broadcast, TV show, movie, book, textbook, and educational institution you have ever read, seen, heard, or attended – yes since you were an infant! These false teachings have been drummed into you for so long and so hard that they are even unconsciously affecting what you think and believe today; in effect, as I said, you have been brainwashed. You may not even be aware of them, as the false teachings are the only things you've ever known as "truth"; you may believe them so deeply that they are actually operating at an unconscious level within you. That's what brainwashing does.

It is beyond the scope or ability of this book to present a rigorous critique/rebuttal of each false teaching, as doing so would fill hundreds of pages (even whole books). You must read and study Scripture for yourself, following the example of the Bereans:

> Now these were more noble-minded than those in Thessalonica, for they received the word with great eagerness, examining the Scriptures daily *to see* whether these things were so. – Acts 17:11

How is one not deceived? It is by being diligent to "grow in the grace and knowledge [understanding]" of the Lord Jesus Christ, "make your calling and election sure," and "work out your own salvation with fear and trembling" – and that takes hard work and determination, you must want to do so. You must "press on to the maturity" in the faith, and this is a never-ending process until death. You must love truth and seek it with all your heart, mind, and soul. Note that this is a vital component of the "Armor of God" (Ephesians 6:10-17, verse 14 in particular). You must diligently read and study Scripture, and you must learn how to read and interpret Scripture for yourself correctly.

Furthermore, one must "ask of God" for His wisdom, "the wisdom from above," and stop relying on the wisdom of man, which only leads to sin, suffering, and death ("There is a way *which seems* right to a person, but its end is the way of death."). And if at first you do not receive wisdom, keep asking – pray again with persistence! This lesson is given to us in the parable of the Unjust Judge (see the chapter on The Power of Prayer). We are to be persistent in prayer with our requests, not in a rude or demanding fashion, but by continually presenting our requests before God. You can also remind God of what His own Word says – yes, it is very profitable and good to do. King David did this often in the psalms, and I've found that doing this greatly helps me – for it is not God who needs to be reminded of Scripture, but us.

SOURCES OF FALSE TEACHINGS

While Satan is the originator of lies, fallen sinful man is all too willing to go along with his schemes as they also further their own lustful worldly pursuits of fame, fortune, wealth, and power. At a high level, there are three distinct sources of false teachings:

1. The secular/atheistic God-denying world,
2. The "wolves" who come into the church intentionally to deceive,
3. Well-meaning but horribly misguided Christian pastors and teachers.

It is helpful to understand more about each of those groups.

1) False teachings arise from the first group, the God-denying secular world, for obvious reasons – for it is written that if you are not of Christ, then "you are of your father the devil." Once you believe in God, the false teachings of this group are somewhat easier for you to spot, although many of them (e.g., the "Theory of Evolution") have been drummed into you since you were a wee infant, so you've already been brainwashed into accepting and believing them as truth and may not even realize it.

2) The second group, the "wolves" (and "vipers," and modern-day "Pharisees"), are much harder to spot, for they are in disguise, camouflaged, if you will. Christ warned of this very subject:

> For such men are false apostles, deceitful workers, disguising themselves as apostles of Christ. No wonder, for even Satan disguises himself as an angel of light. Therefore it is not surprising if his servants also disguise themselves as servants of righteousness [e.g., pastors, elders, and teachers within the church], whose end will be according to their deeds. – 2 Corinthians 11:13-15

Satan disguises himself as an "angel of light" (giving what appears to be the truth but isn't), and his ministers disguise themselves as "servants of righteousness." It is these "wolves" who pretend to serve Christ, appearing (dressed up) as "Christian" ministers and pastors, but they are actually "of their father the devil" (i.e., modern-day "Pharisees"). These "wolves" are also described as "false prophets." They use intentional deception to deceive the unsaved masses into following worthless man-made "religious" rituals, false doctrines and theology, myths, sorcery, superstition, mysticism, "traditions," and nonsense that lead to eternal death instead of eternal life. Jesus warned us about this:

> And He said to them, "Rightly did Isaiah prophesy of you hypocrites, as it is written:
>
> 'THIS PEOPLE HONORS ME WITH THEIR LIPS,
> BUT THEIR HEART IS FAR AWAY FROM ME.
> 'BUT IN VAIN DO THEY WORSHIP ME,
> TEACHING AS DOCTRINES THE PRECEPTS OF MEN.'
>
> Neglecting the commandment of God, you hold to the tradition of men." – Mark 7:6-8

These "wolves" mislead naïve and gullible Christians into departing from the "straight and narrow" path towards eternal life and back into the ways of man and eternal death; Scripture warns us further:

> We are no longer to be children [gullible, infants in Christ], tossed here and there by waves and carried about by every wind of doctrine, by the trickery of men, by craftiness in deceitful scheming. – Ephesians 4:14

These "ravenous wolves" are <u>intentionally</u> deceiving you – as they serve the selfish goals and agendas of man and institutions and do so under the disguise of Christianity and Jesus. They are indeed very slick, subtly twisting and distorting Scripture to support their own false teachings, which lead away from Christ or which outright deny Christ when one looks into them more closely. They do this through lies, half-truths, taking verses out of context, distorting symbolic passages by forcing literal interpretations on them, claiming special prophecy and revelations from God, and so forth.

These "wolves" appear in churches that <u>seem</u> to be Christian, for they may even use Jesus Christ in their names, etc. – but they are not of Christ. They come in many shapes and sizes, from innocent-looking little old ladies to the casual hipster, to the powerful man/pastor/elder/author of authority in a popular church all dressed up in a well-tailored suit with lots of initials and abbreviations placed before and after their name, even having "Doctoral Degrees in Divinity"!

3) The third group are what I believe to be genuine, honest to goodness born-again Christians who think they are following Christ, but they are misguided, gullible and simply go along blindly believing many things they have heard or been taught without properly testing them against Scripture as we are admonished to do. These genuine Christian pastors and teachers should know that they are under a stricter judgment (James 3:1) and that they are called to "accurately handle" the Word of God (2 Timothy 2:15).

What confuses me about this third group is that whenever I've tried to help any of them see the error of their teachings, they flat out refuse even to consider that what they are teaching may not be in agreement with Scripture. I can only speculate that this comes largely from pride, which is something we must constantly guard against – at all times and until death. All I know is that I'm supposed to teach you correct doctrine in accord with Scripture and that I'm responsible for doing so – so that is what I'm doing in this book.

A TIME TO SPEAK

It is written:

> There is an appointed time for everything. And there is a time for every event under heaven—
>
>> A time to give birth and a time to die;
>> A time to plant and a time to uproot what is planted.
>> A time to kill and a time to heal;
>> A time to tear down and a time to build up.
>> A time to weep and a time to laugh;
>> A time to mourn and a time to dance.
>> A time to throw stones and a time to gather stones;

> A time to embrace and a time to shun embracing.
> A time to search and a time to give up as lost;
> A time to keep and a time to throw away.
> A time to tear apart and a time to sew together;
> <u>A time to be silent and a time to speak.</u>
> A time to love and a time to hate;
> A time for war and a time for peace. – Ecclesiastes 3:1-8

So, I am speaking out with this book; I'm not remaining silent. For it is way past time to return to the pure gospel "message of truth" and to put aside all manner of false teachings, myths, superstition, "traditions," wild speculation, and fantasies of the mind of man! It's time for a good dose of solid food – the truth of the New Testament Gospel "faith that was once for all *time* handed down to the saints" in Scripture and as it was practiced in the apostolic era (the years just after Christ's death). If you will, "I am A VOICE OF ONE CRYING IN THE WILDERNESS" of modern, liberal, corrupt, apostate, lukewarm, dead, pretend "Christianity": "MAKE STRAIGHT" the gospel of our Lord and Savior Jesus Christ (See John 1:23)! Amen!

Please know that this section of the book is written in the spirit of love out of concern for your eternal well-being. Because unlike some who think that having you come forward at the end of a church service or dumping you in the middle of a giant stadium means that their job is done, I don't leave you with the job half (or not even) done – and the job at hand is to teach you the full truth of Scripture and help ensure that you reach your ultimate goal, which is eternal life in heaven. You will see for yourself that after you come to Christ and look for a church that actually teaches what is in New Testament Scripture, you will be absolutely bombarded by and inundated with a veritable blizzard, yes, a massive avalanche, of false teachings and fake so-called "Christian" churches in every direction that you look and as far as the eye can see. Furthermore, and most seriously: following many of these wrong teachings will lead you to eternal death! It cannot get any more grave or serious than that. The cults, "isms," sects, and groups that are teaching falsehood should be labeled with a "black box" warning label, just like they do with some medicines which may have fatal side effects: stating that if you follow their teaching, it can lead to eternal death.

In the continued spirit of telling the truth, the whole truth and nothing but the truth, I confess here and now to you that I was also deceived and believed many of these false teachings myself before I wrote this book, for they were the only things I ever heard preached, promoted, taught or published for many years, and they all sound very convincing and "biblical" on the surface. I was a gullible baby Christian (an "infant in Christ"), and I didn't "press on to maturity" by "grow[ing] in the grace and knowledge [understanding]" of God, so I was deceived – and I "fell away," back towards this world and eternal death! But here's the key point you must take away: I pressed on towards truth again until I came out of darkness into light – I "came out of Babylon":

> I heard another voice from heaven, saying, "Come out of her [Babylon], my people, so that you will not participate in her sins and receive of her plagues; for her sins have piled up as high as heaven, and God has remembered her iniquities."
> – Revelation 18:4-5

As a new Christian, I had to wade through this absolute maze of man-made nonsense and doctrinal distortions on my own to find truth which was in agreement with Scripture – for I had no church. It has taken me several years (about three) of study to see through all the false teachings. It was only through determined hard work in reading and studying the Bible, in a persistent and relentless rigorous desire for absolute truth, along with the stunningly gracious wisdom and guidance from God, that I was able to finally extract myself from their grip. What is written in James 1:5 was key: I kept "asking of God" for wisdom, His wisdom – which is truth!

You will soon have read the truth about these false teachings so that you will be without excuse – you will need to come out of Babylon also. You cannot continue to willfully sit in churches under these teachings and under those who teach them while claiming to worship Christ "in spirit and in truth." Scripture asserts that claims of ignorance will not be an excuse on Judgment Day, for we are admonished to always be "growing in the grace and knowledge [understanding] of the Lord," and we are also called to "accurately handle [rightly divide] the word of truth" (see Acts 17:22-32, Romans 4:15, Leviticus 5:17-18, 2 Peter 3:18, 2 Timothy 2:15).

Those of us living today have more light and ready access to truth than at any other time in human history! We also have the complete canon of Scripture widely available as never before. Even further, we have many great writings, commentaries, and testimonies from the saints and martyrs who have come before us to learn from. Therefore, we will be under greater accountability before the Lord for how we respond to having received so much light and truth. How grateful we should be today for having readily available access to the Word of God (in large part, though not in all places, of course). Those who attempt to claim ignorance of the truth of Scripture today are doing so against an overwhelming body of evidence and abundance of light (truth), for it is written:

> For whatever was written in earlier times was written for our instruction, so that through perseverance and the encouragement of the Scriptures we might have hope. – Romans 15:4

It is also written:

> "From everyone who has been given much, much will be required; and to whom they entrusted much, of him they will ask all the more." – Luke 12:48

> "Woe to you, Chorazin! Woe to you, Bethsaida! For if the miracles had occurred in Tyre and Sidon which occurred in you, they would have repented long ago in sackcloth and ashes. Nevertheless I say to you, it will be more tolerable for Tyre and Sidon in *the* day of judgment than for you." – Matthew 11:21-22

These verses speak not only of how you use the material provisions God has given you in grace but also of your level of knowledge and understanding of the truth. You will be judged by the amount of light (truth) you have received and how you responded to that light. Scripture teaches that those who have been given greater light and truth have a greater responsibility to respond to it. Matthew Henry writes on this subject: [93]

> Secondly, In that judgment, all the means of grace that were enjoyed in the state of probation will certainly come into the account, and it will be enquired, not only how bad we were, but how much better we might have been, had it not been our own fault, Isa 5:3, Isa 5:4. Thirdly, Though the damnation of all that perish will be

---

[93] Henry, Matthew. *Exposition of the Old and New Testaments*, London. 1706-1710/1721.

intolerable, yet the damnation of those who had the fullest and clearest discoveries made them of the power and grace of Christ, and yet repented not, will be of all others the most intolerable. The gospel light and sound open the faculties and enlarge the capacities of all that see and hear it, either to receive the riches of divine grace, or (if that grace be slighted) to take in the more plentiful effusions of divine wrath. If self-reproach be the torture of hell, it must needs be hell indeed to those who had such a fair opportunity of getting to heaven. Son, remember that. ... Secondly, That Sodom's ruin will therefore be less at the great day than Capernaum's. Sodom will have many things to answer for, but not the sin of neglecting Christ, as Capernaum will. If the gospel prove a savour of death, a killing savour, it is doubly so; it is of death unto death, so great a death (2Co 2:16); Christ had said the same of all other places that receive not his ministers nor bid his gospel welcome (Mat 10:15); It shall be more tolerable for the land of Sodom than for that city. We that have now the written word in our hands, the gospel preached, and the gospel ordinances administered to us, and live under the dispensation of the Spirit, have advantages not inferior to those of Chorazin, and Bethsaida, and Capernaum, and the account in the great day will be accordingly. It has therefore been justly said, that the professors of this age, whether they go to heaven or hell, will be the greatest debtors in either of these places; if to heaven, the greatest debtors to divine mercy for those rich means that brought them thither; if to hell, the greatest debtors to divine justice, for those rich means that would have kept them from thence.

Proverbs 7 speaks to being naïve (lacking sense) and further reinforces that ignorance of the truth of God's Word (and His commandments), or abandoning that truth in favor of man-made false teachings, leads to eternal death:

> My son, keep my words
> And treasure my commandments within you.
> Keep my commandments and live,
> And my teaching as the apple of your eye.
> Bind them on your fingers;
> Write them on the tablet of your heart.
> Say to wisdom, "You are my sister,"
> And call understanding *your* intimate friend;
> That they may keep you from an adulteress,
> From the foreigner who flatters with her words.
>
> For at the window of my house
> I looked out through my lattice,
> And I saw among the naive,
> *And* discerned among the youths
> A young man lacking sense,
> Passing through the street near her corner;
> And he takes the way to her house,
> In the twilight, in the evening,
> In the middle of the night and *in* the darkness.
> And behold, a woman *comes* to meet him,
> Dressed as a harlot and cunning of heart.
> She is boisterous and rebellious,

The Message of Truth

> Her feet do not remain at home;
> *She is* now in the streets, now in the squares,
> And lurks by every corner.
> So she seizes him and kisses him
> And with a brazen face she says to him:
> "I was due to offer peace offerings;
> Today I have paid my vows.
> "Therefore I have come out to meet you,
> To seek your presence earnestly, and I have found you.
> "I have spread my couch with coverings,
> With colored linens of Egypt.
> "I have sprinkled my bed
> With myrrh, aloes and cinnamon.
> "Come, let us drink our fill of love until morning;
> Let us delight ourselves with caresses.
> "For my husband is not at home,
> He has gone on a long journey;
> He has taken a bag of money with him,
> At the full moon he will come home."
> With her many persuasions she entices him;
> With her flattering lips she seduces him.
> Suddenly he follows her
> As an ox goes to the slaughter,
> Or as *one in* fetters to the discipline of a fool,
> Until an arrow pierces through his liver;
> As a bird hastens to the snare,
> So he does not know that it *will cost him* his life.
>
> Now therefore, *my* sons, listen to me,
> And pay attention to the words of my mouth.
> Do not let your heart turn aside to her ways,
> Do not stray into her paths.
> For many are the victims she has cast down,
> And numerous are all her slain.
> Her house is the way to Sheol,
> Descending to the chambers of death. – Proverbs 7

The harlot represents the false teachers, false religions, false doctrines, fake so-called "Christian" churches, etc., of this world (e.g., see also the great harlot of the book of Revelation). The young man is you. You can have wisdom or not; wisdom is only found by learning and keeping God's Word. You must know it exceedingly well by diligently reading and studying the Bible as if your life depended on it (and it does!). The naïve, those lacking sense, and those with "itching ears" will seek out and follow the schemes, doctrines, and deceptions of man! The choice is yours. It is out of care and concern for your eternal soul that I am trying to warn you about these false teachings and identify anything that might keep you from eternal life. You can see that Jesus did similarly, trying to help and warn those who were going astray:

> Looking at him, <u>Jesus felt a love for him</u> and said to him, "One thing you lack: go and sell all you possess and give to the poor, and you will have treasure in heaven; and come, follow Me." – Mark 10:21

But even further, I also have a duty to warn you about them. In contrast, the enemy (the "wolves" and "vipers") will "kiss you" with their false teachings, which appeal to "itching ears," but in the end, only lead away from Christ (and possibly to eternal death).

> I am amazed that you are so quickly deserting Him who called you by the grace of Christ, for a different gospel; which is *really* not another; only there are some who are disturbing you and want to distort the gospel of Christ. But even if we, or an angel from heaven, should preach to you a gospel contrary to what we have preached to you, he is to be accursed! As we have said before, so I say again now, if any man is preaching to you a gospel contrary to what you received, he is to be accursed! – Galatians 1:6-9

To the brother or sister in Christ who may already believe in some of these false teachings, I hope you recognize that my warnings about such herein are given in the spirit of love and helpful "wounds from a friend" as it is written:

> Faithful are the wounds of a friend,
> But deceitful are the kisses of an enemy. – Proverbs 27:6

> So have I become your enemy by telling you the truth? – Galatians 4:16

A CALL-OUT TO FELLOW BELIEVERS

To the Christian reader who may sincerely believe these false teachings, and to sincere brothers and sisters in Christ who find themselves in churches under pastors who teach these false doctrines, may God grant you grace and wisdom to now see the truth. Are you in Babylon and don't even know it?

We are sent out as "sheep" among "wolves," so please don't continue to be a gullible Christian and sit in churches and under those who teach wrongly – you must "come out of her [Babylon]"! After reading this book, you now know the truth (see also Acts 17:22-32, Romans 4:15, Leviticus 5:17-18, 2 Peter 3:18, 2 Timothy 2:15).

You should be learning Scripture yourself every single day, and you should even know it as well as or maybe even better than your pastor or preacher does, so you are not deceived! May you have "eyes to see" and "ears to hear" the truth:

> Brothers *and sisters*, my heart's desire and my prayer to God for them is for *their* salvation. For I testify about them that they have a zeal for God, but not in accordance with knowledge [i.e., having the correct knowledge and understanding of what is stated in Scripture for salvation]. – Romans 10:1-2

> The Lord's bond-servant must not be quarrelsome, but be kind to all, able to teach, patient when wronged, with gentleness correcting those who are in opposition, if perhaps God may grant them repentance leading to the knowledge of the truth, and they may come to their senses *and escape* from the snare of the devil, having been held captive by him to do his will. – 2 Timothy 2:24-26

> Therefore, beloved, since you look for these things, be diligent to be found by Him in peace, spotless and blameless, and regard the patience of our Lord as salvation;

> just as also our beloved brother Paul, according to the wisdom given him, wrote to you, as also in all *his* letters, speaking in them of these things, in which are some things hard to understand, which the untaught and unstable distort, as *they* do also the rest of the Scriptures, to their own destruction. You therefore, beloved, knowing this beforehand, be on your guard so that you are not carried away by the error of unprincipled men and fall from your own steadfastness, but grow in the grace and knowledge of our Lord and Savior Jesus Christ. To Him *be* the glory, both now and to the day of eternity. Amen. – 2 Peter 3:14-18

> For this reason also, since the day we heard *of it*, we have not ceased to pray for you and to ask that you may be filled with the knowledge of His will in all spiritual wisdom and understanding, so that you will walk in a manner worthy of the Lord, to please *Him* in all respects, bearing fruit in every good work and increasing in the knowledge of God. – Colossians 1:9-10

> "But an hour is coming, and now is, when the true worshipers will worship the Father in spirit and truth; for such people the Father seeks to be His worshipers. God is spirit, and those who worship Him must worship in spirit and truth." – John 4:23-24

> I heard another voice from heaven, saying, "Come out of her [Babylon], my people, so that you will not participate in her sins and receive of her plagues; for her sins have piled up as high as heaven, and God has remembered her iniquities." – Revelation 18:4-5

A CALL-OUT TO PASTORS, TEACHERS & ELDERS

Dear Christian pastor, teacher, or elder: Are you teaching the pure truth of the gospel "faith that was once for all *time* handed down to the saints" in New Testament Scripture, or are you leading others into Babylon and towards eternal death? If so, beware James 3:1! And to those pastors and teachers who choose to continue to preach and teach falsely despite now knowing the truth, please read and pray over the verses given below – and may the Lord open your heart and your mind to see and hear the truth, for these false teachings are in fact "another gospel which is not another." Paul said those teaching such things should be "accursed," and he repeated it twice for emphasis! You too need to come out of her (Babylon), or beware:

> But even if we, or an angel from heaven, should preach to you a gospel contrary to what we have preached to you, he is to be accursed! As we have said before, so I say again now, if any man is preaching to you a gospel contrary to what you received, he is to be accursed! – Galatians 1:8-9

> For such men are false apostles, deceitful workers, disguising themselves as apostles of Christ. No wonder, for even Satan disguises himself as an angel of light. Therefore it is not surprising if his servants also disguise themselves as servants of righteousness [e.g. pastors, elders and teachers within the church], whose end will be according to their deeds. – 2 Corinthians 11:13-15

> Let not many *of you* become teachers, my brethren, knowing that as such we will incur a stricter judgment. – James 3:1

While I do believe that God has children in the many various churches and denominations (despite them not being supported in Scripture) that will be saved to eternal life (for God is a God of amazing mercy and grace), the situation for those church leaders (pastors, teachers, and elders) in the false churches will be quite another matter (see again James 3:1). [Note: Yes, I'm fully aware of James 3:1 myself, and I take it very seriously. But the "message of truth" needs to get out, and if not I, then who? Therefore, I must not shrink back from the task set before me in declaring the truth.]

Also, note that you can sincerely believe that what you are teaching is true, but that doesn't actually make it true, and if you are teaching wrongly, you are still a false teacher regardless of cause or motive even if teaching in ignorance (simply because that's what you were taught, and you are just repeating it).

EXAMINE YOURSELVES

The chapter on perseverance showed you that Scripture admonishes us not to treat our eternal salvation lightly or with carelessness. We are exhorted to "work out your salvation with fear and trembling" and to "test yourselves [examine yourselves!] to see if you are in the faith" (and the truth!):

> So then, my beloved, just as you have always obeyed, not as in my presence only, but now much more in my absence, work out your salvation with fear and trembling; for it is God who is at work in you, both to will and to work for *His* good pleasure. – Philippians 2:12-13

> Test yourselves *to see* if you are in the faith; examine yourselves! Or do you not recognize this about yourselves, that Jesus Christ is in you—unless indeed you fail the test? – 2 Corinthians 13:5

Part of examining ourselves is to (continually) test our beliefs (and teachings) to ensure they are in conformance with New Testament Scripture, for we may have been (or are being) led astray by the wolves. Wayne Jackson writes further on this matter: [94]

> "Examine your own selves, whether you are in the faith; prove your own selves" (2 Cor. 13:5).
>
> This challenge contains an abiding principle that ranges far beyond the immediate context of this rebuke to the Corinthians. From this situation the conscientious student may extract valuable truths to bless his own life.
>
> **Self-examination**
>
> The term "examine" (KJV, ESV) or "try" (ASV) is from the Greek peirazo (found thirty-eight times in the New Testament), which can convey several senses depending upon the context—not the least of which is the idea of endeavoring to discover the nature or quality of something by testing it (Danker et al. 2000, 792 [95]). For instance, the early Christians were subjected to a fiery trial to test their authenticity (1 Pet. 4:12).
>
> In this Corinthian text, the term is a present tense form, suggesting **sustained** examination.

---

[94] Jackson, Wayne. "Examine Yourselves!" ChristianCourier.com. Access date: September 25, 2019. https://christiancourier.com/articles/1445-examine-yourselves

[95] Danker, F. W. et al. 2000. A Greek-English Lexicon of the New Testament. Chicago, IL: University of Chicago.

In order for a spiritual examination to be effective, it must be characterized by certain qualities, none of which may be lacking. These are elements every conscientious person should constantly pursue and cultivate, difficult though the challenge may be.

Personal Examination

Human beings are professional critics of others. We analyze, criticize, stigmatize, and ostracize. While there is a place for "righteous judgment" (Jn. 7:24), critical examination should began in the mirror.

In the Greek Testament the term "yourselves" leads the sentence for emphasis. One will never be able to remove the splinter from another's eye until self-surgery extracts the log from his own (Mt. 7:3-5). There first must be personal scrutiny. Until that is achieved, one can go no further.

Jesus told a parable of two Jews who went to the temple to pray (Lk. 18:9ff). The one, a Pharisee (the strictest sect of Judaism — Acts 26:5), congratulated himself that he stood elevated above others. He cataloged his alleged virtues and drew a sharp line between himself and "this publican" (the phrase drips with disdain) who likewise had entered the environs of the temple.

In glaring contrast, the publican (a Hebrew tax collector on behalf of Rome, thus a despised person) humbly stood "afar off" from the sacred precinct. He would not even lift up his eyes, so conscious was he of his own spiritual flaws. Rather, he "beat his breast" in contrition, and solicited the Lord's merciful propitiation (see ASV fn).

He was a model of self-examination. Those who would please their Creator must be courageous enough to examine themselves and take careful notes.

An Honest Heart

Once one is sufficiently candid to initiate a self-analysis, he must be able to honestly evaluate and acknowledge what he discovers. This demands integrity (Psa. 26:1).

In his parable of the sower, the Lord spoke of the "good" soil that was wonderfully productive. He explained the metaphor as the "heart" (mental disposition) that is "honest and good" (Lk. 8:15).

If a Christian desires God's approval, he must have that level of integrity that operates on the premise: "I long to obey the Lord so passionately that I am willing to make any sacrifice to do so." That is the ideal, however short of it we may fall.

As the Jews steadily resisted believing that Jesus was their Messiah (cf. Jn. 12:37), they had begun already to form murderous plans, claiming he was leading the people astray (Jn. 7:1, 12). Nonetheless, they marveled at his teaching brilliance because he was not a formally trained rabbi (Jn. 7:15).

The solution to that puzzle, he contended, was that his teaching was not strictly human. Rather, it was from God (Jn 7:16). Then he provided the key to faithful discipleship:

"If any man **wills** to do his will, he shall know of the teaching, whether it is of God, or whether I speak from myself" (Jn. 7:17).

The sense is this: "[Y]ou must take care to preserve an honest mind and cultivate a heart that yields itself unquestioningly to God's truth" (Pink 1945, 385).[96]

For pastors, teachers, and elders, I realize that most of you truly love the Lord and believe that you are teaching correctly, but you are not, and isn't it wise and prudent to heed the apostle Paul's advice and examine things more closely. While you may be teaching Christ crucified, that is not enough – you must also honor Christ by teaching His whole gospel message and do so correctly, properly training up the saints so they can make it all the way to eternal life. This is what James 3:1 is about at its core: for if your teaching causes some to "come short of" eternal life, you will be held to account for their lost soul on Judgment Day. For example, if you teach that baptism isn't required for salvation (i.e., that it is just a good work of obedience or whatever) and practice delay in performing them at your church, and if someone under your care and teaching then accepts Christ but delays their baptism for months or even years and then dies before they "get around to it" (after all, you have taught them that it's not required), you will be held to account for their lost soul!

Please don't let pride stand in the way of coming to a better understanding of the truth and correcting any false teachings that may be present. We have the splendid example of Apollos set before us:

> Now a Jew named Apollos, an Alexandrian by birth, an eloquent man, came to Ephesus; and he was mighty in the Scriptures. This man had been instructed in the way of the Lord; and being fervent in spirit, he was speaking and teaching accurately the things concerning Jesus, being acquainted only with the baptism of John; and he began to speak out boldly in the synagogue. But when Priscilla and Aquila heard him, they took him aside and explained to him the way of God more accurately. And when he wanted to go across to Achaia, the brethren encouraged him and wrote to the disciples to welcome him; and when he had arrived, he greatly helped those who had believed through grace, for he powerfully refuted the Jews in public, demonstrating by the Scriptures that Jesus was the Christ. – Acts 18:24-28

Even though Apollos was very well versed ("mighty in the Scriptures") up through John's baptism and spoke out boldly, he was teaching wrongly. The important part, though, is that he humbly accepted (and embraced) correction from Priscilla and Aquila, who gave him a greater revelation of truth, and then he continued on again to be a great warrior for Christ, but now with a greater understanding of truth. What a wonderful example of humility and willingness to continue learning the truth – a process that ideally continues all our lives.

WHY FALSE TEACHINGS MATTER

Some of the false teachings I expose in this book relate directly to matters of salvation and are therefore of critical and eternal importance; others may seem (on the surface) to be of much lesser importance. However, I have already explained that Scripture contains numerous explicit warnings that you can indeed "come short of"

---

[96] Pink, Arthur. 1945. Exposition of the Gospel of John. Vol. 1. Grand Rapids, MI: Zondervan.

eternal life and even be "tricked" out of your "crown of life" by the false teachings of man by not knowing the truth of what is actually written and taught in Scripture:

> My <u>people are destroyed</u> for lack of knowledge. – Hosea 4:6
>
> But the Spirit explicitly says that in later times <u>some will fall away</u> from the faith, paying attention to deceitful spirits and doctrines of demons, by means of the hypocrisy of liars seared in their own conscience as with a branding iron, *men* who forbid marriage *and advocate* abstaining from foods which God has created to be gratefully shared in by those who believe and know the truth. – 1 Timothy 4:1-3
>
> "'Because you have kept the word of My perseverance, I also will keep you from the hour of testing, that *hour* which is about to come upon the whole world, to test those who dwell on the earth. I am coming quickly; hold fast what you have, <u>so that no one will take your crown</u>.'" – Revelation 3:10-11

Case in point, I was talking with an older gentleman at the gym as I was writing this book. This just happened to occur on the very same day that I was finalizing this chapter's introduction. He was raised as a Catholic and attended Catholic schools in childhood. He, therefore, has heard about Jesus his whole life, but he has not accepted Christ by his own admission. When pressed, he does acknowledge that there is a God, although he thinks he will pass into nothingness after death (the false teaching of annihilation). So, although he has known and heard about "religion" and God and even Jesus his whole life, he doesn't believe – in fact, he doesn't even know what to believe. All he has heard taught and preached his whole life are the distortions and false teachings of man, and those were wrapped up in staggering hypocrisy by the ones teaching and preaching them. However, he does know that what he has heard and been taught is "a bunch of hypocrisy and nonsense."

And now we get to the crux of the matter: When I tried to explain the correct gospel "message of truth" to him, I could make no progress whatsoever. He finally just came out and said to me: "You know, I've seen and heard so many things which claim to be Christianity, that very frankly I don't even know what or who to believe anymore. It's all a bunch of crap!" He also again (repeatedly) mentioned the hypocrisy of those who profess to be telling him the truth but then do not act in accord with Scripture themselves.

Yes, every single bit of what he was taught and experienced was from those who call themselves "Christians." That they are not true to the Christianity of the Bible, he could not have known without a lot of diligent Bible reading, but when you're lost to God, that's not what you do. Frankly, he has all but given up, so when I come along and try to explain things all over again correctly to him, he simply doesn't want to hear anymore. He's heard so much nonsense that it has disgusted, overwhelmed, and discouraged him completely. He's given up on it all. And frankly, deep down, he does actually believe that there is a God. How tragic!

So, you see, it <u>does</u> matter. It matters a lot. This guy has been deceived all his life – first by the deception of Roman Catholicism from his childhood, then followed by exposure to the various bizarre, nonsensical and ridiculous stuff that passes today for being "Christian" but which does not lead to eternal life and does not conform to what is actually taught in Scripture. And, on top of all that, he sees an endless parade of self-proclaimed "Christians" around him behaving in abject hypocrisy.

ALL CHRISTIANS SHOULD "JUST GET ALONG"

I continue to hear and have to counter the "we should all just get along" shilling from professing "Christians," which is always accompanied by the statement that "minor doctrinal differences" should just be ignored. Are differences on baptism "minor" or not? What about differences in worshipping the Lord on Saturday or Sunday? What about demanding in a statement of faith that some foods must be rejected as "unclean"? What about keeping the Jewish Saturday Sabbath today or not? What about claiming that someone can be saved to eternal life simply by saying a small prayer at one time in their life (a practice nowhere to be found in the Bible)?

But I ask you, friend and fellow Christian, who are you to decide what "doctrinal differences" are "minor" and which ones are major? Should not the Lord's Word stand as it was given? Jesus prayed for unity because He knew that "wolves" (and wolvettes) and modern-day "Pharisees" would come in to distort the gospel "faith that was once for all *time* handed down to the saints" in NT Scripture and introduce false teachings and false doctrines which would, in fact, divide the church and also lead many astray (to destruction) as they are teaching "another gospel which is not another" – for there is only one Gospel.

Did not Cain in this same way go astray? For he <u>knew</u> what the Lord had commanded as to the way men must worship Him and as to what type of offering was acceptable, and yet Cain simply disregarded that and made up his own opinion as to what he thought was acceptable and what he thought was a "minor difference" – and he suffered the consequences. There are consequences for teaching wrongly, and there are consequences for being led astray by the false teachers and false teachings, whether you think they are minor or not. Let the Lord be found true even if "every man be found a liar." God's Word stands as it was given, with the "sum of thy word is truth" – not selected verses chosen or ignored based on the whims and opinions of man.

Further to the point, did the apostle Paul just "get along" with Peter when Peter was acting hypocritically with respect to the Mosaic Law in the mixed company of Jews and Gentiles (see Galatians 2)? No, he didn't just "get along" – he confronted Peter, and he did so boldly! For Peter's actions and example might have caused others to stumble and fall away from Christ and grace back under Mosaic Law. These are matters of utmost seriousness, for it is a battle for eternal souls!

And lastly, many of the false teachings are outright disrespectful to the Lord Jesus Christ in one way or another – either expressing infidelity or denying Him and His blood on the cross! Just "going along" with these false teachings indicates a lack of understanding of what Jesus did on the cross, of Christ's commands as given in the New Testament, or of the nature of the "Kingdom of God" (which is "not of this world"). I, therefore, disagree with the sentiment that all Christians should "just get along" with each other regardless of doctrinal beliefs and teachings. Wayne Jackson writes correctly on this matter in response to a question that was sent to him: [97]

> "I am sincerely asking whether we need to be loving and accepting towards all religious groups. I have never believed God to be exclusive or vindictive towards those who have different understandings of Him."

---

[97] Jackson, Wayne. "Is It Wrong to Dispute Religious Error?" ChristianCourier.com. Access date: September 14, 2020. https://christiancourier.com/articles/731-is-it-wrong-to-dispute-religious-error

Occasionally it is necessary to dispute certain doctrines that are taught within the religious community.

But some people feel that any religious disagreement with anyone who identifies themselves as a Christian is mean-spirited. They believe opposition to certain teachings is unkind and narrow.

We would respond to this sincere question in the following fashion.

Love and the Acceptance of Error

First, it should go without saying that the Christian is to **demonstrate love** towards all—even those who resist the truth in the most militant fashion.

The love of God for rebellious mankind is portrayed repeatedly in the Scriptures. The Father commended his love toward us by giving his Son for our sins, even while we were hostile and sinful toward him (Rom. 5:8).

That does not mean, however, that he **ignores** how we live or **what we teach**.

In this same context, the lost are described as being weak and ungodly, as sinners, and enemies worthy of divine wrath. (Rom. 5:6, 8, 9-10).

Love offers a remedy for humanity's sinful condition, but it does not **close its eyes** to reality.

The Consequences of Rejecting God's Loving Rebuke

An understanding of Old Testament history forever demolishes the erroneous notion that God is **unconcerned** with whether men and women entertain "different understandings of Him."

For example, many of the nations of the antique world **understood** God to be identified in various idol forms, which they devoutly worshiped. But the prophets rebuked these base activities. And Jehovah destroyed nation after nation that persisted in this evil ideology and practice.

The Honest Compassion of Christ

No informed Bible student will deny that Jesus Christ loved men and women supremely. When they ignorantly languished under the effects of sin, he tenderly sought to reclaim them (cf. Lk. 7:36ff; Jn. 8:1-11). The Savior came not to crush the bruised reed, nor to quench the smoldering wick (cf. Mt. 12:20).

Jesus was the **compassionate** Christ!

On the other hand, the Lord could be (and was) **very severe** in dealing with **corrupt religious leaders**, who should have known better (and frequently did) than to act and teach **contrary to truth**.

He cast out of the temple those who trafficked in religion for commercial purposes (Mt. 21:12-13; Jn. 2:13-17). He informed the corrupt Pharisees that they were not legitimate heirs of Abraham; rather, they were **devilish** in their actions (Jn. 8:33ff).

One can scarcely read the twenty-third chapter of Matthew without **feeling the heat** of Christ's rebuke of certain **corrupt Hebrew leaders**.

It is not, therefore, wrong to **oppose error**.

Further, it is a gross inconsistency to rebuke someone for being a rebuker. Why is it that folks cannot see the flaw in their argument when they are **intolerant** of those with whom they charge intolerance?

May We Disagree About God?

The most stunning component of our reader's complaint, however, is the allegation that it is permissible for people to entertain **different understandings of divine truth** that pertain to the salvation of one's soul!

We must call attention to the following.

God is **infinite in his knowledge** (Psa. 147:5). He is a God of knowledge (1 Sam. 2:3), who knows all things (1 Jn. 3:20). The riches of his knowledge is a reality too deep for human conception (Rom. 11:33).

It is never accurate to say or even to imply that God is **unconcerned with disagreements** among men relative to the **eternal truths** that he has revealed to the human family.

Disputes regarding what the Lord requires men and women to believe and practice is not the result of **different understandings**. It is because of **misunderstandings on the part of misinformed people**, even though they may be very sincere.

God is a being of **truth** (i.e., faithfulness; cf. Deut. 32:4, ASV). All his words are pure (Psa. 12:6). He cannot speak that which is untrue (Tit. 1:2; Heb. 6:18), because his word is truth (Jn. 17:17).

Any disagreement as to what **God requires**, therefore, is a disagreement over the difference between **truth and error**. To suggest that God is not concerned with the difference between truth and non-truth is to cast serious reflection upon the God of truth.

It is **a dangerous thing** to suggest that folks may disagree about what God teaches and at the same time stand approved in his sight.

In his letter to the Roman saints, Paul discussed the advantage that historically had been granted to the Hebrew nation. For one thing, they had been entrusted with the "oracles of God" (i.e., the sacred Scriptures; cf. Rom. 3:1-2).

The question then is raised: "What if some were without faith?"

The meaning of that question is this. What would be the case if some of the Jews proved to be **unfaithful** to Jehovah's plan on their behalf? What if some of the Hebrews decided to **chart their own course**. In other words, they entertained **disagreements** with the faithful about what the Lord required of them?

Would their disagreement or misunderstanding have nullified the divine plan? Would they have exposed God as being unfaithful? Absolutely not!

This stinging rebuke is then offered: "Let God be found true, though every man be found a liar" (Rom. 3:4).

Conclusion

Here is what the inspired apostle is affirming.

Any theory, opinion, or doctrinal position that is adverse to the revealed will of God is a lie.

And those who teach and broadcast such are liars, whether they intend to be or not.

Is that strong language from Paul? Most assuredly it is, but the force of it is designed to preserve the **integrity of the Almighty**.

By implication this text teaches that those who profess to be Jehovah's people, especially teachers (Jas. 3:1), must agree with him and among themselves.

> The Lord expects us to strive for submission to him and a **united teaching** on fundamental truths.
>
> It is exceedingly foolish to suggest that God **does not care** whether people understand his will or not. It is a grave danger to develop the mindset that it really doesn't matter whether what we teach is truth or error.
>
> "Be not foolish, but understand what the will of the Lord is" (Eph. 5:17).

Finally, we also have a duty to correct and admonish others who are in error or who are teaching in error:

> I solemnly charge *you* in the presence of God and of Christ Jesus, who is to judge the living and the dead, and by His appearing and His kingdom: preach the word; be ready in season *and* out of season; reprove, rebuke, exhort, with great patience and instruction. – 2 Timothy 4:1-2
>
> We proclaim Him, admonishing every man and teaching every man with all wisdom, so that we may present every man complete in Christ. For this purpose also I labor, striving according to His power, which mightily works within me. – Colossians 1:28-29
>
> Let the word of Christ richly dwell within you, with all wisdom teaching and admonishing one another with psalms and hymns and spiritual songs, singing with thankfulness in your hearts to God. – Colossians 3:16
>
> All Scripture is inspired by God and profitable for teaching, for reproof, for correction, for training in righteousness; so that the man of God may be adequate, equipped for every good work. – 2 Timothy 3:16-17
>
> …holding fast the faithful word which is in accordance with the teaching, so that he will be able both to exhort in sound doctrine and to refute those who contradict. – Titus 1:9
>
> My brethren, if any among you strays from the truth and one turns him back, let him know that he who turns a sinner from the error of his way will save his soul from death and will cover a multitude of sins. – James 5:19-20

THE DANGER OF COMPLACENCY

Another huge danger that the false teachings pose is creating complacency, as I have already discussed, causing many to procrastinate in accepting Christ or sharing the gospel with urgency. Many of the false teachings are intentionally designed to lull people, both the saved and the lost, into complacency – a lack of determined, daily spiritual growth in oneself (growing in the "grace and knowledge [understanding]" of the Lord), a lack of urgency in sharing the gospel, and a lack of attending to and doing the Lord's business today!

This happens because the false teachings send this message (I'm paraphrasing here): "Don't worry, there's still more time left because here are a bunch of (false) prophecies which we are still waiting to happen before Christ returns, so when you see these (false) prophetic events happening, you can then get serious about all this stuff." Those succumbing to the false teachings are therefore falling into the exact trap they were designed to create, and they do not even realize it!

Scripture warns repeatedly and explicitly about falling into complacency for the great Day of Judgment will arrive like a "thief in the night" when most are thinking "safe and secure," whether you are ready to meet God and His Christ for judgment or not! It is written:

> "Then the kingdom of heaven will be comparable to ten virgins, who took their lamps and went out to meet the bridegroom. Five of them were foolish, and five were prudent. For when the foolish took their lamps, they took no oil with them, but the prudent took oil in flasks along with their lamps. Now while the bridegroom was delaying, they all got drowsy and *began* to sleep. But at midnight there was a shout, 'Behold, the bridegroom! Come out to meet *him*.' Then all those virgins rose and trimmed their lamps. The foolish said to the prudent, 'Give us some of your oil, for our lamps are going out.' But the prudent answered, 'No, there will not be enough for us and you *too*; go instead to the dealers and buy *some* for yourselves.' And while they were going away to make the purchase, the bridegroom came, and those who were ready went in with him to the wedding feast; and the door was shut. Later the other virgins also came, saying, 'Lord, lord, open up for us.' But he answered, 'Truly I say to you, I do not know you.' Be on the alert then, for you do not know the day nor the hour." – Matthew 25:1-13

> "Therefore be on the alert, for you do not know which day your Lord is coming. But be sure of this, that if the head of the house had known at what time of the night the thief was coming, he would have been on the alert and would not have allowed his house to be broken into. For this reason you also must be ready; for the Son of Man is coming at an hour when you do not think *He will*.

> "Who then is the faithful and sensible slave whom his master put in charge of his household to give them their food at the proper time? Blessed is that slave whom his master finds so doing when he comes. Truly I say to you that he will put him in charge of all his possessions. But if that evil slave says in his heart, 'My master is not coming for a long time,' and begins to beat his fellow slaves and eat and drink with drunkards; the master of that slave will come on a day when he does not expect *him* and at an hour which he does not know, and will cut him in pieces and assign him a place with the hypocrites; in that place there will be weeping and gnashing of teeth." – Matthew 24:42-51

> Be of sober *spirit*, be on the alert. Your adversary, the devil, prowls around like a roaring lion, seeking someone to devour. – 1 Peter 5:8

> Now as to the times and the epochs, brethren, you have no need of anything to be written to you. For you yourselves know full well that the day of the Lord will come just like a thief in the night. While they are saying, "Peace and safety!" then destruction will come upon them suddenly like labor pains upon a woman with child, and they will not escape. But you, brethren, are not in darkness, that the day would overtake you like a thief; for you are all sons of light and sons of day. We are not of night nor of darkness; so then let us not sleep as others do, but let us be alert and sober. For those who sleep do their sleeping at night, and those who get drunk get drunk at night. But since we are of *the* day, let us be sober, having put on the breastplate of faith and love, and as a helmet, the hope of salvation. For God has not destined us for wrath, but for obtaining salvation through our Lord Jesus Christ. – 1 Thessalonians 5:1-9

The Message of Truth

> "But of that day [the great Day of Judgment] and hour no one knows, not even the angels of heaven, nor the Son, but the Father alone. For the coming of the Son of Man will be just like the days of Noah. For as in those days before the flood they were eating and drinking, marrying and giving in marriage, until the day that Noah entered the ark, and they did not understand until the flood came and took them all away; so will the coming of the Son of Man be." – Matthew 24:36-39

As you can clearly see, Scripture warns us in no uncertain terms to "be on the alert" and to be "on guard"!

THIS IS JUST A PARTIAL LIST

Also, know that what I've included in this section of the book is only a partial list of the false teachings you will likely encounter. The fact of the matter is that some of the items (e.g., churches and institutions) that I have listed here are themselves comprised of many false teachings within! I also must mention that it is very common that where you find one false teaching, you will almost always find other false teachings within the same group/sect. Like "wolves," false teachings usually travel in packs!

If you want to pick one single false teaching topic to dig into first yourself, I suggest that it be Dispensational Premillennialism (of various forms, with its attendant pre-tribulation, post-tribulation, mid-tribulation, and "secret rapture" false teachings). I've found that deconstructing and understanding that one particular false teaching helps lead one to then be able to discern many of the other false teachings more easily.

Additionally, by studying that one particular false teaching, you will also become aware of the particular groups/sects/cults/churches which are promoting (yes promoting – as in advertising, pushing an agenda for gain or political objective) many of the other false teachings as well. You will also find that as you search for a church that is free from false teachings, one by one, churches will eliminate themselves from your consideration, and you will be left with only one church to pick from – for there is only one which isn't full of false teachings! Amazing! See the Finding a Church chapter.

As I suggested earlier, you should study each of these teachings yourself and draw your own conclusions. I also recommend reading *The Pilgrim's Progress* by John Bunyan. It is a wonderful book that describes Christian's journey from this world to that which is to come. Along the way, he meets many different characters and false teachings which try to "trick" him and turn him out of the "straight and narrow" path to eternal life, cause him to stumble and fall, and cause him to turn back from Christ. You will see that this very highly regarded book reinforces my warnings about the danger of false teachings.

THE TRUTH OF SCRIPTURE PREVAILS

I have presented to you already in this book "the message of truth" as given in Scripture. I have outlined the biblically specified conditions for eternal salvation, which are: being "born again" (through hearing the gospel "message of truth" followed by belief, repentance, confession, and baptism by immersion), obedience to the commands of Christ as given in the New Testament with the natural result of a true saving faith being made manifest through action (i.e., "good works," "bearing fruit" for the Lord) and "persevering" in faith until death. Remember that being born again is a necessary but not sufficient condition for eternal salvation; it is only the start of your journey. Being "born again" is only the first step (but by far the most important step) on your path to eternal life – which is your ultimate goal and destination with God and His Christ in heaven. Amen!

Any teaching which makes claims contrary to the above is a false teaching. Scripture is clear that all of those are components of eternal salvation for the Christian; you cannot omit any of them simply because you don't like them. Remember, the "ravenous wolves" cleverly and subtly mix bits of actual Scriptural/Christian truth in with their false teachings, so it looks all very authentic and "Biblical" on the surface – but it is not. All teachings should be directly tested against Scripture (including anything I write in this book). These lies, distortions, and false teachings aim to take away your "crown of life"!

I pray that "those who have an ear to hear, hear" the warnings I'm giving in this section of the book, and may God give you grace in wisdom and understanding of His truth. Again, I say, be not deceived! The list of false teachings follows after the related Scripture below.

RELATED SCRIPTURE:

NOTE: Scripture given below applies to the entire Wolves section, not just to any single false teaching in particular.

For we are not as many, which corrupt [and peddle] the word of God: but as of sincerity, but as of God, in the sight of God speak we in Christ. – 2 Corinthians 2:17 (KJV)

O Israel, your prophets have been like foxes among ruins. You have not gone up into the breaches, nor did you build the wall around the house of Israel to stand in the battle on the day of the LORD. They see falsehood and lying divination who are saying, 'The LORD declares,' when the LORD has not sent them; yet they hope for the fulfillment of *their* word. Did you not see a false vision and speak a lying divination when you said, 'The LORD declares,' but it is not I who have spoken?"

Therefore, thus says the Lord GOD, "Because you have spoken falsehood and seen a lie, therefore behold, I am against you," declares the Lord GOD. "So My hand will be against the prophets who see false visions and utter lying divinations. They will have no place in the council of My people, nor will they be written down in the register of the house of Israel, nor will they enter the land of Israel, that you may know that I am the Lord GOD." – Ezekiel 13:4-9

Now I urge you, brethren, keep your eye on those who cause dissensions and hindrances contrary to the teaching which you learned, and turn away from them. For such men are slaves, not of our Lord Christ but of their own appetites; and by their smooth and flattering speech they deceive the hearts of the unsuspecting. For the report of your obedience has reached to all; therefore I am rejoicing over you, but I want you to be wise in what is good and innocent in what is evil. The God of peace will soon crush Satan under your feet. – Romans 16:17-20

For the overseer must be above reproach as God's steward, not self-willed, not quick-tempered, not addicted to wine, not pugnacious, not fond of sordid gain, but hospitable, loving what is good, sensible, just, devout, self-controlled, holding fast the faithful word which is in accordance with the teaching, so that he will be able both to exhort in sound doctrine and to refute those who contradict.

The Message of Truth

For there are many rebellious men, empty talkers and deceivers, especially those of the circumcision. – Titus 1:7-10

Then Jesus spoke to the crowds and to His disciples, saying: "The scribes and the Pharisees have seated themselves in the chair of Moses; therefore all that they tell you, do and observe, but do not do according to their deeds; for they say *things* and do not do *them*." – Matthew 23:1-3

Then some Pharisees and scribes came to Jesus from Jerusalem and said, "Why do Your disciples break the tradition of the elders? For they do not wash their hands when they eat bread." And He answered and said to them, "Why do you yourselves transgress the commandment of God for the sake of your tradition? For God said, 'HONOR YOUR FATHER AND MOTHER,' and, 'HE WHO SPEAKS EVIL OF FATHER OR MOTHER IS TO BE PUT TO DEATH.' But you say, 'Whoever says to *his* father or mother, "Whatever I have that would help you has been given *to God*," he is not to honor his father or his mother.' And *by this* you invalidated the word of God for the sake of your tradition. You hypocrites, rightly did Isaiah prophesy of you:

'THIS PEOPLE HONORS ME WITH THEIR LIPS,
BUT THEIR HEART IS FAR AWAY FROM ME.
'BUT IN VAIN DO THEY WORSHIP ME,
TEACHING AS DOCTRINES THE PRECEPTS OF MEN.'" – Matthew 15:1-9

Know this first of all, that in the last days mockers will come with *their* mocking, following after their own lusts, and saying, "Where is the promise of His coming? For *ever* since the fathers fell asleep, all continues just as it was from the beginning of creation." – 2 Peter 3:3-4

And Jesus answered and said to them, "See to it that no one misleads you. For many will come in My name, saying, 'I am the Christ,' and will mislead many. You will be hearing of wars and rumors of wars. See that you are not frightened, for *those things* must take place, but *that* is not yet the end. For nation will rise against nation, and kingdom against kingdom, and in various places there will be famines and earthquakes. But all these things are *merely* the beginning of birth pangs.

"Then they will deliver you to tribulation, and will kill you, and you will be hated by all nations because of My name. At that time many will fall away and will betray one another and hate one another. Many false prophets will arise and will mislead many." – Matthew 24:4-11 [Note: While these verses applied to the period leading up to the events of A.D. 70, they also serve as a caution today, for what has been will be, for there is "nothing new under the sun"!]

"Then if anyone says to you, 'Behold, here is the Christ,' or 'There *He is*,' do not believe *him*. For false Christs and false prophets will arise and will show great signs and wonders, so as to mislead, if possible, even the elect. Behold, I have told you in advance." – Matthew 24:23-25 [Note: These verses applied to the period leading up to the events of A.D. 70, but they also serve as a caution for us not to be misled today.]

Do not be carried away by varied and strange teachings; for it is good for the heart to be strengthened by grace, not by foods, through which those who were so occupied were not benefited. – Hebrews 13:9

"'But the prophet who speaks a word presumptuously in My name which I have not commanded him to speak, or which he speaks in the name of other gods, that prophet shall die.'" – Deuteronomy 18:20

"Woe to the shepherds who are destroying and scattering the sheep of My pasture!" declares the LORD. Therefore thus says the LORD God of Israel concerning the shepherds who are tending My people: "You have scattered My flock and driven them away, and have not attended to them; behold, I am about to attend to you for the evil of your deeds," declares the LORD. – Jeremiah 23:1-2

"For both prophet and priest are polluted;
Even in My house I have found their wickedness," declares the LORD.

"Moreover, among the prophets of Samaria I saw an offensive thing:
They prophesied by Baal and led My people Israel astray.
"Also among the prophets of Jerusalem I have seen a horrible thing:
The committing of adultery and walking in falsehood;
And they strengthen the hands of evildoers,
So that no one has turned back from his wickedness.
All of them have become to Me like Sodom,
And her inhabitants like Gomorrah."

Thus says the LORD of hosts,
"Do not listen to the words of the prophets who are prophesying to you.
They are leading you into futility;
They speak a vision of their own imagination,
Not from the mouth of the LORD." – Jeremiah 23:11, 13-14, 16

"I have heard what the prophets have said who prophesy falsely in My name, saying, 'I had a dream, I had a dream!' How long? Is there *anything* in the hearts of the prophets who prophesy falsehood, even *these* prophets of the deception of their own heart, who intend to make My people forget My name by their dreams which they relate to one another, just as their fathers forgot My name because of Baal?" – Jeremiah 23:25-27

Then the LORD said to me, "The prophets are prophesying falsehood in My name. I have neither sent them nor commanded them nor spoken to them; they are prophesying to you a false vision, divination, futility and the deception of their own minds." – Jeremiah 14:14

"An appalling and horrible thing
Has happened in the land:
The prophets prophesy falsely,
And the priests rule on their *own* authority;
And My people love it so!
But what will you do at the end of it?" – Jeremiah 5:30-31

Put on the full armor of God, so that you will be able to stand firm against the schemes of the devil. For our struggle is not against flesh and blood, but against the rulers, against the powers, against the world forces of this darkness, against the spiritual *forces* of wickedness in the heavenly *places*. Therefore, take up the full armor of God, so that you will be able to resist in the evil day, and having done everything, to stand firm.

Stand firm therefore, HAVING GIRDED YOUR LOINS WITH TRUTH, and HAVING PUT ON THE BREASTPLATE OF RIGHTEOUSNESS, and having shod YOUR FEET WITH THE PREPARATION OF THE GOSPEL OF PEACE; in addition to all, taking up the shield of faith with which you will be able to extinguish all the flaming arrows of the evil *one*. And take THE HELMET OF SALVATION, and the sword of the Spirit, which is the word of God. – Ephesians 6:11-17

"You are of *your* father the devil, and you want to do the desires of your father. He was a murderer from the beginning, and does not stand in the truth because there is no truth in him. Whenever he speaks a lie, he speaks from his own *nature*, for he is a liar and the father of lies." – John 8:44

For this reason God will send upon them a deluding influence so that they will believe what is false, in order that they all may be judged who did not believe the truth, but took pleasure in wickedness. – 2 Thessalonians 2:11-12

If you have died with Christ to the elementary principles of the world, why, as if you were living in the world, do you submit yourself to decrees, such as, "Do not handle, do not taste, do not touch!" (which all *refer to* things destined to perish with use)—in accordance with the commandments and teachings of men? These are matters which have, to be sure, the appearance of wisdom in self-made religion and self-abasement and severe treatment of the body, *but are* of no value against fleshly indulgence. – Colossians 2:20-23

"Behold, I will cause *those* of the synagogue of Satan, who say that they are Jews and are not, but lie—I will make them come and bow down at your feet, and *make them* know that I have loved you." – Revelation 3:9

And the beast was seized, and with him the false prophet who performed the signs in his presence, by which he deceived those who had received the mark of the beast and those who worshiped his image; these two were thrown alive into the lake of fire which burns with brimstone. – Revelation 19:20

That which has been is that which will be,
And that which has been done is that which will be done.
So there is nothing new under the sun. – Ecclesiastes 1:9 [Note: Some might wonder why I've included this verse in this chapter. It reminds you that what has happened in times of old also happens today. So, just as false prophets abounded in Old Testament times, they also abound in New Testament times!]

For this reason we must pay much closer attention to what we have heard, so that we do not drift away *from it*. – Hebrews 2:1

*****

AGAIN, I SAY, BEWARE! DANGER AHEAD! EVERYTHING THAT FOLLOWS IN THIS SECTION OF THE BOOK IS A FALSE TEACHING!

*****

6.1 THE "THEORY" OF EVOLUTION
(And "Millions of Years" For Earth History)

This false teaching/fake science claims that all life originated millions (or billions) of years ago, out of lightning striking some primordial puddle of goo somewhere, and further that man "evolved" from lower animals (e.g., having a common primate ancestor with apes) – basically, that all life subsequently "evolved" from lower forms to higher forms without any Creator (God) involved. This false teaching is brought to you by the secular/atheist world who deny that there is a God, and wow, this lie is a big one. You see, if the forces of evil (led by Satan) can stop you from believing the very first sentence(s) of the Bible, they know that you will not believe (or even read) the rest of the Bible!

That is why this false teaching is shouted far and wide in blaring volume 24/7/365 (all day, every day) from every secular media source on the planet. Nearly every textbook and educational institution, from the preschool/kindergarten level all the way up through university and post-graduate doctoral level have been teaching this "theory" to you nonstop. In fact, this false teaching has been drummed into you since you were just a wee infant. In effect, you are being (or have been) brainwashed!

But realize that their very own evolutionary scientists acknowledge that their <u>theory</u> cannot (and does not) explain where life first came from (i.e., where did that very <u>first</u> "evolutionary step" come from?)! Amazing, eh? And I bet you have never heard that part – yet it is true. Yes, they try to make claims about how "life evolves" and "survival of the fittest" (e.g., natural selection, etc.), but when you press them, they admit they have no answer to that "first" question.

Please also note that it is called the "Theory" of Evolution, not the "Facts" of Evolution! That's right, it's just a "theory" of man, although they try to pass it off as fact, as hard science, when it is nothing of the sort. This false teaching is also intimately tied together with other secular false teachings on many matters of so-called "science" – including dinosaurs, light "redshift," the "Big Bang" theory, tree growth rings, radioactive carbon dating, etc. You see, when you start to unravel the web of lies that they are presenting as facts in these areas of "science," many of the things which you have been taught and accept as scientific facts which claim to disprove the Bible are, in fact, just fanciful "theories" of man. (See also the chapter Science vs. the Bible.)

This false teaching is compounded by Christians who blindly believe it and then keep repeating it themselves, even going so far as to try to bend the Word of God so that it will be in agreement with this secular God-denying false teaching of man! They, therefore, try to shoehorn this "theory" into the Bible and the book of Genesis, chapters 1 and 2 specifically.

So much has been written about this teaching that it's pointless to go into it further here, except to point out if it wasn't already obvious, that if you deny/don't believe the very first sentences in the Bible, why will you believe all the rest? Hence, this is a primary attack vector by which the fallen world and those who deny God (and Christ) try to discredit the Bible. Remember, we are in a spiritual war. Also, just because you read something in a science/school/university textbook doesn't make it true!

In fact, most of the companies that publish the textbooks (for all educational levels – kindergarten to post-graduate levels) are owned or operated by either secular groups who outright deny God or by groups who deny Christ! Literally everything you are taught since childhood from textbooks at all levels is under their control. The hard part of this fake science false teaching is that it's been drilled into us since we were just children, so much so that many just accept it as truth without even giving it a second thought; it's called brainwashing. It's going to lead many (many) billions to eternal destruction.

Realize that there is a Creator, the Lord God of Hosts, who created heaven and earth and all things in it (including you and me), and He created everything in seven (7) literal days – not over "millions of years" as some "theory" claims. No, the "theory" (not facts) of evolution does not disprove the Bible, not even remotely.

6.2 SATAN (THE DEVIL) IS JUST A MYTH

Many try to dismiss the fact that the Bible declares that there is a very real spiritual being called Satan. Various names are given to Satan, including: the "Devil" (Greek diabolos), "serpent/snake," "Abaddon," "Beelzebub," and "Belial." His name means "adversary" and "deceiver." He is also described as "a liar and the father of lies," "a murderer from the beginning," and that "there is no truth in him" (John 8:44). He is your "accuser" before God (Revelation 12:1, Job 1), "the prince of the power of the air [this fallen world]" (Ephesians 2:1-2), "the god of this age [world]" (2 Corinthians 4:4), and "the ruler of this world" (John 12:31). Note, however, that he is not called "Lucifer" (see the Lucifer as the Devil false teaching).

Many claim that the devil is just an idea, a concept, a myth, or a fairy tale. But here's an analogy to help you understand this point: we don't have to know where the Law of Gravity came from, or even need to understand it fully, in order to know that it is very real indeed and that there are dire consequences for ignoring it. The same goes for Satan.

It is interesting to note that in the documented exchange between Satan and Eve in the Garden of Eden (Genesis 3:1-19), Satan uses his tried-and-true tactic (which he still uses today) of deliberately twisting God's Word with the intent to deceive and to spiritually/eternally kill all of the human race which was being born. Satan does this by either adding to, subtly altering, or taking away from God's Word. This is why a Christian is strongly admonished to know the Word of God for themselves, so they are not deceived.

The Bible doesn't tell us exactly when Satan was created, but it does say that he is a very real created spiritual being, an angel. As a created being, he is therefore not omniscient (all-knowing), omnipresent (able to be everywhere at once), or impotent (all-powerful) like God is. And Scripture tells us that he "prowls around like a roaring lion, seeking someone to devour" (1 Peter 5:8). So yes, Satan exists, and he means to destroy you – to kill you eternally. He tries to do this by obfuscating the truth of Scripture, by telling lies, half-truths, and distorting (misquoting) Scripture. He is the "father of lies." Below is an excerpt from *Beyond the Tomb*:[98]

> Sometime, not clearly revealed to us, some "angels sinned," "kept not their first estate, but left their own habitation," and are reserved in "chains of darkness unto the judgment of the great day" (2 Peter 2:4; Jude 6). It is generally believed that Satan and his hosts of demons are the ones referred to. Satan is called the "prince of devils" (Matthew 9:34), "prince of the power of the air" (Ephesians 2:2), "ruler

---

[98] Riggle, H.M. (1929/2018), *Beyond the Tomb*, (The Gospel Trumpet Company/Holy Spirit Prints).

of the darkness of this world" (Ephesians 6:12), and the "power of darkness" (Colossians 1:13; Ephesians 6:12).

He then has a kingdom, has a dominion, and reigns. From Matthew 25:41 we infer that hell was "prepared for the devil *and his angels.*" Then demons are angels, and of course must be fallen angels [also called unclean spirits]. Knowing their final doom, James tells us they "believe and tremble" (James 2:19) This is evident from what the demons said to Jesus: "And, behold, they cried out, saying, What have we to do with thee, Jesus, thou Son of God? Art thou come hither to torment us before the time?" (Matthew 8:29).

So, there are good, holy angels in heaven, and there are evil, fallen angels in hell. The good are "ministering spirits, sent out to render service for the sake of those who will inherit salvation." (Hebrews 1:14) The evil ones are under the direction and rulership of Satan and are sent forth to destroy the souls of men.

Satan opposes everything good and of God. His main weapon today is deception. The false teachings in this section of the book are of his doing, as he attempts to deceive people out of believing in God, in the Bible, in Christ, and then even after they are born again, to try to cause them to stumble and "fall away" from the faith, backslide, go apostate, follow "another gospel which is not another" (i.e., false teachings), or be lured out of the "straight and narrow" path to eternal life and back into bondage under sin to eternal death.

The popular rendition of him as a fanciful cartoon character with horns in red tights and a pitchfork is woefully off the mark and designed again to deceive you into dismissing and underestimating the fact that he is a very real spiritual being and that he means your eternal death. The forces of evil are in a battle with the forces of God and good, and this world is the battleground. We as Christians are on the front line in this spiritual war, with Satan and the angels who sinned on one side and God and His holy angels and saints on the other side. Do not make the mistake of underestimating Satan, nor make the mistake of pretending he doesn't exist. Both mistakes can lead you to eternal death. See also the chapter on The Armor of God.

6.3 ANNIHILATION AFTER DEATH

This false teaching, called "annihilation," claims that when the unsaved/wicked person dies, they simply cease to exist (in both body and soul) and pass away into nothingness. This belief comes from the fact that many people (and even some Christians) do not believe in an eternal hell, regardless of the truth of Scripture.

Two groups that advocate this false teaching: 1) "materialists," who also deny God and proclaim that this material world and this physical life are the only things we have – that when we die, that's it, and 2) some so-called "Christian" churches, sects and denominations (e.g., 7th Day Adventists, Jehovah Witnesses).

The Bible emphatically disagrees with both of those viewpoints, and the Bible teachings on it are clear – you were created with an eternal soul/spirit, and it will continue forever. The only unknown is its eternal destination: heaven or hell. Scripture teaches that both the saved and the lost will be resurrected in immortal bodies! Scripture teaches that the spirit (still conscious) goes to be with the Lord at death for those who are saved ("absent from the body and to be at home with the Lord" – 2 Corinthians 5:8), and for those who die in sin, their spirit (still conscious also) goes to a holding place

("Sheol," "Hades"), reserved for the Day of Judgment, after which they will be cast into hell for eternity.

For a detailed treatment of this topic, please see another book we publish called *Beyond the Tomb*, which presents what Scripture says about your eternal soul and destiny in much greater detail and provides solid Scriptural support for what I'm saying here. Also, did you know that Scripture uses the exact same word to describe both "eternal" life for the saved in heaven and "eternal" torment for the lost in hell – and yet no one argues that eternal life in heaven means we will cease to exist in heaven. A snippet from the book is given below on the subject of annihilation: [99]

> Our position is that sin is such an infinite evil that it will be justly followed by an endless punishment. Our annihilationist friends insist that they believe in eternal punishment but that this punishment is an eternal blotting out of existence, a cessation of being. They deny eternal suffering. Here the issue is drawn. Now, if the wicked can suffer punishment without being conscious of it, why cannot the righteous enjoy eternal happiness unconsciously? The one looks as consistent as the other.
>
> We might ask: Will a person who is annihilated *forever* feel it more than one who is annihilated *for a few thousand years?* Our materialist friends hold that all at death are unconscious, go into utter nonexistence. That is all they claim will happen to the wicked at the resurrection. Why take them out of a non-existent state, and then again suddenly blot them out of existence again? What is the difference? If the righteous at death go into non-existence, what is the difference between them and the wicked who will go into the same state beyond the judgment? If mere physical death, passing into a state of non-existence, is eternal punishment, then will not the death of the brutes also be everlasting punishment? Where is the difference? ...
>
> The next term is *"eternal,"* also derived from *aionios:*
>
> - "But the righteous unto life eternal" (Matt. 25:46).
> - "Eternal salvation" (Heb. 5:9).
> - "Eternal redemption" (Heb. 9:12).
> - "Eternal Spirit" (Heb. 9:14).
> - "Eternal inheritance" (Heb. 9:15).
> - "Eternal glory" (2 Tim. 2:10).
> - "King eternal" (1 Tim. 1:17).
> - "In danger of eternal damnation" (Mark 3:29).
> - "Suffering the vengeance of eternal fire" (Jude 7).
>
> No earthly wisdom can overthrow these solid truths. The same word that measures the life, salvation, redemption, and inheritance of the righteous in heaven, the existence of the Spirit, and the eternal existence of God Himself, measures the damnation of the lost in hell, where they will suffer the "vengeance of eternal fire." As long as the heavens shall stand, as long as the righteous will enjoy their life with Christ, so long shall the damnation of the wicked last. There is no way to evade the plain testimony of the Bible on this point. Eternal truth teaches eternal damnation in eternal fire.

---

[99] Riggle, H.M. (1929/2018), *Beyond the Tomb*, (The Gospel Trumpet Company/Holy Spirit Prints).

We shall now come to the word *"forever,"* from *aiona:*

- "And he shall reign over the house of Jacob forever; and of his kingdom there shall be no end" (Luke 1:33).
- "The Son abideth forever" (John 8:35).
- "Jesus Christ, the same yesterday, and today, and forever" (Heb. 13:8).
- "Thine is the kingdom, and the power, and the glory forever" (Matt. 6:13).
- "To whom be glory forever" (Rom. 11:36).
- "The word of God, which liveth and abideth forever" (1 Pet. 1:23-25).
- "Him that sat on the throne, who liveth forever and ever" (Rev. 4:9).
- "Thy throne, O God, is forever and ever" (Heb. 1:8).
- "They shall reign forever and ever" (Rev. 22:5).

Now, concerning the future of the wicked we read:

- "To whom the mist of darkness is reserved forever" (2 Pet. 2:17).
- "To whom is reserved the blackness of darkness forever" (Jude 13).
- "Shall be tormented day and night forever and ever" (Rev. 20:10).
- "And he shall be tormented with fire and brimstone; ... and the smoke of their torment ascendeth up forever and ever" (Rev. 14:10-11).

As long as God shall reign and His throne shall endure, the torments of Satan and wicked men shall last.

On the strength of all the facts presented in this chapter I affirm in the name of the God of the Bible, that the Scriptures nowhere employ any stronger words to express the endless existence of God Himself and of all that pertains to His eternal life, kingdom, and glory, than it uses to set forth both the never-ending felicities of the righteous in heaven, and the never-ending torments of the wicked in hell, "where their worm dieth not, and the fire is not quenched" (Mark 9:44).

The subject of hell is a related topic (with its own attendant false teaching "Hell Isn't Real") and is also covered extensively in *Beyond the Tomb*. Suffice it to say that hell is a real literal place where sinners will go for all eternity, with various degrees of punishment for their deeds in this world. *Beyond the Tomb* also lays out what the Bible says about spirit, soul, man, God, heaven, hell, angels, death, what happens after death for sinners and saints, the nature of eternity, etc. That book makes a good follow-up/companion to read after this one.

So, in summary, the Bible unequivocally teaches that both the saved and the lost will be raised eternally! The Bible clearly teaches that there is an eternal heaven and an eternal hell. Also, know that the "Christian" churches, sects, and cults that teach wrongly on this subject will also teach wrongly on others as well (e.g., "Soul Sleeping") – false teachings often travel in a pack, like a pack of "ravenous wolves."

6.4 "SOUL SLEEPING"

This false teaching claims that you go to sleep in unconsciousness when you die. This false teaching is popular with certain sects, cults, and "isms" (e.g., 7th Day Adventists). However, Scripture is very clear on the matter: "to be absent from the body, and to be present with the Lord" (2 Corinthians 5:8). This subject is also covered extensively in the *Beyond the Tomb* book. Here is a snippet: [100]

> Death is a separation. "And it came to pass, as her soul was in departing, (for she died) that she called his name Benoni: but his father called him Benjamin" (Genesis 35:18). How plain this declaration from heaven! Death is simply the separation of soul and body. The soul departs when the body dies. Our materialist [soul sleeping] friends tell us that it is simply the breath, or physical life, that leaves the body when we die. It seems to me that there is more implied in this scripture than that. Surely the inspired writer was speaking of more than the mere exhaling from the lungs. "For as the body without the spirit is dead, so faith without works is dead also" (James 2:26). Here we see that it is the body that goes down into decomposition in death. "The body without the spirit is dead." So, when the spirit leaves the body the latter is dead. Death, then, is a separation.
>
> "Then shall the dust return to the earth as it was: and the spirit shall return unto God who gave it" (Eccl. 12:7). It is impossible to mistake the import of this passage. The returning to the dust is not the same thing as returning to God. And mark the fact that in death it is only the dust—the fleshly body—that returns to dust again. The spirit does not go down into decomposition with the body, but is separable from it, survives the stroke of death, and returns to God. ...
>
> "Verily I say to you, That this day thou shalt be with me in paradise" (Luke 23:43, Syriac Version). So, it is clear that the very day of their death Christ and the penitent thief entered the paradise of God.
>
> "Yea, I think it meet, as long as I am in this tabernacle, to stir you up by putting you in remembrance; knowing that shortly I must put off this my tabernacle, even as our Lord Jesus Christ hath showed me. Moreover, I will endeavor that ye may be able after my decease to have these things always in remembrance" (2 Peter 1:13-15).
>
> Peter describes his sojourn upon earth in these words: "As long as I am in this tabernacle." By "this tabernacle" he means his mortal body. Several versions so render it. The body was not Peter, but Peter dwelt in the body. This proves that Peter understood that the soul is distinct from the body. As a man's house is the place where he dwells, so the body is the house where the soul dwells. His decease (death), he describes as the time when "I must *put off* this *my tabernacle.*" Here we have the testimony of an inspired apostle that at death we put off this earthly tabernacle, which is dissolved—goes back to the dust of the earth, while the soul, the inner man, departs and is in a more sacred nearness to Christ, which is "far better." "Absent from the body and present with the Lord" (2 Corinthians 5:8). This testimony concurs with all Scripture.
>
> Only the bodies of men, that part which returns to dust, sleep in the grave: "And many *bodies* of the saints which slept arose, and *came out of the graves*" (Matthew 27:52-53). "And many of them that sleep in the dust of the earth shall awake" (Daniel 12:2). "The dead know not anything" (Ecclesiastes 9:5). This last text refers to participation in things of earth. They know nothing of what is being "done under the sun" (Ecclesiastes 9:6).

---

[100] Riggle, H.M. (1929/2018), *Beyond the Tomb*, (The Gospel Trumpet Company/Holy Spirit Prints).

> Our spirit returns to God (Ecclesiastes 12:7) and continues to exist "absent from the body" (2 Corinthians 5:8), which, to the righteous, is "far better than to abide in the flesh" (Philippians 1:24), "Whether we wake [are alive and remain in the body] or sleep [our body dies], we should live together with him" (1 Thessalonians 5:10). "Your heart shall live forever" (Psalm 22:26). …
>
> Those who have assimilated this [soul sleeping] doctrine err in confounding the *experience* of spiritual life with *eternal existence*. They confound a *condition* of the soul with its *nature*. This is confusion and error. The following are some of the scriptures they use: "The gift of God is eternal life through Jesus Christ our Lord" (Romans 6:23). "He that believeth on the Son hath everlasting life: and he that believeth not the Son shall not see life" (John 3:36). "That whosoever believeth in him should not perish, but have eternal life" (John 3:15). "My sheep hear my voice, and I know them, and they follow me: and I give unto them eternal life" (John 10:27-28). "God hath given to us eternal life, and this life is in his Son" (1 John 5:11).
>
> "Eternal life" implies eternal conscious existence without intermission, and "God *hath given* to us eternal life." This utterly refutes the soul-sleeping theory.

Those who die in Christ go to be with Christ; for those who die in sin, their spirit is held apart from Christ but fully conscious, awaiting the great Day of Judgment. Here is another snippet from *Beyond the Tomb*:[101]

> Peter declares that God has reserved "the unjust unto the day of judgment to be punished" (2 Peter 2:9). In Jude 6 we read, "The angels which kept not their first estate, but left their own habitation, he hath reserved in everlasting chains under darkness unto the judgment of the great day." "God spared not the angels that sinned, but cast them down to hell [Greek *tartarosas,* Tartarus], and delivered them into chains of darkness, to be reserved unto judgment" (2 Peter 2:4). By reference to Matthew 25:41, it will be seen that at the judgment the wicked will be cast into the same hell of torment as that into which "the devil and his angels" are cast.
>
> It is very reasonable then to suppose that at death the souls of the impenitent [the unsaved sinner, unrepentant, not feeling shame or regret about one's sins or actions] go to the same place where these fallen angels or demons are reserved in chains of darkness unto the judgment, when all together will receive their eternal damnation.

On the great Day of Judgment at Christ's Second Coming, everyone's spirit (both the saved and the lost) will be reunited with their eternal (immortal, incorruptible) body, and then judgment will be rendered. Those in Christ will be awarded eternal life with God in heaven; those who died in sin will be cast into eternal death in hell, "which has been prepared for the devil and his angels," separated from God and His Christ forever in eternal "darkness."

6.5 HELL ISN'T REAL

Some falsely teach that hell is not a real place of eternal torment, that it is only a metaphor, a symbol if you will. Others claim there is no hell whatsoever. And still

---
[101] Riggle, H.M. (1929/2018), *Beyond the Tomb*, (The Gospel Trumpet Company/Holy Spirit Prints).

others claim that you disappear into "nothingness" after death (see the Annihilation After Death false teaching above). However, the Bible is clear that hell is both 1) a place and 2) a state of torment – and that its duration is eternal.

The Bible tells us that hell was originally created for "the devil and his angels who sinned" at one time in disobedience and rebellion to God. The Bible doesn't say when that occurred, but it nonetheless occurred. Mankind wasn't supposed to go to hell, but through the disobedience of God by man, sin entered the world, and death through sin. When God restores His creation to a perfect state at the end of time, all things sinful, including those who chose to die in sin not covered by the blood of Christ, will be cast into hell with Satan and his angels for eternity. God will make a full end of sin, banishing it forever from His heavenly kingdom.

The topic of hell is also covered extensively in *Beyond the Tomb*.

6.6 THE DOCTRINE OF "ORIGINAL SIN"

This false teaching claims that everyone is born a sinner (guilty of or marred by sin as an infant straight from the womb) and "totally depraved." The false doctrine known as Calvinism teaches this, as well as other sects/cults/isms. This false teaching comes from misinterpreting verses of the Bible, Psalm 58 in particular, where poetic language is being interpreted literally.

However, Scripture is clear that each of us is born sinless and that we become responsible for our own personal choices and sins after we reach an age of accountability. Further, Scripture is clear that we are not held accountable for Adam and Eve's "original sins"; we are held to account for our own sins! However, this false teaching is still widely believed, and the danger here is that it can lead one to ignore the seriousness of their own sins and forego accepting Christ by blaming their own sins on their ancestors or blaming them on God for "giving them their sinful" nature. Therefore, I want to provide a more complete discussion of it here.

Below is an excellent commentary by Wayne Jackson: [102] [103]

> **Does Psalm 58 Teach "Original Sin"?**
>
> "I've just discovered your web site and all the wonderful Christian articles there. I'm pleased with what I've read, and I appreciate the fact that you are willing to address and discuss some biblical issues that are difficult. I have read your article Original Sin and a Misapplied Passage. I used to think that God considered all babies innocent, and I had heard about 'the age of accountability.' But after learning more about the Bible, I have changed my conclusion on that. It definitely is a very hard thing to think about. Have you read Psalm 58:3ff? It seems to say that babies are seen by God as sinners. Can you explain this passage?"
>
> We appreciate this sincere question. We are quite familiar with Psalm 58. Verses 3-6 read as follows:

---

[102] Jackson, Wayne. "Does Psalm 58 Teach 'Original Sin'?" *ChristianCourier.com*. Access date: November 8, 2018. https://christiancourier.com/articles/793-does-psalm-58-teach-original-sin

[103] Jackson, Wayne. "Are Infants by Nature Children of Wrath?" ChristianCourier.com. Access date: September 14, 2020. https://christiancourier.com/articles/43-are-infants-by-nature-children-of-wrath

"The wicked are estranged from the womb: They go astray as soon as they are born, speaking lies. Their poison is like the poison of a serpent: They are like the deaf adder that stops up her ear, who listens not to the voice of charmers, charming ever so wisely. Break their teeth, O God, in their mouth: Break out the great teeth of the young lions, O Jehovah."

The first thing that the careful Bible student must observe is the fact that this text is a part of that body of Old Testament literature that is highly poetic in nature, and as such, is punctuated with graphic figures of speech.

These four verses contain several vivid figures, e.g., the hyperbole, the simile, and metonymy. Hyperbole is an exaggeration for emphasis' sake; simile is a comparison between two objects by the use of "like" or "as," etc., and metonymy involves the substitution of one name for another in order to stress an important truth.

One of the most significant sources of erroneous views about the Bible is the failure to discern the difference between the literal and the figurative expressions of Scripture. And that is precisely the problem in reading this text and concluding that it provides substance for the doctrine of "original sin" or "hereditary total depravity," i.e., the notion that infants are born in sin. Our response to this question, therefore, involves an understanding of several important principles of interpretation.

First, the Bible teaches — in unambiguous prose — that moral responsibility for sin comes in the "youth" of one's life, and not at the point of one's conception, or birth (see Gen. 8:21; Isa. 7:16, etc.). For a more detailed discussion of this point, we refer the reader to our companion article on Original Sin and a Misapplied Passage [also reprinted here below]. Passages such as Psalm 51:5; 58:3ff, which are highly figurative in composition, must be brought into harmony with the literal language of prose – not the reverse.

Second, when one presses the language of these two Psalms, in order to extract the dogma of "original sin," he encounters some insuperable difficulties. Consider the following points.

A contradiction

If the language of Psalm 51:5 and 58:3-6 is to be pressed literally, then one encounters a contradiction between the two texts. Psalm 51:5 would teach that the child is a sinner from the moment of his conception, whereas Psalm 58:3 would suggest that the infant does not "go astray" until he is born — nine months later. Which is it – if the text is strictly literal?

Going astray

The fact that the sinner is said to "go astray" (Psa. 58:3), rather than being "born astray," reveals the individual's personal culpability, rather than Adam's responsibility (as in the "original sin" theory). Compare Isaiah's declaration: "All we like sheep have gone astray; we have turned every one to his own way" (Isa. 53:6). No one is considered "sinful" on account of the sins of someone else (Ezek. 18:20).

An impossibility

A literal interpretation of Psalm 58:3 involves an impossibility. It has the infant "speaking" lies as soon as it is born, which every parent knows is not the reality. It is the case, however, that we often figuratively (using hyperbole) refer to the language that one has spoken most of his life as the tongue of his "birth" (cf. Acts 2:8).

Similarly, the fact that these "estranged" people are said to have "teeth" at the point of birth (v. 6) is further evidence that the sacred writer is not speaking of a literal, newborn child. Can anyone cite a case of where a day-old child has told a lie?

Kill the baby?

If the text of Psalm 58:3ff is to be pressed literally, these little ones who are "speaking lies" must have their teeth broken (v. 6). And since they are compared to poisonous snakes, the implication is that they should be killed so that their venom will not be deadly to others. Can the reader not see the gross error in pressing this language into a literal mold?

Lions or people?

If the language of Psalm 58:3-6 is literal, one must conclude that the divine writer was not dealing with human beings at all, but with "lions" — and, in fact, lions that spoke lies (v. 6). What is this: an example of figurative language, or some kind of Walt Disney production?

One of the cardinal rules of Bible interpretation is that one must never force a scriptural statement into a situation wherein an absurdity is affirmed. Such certainly would be the case, however, if the "original sin" interpretation of this passage is maintained.

The meaning of the text, then, is simply this. When the panorama of one's life is viewed as a whole, relatively early in life each rational person begins to move away from God into a sinful state of spiritual rebellion. He utters things contrary to the will of God – his speech being a commentary on the disposition of his heart (cf. Mk. 7:21). He does not listen and respond to the voice of the Lord. Such conduct, therefore, if pursed continuously, is worthy of punishment.

As one writer observes, these enemies of the Lord "are so evil, it seems as if they had been born to it (cf. Ps. 51:5). This is literally impossible, and those who use this verse to argue for infant depravity surely miss the author's point" (Ash 1980, 198).[104]

It is not the case that one goes astray and speaks lies from his mother's womb in a literal sense, any more than it was a reality that Job was caring for orphans and widows from his mother's womb (Job 31:18). Why is the Psalms passage considered to be literal, while the Job text is acknowledged to be figurative?

It is interesting to observe that Albert Barnes, the renowned Presbyterian commentator who believed in the dogma of "original sin," conceded that this doctrine could not be sustained from this passage by itself. He said this text spoke of the fact that men "develop a wicked character" fairly "early" in life. He acknowledged that the concept of "original sin" would have to be found elsewhere in Scripture before this context could be said to lend any support to the idea (1980, 138).[105]

---

[104] Ash, Anthony and Clyde Miller. 1980. *Psalms*. Austin, Texas: Sweet.

[105] Barnes, Albert. 1980. *Notes on the Psalms. Vol. 2*. London, England: Blackie & Son.

Note: Barnes' view of "original sin" was somewhat confusing. He once wrote: "The notion of *imputing sin*, is an invention of modern times ... Neither the facts, not any proper inferences from the facts, affirm that I am, in either case, *personally responsible* for what another man did before I had an existence" (1830, 7; emphasis original). [106]

The reality is — the doctrine of "original sin" is not found in Psalm 58, or elsewhere in the Bible.

And: [107]

Original Sin and a Misapplied Passage

The doctrine of original sin—the notion that one is born into this world hereditarily totally depraved—is widely believed in the religious world.

For example, the *Augsburg Confession of Faith* (1530), Lutheranism's creed, asserted:

[A]ll men, born according to nature, are born with sin, that is, without the fear of God, without confidence towards God and with concupiscence, and that this original disease or flaw is truly a sin, bringing condemnation and also eternal death to those who are not reborn through baptism and the Holy Spirit (Article II).

This, of course, explains the practice of infant baptism as advocated by numerous sects.

Likely, the passage that is commonly appealed to in an attempt to justify the concept of original sin is Psalm 51:5.

Behold, I was brought forth in iniquity; And in sin did my mother conceive me.

Does this verse provide a basis for the doctrine of original sin? Assuredly, it does not. But let us carefully study the matter.

Preliminary Principles

First of all, it needs to be initially recognized that this passage is Hebrew poetry. And Hebrew poetry abounds with bold and imaginative figures of speech; it is frequently characterized by a freedom which departs from customary forms of expression. It is, therefore, a mistake of great magnitude to extract statements from poetical literature and thus employ them as a foundation for doctrinal schemes.

This is precisely the error of the materialists (Watchtower Witnesses, Armstrongites, etc.) who dip into Old Testament poetical books, like Psalms and Job, for their doctrines of soul-sleeping and the annihilation of the wicked.

Secondly, one of the primary rules of biblical interpretation suggests: "The language of Scripture may be regarded as figurative, if the literal interpretation will cause one passage to contradict another" (Dungan n.d., 196). [108]

---

[106] Barnes, Albert. 1830. *Sermon*. February 8, 1829. Morristown, New Jersey: Jacob Mann.

[107] Jackson, Wayne. "Original Sin and a Misapplied Passage." *ChristianCourier.com*. Access date: November 8, 2018. https://christiancourier.com/articles/276-original-sin-and-a-misapplied-passage

[108] Dungan, D. R. n.d. *Hermeneutics*. Cincinnati, OH: Standard.

There are numerous Bible verses, in plain, literal language, that affirm the innocency [sic] of infants, and Psalm 51:5 must not be arrayed against these. Consider the following:

(1) Scripture plainly teaches that sin is not inherited. "[T]he son shall not bear the iniquity of the father" (Ezekiel 18:20); every person is responsible for his own conduct (Romans 14:12).

(2) Human sinfulness commences in that period of one's life that is characterized as youth (Genesis 8:21; Jeremiah 3:25).

(3) A child must reach a certain level of maturity before he is able to choose between evil and good (Isaiah 7:15, 16).

(4) The qualities of little children are set forth as models for those who would aspire to enter the kingdom (Matthew 18:3; 19:14) and for those already in the church (1 Corinthians 14:20). Surely the Lord was not suggesting that we emulate little, totally corrupt sinners!

(5) The human spirit is not inherited from one's parents; rather, it is given by God (Ecclesiastes 12:7; Hebrews 12:9). Hence, at birth it must be as pure as the source from whence it comes.

Clearly, babies are not born in sin.

Psalm 51:5 Analyzed

Having shown what Psalm 51: 5 cannot mean, we now turn to some possible views of the passage that do not violate portions of Scripture found elsewhere.

(1) Since Psalm 51 is one of David's penitent psalms revealing the anguish resulting from his adulterous conduct with Bathsheba, some have felt that verse five contains words that are figuratively put into the mouth of the child conceived by that illicit union (2 Samuel 11:5), thus acknowledging the sinfulness of that relationship. The sinfulness is therefore attributed to the parent and not the child.

T. W. Brents commented:

Whatever may be the meaning of this passage, it can not be the imputation of sin to the child. 'In sin did my mother conceive me:' that is, she acted wickedly when I was conceived. Were the wife to say, 'In drunkenness my husband beat me,' or the child that 'in anger my father whipped me,' surely no one would attribute drunkenness to the wife or anger to the child; neither can they impute the sin of the mother to the child (1957, 133, 134). [109]

(2) Others have suggested that David alludes to an incident in his ancestral lineage, an adulterous affair (Genesis 38), whereby he was considered ceremonially defiled because he was of the tenth generation of that unlawful intercourse (Deuteronomy 23:2). This is probably a rather remote possibility.

(3) Most likely, however, Psalm 51:5 merely refers to the fact that David was born into a sinful environment. We all are conceived in and brought forth into a sinful world. But we do not actually sin until we arrive at a stage of spiritual responsibility.

Perhaps David also, by the use of dramatic language, alludes to the fact that sin had characterized his whole life, relatively speaking.

In a similarly poetic section, for example, Job, in denying that he had neglected his benevolent responsibilities, affirmed that he had cared for the orphan

---

[109] Brents, T. W. 1957. *The Gospel Plan of Salvation*. Nashville, TN: Gospel Advocate.

The Message of Truth

and the widow from his mother's womb! Surely, no one believes that on day one of Job's existence that he was out ministering to the needy! In fact, the Hebrew parallelism of this verse (Job 31:18), clearly indicates that the word "womb" is used in the sense of youth.

A Concluding Problem

Those who employ Psalm 51:5 to buttress the doctrine that sin is inherited from one's mother are faced with a serious problem. Jesus was both conceived by and brought forth from a human mother (Luke 1:31). If original sin is inherited from one's mother, Christ had it. If, however, someone should suggest that depravity is received only from the father, Psalm 51:5 cannot be used to prove it, for it mentions only the mother!

The truth of the matter is, the doctrine of original sin is not biblical. It had its origin in the writings of the so-called "church fathers" in the post-apostolic era. Such men as Tertullian (160-220) and Cyprian (200-258) first formulated the doctrine and it was later popularized by Augustine and John Calvin.

Those who accept the plain testimony of the sacred Scriptures will reject this error.

And finally, Wayne Jackson correctly writes: [110]

> …there is absolutely nothing that would suggest that anyone was tainted hereditarily, so that his sinfulness was a condition for which he was not responsible. The doctrine of inherited guilt is of human invention, with no basis in scripture (see Ezekiel 18:20).

6.7 SABBATH KEEPING
(A Form of Legalism)

This false teaching claims that Christians today are still obligated to observe and keep the ancient Jewish Sabbath day of Saturday rest. Legalism (which is an extended variation of this Sabbath keeping false teaching) tries to trap people back under bondage to the entire Mosaic Law of the ancient Hebrews along with required observance of other Jewish customs, food restrictions, feasts, holy days, "traditions," etc.

Those who preach and teach this false teaching today are called "Sabbatarians," and beware that they are very smooth and polished in the extreme! The "wolves" and "vipers" they are, for they are preaching "another gospel which is not another" – as there is only one gospel and these "wolves" and "vipers" should be condemned ("accursed") just like the apostle Paul wrote: "But even if we, or an angel from heaven, should preach to you a gospel contrary to what we have preached to you, he is to be accursed!" (Galatians 1:8). They have all kinds of tricks they use to attempt to justify their false teaching.

First, they claim that the seventh day of Creation was a "Sabbath" and that the early saints and patriarchs in Genesis kept the Sabbath. There is not one single solitary verse or syllable found in the Bible about keeping the Sabbath until it was first introduced, defined, and given specifically to Moses and the Jews who were led out of

---

[110] Jackson, Wayne. "Is Accountability 'Hereditary'?" *ChristianCourier.com*. Access date: January 15, 2019. https://christiancourier.com/articles/925-is-accountability-hereditary

Egypt. It was given specifically to the Jews as a sign of remembrance of God having brought them out of bondage in Egypt (Exodus 31:13, Deuteronomy 5:15).

Next, the teachers of this false doctrine make the claim that Christ did not come to "abolish" this law, so it is therefore still binding on us today. They make this claim while conveniently ignoring the other part of the exact same verse where it also states that Christ "fulfilled" the law for us (because no man could ever do so)!

Even further, the churches and groups that claim to be keeping the "Sabbath" today are doing so in abject hypocrisy and not even doing so according to the rules and instructions that were explicitly given in Old Testament Scripture. They have devised artificial man-made rules and interpretations on how to keep the "Sabbath" today (e.g., the exact starting and ending times, what you may or may not eat, what you may and may not do for work, and even selecting which excuses are allowed for having to work on a Saturday, etc.). The Old Testament penalty for breaking the Sabbath was death; to my knowledge, in true hypocritical fashion, the groups teaching Sabbath keeping today have yet to put a single one of their members to death for breaking their make-believe Sabbaths! No, they do not even keep the Sabbath as it was commanded, and their own hypocritical observance of "Sabbath keeping" proves their actions and teachings to be false.

And still yet further, in an even more futile attempt to justify their false teachings, these groups then resort to the claim that we are only under the Ten Commandments today (but not the other parts of the Mosaic Law). They claim that "one part (of the law) is sacrificial" and "one part is ceremonial." This is simply more obfuscation in their pretend justification. Nowhere in Scripture is it specified that there is a distinction between the two, in that an ancient Jew who performed one set of laws didn't have to perform both sets of laws. They are all part of "the law," as given in the Old Testament. As I mentioned, it is written that if you choose to keep the law, you must keep the entire law – failure to break even the smallest part of the law was equivalent to breaking the entire law (see Galatians 5:3, James 2:10)! Somehow, this explicit teaching of Scripture also seems to elude the "wolves" who teach Sabbath keeping.

And finally, Sabbatarians claim that it was Roman Catholic Church that changed the Sabbath to Sunday and that the early apostolic Christian church honored the Lord's Day (which is correctly Sunday) on the Saturday Sabbath. Once again, there is not a shred of biblical or historical support for this.

To top it all off, the groups, cults, and ism's which espouse this false teaching also tend to have many other false teachings as well, such as: believing in "newly inspired" extra-biblical writings by their own sects' specially "anointed prophets," commanding you to abstain from certain foods (see the very next false teaching), etc. You cannot get a better example of where you find one false teaching, you will almost always find others with it!

This false teaching was also prevalent in the very early days of the church, and it is also being preached far and wide again today, deceiving millions of people! By accepting and adhering to this false teaching, you are re-crucifying Christ! Let me repeat that so it's crystal clear: In returning to the observance of the Mosaic Law (even one little part of it), you are re-nailing Jesus Christ again to the cross by doing so! Furthermore, if you are putting yourself back under even just one single part of the Mosaic Law, you will be back under all of it (see James 2:10), and you must keep it perfectly from birth to death – which no person has ever done nor will ever do, except Jesus Christ Himself! Beware!

Let's stop right here and take a minute to reflect deeply on just this one verse before continuing:

> You have been severed from Christ, you who are seeking to be justified by the Law; you have fallen from grace. – Galatians 5:4

That one verse puts a full stop to this false teaching – for it is beyond abundantly clear that if you choose to continue with observing this Sabbath keeping false teaching, that you are now knowingly and fully binding yourself again to the entire law and also "severing yourself from Christ!"

Judaism (as defined by the Mosaic Law, with its sacrifices, rituals, traditions, feasts, holidays, etc.) ended at the cross. The Mosaic Law was used to prepare the Jewish people for the coming of the Messiah, and it looked forward to Jesus' perfect, ultimate and final sacrifice on the cross –it "was a shadow of things to come." After Christ's death on the cross (and resurrection), we now live under the Law of Grace, and we are all united as one body of believers in Christ (the "Church of Christ"). For "There is neither Jew nor Greek [Gentile], there is neither slave nor free, there is neither male nor female; for you are all one in Christ Jesus" – there are only those who are unified together in Christ and those who are not in Christ (opposed to Him), for it is written:

> For you are all sons of God through faith in Christ Jesus. For all of you who were baptized into Christ have clothed yourselves with Christ. There is neither Jew nor Greek [Gentile], there is neither slave nor free man, there is neither male nor female; for you are all one in Christ Jesus. And if you belong to Christ, then you are Abraham's descendants, heirs according to promise [i.e., Spiritual Jews]. – Galatians 3:26-29

> For there is no distinction between Jew and Greek; for the same *Lord* is Lord of all, abounding in riches for all who call on Him; for "WHOEVER WILL CALL ON THE NAME OF THE LORD WILL BE SAVED." – Romans 10:12-13

> For in Christ Jesus neither circumcision nor uncircumcision means anything, but faith working through love. – Galatians 5:6

> For He [Jesus] Himself is our peace, who made both *groups into* one and broke down the barrier of the dividing wall, by abolishing in His flesh the enmity, *which is* the Law of commandments *contained* in ordinances, so that in Himself He might make the two into one new man, *thus* establishing peace, and might reconcile them both in one body to God through the cross, by it having put to death the enmity. – Ephesians 2:14-16

> Wayne Jackson writes: [111] [112]

---

[111] Jackson, Wayne. "God and the Nation of Israel." ChristianCourier.com. Access date: September 25, 2019. https://christiancourier.com/articles/28-god-and-the-nation-of-israel

[112] Jackson, Wayne. "A Common Faith and Common Salvation." ChristianCourier.com. Access date: September 25, 2019. https://christiancourier.com/articles/1389-common-faith-and-common-salvation-a

As a consequence of Israel's rejection of the Messiah, God has replaced physical Israel with a new nation, **spiritual Israel**. Today, the "Jew" is not one who is so physically, but one who is so inwardly, i.e., spiritually (Rom. 2:28-29).

In this age, those who submit to the gospel plan of redemption—whether Jew or Gentile (Rom. 1:16)—become children of God, and thus are constituted as the true "seed of Abraham" (Gal. 3:26-29).

In effect, Christians are "spiritual Jews," and the Bible defines the true Jew of today as one who has accepted inwardly ("circumcision of the heart") the perfect and complete and final sacrifice of Christ on the cross:

> For he is not a Jew who is one outwardly, nor is circumcision that which is outward in the flesh. But he is a Jew who is one inwardly; and circumcision is that which is of the heart, by the Spirit, not by the letter; and his praise is not from men, but from God. – Romans 2:28-29

Today, believers in Christ are called "Christians" (and "spiritual" Jews according to Romans 2:28-29). Matthew Henry writes: [113]

> The name of God's chosen shall become a blessing: He shall call his servants by another name. The children of the covenant shall no longer be called Jews, but Christians; and to them, under that name, all the promises and privileges of the new covenant shall be secured. This other name shall be an honorable name; it shall not be confined to one nation, but with it men shall bless themselves in the earth, all the world over. God shall have servants out of all nations who shall all be dignified with this new name.

Furthermore, when Christ said to "keep my commandments," He is referring to His commands as given in the New Testament books of the Bible, not the Mosaic Law that was specifically given to the ancient Jews under Moses! I cannot stress this strongly enough. Today, we look back at the cross and move forward in compliance with the Son of God's commandments as given in the New Testament. We are not to return to Old Testament practices or the Mosaic Law or Sabbath Keeping on Saturdays. The book of Galatians (among other Scripture) specifically addresses the issue of returning to Mosaic Law legalism and strongly warns and commands against it ("O foolish Galatians...").

And while we must strongly rebuke the Sabbath keeping false teaching (while correctly teaching New Testament doctrine), we must also always remember and be thankful that "salvation is from the Jews," and even further, that our "King of Kings" and "Lord of Lords" Jesus Christ was a Jew (the "King of the Jews"), and that all who are in Christ are also spiritual Jews for we "are Abraham's descendants, heirs according to promise." Wayne Jackson further, therefore, correctly writes: [114]

> No Christian can be anti-Semitic toward the Jews [note: or racist towards anyone in general. Remember that the family of God includes people from every race, tribe and tongue, and they are your brothers and sisters in Christ]. Christ was

---

[113] Henry, Matthew. *Exposition of the Old and New Testaments*, London. 1706-1710/1721.

[114] Jackson, Wayne. "Salvation Is from the Jews." ChristianCourier.com. Access date: September 25, 2019. https://christiancourier.com/articles/1425-salvation-is-from-the-jews

a Jew, and that by divine intent. In a conversation with a Samaritan woman, Jesus declared: "[S]alvation is from the Jews" (John 4:22). The focus, of course, was upon his personal identity as the Messiah (vv. 25-26). All people are indebted to the Hebrew nation for the Savior.

Christians are to love all people, but that does not mean that they are permitted to ignore history. The Jews have both a positive and negative history concerning Christ. What did Jesus mean by his statement: "[S]alvation is from the Jews"?

There are two important preliminary points. First:

> *The affirmation, "It is from the Jews that salvation proceeds," stands as an effective answer to the charge of anti-Jewish bias frequently laid against the Evangelist [John] nowadays (Bruce 1983, 110).* [115]

Jesus acknowledged his Jewish heritage, and Christians should rejoice in this fact as well.

In closing this false teaching, never forget that we are today under the stunning grace of Christ, not the Mosaic Law. This Sabbath keeping false teaching leads to death; Christ and His gospel of grace lead to life. This teaching tramples the cross of Christ underneath it and leads one back to bondage under the law and death. Even the ancient book *The Pilgrim's Progress* warns against turning back to legalism, i.e., the way to death. And yet still, this false teaching is more rampant today than at almost any time in history.

See also the "Third Temple" false teaching.

6.8 ABSTAINING FROM CERTAIN FOODS

Some groups/sects/cults claim you cannot eat meat or caffeine or tea (or whatever food or drink they somehow declare to be bad). However, the Lord declared all foods clean in the New Testament. Furthermore, the whole idea of "Kosher" food today is not supported by the New Testament. I am speaking here of foods consumed in the normal course of life, not the partaking of substances that may induce sinful behavior or vices (e.g., alcohol, tobacco, drugs, etc.) or abstaining from certain foods due to medical reasons (e.g., food allergies). A discussion of such topics is beyond the scope of this book.

Even one verse that proves this teaching false is enough, so I present it here:

> And He said to them, "Are you so lacking in understanding also? Do you not understand that whatever goes into the man from outside cannot defile him, because it does not go into his heart, but into his stomach, and is eliminated?" (*Thus He* declared all foods clean.) – Mark 7:18-19

Please note that I did not add the words in parenthesis; they are in the inspired record. Why such crystal-clear literal words of the Bible are ignored or cannot be understood, especially by those who profess to be "Christian," is truly mind-boggling. The apostle Paul further warns that when a group/sect/cult makes artificial restrictions on foods, that very act in itself is a sign of apostasy:

---

[115] Bruce, F. F. 1983. The Gospel and Epistles of John. Grand Rapids, MI: Eerdmans.

But the Spirit explicitly says that in later times some will fall away from the faith, paying attention to <u>deceitful spirits and doctrines of demons,</u> by means of the hypocrisy of liars seared in their own conscience as with a branding iron, <u>men who forbid marriage *and advocate* abstaining from foods</u> which God has created to be gratefully shared in by those who believe and know the truth. For everything created by God is good, and nothing is to be rejected if it is received with gratitude; for it is sanctified by means of the word of God and prayer. – 1 Timothy 4:1-4

Matthew Henry writes on the above verses: [116]

> Having mentioned their hypocritical fastings, the apostle takes occasion to lay down the doctrine of the Christian liberty, which we enjoy under the gospel, of using God's good creatures, - that, whereas under the law there was a distinction of meats between clean and unclean (such sorts of flesh they might eat, and such they might not eat), all this is now taken away; and we are to call nothing common or unclean, Act 10:15. Here observe,
>
> 1. We are to look upon our food as that which God has created; we have it from him, and therefore must use it for him.
>
> 2. God, in making those things, had a special regard to *those who believe and know the truth,* to good Christians, who have a covenant right to the creatures, whereas others have only a common right.
>
> 3. What God has created is to be *received with thanksgiving.* We must not refuse the gifts of God's bounty, nor be scrupulous in making differences where God has made none; but receive them, and be thankful, acknowledging the power of God the Maker of them, and the bounty of God the giver of them: *Every creature of God is good, and nothing to be refused,* 1Ti 4:4.
>
> This plainly sets us at liberty from all the distinctions of meats appointed by the ceremonial law, as particularly that of swine's flesh, which the Jews were forbidden to eat, but which is allowed to us Christians, by this rule, *Every creature of God is good,* etc. Observe, God's good creatures are then good, and doubly sweet to us, when they are received with thanksgiving. - *For it is sanctified by the word of God and prayer,* 1Ti 4:5. It is a desirable thing to have a sanctified use of our creature-comforts. Now they are sanctified to us,
>
> (1.) By the word of God; not only his permission, allowing us the liberty of the use of these things, but his promise to feed us with food convenient for us. This gives us a sanctified use of our creature-comforts.
>
> (2.) By prayer, which blesses our meat to us. The word of God and prayer must be brought to our common actions and affairs, and then we do all in faith. Here observe,
>
> [1.] Every creature is God's, for he made all. *Every beast in the forest is mine* (says God), *and the cattle upon a thousand hills. I know all the fowls of the mountains, and the wild beasts of the field are mine,* Psa 50:10, Psa 50:11.
>
> [2.] Every creature of God is good: when the blessed God took a survey of all his works, God saw all that was made, and, behold, it was very good, Gen 1:31.

---

[116] Henry, Matthew. *Exposition of the Old and New Testaments*, London. 1706-1710/1721.

> [3.] The blessing of God makes every creature nourishing to us; man lives not by bread alone, but by every word that proceeds out of the mouth of God (Mat 4:4), and therefore nothing ought to be refused.
>
> [4.] We ought therefore to ask his blessing by prayer, and so to sanctify the creatures we receive by prayer.

To summarize, the New Testament declares all foods clean, and we may eat all foods today with thanksgiving and prayer. The only restriction is that we should restrain from partaking of certain foods at certain times in certain company if it might cause a weaker brother or sister in Christ to stumble, where their (more sensitive) conscience is troubled by a particular food (perhaps due to their upbringing, etc.) – see 1 Corinthians 8:1-8. As a side note, a Christian should not, of course, participate in any pagan (or other) idol ceremony (whether meat is used in it or not, Acts 15:29). And once again, where you find this false teaching, other false teachings will also be found! See also Colossians 2:20-22, 1 Timothy 4:1-4.

6.9 FALSE TEACHINGS ON BAPTISM

I have given you the correct teaching about baptism in the main chapter of this book. However, you will find much (seemingly endless) debate, discussion, and disagreement about whether baptism is a required element for salvation. The minds of men love to make (false) doctrinal mountains out of molehills by distorting, diluting, and obfuscating the very simple teachings of the Bible. Some also falsely teach and perform "infant" baptism and baptism by "sprinkling." Neither is in agreement with Scripture.

Some Christian churches and groups falsely teach that baptism is not a required element of salvation, that it is a "good work" done by man. They then build that incorrect position into a dispute of monumental and biblical proportions (pun intended). In fact, arguments over this one simple teaching of the Bible have led to serious and seemingly endless divisions within the church, and hundreds of books have been written to defend whatever doctrine a particular group thought was right. Amazing the folly of man, yes? But we are called to "contend earnestly for the faith that was once for all *time* handed down to the saints" in Scripture and not be deceived by the doctrines invented by man. Because baptism is such a fundamental and important part of the gospel message and the plan of redemption/salvation for a Christian, I, therefore, want to go into this subject in some detail.

Some of the reasons various groups give as to why baptism is not a required element of salvation are listed below, along with my response:

1. **Baptism is a "good work":** First, this shows a complete misunderstanding of what a "good work" is. A good work is something that is done (after conversion and in obedience to the teachings/commands of Christ) that benefits someone else, not yourself. Second, how can having someone else immerse you in water be considered a "good work" on your part at all? It is not even you who is doing the work of dunking yourself! Third, and most importantly, it is Christ (not you) who is actually doing all the work at your baptism. It is He who is forgiving your sins, not you! He is the one who is redeeming you and cleansing you of sin by His shed blood on the cross – there is nothing anyone can do to buy or earn forgiveness of sins (e.g., through good

works, or any works whatsoever). So, give glory to Jesus and let Him do His work in you at baptism.
2. **The second half of Mark 16:16 doesn't mention baptism:** This claim asserts that since the first half of Mark 16:16 mentions baptism but the second half doesn't; therefore, baptism is not a required element of salvation. In response, I say, please use logic and common sense: there is no need to mention baptism (or repentance, confession, obedience, perseverance, etc.) in the second part of the verse because without faith, one is condemned regardless of whether one is dunked in water or not, so it would be completely redundant to mention it in this part of the verse - it is simply not needed. Wayne Jackson writes [117]: "After introducing the person who 'believes not,' why in the name of common sense would it be necessary for the Lord to list additional items of rebellion, in order to emphasize the unbeliever's state of condemnation?" Furthermore, if one adopts their (wrong) logic, one must also say that since the first part of Mark 16:16 doesn't mention repentance, that repentance, therefore, isn't required for salvation either! I think (and hope) no clear-thinking Christian will adopt that position. As you can see, they are using different (and inconsistent) rules of logic for the two parts of Mark 16:16. When you point this out to those who deny baptism on this basis, they don't seem to be able to see their error in logic and resulting inconsistency. Even beyond the simple logic error, one must consider the <u>sum total</u> of what Scripture teaches on any particular subject in order to arrive at truth and correct doctrine (Psalm 119:160). It is true that various verses call out and stress certain elements of salvation at times for various reasons, but you cannot create a gospel doctrine that agrees with some verses and contradicts with others – your doctrine must harmonize true across all of Scripture, for Scripture is 100% correct and never contradicts itself. No matter what you think or believe, if it contracts even so much as one single clear and unambiguous verse of Scripture, it is not Scripture that is wrong; it is your interpretation that is wrong. This is one of the most common causes of doctrinal errors.
3. **The Cornelius conversion (Acts 10:1-23):** The claim made here is that since Cornelius et al. received the Holy Spirit before they were baptized, this also applies to all believers today, and therefore baptism isn't required for salvation (or to receive the Holy Spirit). What this fails to recognize is that the Cornelius conversion <u>was</u> a special case – it signified the expansion of the gospel message to the gentiles. In this Cornelius case, the Spirit was specifically given here as a sign to Peter that salvation is now also to the gentiles. Without such a sign, Peter (et al.) would not have started giving the gospel to the gentiles, so this event <u>was</u> a special and unique confirmation by the Spirit and recorded for us in Scripture.
4. **Paul did not go to baptize, so baptism isn't required:** This is a generalization from 1 Corinthians 1:14-16 that isn't warranted in Scripture or supported by logic. The context of those verses is concerning a problem that some in Corinth were being puffed up (proud) because they were baptized by

---

[117] Jackson, Wayne. "The Assault upon Mark 16:16." ChristianCourier.com. Access date: May 17, 2021. https://christiancourier.com/articles/605-the-assault-upon-mark-16-16

the great apostle Paul and hence felt superior to others – they were unduly identifying with Paul instead of with the gospel as a whole and with Christ. What Paul is trying to get across here is that it is the gospel message itself that is important (including baptism!), not the particular person who happens to immerse you in the water! Nothing about this section of Scripture contradicts or denies the very clear and unambiguous teachings on baptism given elsewhere. Even further, let's press this false interpretation to the ultimate pinnacle: In exactly similar fashion in John 4:1-2, it is noted that Jesus Himself didn't personally baptize anyone (His disciples did), so by way of analogy, one would have to conclude that by John 4:1-2 baptism isn't necessary either – despite Jesus clear teaching to the contrary! Once again, it is the pride of man which is in focus here, not whether baptism is required. Please think about this using yourself as a test case – imagine if Jesus personally baptized you Himself, do you not see how pride could result and that you might feel superior to others, even other brothers and sisters in Christ? I do! That is the point being made here in both passages of Scripture. These verses have nothing whatsoever to do with the removal of baptism as a required element for salvation. Jesus, and Paul, wanted to avoid pride resulting from an association with who (or Who) did the baptismal immersion...that is all.

5. **The deserted island (or middle of a desert) straw-man argument:** Some make the argument: Since a person stranded on a deserted island (or in the middle of a desert without water) can't be baptized; therefore, baptism is not required for salvation by anyone. This argument doesn't really need a response, as it's completely ridiculous, spurious, and does absolutely nothing to defend their teaching. However, if you find yourself in one of those locations and accept Christ there, rest assured that Christ will find a way to allow you to be saved properly. Franky, I'm surprised they don't also argue: "What if you are on the moon and accept Christ?" as a proof case against baptism. Instead of worrying about a hypothetical fictional case that applies to literally no one, the focus should be on the clear Scriptures that do apply to you.

6. **The thief on the cross wasn't baptized, so it's not required:** First of all, the thief on the cross who accepted Christ actually did so and died under Old Testament Mosaic Law – the New Covenant didn't take effect until Christ's death and resurrection. Furthermore, he may have been baptized; we do not know. Scripture doesn't say whether he was or wasn't. The thief seems to be familiar with Christ and His teachings, at least to some extent. But let's assume for argument's sake that he wasn't. Christ, who is God Almighty Himself, can do whatever He pleases, whenever He pleases! He can make any special exceptions He deems necessary or pleasing to His will – who are we to say otherwise? While on earth, Jesus repeatedly forgave the sins of various people, like the thief. But to make a general case of this wonderful special conversion and demonstration of grace is a travesty of logic and flies in the face of other clear and unambiguous verses about baptism. Now let's press this argument to its logical conclusion – I'm willing to concede that if a) you find yourself hanging on a cross, and b) you are hanging right next to Christ at the same time, then yes, you too may be saved simply by Christ's proclamation over you without baptism. But that simply doesn't apply to any of us today, does it?

So why use this case to deny baptism in the face of clear Scripture to the contrary?

7. **It's what we've been teaching for a long time, so it must be correct.** Yes, I have actually run across this claim, which goes like this (paraphrasing): "Well, we have been teaching that baptism is not required for many hundreds of years, so we must be right." Yes, some actually think that somehow saying this adds credibility to their position, but the fact that they have been teaching something (wrongly) for any period of time does absolutely nothing whatsoever to bolster their defense that the teaching is correct. If one adopts their own logic here, then they must also concede that the Roman Catholic Church could therefore come along right after them and say: "Well, since we have been teaching (falsely) on matters of doctrine for nearly 2000 years, our teachings must be even more correct"! I hope you can see the ridiculousness of this argument.

It is interesting to note that those who adopt the position that baptism isn't required also teach that one can casually and nonchalantly decide to wander in and get baptized whenever you want to, any time after you accept Christ – even days, weeks, months, and years later! I'm paraphrasing their teaching again, but you understand the point. After all, since they teach that baptism is not required, there is, therefore, no rush or urgency about doing it. But be not deceived; there is not a single instance in Scripture that supports this position. In every single case, without exception, those who received and accepted the good news of the gospel in Scripture were <u>immediately</u> baptized! There are no exceptions.

Please do not be confused or deceived by those using strange logic. Adhere to the simple gospel message and its clear teaching about baptism: one is not born again until after one has: heard the gospel message, believed in Christ, repented of their sins, confessed Christ, and is baptized by immersion for the forgiveness of sins. It is at baptism that you die (are buried) to your old self and are raised to life a new creature in Christ. It is also at baptism when you receive the gift of the Holy Spirit.

The bottom line (in truth) is: if you've just believed, repented, and confessed Christ, get baptized as soon as possible by immersion for the forgiveness of sins! It's just that simple. There's no valid excuse not to be baptized or to keep putting it off. Scripture speaks very simply, explicitly, and plainly for itself regarding baptism.

Wayne Jackson also writes on the topic of baptism:[118]

> ### THE SIMPLICITY OF MARK 16:16
>
> It is a fundamental fact of Bible interpretation that those passages that are most crucial to one's salvation are the easiest to understand. That is why Mark's account of the "great commission" is so incredibly simple. One of the great mysteries of modern "Christendom" is why certain clergymen have so obscured this wonderful text [that of Mark 16:16]. ...
>
> **The Conditions Mentioned**
>
> In Mark 16:16, two conditions of the divine plan of redemption are mentioned — belief and baptism. These are preliminary to the reception of

---

[118] Jackson, Wayne. "The Assault upon Mark 16:16." *ChristianCourier.com*. Access date: November 8, 2018. https://christiancourier.com/articles/605-assault-upon-mark-16-16-the

salvation. Surely even the most amateur student can see that these items are but representative of the fuller complement of sacred requirements. There is, for example, no reference to repentance, though this change of disposition — which results in a reformation of life — clearly is requisite for redemption (Lk. 13:3,5; Acts 2:38; 17:30). Nor is the "good confession" included (cf. 1 Tim. 6:13), though it is combined with belief elsewhere (Rom. 10:9-10). It is common in the New Testament for a writer to emphasize occasionally certain conditions relating to salvation, without citing the entire catalog of requirements (cf. Jn. 3:16; Acts 17:30; 1 Pet. 3:21). How wonderful it would be if those who argue for "salvation by faith alone" could learn this simple principle. ...

Sectarian Evasion

Due to the fact that some religionists are so saturated with the notion that salvation is by "faith alone" (a doctrine alien to the New Testament, and specifically repudiated therein — see Jas. 2:24), they resort to various interpretative contortions in an effort to evade the transparent instruction of this passage. Typical of this maneuver was prominent Baptist scholar, A.T. Robertson, who, in his massive Grammar of the Greek New Testament, asserted that sometimes grammar must yield to theology (389). [119] The practical meaning of that statement is this: Sometimes it becomes necessary to ignore what the text actually says, and in its place substitute one's opinion! The fact is, the grammar is inspired; one's personal theology is not!

And so, relative to Mark 16:16, Robertson, in his Word Pictures, wrote: [120]

"The omission of baptized with 'disbelieveth' [16:16b] would seem to show that Jesus does not make baptism essential to salvation. Condemnation rests on disbelief, not on baptism" (1.405).

Quite frankly, that is pathetic. After introducing the person who "believes not," why in the name of common sense would it be necessary for the Lord to list additional items of rebellion, in order to emphasize the unbeliever's state of condemnation? Besides, elsewhere in the divine record Jesus did warn of the consequences of rejecting baptism. Such rejection, according to Luke's record, is the reflection of an attitude that repudiates the very "counsel of God" (see Lk. 7:29-30).

And further: [121]

Is Baptism a Work of Merit?

The truth is, most denominational folks have little difficulty in acknowledging that both faith and repentance are requirements for the remission of sins, even though they are classified as works in the Scriptures. The real point of contention is baptism. Sectarians feel that if it were conceded that baptism is essential to salvation, this would be equivalent to arguing that forgiveness is

---

[119] Robertson, A.T. (1919), A Grammar of the Greek New Testament in the Light of Historical Research (London: Hodder & Stoughton).

[120] Robertson, A.T. (1930), Word Pictures in the New Testament (Nashville: Broadman).

[121] Jackson, Wayne. "The Role of 'Works' in God's Plan of Redemption." ChristianCourier.com. Access date: November 8, 2018. https://christiancourier.com/articles/729-role-of-works-in-gods-plan-of-redemption-the

earned. Baptism, it is charged, is a work of human merit. Under this assumption, it is thus (by many sincere people) excluded as a requirement for salvation. But this reasoning is fallacious.

In the first place, the only passage in the New Testament that even remotely identifies baptism as a "work" is found in the book of Colossians. There, Paul says "[H]aving been buried with him in baptism, wherein you were also raised with him through faith in the working of God, who raised him from the dead" (Col. 2:12, ASV). The act of submitting to immersion is not meritorious; the operation is a "working of God" designed to provide pardon upon the basis of Jesus' death. One is spiritually blessed by the working of God when he submits to the sacred ordinance. Nowhere does scripture come anywhere near suggesting that submission to God's command, "be baptized" (Acts 2:38; 22:16), is a meritorious work.

Second, the Bible specifically excludes baptism from that type of works that have no relationship to salvation. Paul, in his letter to Titus, affirmed that we are "not [saved] by works done in righteousness which we did ourselves," i.e., which we contrived and implemented as a means of justification. Rather, "according to his mercy he saved us, through the washing of regeneration and renewing of the Holy Spirit" (3:5). The "washing of regeneration" (an indisputable allusion to baptism) is plainly placed in contrast to those human "works" that are ineffectual to save.

The conscientious Bible student needs to eradicate from his mind the false notion that "works" are wholly alien to God's plan of salvation. If you have been confused about the role of works in the divine pattern of conversion, why not give the matter fresh consideration?

And to those who teach and preach false doctrine regarding baptism, I say you now know better having read the truth of what Scripture actually teaches, so if you continue to teach and preach in contradiction to Scripture, you must beware (James 3:1). Wayne Jackson echoes the same sentiment succinctly: [122]

> "Those who speak in opposition to New Testament baptism, contradicting the sacred writings, will have a heavy judgment to bear."

I next present this commentary by Matthew Henry (on Acts 2:38), where I think he summarizes things nicely: [123]

> He here shows them the course they must take.
> (1.) Repent; this is a plank after shipwreck. "Let the sense of this horrid guilt which you have brought upon yourselves by putting Christ to death awaken you to a penitent reflection upon all your other sins (as the demand of some one great debt brings to light all the debts of a poor bankrupt) and to bitter remorse and sorrow for them" This was the same duty that John the Baptist and Christ had preached, and now that the Spirit is poured out is it still insisted on: "Repent, repent; change your mind, change your way; admit an after-thought."

---

[122] Jackson, Wayne. "What Is Baptismal Regeneration?" *ChristianCourier.com*. Access date: November 8, 2018. https://christiancourier.com/articles/416-what-is-baptismal-regeneration

[123] Henry, Matthew. *Exposition of the Old and New Testaments*, London. 1706-1710/1721.

> (2.) Be baptized every one of you in the name of Jesus Christ; that is, "firmly believe the doctrine of Christ, and submit to his grace and government; and make an open solemn profession of this, and come under an engagement to abide by it, by submitting to the ordinance of baptism; be proselyted to Christ and to his holy religion and renounce your infidelity." They must be baptized in the name of Jesus Christ. They did believe in the Father and the Holy Ghost speaking by the prophets; but they must also believe in the name of Jesus, that he is the Christ, the Messias [Messiah] promised to the fathers. "Take Jesus for your king, and by baptism swear allegiance to him; take him for your prophet, and hear him; take him for your priest, to make atonement for you," which seems peculiarly intended here; for they must be baptized in his name for the remission of sins upon the score of his righteousness.
>
> (3.) This is pressed upon each particular person: Every one of you. "Even those of you that have been the greatest sinners, if they repent and believe, are welcome to be baptized; and those who think they have been the greatest saints have yet need to repent, and believe, and be baptized. There is grace enough in Christ for every one of you, be you ever so many, and grace suited to the case of everyone. Israel of old were baptized unto Moses in the camp, the whole body of the Israelites together, when they passed through the cloud and the sea (see 1 Corinthians 10:1-2), for the covenant of peculiarity was national; but now every one of you distinctly must be baptized in the name of the Lord Jesus and transact for himself in this great affair."

To the above, I say Amen! And two further examples are now given. 1) It is written:

> For all of you who were baptized into Christ have clothed yourselves with Christ. – Galatians 3:27

Or to state the inverse of that verse to draw out the inescapable logical conclusion: you who have not been baptized have not clothed yourselves with Christ. Conclusion: baptism is not optional.

And 2) Ananias, under direction from the Lord, says to Paul (formerly Saul) as a just converted apostle after his experience on the road to Damascus:

> '…Get up and be baptized, and wash away your sins by calling on His name.' – Acts 22:16

So, I ask you, how can one "wash away" their sins without being baptized? Further, if it wasn't required, why would it be given as a command at all? Therefore, I ask you again, can you "wash away" your sins without being baptized? Clearly, Scripture says no.

I want to close this false teaching with a note of encouragement and understanding for those who are reading this book after being taught and believe that baptism is not required for salvation. Please know that I understand how difficult you will struggle with this topic. You see, I was once like you, having the same belief that baptism is not required for salvation and that it was a "good work" of man, as that was the only thing I was ever taught or had heard preached (or read). It was a MIGHTY struggle indeed to concede that my beliefs were not in agreement with Scripture. So, I understand the tremendous difficulty you will have in breaking free from this false teaching. It's not unlike the extraordinary difficulty one has in trying to break the flesh free from a sinful habit or addiction. It's extremely hard, and it takes the power of God; it will be the same with this topic.

I also understand that you might resist the correct teaching on baptism as explained in this book because you are afraid that by doing so, you would be diminishing what Christ did on the cross. However, if you persevere in truth, you will come to see that the correct teaching on baptism doesn't diminish the cross or Christ one iota. In fact, it is further glorifying the Lord as you will have come to a correct knowledge and understanding of the truth of Scripture.

6.10 SAYING A "SINNER'S PRAYER" SAVES YOU

This false teaching proclaims that one is born-again (accepts Christ) by simply making a one-time profession of faith, often called the "sinner's prayer." You have surely seen the big revival events on TV or held in giant sports stadiums, where at the end of the program, people are invited to come forward and "accept Christ" and be "saved" by saying a simple prayer. Similarly, many churches perform an "altar call" at the end of their service where people are invited to come forward and "accept Christ" and be "saved" by saying a simple prayer. And their use of the word "saved" usually conveys the notion of being saved to eternal life.

This practice is not biblical – the "sinner's prayer" teaching and practice are not found in Scripture anywhere! Contrary to popular belief, you are neither born-again nor saved to eternal life by saying a magical set of words at one time in your life. This book has properly explained that one is born again in accordance with Scripture through belief, repentance, confession, and baptism! At best, and I hesitate even to concede this much, the "sinner's prayer" that you may be led to speak by your church or pastor is only a way to help you verbalize steps 1.2-4 listed in the chapter on The Path to Eternal Life, although nowhere does the Bible prescribe a certain set of words that must be used.

I'm all for people coming to accept Christ, but let's do so as prescribed in Scripture, not according to the folly and particular (wrong) interpretations and rules made up by man. It is fantastic that the Holy Spirit is working on your heart and you are feeling called to Jesus, but please be diligent in being born again in the manner as prescribed in Scripture (and explained in this book)! If you thought that you accepted Christ by simply saying a "sinner's prayer" at your local church, while listening to the radio in the car, or maybe at a big convention or stadium revival event, please re-read The New Testament Plan of Salvation section of this book very carefully and make sure you have truly been born again according to the instructions as given in the New Testament.

Furthermore, this book has explained to you the difference between initial salvation (forgiveness of sins) and final salvation (eternal life). This book has also explained to you the role of obedience, works, and perseverance in the plan of salvation for a Christian. Realize that being born again is only the first step (but by far the most important step) on your path to eternal life – which is your ultimate goal and destination.

Christ said that there is a cost in following Him. It is written:

> "Whoever does not carry his own cross and come after Me cannot be My disciple. For which one of you, when he wants to build a tower, does not first sit down and calculate the cost to see if he has enough to complete it? Otherwise, when he has

laid a foundation and is not able to finish, all who observe it begin to ridicule him, saying, 'This man began to build and was not able to finish.' Or what king, when he sets out to meet another king in battle, will not first sit down and consider whether he is strong enough with ten thousand men to encounter the one coming against him with twenty thousand? Or else, while the other is still far away, he sends a delegation and asks for terms of peace. So then, none of you can be My disciple who does not give up all his own possessions." – Luke 14:27-32

So, to those who teach and believe this "sinner's prayer" false teaching, I ask you: Where is the "cost" in saying a simple one-time prayer and then being magically saved to eternal life by it? There is no cost!

While I've done my best to untangle and explain this and other false teachings for you in this book, in reality, false teachings are interrelated and interwoven together in a giant tangled web or knot. Therefore, realize that this false teaching is almost always accompanied by other false teachings, such as: you are saved by "faith alone/only," false teachings on baptism, and the "once saved always saved" false teaching. I'm trying to show you these false teachings are all wound up together in a knot so tight you can't even figure out where one false teaching ends and the next one begins. For example, can you really say that you were "saved" by saying a "sinner's prayer" without also implying (whether you realize it or not) that you also believe in "once saved always saved" and even further that you are also saved by (a simple profession) of "faith alone/only?" By conceding that the "sinner's prayer" saves them, aren't they also therefore implicitly denying the role of baptism, whether they admit to it or not? Similarly, can one really believe they are saved by "faith only/alone" without also (perhaps even unknowingly) believing that being born again is all one must do to receive eternal life?

To say one often implies another as an inescapable consequence. And in my experience, as a general rule, whenever you see someone (a church, group, book, etc.) leading off with the "sinner's prayer" false teaching, you can rest assured that you will find many of the other false teachings in their materials as well. It's a sad fact that when you hear someone today in modern American Christendom say that they are "saved," in the vast majority of cases, they are indicating that these four false teachings are what they believe and that they believe that they were "saved to eternal life" simply by saying a one-time "sinner's prayer."

See also The Path to Eternal Life chapter of this book for more information, including an example of how the "sinner's prayer" false teaching is commonly encountered in real life.

6.11 YOU ARE SAVED BY "FAITH ALONE/ONLY"

This false teaching denies that obedience and works (action on the part of the believer) have any part whatsoever in the plan of salvation – and that a simple profession of faith alone saves one to eternal life. Those who proclaim this false teaching almost always also falsely teach that: 1) baptism is a "good work" of man and 2) that baptism is therefore not a requirement for salvation.

Because this false teaching is so widespread today, infecting the vast majority of so-called "Christian" churches (at least in America), it has already been addressed throughout the main chapters of this book (see The Path to Eternal Life, Be Baptized, Obedience and Bearing Fruit). However, further information is given here for those who are still deceived by this false teaching – in fact, writing this book has helped me understand just how pervasive this false teaching is today. This book is showing you that those who proclaim this "faith alone/only" false teaching are, therefore, actually triply wrong because:

1) Baptism is not a "good work" of man,
2) It is required for salvation (to be born again), and
3) Scripture clearly teaches us that works do play an important role in the biblical plan of salvation.

This false teaching comes primarily from those who call themselves "Reformed" Protestants and those who call themselves "Calvinists." And as you will soon read, Calvinism is yet another false theology of man, which is chock full of false teachings from start to finish. But it doesn't matter what fancy names they give to their own man-made interpretations of Scripture and rules (e.g., Arminianism, Calvinism, "Reformed" Protestantism, Whatever-ism, etc.). They are still man-made interpretations, and they are not in agreement with Scripture.

To support this false teaching, Paul's writing in the letter to the Ephesians 2:8-10 is widely distorted and taken out of context. Furthermore, it's as if the entire book of James was torn out of the Bibles of those who proclaim this errant theology. It is also a historical fact that Martin Luther added the word "only" into his rewrite of Romans 3:28! Yes, he actually rewrote Scripture to change it to match his own opinion! Luther also denied the inspiration of the book of James – simply because it didn't fit his own theology. Those two facts are commonly ignored (and certainly not publicized much) by those who promote this false teaching.

Scripture is clear that the life of a true child of God is marked by continued "obedience" to Christ and "bearing fruit" for the Lord (the role of works) as a bondservant of Christ. True Christianity is as much about action and a life of service as it is about profession of faith. It is written: "faith without works is dead." So, I ask you: Can a "dead" faith save you to eternal life? You cannot have one (faith) without the other (action) and obtain eternal life. Wayne Jackson writes that faith is not an idle concept, devoid of obedience and action on the part of the believer: [124]

> **A Perversion of Biblical Faith**
>
> One of the great tragedies of ecclesiastical history is the fact that so many have failed to find a balanced view of human redemption as this concept is set forth in the biblical record.
>
> On the one hand there is Roman Catholicism, arrogantly contending that salvation is conferred upon the basis of meritorious acts. The Council of Trent declared that good works, done to the honor of God, have "truly merited the attainment of eternal life in due time" (session vi, chapter xvi.).
>
> On the other hand, Protestant reformers, reacting against this unscriptural ideology, gravitated to an equally indefensible position, alleging that salvation is bestowed by means of "faith alone." The French reformer Jacobus Faber (1455-1536) argued that salvation is upon the basis of faith without works. And Martin

---

[124] Jackson, Wayne. "A Perversion of Biblical Faith." *ChristianCourier.com*. Access date: May 23, 2019. https://christiancourier.com/articles/190-perversion-of-biblical-faith-a

Luther's obsession with this theme led him to alter the text of Romans 3:28 so that his translation read: "[A] man is justified by faith only." It is rather well known that he rejected the divine character of the book of James due to the inspired writer's affirmation that "faith apart from works is dead." ...

It will be the burden of this study to demonstrate that "faith," as that term is employed in contexts in which the subject is commended, is never a mere intellectual or emotional disposition divorced from devout obedience. Valid faith is never passive. It becomes a redemptive quality only when it responds in implementing the will of Jehovah.

"Faith"—A Word of Action

One of the most absurd statements that we ever read was from a denominationalist who declared: "Faith is the only thing that one can do without doing anything." The affirmation is a textbook case of contradiction.

The following examples will clearly reveal that genuine faith is not a mere attitude; rather, it is a word of action.

(1) Jesus was teaching in the city of Capernaum. The crowds so pressed around him that some who sought his presence could not gain access to the Lord. Four enterprising men brought a lame friend, climbed to the rooftop of the house wherein Christ was teaching, and lowered their impotent companion through the ceiling. Significantly, the inspired writer comments: "And Jesus seeing their faith said unto the sick of the palsy, Son, your sins are forgiven" (Mark 2:5).

What did Christ see? He literally saw the action of these men (including the sick man who obviously endorsed the activity). But the action is called faith. In a similar vein, James challenged: "Show me your faith apart from your works, and I by my works will show you my faith" (James 2:18).

(2) John 3:16 is perhaps the best-known verse in the Bible; but it is one of the most misunderstood: "For God so loved the world, that he gave his only begotten Son, that whosoever believeth on him should not perish, but have eternal life."

Does the "belief" of this passage include obedience, or exclude it? A comparison of this verse with Hebrews 5:9 reveals that the former is the case. In John 3:16, believing results in eternal life. In Hebrews 5:9, eternal salvation is said to issue from obedience to Christ. It thus should be quite clear that the belief that saves is one that manifests itself in obeying the Son of God. True faith is not just a mental process.

(3) Note this declaration from the Lord: "He that believeth on the Son hath eternal life; but he that obeyeth not the Son shall not see life, but the wrath of God abideth on him" (John 3:36, ASV).

We have cited the American Standard Version here because it is more accurate in its rendition of the original language than is the King James Version. The term in the latter portion of the verse is apeitheo, which, according to Balz and Schneider, literally means "to disobey" (1990, 118). In this passage "believing" is set in vivid contrast to disobedience.

Is not Christ suggesting that the one who obeys the Son is promised life, but the person who disobeys will not receive such? ...

The Bible knows nothing of true faith that is divorced from obedience.

(4) When a jailor in the city of Philippi feared for his life during an earthquake that rocked the prison, he pled with Paul and Silas: "Sirs, what must I

do to be saved?" God's messengers proclaimed to him the gospel. Evincing repentance (for having beaten his prisoners), the jailor washed their stripes. Subsequently, he and his family were immersed (Acts 16:31-33).

Significantly, this entire process is summed up in this fashion: "And he…rejoiced greatly, with all his house, having believed in God" (v. 34). It is clear that the participle, "having believed," includes the jailor's repentance and his baptism. …

(7) James shows the connection between faith and obedience when he writes: "Was not Abraham our father justified by works [obedience], in that he offered up Isaac his son upon the altar? You see that faith operated with his works [obedience], and by works [his obedience] was [his] faith made complete; and the scripture was fulfilled which says, And Abraham believed God, and it was reckoned unto him for righteousness; and he was called the friend of God" (James 2:21-23). …

It is this type of biblical evidence that has compelled leading New Testament language authorities to acknowledge that faith is more than a mere philosophy of belief. Genuine faith cannot be separated from submission to the Lord.

Conclusion

The doctrine of salvation by "faith alone" does not have the support of Scripture. It has resulted from a sincere but misguided reaction to Roman Catholicism. Those who have embraced this philosophy should carefully restudy the question of salvation.

And further: [125]

Justified by Faith

The text is thrilling beyond the human tongue to express:

Being therefore justified by faith, we have peace with God through our Lord Jesus Christ; through whom also we have had our access by faith into this grace wherein we stand; and we rejoice in hope of the glory of God (Romans 5:1-2).

The Exegesis

Bible passages brim with inspired information worthy of careful examination. Unfortunately all too often the holy words are treated superficially. It is a tragedy of no small magnitude that this lovely citation is so seriously misunderstood by a sizable segment of "Christendom." Let us give it a focused investigation.

The Contextual Background

It should be noted first that the text is prefaced with the conjunction "therefore" (oun), the design of which is to draw a logical conclusion from previously stated premises. Though we cannot develop the entire preceding context in this brief article, we must note two important facts set forth in the final verse of chapter four. Christ "was delivered up for our trespasses, and was raised for our justification."

---

[125] Jackson, Wayne. "Justified by Faith." *ChristianCourier.com*. Access date: May 23, 2019. https://christiancourier.com/articles/1374-justified-by-faith

These compound phrases set forth two great acts in the divine plan of human redemption. (a) Christ was "delivered up" to death (cf. Acts 2:23) for our "trespasses." A trespass is an infraction of divine law—an action against either God or man. The human family has been ruined by sin (cf. Romans 5:12), and there is no remedy for such apart from Christ (Acts 4:12). (b) Jesus was "raised for our justification." Both the death of Christ and his subsequent resurrection were key elements in the sacred program enacted for humanity's salvation. From this foundation springs the important passage cited above.

Justification

The noun, "justification," is found ninety-two times in the New Testament (fifty-eight times in Paul's letters), while the verb "justify" occurs thirty-nine times (twenty-seven times in Paul's writings). Justification is the legal **standing** that results from the **process** of "being justified." To say that one is justified from sin is not to claim that he is **innocent** of the crime; far from it. Rather, the term suggests that the offender has been exempted from the penalty he justly deserves. The "death sentence" (cf. Romans 5:12; 6:23) has been set aside, consistent with the righteous Judge's system of justice.

In the case of the sin-guilt of a rebellious people (which all accountable souls have been – Romans 3:10,23), both the problem and the solution are set forth in Romans chapter three. The issue is this: how may God be **just**, and yet **justify** sinners (cf. 3:26). The answer is found in the gift of Christ. God set forth his Son to be the "propitiation" for sin (hilasterion), i.e., an offering of atonement, a covering for sin (cf. Hebrews 9:5). The sinless "lamb of God" takes the penalty for the sinful individual who submits to the conditions imposed by the Judge, God (cf. Isaiah 53:4-6). Paul affirms that these "beloved of God...saints" in the city of Rome have been "justified" (a past tense act with an abiding result). Practically speaking, justification is the equivalent of forgiveness, as well as the "in Christ" relationship (cf. Romans 6:3-4; Galatians 3:27).

By Faith

The battleground on this passage, and numerous others of similar import, is the meaning of "by faith" (ek pisteos). The preposition ek has been variously translated as "by" (KJV, ASV) or "through" (NIV). The term basically means "out of" and it reveals the human side of the salvation equation. Out of a genuine faith flows submission to God in response to sacred instruction (Romans 10:17). The sinner's "faith" is essential to his justification. This affirmation, of course, negates the baseless theories of "universal salvation" and "unconditional election."

The major controversy, however, is over the meaning of "faith." Is this merely the willingness of the sinner to accept the historical facts about Christ, and the surrender of one's soul to "trust" the Lord for his salvation? This is a common perception, but is it accurate? Though this view gained the strong support of the early Protestant Reformation in its opposition to the Roman Catholic dogma of justification upon the basis of meritorious works, the theory has no support in the larger context of the book of Romans, or, for that matter, elsewhere in the New Testament. In J.H. Thayer's discussion of the verb pisteuo ("believe"), he supplements the idea of trust with that of "obedience to Christ" (1958, 511), and this is amply supported by the biblical text. Note the following facts:

1. In his letter to the Romans (and elsewhere), Paul never divorces faith from obedience. Valid faith is that which yields obedience, and obedience derives its genesis from faith (1:5; 16:26). This is such an established biblical principle that gospel obedience in the book of Acts is characterized as being "obedient to the faith" (6:7). Faith, aloof from submission to God, is simply viewed as non-faith, redemptively speaking (cf. James 2:24).
2. In chapter six, Paul aligns himself with the Christians in Rome and characterizes all as "we who died to sin" (v. 2). Later, the apostle complements the earlier affirmation by this supplementary phrase: "for he who has died is justified" (v. 7). If, therefore, one learns what transpired between verses two and seven, he will know precisely how justification was effected. Paul's explanation is clear. He contends that dying to sin essentially is a resolution to no longer live the unrestrained life of sin (v. 2). The one who dies to the love and reckless practice of sin will submit to being buried in baptism, just as Christ was buried following his death. Moreover, as Jesus was "raised," so it is the case that when one emerges from immersion, he enjoys "newness of life" (v. 4), i.e., justification from sin (v. 7). Later, in the same context, the apostle describes the process as being "obedient from the heart," hence being "delivered" and "made free from sin" (vv. 17-18).
3. Since Paul uses the plural "we" to join himself with the Romans, in terms of what each did in procuring justification, and inasmuch as we elsewhere learn that Saul's sins were "washed away" at the point of baptism (Acts 22:16), one must conclude that justification occurs at the point of immersion. This is a part of the broader process of being "justified by faith." One has not the liberty, therefore, to isolate the initial act of belief/trust from the full complement of conditions (e.g., "repentance" and "confession" of one's faith – 2:4; 10:9-10) that lead to the point of actual justification.
4. In chapter ten of this book, the apostle discusses the problem of Jewish disbelief. What was at the core of that problem? They sought to make themselves right with God by adopting a mode of "righteousness" on their own, rather than submitting themselves to the "righteousness of God," i.e., God's plan for constituting one as righteous (10:1-3). When one obeys the first principles of the gospel, he is accounted to be "righteous" (dikaios – see Matthew 25:37), which is the equivalent of "justified" (dikaioo). Subsequently in this chapter the apostle quotes scripture (Isaiah 28:16) to the effect that whosoever "believes on him" [Christ] "shall not be put to shame" (v. 11). This last phrase is the negative form of the positive terms "saved" or "justified." He then references a parallel sentiment from Joel (2:32), "Whosoever shall call upon the name of the Lord shall be saved" (v. 13). From the book of Acts one learns that "calling upon the name of the Lord" in order to receive salvation, occurs when one repents of sins and is immersed in the name of Christ—at which point he receives "forgiveness of sins" (cf. Acts 2:21,38). But, by way of contrast, what was the plight of many of the Jews? Tragically, "they did not all obey the gospel" (10:16). Thus, "believing" (v. 11), and "calling upon the name" (v. 13), are the equivalents of obeying the gospel. Faith obeys!

Clearly, a full consideration of all the facts leads the careful and honest student only to the conclusion that while being justified is by faith, the initial act of believing does not represent the total plan of justification. Faith is the guiding principle of obedience; it is, however, only the beginning of the process that leads to further obedience. Faith does not justify without that submission.

Grace Accessed

Grace is a wonderful, though much misunderstood, theme. The term charis occurs about 155 times in the New Testament. The word is related to the Greek, chairo, meaning "to rejoice." Grace conveys the ideas of favor, gratification, or gratitude, depending upon the context. There is significant stress upon the fact that salvation is the result of God's grace (Ephesians 2:8-9), but there are several important aspects to this matter.

1. Heaven's grace is made available to "all men" (Titus 2:11), contrary to the claims of Calvinism, which alleges it is bestowed only upon certain "elect" ones.
2. Divine grace is accessed by means of a system of intellectual instruction (Titus 2:12; cf. John 6:45); it is not arbitrarily bestowed.
3. Grace is extended conditionally (cf. Genesis 6:8; Hebrews 11:7)—again, contra Calvinism. The Ephesian Christians had been saved "by grace" (Ephesians 2:8), but their salvation occurred at that point in time when they were "cleansed by the washing of water" (5:26). This is a reference to their baptism—a fact almost universally conceded by scholars.
4. Grace excludes merit; salvation can never be earned (Romans 6:23; cf. Matthew 18:24-27). On the other hand, the offer of grace must be "received" (2 Corinthians 6:1; cf. John 1:11-12), and it is received by responding to certain divinely required conditions (Titus 3:4-7; cf. John 3:3-5).
5. As noted already, within the sphere of grace one can be at peace with God, and in achieving that, he becomes an heir of "the grace of life" (1 Peter 3:7).

Truth be told, I used to believe this false teaching because it was the only thing I had ever heard taught and preached in every single one of the churches I attended! Also, realize that other false teachings almost always accompany this false teaching (see the "sinner's prayer," "once saved always saved," false teachings on baptism, etc.), which are all interwoven together into a giant, intricate knot and tangled web of deception.

See the chapters on The Path to Eternal Life, Be Baptized, Obedience, and Bearing Fruit (The Role of Works) for information on the truth of what Scripture actually teaches.

6.12 ONCE SAVED ALWAYS SAVED
(a.k.a. "Perseverance of The Saints" Under Calvinism)

Another enormously popular false teaching today proclaims that once someone has accepted Christ (i.e., is born again), they can never lose their salvation regardless of how one subsequently lives the rest of their life (i.e., once saved, you are always saved to eternal life no matter what). This false teaching is also called "perseverance of the saints" by Calvinists.

This false teaching asserts that the believer in Christ can choose to keep (obey) the commands of Christ or freely ignore them without any peril, and even choose to live a life of reckless abandon and deliberate/wanton sinful behavior, and yet no matter what, eternal salvation is still ensured. And in the extreme, this false teaching declares that even if one were to deny Christ (after they were born again), they are still saved to eternal life! Now that I understand what Scripture actually says for myself (not just blindly believing whatever I heard taught or preached), I see this for the false teaching that it is!

In this false teaching, it is asserted that your final eternal salvation occurred at an instant of time when you first accepted Christ. However, this book has explained to you the difference between initial salvation (forgiveness of sins) and final salvation (eternal life); it is at final salvation when you receive your "crown of life." I have also explained that salvation (and sanctification) is a process that starts when you are born again but continues throughout the rest of your life. This book has also explained to you the role that obedience, works, and <u>perseverance</u> has in the plan of salvation. Realize that being born again is only the first step (but by far the most important step) on your path to eternal life – which is your ultimate goal and destination.

In the chapter on Persevering in Faith, I showed you that Scripture is adamant and abundantly clear that one must persevere in faith until death, with numerous repeated and explicit warnings about "falling away," going apostate, "backsliding," "turning back," "quitting [abandoning] the faith," and even being "tricked" or "deceived" out of your "crown of life" by the false teachings of man (the "wolves" and "vipers") – even after you are born again. While it is true that God will never forsake or leave you, Scripture is abundantly clear that you can still choose to leave/quit Him, even after you have been born again – and that some will do just that! It is written:

> But the Spirit explicitly says that in later times <u>some will fall away</u> from the faith, paying attention to deceitful spirits and doctrines of demons, by means of the hypocrisy of liars seared in their own conscience as with a branding iron, *men* who forbid marriage *and advocate* abstaining from foods which God has created to be gratefully shared in by those who believe and know the truth. – 1 Timothy 4:1-3

In order to fall away, one must have first been part of that faith to begin with. So those who claim that this verse indicates that those who fell away were never truly born-again to begin with are therefore using false logic. Wayne Jackson writes: [126]

> We would encourage those who have been led to believe the erroneous notion that the Christian may never forfeit his redemption, to restudy this issue with the greatest of care. One does not lose his "freedom of choice" when he becomes God's child. As he once chose to identify with the Lord, he may choose to renounce him. And if he does, and remains in an impenitent state, his destiny will be horrible and eternal.

It should also be noted that those who proclaim this false teaching often also falsely teach the conditions for how one is to be born again; therefore, this false teaching is almost always accompanied by the "sinner's prayer" and the "faith alone/only" false

---

[126] Jackson, Wayne. "But Were They Really Saved?" ChristianCourier.com. Access date: February 20, 2021. https://christiancourier.com/articles/1275-but-were-they-really-saved

teachings – all three of these false teachings usually come together as an Unholy Trinity pack (where there is one false teaching, others are surely lurking nearby).

6.13 PREDESTINATION
(a.k.a. "Unconditional Election" Under Calvinism)

Those who call themselves Calvinists (Calvinism) claim that God has predestined ("unconditionally elected") some people (individually) to be saved and others (individually) to be lost before the world began, and that not even faith itself is required for salvation (nor repentance, nor confession, nor baptism, nor perseverance, nor obedience, … nor anything whatsoever). It's astonishing that some "Christian" pastors actually believe and teach this.

This false teaching, which comes along with the other Calvinism and "Reformed" Protestantism false teachings, says that God has already chosen who to save before the foundation of the world (and also thereby who will be lost) and that man has no choice nor say nor free will nor responsibility to accept Christ in the matter. I must immediately, therefore, point out that in light of their own teaching, it is ironic and hypocritical in the extreme why this group still has pastors, ministers, elders, and even churches at all today preaching the gospel; for according to their own beliefs, there is no point nor effect in preaching the gospel to anyone, because God has already selected everyone to either save or condemn, and it was all predetermined long before the world began! They can all therefore close up shop, stop begging for donations, and go home, right? But they don't do that. Hmmm…is the hypocrite alarm going off for anyone else besides me on this? Why do they even need preachers of their theology if men cannot choose whether to accept the gospel or not? They could just as soon play reruns of *Gilligan's Island* at their church services and have the same result, yes?

And not only that, but this group compounds their error even further by also teaching what they call the "perseverance of the saints," i.e., a fancy name for the "once saved always saved" false teaching, which claims that a person can never lose his salvation after confessing Christ, regardless of how he lives the rest of his life, and regardless of whether he is obedient to the commands of Christ or not. As I've mentioned, false teachings come in packs: where there is one, others abound.

Wayne Jackson gives the following rebuttal to this false teaching:[127]

> As he commences his letter to the saints in Ephesus, Paul declares that God: "chose us in him [Christ] before the foundation of the world…having foreordained [predestinated – KJV] us unto adoption as sons through Jesus Christ unto himself?" (1:4-5).
>
> Does this passage teach that our salvation is strictly a matter of God's arbitrary election, settled before the world was made, irrespective of any choice that we might exercise in the matter?
>
> That was the philosophy of John Calvin. The Presbyterian *Westminster Confession of Faith* stated: "By the decree of God, for the manifestation of His glory, some men and angels are predestinated unto everlasting life, and other foreordained to everlasting death" (Article III).

---

[127] Jackson, Wayne. "Ephesians 1:4 – Predestination." *ChristianCourier.com*. Access date: June 24, 2018. https://christiancourier.com/articles/784-ephesians-1-4-predestination

This concept makes void every passage in the Bible that teaches human responsibility. If one's eternal destiny was sealed from the beginning of time, what is the purpose of preaching to the lost?

The key phrase in Ephesians 1:4 is "in him." It was not the case that God chose certain individuals to be either saved or lost; rather, the Lord foreordained that a certain *class of persons* would be saved.

What sort of class? Those who submit to Heaven's divine plan of redemption, which, in this dispensation, involves obeying Jesus Christ (Hebrews 5:8-9), and entering into that relationship that is described as being "in him" (cf. Galatians 3:26-27).

To say the same thing in another way, before the world's foundation, God elected to save those who would be obedient to His Son. Underline "chose us in him," and record this comment: *Not individual election, but class election.*

Please also see the "Calvinism" false teaching section which follows.

6.14 CALVINISM
(i.e., So-called "Reformed Protestantism")

"Calvinism" is yet another man-made theology and set of doctrines chock full of false teachings from top to bottom, which are shouted from the pulpits, seminaries, and so-called "Christian" publications, media, television, and radio with extreme force and volume today.

While there may have been good and noble intentions involved regarding this teaching when it evolved (I don't know, I wasn't there), it nonetheless is deceiving millions today, giving them a false sense of eternal security, and preaching a "gospel which is not another" and which is in contradiction with what the Bible actually teaches.

This system of theology is derived from what are called the "five points" of Calvinism, often given the name/acronym: "TULIP" (as to the first letter in each of the following items). Calvinism is therefore actually comprised of a bunch of false teachings all grouped together under one name, as each of these "five points" is itself also a false teaching. As I've repeatedly warned, where you find one false teaching, you will surely find others lurking nearby with it; you simply cannot have a better example of this than with Calvinism.

Here are the five false teachings of Calvinism:

1) "Total Depravity" – This false teaching claims that humans (and children) are all born sinful. This is very closely related to the "original sin" false teaching discussed elsewhere in this book. Now, I can see how they might have arrived at this conclusion by looking at how people behave (yes, even infants), but it is not in agreement with Scripture, and therefore must be rejected.
2) "Unconditional Election" (i.e., Predestination) – This teaching claims that God "predestines" (chose) all those (individually) who will be saved, and also all those who (individually) will be condemned, and He did this before time began and there is nothing anyone can do or really does of their own free will to choose their destiny. This teaching, therefore, denies that there is free will. Staggeringly, this false teaching also implies that even faith isn't a requirement

for salvation (nor repentance, nor baptism, nor anything whatsoever). See the Predestination false teaching discussed prior for more information.
3) "Limited Atonement" – this claims that Christ didn't die for the sins of everyone, that He only died for the sins of those who were (predestined) to be saved. This again contradicts Scripture which clearly asserts that man has free will and that God wishes that "all" men would come to repentance. They make this claim on the basis that they think God wouldn't "waste" Jesus' blood on those who were predestined to be lost. Jesus died for the sins of "all" men (1 Timothy 2:5-7), and when they stand before Christ on Judgment Day, every single person who has ever lived will know and see that Christ died for them also – and that had they chosen to accept Christ, their sins would have been forgiven, for Christ died for all. This is so that all men will be without excuse on that day. Do you really think that the Lord would allow anyone to stand up on that Day of Judgment and be able to make a valid claim like the following: "See, even if I had believed in your Son, He didn't die for my sins, so I wouldn't have been saved anyway!"? It will be very clear to all at that time, and everyone will be without excuse of any kind; because if anyone is condemned to hell, it will have been by their own choice, not that "Jesus did not die for them." Jesus died so that all men could come to eternal life, not just some. Wayne Jackson succinctly summarizes this as: "God so loved the entire world and gave his Son as a potential redeeming sacrifice for all who avail themselves of His gift (John 3:16). He is the loving benefactor to everyone who submits to his will in faithful obedience (1 Timothy 2:4; Hebrews 5:8-9; cf. 2 Peter 3:9)."[128]
4) "Irresistible Grace" – This is yet another false teaching tied to the Unconditional Election/Predestination false teaching that says no one can "resist" the will of God. Apparently, we are all robots according to Calvinism, devoid of free will to choose to accept or reject Christ. As I've said, if this is the case, their very own preachers and churches can close up shop because there is no need to preach the gospel to anyone (or beg for donations either).
5) "Perseverance of the Saints" – this is the fancy name they give to the "once saved always saved" false teaching already discussed in this book.

As you can see, every single one of the pillars of Calvinism is a false teaching! This Calvinism is such a staggering ecclesiastical horror house of mirrors, a bag of doctrinal errors and tricks, that it is astounding that it actually passes for being Christian. Please don't just accept my word on this; do your own Bible study and diligently seek out the truth. That's what I had to do.

Calvinism seems to have obtained its doctrine by picking and choosing some verses in Scripture and making an interpretation of those verses, but then ignoring the fact that their interpretation is in direct contradiction to (many) other verses in Scripture. But you just cannot do that – you must consider the <u>sum</u> of what Scripture says in aggregate (Psalm 119:160). If your interpretation of one verse contradicts other literal and unambiguous verses, then it's your interpretation that is wrong, not Scripture. And further, you must know Scripture for yourself, and, in fact, you must know it as well as (or better than) your own Pastor does (and better than Satan does)!

---

[128] Jackson, Wayne. "Did the Ancient Gentiles Have the Hope of Salvation?" *ChristianCourier.com*. Access date: November 8, 2018. https://christiancourier.com/articles/1475-did-the-ancient-gentiles-have-the-hope-of-salvation

As you have seen in this book, so-called "Reformed" Protestantism, as well as Calvinism, is as chock full of doctrinal errors as many other cults, including Roman Catholicism, which it was created to "reform." Very frankly, if one is following Scripture to begin with, there is no need for it to be "reformed" at all. To those who are sitting in churches and under "Christian" pastors who teach this nonsense, come out of "Babylon" (Revelation 18:4)! And to those "ravenous wolves" and "vipers" who teach this non-biblical nonsense, also come out of her ("Babylon") or beware James 3:1!

6.15 THE "SECRET RAPTURE"

This false teaching proclaims that the Church will be "raptured" (caught up in the air) to be with Christ, while unbelievers are "left behind" here on Earth to face a "7-year great tribulation" period where "The Antichrist" person of political and national power will lead the world against Christ (or more accurately, against the Jews and Israel) in the Battle of Armageddon, etc.

This "secret rapture" comes in various flavors, such as "pre-tribulation" rapture, "mid-tribulation rapture," "post-tribulation rapture," "pre-wrath rapture," etc. (see also the "7-Year Great Tribulation" false teaching). I'm not going to take the time to discuss them all here, as they are all equally wrong. There is not a shred of biblical support for this theory. This theory is enormously popular and widespread today and is shouted in blaring volume 24/7/365 from the pulpits of nearly every so-called "Christian" church today!

The only "rapture" Scripture talks about is in 1 Thessalonians 4:17, where it describes events happening <u>at the end of time</u> "when the Lord Jesus will be revealed from heaven with His mighty angels in flaming fire, dealing out retribution to those who do not know God and to those who do not obey the gospel of our Lord Jesus" (2 Thessalonians 1:7-8). As you can plainly see from that verse, this will definitely not be a "secret" event – it will be massively visible to everyone worldwide. Furthermore, it will be visible to all who have ever lived, both the living and the dead!

This event also coincides with (occurs on) the great Day of Judgment, not to start a further "7-year great tribulation" period which is to be even further followed by yet another "1000-year earthly millennial reign of Christ in Jerusalem" period. Those are all false teachings made up by man!

On the Last Day, when the skies open up in flaming fire above, and you see the Lord Jesus with all His holy angels and saints, it will be too late to be saved if you do not already believe in Him! For the great Day of Judgment will have arrived, and you will be woefully unprepared to stand before God in Judgment unless you are covered by the blood and righteousness of Jesus Christ! This false teaching is therefore leading millions to eternal death as it causes them to procrastinate in coming to Christ by implying the promise of "more time," and yet again "more time" – i.e., it causes people to think to themselves (and I'm paraphrasing here): "See, you haven't been raptured away yet, so I still have more time to get serious about all this Jesus and Bible stuff." Furthermore, the believing spouse or friend also procrastinates in sharing the gospel message with a friend or loved one, thinking to themselves: "Well, when you see me raptured away, then you will believe!" But be not deceived, for that will not be possible! Time will have run out on your friend or loved one, and the Great Day of Judgment will have already arrived simultaneously with the return of Christ.

Therefore, this false teaching is Satanic in nature! The fact that myriads of "Christian" pastors, teachers, and even seminary schools teach and preach this false teaching is mind-boggling and bizarre to me. See also the "7-Year Great Tribulation" Period, the "Third Temple," the "Dispensational Premillennialism," and the "Distortions of Matthew 24" false teachings also, as they are all intimately and cleverly woven together with this one.

As a side note, most Christians that I have met who espouse this false teaching also want to be raptured away right now instead of staying here for a while and doing hard work to help build the kingdom of God.

6.16 THE "7-YEAR GREAT TRIBULATION" PERIOD
(The 70-Weeks of Daniel Distorted)

This false teaching makes the claim that there is still a "missing week" of years from the Daniel 9 prophecy that has yet to unfold in the world, minus the church which was "raptured" to heaven beforehand (see the "Secret Rapture" false teaching). They claim this period will begin after "the Antichrist" person rises to worldwide political power and that this period will be the "7-year great tribulation period" before Jesus returns (but only to set up his earthly "millennial" reign in Jerusalem on earth for another 1000 years). This false teaching is one of the pillars used to "prove" the Dispensational Premillennialism false teaching.

They justify this false teaching by distorting and misinterpreting the visions of Daniel 9 and then combine that misinterpretation with other bizarre interpretations of the book of Revelation (yes, even more false teachings). I hope you are seeing the pattern here how false teachings work: One false teaching is used to justify the next false teaching, and on and on it goes until you are so far away from the actual truth of Scripture that you cannot even recognize it any longer!

The great tribulation spoken of in Matthew 24 occurred in A.D. 70, when the Jews were nearly wiped out with only a small remnant remaining when the Romans destroyed Jerusalem. This was in judgment for rejecting Jesus Christ. Jesus came the first time, right on schedule according to the prophecy given in Daniel and He was "cut off" (crucified) in the middle of the last week of years. There is no "missing week" of years from the book of Daniel.

6.17 DISPENSATIONAL PREMILLENNIALISM
(i.e., Earthly Millennial Reign of Christ)

This false teaching views most New Testament "end-times" Bible prophecy (especially the book of Revelation) from a "futurist" perspective – meaning that fulfillment is still in our future. Christians today, in large part (especially in America), are almost completely ignorant of early church history and of the intense suffering and persecution unto death that the early Church suffered at the hands of Rome Pagan and Rome Papal. This ignorance is then preyed upon and serves as fertile ground for the "wolves" to plant sensationalistic futuristic seeds of Bible prophecy, which are further lapped up by "itching ears" who find it all emotionally exciting and titillating. This is how the false prophets capture the imagination.

This false teaching in particular claims that Christ will come to rule and reign on the earth again from Jerusalem in a rebuilt "Third Temple" (with resumed sacrifices!)

for a literal "thousand years" (i.e., millennial) reign. They claim that the church age will have ended (the church will have been "raptured" off the earth, see the "Secret Rapture" false teaching) and that the nation of Israel will be restored with the Messiah (again, not necessarily Jesus!) ruling worldwide from Jerusalem with a restored Jewish temple (see the "Third Temple" false teaching) along with its priesthood, and that it will be a state of Jewish domination over all the world. They claim this millennial reign will start after some specific nationalistic, political "Antichrist" person has risen to worldwide power and control and torments the world in the "7-year great tribulation period" followed by the literal "Battle of Armageddon" on earth (yes, those are still yet three more false teachings!).

The proponents of this false teaching also argue violently among themselves about whether the "secret rapture" comes at the beginning of the supposed "7-year great tribulation" period (pre-tribulation), in the middle of it (mid-tribulation), before the wrath period (pre-wrath) and even after it (post-tribulation). These are all wrong – you simply have the blind arguing with the blind over who is more wrong than the other!

This false teaching is primarily based on Revelation 20:4, where a figurative phrase of "a thousand years" is interpreted literally when it is actually symbolic, representing a long period of time which is up to the discretion of God (i.e., this church age). The "wolves" who proclaim this false teaching wrongfully interpret that symbolic verse literally, despite there being many verses elsewhere in Scripture that contradict their teaching! Amazing, eh?

What Revelation 20 with its "thousand years" verse and also 2 Peter 3:8 is describing is symbolism, as if someone were making a wide sweeping gesture with their arms saying, "that with the Lord one day is like a thousand years, and a thousand years like one day" (i.e., it is just a long period of time, which isn't exactly specified). Both verses are symbolic, not literal! In fact, please realize that nearly all numbers used in the book of Revelation are symbolic! Those verses were meant to give you a sense of the scale and magnitude of the time period on which the Lord operates. Remember, God lives outside of (beyond) time as we know it and that we shouldn't judge God or place our own preconceived notions of time on Him about what is "long enough." This is why Scripture also indicates that while we think the Lord is "tarrying" (2 Peter 3:9, Hebrews 10:37, Revelation 10:6, Revelation 6:10, etc.), He is, in fact, exactly right on time – His time, not ours. We are to be living each and every day as if we were expecting His return today (see Matthew 25, Romans 13:11-12, Hebrews 10:37, Revelation 3:11, Revelation 22:12, Revelation 22:20, etc.).

This particular false teaching/deception is enormously popular today, being widely taught, preached, published, and broadcast in absolutely deafening volume from nearly every single pulpit, radio or media station, book, internet site, so-called "Christian" movie, etc. – nonstop, 24 hours a day, 7 days a week, and 365 days a year, from both heathen (secular) and Christian sources! The fact that secular God-denying factions support this false teaching should tell you all you need to know about it.

I hope you noticed how this one false teaching is intimately tied together with a whole PLETHORA of other false teachings, all woven together into an intricate fabric/web of lies and deception. Yes, the "wolves" and "vipers" combine together bizarre and mind-bending distortions of clear and straightforward scripture verses in an effort to support their false teachings, which in actuality are nothing more than the schemes of man in disguise. As indicated previously, where you find one false teaching, you will surely find others with it.

Do not be such a gullible Christian to just go along with all of these false teachings, and this one is at the center of them all when it comes to matters of eschatology. In fact, it is the fulcrum. That's why I suggested earlier that if you pick one false teaching to dig into first, this is the one – for when you untangle its web of lies, many other areas of Scripture suddenly become clear, and you can see the truth, and you also start to see the cults/sects/groups/churches which are the source of these lies.

The "wolves" and "vipers" who are espousing this false teaching claim that Christ will return to the earth a second time only to "rapture" the church (See the "Secret Rapture" false teaching), and then come back a third time to reign on earth from Jerusalem, with restored Israel as ruler over all nations, with a mixture of half-saved saints in eternal bodies living on earth along with unbelievers still in their fleshly, sinful bodies, and a whole jumbled up mess of other nonsense.

But I ask you, where in the Bible does it mention a third (or even fourth) coming of Christ? And most importantly, this false teaching shows a clear lack of understanding of Christ's kingdom – which we are in right now! Yes, this very second, Christ is "seated at the right hand" of the Father in heaven, "ruling and reigning" in His Kingdom! The earthly millennialists deny this rule and reign. They are denying that their own Lord and King is ruling this very day; they do not even seem to understand the Kingdom of God and His Christ. What about Christ's clear and explicit statement that "My kingdom is <u>not of this world</u>" (John 18:36) do they not understand? It is further written:

> Now having been questioned by the Pharisees as to when the kingdom of God was coming, He answered them and said, "The kingdom of God is not coming with signs to be observed; nor will they say, 'Look, here *it is*!' or, 'There *it is*!' For behold, the kingdom of God is in your midst." – Luke 17:20-21 [i.e., The Kingdom is among you, within each of you, for that is where Christ dwells, and it is also His Church.]

This earthly millennial reign false teaching also leads (or stems from) a distorted understanding of the meaning of Isaiah 11, in particular the verse: "the wolf will dwell with the lamb." That verse does not mean that literal lamb and wolf animals will co-habitat a future renovated Earth during a literal 1000-year reign of Christ on Earth. Scripture often utilizes various animals to represent the different characters/natures of various types of men. The Isaiah verse speaks prophetically of how men who are lambs (Christians, followers of Jesus) will get along (through the power of the Gospel/Christ) with those who were formerly wolves (men who denied God, persecuted Christians, etc.) during the Kingdom of Christ, which is this age of grace, this church age we are in now. The apostle Paul was a great example of this prophecy: he was first a wolf devouring and persecuting the early church saints, but when converted to Christ, he became like a lamb and peacefully dwelt together with the apostles/disciples in the Kingdom of Christ. The power of Christ converted him from a "wolf" type of man to a "lamb" type of man.

Scripture also declares that the kingdom of heaven is not to be seen with visible signs and wonders, nor is it to be found among the nations of this world or the political agendas of man; the kingdom of God resides where Christ is – which is in heaven (where Christ is seated at the right hand of the Father ruling and reigning right now) and also inside the heart of each believer, where Christ is abiding (Luke 17:20-21, John 15:4, Ephesians 1:20-21, Colossians 3:1).

And while I do think that there will be those of differing "millennial" kingdom beliefs in heaven (i.e., I agree that having a correct understanding of this subject is not a condition for eternal salvation), I strongly disagree with those who say that it is just a minor matter. First, this false teaching is disrespectful to Christ, for how someone can claim Christ as their King and not even know that He is ruling right now in His kingdom?

Secondly and much more importantly, while a correct understanding of this matter may not affect your eternal destiny, it can greatly affect the eternal destiny of others – especially those who don't yet know Christ. Let me explain why. This false teaching is designed by Satan to mislead and deceive millions of souls by causing them to procrastinate in coming to know Christ – because the false teaching implies that there is "more time"! If you are not sharing the gospel message with your family, friends, loved ones, and co-workers because you are counting on them to finally "get serious about all this Jesus stuff" when they see you "raptured," you are horribly deceived. At Jesus' return, the great Day of Judgment will have arrived – there will not be "more time."

At its core, this false teaching is a complete rejection of what He did at the cross when taken to its fullest extent, for this false teaching indicates a resumption of sacrifices in a "Third Temple." As Wayne Jackson writes, it is a "system of infidelity." [129] So, no matter whether you think it's fundamental to the faith or not, you are teaching wrongly about it and greatly impacting others by leading them astray – possibly even to eternal death.

The truth is that we are currently in the "thousand year" reign of Christ today as He rules and reigns on His throne. This (correct) interpretation of Revelation 20 is sometimes given the name "amillennialism" – although I do not use that term myself because it literally means that there is "no" millennial period. If you must give a name to the correct teaching, I prefer to use now-millennial, as we are right now this very day in the "thousand years" (symbolically speaking), which coincides with this church age and the age of grace. These are also called the "last days" in Scripture.

I'll end with what Wayne Jackson has written: [130]

> The premillennial concept is the result of literalizing a few symbolic verses in the book of Revelation, coupled with a considerable disregard for scores of Bible passages of clearest import. The word "premillennial" itself is derived of two components – "pre" signifies **before**, and "millennium" denotes a period of **one thousand years**. The theory thus suggests that Christ will return to the earth **just prior to a one-thousand-year reign**.
>
> The premillennial theory is advanced in several different ways. It is, therefore, not an easy task to generalize regarding this system of doctrine. We will focus mainly on that branch of millennialism that is known as dispensational premillennialism. The following quotations are introduced to bring some of the main points into focus:

---

[129] Jackson, Wayne, *Premillennialism, A System of Infidelity*, Christian Courier Publications

[130] Jackson, Wayne. "Examining Premillennialism." *ChristianCourier.com*. Access date: April 1, 2019. https://christiancourier.com/articles/322-examining-premillennialism

It is held that the Old Testament prophets predicted the re-establishment of David's kingdom and that Christ himself intended to bring this about. It is alleged however, that because the Jews refused his person and work he postponed the establishment of his kingdom until the time of his return. Meanwhile, it is argued, the Lord gathered together "the church" as a kind of interim measure (Kevan 1999, 352).[131]

Generally, premillennialists believe that shortly before the second coming the world will be marked by extraordinary tribulation and evil and the appearance of the Anti-Christ. At his coming, Christ will destroy this anti-Christ and believers will be raised from the dead. There will then follow a millennium of peace and order over which Christ will reign with his saints. At the close of this time, Satan will be loosed and the forces of evil will once again be rampant. The wicked will then be raised, and a final judgment will take place in which Satan and all evil ones will be consigned to eternal punishment (Harvey 1964, 151).[132]

For centuries the Jews have been scattered among many nations. In preparation for the return of Christ and the beginning of the millennium, they are being gathered back to their own land, according to prophecy, in a national restoration. David's throne will be re-established at Jerusalem, and through these restored people as a nucleus Christ will reign with his immortal saints over the whole world (Nichols n.d., 279).[133]

To summarize, the premillennial view asserts that Christ came to this earth for the purpose of setting up his kingdom. He was, however, surprisingly rejected by the Jews. Hence, he postponed the kingdom plans and set up the church instead—as sort of an emergency measure. When he returns, he allegedly will raise only the righteous dead, restore national Israel, sit upon David's literal throne in Jerusalem, and then reign for a span of one thousand years—after which comes the resurrection of the wicked and the judgment.

One of the primary fallacies of the premillennial concept is a **materialistic** view of the reign of Christ. This same notion was entertained by the ancient Jews and actually was responsible for their rejection and crucifixion of the Messiah. The fact is, this mistaken Jewish expectation of a literal, material kingdom spawned the millennial doctrine that was taught in the early post-apostolic age. As one historian observed:

The idea of a millennial reign proceeded from Judaism, for among the Jews the representation was current, that the Messiah would reign a thousand years on earth, and then bring to a close the present terrestrial System. This calculation was arrived at, by a literal interpretation of Psalm 90:4, "A thousand years are in thy sight as one day." It was further argued that as the World was created in six days, so it would last six thousand years, the seventh thousand would be a period of repose, a sabbath on Earth to be followed by the destruction of the World (Neander 1858, 248).[134]

The necessary implications of the premillennial doctrine are grave indeed. This teaching strikes treacherously at numerous facets of biblical truth.

---

[131] Kevan, Ernest F. 1999. *Wycliffe Dictionary of Theology*. E. F. Harrison, G. W. Bromiley, C. F. Henry, eds. Peabody, MA: Hendrickson.

[132] Harvey, Van A. 1964. A Handbook of Theological Terms. New York, NY: Macmillan.

133 Nichols, James A., Jr. n.d. Christian Doctrine—A Presentation of Biblical Theology. Nutley, NJ: Craig.

134 Neander, Augustus. 1858. History of Christian Dogmas. Vol. 1. London, England: Bohn.

I've pointed you towards truth herein; now you need to also take some steps towards it on your own. God will lead you into all truth, but you must want it. This false teaching is brought to you by those who scheme endlessly in the lustful pursuit to glorify man and political and nationalistic power and control, not God. I really hope you are starting to see the massive sea of lies and deceptions that you are being taught and fed to you, and maybe you also have believed? Wake up, fellow brother or sister in Christ! While I also used to believe many of these lies, I have woken up to the truth and come out of "Babylon"!

6.18 DISPENSATIONAL POSTMILLENNIALISM
(i.e., Widespread Peace on Earth before Jesus Returns)

This false teaching claims that Christ's Second Coming will only occur after the gospel has spread to all the world, and there has been a thousand-year (millennium) "golden age" of worldwide peace and harmony under Christian ethics, morals, prosperity, and dominance. This false teaching also claims that most people will be saved during this "golden age" of Christianity (although, of course, it says nothing about those who lived before this period). Supposedly, Jesus will only return for Judgment and usher in eternity after this so-called "golden age" on Earth has occurred.

This is yet another false teaching in clear and direct opposition to Scripture, satanically designed to get you to procrastinate and delay in accepting Christ or delay in sharing the gospel message with your family, friends, and loved ones. Scripture tells us that:

> "The coming of the Son of Man will be just like the days of Noah. For as in those days before the flood they were eating and drinking, marrying and giving in marriage, until the day that Noah entered the ark, and they did not understand until the flood came and took them all away; so will the coming of the Son of Man be." – Matthew 24:37-39

> Now as to the times and the epochs, brethren, you have no need of anything to be written to you. For you yourselves know full well that the day of the Lord will come just like a thief in the night. While they are saying, "Peace and safety!" then destruction will come upon them suddenly like labor pains upon a woman with child, and they will not escape. But you, brethren, are not in darkness, that the day would overtake you like a thief. – 1 Thessalonians 5:1-4

We know from Scripture that in the days of Noah:

> The LORD saw that the wickedness of man was great on the earth, and that every intent of the thoughts of his heart was only evil continually. – Genesis 6:5

> The earth was corrupt in the sight of God, and the earth was filled with violence. God looked on the earth, and behold, it was corrupt; for all flesh had corrupted their way upon the earth. – Genesis 6:11-12

> He went and made proclamation to the spirits *now* in prison, who once were disobedient, when the patience of God kept waiting in the days of Noah, during the construction of the ark, in which a few, that is, eight persons, were brought safely through *the* water. – 1 Peter 3:18-20

Now, does that sound like a period of global peace, harmony, and a "golden age" of salvation to you? No, the world was going about its daily business of sin and corruption with no thought whatsoever of God or the judgment to come. In fact, Noah preached of the coming judgment by flood for 120 years, and all the while, God waited patiently for anyone to come to repentance, but <u>not a single person</u> outside of his own family believed Noah.

Further, Scripture explicitly tells us what men will be like in these "last days," which is this gospel/church age and the last period of human history before Christ returns for Judgment Day:

> But realize this, that in the last days difficult times will come. For men will be lovers of self, lovers of money, boastful, arrogant, revilers, disobedient to parents, ungrateful, unholy, unloving, irreconcilable, malicious gossips, without self-control, brutal, haters of good treacherous, reckless, conceited, lovers of pleasure rather than lovers of God, holding to a form of godliness, although they have denied its power. – 2 Timothy 3:1-5

Again, if a theory or teaching of man contradicts even so much as one clear and direct verse of Scripture, it is man's theory that is wrong, not Scripture. See also the Dispensational Premillennialism false teaching.

6.19 A THIRD TEMPLE

Some teach that a literal, physical "3rd Temple" will be built in Jerusalem so the Messiah (not necessarily Jesus) can reign on earth. I give below the Scripture which calls for a literal physical third temple to be built in Jerusalem:

> (This area intentionally left blank)

That's right; there is not a single verse of Scripture that calls for a literal physical third temple to be built in Jerusalem (or anywhere else). A resumption of sacrifices (of any kind) denies the sacrifice of Christ on the cross. Scripture is clear that the Old Testament Mosaic Law system of temple sacrifices (and the Mosaic Law) ended (was fulfilled in and by Christ) at the cross.

In fact, we who are Christians are "living stones" in the temple of Christ (1 Peter 2:5), which is also the body of Christ of which we are all members – which is also the "Church of Christ":

> So then you are no longer strangers and aliens, but you are fellow citizens with the saints, and are of God's household, having been built on the foundation of the apostles and prophets, Christ Jesus Himself being the corner *stone*, in whom the whole building, being fitted together, is growing into a holy temple in the Lord, in whom you also are being built together into a dwelling of God in the Spirit. – Ephesians 2:19-22

> And coming to Him as to a living stone which has been rejected by men, but is choice and precious in the sight of God, you also, as living stones, are being built up as a spiritual house for a holy priesthood, to offer up spiritual sacrifices acceptable to God through Jesus Christ. – 1 Peter 2:4-5

To support this false teaching, Ezekiel 37:26-28 is distorted into meaning that a "Third Temple" will be built by the Messiah. However, this is not a correct interpretation, as Wayne Jackson writes: [135]

> "Ezekiel 37:26-28 seems to imply that the Messiah would rebuild the temple for the third time. Since Christ did not rebuild the temple, how does one reconcile the Ezekiel passage with Christ being identified as the Messiah?"
>
> The "sanctuary" or "tabernacle" to which the prophet alluded is not a literal temple; rather, the declaration foretells the establishment of the Christ's church, which is characterized by inspired New Testament writers as a "temple" or "house of God" (cf. 1 Corinthians 3:16; 2 Corinthians 4:16; Ephesians 2:21; 1 Timothy 3:15; 1 Peter 2:5).
>
> The preceding verses (21ff) have to do with the uniting of the people of God in the new regime, the Christian age (cf. John 10:16; Ephesians 2:16). While these passages allude to the call of the Gentiles, the same unity principle applies to once-divided Israel as well. Notice also that "David" is said to be their king. This cannot refer to the literal "David," for David was still to be sleeping with the "fathers" when the Messiah's kingdom was established (2 Samuel 7:12).
>
> In chapter 42, Ezekiel again discusses the building of a "temple." Its "outer court" measured 500 "reeds" on each side (42:15ff). Each "reed" was 6 Babylonian cubits (a minimum of 21 inches each). This would indicate that the temple court was about 1 mile in each direction — which would be larger than the entire city of Jerusalem (see McClintock & Strong, Cyclopedia, Vol. X, p. 258). This nullifies a literal interpretation.
>
> Additionally, Ezekiel's prophetic temple was to be located in the center of a sacred parcel that measures 25,000 "reeds" on each side. According to the figures provided in 45:5 (1 reed = 6 cubits), this would make the holy area almost 50 miles in each direction. There is not enough room in Palestine to accommodate such a large region, with Jerusalem at its center.
>
> Quite obviously, then, the narrative, as portrayed in this section of the prophet's document, is very symbolic. Millennialists who force this language into a literal temple do so at the sacrifice of sound interpretative methodology.

In summary, a "Third Temple" is not indicated or called for in Scripture. The Old Testament Mosaic Law was nailed to the cross – not abolished, but completely "fulfilled" in the person of Jesus Christ. Today, a true Jew is one who worships Christ in "spirit and in truth" according to New Testament Scripture by accepting Christ as their Lord and Savior (not by observing the Mosaic Law or other mystical rituals, rites, holidays, or "traditions"). [136] [137] See also the "Sabbath Keeping" false teaching.

---

[135] Jackson, Wayne. "What About Judging Angels, Godfathers and Ezekiel's Temple?" *ChristianCourier.com*. Access date: January 15, 2019. https://christiancourier.com/articles/1029-what-about-judging-angels-godfathers-and-ezekiels-temple

[136] See also: Jackson, Wayne. "Was the Lord's "Second Coming" in A.D. 70?" *ChristianCourier.com*. Access date: November 8, 2018. https://christiancourier.com/articles/449-was-the-lords-second-coming-in-a-d-70

[137] See also: Jackson, Wayne. "Genesis 15:18 – Will Israel Once Again Possess the Promised Land?" *ChristianCourier.com*. Access date: November 8, 2018. https://christiancourier.com/articles/402-genesis-15-18-will-israel-once-again-possess-the-promised-land

6.20 DISTORTIONS OF MATTHEW 24
(The Olivet Discourse)

There are so many popular (and grossly incorrect) interpretations of Matthew 24, called the "Olivet Discourse," that it boggles the mind. Jesus gave this discourse shortly before His crucifixion. Suffice it to say that nearly all popular and widely accepted interpretations are wrong because they are based on other false teachings such as Dispensational Premillennialism or based on misinterpretations of the books of Daniel and Revelation.

The verses of Matthew 24:4-34 are speaking of the Great Tribulation, which was what happened to the Jews in A.D. 70 when Jerusalem was destroyed by the Roman armies and over 1 million Jews perished. That was the "great tribulation" indicated in Matthew 24:21…it is not some fanciful man-conjured 7-year period of time still yet to come in the future after some mythical Anti-Christ nationalistic/political figurehead person emerges. Matthew 24:36-51 is about the second coming of Jesus, as is all of Matthew 25.

See also the "Secret Rapture," "7-Year Great Tribulation," "Third Temple," the "Antichrist Person," and "Earthly Millennial Reign" false teachings and be not deceived.

6.21 MODERN/POPULAR ESCHATOLOGY
(Distortions of The Book of Revelation)

Now, if you want a real headache, read some of the things written about the book of Revelation, not only from secular sources but also from "Christian" sources. You will quickly realize how the foolish mind of man truly excels in conjuring up sheer nonsense and rubbish when it comes to interpreting Scripture.

False teachings from this book of Scripture come in many forms and are given various names: Preterist (in its various forms and reincarnations: Radical Preterism, the "A.D. 70 Doctrine," "Realized Eschatology"), Idealist, Dispensational Futurist, Progressive Dispensationalist, and Historist. Suffice it to say, probably 99.9% of everything that you hear or read on the Book of Revelation (yes, nearly all of it) shouted from the pulpits (and the secular world) today is blatantly wrong – all created in support of the agendas of man, not God. This includes teachings on the "Battle of Armageddon," "Gog and Magog" (i.e., the big bad Russians and Chinese, etc.), the "Mark of the Beast" (666), the nationalistic, political super-villain "Antichrist Person" yet to come, etc. [138] [139]

The false teachings about the book of Revelation are intricately woven together by the "wolves" into a web of deception with many other false teachings as well (Dispensational Premillennialism in particular). In fact, once you dismantle that one false teaching façade of lies, many of the others come tumbling down with it (i.e., the "7-Year Great Tribulation Period," "The Secret Rapture," a "Third Temple," etc.). Some of these fanciful man-made false interpretations of eschatology (end-times prophecy) are so popular that they've been published in books selling many millions of

---

[138] See also: https://christiancourier.com/articles/434-1-john-2-18-who-is-the-antichrist
[139] See also: https://christiancourier.com/articles/677-who-is-pauls-man-of-sin

copies and are used to make Hollywood movies. That alone should tell you much about them: they appeal to "itching ears" and are not sound biblical doctrine.

Also, be aware that study Bible notes (and even chapter headings and illustrations) reflect the viewpoint of the publisher or group who printed the book – they are words of man added to Scripture! Be especially wary, therefore, of any items or notes added relating to eschatological (end-times) matters and Bible prophecy, as nearly all Bibles, books, and commentaries printed after the late 1800s (approximately) are infected with the Dispensational Premillennialism false teaching.

The book of Revelation is highly symbolic; trying to read it literally or as literal history results in errors and false teachings. Do you know that the word "antichrist" doesn't even appear anywhere in the book of Revelation? Be not deceived.

According to Scripture:

- No Third temple is indicated or called for: there is to be no resumption of sacrifices (unless you desire to deny Christ's sacrifice on the cross!),
- There is no "missing week of years" yet to unfold in Bible prophecy from the book of Daniel,
- There is no specific political, nationalistic "Antichrist Person" that we are still waiting to arise,
- There is no "pre-tribulation rapture" of the Church (or "mid-trib" or "post-trib," etc.), and
- There is no literal "Battle of Armageddon," usually postured as a nuclear war perpetrated by the "big bad" Russians (or Chinese) against Israel.

And it shouldn't need to be pointed out, but if someone can't even get the core gospel doctrine correct, why in the world would you ever listen to anything they say regarding Bible prophecy? That makes zero sense. Once someone has gospel truth down, only then does it make sense to consider their beliefs and opinions regarding prophecy.

I cannot waste much more space in this book trying to list, let alone refute, all the nonsense and rubbish that is conjured up in this area as it would take many more hundreds, even thousands of pages, but a couple of topics are discussed in more detail to help you a bit further (the "mark of the beast" and the "two witnesses"). It is then left as an exercise for the reader to seek truth – but you must really want to find truth and seek it diligently with much hard work and possibly years of Bible study. That is what was required for me to be able to see the false teachings for what they are.

6.22 BIZARRE INTERPRETATIONS OF THE "MARK OF THE BEAST"

This topic is about the "mark of the beast" referred to in the book of Revelation. The mark is given by the second "beast" of Revelation 13, which is also identified by the number "666." There is probably more rubbish, complete nonsense, wild speculations, mystical notions, fanciful theories, and fantastical conjurings of man written about this topic than anything else in the entire Bible. Even those who don't read or believe the Bible or even believe in God seem to know what this mark is, and they are happy to tell you all about it – and it's almost always wrong, of course. The wildly popular (among both heathens and Christians) teachings and musings are that this mark will be a chip implant, tattoo, or barcode on your forehead or hand; these are complete nonsense. This brings up a good point, which shouldn't even have to be said, but seems necessary: do not get your Christian doctrine and Bible interpretation from secular sources! You're in for a world of trouble and deception if you do so, and yet I see it happening all the time.

First, let's talk about the symbolism and meaning of this passage; only after that is established can we then talk about the possible fulfillments (near and far) of this mark and discuss its applicability to us today.

When you accept Christ, you are born-again of the Holy Spirit who resides in you; this is how you abide in Christ and He in you. Scripture refers to this as being "sealed" with the Holy Spirit. It is symbolically and figuratively described as having a "mark" placed on your forehead, and this mark identifies you as being a child of God. The mark is spiritual – it is not a literal physical mark! King David writes about this as "You have anointed my head with oil" (Psalm 23:5). Revelation 7:3 states that the "bond-servants of [our] God" were "sealed on their foreheads."

In contrast, for those who reject Christ, the Bible also symbolically speaks about them as having a mark placed on their forehead (or their hand), which signifies that they are following after Satan, the devil, in mind (forehead – heart and mind) and in action/deed (on the hand – doing his works and the deeds of this sinful world). The Bible also refers to this marking as those who have "His [Jesus] name will be on their foreheads" vs. those who have the name of the world ("BABYLON THE GREAT, THE MOTHER OF HARLOTS AND OF THE ABOMINATIONS OF THE EARTH") written on their foreheads. The symbolism is obvious and the same: followers of Christ or followers of Satan (i.e., this world/man). Those are the only two families of people on Earth, and everyone who has ever lived will be in one or the other. Correspondingly, there are two marks; you are marked either as:

1) Belonging to Christ, or
2) Belonging to this world (which is of Satan and those who follow him, including apostate churches and governments of man, i.e., the "beasts" of Revelation)

Furthermore, these marks are constantly being given out during this gospel and church age to those who choose Christ as Lord and those who do not. So, if you are following man and the ways of the world ("for the ways of man lead to death," Proverbs 14:12), then you have the mark of the beast (who is of Satan, and this world); if you are following Jesus, then you have the mark/anointing of the "Oil of Gladness" (The Holy Spirit) sealing you as a child of God. Once again, that is the symbolism described.

I encourage you to read a couple (or three or four) books on early Christian church history to cure any ignorance of the horrendous persecution that they endured at the hands of the Jews, Romans, and Roman Catholics. It is narcissistic and egocentric to think that all Bible "end-times" prophecy is written to us and applies only to our own future. The book of Revelation would have been immensely helpful to those early Christians, to whom it was expressly written.

Let us now look at the likely specific historical fulfillments of this mark. Contrary to popular opinion today, which by and large thinks that all end-times Bible prophecy (e.g., the book of Revelation) has fulfillment and application only to us who are alive now or in the future, much of the prophecy of the book (but not all) was fulfilled in the early days of the church, when they suffered extreme persecution. The hope that the book of Revelation offers would have been very necessary during the early church.

The mark likely had fulfillment during the early years of the church, where taking the mark meant declaring or proclaiming any man or institution of man (e.g., Roman Caesar, or the Pope) as Lord and God (i.e., worshiping him), thereby denying "the living and true God," Jesus Christ. That worship was coerced with threats of death, persecution, and economic starvation during the extreme persecution of the early church, first under Rome Pagan (i.e., Caesar) and then under Rome Papal (i.e., the Roman Catholic Church).

In the first case, if a Christian didn't confess Caesar as Lord and God, they would be burned alive, sent to the arena to be torn apart by lions, or suffer a similar fate. Many Christians refused to take this "mark" of Caesar. Subsequently, under Rome Papal, the Roman Catholic Church was in full power, and if you didn't confess the Pope as Lord and God, you would be excommunicated (put out of the church), and you would effectively have been cut off from all means of economic livelihood and support (i.e., can't buy or sell), for the church had an iron grip on nearly all aspects of society. Many faithful Christians refused the "mark" of Papacy.

I value the commentary from biblical scholars not infected with false teachings (such as Dispensational Premillennialism, Postmillennialism, Radical Preterism, the "A.D. 70 Doctrine," "Realized Eschatology," etc.), but I also weigh whether they are teaching correct doctrine in other areas as well because, as I've indicated, false teachings travel in packs. Reputable commentaries agree that this prophecy likely described (specifically) the persecution of early Christians by the Roman Catholic Church in the centuries after the apostolic/early church age. Note that this was coincident with the rise of Roman Catholicism (the great apostasy mentioned in 2 Thessalonians 2, the "man of sin," the "lawless one," i.e., the Pope).

On the second beast of Revelation 13, Matthew Henry writes: [140]

> Those who think the first beast signifies Rome pagan by this second beast would understand Rome papal, which promotes idolatry and tyranny, but in a more soft and lamb-like manner: those that understand the first beast of the secular power of the papacy take the second to intend its spiritual and ecclesiastical powers, which act under the disguise of religion and charity to the souls of men. Here observe,
>
> I. The form and shape of this second beast: He had two horns like a lamb, but a mouth that spoke like the dragon. All agree that this must be some great impostor, who, under a pretence of religion, shall deceive the souls of men. The papists would have it to be Apollonius Tyranaeus; but Dr. More has rejected that opinion, and fixes it upon the ecclesiastical powers of the papacy. The pope shows the horns of a lamb, pretends to be the vicar of Christ upon earth, and so to be vested with his power and authority; but his speech betrays him, for he gives forth those false doctrines and cruel decrees which show him to belong to the dragon, and not to the Lamb.
>
> II. The power which he exercises: All the power of the former beast (Rev 13:12); he promotes the same interest, pursues the same design in substance, which is, to draw men off from worshipping the true God to worshipping those who by nature are no gods, and subject the souls and consciences of men to the will and authority of men, in opposition to the will of God. This design is promoted by the

---

[140] Henry, Matthew. *Exposition of the Old and New Testaments*, London. 1706-1710/1721.

popery as well as by paganism, and by the crafty arts of popery as well as by the secular arm, both serving the interests of the devil, though in a different manner.

> III. The methods by which this second beast carried on his interests and designs; they are of three sorts: - 1. Lying wonders, pretended miracles, by which they should be deceived, and prevailed with to worship the former beast in this new image or shape that was now made for him; they would pretend to bring down fire from heaven, as Elias did, and God sometimes permits his enemies, as he did the magicians of Egypt, to do things that seem very wonderful, and by which unwary persons may be deluded. It is well known that the papal kingdom has been long supported by pretended miracles.

On the "buying and selling" restriction, he writes:

> 2. Excommunications, anathemas, severe censures, by which they pretend to cut men off from Christ, and cast them into the power of the devil, but do indeed deliver them over to the secular power, that they may be put to death; and thus, notwithstanding their vile hypocrisy, they are justly charged with killing those whom they cannot corrupt.
> 3. By disfranchisement, allowing none to enjoy natural, civil, or municipal rights, who will not worship that papal beast, that is, the image of the pagan beast. It is made a qualification for buying and selling the rights of nature, as well as for places of profit and trust, that they have the mark of the beast in their forehead and in their right hand, and that they have the name of the beast and the number of his name. It is probable that the mark, the name, and the number of the beast, may all signify the same thing - that they make an open profession of their subjection and obedience to the papacy, which is receiving the mark in their forehead, and that they oblige themselves to use all their interest, power, and endeavour, to promote the papal authority, which is receiving the mark in their right hands. We are told that pope Martin V. in his bull, added to the council of Constance, prohibits Roman Catholics from suffering any heretics to dwell in their countries, or to make any bargains, use any trades, or bear any civil offices, which is a very clear interpretation of this prophecy.

In summary, the buying and selling restriction likely had an exact literal fulfillment under either the Rome Pagan or Rome Papal persecution of Christians in the early Church. However, this doesn't change its application, meaning, and purpose to us today, which is: if someone asks you to worship any man, or idol, or any institution of man instead of Christ (or they ask you to deny Christ), simply say no, even in matters of life and death through persecution! You'll therefore never have to worry about this "mark of the beast." In effect, if you are worshiping the things of man and this world, you already have the mark of the beast. If you are worshiping Christ in "spirit and in truth," you do not have the mark of the beast.

And a final note is warranted. Bible prophecies can have both a near and a far fulfillment. So, while this prophecy was likely fulfilled in the persecution of the early Church under Rome Pagan (Caesar) and/or Rome Papal (Roman Catholic Church), Satan (working through the men who choose to follow him) loves to mimic/imitate what is written in Scripture, so there may once again be a time when he tries to recreate what appears to be a far fulfillment of this prophecy in today's age. But be not deceived.

Also, it is wise to study church history, for one can learn much from those who have gone before us.

6.23 THE "TWO WITNESSES" OF REVELATION

In the book of Revelation, chapter 11 mentions "two witnesses" that appear for a time and then are killed and taken up to heaven. This false teaching could have been grouped with the modern/popular eschatology false teaching, but I wanted to call it out separately since it's so widely distorted.

There is widespread speculation and fantastical conjurings of man as to the identity of these "two witnesses," based largely on "futurist" and so-called literal interpretations of the book of Revelation. I say so-called literal interpretations because despite claiming to interpret all Scripture literally, they (the "ravenous wolves") do so in an arbitrarily inconsistent and hypocritical manner.

These "futurist" interpreters of Revelation proclaim that these "two witnesses" will be two literal men who stand in the literal streets of literal Jerusalem with literal fire coming out of their literal mouths. Others further proclaim that the two men will be Enoch and Elijah (or Enoch and Moses, or Moses and Elijah) returned from heaven again to earth. Such false interpretations are the result of treating symbolic biblical language literally.

Scripture states that it is by the mouth (testimony) of at least two (2) witnesses that all truth is to be established (Deuteronomy 17:6, 2 Corinthians 13:1). God has also always maintained at least two (2) witnesses to testify about His truth to man. In the Old Testament, they were the Law and the Prophets. In the New Testament age, there are also witnesses for God (and Christ); these are The Word, The Spirit, and the Church (for we are all witnesses of Christ). See John 15:26-27.

It is of these witnesses which the book of Revelation is referring to in a symbolic manner, for the text even tells us who these witnesses are: "These are the two olive trees and the two lampstands that stand before the Lord of the earth." One can therefore let Scripture interpret Scripture and simply go read what Scripture tells us about what the two "olive trees" and two "lampstands" represent (symbolically). Scripture defines these for us as The Holy Spirit and the Church (we are to be a "light of [to] the world…a city set on a hill," "a lamp/lampstand," we are to "shine before people," etc.).

As a side note, God has also provided a third witness for Himself at all times: nature (creation and the heavens, rains, food, etc., see Psalm 19:1-4, Romans 1:18-23, Acts 14:15-17).

6.24 PREDICTIONS OF JESUS' RETURN
(And Other "End of World" Prophesies)

This one is easily handled: any person or church/group/sect/cult that is making End-of-World prophesies, setting specific dates for Jesus' return, etc., is not a true Christian church – period! Scripture is clear that God, and God alone, knows the date and timing of Christ's return and the Day of Judgment. Scripture, and all prophesy, was finalized and sealed long ago.

Many of the things which you hear proclaimed to be so-called "end-times" prophecies (as in related to the second coming of Christ) aren't, in fact, even "end-times" prophecies at all – for they have already fulfillment hundreds of years ago during the persecutions of the early church under Rome Pagan and Rome Papal.

The Message of Truth 491

Whenever you see end-of-world prophesies or other teachings which claim to be inspired by "secret new revelations" or "visions" from God that someone has had, run as fast and as far away from that person or group as you can. They are of the devil, not of the Lord. Additionally, wherever you find this false teaching, you will surely find other false teachings from the same group as well.

6.25 LUCIFER AS THE DEVIL

Many Christians mistakenly believe that "Lucifer" is the name of the devil (Satan). They believe this simply because they hear others repeating it. The secular world also loves to repeat this, for they do not know any better. However, this is a false interpretation of Isaiah 14:12 (KJV translation). The context of the verse mentioning "Lucifer" is speaking of a specific man, a king/ruler, not Satan.

Various names are given to Satan, including: the "Devil" (Greek diabolos), "serpent/snake," "Abaddon," "Beelzebub," and "Belial." His name means "adversary" and "deceiver." He is also described as "a liar and the father of lies," "a murderer from the beginning," and that "there is no truth in him" (John 8:44). He is your "accuser" before God (Revelation 12:1, Job 1), "the prince of the power of the air [this fallen world]" (Ephesians 2:1-2), and "the ruler of this world" (John 12:31). Note, however, that he is not called "Lucifer."

You might be wondering why I am spending time addressing such a silly and unimportant false teaching (for it obviously is not a matter of salvation). I am doing so to teach you that you need to watch for a pattern, which is: where you find one false teaching, you will almost always find others lurking nearby from the same group, sect or cult. So, when you hear the name "Lucifer" being bandied about as the name for Satan, you know to be on the alert for other false teachings as well![141]

6.26 ALL BIBLE PROPHECY MUST BE LITERALLY FULFILLED

Many false teachers (yes, the "ravenous wolves" again, for they are extraordinarily busy) teach and preach that all Bible prophecy must be fulfilled literally. A couple of simple examples should suffice to show you that their claim is false:

1) Malachi 4:5: Did Elijah come back physically in person? No. Jesus said that "John [the Baptist] himself is Elijah who was to come" (Matthew 11:14) and indicated that was the fulfillment of the Malachi prophecy. Luke writes further that John the Baptist came "…as a forerunner before Him [Jesus] in the spirit and power of Elijah" (Luke 1:17). The Malachi prophecy had a spiritual, not literal, fulfillment.
2) Christ Prophesied in John 2:19: "Destroy this temple, and in three days I will raise it up." Was the literal Jewish temple literally torn down and rebuilt in three days? No, the prophecy was symbolic of Christ's body undergoing death and resurrection; the fulfillment of that prophecy was not literal.
3) In the very first prophecy of the Bible (Genesis 2), where Adam and Eve were forbidden to eat from the Tree of the Knowledge of Good and Evil, it was

---

[141] See also: Jackson, Wayne. "Who Is Lucifer?" *ChristianCourier.com*. Access date: November 8, 2018. https://christiancourier.com/articles/158-who-is-lucifer

written: "In the day that you eat from it you will surely die." Now, did they literally drop dead and fall to the ground on the day they ate the fruit? No, they died spiritually. It is also true that on that day, sin (and physical death) entered the world (and they did ultimately die physically), so the prophecy had both a physical and a spiritual aspect to it.

Another early prophecy of the Bible is given in Genesis 3, where it is written that: "He shall bruise you on the head, and you shall bruise him on the heel" when speaking about Jesus and Satan. This is perhaps the most significant prophecy in the entire Bible. Now, did Satan literally give Jesus a single actual black and blue bruise on his foot? No – it was symbolic of Christ being crucified on the cross (bruised) but then being raised to life again. Some of the prior false teachings have also shown you that literal interpretations of Bible prophecy are often wrong (e.g., Dispensational Premillennialism, a "Third Temple," etc.).

6.27 THE "ONE TRUE END-TIMES CHURCH"

Some denominations, sects, and cults today claim to be the "one true church" through which one is exclusively saved at the end of time. This is another false teaching conjured up by the very same denominations/sects that also have an abundance of other false teachings. Some of these groups/cults even claim that their church is the "144,000" chosen Jews mentioned in Revelation 7 (i.e., they are the "lost tribe") – more ridiculous nonsense. All followers of Christ are part of the worldwide "Church of Christ," regardless of where they are physically located. Sectarian and denominational divisions have no Scriptural support and are against the commands (and prayers) of Jesus. See also the Chapter on Finding a Church.

6.28 UNIVERSALISM
(Everyone Will Ultimately be Saved)

The false teaching called Universalism, or "Universal Reconciliation," comes in a few different flavors, but it generally teaches that God will ultimately save every human who has ever lived to be with Him in heaven. Universalism is a modern liberal attempt to legitimize all religions as valid, regardless of whatever they make up and believe, claiming there are many paths to heaven. This teaching is in clear contradiction to the direct (and literal) statements of Jesus: "for there is one God, and one mediator also between God and men, the man Christ Jesus, who gave Himself as a ransom for all" (1 Timothy 2:5-6), "I am the way, and the truth, and the life; no one comes to the Father but through Me" (John 14:6), and "there is salvation in no one else; for there is no other name [the name of Jesus] under heaven that has been given among men by which we must be saved" (Acts 4:12). Choose wisely which to believe: the opinions of man or the Word of God.

6.29 ECUMENISM
(All Denominations, Sects, and Cults Should "Just Get Along")

This is a modern liberal interdenominational initiative/attempt to convince the various sects/denominations of "Christianity," which have evolved over the last 2000 years, to come together with themselves (and even with all of the other world's religions) under the (false) umbrella of unity and compromise, regardless of whatever core beliefs (and false teachings) each group has. Since the sects/denominations that are being brought together here are themselves apostate from true Christianity, it's just another hoax, brought to you by the men who bring many of these other false teachings to you, all done in an attempt to consolidate their power over others.

6.30 YOU GET A "2nd CHANCE" AFTER DEATH

Some teach that those who die without accepting Christ will have a second chance to do so after death (or when He returns, or on Judgment Day). As with any false teaching, if we can provide even one clear and unambiguous verse that contradicts the teaching, you can see that it is indeed a false teaching. So, I present:

> And inasmuch as it is appointed for men to die once and after this *comes* judgment. – Hebrews 9:27

Scripture is clear that the state of your spirit/soul is fixed at your death for all eternity, with no second chance at redemption – in sin if you die without Christ, or in righteousness if you die in Christ. See the *Beyond the Tomb* book for more information about your eternal soul and what happens after death.

6.31 ROMAN CATHOLICISM MASQUERADING AS CHRISTIANITY

Roman Catholicism gives the appearance of being the Christianity of the Bible, but it is not. The Roman Catholic Church (along with its Eastern Orthodox brethren) teaches and preaches doctrines that are designed to trap people within a man-made system of false worship, false teachings, vain repetitious babbling, rites, rituals, sacraments, traditions, idol worship, mysticism, occult and pagan practices, beliefs and blasphemous claims, with all of those mixed together and masquerading behind a thin veneer of pretend/fake Christianity!

The many false teachings of Roman Catholicism include (but are not limited to):

- Purgatory,
- The Eucharist being Christ's body literally,
- Paying penance,
- Selling "indulgences" (sins),
- The Pope as "God" on earth (blasphemy),
- Mandated celibacy,
- Salvation is earned by "meritorious acts,"
- Other man-made rituals, ordinances, sacraments, and deceptions which are too long to even list here.

However, it is written:

> I am amazed that you are so quickly deserting Him who called you by the grace of Christ, for a different gospel; which is *really* not another; only there are some who are disturbing you and want to distort the gospel of Christ. But even if we, or an angel from heaven, should preach to you a gospel contrary to what we have preached to you, he is to be accursed! As we have said before, so I

say again now, if any man is preaching to you a gospel contrary to what you received, he is to be accursed! – Galatians 1:6-9

For many hundreds of years, the Roman Catholic Church worked to suppress the truth of Scripture, even corrupting Scripture (in the form of the Latin Vulgate) to support church doctrines. This so-called "Christian church" even tortured and massacred those who would dare to translate the Bible in their own language or even just read it in their own language! Understandably, many people were deceived by the Church of Rome during the dark ages, as the truth of Scripture was withheld from the common man, but with abundant access to the truth of God's Word today, I'm not sure how anyone mistakes Roman Catholicism for true Christianity as defined in Scripture.

Keep in mind that Roman Catholicism evolved out of mixing pagan beliefs with elements of Christianity, and Catholicism began hundreds of years after Christ. Part of the deception is their claimed association with the early saints and apostles such as Peter and Paul, giving the appearance that they are associated with the early apostolic Christian church. In an excerpt from *The Christian Church, Its Rise and Progress,* H. M. Riggle helps shed more light on this by comparing the true church of the New Testament (the one universal Church of God, the Church of Christ) vs. the Church of Rome: [142]

> The apostate church is brought to view in Revelation 17 under the symbol of a corrupt woman having a golden cup in her hand, full of abominations and filthiness of her fornications. She is called "Babylon the great, the mother of harlots." This corrupt woman is not the (pure) bride of Christ. There is no communication with the living head (Christ). She apostatized— separated from the truth, played the harlot— and at last she will have her portion in the lake of fire and brimstone. This is the great apostasy.
>
> **The Primitive Church and the Church of Rome Compared**
>
> The true church is characterized by its receiving and retaining the doctrine and faith of the apostles. It is "built upon the foundation of the apostles and prophets, Jesus Christ himself being the chief cornerstone" (Eph. 2:20). "And they were persevering in the doctrine of the apostles" (Acts 2:42). The church must hold the same doctrines which the inspired apostles and prophets taught, and which are contained in the Holy Scriptures. This is the test laid down by Jesus himself: "My sheep hear my voice: ...and they follow me"; "A stranger they follow not." Hear the apostle on this point: "Whosoever revolteth, and continueth not in the doctrine of Christ, hath not God. He that continueth in the doctrine, the same hath both the Father and the Son."
>
> It is not, then, the sentiments of fathers, or pontiffs, or bishops, or councils, but only those of prophets and apostles, that constitute the foundation of the church's faith. Its apostolic doctrine is the first test of the church, which is emphatically entitled "the pillar and ground of the truth." If this quality is wanting, nothing else can avail.
>
> The Church of Rome fulfils the prediction of Paul that "some shall depart from the faith, giving heed to spirits of error, and doctrines of devils" (1 Tim. 4:1). She has departed from the apostolic doctrine that salvation is obtainable through

---

[142] Riggle, H.M. (1912), *The Christian Church, Its Rise and Progress*, (The Gospel Trumpet Company).

repentance faith (Mark 1:15; Rom. 4:16; Rom. 10:9; Eph. 2:8, 9) and substituted a religion of works, including indulgences, the confessional, mass, extreme unction, purgatory, etc. Not a single one of these has any foundation in Holy Writ.

She has departed from the apostolic doctrine of holiness of heart and life (Matt. 5:8; Tit. 2:11, 12; Luke 1:74, 75; 1 John 4:17; 1 John 3:3, 6) and substituted a mere external holiness, which she has restricted to certain orders and individuals, such as monks, nuns, sisters of charity, prelates, and popes; thus has come the appellation, "His Holiness the Pope." In the primitive church all the brethren were holy, because they were saved from sin.

She has departed from the apostolic doctrine of a sinless life (1 John 3:6, 8, 9; 1 John 5:18), and in the following quotations from her standard authors acknowledges and teaches that her members are full of sin. In fact, a sinless life is nowhere taught by the priesthood of Rome.

The Call to Leave Babylon

We have seen that "Babylon the great" of Revelation 17 consists of a family, a mother and her harlot daughters. The mother is the Church of Rome, while the daughters are in particular the Protestant sects. This fraternity of so-called churches, from Rome down to the latest born daughter, does not represent the pure bride, "the Lamb's wife." Of his bride the Lord said, "Thou art all fair, O my love, and there is not a spot in thee." "One is my dove, my perfect one is but one." "And it is granted to her that she should clothe herself with fine linen, glittering and white. For the fine linen are the justifications of saints." "That I may present you as a chaste virgin to Christ." God has but one family, his household. Since no man can rightly have two families, God has but one church, which is the holy family.

Ignorantly many honest souls, as well as true children of God, have been led to join these apostate institutions. We do not doubt that the Church of Rome holds within her fold many sincere and honest people whose hearts are longing for better things. We have a warm and tender feeling for these dear people. It is not them that we antagonize, but the apostate, corrupt religion and teaching that is destroying their souls.

There are many books and resources which discuss the errors of Roman Catholicism in greater detail, so please seek them out. See also Denominationalism and the chapter on Finding a Church.

6.32 THE "KJV ONLY" BIBLE MOVEMENT

This group falsely proclaims that the 1611 King James Bible is the only accurate and inerrant English language translation Bible ever made. This "KJV Only" sect claims (loudly and ferociously) that all other English language Bibles are completely corrupt and not to be trusted or used at all. They also condescendingly issue a lot of very vocal threats and noise about your condemnation and damnation to hell if you read or use any other English language Bible today! While I appreciate (and strongly support) their desire to keep the Word of God free from error and corruption, their argument and teaching are without merit and logically inconsistent. Their claim is not only false, but it also cannot even be defended by well-formed logical reasoning. And are we really to believe that the Sovereign Lord God Almighty of the entire universe stopped protecting the sanctity of His Holy Word in the year 1611? And only in the English language?

Ridiculous! Preposterous! Please use just a little common sense here: does it sound logical to you that the Lord would stop protecting the sanctity of His Word in 1611 and only in the English language? I hope you see the absurdity of their position.

Furthermore, and here their own logic fails even further: what about readers of other languages? Are they all just left out in the dark by God? How does the Spanish, German, or French language reader handle the claim that the KJV Bible is the only Bible that can ever be used? Must they learn English if they want to read the Word of God? It always amazes me when I ask them that question. They look at me like I have three eyes and two heads and just spoke to them in an unknown tongue – because they, of course, have no logical answer to that question.

It's also a historical fact that there were publishing/printing errors in the 1611 KJV Bible, and a number of unfortunate word translation choices were made in it. With just a little research, you can find these errors documented for yourself. In fact, subsequent revisions of the 1611 KJV were made specifically to correct many of these printing errors. Here is an example regarding the "unicorn" word used in the KJV Bible: [143]

> The term "unicorn" is found nine times in the King James Version of the Bible (Num. 23:22; 24:8; Dt. 33:17; Job 39:9-10; Psa. 22:21; 29:6; 92:10; Isa. 34:7). However, unicorn does not appear at all in the American Standard Version, nor in most other more modern versions. This should be a signal that the "problem" is one of translation, rather than a problem with the original, biblical text.
>
> In ancient mythological literature, the unicorn was a horse-like animal with a prominent horn protruding from the center of its forehead. There is no evidence that this creature is alluded to in the scriptures.
>
> In the Hebrew Old Testament, the word that is found in the texts referenced above is re'em, which is translated "wild ox" in the later versions. Most scholars believe the term refers to a large, fierce ox of the ancient world — a beast that now is extinct.
>
> The translators of the Greek Old Testament (Septuagint) rendered re'mes by the Greek term monokeros ("one horn"), on the basis of certain pictographs which were among the ruins of ancient Babylon. The carvings depicted the "wild ox" in profile form, thus seeming to suggest that the creature had but a single horn (Pfeiffer et al, 1999, p. 83). [144] Out of this background derived the "one horn" perception.
>
> Biblical evidence, however, indicates otherwise. Note that in Deuteronomy 33:17, the re'em is described as having "horns" (plural), not a single horn.

So, while I recognize that the KJV Bible was nearest (temporally) to the Protestant Reformation, a time when many of the translators and publishers of the Bible paid for their faith (and their Bible translations) with their own lives, that is not a valid defense for the "KJV only" claim. It is true that the Word of God has always been under attack by men who seek to discredit it or twist it to suit their own agendas. So, I do agree they have a valid concern that modern Bibles are subject to corruption. I also agree with them that the threat of corruption is high today as the message of Christ faces increased hostility from the world, and it is also true today that nearly all of the publishers of

---

[143] Jackson, Wayne. "What Are the Unicorns and Satyrs Mentioned in the Bible?" *ChristianCourier.com*. Access date: March 18, 2019. https://christiancourier.com/articles/880-what-are-the-unicorns-and-satyrs-mentioned-in-the-bible

[144] Pfeiffer C., Vos H., & Rea J., Eds. 1999. *Wycliffe Bible Dictionary*. Peabody, MA: Hendrickson.

Bibles have non-Christian owners, which further increases the risk of corruption of God's Holy Word. For an example of this, compare Colossians 1:14 across multiple modern versions and notice how the mention of the blood of Christ has been suppressed in many of them. However, this concern of corruption by translators, editors, and publishers is not suddenly a new concern that started after the year 1611 – witness the corruption of the Latin Vulgate (which happened way before the KJV version) to support the peculiar doctrines of the Roman Catholic church.

We must remember that language continually evolves. What English words used to mean several hundred years ago doesn't always match what they mean now. For a dramatic example, see the snippet below from the original Old English version of the *Beowulf* poem:[145]

> Hwæt! Wé Gárdena
> þéodcyninga
> hú ðá æþelingas
> Oft Scyld Scéfing
> monegum maégþum
> egsode Eorle
> féasceaft funden
> wéox under wolcnum·
> oð þæt him aéghwylc

Yes, that is written in English – more specifically, it is written in what is called "Old English" of A.D. 1000. I think you will agree that you can scarcely recognize even one single word of it, let alone understand it. Later translations of that same poem are also available, but even they are starting to become harder for many to read today. Aren't we glad that the Lord didn't arbitrarily decide to stop protecting His Holy Word in only the Old English language and only in the year 1000 A.D.! Now, what makes the year 1611 any different? I think you already know the answer...nothing whatsoever.

One final counterargument to the "KJV Only" claim is that as time passes, archeologists have uncovered new finds of more ancient scripture texts and scrolls which were previously unknown; these can be used to actually increase the accuracy of newer Bible translations.

So, while there is a certain regal nature to the 1611 KJV Bible, and I use it myself, it is just <u>one of several translations</u> that a careful student of the Bible should be using. If you are happy speaking the King's English of 1611, then the KJV Bible is a good choice for you, but it is important to get a version of the Bible that you can actually read and understand. My first Bible was a NASB Bible. That is the Bible I used when I first accepted Christ, and it is also the one I still read the most today. Please see the chapter on Choosing a Bible for more information; that chapter also explains how to address the issue of Bible corruption. It must again be noted that the adage where you find one false teaching, you will almost always find others as well, has been born out in my experience with the "KJV Only" advocates. Therefore, when I see the "KJV Only" false teaching, I know other false teachings (often of a much more serious nature) are lurking nearby from the same group!

---

[145] Dr. Benjamin Slade, University of Utah, "Beowulf", http://www.heorot.dk/beowulf-rede-text.html

6.33 DEMONIC POSSESSION/EXORCISM TODAY

At the time Jesus lived, demon possession was prevalent and demonic spirits entered into and possessed both humans and animals. However, this phenomenon was temporary and localized to the time of Jesus' ministry on earth, solely to demonstrate His authority over the powers and forces of darkness and evil (Satan and his demons).

The modern superstition and belief in demon possession and the practice of "exorcism" today are not Scriptural. The Roman Catholic Church and Pentecostal (charismatics) churches, in particular, are known for this type of sensationalism and superstitious practices; but it is simply yet one more of their many false doctrines/false teachings which come from paganism, not the true Christianity of the New Testament Bible.

Wayne Jackson writes: [146]

> Do evil spirits enter into human bodies and afflict people today? I confidently affirm they do not. Unfortunately, though, some modern writers have argued that demon activity is still a part of Earth's environment.
>
> Charles Ryrie contended that certain "fallen angels" are "still free to roam the earth as demons carrying out Satan's designs" (1959, 296). [147] Merrill Unger, a respected scholar, subtitled his book, Biblical Demonology, "A Study of the Spiritual Forces Behind the Present World Unrest." [148]
>
> And several years ago a book titled UFOs, Satan and Evolution enjoyed a limited circulation in the evangelical community. Therein the author claimed that hundreds of UFO visits to Earth represented an invasion of demons. He cited one "example" where a demon raped a woman—an interesting feat for a spirit! The fact that a prominent creationist wrote the foreword for this literary fiasco remains an inexplicable mystery.
>
> The position that demon possession does not exist today can be argued from a twofold base. First, a thoughtful study of the details associated with the so-called modern examples of demon habitation reveals that these cases bear no resemblance to the genuine examples of spirit possession described in the New Testament. The contrast is dramatic.
>
> Second, a consideration of certain data set forth in the New Testament leads only to the conclusion that demon possession was a first-century experience; it was allowed for a very specific reason, and the divine concession was suspended near the end of the apostolic era.

6.34 TOUCHING VIPERS (SNAKES)

This false teaching takes two verses of the bible (Mark 16:18 and Luke 10:19) and misapplies them today in an attempt to sensationalize and justify preachers handling snakes. This false teaching often coincides with the "Charismatic" church teachings (e.g., Pentecostals). While it is true the early apostles were gifted with signs and

---

[146] Jackson, Wayne. "Demons: Ancient Superstition or Historical Reality?" *ChristianCourier.com*. Access date: November 8, 2018. https://christiancourier.com/articles/21-demons-ancient-superstition-or-historical-reality

[147] Ryrie, Charles C. 1959. Biblical Theology of the New Testament. Chicago, IL: Moody.

[148] Unger, Merrill F. 1952. Biblical Demonology. Wheaton, IL: Scripture Press.

wonders that are no longer active, that doesn't justify misapplying Scripture to teach or perform snake-handling actions today.

Animals (snakes, serpents, wolves, lions, etc.) are often used in Scripture in a symbolic sense (e.g., Psalm 91:13) as a simile or metaphor; snakes and serpents represent wicked, sinful men and their sinful natures, personality, schemes, and actions. When we "tread" on them, we are overcoming them (their evil plans and actions) by the power of the Word of God through the preaching of the (correct) gospel; we are not literally stepping on the top of a snake. There is no Scriptural basis for touching or handling serpents or snakes today as part of Christianity![149]

See also the false teaching on wrongfully interpreting symbolic or figurative language literally.

6.35 SPEAKING IN TONGUES TODAY

Similar to miracle healings (largely), demonic possession, and "snake handling," the gift of speaking in tongues was localized to the early apostolic church period and has ceased today. This capability/gift was given at times and places through the power of the Holy Spirit to early apostles to help the early church grow rapidly and also as a sign of the early apostolic authority derived from Christ.

Furthermore, the languages spoken were not made up of gibberish or "alien" utterings as is often contended. The tongues spoken were simply other human languages in order to help spread the gospel message beyond the initial Jewish Christians. There is no scriptural basis whatsoever that speaking in tongues occurs today. Those who claim to practice this today do not even do so in accord with Scripture (i.e., providing interpretation coincident with the tongue speaking); this makes them hypocrites on top of deceivers.[150]

6.36 MIRACLE HEALERS TODAY

I recognize that this can be a very emotional topic. God is completely sovereign, and He (through Christ) is the "Prince" and author of all life (Acts 3:15). He may, of course, act supernaturally and providentially today in matters of His own time and choosing. But also realize that miracle healings were numerous and widespread while Jesus was here on earth because they served to confirm His authority over all things (nature, health, and even death itself) and to confirm His claim of deity. The miracle healings also served to demonstrate His ability to reverse the fall of mankind (the curse, see Genesis 3). Miracle healings continued for a period of time in the early church and once again served the following purposes:

- Confirmed the authority of the apostles,
- Demonstrated continuity of both the message and power of Christ (i.e., His death didn't affect His power), and
- They continued to serve as a physical manifestation of Jesus restoring all things (i.e., reverse the fall/curse of humanity).

---

[149] See also: Jackson, Wayne. "Sincere but Wrong--Dead Wrong." *ChristianCourier.com*. Access date: November 8, 2018. https://christiancourier.com/articles/27-sincere-but-wrong-dead-wrong

[150] See also: Jackson, Wayne. "Can Christians 'Speak in Tongues' Today?" *ChristianCourier.com*. Access date: November 8, 2018. https://christiancourier.com/articles/626-can-christians-speak-in-tongues-today

Note also that the disciples were very careful and clear to attribute all miracles (and the power to perform them) to Christ, not to themselves or done by their own power or piety. From some of the early saints' writings, we see that miracles continued in various places at various times for about the next 200 years. But we must recognize that such events today are the exception rather than the rule. Hopefully, one is not deceived by the "miracle healers" performed on TV (or elsewhere).[151]

6.37 THE "PROSPERITY GOSPEL"

We all know who they are: they teach to widespread audiences with popular approval that you should "believe and receive" – abundance in all things material: money, wealth, possessions, fame, power, prestige, etc. These false teachings come in various forms and are often promoted with glitzy/cool slogans attached and lots of slick marketing and visual effects for the gullible. Remember, it is written:

> But false prophets also arose among the people, just as there will also be false teachers among you, who will secretly introduce destructive heresies, even denying the Master who bought them, bringing swift destruction upon themselves. Many will follow their sensuality, and because of them the way of the truth will be maligned; and in *their* greed they will exploit you with false words; their judgment from long ago is not idle, and their destruction is not asleep. – 2 Peter 2:1-3

It should shock no one whatsoever that these prosperity gospel false teachings are in direct and complete contradiction to the teachings of Scripture and the behavior of Jesus Himself while He was here on earth. The lifestyle of a Preacher/Pastor tells you what he values. We are told to "seek the things which are above" (i.e., heavenly things) and not seek the things of this world (money, fame, power, etc.). Enough said.

6.38 A "SECOND FILLING" OF THE HOLY SPIRIT

Some groups advocate that there is a "second filling" or a "Holy Spirit baptism" that believers will get after they have been born again (at some unspecified later time). There is no Scriptural support for this claim.

While Cornelius experienced a special "baptism" by the Holy Spirit, it was done as a special sign to the early church to show that Gentiles were also now to receive the Holy Spirit. This was a one-time special case event to show the early apostles (who were nearly all Jews) that God's grace now extended to the Gentiles. From the cited reference:[152]

> The purpose for which Cornelius was granted the Spirit was to demonstrate to the Jews that God was ready for the gospel to be offered to the Gentiles — which circumstance constituted a problem in the thinking of the Hebrews.

---

[151] See also: Jackson, Wayne. "What Does the Bible Say About Miracles?" *ChristianCourier.com*. Access date: November 8, 2018. https://christiancourier.com/articles/5-what-does-the-bible-say-about-miracles

[152] See also: Jackson, Wayne. "Is Holy Spirit Baptism Available Today?" *ChristianCourier.com*. Access date: November 8, 2018. https://christiancourier.com/articles/519-is-holy-spirit-baptism-available-today

In effect, the Holy Spirit baptism given to Cornelius was analogous to the pouring out of the Holy Spirit upon the Jewish apostles at Pentecost. So, the gospel thereby and thereafter spread out to go to the Gentiles also. Amen!

6.39 FEET WASHING

The example of Jesus washing the feet of the disciples was a symbolic act of humility. The incident was set in the all-important context of the disciples' selfish and prideful jockeying for position as top dog in the kingdom, and even doing so on the very eve that Jesus was to be handed over for crucifixion. So, Jesus Himself, the true Top Dog, to counter their misplaced aspirations and to teach them a lesson, humbled Himself by taking the lowest place of a servant and washed their feet.

However, some churches and groups teach that this "foot washing" must be performed literally even today. Is one really to believe that Christ taught His followers to literally wash the dirt off of millions of each other's feet every Sunday? Ridiculous, and yet that's what some contend. The act was symbolic.

Even further, those who interpret this Scripture literally do so inconsistently, for they do not perform their "foot washing" in literal agreement with Scripture as Jesus did: for they do not strip down themselves and put on a towel as Jesus did when doing the washing. If they were consistent in their literal treatment of this symbolic act, they would also perform the feet washing literally exactly as Christ did. [153]

6.40 MORMONISM MASQUERADING AS CHRISTIANITY

The Church of Jesus Christ of Latter-Day Saints, also referred to as "LDS" or "Mormons," contains foundational beliefs which deny the deity of Christ. This puts the Mormons squarely in opposition with Holy Scripture. A partial list of their false teachings includes: [154] [155]

1) Baptism for the dead (vicarious baptism),
2) Jesus is an angel, the brother of Satan (but not God),
3) We can all become "Gods" ourselves,
4) False prophets and prophecy with "special revelations" from God,
5) False books added to the Holy Bible,
6) That they are the "lost tribe" of Israel,
7) God is not eternal,
8) They deny the virgin birth of Jesus Christ,
9) Jesus was a polygamist,
10) Among others.

It is written:

---

[153] See also: Jackson, Wayne. "Did Jesus Institute Ceremonial 'Feet-Washing'?" *ChristianCourier.com*. Access date: November 8, 2018. https://christiancourier.com/articles/796-did-jesus-institute-ceremonial-feet-washing

[154] See also: Jackson, Wayne. "The Mormons Seek a Face Lift." *ChristianCourier.com*. Access date: November 8, 2018. https://christiancourier.com/articles/357-mormons-seek-a-face-lift-the

[155] See also: Jackson, Wayne. "Is the Mormon Church the Restored Church?" *ChristianCourier.com*. Access date: November 8, 2018. https://christiancourier.com/articles/204-is-the-mormon-church-the-restored-church

I am amazed that you are so quickly deserting Him who called you by the grace of Christ, for a different gospel; which is *really* not another; only there are some who are disturbing you and want to distort the gospel of Christ. But even if we, or an angel from heaven, should preach to you a gospel contrary to what we have preached to you, he is to be accursed! As we have said before, so I say again now, if any man is preaching to you a gospel contrary to what you received, he is to be accursed! – Galatians 1:6-9

To any who find themselves in this church, I pray that you will seek the truth of Scripture, and God's truth, for yourself.

6.41 DENOMINATIONALISM

There is only one true Christian Church, which was founded by Jesus, and which is comprised of all believers in Christ worldwide, called the "Church of God" or the "Church of Christ" – all other so-called "Christian churches" are counterfeits. And all the man-made divisions into the sects and denominations that we see today (Methodists, Baptists, Lutherans, Adventists, etc. ad nauseum…), each with different beliefs, doctrines, and teachings, is not Scriptural. Wayne Jackson writes: [156]

> What was the first century church called? How were the early disciples designated?
>
> There were several appellations employed to describe the first-century believers, e.g., disciples, saints, brethren, etc. But beginning in Acts 11, the early disciples were formally called Christians — first at Antioch of Syria (Acts 11:26; cf. 26:28; 1 Pet. 4:16).
>
> And interestingly enough, the word "called" in Acts 11:26 is a very special word that has to do only with a **divine** sort of calling. It is a calling that issues from God as its source. They were **divinely called** "Christians."
>
> Why would men set aside that name, and designate themselves by human heroes (e.g., Lutheran)? Or name themselves after some form of organization, (e.g., Presbyterian)? Or adopt titles according to some individual point of doctrine they espouse, (e.g., Baptist)? There is no scriptural basis for this common practice.
>
> Tell me please, why are those who profess allegiance to Jesus Christ dissatisfied with simply wearing the name "Christian"? Why are they not known as just "churches of Christ" (Rom. 16:16) or "churches of God" (1 Cor. 1:2) — either appellation being entirely scriptural. There is no solitary, **exclusive** name for the church. But whatever you call it, you need to call it what it **is**, and not what it is **not**.
>
> The church is not a Pentecostal church just because it was established on the day of Pentecost. The church is not a Baptist church just because it advocates baptism. The church is not a Congregational church just because it is organized congregationally. The church is the church of God (1 Cor. 1:2), because God planned it.
>
> Congregations are the churches of Christ (Rom. 16:16), because Christ gave his life in order to bring them into existence. The New Testament indicates that we

---

[156] Jackson, Wayne. "Identifying the Church of the New Testament." *ChristianCourier.com*. Access date: May 15, 2019. https://christiancourier.com/articles/470-identifying-the-church-of-the-new-testament

ought to speak as the oracles of God (1 Pet. 4:11), which means we ought to express biblical concepts with biblical terms whenever possible.

Christ prayed specifically for unity among Christians (see John 17), and it is written: "There is one body and one Spirit, just as also you were called in one hope of your calling; one Lord, one faith, one baptism, one God and Father of all who is over all and through all and in all" (Ephesians 4:4-6). The sectarians and denominations of today disregard that prayer of Christ for unity.

An excerpt from *The Christian Church, Its Rise and Progress* by H.M. Riggle is helpful here: [157]

> The church of God includes the family of God, and it is but one family in Heaven and on earth; therefore, it includes in its membership every Christian, all the redeemed in paradise and all the saved on earth. Including all Christians, it is not a sect, but is the whole. Now, a church that does not include in its membership all Christians in Heaven and earth cannot be God's church, and hence it is a sect. All the religious denominations taken together come far short of including all Christians. Before any of these institutions arose, there were millions of Christians. None of the blood-washed saints in paradise are now members of any of these earth-born institutions; and right here upon earth there are tens of thousands of happy saints in robes of righteousness who have come out and stand clear of creed-bound churches, and there are many thousands of others who are saved from sin and have never joined any of them. Therefore, all denominations put together, both Roman, Greek, and Protestant, do not constitute the universal church, but are only sects.
>
> In holding membership in the one universal church and in no other, we stand clear of the sin of division; are members of no sect, but members of that church to which all the saved in Heaven and earth belong.

And more: [158]

> So the church of God stands out before us the most beautiful, visible institution on earth.
>
> Sects, then, are not necessary to make the church visible. In this respect they are worthless. This theory is generally circulated by sectarians in defense of their own rival organizations, that the constitution of sects is essential to the visible manifestation of the church. A sect is a portion "cut off." Is there any sense, reason, or divine truth in the teaching that an invisible body is made visible by cutting off a portion of it? None of the present sects came into existence until the third century. Was God's church an invisible thing on earth for nearly three hundred years? Who can affirm that the multitude of sects have made visible the church of God, from which they are severed by their particular creeds? We affirm in the presence of the Judge of all men, with a clear consciousness of His truth to support our proposition, that the creation of the sects of Christendom have had exactly the opposite effect.
>
> Their traditions have made "the Word of God of none effect." Their confusing creeds, heaps of rubbish, and interminable machinery have utterly

---

[157] Riggle, H.M. (1912), *The Christian Church, Its Rise and Progress*, (The Gospel Trumpet Company).

[158] Riggle, H.M. (1912), *The Christian Church, Its Rise and Progress*, (The Gospel Trumpet Company).

subverted and well-nigh hidden the church that Jesus built. As the historian D'Aubigne says, in the third century an "earthly association," "an external organization," was gradually substituted for "the interior and spiritual communion which is the essence of the religion of God." Then, says the historian, "the living church retired gradually within the lonely sanctuary of a few solitary hearts"; that is, the real church of God was almost hidden from view by the overspread pomp of the false. So, then, men's sects do not make visible God's church, but, on the contrary, obstruct her life and obscure her glory. These are facts of the history that no honest and intelligent man can deny.

The Babel of human sects long obscured the sight of the church of the first-born.

Wayne Jackson writes: [159]

Denominationalism

The word "denominate" means "to give a name to, to designate." It is a perfectly respectable term. If one cashes a two-hundred-dollar bank draft, he may request currency in "denominations" of tens and twenties. In this sense the word merely signifies a separation into various divisions by name. And so the term itself is not "tainted."

"Denomination" takes on a less-than-ideal sense when one considers its popular use in the lexicon of "Christendom." "Christendom" is a term that embraces the entire religious terrain that professes any identification – however remote the connection may be – with Jesus Christ. This would include every kind of organism, from the Unitarian Universalist Church, to the various cults that allege an association with Christ (e.g., Christian Science, the Watchtower movement, etc.).

One authority defines denominationalism in the following fashion.

"The system and ideology founded on the division of the religious population into numerous ecclesiastical bodies, each stressing particular values or traditions and each competing with the other in the same community under substantial conditions of freedom" (Brauer, pp. 262-263). [160]

Within this definition several flaws are revealed that mar the system.

(1) Denominationalism is the result of division – a division, incidentally, that frequently is applauded.

(2) The ideology accommodates variant "ecclesiastical [church] bodies" with distinctive, doctrinal differences.

(3) Denominationalism tends to focus more upon tradition and preferential values than Scripture.

(4) The system engenders a spirit of adversarial rivalry rather than cooperation.

(5) The denominational concept encourages the idea that the freedom to differ on major points of doctrine is a healthy spiritual phenomenon.

---

[159] Jackson, Wayne. "Denominationalism – Permissible or Reprehensible?" *ChristianCourier.com*. Access date: November 9, 2018. https://christiancourier.com/articles/798-denominationalism-permissible-or-reprehensible

[160] Jerald C. Brauer, Ed., *The Westminster Dictionary of Church History*, Philadelphia: The Westminster Press, 1971

Each of these propositions is antagonistic to biblical truth. …

Conclusion

The spirit of denominational compromise is steadily invading more and more churches that once repudiated the disposition. Prominent personalities openly advocate that the "mode" of baptism is irrelevant, or that the rite, in terms of its purpose, may be received either as "for" the remission of sins, or "because of" the remission of sins; it does not matter. Doors of fellowship are flung open, and sectarian groups are embraced.

Far too many imagine that the church is a "democracy" in which the people decide what is permissible procedure, rather than recognizing that Christ's church is a kingdom. And the King is the author of its law (1 Cor. 9:21; Gal. 6:2).

Denominationalism is wrong. There must be no compromise on this issue. Christians can and should oppose the system compassionately and courteously, but it must be resisted relentlessly. To neglect to do so is to fail in one's responsibility.

Wayne Jackson further writes: [161]

> The New Testament is the only place to which we can turn to learn about the church of Christ. We recall that the church is described as the eternal purpose of God (Eph. 3:9-11). It is obviously very important. It is necessary, therefore, that we are educated by the New Testament and not by the ideas of men.
>
> The New Testament teaches us what the church is, and what the church should be today, according to the plan of God.
>
> First, the church was built and purchased by Christ (Matt. 16:18; Acts 20:28). No one has the right to start a church as a divinely approved institution (cf. 1 Cor. 1:10-13). Christ, the Son of God, is the only one qualified, and he has established his church (cf. Eph. 4:4; 1:22-23).
>
> After religious division arose within the church at Corinth, Paul asked some probing questions. "Is Christ divided? Was Paul crucified for you? Or were you baptized in the name of Paul?" (1 Cor. 1:13). The church belongs to Christ on the basis of these gospel truths. He died for it. He built it. He lays down requirements through which we can belong to him. The church belongs to Christ. He is the head of the church (Col. 1:18).
>
> Second, the church that belongs to Christ began on the day of Pentecost as recorded in Acts 2. Religious bodies that have their origin in Rome, Zurich, London, or any other place but Jerusalem, are ones that started in the wrong places. The Lord's church was founded by Christ through the preaching of the apostles in Jerusalem, corresponding to Old Testament prophecy (Is. 2:2-4).
>
> When the gospel was preached by Paul, and others, throughout the ancient world, different denominations were not set up. Whenever the pure gospel of Christ was taught, just as it was preached for the first time in Jerusalem, the result was simply Christians who belonged to Christ — collectively the church of Christ — when people obeyed the gospel.
>
> If there was no congregation of the Lord's church in your hometown, and you started teaching others about the death of Jesus, the benefits of his redemptive blood, and the requirements of the New Testament to have the forgiveness of sins

---

[161] Jackson, Jason. "What Is the Church of Christ?" *ChristianCourier.com*. Access date: May 15, 2019. https://christiancourier.com/articles/1205-what-is-the-church-of-christ

— you would not be setting up a denomination. Rather, you would be following the New Testament pattern, and those who obey the gospel would be a part of the Lord's church. The church of Christ would then exist in your hometown, and the New Testament alone would be its guide for work and worship.

Third, only divinely appointed names were worn by the church. Such designations like church of Christ (Rom. 16:16) and church of God (1 Cor. 1:2) are scriptural names that describe the church as belonging to Christ and God.

"The church of Christ" is not a denominational title that describes a religious institution established by men. Rather, it is the collective reference to the people of God in the world — people who follow the New Testament teaching regarding the church.

See also the chapter on Finding a Church.

6.42 12-STEP RECOVERY PROGRAMS

There are many "12-step" programs for dealing with addictions. While these man-made programs might work for a few people (often only for a short time), there is only one way to completely 100% cure/heal any addiction: and that is through Christ. It is only by coming to Jesus and turning your life over to Him completely every single day that the grip of addiction is broken. Once you come to Christ and fully commit (dedicate) your life to Him, He removes the addiction. We are, of course, not absolved of our own responsibility for choosing not to drink, even after we have dedicated our lives to the Lord, but you will now be able to do that by the power of Christ living in you!

Many are unaware that most of the 12-step programs were originally based and founded upon Christian principles. However, once again, as with the ways of man, those have since been abandoned and "liberalized," and they have pushed God and Jesus completely out of the program. But know that it is not the 12-step program that cures the addiction; it is the power of God Almighty living inside you, abiding in you, which casts out the addiction! Friend, or brother or sister in Christ, I know what I'm talking about here – I've been there personally, for I have lived this myself. Please see my testimony at the end of this book.

Furthermore, those who are trapped in an addiction are doubly lost: first to the addiction and second to Christ (eternally). Even if by some slim chance you manage to overcome (control) an addiction through one of these programs (or by sheer willpower), you will still be under bondage to sin and death without Christ. When you come to Christ, you fully break BOTH your bondage under sin and the addiction at the same time – and you do so by the power of Christ living in you, not by your own willpower or "12-step" programs:

> "'Not by might nor by power, but by My Spirit,' says the LORD of hosts." – Zechariah 4:6

6.43 JESUS ALREADY RETURNED IN A.D. 70
(The "A.D. 70 Doctrine," "Realized Eschatology," or Full/Radical Preterism)

This false teaching claims that all of the prophecy given in the book of Revelation (and indeed, the entire New Testament) was fulfilled in and by the year A.D. 70 with the destruction of Jerusalem – and that Christ returned at that time! They therefore falsely teach that there is no future return of Christ, ever. Frankly, it's too lengthy to debate and refute this false teaching here. The reader is encouraged to seek truth. Please note that the Book of Revelation was written to Christians (the "bond-servants of Christ"), not to the Jews; the Jews had many prior OT writings and some of the NT writings (e.g., the first part of Matthew 24) to warn them, they didn't need any more warnings.

This false teaching goes by several names (with slight variations) such as: Preterism, Radical Preterism, the "A.D. 70 Doctrine," "Realized Eschatology," etc., and has been around for a very long time. It seems to get reincarnated every few decades and given a shiny new name, so it all appears new again to the uninformed – but be not deceived.

6.44 MYSTICAL SIGNS BEFORE/PREDICTING CHRIST'S RETURN

Many of those who teach and preach the false teachings identified in this book also watch, track and even prophesy about various heavenly events as if they were literal fulfillment of Biblical prophecy (i.e., astrology, movements in the comets, planetary alignments, "blood moons," etc.). This is nothing less than pagan mysticism, witchcraft, and sorcery – all of which are strongly condemned in the Bible.

It's not uncommon for those who engage in such things to also have false teachings on the book of Revelation, the kingdom of God, the "Secret Rapture," the "Third Temple," etc. They all seem to go hand in hand – where there is one of these false teachings, others almost always abound also. Again, I say, this is simply mysticism and sorcery and is strongly condemned in the Bible; and those who practice such will not inherit the Kingdom of Heaven.

No more signs and wonders will be given to this generation until Christ returns, literally and visibly for all to see worldwide "when the Lord Jesus will be revealed from heaven with His mighty angels in flaming fire" (2 Thessalonians 1:7), which is also the great Day of Judgment.

6.45 WRONGFULLY INTERPRETING SYMBOLIC OR FIGURATIVE LANGUAGE LITERALLY

The Bible is composed of many different styles of writing. Some parts of Scripture (including Bible prophecy) are written in symbolic/figurative language instead of literal language. Furthermore, Bible prophecy can also have literal or spiritual fulfillment. Wrongfully interpreting symbolic/figurative statements in Scripture as literal is the source of many false teachings and results in bizarre interpretations of Bible prophecy (particularly related to matters of end-times eschatology). For example, many false teachers (yes, the "wolves" again) teach and preach that all Bible prophecy must be fulfilled literally; however, I have already shown you that this is not the case.

The practice of wrongful interpretation goes way beyond just Bible prophecy, as discussed by Wayne Jackson:[162]

An Introduction to Bible Figures of Speech

How dreary human communication would be were it not for the figures of speech that adorn language. In fact, it scarcely would be possible to convey ideas meaningfully if figurative speech were not a part of our vocabulary.

Adam's first recorded words contain some thought figures. Of Eve he said, "This is now bone of my bones, and flesh of my flesh..." (Genesis 2:23). This delightful creation was much more than mere "flesh" and "bones," but on this occasion she was represented by two principal elements of her physical composition.

Some of the initial words of the Creator to Adam were of a figurative thrust. To the first man the Lord warned (with reference to the forbidden fruit): "... in the day that you eat thereof, you shall surely die" (Genesis 2:17). That Adam did not literally die the day of his sin (though the aging process commenced from the time of his expulsion from Eden) is apparent, for he ultimately lived to the age of 930 years (Genesis 5:5). The expression "die" doubtless had a spiritual significance beyond that of physical degeneration. "Death" also signifies a religious or moral separation from fellowship with God (cf. Isaiah 59:1-2; Ephesians 2:1).

One should not be surprised, therefore, that the Holy Scriptures abound with figures of speech. This reality does not detract from the value of divine communication through the Scriptures; rather, it enhances the power and beauty of God's Word.

The Bible abounds with a great variety of figures of speech. In 1899 E.W. Bullinger produced a massive work of more than 1,100 pages dealing with biblical figures of speech. Therein he classified some 200 different figures, many of which were subdivided into different variations, so that the total number finally catalogued was more than 500 terms (Bullinger, p. ix).[163]

And:[164]

How Do I Distinguish the "Literal" from the "Figurative"?

"I do not understand why ministers will teach that one passage in the Bible is 'literal,' while they say that another one is 'figurative.' For instance, in one of your articles you argue that the 'days' of the creation week are literal (twenty-four-hour days). On the other hand, you say that the '1,000 years' mentioned in Revelation, chapter 20, is 'figurative.' Why do you go back and forth from literal to figurative?"

Your question is a very reasonable one and we are happy to clarify this matter.

---

[162] Jackson, Wayne. "An Introduction to Bible Figures of Speech." *ChristianCourier.com*. Access date: March 18, 2019. https://www.christiancourier.com/articles/1114-introduction-to-bible-figures-of-speech-an

[163] Bullinger, E. W. 1968. *Figures of Speech Used in the Bible*. Grand Rapids, MI: Baker.

[164] Jackson, Wayne. "How Do I Distinguish the 'Literal' from the 'Figurative'?" *ChristianCourier.com*. Access date: March 18, 2019. https://christiancourier.com/articles/694-how-do-i-distinguish-the-literal-from-the-figurative

The Scriptures abound with a great variety of figures of speech. In 1899, E.W. Bullinger produced a massive work of more than 1,100 pages dealing with biblical figures of speech. Therein he classified some 200 different figures, many of which were subdivided into different variations, so that the total number catalogued finally was more than 500 (Bullinger, p. ix).[165]

A Figure Defined

A figure of speech occurs when a word, phrase, or sentence is employed in a sense other than the usual or literal sense it has naturally. The purpose behind the use of a figurative expression is to intensify the idea being conveyed. The figure adds emphasis, feeling, and color to the thought presented. It is a mistake to assume that when a figure of speech is utilized the force of the statement or argument is weakened; actually, just the reverse is true.

It is very important, however, to be able to distinguish the figurative from the literal. A failure to discern the difference, in various biblical contexts, has resulted in much error.

How to Identify Figurative Language

Just as "beauty" is said to be "in the eye of the beholder," unfortunately the identification of figurative language in the Scriptures is sometimes "in the eye" of the interpreter. By this we mean there is considerable confusion in the religious world in the matter of distinguishing between literal and symbolic terminology. There are, however, some common sense principles which may (and must) be employed in the identification process.

Words must be interpreted literally unless the sense implies an *impossibility*.

For example, John closes his Gospel account with the declaration that should all the deeds of Jesus, during his earthly ministry, be fully recorded, not even the world itself could hold the books that might catalog them (Jn. 21:25). This language is acknowledged as "hyperbole," "hyperbolic."

A hyperbole (meaning "to throw above") is an exaggeration for the purpose of emphasis. John's design was to show that the miracles delineated in his inspired narrative were merely representative of what the Savior did; the list of only seven signs that the apostle mentioned was far from exhaustive.

Words must be interpreted literally unless the sense implies a *contradiction*.

In the book of Revelation, the final abode of the redeemed is depicted as a "holy city" (cf. Heb. 11:10,16). One of the features of that city was its wall, that rested on "twelve foundations," upon which were written the names of the "twelve apostles" (Rev. 21:14). The numeral "twelve," as used here, cannot be literal, for there were thirteen apostles (the original twelve, minus Judas, plus Matthias, plus Paul). The number "twelve" came to be used as a symbol of the apostolic group, even when the number "twelve" was not precise. After Judas died, yet before Matthias was chosen, Jesus (following his resurrection) appeared to "the twelve" (1 Cor. 15:5). "Twelve," therefore, in Revelation 21:14 is employed symbolically for the apostolic company, without literal, mathematical precision.

---

[165] Bullinger, E. W. 1968. *Figures of Speech Used in the Bible*. Grand Rapids, MI: Baker.

Words must be interpreted literally unless the sense implies an *absurdity*.

The Scriptures use the term "face" dozens of times in a figurative sense, e.g., face of the deep (Gen. 1:2), face of the earth (Gen. 1:29), face of the ground (Gen. 2:6), etc. Obviously, to press the word "face," in a literal sense, would imply an absurdity with reference to the sea, the earth, etc. Clearly, then, these uses are figurative.

The *nature* of a biblical book may provide a clue, suggesting that the student is to watch for an abundance of figures of speech.

This is true of certain Old Testament books, such as portions of Ezekiel, Daniel, and Zechariah. But there is no clearer example of this than that of the concluding book of the New Testament, Revelation.

The apocalyptic document begins with the notation that Christ "signified" the message, via his messenger, to the apostle John (1:1). The verb "signified" derives from semaino, which in early Greek meant "to show by a sign, indicate, make known, point out" (Liddell-Scott, p. 1448).[166]

Vincent cites John's use of the term in his Gospel (12:33) where Jesus, in symbolic fashion, identified the method of his death by means of the expression "lifted up," which hinted of the crucifixion (cf. also Jn. 21:19). He further notes that the term "signified" is "appropriate to the symbolic character of the revelation" (Vincent, p. 564).[167]

What About the "Days" of Genesis?

Now regarding the original question, how is one able to say that the "days" of the creation week are literal days, while the "1,000 years" of Revelation 20:1ff represents a figure of speech? The answer is this: by the respective contexts of the two portions of Scripture, and the language considerations found therein.

1. The "days" of the creation week are divided into periods of light and darkness (vv. 4-5). The "days" are distinguished from "years" (v. 14). And the "days" are subsequently defined by Moses as the same type of "day" as the Sabbath which the Hebrews were required to observe (Ex. 20:11). There are other reasons for the view that the creation days must be literal, but this should suffice for the present. See our "Archives" section for June 15, 2000 (The Creation "Days" —Literal or Figurative.

2. Regarding the "thousand years" of Revelation 20, it should be observed that the opening of the book itself provides caution that this is a document characterized by symbols (see "signified" – 1:1). In addition, the "thousand years" of Revelation 20 is nestled in the midst of a number of other dramatic figures —a pit, a great chain, the dragon/serpent, thrones, a beast, a mysterious "mark," resurrections, etc. Why should the pit, chain, dragon, etc., be viewed as figures, and yet the "thousand years" be singled out as literal? That defies common sense. The fact is, the numeral "thousand" is found more than twenty times in Revelation, and not once is it employed in a literal sense. In Chapter 20, the most likely interpretation of the number is that of "completeness." As William

---

[166] Liddell-Scott, *A Greek-English Lexicon*, Oxford: Clarendon, 1869.

[167] Vince, M.R.. *Word Studies in the New Testament*, Wilmington, DE: Associated Publishers, 1972.

Milligan observed: "'[T]he thousand years' mentioned in the passage express no period of time. They embody an idea; and that idea, whether applied to the subjugation of Satan or to the triumph of the saints is the idea of completeness or perfection" (Milligan, p. 913).[168]

There are, therefore, sound exegetical reasons for making a distinction between the literal "days" of Genesis 1, and the figurative "years" of Revelation 20.

The reader who pursues truth must be able to discern for themselves where wrongful symbolic/figurative interpretation is being made and not just blindly believe whatever they hear taught or preached as biblical truth. As I said, this only touches on this subject. I highly recommend reading the book *Biblical Figures of Speech* by Wayne Jackson.

6.46 ALIENS AND THE NEPHILIM

Fanciful theories and bizarre interpretations of Scripture lead to assertions that angels "mated" with human females producing half-alien/half-human offspring. This is all false nonsense conjured up by the mind of mystical man. These false teachings mesmerize those with "itching ears" (2 Timothy 4:3-4).

The "Sons of God" identified in Genesis 6:4 were those human males who followed God. They then intermarried with disobedient/heathen women who did not follow God. This is exactly analogous to what the ancient Jews did when they married foreign women, who subsequently turned them away from God. The "Nephilim" were men of "renown," they were not gigantic monsters or half-alien/half-human beings. Renown simply means that they were men of great reputation. Much like today, when we say that the CEO of a Big Corporation is a man of renown, or that the President of the United States is a man of renown, we mean that they are well and widely known – that they have a wide reputation (and not always a good one). That reputation often conveys some characteristic about those people (for good or bad, for God or away from God).

This false teaching of bizarre alien-like half-angel/half-man creatures then morphs its way into further mysticism and fantasies of man, including UFOs, aliens from outer space, creatures from Antarctica, etc. There simply is no end to the folly and madness of the mind of man!

6.47 CULTS THAT DENY CHRIST

Have you ever read the foundational documents and/or statement of faith/belief of the church you attend? I ask this because many, in fact, have never done so. Some who are reading this book may therefore already be part of a church that claims to be "Christian," a church of Christ if you will, but when you learn their true fundamental beliefs and statement of faith, you realize that it's not really Christian at all. These cults look (to the casual observer) like they believe in the gospel message of Scripture, but when you actually go read their foundational beliefs (which are available if you seek them out), you will find that they simply believe in a scheme of man.

---

[168] Milligan, William. *An Exposition of the Bible, Vol. VI*, Hartford, CT: S.S. Scranton, 1903

Many of these cults use the name of Jesus (or Jesus Christ) in their own church names and in their teachings. They may even <u>appear</u> to believe in the Jesus of the Bible, but upon closer examination, you will see that their core beliefs deny Christ in one way or another, such as:

- Denying that Jesus is God,
- Denying that Jesus has existed eternally (i.e., Jesus was a created being, and that Jesus had a beginning),
- Claiming that Jesus is just "an angel" (e.g., Michael) or the "brother of Satan,"
- Claiming that God is "flesh and bones" (instead of spirit),
- Claiming that there are other ways to heaven,
- Claiming man can become "a god" (apparently, one of many gods),
- Or other heresies

However, it is written:

> I am amazed that you are so quickly deserting Him who called you by the grace of Christ, for a different gospel; which is *really* not another; only there are some who are disturbing you and want to distort the gospel of Christ. But even if we, or an angel from heaven, should preach to you a gospel contrary to what we have preached to you, he is to be accursed! As we have said before, so I say again now, if any man is preaching to you a gospel contrary to what you received, he is to be accursed! – Galatians 1:6-9

I therefore strongly encourage you to seek out and read (or re-read) the core beliefs of your church. Know that some cults go to great lengths to hide their true core statements/beliefs from you. And after doing so, you may need to confront the cold hard reality that you are indeed in a cult that doesn't actually worship "the living and true God" – Jesus of Nazareth, the Christ, the Son of God, and the Son of Man, eternally existing, second Person of the Holy Trinity.

You may also find that your church has writings that either add to or take away from the Word of God as given in Scripture. Many of these cults even have their own special prophet(s) who claim to have received special (and private) messages, inspiration, and revelations directly from God. Such things have no support from Scripture. Scripture says that God must be worshipped "in spirit and in truth"; Scripture also teaches us that the canon of Scripture was completed and closed up and that special prophecy, visions, and dreams have ceased.

These cults combine and utilize multiple false teachings that appear to be very "biblical" on the surface, but which actually are a man-made façade of lies, myths, superstitions, rituals, rites, "traditions," and false teachings. Woe to any group/sect/cult that denies the deity of Christ and/or His sacrifice on the cross! Any cults or church which denies the deity of Christ is not Christian – no matter how hard they try to convince you that they are, or how boldly they use His holy name in their church name, or how clever their arguments are in support of their denial of Jesus' divinity.

6.48 SALVATION IS A FREE GIFT OF GOD, SO NO HUMAN ACTION IS REQUIRED

Some contend that since Scripture describes salvation as a "free gift" of God (Romans 3:24, Romans 6:23), man isn't under obligation to do anything to receive it – such as being baptized, being obedient to Christ, etc. Wayne Jackson has written on this matter:[169]

> Salvation is wonderfully described in the New Testament as a **free gift**. This terminology is employed in order to emphasize that God is under no **compulsion** to offer it.
>
> Man, by his choice, has rebelled against the Lord. He thus has **earned** the penalty of death (cf. "wages" in Rom. 6:28).
>
> Was the Creator morally obligated to offer salvation? No he was not. However, he has extended redemption to his creation as a matter of pure love and grace (Jn. 3:16; Eph. 2:8-9).
>
> From this perspective, forgiveness is depicted as a gift.
>
> **A Gift Can Be Conditional**
>
> The term "gift" (even "free gift"), however, does not necessarily exclude the idea of a condition being imposed. Note the following:
>
> **Jericho: A Conditional Gift**
>
> God promised the city of Jericho to the Hebrews as a gift (Joshua 6:2, 16), yet the Israelites were required to submit to several conditions in order to receive the gift (Josh. 6:3ff; Heb. 11:30).
>
> **Saved from Shipwreck: On Condition**
>
> During Paul's voyage to Rome, the ship upon which he sailed encountered a life-threatening storm. It was feared that all would be lost.
>
> Yet God, on account of Paul's fidelity, "granted" (charizomai — to give freely) to him the lives of all that sailed with him (Acts 27:24).
>
> In spite of that promise, the apostle later informed the centurion in charge of the vessel:
>
> "Except [a condition] these abide in the ship, you [plural] cannot be saved" (27:31).
>
> **Work for the Gift**
>
> Jesus himself had clearly taught this principle. To the disciples he admonished:
>
> "Work not for the food which is perishing, but [work—the verb is understood] for the food which is abiding unto eternal life, which the Son of man shall give unto you" (Jn. 6:27).
>
> A gift, then, does not exclude the necessity to lovingly accept or "receive" that gift (cf. Jn. 1:11-12). And this is accomplished in obeying the Lord, and at the point of one's immersion in water (Acts 2:38; 22:16).

---

[169] Jackson, Wayne. "Must We Do Something To Receive the Free Gift of Salvation?" *ChristianCourier.com*. Access date: May 23, 2019. https://christiancourier.com/articles/176-must-we-do-something-to-receive-the-free-gift-of-salvation

Salvation a Free Gift Received by Obedient Heart

Even within the book of Romans this truth is apparent.

While salvation is therein represented as that which is "freely given," the apostle nonetheless forcefully argues that these saints were "delivered" and "made free from sin" by virtue of their having "obeyed from the heart that form of teaching" which had been proclaimed to them (Rom. 6:17).

Earlier, in this same chapter, the apostle, with greater specificity, affirms that the Roman Christians began to walk in **newness of life** (i.e., salvation) at the point of their having been **united with Christ in the likeness of his burial and resurrection**.

This occurred when they were buried in baptism and raised therefrom (Rom. 6:3-10).

It is thus quite clear that salvation, as a free gift, and the need to obey the Lord, are not mutually exclusive propositions.

Let men then receive God's free gift by submitting to his will.

6.49 A CHRISTIAN NO LONGER SINS

Some claim and teach that a Christian no longer commits any sin (ever) after they are born again. This is a false teaching, for the life of a Christian is one of continued repentance. We will still sin while we are short of glory here on earth, even after being born again of the Spirit, for we are still in fleshly bodies in this fallen world. Others misconstrue 1 John 3:9 to mean that a born-again Christian never sins. Wayne Jackson writes on this misconception:[170]

> In one of his epistles, the apostle John writes:
>
> *"Whosoever is begotten of God does not sin, because his [God's] seed abides in him: and he cannot [ou dunamai] sin, because he is begotten of God"* (1 John 3:9).
>
> The apostle is not suggesting that it is impossible for the child of God to sin (cf. 1 John 1:8-9; 2:1-2); rather, he is stating that when divine truth becomes resident in the heart, one will choose not to yield ourselves to a habitual, unrestrained life of sin. The term "cannot" is used in the sense of a **moral imperative**.

A Christian's life is one of continued repentance and continued avoidance of deliberate, willful sin. That we may stumble and fall at times is normal, for we are human; and in that case, the apostle John reassures us that we have a faithful Advocate in Christ:

> My little children, I am writing these things to you so that you may not sin. And if anyone sins, we have an Advocate with the Father, Jesus Christ the righteous. – 1 John 2:1

> If we say that we have no sin, we are deceiving ourselves and the truth is not in us. If we confess our sins, He is faithful and righteous to forgive us our sins and to

---

[170] Jackson, Wayne. "Why Couldn't Jesus Perform Miracles in His Hometown?" *ChristianCourier.com*. Access date: May 15, 2019. https://christiancourier.com/articles/983-why-couldnt-jesus-perform-miracles-in-his-hometown

cleanse us from all unrighteousness. If we say that we have not sinned, we make Him a liar and His word is not in us. – 1 John 1:8-10

Matthew Henry writes on 1 John 1:8-10: [171]

> Here, I. The apostle, having supposed that even those of this heavenly communion have yet their sin, proceeds here to justify that supposition, and this he does by showing the dreadful consequences of denying it, and that in two particulars: - 1. If we say, We have no sin, we deceive ourselves, and the truth is not in us, 1Jn 1:8. We must beware of deceiving ourselves in denying or excusing our sins. The more we see them the more we shall esteem and value the remedy. If we deny them, the truth is not in us, either the truth that is contrary to such denial (we lie in denying our sin), or the truth of religion, is not in us. The Christian religion is the religion of sinners, of such as have sinned, and in whom sin in some measure still dwells. The Christian life is a life of continued repentance, humiliation for and mortification of sin, of continual faith in, thankfulness for, and love to the Redeemer, and hopeful joyful expectation of a day of glorious redemption, in which the believer shall be fully and finally acquitted, and sin abolished for ever. 2. If we say, We have not sinned, we make him a liar, and his word is not in us, 1Jn 1:10. The denial of our sin not only deceives ourselves, but reflects dishonour upon God. It challenges his veracity. He has abundantly testified of, and testified against, the sin of the world. And the Lord said in his heart (determined thus with himself), I will not again curse the ground (as he had then lately done) for man's sake; for (or, with the learned bishop Patrick, though) the imagination of man's heart is evil from his youth, Gen 8:21. But God has given his testimony to the continued sin and sinfulness of the world, by providing a sufficient effectual sacrifice for sin, that will be needed in all ages, and to the continued sinfulness of believers themselves by requiring them continually to confess their sins, and apply themselves by faith to the blood of that sacrifice. And therefore, if we say either that we have not sinned or do not yet sin, the word of God is not in us, neither in our minds, as to the acquaintance we should have with it, nor in our hearts, as to the practical influence it should have upon us.
>
> II. The apostle then instructs the believer in the way to the continued pardon of his sin. Here we have, 1. His duty in order thereto: If we confess our sins, 1Jn 1:9. Penitent confession and acknowledgment of sin are the believer's business, and the means of his deliverance from his guilt. And, 2. His encouragement thereto, and assurance of the happy issue. This is the veracity, righteousness, and clemency of God, to whom he makes such confession: He is faithful and just to forgive us our sins, and to cleanse us from all unrighteousness, 1Jn 1:9. God is faithful to his covenant and word, wherein he has promised forgiveness to penitent believing confessors. He is just to himself and his glory who has provided such a sacrifice, by which his righteousness is declared in the justification of sinners. He is just to his Son who has not only sent him for such service, but promised to him that those who come through him shall be forgiven on his account. By his knowledge (by the believing apprehension of him) shall my righteous servant justify many, Isa 53:11. He is clement and gracious also, and so will forgive, to

---

[171] Henry, Matthew. *Exposition of the Old and New Testaments*, London. 1706-1710/1721.

the contrite confessor, all his sins, cleanse him from the guilt of all unrighteousness, and in due time deliver him from the power and practice of it.

So, if you sinned yesterday, confess it and repent and let His peace guard your heart. Stay focused only on Jesus each day. Remember we have these powerful verses to help remind us that:

> The LORD'S lovingkindnesses indeed never cease,
> For His compassions never fail.
> *They* are new every morning;
> Great is Your faithfulness.
> "The LORD is my portion," says my soul,
> "Therefore I have hope in Him."
> The LORD is good to those who wait for Him,
> To the person who seeks Him.
> *It is* good that he waits silently
> For the salvation of the LORD. – Lamentations 3:22-26

Wayne Jackson further writes on 1 John 2:1-2:[172]

> There are several points in this passage that are worthy of notation. Let us briefly concentrate upon them and the meaning they contain for our lives.
>
> 1) The phrase "little children" is found nine times in this epistle. It reflects the tender love that the apostle had for his fellow Christians. Would it not be wonderful if more of God's children would treat one another as "family"? This disposition is possible—even when we disagree. Can we not consider each other as "brothers," rather than "enemies" (2 Thes 3:15)? This does not mean that we are allowed to ignore error; it does address the attitude we should adopt in dealing with our spiritual kinsmen.
>
> 2) The text underscores the power of the written word; John hopes that his message will inoculate against sin in his brethren's lives. There are those who believe that an inward, supernatural operation of the Holy Spirit guards them against wrongdoing. John knows nothing of the "zap" ideology. In fact, if such were the case, one could only conclude that the Holy Spirit is doing a mediocre job—since even Christians cannot live above sin. According to the apostle, the *written word* is the antidote against evil (Psa. 119:11). And when there is failure, the flaw is with *us*—not the Spirit of God.
>
> 3) John acknowledges human weakness; he takes note of the fact that sin will overtake us on occasion (see: 1:8; cf. Rom. 7:15; 1 Cor. 10:12). I shall never forget the conversation that I once had with a Christian brother who, deadly serious, stated that he had finally graduated to the level where he sinned no more! I could only listen in stunned amazement, noting that he had eclipsed even God's apostle. Perhaps John anticipated such arrogance when he wrote, "If we say that we have [present tense] no sin, we deceive ourselves, and the truth is not in us" (1 Jn. 1:8). When we do yield to sin, if the evil is not remedied

---

[172] Jackson, Wayne. "A Message from John." *ChristianCourier.com*. Access date: May 16, 2019. https://christiancourier.com/articles/698-message-from-john-a

in the biblical way, even Christians can be cut off from Heaven's grace (Gal. 5:4)—contrary to the dogma of Calvin.
4) When the child of God does sin, however, he need not feel that his situation is hopeless. If he confesses his wrongdoing (1:9), and attempts to turn from such in repentance (Acts 8:22), his "Advocate" (*parakletos* – a term meaning, "to call to one's side") is available to help him. The idea suggested is a legal one; Jesus is the "counsel for the defense" on our behalf. Based upon his own flawless record (cf. "righteous" v.1b), and his atoning mission (1:7), he is qualified to plead our cause. If we practice "walking in the light" (the grammatical tense implies sustained activity), our case will not be lost!

6.50 THE NICENE CREED

Many people (even Christians) simply accept whatever they have heard repeated often, frequently, and loudly (usually over an extended period of time) as truth and assume it to be correct without challenging it, inspecting it, studying it, and being like the Bereans – checking to see if what is being repeated actually matches the truth of Scripture.

One such example of this happening has been the "sinner's prayer" false teaching which is constantly and loudly repeated as the way to salvation by nearly all so-called "modern" American Christian churches, and yet this book has shown you that this "sinner's prayer" teaching is nowhere to be found in the Bible.

I now present another example, the so-called "Nicene Creed," which is a widely repeated, accepted, and believed statement of Christian faith/doctrine. The creed was formed at the First Council of Nicaea in A.D. 325 and has been blindly (for the most part) accepted as valid and true by most Christians ever since.

I had actually never heard of this creed until I came across it after I had finished the first edition of this book and was looking for ways to market it. One such marketer required me to accept the "Nicene Creed" by clicking a little checkbox on their website before I could submit the book for consideration. So, I did what a Berean should do…I researched the creed, where it came from, and what it says. It all sounded very "Biblical" (yes, even after writing this book, it wasn't immediately obvious to me there were any problems in it), but I decided to do further research before just blindly accepting it. I also, therefore, went to read and study what other trusted sources had to say on it, and lo and behold, I found I cannot simply and blindly accept the little innocuous looking creed agreement checkbox on that marketer's site.

I'll leave it as an exercise to the reader to do their own research into the Creed, but the below snippet from Wayne Jackson gives you a solid start: [173]

> But there is one novel theory regarding Christ that was embraced by the evolving apostasy that eventually manifested as Catholicism in its various forms. Later, a majority within the Protestant movement also adopted the idea.
>
> And what is this false idea regarding Jesus?
>
> It is the notion that Christ in eternity past **always was** the "Son of God." That he was "eternally begotten" or "generated" by the Father and "proceeding from" him.

---

[173] Jackson, Wayne. "Was Jesus the Son of God Eternally?" ChristianCourier.com. Access date: April 15, 2020. https://christiancourier.com/articles/1359-was-jesus-the-son-of-god-eternally

Today, it is hard to find many volumes on systematic theology that do not advocate the dogma of the eternal sonship of Jesus.

Origin and Growth of the Eternal Sonship Theory

Several of the church fathers occasionally used language that hinted of the **eternal generation** doctrine, but it appears to have had its most vocal introduction with Origen (c. 185-254), a scholar in Alexandria whose mind "shot off ideas like a Roman candle" as someone has said.

Here's what he wrote:

"Jesus Christ Himself, who came (into the world), was **born of the Father** before all creatures; that, after He had been the servant of the Father in the creation of all things — "for by Him were all things made" — He in the last times, divesting Himself (of his glory), and became a man, and was incarnate although God" (De Principiis Preface 4, emphasis added).

The theory obviously gained momentum because it was incorporated in the Nicene Creed in A.D. 325. Christ is described as "Son, only begotten, Firstborn of all creation, **begotten of the Father before all the ages**" (Bettenson, 35, emphasis added).

Later, Augustine (354-430) provided the notion with considerable notoriety. Philip Schaff described Augustine as one who possessed a "speculative spirit" — a depiction that certainly holds true with reference his thoughts on the Godhead. Schaff notes that: "by his discriminating speculation he exerted more influence upon the scholastic theology and that of the Reformation, than all the Nicene divines."

Not only did Augustine repudiate the concept that Father, Son and Holy Spirit are "three separately subsisting individuals," he vigorously advocated the theory which contends the Son was eternally begotten of the Father. His view "gradually met universal acceptance in the West" (III.684-687). Augustine significantly impacted both Roman Catholicism and modern Protestantism.

It is utterly amazing how, on occasion, the influence of very few personalities have channeled almost the entire stream of history. ...

Begotten Is Not Eternal

If it is the case that the Second Person of the Godhead was begotten, he is not eternal God, for eternality is an intrinsic quality of deity. God is from "everlasting to everlasting" (Psa. 90:2). So here is a very important implication. If a doctrine by necessary implication negates the deity of Jesus Christ can one be considered faithful who espouses it?

Contradictory Language

The dogma is discredited logically by self-contradiction. To contend that the Son was eternally begotten is a manifest contradiction of terms. It is the equivalent of saying, "Christ had an eternal beginning." Can an object both begin and not have been begun?

Mumbo-Jumbo Theology

Advocates of the eternal Sonship dogma are forced to resort to some of the most discombobulated jargon to explain their position. One writer says:

"If God is the perfect Mind, action of the same nature with this will enter into his self-consciousness also. He too will reproduce himself in thought, and recognize the reproduction as identical with the Mind that thought it forth" (W. Clarke, 173). Another says: "there must be in God a producing not subject to time, and productions which have no beginning" (McClintock, IX.889). When the language employed in an attempt to explain an issue becomes such a linguistic maze that not even the zealous advocate for the theory can convey it rationally, you can be assured that the idea behind it is suspect.

The lesson I'm trying to teach you here by calling out this Nicene Creed false teaching is to hopefully train you to challenge every single thing you read and hear, even when it sounds very "Biblical" on the surface. It would have been a simple matter for me just to accept the little checkbox of this very Biblically sounding statement on the market's website and get on with life, but it turns out that while objections to the Creed's language may seem minor at first, they hit at the very heart of the deity and eternality of Christ, so it's not something one should just "blindly accept."

It is through these very small errors (in wording) that much larger apostasy arises later on. Do not give your enemy (Satan) any openings whatsoever! So please, dear brother or sister in Christ, don't just go along blindly accepting whatever you hear or read being taught or preached – regardless of the source, regardless of how often they repeat it or how loudly they proclaim it, or how many distinguished initials they place before or after their names or the size and pomp of their church or congregation. See also the example given earlier in this book about the "Biblically sounding" Christian tract/pamphlet which was being passed out by "an old fashioned, independent, Baptist Church that believes, preaches, and practices the Bible."

PART VII:

CLOSING ITEMS

7.0 QUESTIONS & DOUBTS

The fear of the Lord is the beginning of wisdom. – Proverbs 9:10

If you're like me, even after reading this book, you may still have thousands of questions (ok, maybe hundreds), doubts, etc., about God, the Bible, and Christianity. Perhaps lingering questions like:

- How can the Bible possibly be true?
- Is there really a God?
- What about evolution? Didn't we "evolve" from apes?
- What about the dinosaurs?
- Doesn't science, carbon dating, and the "big bang" theory prove humans "evolved" billions of years ago from "primordial goo"?
- Why did God create us knowing we would sin and suffer?
- If Satan is evil, why did God create him?
- Why is there pain and suffering if God is a loving God?
- Why does God allow evil to continue to exist now?
- And…what about {___fill in the blank here___}.

Know that you are not alone! I was just like you – I questioned everything. It was hard searching for answers and truth amidst a veritable worldwide sea of lies, delusions, fake science, false teachings, and deceptions in nearly every direction you look!

But I urge you: please deal with your questions, doubts, and fears head-on, with brutal candor and honesty. Don't ignore or pretend that they don't exist as I did for years. And above all, do not let them cause you to stumble and fall, or worse, to not believe in God and in Jesus. Please do not let them stop you from pursuing truth and eternal life – for it is your eternal destiny that is at stake! There is additional information on our website, including links to helpful resources, which address topics that couldn't be covered in this book. May God lead you into all truth and help you to grow in the grace and knowledge (understanding) of our Lord and Savior Jesus Christ. Amen.

https://eachday.org

7.1 PSALM 1

How blessed is the man who does not walk in the counsel of the wicked,
Nor stand in the path of sinners,
Nor sit in the seat of scoffers!
But his delight is in the law of the LORD,
And in His law he meditates day and night.
He will be like a tree *firmly* planted by streams of water,
Which yields its fruit in its season
And its leaf does not wither;
And in whatever he does, he prospers.

The wicked are not so,
But they are like chaff which the wind drives away.
Therefore the wicked will not stand in the judgment,
Nor sinners in the assembly of the righteous.
For the LORD knows the way of the righteous,
But the way of the wicked will perish.

7.2 PSALM 2

Why are the nations in an uproar
And the peoples devising a vain thing?
The kings of the earth take their stand
And the rulers take counsel together
Against the LORD and against His Anointed, saying,
"Let us tear their fetters apart
And cast away their cords from us!"

He who sits in the heavens laughs,
The Lord scoffs at them.
Then He will speak to them in His anger
And terrify them in His fury, saying,
"But as for Me, I have installed My King
Upon Zion, My holy mountain."

"I will surely tell of the decree of the LORD:
He said to Me, 'You are My Son,
Today I have begotten You.
'Ask of Me, and I will surely give the nations as Your inheritance,
And the *very* ends of the earth as Your possession.
'You shall break them with a rod of iron,
You shall shatter them like earthenware.'"

Now therefore, O kings, show discernment;
Take warning, O judges of the earth.
Worship the LORD with reverence
And rejoice with trembling.
Do homage to the Son, that He not become angry, and you perish *in* the way,

For His wrath may soon be kindled.
How blessed are all who take refuge in Him!

7.3 PSALM 23

The LORD is my shepherd,
I shall not want.
He makes me lie down in green pastures;
He leads me beside quiet waters.
He restores my soul;
He guides me in the paths of righteousness
For His name's sake.

Even though I walk through the valley of the shadow of death,
I fear no evil, for You are with me;
Your rod and Your staff, they comfort me.
You prepare a table before me in the presence of my enemies;
You have anointed my head with oil;
My cup overflows.
Surely goodness and lovingkindness will follow me all the days of my life,
And I will dwell in the house of the LORD forever.

7.4 PSALM 31

In You, O LORD, I have taken refuge;
Let me never be ashamed;
In Your righteousness deliver me.
Incline Your ear to me, rescue me quickly;
Be to me a rock of strength,
A stronghold to save me.
For You are my rock and my fortress;
For Your name's sake You will lead me and guide me.
You will pull me out of the net which they have secretly laid for me,
For You are my strength.
Into Your hand I commit my spirit;
You have ransomed me, O LORD, God of truth.

I hate those who regard vain idols,
But I trust in the LORD.
I will rejoice and be glad in Your lovingkindness,
Because You have seen my affliction;
You have known the troubles of my soul,
And You have not given me over into the hand of the enemy;
You have set my feet in a large place.

Be gracious to me, O LORD, for I am in distress;
My eye is wasted away from grief, my soul and my body *also*.
For my life is spent with sorrow
And my years with sighing;
My strength has failed because of my iniquity,

And my body has wasted away.
Because of all my adversaries, I have become a reproach,
Especially to my neighbors,
And an object of dread to my acquaintances;
Those who see me in the street flee from me.
I am forgotten as a dead man, out of mind;
I am like a broken vessel.
For I have heard the slander of many,
Terror is on every side;
While they took counsel together against me,
They schemed to take away my life.

But as for me, I trust in You, O LORD,
I say, "You are my God."
My times are in Your hand;
Deliver me from the hand of my enemies and from those who persecute me.
Make Your face to shine upon Your servant;
Save me in Your lovingkindness.
Let me not be put to shame, O LORD, for I call upon You;
Let the wicked be put to shame, let them be silent in Sheol.
Let the lying lips be mute,
Which speak arrogantly against the righteous
With pride and contempt.

How great is Your goodness,
Which You have stored up for those who fear You,
Which You have wrought for those who take refuge in You,
Before the sons of men!
You hide them in the secret place of Your presence from the conspiracies of man;
You keep them secretly in a shelter from the strife of tongues.
Blessed be the LORD,
For He has made marvelous His lovingkindness to me in a besieged city.
As for me, I said in my alarm,
"I am cut off from before Your eyes";
Nevertheless You heard the voice of my supplications
When I cried to You.

O love the LORD, all you His godly ones!
The LORD preserves the faithful
And fully recompenses the proud doer.
Be strong and let your heart take courage,
All you who hope in the LORD.

7.5 PSALM 34

I will bless the LORD at all times;
His praise shall continually be in my mouth.
My soul will make its boast in the LORD;
The humble will hear it and rejoice.

O magnify the LORD with me,
And let us exalt His name together.

I sought the LORD, and He answered me,
And delivered me from all my fears.
They looked to Him and were radiant,
And their faces will never be ashamed.
This poor man cried, and the LORD heard him
And saved him out of all his troubles.
The angel of the LORD encamps around those who fear Him,
And rescues them.

O taste and see that the LORD is good;
How blessed is the man who takes refuge in Him!
O fear the LORD, you His saints;
For to those who fear Him there is no want.
The young lions do lack and suffer hunger;
But they who seek the LORD shall not be in want of any good thing.

Come, you children, listen to me;
I will teach you the fear of the LORD.
Who is the man who desires life
And loves *length of* days that he may see good?
Keep your tongue from evil
And your lips from speaking deceit.
Depart from evil and do good;
Seek peace and pursue it.

The eyes of the LORD are toward the righteous
And His ears are *open* to their cry.
The face of the LORD is against evildoers,
To cut off the memory of them from the earth.
The righteous cry, and the LORD hears
And delivers them out of all their troubles.
The LORD is near to the brokenhearted
And saves those who are crushed in spirit.

Many are the afflictions of the righteous,
But the LORD delivers him out of them all.
He keeps all his bones,
Not one of them is broken.
Evil shall slay the wicked,
And those who hate the righteous will be condemned.
The LORD redeems the soul of His servants,
And none of those who take refuge in Him will be condemned.

7.6 PSALM 46

God is our refuge and strength,
A very present help in trouble.
Therefore we will not fear, though the earth should change

And though the mountains slip into the heart of the sea;
Though its waters roar *and* foam,
Though the mountains quake at its swelling pride. *Selah.*

There is a river whose streams make glad the city of God,
The holy dwelling places of the Most High.
God is in the midst of her, she will not be moved;
God will help her when morning dawns.
The nations made an uproar, the kingdoms tottered;
He raised His voice, the earth melted.
The LORD of hosts is with us;
The God of Jacob is our stronghold. *Selah.*

Come, behold the works of the LORD,
Who has wrought desolations in the earth.
He makes wars to cease to the end of the earth;
He breaks the bow and cuts the spear in two;
He burns the chariots with fire.
"Cease *striving* and know that I am God;
I will be exalted among the nations, I will be exalted in the earth."
The LORD of hosts is with us;
The God of Jacob is our stronghold. *Selah.*

7.7 PSALM 69

Save me, O God,
For the waters have threatened my life.
I have sunk in deep mire, and there is no foothold;
I have come into deep waters, and a flood overflows me.
I am weary with my crying; my throat is parched;
My eyes fail while I wait for my God.
Those who hate me without a cause are more than the hairs of my head;
Those who would destroy me are powerful, being wrongfully my enemies;
What I did not steal, I then have to restore.

O God, it is You who knows my folly,
And my wrongs are not hidden from You.
May those who wait for You not be ashamed through me, O Lord GOD of hosts;
May those who seek You not be dishonored through me, O God of Israel,
Because for Your sake I have borne reproach;
Dishonor has covered my face.
I have become estranged from my brothers
And an alien to my mother's sons.
For zeal for Your house has consumed me,
And the reproaches of those who reproach You have fallen on me.
When I wept in my soul with fasting,
It became my reproach.
When I made sackcloth my clothing,
I became a byword to them.

The Message of Truth

Those who sit in the gate talk about me,
And I *am* the song of the drunkards.

But as for me, my prayer is to You, O LORD, at an acceptable time;
O God, in the greatness of Your lovingkindness,
Answer me with Your saving truth.
Deliver me from the mire and do not let me sink;
May I be delivered from my foes and from the deep waters.
May the flood of water not overflow me
Nor the deep swallow me up,
Nor the pit shut its mouth on me.

Answer me, O LORD, for Your lovingkindness is good;
According to the greatness of Your compassion, turn to me,
And do not hide Your face from Your servant,
For I am in distress; answer me quickly.
Oh draw near to my soul *and* redeem it;
Ransom me because of my enemies!
You know my reproach and my shame and my dishonor;
All my adversaries are before You.

Reproach has broken my heart and I am so sick.
And I looked for sympathy, but there was none,
And for comforters, but I found none.
They also gave me gall for my food
And for my thirst they gave me vinegar to drink.

May their table before them become a snare;
And when they are in peace, *may it become* a trap.
May their eyes grow dim so that they cannot see,
And make their loins shake continually.
Pour out Your indignation on them,
And may Your burning anger overtake them.
May their camp be desolate;
May none dwell in their tents.
For they have persecuted him whom You Yourself have smitten,
And they tell of the pain of those whom You have wounded.
Add iniquity to their iniquity,
And may they not come into Your righteousness.
May they be blotted out of the book of life
And may they not be recorded with the righteous.

But I am afflicted and in pain;
May Your salvation, O God, set me *securely* on high.
I will praise the name of God with song
And magnify Him with thanksgiving.
And it will please the LORD better than an ox
Or a young bull with horns and hoofs.
The humble have seen *it and* are glad;
You who seek God, let your heart revive.

For the LORD hears the needy
And does not despise His *who are* prisoners.

Let heaven and earth praise Him,
The seas and everything that moves in them.
For God will save Zion and build the cities of Judah,
That they may dwell there and possess it.
The descendants of His servants will inherit it,
And those who love His name will dwell in it.

7.8 PSALM 91

He who dwells in the shelter of the Most High
Will abide in the shadow of the Almighty.
I will say to the LORD, "My refuge and my fortress,
My God, in whom I trust!"
For it is He who delivers you from the snare of the trapper
And from the deadly pestilence.
He will cover you with His pinions,
And under His wings you may seek refuge;
His faithfulness is a shield and bulwark.

You will not be afraid of the terror by night,
Or of the arrow that flies by day;
Of the pestilence that stalks in darkness,
Or of the destruction that lays waste at noon.
A thousand may fall at your side
And ten thousand at your right hand,
But it shall not approach you.
You will only look on with your eyes
And see the recompense of the wicked.
For you have made the LORD, my refuge,
Even the Most High, your dwelling place.
No evil will befall you,
Nor will any plague come near your tent.

For He will give His angels charge concerning you,
To guard you in all your ways.
They will bear you up in their hands,
That you do not strike your foot against a stone.
You will tread upon the lion and cobra,
The young lion and the serpent you will trample down.

"Because he has loved Me, therefore I will deliver him;
I will set him *securely* on high, because he has known My name.
"He will call upon Me, and I will answer him;

I will be with him in trouble;
I will rescue him and honor him.
"With a long life I will satisfy him
And let him see My salvation."

7.9 PSALM 107

Oh give thanks to the LORD, for He is good,
For His lovingkindness is everlasting.
Let the redeemed of the LORD say *so*,
Whom He has redeemed from the hand of the adversary
And gathered from the lands,
From the east and from the west,
From the north and from the south.

They wandered in the wilderness in a desert region;
They did not find a way to an inhabited city.
They were hungry and thirsty;
Their soul fainted within them.
Then they cried out to the LORD in their trouble;
He delivered them out of their distresses.
He led them also by a straight way,
To go to an inhabited city.
Let them give thanks to the LORD for His lovingkindness,
And for His wonders to the sons of men!
For He has satisfied the thirsty soul,
And the hungry soul He has filled with what is good.

There were those who dwelt in darkness and in the shadow of death,
Prisoners in misery and chains,
Because they had rebelled against the words of God
And spurned the counsel of the Most High.
Therefore He humbled their heart with labor;
They stumbled and there was none to help.
Then they cried out to the LORD in their trouble;
He saved them out of their distresses.
He brought them out of darkness and the shadow of death
And broke their bands apart.
Let them give thanks to the LORD for His lovingkindness,
And for His wonders to the sons of men!
For He has shattered gates of bronze
And cut bars of iron asunder.

Fools, because of their rebellious way,
And because of their iniquities, were afflicted.
Their soul abhorred all kinds of food,
And they drew near to the gates of death.
Then they cried out to the LORD in their trouble;
He saved them out of their distresses.

He sent His word and healed them,
And delivered *them* from their destructions.
Let them give thanks to the LORD for His lovingkindness,
And for His wonders to the sons of men!
Let them also offer sacrifices of thanksgiving,
And tell of His works with joyful singing.

Those who go down to the sea in ships,
Who do business on great waters;
They have seen the works of the LORD,
And His wonders in the deep.
For He spoke and raised up a stormy wind,
Which lifted up the waves of the sea.
They rose up to the heavens, they went down to the depths;
Their soul melted away in *their* misery.
They reeled and staggered like a drunken man,
And were at their wits' end.
Then they cried to the LORD in their trouble,
And He brought them out of their distresses.
He caused the storm to be still,
So that the waves of the sea were hushed.
Then they were glad because they were quiet,
So He guided them to their desired haven.
Let them give thanks to the LORD for His lovingkindness,
And for His wonders to the sons of men!
Let them extol Him also in the congregation of the people,
And praise Him at the seat of the elders.

He changes rivers into a wilderness
And springs of water into a thirsty ground;
A fruitful land into a salt waste,
Because of the wickedness of those who dwell in it.
He changes a wilderness into a pool of water
And a dry land into springs of water;
And there He makes the hungry to dwell,
So that they may establish an inhabited city,
And sow fields and plant vineyards,
And gather a fruitful harvest.
Also He blesses them and they multiply greatly,
And He does not let their cattle decrease.

When they are diminished and bowed down
Through oppression, misery and sorrow,
He pours contempt upon princes
And makes them wander in a pathless waste.
But He sets the needy securely on high away from affliction,
And makes *his* families like a flock.
The upright see it and are glad;
But all unrighteousness shuts its mouth.

Who is wise? Let him give heed to these things,
And consider the lovingkindnesses of the LORD.

7.10 PSALM 116

I love the LORD, because He hears
My voice *and* my supplications.
Because He has inclined His ear to me,
Therefore I shall call *upon Him* as long as I live.
The cords of death encompassed me
And the terrors of Sheol came upon me;
I found distress and sorrow.
Then I called upon the name of the LORD:
"O LORD, I beseech You, save my life!"

Gracious is the LORD, and righteous;
Yes, our God is compassionate.
The LORD preserves the simple;
I was brought low, and He saved me.
Return to your rest, O my soul,
For the LORD has dealt bountifully with you.
For You have rescued my soul from death,
My eyes from tears,
My feet from stumbling.
I shall walk before the LORD
In the land of the living.
I believed when I said,
"I am greatly afflicted."
I said in my alarm,
"All men are liars."

What shall I render to the LORD
For all His benefits toward me?
I shall lift up the cup of salvation
And call upon the name of the LORD.
I shall pay my vows to the LORD,
Oh *may it be* in the presence of all His people.
Precious in the sight of the LORD
Is the death of His godly ones.
O LORD, surely I am Your servant,
I am Your servant, the son of Your handmaid,
You have loosed my bonds.
To You I shall offer a sacrifice of thanksgiving,
And call upon the name of the LORD.
I shall pay my vows to the LORD,
Oh *may it be* in the presence of all His people,
In the courts of the LORD'S house,
In the midst of you, O Jerusalem.
Praise the LORD!

7.11 PSALM 145

I will extol You, my God, O King,
And I will bless Your name forever and ever.
Every day I will bless You,
And I will praise Your name forever and ever.
Great is the LORD, and highly to be praised,
And His greatness is unsearchable.
One generation shall praise Your works to another,
And shall declare Your mighty acts.
On the glorious splendor of Your majesty
And on Your wonderful works, I will meditate.
Men shall speak of the power of Your awesome acts,
And I will tell of Your greatness.
They shall eagerly utter the memory of Your abundant goodness
And will shout joyfully of Your righteousness.

The LORD is gracious and merciful;
Slow to anger and great in lovingkindness.
The LORD is good to all,
And His mercies are over all His works.
All Your works shall give thanks to You, O LORD,
And Your godly ones shall bless You.
They shall speak of the glory of Your kingdom
And talk of Your power;
To make known to the sons of men Your mighty acts
And the glory of the majesty of Your kingdom.
Your kingdom is an everlasting kingdom,
And Your dominion *endures* throughout all generations.

The LORD sustains all who fall
And raises up all who are bowed down.
The eyes of all look to You,
And You give them their food in due time.
You open Your hand
And satisfy the desire of every living thing.

The LORD is righteous in all His ways
And kind in all His deeds.
The LORD is near to all who call upon Him,
To all who call upon Him in truth.
He will fulfill the desire of those who fear Him;
He will also hear their cry and will save them.
The LORD keeps all who love Him,
But all the wicked He will destroy.
My mouth will speak the praise of the LORD,
And all flesh will bless His holy name forever and ever.

7.12 MY TESTIMONY

I was raised Methodist as a young child, although I'm not sure that much of anything about that upbringing sunk in or stuck with me. I didn't like church, didn't want to be there, didn't remember any of it, and then went for many years without darkening any church doorway. However, looking back now, I'm still very grateful that my mom "dragged" me to church.

I didn't have any continued association with religion, faith, or church from those early years on up through college and beyond. In high school and college, I pursued science actively and loved math, physics, astronomy, and cosmology (the study of the universe and its origins amazed me), and I, therefore, attended university for physics (and graduated, yay!). But I eventually lost interest in cosmology, as I started to realize that science would never be able to answer with 100% certainty where the universe came from and how it all came about. It was just theory after theory after theory. Little did I know then, but I was actually right for coming to that realization, but for a very different reason. The reason is that science is not looking in the right area – the Bible has the answers, not man. Until science looks there, it will simply be one "theory" of man after another in an endless parade of futility and wild speculation.

I then married and continued living without any "religion" or God for about 13 years. I just did what the world did: got married, got a good job, worked hard, etc....and I surely considered myself to be a "good person" and not "as bad as others." I didn't do drugs or steal (much) and was (generally) honest (I thought). I thought that religion and God and all that "spiritual" stuff was utter rubbish and nonsense. Having a scientific mind, I was all about logic and factual proofs based on evidence.

Then at about age 35, I got divorced; that was a difficult time for me. It was also at that time that I started drinking alcohol (I got a late start on it). Little did I know where that would lead. Then while I was driving home from work one day, suddenly, out of the blue, I felt a "desire" to turn into this church parking lot and get some information. I had no clue what the church was; it just happened to be on my way to and from work, and I had driven by it hundreds of times without even noticing it. Even looking back now on this incident, there is no other way to describe what happened other than to say it was simply a "hey, let's turn in there" desire that came suddenly and without any prior warning. I certainly don't take any credit for it.

So, after getting some information, I decided to attend church there a few times and "just see what it's about" and "who knows, maybe I'll meet a nice church girl" also. I came to understand and realize that there IS a God – and I also came to believe in Christ. I'm very thankful to Pastor Darryl DelHousaye for his ability to explain difficult topics that had prior caused me to stay far away from "religion." After all, I was a scientist needing facts and proof, and all this "God" stuff was just made-up nonsense, or so I had thought.

I got a Bible, but I didn't read it much except for a few Bible studies here and there that I went to occasionally. I do remember beginning to notice Scripture starting to reveal itself to me (I now know that was by the Spirit), but I didn't follow through or keep at it, not at all. I was also baptized at the church, but it turns out (looking back), I never really turned my life over to the Lord!

In fact, it was after this point that I started working more than ever. I got remarried and just carried on with life as usual, as if nothing had happened, as if nothing had changed. I ended up working 15+ hrs./day, seven days/week for 10+ years straight. I didn't realize it at the time, but I had become an alcoholic, although it wasn't a problem at that time (and we are always the last to realize that fact anyway). No one told me either until many years later, but even if they had, I wouldn't have believed them or listened to them.

Then came a move to a different city, and finally, the addiction took over, and things went downhill pretty quickly from that point. I sunk pretty low with depression, anxiety, another divorce, etc. Luckily for me, I never even once touched hard drugs, or it probably would have been all over for me. However, alcohol is more insidious and sneakier/silent, but it is nonetheless just as dangerous, destructive, and deadly in its end result.

So even after I had accepted Christ, I was thereafter almost immediately (within a year or so) prodigal, apostate and backsliding for about 13 years because I was also trapped in an addiction that I didn't realize I had. It was also because I just continued living life as I had always lived it before…for another 15+ years actually! I drifted away from going to church, stopped reading the Bible, stopped thinking about God, or Jesus, or anything related to it all – I just focused on work, work, work, and earning money. Finally, things climaxed as I hit bottom.

I want to point out that those who are unsaved and who are also caught in an addiction don't realize it, but they are actually <u>doubly</u> lost! First, they are lost to the addiction, and secondly, to God and eternal life. For even if you somehow manage to get out of the addiction by yourself (or the help of others, e.g., a "12-step" program), you will still "come short of" eternal life. But Christ solves both – He will save you from the addiction and He will also restore you to eternal life at the same time! How amazing is that!

Please note that I had, in fact, accepted Christ at one time in my life as I indicated, but I then went apostate. Yes, I had departed or "fell away" from the faith. It IS possible to fall away! The "once saved always saved" teaching you commonly hear taught and preached is completely false (as I've shown you in this book). I had been born again at one time as best I knew how. However, by not growing and maturing in my faith, by returning to my old ways of pursuing the things of this world, and through sheer neglect of seeking Christ daily, I fell away. I know now that I was what the Bible calls "thorny soil": where the cares of this world choke Jesus out of your life. I also now know that I fell away also in large part due to not reading and *really* studying (desiring) the Word of God every single day. I now hope to be fertile soil, producing a crop 30-fold for the Lord.

If you are not living and working your Christian faith every single day and reading the Word of God every single day, you are placing yourself in great danger of falling away from Christ and back towards sin and the world. Do NOT underestimate the attraction and pull that this world exerts on you even after you are born again – for this mistake can be eternally deadly! This is why I have advised you repeatedly in this book to read the Bible every single day because when you are born again, your new spirit actually feeds on the Word of God, just as your body feeds on food. So, if you are not feeding your new spirit with the Word, you are literally starving it, as it is written: "Man shall not live on bread alone but on every word that proceeds out of the mouth of God" (Matthew 4:4).

In His unimaginable lovingkindness, patience, slowness to anger, and awesome mercy, Christ drew me back again. Yes, He called out to me again, and it was crystal clear to me! Imagine that! He chased after me in an attempt to draw me back, and I am forever thankful and grateful to Him for doing so. For I was indeed one of the lost sheep which had gone astray – I had left the fold, and He came after me to find me again. I need to emphasize that I can't take credit for any of this, as I didn't reach out to Him at all. It was He who came after to me (again)! I still don't fully understand it. I had completely discarded Him even after being born again, as the world and addiction slowly dragged me back into its net of destruction. That's how the world and Satan work. Again, I say, beware!

I've examined myself hard to see if I was really and truly born again at that prior time (15 years ago), and I have to say yes. At that time in my life, I confessed Jesus with all my heart, mind, and soul. I didn't just pretend to confess Christ; it was completely genuine and real. Some will argue that I wasn't truly born again, but why don't we ask Jesus when we see Him, for only God knows a man's heart.

I did learn this huge lesson, however, that unless you start to walk like a Christian (and bear fruit) and truly turn your life over to Him every single day as Lord, the world and sin will again seek you out and draw you back in and try to destroy you, for it is written: "Sin is crouching at the door; and its desire is for you" (Genesis 4:7). I've seen this verse play out in my own life. In fact, I now see that the Holy Bible and God and His Christ ARE truth. Nearly everything else, including this material world and all the ways and wisdom of man, are completely corrupt, lies, and are passing away – nothing of them will survive the great Day of Judgment. He is the only thing that stands solid through eternity.

I can't stress enough that it wasn't until I finally <u>turned my life over to Christ and submitted to the will of God</u> that things changed for me for the better – and they changed almost instantly the very day I did that (yes, that very day). The addiction was gone instantly, banished, never to return. I had believed in God and Jesus years prior, but I had never really submitted to Him. Also, no one had taught me how to walk as a Christian. That is another reason why I'm writing this book, so I can help others avoid doing what I did and making the same mistakes I made. Perhaps I can help others from falling away as I had. The steps are very simple: get on your knees at least twice daily (morning and evening), really turn your life over to and submit to God, pray constantly, read the Bible, love and serve God and love and serve others. If you do these things, Christ does the rest.

Since that one day a few years back, I've gone from being trapped in the throes of addiction and clutching a bottle to being sent nearly around the world twice doing photography (hopefully to glorify the Lord). I've gone from bondage under sin, Satan and death to the hope of eternal life in Christ. But the key is staying close to Jesus and seeking Him each day, no matter what! – RJA

7.13 HELPFUL RESOURCES

We are very blessed to have available to us today the good works and writings of many wonderful men of God who have come before us, true saints of the faith, many of whom also gave their lives for Christ as martyrs. Today, at more than at any time in history, we have a wealth of information available to read and learn from, along with the freedom to read and have access to these materials.

I've found the resources/books listed below to be helpful and predominantly free of false teachings. However, please note that I do not completely agree with or endorse all content in these resources. Great discernment must be used when reading, recommending, and using any non-inspired resources written by man. While many other wonderful resources are available, I've only included those I can vouch for personally as ones that will not lead you astray.

As mentioned in the Choosing a Bible chapter, be especially wary of all commentaries, notes contained in study Bibles, and even the headings in your Bible which have been added by man (the ones inserted in between chapters/sections of the Bible by the publishers) – these are all simply the words of man and not inspired, and they offer a great opportunity for the authors/editors/publishers to inject their own particular bias, doctrines, and false teachings. This warning applies especially to any notes, commentary, and headlines dealing with Bible prophecy and eschatology (end-times matters) that have been published after the late 1800s, for they are infected and corrupted badly with the Dispensational Premillennialism false teaching (with very few exceptions).

Some of the books are out of print and may therefore be difficult to find. But I strongly recommend that you try to find and read editions that were printed as closest to the original author's first date of publication as possible, as newer revisions offer an opportunity once again for editors and publishers to twist, distort, or even rewrite the original author's content and introduce their own false doctrines and teachings.

And lastly, before purchasing any book, look to see what other books that same author (and publisher) has produced, as doing so will help you understand if their books can be trusted to be in agreement with the Divine "message of truth" (not the false doctrines of man).

BOOKS:

- *The Message of Truth*, by R. John Anderson, Holy Spirit Prints, 2019 (También disponible en Español *La Palabra de Verdad*)
- *Jesus > Addiction*, by R. John Anderson, Holy Spirit Prints, 2020 (También disponible en Español)
- *Jesus > Anxiety*, by R. John Anderson, Holy Spirit Prints, 2020 (También disponible en Español)
- *The Commands of Christ*, by R. John Anderson, Holy Spirit Prints, 2020 (También disponible en Español)
- *The Last Day*, by R. John Anderson, Holy Spirit Prints, 2020 (También disponible en Español)
- *Pilgrim's Progress*, by John Bunyan, Republished by Holy Spirit Prints, 1678/2018
- *Exposition of the Old and New Testaments*, by Matthew Henry, 1706-1710/1721 [Note: this work was completed in 1721 after his death by others who tried to complete his work. There are also many revisions titled *Matthew Henry's Bible Commentary*, either complete or concise/abridged. The later versions are marked as "carefully revised and corrected" or "new modern edition," however, I strongly recommend you find and use his original exposition version (up to the date 1721), which hasn't been altered by those who wanted to change doctrine. What I've learned is that when someone says "revised" or "corrected," it means that they have altered it to fit their own theology in nearly all cases!]
- *A New Testament Commentary*, by Wayne Jackson, Christian Courier Publications, 2011
- *The Prophets, An Old Testament Commentary*, by Wayne Jackson, Christian Courier Publications, 2015
- *The Acts of the Apostles*, by Wayne Jackson, Christian Courier Publications, 2005
- *Jesus Christ The Master Teacher*, by Wayne Jackson, Christian Courier Publications, 2013
- *Beyond the Tomb*, by H. M. Riggle, The Gospel Trumpet Company/Holy Spirit Prints, 1929/2018
- *The Sabbath and the Lord's Day*, by H. M. Riggle, The Gospel Trumpet Company, 1918
- *The New Answers Books (1-4)*, by Ken Ham et al., Answers in Genesis, 1982
- *The Bible on Trial*, by Wayne Jackson, Christian Courier Publications, 2009
- *The Bible and Science*, by Wayne Jackson, Christian Courier Publications, 2000
- *The Parables in Profile*, by Wayne Jackson, Christian Courier Publications, 1978
- *The Human Body, Accident or Design*, by Wayne Jackson, Christian Courier Publications, 2000
- *Science Speaks*, by Peter W. Stoner, Robert C. Newman, The Moody Bible Institute of Chicago, 1969/1976
- *Biblical Figures of Speech*, by Wayne Jackson, Christian Courier Publications, 2005

- *Why Did My Savior Have To Die?*, by Wayne Jackson, Christian Courier Publications
- *The Church of Christ, A Biblical Ecclesiology for Today*, by Everett Ferguson, William B. Eerdmans Publishing Company, 1996
- *The Faith Once for All: Bible Doctrine for Today*, by Jack Cottrell, College Press Publishing, 2002
- *Faith's Fundamentals*, by Jack Cottrell, Wipf and Stock Publishers, 1995
- *Baptism, A Biblical Study*, by Jack Cottrell, College Press Publishing Co., 1989
- *The Momentous Event*, by W. J. Grier, Evangelical Bookshop, 1945
- *Christ's Triumphal Reign*, by H. M. Riggle, Gospel Trumpet Company, 1930
- *Premillennialism, A System of Infidelity*, by Wayne Jackson, Christian Courier Publications
- *Bible Words and Theological Terms Made Easy*, by Wayne Jackson, Christian Courier Publications, 2002
- *The Kingdom of God*, by H. M. Riggle, The Gospel Trumpet Company, 1903
- *Christ's Second Coming and What Will Follow*, by H. M. Riggle, 1872
- *Jesus Is Coming Again*, by H. M. Riggle, The Gospel Trumpet Company, 1943
- *Foxe's Book of Martyrs (The Actes and Monuments)*, by John Foxe, 1563 (English version).
- *Creation, Evolution and the Age of the Earth*, by Wayne Jackson, Christian Courier Publications, 1989
- *The book of Job*, by Wayne Jackson, Christian Courier Publications, 1983
- *Revelation*, by Wayne Jackson, Christian Courier Publications, 2004
- *The Christian Church, Its Rise and Progress*, by H. M. Riggle, The Gospel Trumpet Company, 1912
- *The Jewish War*, by Titus Flavius Josephus
- *Antiquities of the Jews*, by Titus Flavius Josephus
- *The Church History*, by Eusebius of Caesarea
- *The Heavenly Footman*, by John Bunyan, 1698
- *The New Testament of our Lord and Saviour Jesus Christ. With a Commentary and Critical Notes* (Adam Clarke's commentary), by Adam Clarke, 1831
- *Nobody Left Behind*, by David Vaughn Elliot, 2004

WEBSITES:

- https://eachday.org
- https://christiancourier.com
- http://www.biblestudytools.com
- http://www.biblegateway.com
- http://www.biblehub.com
- http://www.e-sword.net
- http://www.christianbook.com
- https://truthbooks.com
- http://apologeticspress.org
- https://www.focuspress.org
- http://wvbs.org
- http://oabs.org
- https://insightintobibletruth.net/

The following websites are recommended <u>only</u> for their scientific content, not their Christian doctrine:

- http://www.answersingenesis.org
- http://www.icr.org

BENEDICTION

Be still, and know that I am God. – Psalm 46:10 (ESV)

God does not grow tired.
He does not grow weary.
He does not need a day off.
He does not need to call in sick.
He does not need a vacation.
He does not need to stop and rest.
He does not need a timeout.
He does not need to stop and catch His breath.
He does not need to sleep.
He does not give up.
He does not need a second chance to get it right.

He does not hope He can. He does not hope it may.
He does not hope He might; He is might.

He does not wish He could.
He does not wonder if He will;
It is His will.

He is not surprised. He is not caught unaware.
He sees all. He knows all. He is everywhere.
He is omniscient. He is omnipresent. He is omnipotent.
And He will judge all.

He doesn't need to ask permission.
He doesn't need to pay better attention.
He doesn't need to take more classes.
He doesn't need to learn anything new.
He doesn't need to wait to see what will happen.
He doesn't depend on mere man for His will to be done.

The Message of Truth

He is not ignored.
He is not disrespected.
He is not mocked.

He doesn't lie. He doesn't omit truth.
He doesn't tell half-truths. He doesn't change His mind.
He doesn't break His promises.
He doesn't forget you. He will not forsake you.
Ever, and forever.

He is patient. He is loving. He is kind.
He is slow to anger. He is merciful. He is righteous.
He is holy. He is glorious.
He is just. He just is.

He is who He always was.
He is who He is right now.
He is who He will be for all eternity.

He is not overcome.
He will prevail.
He has prevailed.
He is with you this very instant,
Right now, right where you are at.

For He is Creator of all, before all, for all, in all, through all,
upholds all, after all, above all, and all in all.

Rest in the eternal peace of our Lord and Savior Jesus Christ,
today and forevermore. Amen.

BOOKS BY HOLY SPIRIT PRINTS

Visit https://holyspiritprints.com

The Truth Can Set You
FREE...

This book presents the central message of the Holy Bible - the gospel, which means "good news." This book can also help you understand how we "got here" — a sinful fallen world with death, destruction, disease, famine, war, lying, cheating, stealing, murder, killing and other sinful behavior with misery all around us. God's great Day of Judgment awaits us all! You will also read that our hope is in Jesus Christ, the one true and living God, the Lord our Savior.

Visit http://www.holyspiritprints.com to order

Where Will You Spend ETERNITY...

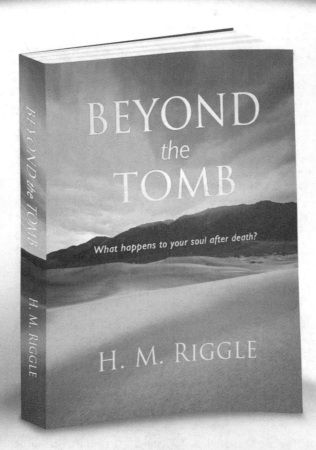

Do you know what happens to your soul after death? Are you curious about heaven and hell? How long is eternity anyway? What happens at the moment of death, for those saved and those lost? While there are many opinions, speculations, myths and superstitions about what happens to the human soul after death, *Beyond the Tomb* presents what the holy Bible, the inerrant inspired word of God, has to say on the matter.

Visit http://www.holyspiritprints.com to order

An All-Time Christian
CLASSIC...

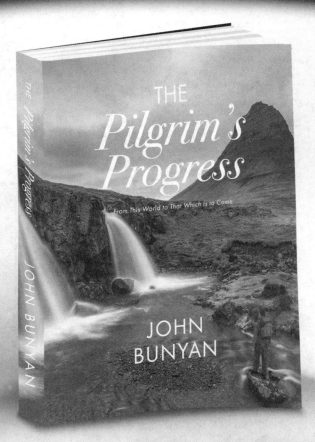

One of the most popular Christian novels of all time. Follow the journey of Christian, and his wife Christiana, as they travel from the City of Destruction to the Heavenly City, facing trials and tribulations, and meeting evil characters of all kinds as well as other pilgrims along the way. It's a book you'll want to read over and over again.

Visit http://www.holyspiritprints.com to order

Anxious for NOTHING...

Is your life marked by a state of continual peace or one of constant uneasiness, worry and anxiety? Anxiety today is of epidemic proportions. But that just should not be – anxiety has no part in the life of a Christian. For the Christian, anxiety is caused by a lack of faith and trust in the Lord. This book shows you how to overcome anxiety by trusting in the LORD.

Visit http://www.holyspiritprints.com to order

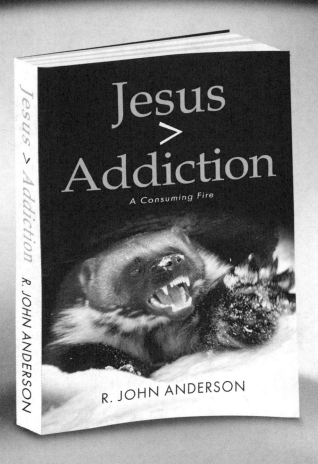

Are you or a friend or loved one trapped in an addiction with seemingly no way out? Know that the power of Christ overcomes any and all addictions. Return to God, and to Christ, and He will give you His power to fully and completely break free from any addiction.

Visit http://www.holyspiritprints.com to order

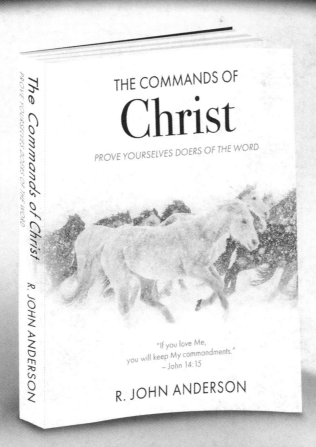

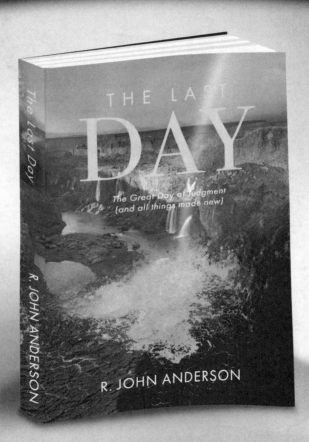

RAYS OF HOPE

Booklet contains 20 tear-out photo & verse cards about hope. Rays of Hope was created to help share the messages of assurance and hope that can be found in the Lord Jesus Christ with those who may find themselves in a lonely, dark, faraway or dangerous place.

Visit http://www.holyspiritprints.com to order

His Perfect
STRENGTH...

Booklet contains 20 tear-out photo & verse cards about strength and courage. Created to help share the message of God's holy and perfect strength that can be found in the Lord Jesus Christ with those who may find themselves in a lonely, dark, faraway or dangerous place.

Visit http://www.holyspiritprints.com to order

FAITH CARDS

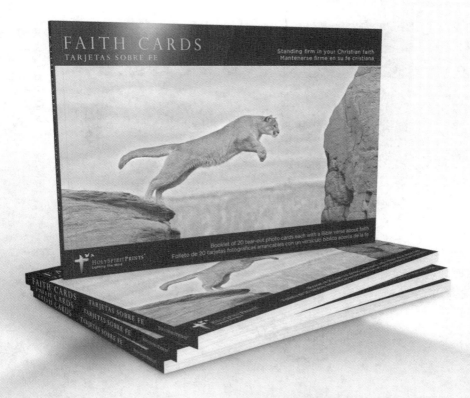

Booklet contains 20 tear-out photo & verse cards about faith. Faith Cards was created to provide simple reminders of the core of Christian faith. Great gift for loved ones in: armed forces, prison/jail, addiction/rehab, recovery centers, or others stranded or posted away from home whose faith is being tested in time of trial or tribulation.

Visit http://www.holyspiritprints.com to order

Booklet contains 20 tear-out photo & verse cards about the peace of God. The Peace of God was created to provide inspirational reminders about God's peace found in the Lord Jesus Christ. This may be especially helpful for those who find themselves in a lonely, dark, faraway or dangerous place.

Visit http://www.holyspiritprints.com to order

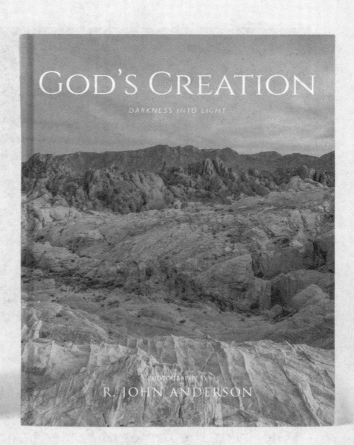

A book showcasing the names of the Lord accompanied by stunning photography. Glorifying the names of Father, Son and Spirit.

Holy, holy, holy is the Lord!

Visit http://www.holyspiritprints.com to order